The Law of Fundraising

WILEY NONPROFIT LAW, FINANCE, AND MANAGEMENT SERIES

The Art of Planned Giving: Understanding Donors and the Culture of Giving by
     Douglas E. White
Beyond Fund Raising: New Strategies for Nonprofit Investment and Innovation by
     Kay Grace
Budgeting for Not-for-Profit Organizations by David Maddox
Careers in Fundraising by Lilya Wagner
The Complete Guide to Fundraising Management, Second Edition by Stanley Weinstein
The Complete Guide to Nonprofit Management by Smith, Bucklin & Associates
Critical Issues in Fund Raising edited by Dwight Burlingame
Cultivating Diversity in Fundraising by Janice Gow Pettey
*Faith-Based Management: Leading Organizations That Are Based on More Than Just
     Mission* by Peter C. Brinckerhoff
Financial and Accounting Guide for Not-for-Profit Organizations, Sixth Edition by
     Malvern J. Gross, Jr., Richard F. Larkin, John H. McCarthy,
     PricewaterhouseCoopers LLP
Financial Empowerment: More Money for More Mission by Peter C. Brinckerhoff
Financial Management for Nonprofit Organizations by Jo Ann Hankin, Alan Seidner,
     and John Zietlow
The First Legal Answer Book for Fund-Raisers by Bruce R. Hopkins
Fund-Raising Fundamentals: A Guide to Annual Giving for Professionals and Volunteers
     by James M. Greenfield
Fundraising Cost Effectiveness: A Self-Assessment Workbook by James M. Greenfield
*Fund-Raising Regulation: A State-by-State Handbook of Registration Forms,
     Requirements, and Procedures* by Seth Perlman and Betsy Hills Bush
Grantseeker's Budget Toolkit by James A. Quick and Cheryl S. New
Grantseeker's Toolkit: A Comprehensive Guide to Finding Funding by Cheryl S. New
     and James A. Quick
Grant Winner's Toolkit: Project Management and Evaluation by James A. Quick and
     Cheryl S. New
*High Impact Philanthropy: How Donors, Boards, and Nonprofit Organizations Can
     Transform Nonprofit Communities* by Kay Sprinkel Grace and Alan L. Wendroff
High Performance Nonprofit Organizations: Managing Upstream for Greater Impact by
     Christine W. Letts, William P. Ryan, and Allen Grossman
*Improving the Economy, Efficiency, and Effectiveness of Nonprofits: Conducting
     Operational Reviews* by Rob Reider
Intermediate Sanctions: Curbing Nonprofit Abuse by Bruce R. Hopkins and D. Benson
     Tesdahl
International Fund Raising for Nonprofits by Thomas Harris
International Guide to Nonprofit Law by Lester A. Salamon and Stefan Toepler &
     Associates
Joint Ventures Involving Tax-Exempt Organizations, Second Edition by
     Michael I. Sanders
The Law of Fundraising, Third Edition by Bruce R. Hopkins
The Law of Tax-Exempt Healthcare Organizations, Second Edition by Thomas K. Hyatt
     and Bruce R. Hopkins
The Law of Tax-Exempt Organizations, Seventh Edition by Bruce R. Hopkins
The Legal Answer Book for Nonprofit Organizations by Bruce R. Hopkins
The Legal Answer Book for Private Foundations by Bruce R. Hopkins and Jody Blazek

The Legislative Labyrinth: A Map for Not-for-Profits, edited by Walter P. Pidgeon, Jr.

Managing Affordable Housing: A Practical Guide to Creating Stable Communities by Bennett L. Hecht, Local Initiatives Support Corporation, and James Stockard

ManagingNonprofits.org by Ben Hecht and Rey Ramsey

Mission-Based Management: Leading Your Not-for-Profit in the 21st Century, Second Edition by Peter C. Brinckerhoff

Mission-Based Management: Leading Your Not-for-Profit in the 21st Century, Second Edition, Workbook by Peter C. Brinckerhoff

Mission-Based Marketing: How Your Not-for-Profit Can Succeed in a More Competitive World by Peter C. Brinckerhoff

Nonprofit Boards: Roles, Responsibilities, and Performance by Diane J. Duca

Nonprofit Compensation and Benefits Practices by Applied Research and Development Institute International, Inc.

The Nonprofit Counsel by Bruce R. Hopkins

The Nonprofit Guide to the Internet, Second Edition by Michael Johnston

Nonprofit Investment Policies: A Practical Guide to Creation and Implementation by Robert Fry, Jr.

The Nonprofit Law Dictionary by Bruce R. Hopkins

Nonprofit Compensation, Benefits, and Employment Law by David G. Samuels and Howard Pianko

The Nonprofit Handbook, Third Edition: Management by Tracy Daniel Connors

The Nonprofit Handbook, Third Edition: Fund Raising by James M. Greenfield

The Nonprofit Manager's Resource Dictionary, Second Edition by Ronald A. Landskroner

Nonprofit Organizations' Business Forms: Disk Edition by John Wiley & Sons, Inc.

Planned Giving: Management, Marketing, and Law, Second Edition by Ronald R. Jordan and Katelyn L. Quynn

Private Foundations: Tax Law and Compliance by Bruce R. Hopkins and Jody Blazek

Program Related Investments: A Technical Manual for Foundations by Christie I. Baxter

Reengineering Your Nonprofit Organization: A Guide to Strategic Transformation by Alceste T. Pappas

Reinventing the University: Managing and Financing Institutions of Higher Education by Sandra L. Johnson and Sean C. Rush, PricewaterhouseCoopers LLP

The Second Legal Answer Book for Fund-Raisers by Bruce R. Hopkins

The Second Legal Answer Book for Nonprofit Organizations by Bruce R. Hopkins

Social Entrepreneurship: The Art of Mission-Based Venture Development by Peter C. Brinckerhoff

Special Events: Proven Strategies for Nonprofit Fund Raising by Alan Wendroff

Starting and Managing a Nonprofit Organization: A Legal Guide, Third Edition by Bruce R. Hopkins

Strategic Communications for Nonprofit Organizations: Seven Steps to Creating a Successful Plan by Janel Radtke

Strategic Planning for Nonprofit Organizations: A Practical Guide and Workbook by Michael Allison and Jude Kaye, Support Center for Nonprofit Management

Streetsmart Financial Basics for Nonprofit Managers by Thomas A. McLaughlin

A Streetsmart Guide to Nonprofit Mergers and Networks by Thomas A. McLaughlin

Successful Corporate Fund Raising: Effective Strategies for Today's Nonprofits by Scott Sheldon

Successful Marketing Strategies for Nonprofit Organizations by Barry J. McLeish

The Tax Law of Colleges and Universities, Second Edition by Bertrand M. Harding

Tax Planning and Compliance for Tax-Exempt Organizations: Forms, Checklists, Procedures, Third Edition by Jody Blazek

The Universal Benefits of Volunteering: A Practical Workbook for Nonprofit Organizations, Volunteers and Corporations by Walter P. Pidgeon, Jr.

Trade Secrets for Every Nonprofit Manager by Thomas A. McLaughlin

Values-Based Estate Planning: A Step-by-Step Approach to Wealth Transfers for Professional Advisors by Scott Fithian

The Law of Fundraising

Third Edition

BRUCE R. HOPKINS

John Wiley & Sons, Inc.

ISBN 0-471-20612-1

Printed in the United States of America.

10 9 8 7 6 5 4 3 2 1

This book is dedicated to all in the fundraising profession,
particularly those who are members of the
Association of Fundraising Professionals,
with the admonition that messengers are not to be blamed.

About the Author

Bruce R. Hopkins is a lawyer in Kansas City, Missouri, with the firm of Polsinelli Shalton Welte, P.C., having previously practiced law in Washington, D.C., for 26 years. He specializes in the representation of charitable and other nonprofit organizations. His practice ranges over the entirety of legal matters involving nonprofit organizations, with emphasis on fundraising law issues, charitable giving (including planned giving), the formation of nonprofit organizations, acquisition of recognition of tax-exempt and public charity status, unrelated business planning, application of intermediate sanctions, use of nonprofit and for-profit subsidiaries, and review of annual information returns.

Mr. Hopkins serves as chair of the Committee on Exempt Organizations, Tax Section, American Bar Association; chair, Section of Taxation, National Association of College and University Attorneys; and president, Planned Giving Study Group of Greater Washington, D.C. He was accorded the Assistant Commissioner's (IRS) Award in 1984.

Mr. Hopkins is the series editor of Wiley's Nonprofit Law, Finance, and Management Series. In addition to *The Law of Fundraising, Third Edition,* he is the author of *The Tax Law of Charitable Giving, Second Edition; The First Legal Answer Book for Fund-Raisers; The Second Legal Answer Book for Fund-Raisers; The Legal Answer Book for Nonprofit Organizations; The Second Legal Answer Book for Nonprofit Organizations; The Law of Tax-Exempt Organizations, Seventh Edition; Charity, Advocacy, and the Law; The Nonprofit Law Dictionary; Starting and Managing a Nonprofit Organization; A Legal Guide, Third Edition;* and is the co-author, with Jody Blazek, of *Private Foundations: Tax Law and Compliance* and of *The Legal Answer Book for Private Foundations;* with D. Benson Tesdahl, of *Intermediate Sanctions: Curbing Nonprofit Abuse;* and with Thomas K. Hyatt, of *The Law of Tax-Exempt Healthcare Organizations, Second Edition.* He also writes *The Nonprofit Counsel,* a monthly newsletter, published by John Wiley & Sons.

Mr. Hopkins earned his J.D. and LL.M. degrees at the George Washington University and his B.A. at the University of Michigan. He is a member of the bars of the District of Columbia and the state of Missouri.

Preface

This book, the third edition of *The Law of Fundraising,* is the culmination of an effort over 22 years to capture the essence of this body of law in one volume. The book reflects what many in the fundraising profession already painfully know: federal, state, and local regulation of fundraising just keeps growing. When the book originated, as *Charity Under Siege: Government Regulation of Fund-Raising* (1980), it was less than an inch thick, yet it was thought the siege was on even then. The first edition of *The Law of Fund-Raising* (1991) (over 1½ inches) encompassed far more law, as did the second edition (1996) (over 2¼ inches). Thus, each of these books contains more elements of law than its predecessor; there is no reason to believe this trend will be changing. Three unfolding developments alone guarantee more government regulation in the realm of fundraising: solicitations by means of the Internet, the intermediate sanctions rules, and privacy concerns.

* * *

Any lawyer whose practice specialty is, like mine, tax, corporate, and other law as it applies to charitable and other nonprofit organizations, cannot avoid entanglement in the legal morass that constitutes federal, state, and local law regulating fundraising by charities. My representation of charitable organizations started more than 30 years ago (in 1969), and the law of fundraising has been a significant component of my practice almost from that beginning.

I remember vividly how it all began. The day was January 20, 1973, a Saturday. A colleague at a client charitable organization telephoned me at my office in Washington, D.C. He excitedly told me about a "hearing" that was to be held in a few days, before a subcommittee of the House of Representatives chaired by Congressman Lionel Van Deerlin. This impending hearing, I was told, concerned "proposed legislation" that would create a system of federal regulation of fundraising by charitable organizations. I was asked to look into this and report back. Knowing nothing of the proposed legislation or the upcoming hearing or Rep. Van Deerlin (or, for that matter, regulation of fundraising in general), I promised my colleague I would explore the matter.

I then telephoned Rep. Van Deerlin's office, hoping to find some dedicated staff person toiling there on a Saturday morning. Times were much different then: my call was answered by the Congressman himself. It turned out that there was no hearing; rather, an informal briefing on a proposed bill was scheduled to be conducted, in Van Deerlin's office, for interested (and concerned) persons. I attended the briefing the following week, spoke up, found myself appointed to an ad hoc group deputed to rewrite the proposal, and thus nearly inadvertently wandered into the ambit of government regulation of fundraising for charity.

As the result of that innocent call, there unfolded innumerable meetings, telephone calls, hours of research, hearings, task forces, new nonprofit organizations, proposals, legislation, and a swirl of other developments that have evolved into today's substantial body of regulatory law directed at solicitations of contributions for charitable purposes. Nearly three decades later, the pace and range of this form of regulation have, as noted, not abated but instead are intense and growing. To say that the contemporary law of fundraising is far more extensive than it was in the days of Congressman Van Deerlin's failed effort to legislate national charitable solicitations law is a gross understatement.

* * *

When I started to familiarize myself with this aspect of the law, then, nearly all of today's federal law on the subject did not exist. The first of the U.S. Supreme Court decisions that would so dramatically shape this field was years away (issued in 1980), and much of the state law we face today had not been written. The fundraising regulation that did exist back then was at the state, and sometimes local, level. Enforcement of these various statutes and ordinances was casual and uneven; punitive action was rare. Federal law on the point was confined to the rules concerning the charitable contribution deduction and some postal laws.

Expansion of state law came about because of occasional abuses that attracted the regulators' (and sometimes the public's) attention. As the climate became more consumer oriented, a few well-publicized fundraising misdeeds fed the states' appetite for regulation. Today, nearly all of the states have statutory law, rules and regulations, and case law on the subject; many of them have massive and intrusive charitable solicitation acts. No letup is in sight on this front. States continue to write and rewrite charitable solicitation acts. With the advent of Internet solicitations, the number of instances where a charity has to comply with the laws of more than one state (or locality) is on the rise.

The federal government—the explorations of Rep. Van Deerlin and others of his ilk notwithstanding—was slow to join the march of inexorable and intensifying regulation but, once engaged, quickly compensated for its initial inattentiveness. The Internal Revenue Service, in particular, has exhibited considerable adventuresomeness in the realm of charitable fundraising regulation by, among other approaches, promulgating regulations in fields such as donor recognition, gift solicitation disclosure, intermediate sanctions, and corporate sponsorships. Other federal agencies, such as the U.S. Postal Service, are playing an increasing role.

Congress has entered this fray, significantly adding to the law of fundraising with legislation concerning such topics as charitable gift substantiation, quid pro quo contributions, intermediate sanctions, corporate sponsorships, charitable remainder and charitable lead trusts, and document disclosure and dissemination. Additional law may be anticipated, with emphasis on disclosure by charitable organizations and revision of the annual information returns they must file.

PREFACE

Court opinions on the subject of fundraising law, direct and indirect, reflect a continuation of the development of this body of law by the judiciary. Decisions on subjects such as private benefit, private inurement, unrelated business activities, joint ventures, planned giving, and the scope of the charitable deduction impact on fundraising.

* * *

A student of the development of the federal and state law of fundraising must be puzzled over the way and direction it has grown and spread. (This perplexity may soon be extended to the breeding of local law on the subject.) Why are these laws blossoming the way they are? What fuels the ongoing ferment? Should some answers to those questions be found, even partially, one must ask: Are these laws effective? Are the rationales for the charitable solicitation acts valid?

From this lawyer's perspective, the extent of abuses does not warrant the crush of legislation and regulations that have been generated. (Intellectually, all of this law is fascinating, bringing interesting constitutional, tax, and other law policy issues.) The consumer protection movement provides an explanation for some of this law. Posturing politicians have made their contribution. Regulation breeds regulation; some of the state and federal law has been engendered and grown in accordance with the principle that vacuums are to be abhorred.

All of this is good news for those who practice law, and write and speak on the subject, or who are employed in a regulatory system. Yet one wonders whether all of this regulation, with the requisite paperwork and drain on charities' staff time, money, and other resources, is worth the effort. It is a marvel that the world of philanthropy manages to fulfill its mission to the extent that it does while laboring under the considerable burden of these laws.

* * *

The state charitable solicitation acts cause manifold problems. Many of them are complex and impose a battery of registration, reporting, bonding, and other requirements. A charitable organization that raises its funds in several states finds these problems compounded; it is confronted with a bewildering array of differing legal requirements, forms and due dates for filings, bonds, accounting principles, and more. Efforts toward uniform reporting, however, have somewhat ameliorated these headaches. Still, some charities "solve" this dilemma by failure to comply with the laws in one or more states.

These laws apply to fundraising of all types: solicitation by direct mail, personal contact, telephone, facsimile, and e-mail. (The book examines the festering federal and state law issues surrounding Website solicitations.) The rules encompass fundraising through capital campaigns, planned giving programs, special events, annual fund drives, corporate giving efforts, bequest programs, and in some instances grant-seeking. The regulatory requirements apply (with exceptions) to churches and other religious organizations; schools, colleges, and universities; hospitals and other health care entities; assorted related "foundations"; publicly supported charities; civic and patriotic groups; and many other types of nonprofit organizations seeking contributions. These bodies of law apply equally to old and new entities—those that are bastions of the philanthropic scene and those that are unpopular, controversial, or espouse what may be perceived as trivial or unnecessary causes. They apply to charities with an existing constituency and those newly building a donor base.

* * *

Many managers of charitable organizations—along with their consultants, fundraisers, lawyers, accountants, and the like—are not aware of the many difficulties, including the immense cost (measured in every way) of compliance, imposed by the burgeoning number of laws, regulations, and rules regarding charitable fundraising. (Chapter 5, summarizing federal law, has 23 sections.) Thus, these managers require background information and a general understanding of the various federal and state laws and their application to multitudinous philanthropic institutions. The principal purpose of this book is to detail this regulatory picture. (I have also approached this subject from other angles, as reflected in *The First Legal Answer Book for Fund-Raisers* (2000) and *The Second Legal Answer Book for Fund-Raisers* (2000), both published by John Wiley & Sons.)

Many organizations and their fundraisers are willing to make a reasonable effort to comply with these laws but do not know where to begin. Thus, another purpose of this book is to describe means by which charitable organizations and their fundraising professionals can rationally approach these laws and develop a procedure for effective compliance with them. Some charitable organizations are in basic adherence with applicable laws but need guidance about protective steps to take when an aspect of their fundraising program is being examined by governmental authority or perhaps threatened. A purpose of the book, then, is to describe the process and the available rationales for keeping an organization in—or bringing it into—regulatory compliance.

Several legal problems, for charitable organizations and fundraising professionals, are inherent in the administration and enforcement of the laws that regulate charitable fundraising. Fundamental constitutional, administrative, tax, and other law issues are involved, and some of them are thorny and unresolved. These legal aspects are discussed and analyzed in the book, to provide a guide to fundraising organizations and their advisors regarding the reach of various statutory and other regulatory law requirements.

The law at the state level is analyzed and compared. (Unlike the first and second edition of this book, the various state statutes are not summarized as such. Change is too frequent for this law to be part of a book. The deletion of this material has caused the book to return to a more normal size, reversing the trend of the growing thickness of the book.) The book also provides a summary of federal law regulation—largely in the tax area—of charitable fundraising. It surveys the issues to be faced in any effort to design a federal statute in this area and summarizes the several items of legislation introduced over the years by members of Congress in attempts to create comprehensive schemes to regulate charitable fundraising at the federal level.

Given the blasts of new state and federal regulation, and the changes in fundraising law in recent years, it became clear that analysis and guidance for the regulated, in the form of a third edition, was necessary. Of particular concern to the fundraising community in this regard is the emergence of Internet fundraising, the intermediate sanctions rules, and privacy regulations. The updated volume has been written to assist fundraising charitable organizations, and their employees and consultants, in coping with this continually growing body of law and regulation.

*   *   *

I have attempted to keep my personal views on this subject to a minimum, wanting the book to be an objective compendium of the law of fundraising. Yet, unlike other aspects of the law that I am privileged to be able to write about (such as the law of tax-exempt organizations and charitable giving), the law of fundraising contains too many absurdities and extremes to let pass without mention. Thus, in Chapter 7 and to an extent in Chapter 8, some of these views have crept in.

In general, I believe that some of this law, particularly at the state level, is repressive, suffocating, unreasonable, unnecessary, and overkill. As Helmer Ekstrom, in his capacity as president of the American Association of Fund Raising Counsel, observed, enforcement of these laws is the equivalent of trying to kill a fly with an elephant gun. The watch-dog agencies continue their pesky practice of causing more harm than good. (The demise of the National Charities Information Bureau—a misnomer of the first order anyway—was celebrated in this quarter.)

Abuses in the world of fundraising occur, to be sure, but nothing to warrant the volume of law crashing down on the nation's charitable organizations, who, after all, are working for the benefit of society and are a core component of our national decision-making and problem-solving structure. Fighting the underbelly of philanthropy is not worth maiming the entire body.

*   *   *

Fundraising professionals tend to be personable, outgoing, and intelligent. They usually are more interesting to be around than those in other fields (lawyers, for example). But many of them collectively have a flaw: a deep desire and ability to avoid, ignore, and deny the law that regulates what they do. Why this is the case is not clear because others serving nonprofit organizations (such as accountants and management consultants) do not share this antipathy. This approach is understandable—few persons like to be regulated by the hand of government—but it is not realistic, given the volume of the regulation with which the fundraising professional (employee or consultant) and the soliciting charitable organizations are required to cope.

As mentioned previously, state law enforcement in this field has become a major regulatory force, and federal regulation on a massive scale has arrived— and few of those affected by all of this seem to understand or even to care!

The fact that this onslaught of regulation and expanded enforcement has not attracted nearly the general attention and concern of fundraising professionals that, in my view, are warranted is partially explicable because of its insidious nature. Some of the philanthropic community's passivity in this regard is forgivable because it has become conditioned to receiving its jolts of new regulation by enactment of federal legislation—usually, tax laws. Fundraising regulation, however, has not always been imposed on the charitable sector by means of a single law. Instead, federal, state, and local legislation, ordinances, and administrative regulation have seeped in, accumulating slowly until they now threaten to reach flood stage. (Will there be regulation by hundreds of counties? Will Website fundraising require multistate registrations?) It is hard to fend off these sources of regulation. They are many and they are powerful (with the regulators thinking always of the public interest, of course).

The fundraising community has yet to launch a coordinated frontal attack on this exploding mass of regulation. From the fundraisers' standpoint, apparently matters will have to get worse before getting better. (Don't expect lawyers to complain.) Hope remains that the world of charitable fundraising will mobilize and successfully fight and squelch this rapacious regulatory impulse.

* * *

Two accolades received as the result of publication of the first edition of *The Law of Fund-Raising* remain too irresistible to not acknowledge here. That book garnered the first annual National Society of Fund Raising Executives (NSFRE)/Staley/Robeson/Ryan/St. Lawrence Research Award, presented in 1991 through the auspices of the NSFRE's Foundation. (The organization now is the Association of Fundraising Professionals [AFP].) This award provided me with the opportunity to address the annual International Conference on Fund Raising of the NSFRE [AFP] that year on the subject of fundraising regulation and its perils. Despite the negativism inherent in the subject, it was a magnificent experience. Then, a year or so later, I received a marvelous letter from a priest at a college who found the book to be "God-sent." (I presume he meant useful.)

I have been presenting some audioconferences for the AFP on the subject of federal and state fundraising regulation. The book reflects the questions that callers have raised and the concerns they have voiced on those occasions.

With this type of support from fundraising professionals and from on high, I have written the third edition of *The Law of Fundraising*, with grand hopes for the fundraising profession as it struggles with the law of fundraising and for the charitable organizations that are fortunate to receive assistance from those in the profession.

* * *

My thanks go to those who have made their interesting and useful contributions to the book: James J. Bausch, James M. Greenfield, Richard F. Larkin, Paul E. Monaghan, Jr., David Ormstead, and Del Staecker. Analysis and commentary I have unburdened myself of in the book should not necessarily be attributed to them.

Thanks as well to those at John Wiley & Sons who have, over the years, seen the editions of this book to completion. In the past, my gratitude has been extended to Marla Bobowick and Martha Cooley. This time, I thank Susan McDermott for everything she has done to facilitate this, the third, edition.

March 2002   BRUCE R. HOPKINS

Contents

**Chapter One   Government Regulation of Fundraising for
Charity: Origins and the Contemporary Climate**   1

§ 1.1   Charitable Sector and American Political Philosophy   2
§ 1.2   Charitable Fundraising: A Portrait   8
§ 1.3   Evolution of Government Regulation of Fundraising   10
§ 1.4   Contemporary Regulatory Climate   14

Chapter Two   Anatomy of Charitable Fundraising   19

§ 2.1   Scope of Term *Charitable* Organization   20
§ 2.2   Methods of Fundraising   23
§ 2.3   Role of Fundraising Professional   32
§ 2.4   Role of Accountant   36
§ 2.5   Role of Lawyer   38
§ 2.6   Viewpoint of Regulators   39
§ 2.7   Viewpoint of a Regulated Professional   46
§ 2.8   Coping with Regulation: A System for the
         Fundraising Charity   48

Chapter Three   States' Charitable Solicitation Acts   51

§ 3.1   Summary   52
§ 3.2   Definitions   52
§ 3.3   Preapproval   61
§ 3.4   Annual Reporting   64
§ 3.5   Exemptions   65
§ 3.6   Regulation of Professional Fundraisers   72
§ 3.7   Regulation of Professional Solicitors   72
§ 3.8   Regulation of Commercial Co-Venturers   73
§ 3.9   Limitations on Fundraising Costs   73
§ 3.10   Availability of Records   75
§ 3.11   Contracts   76
§ 3.12   Registered Agent Requirements   76
§ 3.13   Prohibited Acts   77
§ 3.14   Regulatory Prohibitions   78
§ 3.15   Disclosure Statements and Legends   79

§ 3.16 Reciprocal Agreements   80
§ 3.17 Solicitation Notice Requirements   80
§ 3.18 Fiduciary Relationships   81
§ 3.19 Powers of Attorney General   82
§ 3.20 Miscellaneous Provisions   82
§ 3.21 Sanctions   83
§ 3.22 Other Laws   84

Chapter Four   State Regulation of Fundraising: Legal Issues   **86**

§ 4.1 Regulation of Fundraising Costs   87
§ 4.2 Police Power   106
§ 4.3 Fundraising as Free Speech   110
§ 4.4 Due Process Rights   141
§ 4.5 Equal Protection Rights   143
§ 4.6 Delegation of Legislative Authority   146
§ 4.7 Treatment of Religious Organizations   150
§ 4.8 Other Constitutional Law Issues   161
§ 4.9 Exemption for Membership Groups   162
§ 4.10 Defining *Professional Fundraiser* and *Professional Solicitor*   164
§ 4.11 Direct-Mail Fundraising Guidelines   166
§ 4.12 Registration Fees   169
§ 4.13 Fundraising Over Internet and State Law Restrictions   173
§ 4.14 Conclusions   178

Chapter Five   Federal Regulation of Fundraising   **179**

§ 5.1 IRS Audit Guidelines   181
§ 5.2 Fundraising Disclosure by Charitable Organizations   188
§ 5.3 Charitable Gift Substantiation Requirements   192
§ 5.4 Quid Pro Quo Contribution Rules   199
§ 5.5 Fundraising Disclosure by Noncharitable Organizations   202
§ 5.6 Intermediate Sanctions   205
§ 5.7 Unrelated Business Rules   214
§ 5.8 Exemption Application Process   250
§ 5.9 Reporting Requirements   257
§ 5.10 Lobbying Restrictions   264
§ 5.11 Public Charity Classifications   268
§ 5.12 School Record-Retention Requirements   270
§ 5.13 Fundraising Compensation Arrangements   272
§ 5.14 Charitable Deduction Rules   279
§ 5.15 Commensurate Test   297
§ 5.16 Special Events and Corporate Sponsorships   301
§ 5.17 IRS College and University Examination Guidelines   305
§ 5.18 Postal Laws   308
§ 5.19 Antitrust Laws   316
§ 5.20 Securities Laws   318
§ 5.21 FTC Telemarketing Rule   320
§ 5.22 Internet Communications   321

CONTENTS

§ 5.23   Health Insurance Portability and Accountability
         Act Regulations   325

Chapter Six   Prospective Federal Regulation of Fundraising:
Proposals and Issues   **328**

§ 6.1   Introduction   329
§ 6.2   Major Legislative Proposals   331
§ 6.3   Emerging Issues   336
§ 6.4   Contemporary Developments and Prospects   351

Chapter Seven   Overviews, Perspectives, and Commentaries   **357**

§ 7.1   Charitable Fundraising and the Law   358
§ 7.2   Defining a Fundraising Professional   370
§ 7.3   Professional Solicitors: Role of Telemarketing   374
§ 7.4   Charitable Sales Promotions   376
§ 7.5   Regulation Unlimited: Prohibited Acts   381
§ 7.6   Fundraiser's Contract   385
§ 7.7   A Model Law   391
§ 7.8   State Charity Officials' Concerns about Fundraising Laws   396
§ 7.9   Studies of Fundraising by Professional Solicitors   401
§ 7.10   Charity Auctions   407
§ 7.11   Court Opinion Concerning Sliding-Scale Registration Fees   413
§ 7.12   Fundraising and Private Inurement Doctrine   416
§ 7.13   IRS and Gifts of Used Vehicles   420
§ 7.14   Some Proposals for Relief   423
§ 7.15   A Look Ahead   425

Chapter Eight   Standards Enforcement by Watchdog Agencies   **431**

§ 8.1   Nongovernmental Regulation   431
§ 8.2   Role of an Independent Third-Party
         Monitoring Organization   433
§ 8.3   Standards Applied by Watchdog Agencies   436
§ 8.4   Philanthropic Advisory Service Standards   438
§ 8.5   Evangelical Council for Financial
         Accountability Standards   440
§ 8.6   American Institute of Philanthropy Standards   441
§ 8.7   Standards Enforcement   442
§ 8.8   Commentary   445
§ 8.9   A Watchdog Agency's Response to Commentary   449
§ 8.10   Reply to Response   451

Appendices   **453**

   A   Sources of the Law   453
   B   IRS Form 1023: Application for Recognition
         of Tax Exemption   460

CONTENTS

C   IRS Form 990: Return of Organization Exempt from
Income Tax   469

D   Inflation-Adjusted Insubstantiality
Threshold—$50 Test   488

E   Inflation-Adjusted Insubstantiality
Threshold—$25 Test   489

F   Inflation-Adjusted Low-Cost Article Definition   490

Table of Cases   **491**

Table of IRS Pronouncements   **495**

Table of Cases Discussed in *The Nonprofit Counsel*   **496**

**Table of Private Letter Rulings and Technical Advice
Memoranda Discussed in *The Nonprofit Counsel***   **498**

Index   **499**

Government Regulation of Fundraising for Charity: Origins and the Contemporary Climate

§ 1.1 Charitable Sector and American
     Political Philosophy
§ 1.2 Charitable Fundraising: A Portrait

§ 1.3 Evolution of Government
     Regulation of Fundraising
§ 1.4 Contemporary Regulatory Climate

Charitable organizations are an integral part of U.S. society, and most of them must engage in the solicitation of contributions to continue their work, which benefits that society. Yet both these organizations and their fundraising efforts are under constant criticism and immense regulation. Some of this regulation comes from the many state *charitable solicitation acts*—statutes that are designed to regulate the process of raising funds for charitable purposes. Other aspects of this regulation are found in the federal tax law, with mounting legislation and application of legal principles by the Internal Revenue Service[1] and the courts. Increasingly, other federal laws are contributing to the overall mass of regulation of charitable fundraising.

One of the pressing questions facing philanthropy in the United States is whether this form of regulation is on the verge of stifling or even smothering the nation's independent and voluntary sector. A conflicting attitude is that charity, and fundraising for it, has become a major "industry," and warrants regulation to minimize abuse, protect prospective and actual donors from fraud and other forms of misrepresentation, and reduce waste of the charitable dollar.

Before examining the extent of this regulation, and the accompanying contemporary issues and trends, the role of charitable organizations must be placed in its historical and public policy context.

---

[1] Throughout this book, the Internal Revenue Service is referred to as the IRS.

§ 1.1 CHARITABLE SECTOR AND AMERICAN POLITICAL PHILOSOPHY

Because modern U.S. charity evolved out of the common law of charitable trusts and property, and has been accorded exemption from income taxation since the beginning of federal tax policy and gifts to charity are tax-deductible, the contemporary treatment of charitable organizations is understandably fully reflected in the federal tax laws.

The public policy rationale for exempting organizations from tax is illustrated by the category of organizations that are charitable, educational, religious, scientific, literary and similar entities,[2] and, to a lesser extent, social welfare organizations.[3] The federal tax exemption for charitable and other organizations may be traced to the origins of the income tax,[4] although most of the committee reports accompanying the 1913 act and subsequent revenue acts are silent on the reasons for initiating and continuing the exemption.

One may nevertheless safely venture that the exemption for charitable organizations in the federal tax statutes is largely an extension of comparable practice throughout the whole of history. Congress believed that these organizations should not be taxed and found the proposition sufficiently obvious as not to warrant extensive explanation. Some clues may be found in the definition of charitable activities in the income tax regulations,[5] which include purposes such as relief of the poor, advancement of education or science, erection or maintenance of public buildings, and lessening of the burdens of government. The exemption for charitable organizations is clearly a derivative of the concept that they perform functions which, in the organizations' absence, government would have to perform; therefore, government is willing to forgo the tax revenues it would otherwise receive in return for the public services rendered.

Since the founding of the United States, and earlier in the colonial period, tax exemption—particularly with respect to religious organizations—was common.[6] Churches were openly and uniformly spared taxation.[7] This practice has been sustained throughout the nation's history—not only at the federal but also at the state and local levels, most significantly with property

---

[2] These are the organizations described in section ("§") 501(c)(3) of the Internal Revenue Code of 1986, as amended, Title 26, United States Code ("IRC").

[3] These are the organizations described in IRC § 501(c)(4).

[4] 38 Stat. 166. The income tax exemption for charitable organizations originated in the 1894 statute (28 Stat. 556, § 32), which was declared unconstitutional in *Pollock* v. *Farmers' Loan and Trust Co.*, 157 U.S. 429 (1895). In general, see McGovern, "The Exemption Provisions of Subchapter F," 29 *Tax Law.* 523 (1976); Bittker & Rahdert, "The Exemption of Nonprofit Organizations from Federal Income Taxation," 85 *Yale L. J.* 299 (1976).

A companion book by the author describes the federal tax law as it applies to nonprofit organizations. Chapter 1 of *The Law of Tax-Exempt Organizations*, 7th ed. (New York: John Wiley & Sons, Inc., 1998), contains a fuller analysis of this aspect of public policy and of the independent sector. Throughout this book, the volume on tax-exempt organizations law is referred to as *Law of Tax-Exempt Organizations*.

[5] Income Tax Regulations ("Reg.") § 1.501(c)(3)-1(d)(2).

[6] Cobb, *The Rise of Religious Liberty in America* 482–528 (1902); Lecky, *History of European Morals* (1868).

[7] Torpey, *Judicial Doctrines of Religious Rights in America* 171 (1948).

taxation.[8] The U.S. Supreme Court, in upholding the constitutionality of the religious tax exemption, observed that the "State has an affirmative policy that considers these groups as beneficial and stabilizing influences in community life and finds this classification [exemption] useful, desirable, and in the public interest."[9]

The Supreme Court early concluded that the foregoing rationalization was the basis for the federal tax exemption for charitable entities. In one case, the Court noted that "[e]vidently the exemption is made in recognition of the benefit which the public derives from corporate activities of the class named, and is intended to aid them when not conducted for private gain."[10]

The U.S. Court of Appeals for the Eighth Circuit observed, as respects the exemption for charitable organizations, that "[o]ne stated reason for a deduction or exemption of this kind is that the favored entity performs a public service and benefits the public and relieves it of a burden which otherwise belongs to it."[11] One of the rare congressional pronouncements on this subject is further evidence of the public policy rationale. In its committee report accompanying the Revenue Act of 1938, the House Ways and Means Committee stated:

> The exemption from taxation of money or property devoted to charitable and other purposes is based upon the theory that the government is compensated for the loss of revenue by its relief from financial burden which would otherwise have to be met by appropriations from public funds, and by the benefits resulting from the promotion of the general welfare.[12]

One federal court observed that the reason for the charitable contribution deduction has "historically been that by doing so, the Government relieves itself of the burden of meeting public needs which in the absence of charitable activity would fall on the shoulders of the Government."[13]

Other aspects of the public policy rationale are reflected in case law and the literature. Charitable organizations are regarded as fostering voluntarism and pluralism in the American social order.[14] That is, society is regarded as benefiting not only from the application of private wealth to specific purposes in the public interest but also from the variety of choices made by individual philanthropists as to which activities to further.[15] This decentralized choice-making is arguably more efficient and responsive to public needs than the cumbersome and less flexible allocation process of government administration.[16]

---

[8] *Trustees of the First Methodist Episcopal Church* v. *City of Atlanta*, 76 Ga. 181 (1886); *Trinity Church* v. *City of Boston*, 118 Mass. 164 (1875).

[9] *Walz* v. *Tax Commissioner*, 397 U.S. 664, 673 (1970).

[10] *Trinidad* v. *Sagrada Orden de Predicadores*, 263 U.S. 578, 581 (1924).

[11] *St. Louis Union Trust Company* v. *United States*, 374 F.2d 427, 432 (8th Cir. 1967). Also *Duffy* v. *Birmingham*, 190 F.2d 738, 740 (8th Cir. 1951).

[12] H. R. Rep. No. 1860, 75th Cong., 3d Sess. 19 (1939).

[13] *McGlotten* v. *Connally*, 338 F. Supp. 448, 456 (D.D.C. 1972).

[14] *Green* v. *Connally*, 330 F. Supp. 1150, 1162 (D.D.C. 1971), *aff'd sub nom. Coit* v. *Green*, 404 U.S. 997 (1971).

[15] Rabin, "Charitable Trusts and Charitable Deductions," 41 *N.Y.U.L. Rev.* 912. 920–925 (1966).

[16] Saks, "The Role of Philanthropy: An Institutional View," 46 *Va. L. Rev.* 516 (1960).

The principle of pluralism was stated by John Stuart Mill, in *On Liberty* (1859), as follows:

> In many cases, though individuals may not do the particular thing so well, on the average, as the officers of government, it is nevertheless desirable that it should be done by them, rather than by the government, as a means to their own mental education—a mode of strengthening their active faculties, exercising their judgment, and giving them a familiar knowledge of the subjects with which they are thus left to deal. This is a principal, though not the sole, recommendation of jury trial (in cases not political); of free and popular local and municipal institutions; of the conduct of industrial and philanthropic enterprises by voluntary associations. These are not questions of liberty, and are connected with that subject only by remote tendencies; but they are questions of development. . . . The management of purely local businesses by the localities, and of the great enterprises of industry by the union of those who voluntarily supply the pecuniary means, is further recommended by all the advantages which have been set forth in this Essay as belonging to individuality of development, and diversity of modes of action. Government operations tend to be everywhere alike. With individuals and voluntary associations, on the contrary, there are varied experiments, and endless diversity of experience. What the State can usefully do is to make itself a central depository, and active circulator and diffuser, of the experience resulting from many trials. Its business is to enable each experimentalist to benefit by the experiments of others; instead of tolerating no experiments but its own.

This same theme was echoed by then-Secretary of the Treasury George P. Shultz, in testimony before the House Committee on Ways and Means in 1973, when he observed:

> These organizations ["voluntary charities, which depend heavily on gifts and bequests"] are an important influence for diversity and a bulwark against over-reliance on big government. The tax privileges extended to these institutions were purged of abuse in 1969 and we believe the existing deductions for charitable gifts and bequests are an appropriate way to encourage those institutions. We believe the public accepts them as fair.[17]

The principle of voluntarism in the United States was expressed by another commentator as follows:

> Voluntarism has been responsible for the creation and maintenance of churches, schools, colleges, universities, laboratories, hospitals, libraries, museums, and the performing arts; voluntarism has given rise to the private and public health and welfare systems and many other functions and services that are now an integral part of the American civilization. In no other country has private philanthropy become so vital a part of the national culture or so effective an instrument in prodding government to closer attention to social needs.[18]

---

[17] "Proposals for Tax Change," Department of the Treasury, Apr. 30, 1973, at 72.
[18] Fink, "Taxation and Philanthropy—A 1976 Perspective," 3 *J. C. & U. L.* 1, 6–7 (1975).

Charitable organizations, maintained by tax exemption and nurtured by the ability to attract deductible contributions, are reflective of the American philosophy that all policymaking should not be reposed in the governmental sector. Philanthropy, wrote one jurist,

> is the very possibility of doing something different than government can do, of creating an institution free to make choices government cannot— even seemingly arbitrary ones—without having to provide a justification that will be examined in a court of law, which stimulates much private giving and interest.[19]

The public policy rationale for tax exemption (particularly for charitable organizations) was reexamined and reaffirmed by the Commission on Private Philanthropy and Public Needs in its findings and recommendations in 1975.[20] The Commission observed:

> Few aspects of American society are more characteristically, more famously American than the nation's array of voluntary organizations, and the support in both time and money that is given to them by its citizens. Our country has been decisively different in this regard, historian Daniel Boorstin observes, "from the beginning." As the country was settled, "communities existed before governments were there to care for public needs." The result, Boorstin says, was that "voluntary collaborative activities" were set up to provide basic social services. Government followed later.
>
> The practice of attending to community needs outside of government has profoundly shaped American society and its institutional framework. While in most other countries, major social institutions such as universities, hospitals, schools, libraries, museums and social welfare agencies are state-run and state-funded, in the United States many of the same organizations are privately controlled and voluntarily supported. The institutional landscape of America is, in fact, teeming with nongovernmental, noncommercial organizations, all the way from some of the world's leading educational and cultural institutions to local garden clubs, from politically powerful national associations to block associations—literally millions of groups in all. This vast and varied array is, and has long been widely recognized as, part of the very fabric of American life. It reflects a national belief in the philosophy of pluralism and in the profound importance to society of individual initiative.
>
> Underpinning the virtual omnipresence of voluntary organizations, and a form of individual initiative in its own right, is the practice—in the case of many Americans, the deeply ingrained habit—of philanthropy, of private giving, which provides the resource base for voluntary organizations. Between money gifts and the contributions of time and labor in the form of

---

[19] Friendly, "The *Dartmouth College* Case and the Public–Private Penumbra," 12 *Tex. Q.* (2d Supp.) 141, 171 (1969).
[20] *Giving in America—Toward a Stronger Voluntary Sector* (1975). All quotations herein from the Commission's report are by permission.

volunteer work, giving is valued at more than $50 billion a year, according to Commission estimates.

These two interrelated elements, then, are sizable forces in American society, far larger than in any other country. And they have contributed immeasurably to this country's social and scientific progress. On the ledger of recent contributions are such diverse advances as the creation of noncommercial "public" television, the development of environmental, consumerist and demographic consciousness, community-oriented museum programs, the protecting of land and landmarks from the often heedless rush of "progress." The list is endless and still growing; both the number and deeds of voluntary organizations are increasing. "Americans are forever forming associations," wrote de Tocqueville. They still are: tens of thousands of environmental organizations have sprung up in the last few years alone. Private giving is growing, too, at least in current dollar amounts.[21]

Exemption from taxation for certain types of nonprofit organizations is a principle that is larger than the Internal Revenue Code. Citizens combating problems and reaching solutions on a collective basis—in "association"—are inherent in the very nature of American societal structure. Nonprofit associations are traditional in the United States, and their role and responsibility are not diminished in modern society. Rather, some contend that the need for the efforts of nonprofit organizations is greater today than previously, in view of the growing complexity and inefficiency of government. To tax these entities would be to flatly repudiate and contravene this doctrine that is so much a part of the nation's heritage.

This view of nonprofit associations operating in the United States has been most eloquently stated by Alexis de Tocqueville. He, too, espoused the principle of pluralism, as expressed in his *Democracy in America*:

Feelings and opinions are required, the heart is enlarged, and the human mind is developed only by the reciprocal influence of men upon one another. I have shown that these influences are almost null in democratic countries; they must therefore be artificially created, and this can only be accomplished by associations. . . . A government can no more be competent to keep alive and to renew the circulation of opinions and feelings among a great people than to manage all the speculations of productive industry. No sooner does a government attempt to go beyond its political sphere and to enter upon this new track than it exercises, even unintentionally, an insupportable tyranny; for a government can only dictate strict rules, the opinions which it favors are rigidly enforced, and it is never easy to discriminate between its advice and its commands. Worse still will be the case if the government really believes itself interested in preventing all circulation of ideas: it will then stand motionless and oppressed by the heaviness of voluntary torpor. Governments, therefore, should not be the only active powers; associations ought, in democratic nations, to stand in lieu of those powerful private individuals whom the equality of conditions has swept away.

[21] *Id.* at 9–10.

But de Tocqueville's classic formulation on this subject came in his portrayal of the use by Americans of "public associations" in civil life:

> Americans of all ages, all conditions, and all dispositions constantly form associations. They have not only commercial and manufacturing companies, in which all take part, but associations of a thousand other kinds, religious, moral, serious, futile, general or restricted, enormous or diminutive. The Americans make associations to give entertainments, to found seminaries, to build inns, to construct churches, to diffuse books, to send missionaries to the antipodes; in this manner they found hospitals, prisons, and schools. It is proposed to inculcate some truth or to foster some feeling by the encouragement of a great example, they form a society. Wherever at the head of some new undertaking you see the government in France, or a man of rank in England, in the United States you will be sure to find an association.

One distinguished philanthropist believed that if the leadership of the government and business sectors of U.S. society were to assume the responsibility for support of the private sector, "[w]e would surprise ourselves and the world, because American democracy, which all too many observers believe is on a downward slide, would come alive with unimagined creativity and energy."[22]

Contemporary writing is replete with examples of these fundamental principles. Those who have addressed the subject include:

> . . . the associative impulse is strong in American life; no other civilization can show as many secret fraternal orders, businessmen's "service clubs," trade and occupational associations, social clubs, garden clubs, women's clubs, church clubs, theater groups, political and reform associations, veterans' groups, ethnic societies, and other clusterings of trivial or substantial importance.—Max Lerner

> . . . in America, even in modern times, communities existed before governments were here to care for public needs.—Daniel J. Boorstin

> . . . voluntary association with others in common causes has been thought to be strikingly characteristic of American life.—Merle Curti

> We have been unique because another sector, clearly distinct from the other two [business and government], has, in the past, borne a heavy load of public responsibility.—Richard C. Cornuelle

> The third sector is . . . the seedbed for organized efforts to deal with social problems.—John D. Rockefeller

> . . . the ultimate contribution of the Third Sector to our national life—namely, what it does to ensure the continuing responsiveness, creativity and self-renewal of our democratic society. . . . —Waldemar A. Neilsen

---

[22] Rockefeller 3d, "America's Threatened Third Sector," *Reader's Digest*, Apr. 1978, at 105, 108.

> . . . an array of its [the independent sector's] virtues that is by now fairly familiar: its contributions to pluralism and diversity, its tendency to enable individuals to participate in civil life in ways that make sense to them and help to combat that corrosive feeling of powerlessness that is among the dread social diseases of our era, its encouragement of innovation and its capacity to act as a check on the inadequacies of government.—Richard W. Lyman

> The problems of contemporary society are more complex, the solutions more involved and the satisfactions more obscure, but the basic ingredients are still the caring and the resolve to make things better.—Brian O'Connell[23]

Tax exemption for charities and the charitable contribution deduction, therefore, are not anachronisms, nor are they loopholes. Rather, they are a bulwark against overdomination by government and a hallmark of a free society. These elements of tax law help nourish the voluntary sector of this nation, preserve individual initiative, and reflect the pluralistic philosophy that has been the guiding spirit of democratic America. The charitable deduction has been proven to be fair and efficient, and without it the philanthropic sector of U.S. society would be rendered unrecognizable by present standards.

In sum, there needs to be a realization that the charitable deduction and exemption are predicated on principles that are more fundamental than tax doctrines and are larger than technical considerations of the federal tax law. The federal tax provisions that enhance charity exist as a reflection of the affirmative national policy of not inhibiting by taxation the beneficial activities of qualified organizations striving to advance the quality of the American social order.

Likewise, in the zeal to regulate charitable solicitations, government must take care not to destroy the very institutions that compose the essence of the American societal fabric.

§ 1.2 CHARITABLE FUNDRAISING: A PORTRAIT

About the time the first edition of this book was being written, which largely was during the course of 1989, total giving to charity in the United States was $114.7 billion.[24] Living individuals provided $96.43 billion of this giving, with bequests yielding $6.57 billion; private foundations, $6.7 billion; and corporations, $5 billion. This $114.7 billion was allocated as follows: $54.32 billion for religion, $11.39 billion for human services, $10.69 billion for education, $10.04

---

[23] These quotations in fuller form, and others, are collected in O'Connell, *America's Voluntary Spirit* (New York: The Foundation Center, 1983).

A companion book by the author addresses this point in additional detail, and traces the origins and development of a hypothetical charitable organization to illustrate applicability of the various laws, including fundraising regulation requirements. The book, *Starting and Managing a Nonprofit Organization: A Legal Guide* (3d ed.) (New York: John Wiley & Sons, Inc., 2001), is referred to in this book as *Starting and Managing a Nonprofit Organization*.

[24] *Giving USA* (AAFRC [American Association of Fund Raising Counsel] Trust for Philanthropy, 1990).

billion for health, $7.49 billion for the arts and humanities, $3.62 billion for civic and public causes, and $17.15 billion for other purposes.

By the time this edition of the book was in preparation, total annual charitable giving in the United States was nearly double the 1989 amount. Giving escalated in 2000 to an estimated $203.45 billion. This is growth of 6.6 percent (3.2 percent in inflation-adjusted terms) compared to 1999. Total giving represented 2 percent of the nation's gross domestic product in 2000.

Giving by individuals in 2000 totaled $152.07 billion, an increase from the prior year of 4.9 percent (1.5 percent in inflation-adjusted terms). Gifts from individuals represented 1.8 percent of personal income in 2000. Individual giving constituted 75 percent of total giving in 2000.

Bequests in 2000 were estimated to be $16.02 billion, an increase of 2.6 percent (but −0.7 percent when adjusted for inflation). Gifts by means of bequests represented 8.2 percent of all contributions made in 2000.

Grant-making by private foundations (other than corporation-related foundations) was $24.5 billion in 2000. This represents an increase of 19.6 percent (15.7 percent when adjusted for inflation). These foundation grants accounted for 10.7 percent of total giving in 2000.

Gifts from corporations in 2000 totaled 10.86 billion in 2000, a growth of 12.1 percent (8.4 percent when adjusted for inflation). In that year, corporate charitable contributions were 1.2 percent of corporate pretax income.

Giving to religious organizations reached $74.31 billion in 2000, an increase of 4.3 percent (0.9 percent when adjusted for inflation). Contributions for religious ends accounted for 36.5 percent of all giving in 2000.

In the realm of education, giving totaled $28.18 billion in 2000, an increase of 2.6 percent (−0.7 percent adjusted). Giving to education accounted for 13.9 percent of total giving in 2000.

Giving to health entities in 2000 totaled $18.82 billion, which is a gain of 4.9 percent (1.4 percent adjusted). In 2000, gifts for health purposes represented 9.3 percent of all gifts.

Giving to human services was $17.99 billion in 2000, an increase of 3.6 percent (0.3 percent adjusted). Human services received 8.8 percent of all charitable contributions in 2000.

Giving to the arts, culture, and the humanities reached $11.5 billion in 2000, an increase of 3.9 percent (0.5 percent adjusted). Contributions for these purposes were 5.7 percent of all giving in 2000.

Giving to "public/society benefit" organizations in 2000 was $11.59 billion, an increase of 5.9 percent (2.4 percent adjusted). Giving for these purposes accounted for 5.7 percent of all gifts in 2000.

Giving to environment and wildlife entities increased by 5.7 percent (2.2 percent adjusted), totaling $6.16 billion in 2000. These organizations received 3 percent of all charitable contributions in 2000.

Giving to international affairs reached $2.71 billion in 2000, an increase of 2.6 percent (−0.8 percent adjusted). Giving for international charitable purposes represented 1.3 percent of all giving in 2000.[25]

---

[25] The foregoing data is from *Giving USA 2001* 18–19 (AAFRC Trust for Philanthropy 2001).

As of mid-2001, there were more than 25,000 members of the Association of Fundraising Professionals. The preponderance of these individuals are female (about 17,000) and caucasian (about 19,000). About 2,000 of these members are consultants. Many of those who are employees serve in the fields of education (more than 5,000), human services (about 5,000), health (about 5,000), arts (about 2,000), and religion (more than 1,000). Most members providing data have operating budgets in excess of $1 million; more than 1,000 individuals reported operating budgets exceeding $50 million. Those reporting stated that about 3,500 of them raised between $1–$5 million; about 1,000 members raised $5–$10 million; more than 1,000 members raised $10–$50 million, and about 500 members raised in excess of $50 million.[26]

§ 1.3 EVOLUTION OF GOVERNMENT REGULATION OF FUNDRAISING

"'Helping' Children" was the first line of a front-page *Washington Post* headline, which continued: "Va. Charity Raised Nearly $1 Million, but 93 Percent Went for Expenses."[27] That headline encapsulates one of the prime issues facing America's philanthropic community today: the reasonableness of fundraising costs, as perceived by federal and state legislators and regulators and by the general public—as well as those who manage or are generally responsible for the charities involved. Government regulation of fundraising for charity, while encompassing other matters, is fixed on the single issue of fundraising expenses: their measurement, reporting, and "proper" amount.[28] In fact, the origin of government regulation of fundraising is traceable to the fundraising cost issue; the history of this field of regulation reflects reaction to a pageant of alleged abuses by charities soliciting gifts, each of which featured an ostensibly "high" percentage of fundraising costs.

The *Washington Post* article detailed the direct mail fundraising activities of Children's Aid International (CAI), an organization headquartered in Alexandria, Virginia. According to the account, the organization raised nearly $1 million over a two-year period—"money it promised to spend on packages of high-protein food for malnourished children around the world"—yet expended on "food for children" less than 7 cents out of each dollar raised. The breakdown on CAI's expenditures: 25 percent for management fees, 17 percent for other administrative costs, 51 percent for fundraising, and the balance—7 percent—for "starving children."

---

[26] Data (as of September 6, 2001) provided by the Resource Center of the Association of Fundraising Professionals.

[27] *Wash. Post,* Feb. 7, 1980, at A1. Also see "Correction," *Wash. Post,* May 11, 1980, at 2.

[28] One commentator observed that many states "are beginning to reexamine laws regulating charitable solicitations in the wake of recent disclosures revealing the actual expenditure patterns of many organizations" and concluded: "Of primary concern have been the revelations that in many instances only a small percentage of the money given to further a charitable cause is expended on that cause." Quandt, "The Regulation of Charitable Fundraising and Spending Activities," 1975 *Wis. L. Rev.* 1158, 1159 (1975).

The clear implication gained from the article is that a 93 percent fundraising cost experienced by a charity is "improper," may be close to "fraudulent," and is certainly "wrong." The closest the article came to expressing criticism was its observations that CAI's fundraising costs are "high in comparison with . . . many established charities," and that the fundraising costs of the local United Way agency are less than 7 percent. The organization's defense—unavoidably high startup costs—went unanalyzed and was buried deep in the story. It may be safely assumed that the article helped fuel public suspicion about charitable institutions generally.

Some months before, another *Washington Post* headline had announced: "Pallottines Say Nearly 75% Spent for Fund-Raising."[29] This story featured the celebrated case of the Pallottine Fathers, a Catholic order based in Baltimore, Maryland, that conducted a massive direct-mail fundraising effort and allegedly devoted, in one 18-month period, 2½ cents out of every dollar received for missionary work. Apparently, in 1976, the order raised $7.6 million and spent $5.6 million to do so. This undertaking eventuated in a grand jury investigation, which developed evidence of extensive real estate dealings by the order and a loan to the then governor of the state to help finance his divorce. Little of the proceeds of the order's solicitations went to support Pallottine missions in underdeveloped countries as claimed. The publicity became so intense that the Vatican rector general of the order commanded that Pallottine fundraising activities cease and formed a special investigating commission; the priest who headed the order's fundraising operations was banished from Maryland by the archbishop of Baltimore.

The public had been exposed to a fundraising abuse that was framed in terms of high expenses in relation to contributions received.

Another well-publicized instance of this nature concerned the Freedom Forum International, Inc., formerly the Gannett Foundation. Although this matter did not involve fundraising costs, it focused on ostensibly high administrative expenses; the organization was under investigation by the office of the state attorney general in New York to determine whether these expenses were "imprudent or excessive." A front-page *Washington Post* headline stated: "Neuharth Foundation Spares No Expense," with an inside-page headline trumpeting that "Freedom Forum's Expenses Far Outstrip Its Contributions, Grants."[30] According to this account, in 1991, the foundation incurred expenses of $34.4 million and made grants in the amount of $20.2 million. Office expenses were $17 million and a rooftop conference center accounted for $5.4 million; trustees' fees were higher than the norm, and the chairman's compensation was said to be "more than 10 times greater than is typical in large private foundations."[31] The article related trips of the board of trustees to resort areas for meetings, air travel on first class, and payment of travel expenses of board members and some of their spouses. The newspaper concluded that the organization's "spending

---

[29] *Wash. Post*, Nov. 3, 1977, at C1.

[30] *Wash. Post*, Mar. 23, 1993, at A1. The reference to the "Neuharth Foundation" (not its formal name) reflects the fact that the chairman of the board of the foundation is Allen H. Neuharth, formerly the chief executive of the Gannett Co.; the foundation was established in 1935 by New York newspaper publisher Frank E. Gannett.

[31] *Id.* at A6.

is unusual compared with similar-sized foundations—or even those twice or more its size—which . . . receive their funding from endowments, not from public donations."[32]

Another of these reports focused on the use of candy, gum, and other vending devices by charitable organizations as a fundraising technique. Apparently, the charities often receive small amounts of money in the form of licensing fees, while the vast bulk of the funds flows to those who sell and operate the devices. The arrangement spawned this front-page *Washington Post* headline: "For Charity, Just Drops in the Bucket," followed by "Most of Public's Donations Go to Marketers, Vendors."[33] Although one national charitable organization was said to have received 10 percent of the amount received from dispensers in 1992 ($1.4 million), many receive little or nothing in this fashion. When the charities own the devices directly or in partnership with a vending company, it seems that they regularly receive as much as 15 percent of the gross receipts.[34]

Still another of these episodes, this one involving the Marine Toys for Tots Foundation, was splashed across the front page of the *Washington Post*: "Marines' Toys for Tots Spent Millions on Itself," with the subheadline stating: "Donations Used to Run Charity, Not Buy Gifts."[35] This organization was said to have "collected nearly $10 million in the last two years through a direct-mail campaign, but foundation officials acknowledge that none of the money has gone to buy toys for needy children."[36] When contributions from other sources are taken into account, however, the report added, the three-year-old foundation expended 10 percent of the money raised in its most recent fiscal year for toys for children; the balance was spent on management, fundraising expenses, and promotional materials. The new head of the foundation was quoted as saying that "[m]y goal, and it is an optimistic one, is to have 75 percent of the money raised in the next mailing go toward program expenses, with most of that going to buy toys."[37] Other program activities of the foundation included education of the public on the needs of poor children.

These episodes are, unfortunately, only a few in a series of similar exposés that have haunted legitimate charities for years and helped taint the term *fundraising*.[38] These events also fueled the machinery that has been built

---

[32] *Id.* The three-year investigation of the spending practices of the Forum culminated in an agreement by its trustees to pay to the organization about $174,000 in settlement of claims as to lavish spending; the specifics of the settlement are detailed in XII *Nonprofit Counsel* (No. 2) 1 (Feb. 1995).

[33] *Wash. Post*, Oct. 2, 1993, at A1.

[34] *Id.* at A8. According to this account, some states are investigating this practice, either on the basis of fraud, to force the marketers and vendors to register as professional fundraisers (see § 3.6), or to cause the charities to disclose the percentage of their receipts from this source (see § 3.15).

[35] *Wash. Post*, Feb. 10, 1994, at A1.

[36] *Id.*

[37] *Id.* at A16. Far into the article is this statement: "Part of the problem, according to the foundation, is that it is very expensive to initiate a direct-mail campaign" (*id.*).

[38] Also, "Charity Fund-Raiser, Client Target of Md. Grand Jury Probe." *Wash. Post*, Dec. 12, 1991, at D1; "Solicitors Cash In on Budget Pinch Felt by Nonprofit Groups," *Wash. Post*, Oct. 18, 1982 (Washington Business), at 19; "Many Charity Shows Benefit Mostly the Fundraiser," *Charlotte Observer*, Mar. 22, 1981, at 1.

by and for government to regulate fundraising by charitable organizations. Many an aspiring or practicing politician has parlayed a probe of a charity "scandal" into high office. Thus *Time* magazine, for example, was moved to characterize the Pallottine order scandal as indicative of widespread wrongdoing: "The Pallottine mess provides Americans with one more excuse not to give money to church agencies, even those that make full public accountings"[39] and the "Pallottines were not the only agency that used 80% or more of their [sic] gifts to cover the exorbitant costs of direct mail."[40]

Other episodes—isolated instances having major impact on public and regulatory attitudes—include the solicitation activities of Father Flanagan's Boys Town, the Sister Kenny Foundation, the Police Hall of Fame,[41] the Freedom for All Forever Foundation, the Korean Cultural and Freedom Foundation,[42] and the Children's Relief Fund.[43] Thus, the public media remain alive with one report after another of the alleged misdeeds of charities. Invariably, the scandals involve solicitations of charitable contributions from the general public, by or for organizations that derive their principal support from public giving,[44] with an ostensibly excessive amount of funds devoted to direct-mail campaigns, questionable investments, or administration.[45] At the same time, these developments should be kept in perspective, in that the organizations involved represent only a very small segment of the charitable community.

Thirty-five years ago, federal regulation of fundraising for charity did not exist (other than by means of the charitable contribution deduction), and state regulation in the field was just beginning to flower. Before that time, fundraising regulation (such as it was) was a combination of occasional IRS audits and state attorneys general inquiries, the latter predicated on their historical role of enforcing the requirements imposed on the administration of

[39] "Radix Malorum Est Cupiditas?" *Time,* Jan. 23, 1978, at 75.

[40] "Wrist Tap," *Time,* May 22, 1978, at 64.

[41] In this matter, the Circuit Court of Cook County, Illinois, ordered fundraisers to pay $528,231.52 (including $150,000 in punitive damages) into a trust fund for widows and children of slain law enforcement officers, as the result of a fundraising effort that generated $785,731, of which the fundraisers received $622,000 for costs and compensation. One contract allowed up to 75 percent of total contributions to be consumed in fundraising expenses; the court characterized this and other contracts as authorizing "illegitimate commissions and expenses and were outrageous, unconscionable and an assault upon the public conscience in violation of public policy and Illinois law relating to charitable solicitations." *People of the State of Illinois* v. *Police Hall of Fame, Inc.,* No. 74 CH 5015 (order dated Oct. 19, 1976).

[42] In one instance, the Attorney General of the State of New York charged the Foundation with raising $1,508,256 and expending only $95,674 (6.3 percent) for charitable purposes, and characterized the Foundation as "perpetrating a fraud upon the contributing public." News release dated Feb. 16, 1977.

[43] For a litany of fundraising "abuses," see *Hearing on Children's Charities Before the Subcommittee on Children and Youth of the Senate Committee on Labor and Public Welfare,* 93d Cong., 2d Sess. (1974), chaired by then-Senator Walter F. Mondale. Also *Hearings on Fund Raising By or In Behalf of Veterans Before the House Committee on Veterans' Affairs,* 85th Cong., 2d Sess. (1958); *Hearings on Federal Agencies and Philanthropies Before a Subcommittee of the House Committee on Government Operations,* 85th Cong., 2d Sess. (1958).

[44] E.g., Baldwin, "Ideology By Mail," *New Republic,* July 7 and 14, 1979, at 19.

[45] These developments have spawned articles in the popular media, such as Smith, "New Guidelines for Giving" (subtitled "Our 10 commandments help you separate top charities from wastrels"), *Money,* Dec. 1989, at 141.

charitable trusts.[46] These efforts were based on one premise, and today's vast and growing governmental apparatuses overseeing charitable fundraising continue to be guided by that premise: "The greatest possible portion of the wealth donated to private charity must be conserved and used to further the charitable, public purpose; waste must be minimized and diversion of funds for private gain is intolerable."[47] Out of the inadequacies of common law principles and tax enforcement efforts has grown—and is still growing—a comprehensive supervisory and regulatory program governing the fundraising efforts by charitable organizations at the federal, state, and local levels.

Statutory regulation of fundraising for charity began with codification of the supervisory and investigatory authority of state attorneys general. Thereafter, there came into being provisions seeking to prevent fraud in charitable solicitations or to promote disclosure of information about these solicitations, or both. Municipal ordinances earlier introduced the concepts of licensing and periodic reporting of charities' fund collection activities, and this approach was adopted by the states as their charitable solicitation acts were written. As the years passed, the statutes became more extensive and stringent, the staffs of the regulatory agencies increased, and regulations, rules, and forms unfolded. In general, the call of one observer, who declaimed that the "evils of inefficient or unscrupulous charitable organizations must be attacked head on by strong government regulation,"[48] was heard.

The process is by no means wholly an instance of government regulation increasing merely for the sake of increase. The nature of organized philanthropy and the perception of it by the public, lawmakers, and regulators, have altered dramatically over the past three decades.

§ 1.4 CONTEMPORARY REGULATORY CLIMATE

The number of nonprofit organizations remains steadily on the rise. Most of these are exempt from federal and state income and property taxation, many are eligible to attract tax-deductible contributions, and many utilize preferred postal rates. The involvement of these groups in the day-to-day management and change of American life has never been greater.

Concurrent with the rise in state regulation of fundraising for charity has been a significant upsurge in regulatory activity at the federal level by means of administration of the nation's tax and other laws. The process got under way in 1950, when Congress enacted laws taxing the unrelated business income of otherwise tax-exempt organizations. In 1969, the Internal Revenue Code was sizably thickened by a battery of rules defining, regulating, and taxing private foundations, seeking to prevent self-dealing and large stockholdings and to increase grant-making and public involvement in the affairs of foundations. In

---

[46] Bogert, "Proposed Legislation Regarding State Supervision of Charities," 52 *Mich. L. Rev.* 633 (1954).

[47] Karst, "The Efficiency of the Charitable Dollar: An Unfulfilled State Responsibility," 73 *Harv. L. Rev.* 433–434 (1960).

[48] Quandt, *supra* note 28, at 1187.

1974, Congress authorized the formation, within the IRS, of a formal administrative and regulatory structure, which has stepped up federal oversight and audit of the nation's nonprofit, including charitable, organizations. In 1987, Congress enacted disclosure laws for noncharitable tax-exempt organizations engaged in fundraising; in 1989, the IRS launched a renewed effort to require disclosures in the course of fundraising for charitable organizations; and, in 1993, Congress enacted substantiation and disclosure laws applicable to tax-exempt charitable organizations engaged in fundraising.

Still, notwithstanding this rise in government regulation, all is not well. The malady was evidenced several years ago by a blast from a normally rather staid publication, hurling the following charges against some nonprofit organizations—they:

- Pay their executives fat salaries and allow them generous fringe benefits.

- Award contracts to their trustees and board members.

- Serve as fronts for commercial enterprises with which they have "sweetheart" deals.

- Enjoy special mailing privileges and property tax breaks that give them a competitive edge against tax-paying establishments.

- Engage in wasteful and sometimes fraudulent fundraising with little accountability to the public.[49]

The last allegation is the most immediate concern in relation to this book, but this inventory of wrongdoings is indicative of the state of the nonprofit sector as perceived by some. Public regard is essential to the successful functioning of charitable groups; this regard—which has remained high throughout the country's existence—may be eroding in the face of well-publicized abuses and other pressures.

This, then, is the dilemma of the charities: abuses appear to be on the increase, triggering greater governmental regulation, which makes operations more difficult for authentic charitable undertakings and creates a public climate that is more critical of these undertakings. The inroads being made by a few unscrupulous and fraudulent operators in tapping the resources of philanthropy are threatening to undermine the seriously needed solicitation programs conducted by legitimate charitable organizations.

Coincidentally, the public is demanding greater accountability from nonprofit, principally charitable, organizations. The consumerism movement is causing individual and corporate donors to be more concerned and sophisticated about the uses of their gift dollars. The emphasis now is on disclosure; donors—prospective and actual—are demonstrating greater proclivity to inquire of federal, state, and local agencies, lawmakers, independent "watchdog" agencies, and the philanthropic community itself about the fundraising and fund-expenditure practices of charitable organizations.

---

[49] "For Many, There Are Big Profits in 'Nonprofits,'" *U.S. News & World Rep.*, Nov. 6, 1978, at 45.

GOVERNMENT REGULATION OF FUNDRAISING FOR CHARITY

In this age when the tax bills being levied are rising annually, taxpayers often lack sympathy for and even resent organizations that do not pay tax. Greater understanding of the principle that taxes forgone by one entity must be made up by others may be fostering a public attitude toward nonprofits that is somewhat less lofty than that captured by concepts of voluntarism and pluralism. Likewise, the lure of the standard deduction (now used by a substantial majority of taxpayers) is pulling people away from deductible charitable giving, thereby severing still another traditional nexus between Americans and their charities. The ongoing interest in a flat (or flatter) tax, a national sales or other consumption tax, or a value-added tax is reflective of public interest in a simpler tax system, even though it may lack incentives for charitable giving.

Therefore, in the face of seemingly inadequate disclosure of meaningful information to the public, excessive administrative and fundraising costs, and insufficient portions of the proceeds of charitable gifts passing for charitable purposes, government regulation of fundraising for charity is thriving. Some of the few states that currently lack a comprehensive charitable solicitation act are engaged in the process of trying to enact one. Many states with such a law are contemplating toughening it, either by amending the act or by increasing reporting and similar regulatory burdens. Although the drive for a federal charitable solicitations law has temporarily slowed, the IRS, expanding its administrative capabilities, is quietly but assuredly embarking on a program of substantial regulation in this field, augmented from time to time by Congress. Other federal agencies are creeping into the realm of fundraising regulation.

Despite all this activity, the pressure for still more regulation continues, perhaps ultimately to be manifested in some form of a federal charitable solicitations statute. The drive for such a law, now dormant, may be awaiting only the spark of a well-publicized charity scandal to trigger action by Congress. Part of the interest in a federal law in this field derives from dissatisfaction with the present state-by-state regulatory scheme. Critics voice a variety of complaints about the present reach of federal and state regulation:

- There is no requirement (as there is for private foundations) that public charities annually distribute a portion of their funds for charitable purposes.

- There is no requirement that charities disclose to potential contributors the portion of their funds actually devoted to charitable purposes.

- There are no common requirements regarding state registration, licensing, periodic reporting, disclosure of financial information, and limitations on compensation of fundraisers.

- There are no uniform accounting standards for public charities imposed by law.

- Some charitable and other nonprofit organizations are escaping taxation of unrelated activities, in part by portraying those activities as *fundraising*.

Certain legislative and nonlegislative developments (all discussed in subsequent chapters), however, may mute some of this criticism—for example, development of a new federal annual information return and the mandatory document distribution rules. Also, efforts going forward under the auspices of the National Association of State Charity Officials may result in significant progress toward uniformity of administration and enforcement in this area.

Some parallel developments may also introduce federal law governing charitable solicitations. These concern the fact that, in the wake of more than three decades of experience in strenuously regulating the operations and activities of private foundations, many in the IRS and the Department of the Treasury, and some in Congress, are seriously contemplating comparable regulation of the affairs of one or more categories of public charities.

Unlike the torrents of alleged scandals that preceded the revolution in the federal tax laws pertaining to private foundations, which culminated in a major portion of the Tax Reform Act of 1969, there has been no parade of ostensible abuses warranting strict supervision of public charities. Rather, it appears that this is a last frontier for reformers in the field of charitable organizations and that most of the reforms are being advocated because the statutory basis for the rules is already in place;[50] furthermore, the imposition of these rules on public charities strikes many as the thing to do as a logical extension of existing regulation. Hence, the not-too-far-distant future may well see extension of some of the private foundation restrictions to some or all public charities. (This process got underway in 1996 when Congress enacted the intermediate sanctions rules, which are, in many ways, patterned after the private foundation self-dealing rules.) In this context, the recent attention to the matter of government supervision or regulation of solicitations for charitable contributions may bring some new federally enforced rules to govern the fundraising activities of public charities, that is, as part of a comprehensive effort to regulate public charities to the same degree as is at present the case for private foundations.[51]

Whatever happens, one aspect of the matter is clear: both state and federal regulation are on the rise. The former is not likely to be preempted by the latter, at least not any time soon. Students of this regulatory scene have astutely observed that, "[a]s legislators continue efforts to devise schemes which comply with the [Supreme Court] decision [finding a state charitable solicitation act unconstitutional as violating free speech rights], they will certainly not renounce long-standing views on the important role of state regulation of charitable solicitation."[52]

Probably the most difficult issue to cope with is what all of this regulation is and will be doing to the philanthropic sector. Will fundraising regula-

---

[50] IRC ch. 42.

[51] In early 1989, a task force at the IRS recommended that many of the federal tax rules that are presently applicable only to private foundations be extended to apply to some or all public charities (Report of the IRS Commissioner's Executive Task Force on Civil Penalties). A summary of and commentary on these recommendations appears in VI *Nonprofit Counsel* (No. 5) 1 (1989).

[52] Harris, Holley, & McCaffrey, *Fundraising Into the 1990's: State Regulation of Charitable Solicitation After* Riley 90 (New York: NYU School of Law, 1989).

tion improve the solicitation picture for legitimate charitable groups or will it unduly burden legitimate charitable fundraising efforts? Is there actually sufficient abuse taking place in this area to warrant the massive costs of compliance? Is the overall panoply of nonprofit organizations, tax exemption, and charitable giving becoming an anachronism, in the process of evolutionary departure in the face of the growth of the state? Is fundraising for charity the wave of the past, because charity itself is becoming obsolete?[53]

Although no one knows the answers to these questions, the march of government regulation of fundraising for charity continues inexorably. This new form of regulation, arising from humble origins only a few years ago, is now one of philanthropy's major concerns. How and whether these new governmental policies and philanthropy can coexist will say much about the nature of the charitable sector in the coming years.[54]

[53] See Cook, "Is Charity Obsolete?" *Forbes*, Feb. 5, 1979, at 45. Also Mayer, "End of an Era," *Progressive*, Oct. 1979, at 32; Morganthau, "The Charity Battle," *Newsweek*, May 7, 1979, at 33; Delloff, "Private Philanthropy and the Public Interest," *Christian Century*, Feb. 21, 1979, at 188.
[54] See § 7.15; Hopkins, "Coming: New Law, More Regulation," 20 *Fund Raising Mgmt.* (No. 11) 28 (1990); Hopkins, "Fund-Raisers and The Tax Law: 20 Years' Experience," 20 *Fund Raising Mgmt.* (No. 2) 32 (1989).

CHAPTER TWO

Anatomy of
Charitable Fundraising

§ 2.1 **Scope of Term** *Charitable*
Organization

§ 2.2 **Methods of Fundraising**
   (a) Annual Giving Programs
   (b) Special-Purpose Programs
   (c) Estate Planning Programs
   (d) Reasonable Costs of
       Fundraising
       (i)   Direct Mail Acquisition
       (ii) Direct Mail Renewal
       (iii) Special Events and
             Benefits
       (iv) Corporations and
             Foundations
       (v)   Planned Giving
       (vi) Capital Campaigns

§ 2.3 **Role of Fundraising Professional**
   (a) Types of Professional
       Fundraisers
   (b) Growth toward a Profession
   (c) Professional Associations and
       Societies
   (d) Accreditation and
       Certification
   (e) Standards of Conduct and
       Professional Practice

§ 2.4 **Role of Accountant**
   (a) Generally Accepted
       Accounting Principles
   (b) Financial Reporting
       Requirements
   (c) Financial Management

§ 2.5 **Role of Lawyer**

§ 2.6 **Viewpoint of Regulators**
   (a) 1990 Commentary
   (b) 1992 Commentary
   (c) 2000 Commentary

§ 2.7 **Viewpoint of a Regulated
Professional**

§ 2.8 **Coping with Regulation: A
System for the Fundraising
Charity**
   (a) Monitoring of Compliance
       Requirements
   (b) Public Relations
   (c) Record Keeping and Financial
       Data

Certain basic factual aspects of fundraising for charity warrant summary before an analysis of federal and state governmental regulation of this type of fundraising.[1] These aspects include the types of organizations encompassed by the various laws, the many fundraising techniques, and the roles of those individuals (other than the regulators) who are, along with the charitable organizations themselves, enmeshed in this regulatory process: the fundraising professionals, the lawyers, and the accountants.

---

[1] There are, of course, other forms of fundraising, such as fundraising for political parties and candidates; the governmental regulation of these forms of fundraising is outside the scope of this book.

§ 2.1 SCOPE OF TERM *CHARITABLE* ORGANIZATION

The many laws governing the process of soliciting gifts for charitable purposes principally apply, of course, to charitable organizations and those who raise funds for them. Thus, it is necessary to understand the scope of the term *charitable* organization as it is employed in these laws.

The term *charitable* organization as used in the state charitable solicitation acts has a meaning considerably broader than that traditionally employed under state law and under the federal tax law.[2] Therefore, the soliciting organizations encompassed by the federal definition of what is charitable must comply with the requirements of federal regulation governing fundraising for charity as well as those of the various states (unless specifically exempted). Some organizations, however, are tax-exempt under federal law for reasons other than advancement of charitable purposes but are still obligated to comply with the panoply of state and local charitable solicitation laws.

The federal tax law definition of the term *charitable* is based on the English common law and charitable trust law precepts. The federal income tax regulations recognize this fact by stating that the term is used in its "generally accepted legal sense."[3] At the same time, court decisions continue to expand the concept of *charity* by introducing additional applications of the term.[4] As one court observed, evolutions in the definition of the word *charitable* are "wrought by changes in moral and ethical precepts generally held, or by changes in relative values assigned to different and sometimes competing and even conflicting interests of society."[5]

For the most part, the institutions and other organizations that are subject to these laws are those that have their federal tax status based on their classification as charitable organizations. These are the entities categorized as *charitable, religious, educational, scientific,* or *literary,* or certain organizations that are engaged in fostering national or international amateur sports competition.[6] Each one of these terms is defined in the federal tax law.

The term *charitable* in the federal income tax setting embraces a variety of purposes and activities. These include the relief of the poor and distressed or of the underprivileged,[7] the advancement of religion,[8] the advancement of

---

[2] See § 3.1.

[3] Reg. § 1.501(c)(3)-1(d)(2).

[4] See *Law of Tax-Exempt Organizations,* § 5.5(c), Chapter 6.

[5] *Green* v. *Connally,* 330 F. Supp. 1150, 1159 (D.D.C. 1971), *aff'd sub nom. Coit* v. *Green,* 404 U.S. 997 (1971).

[6] IRC §§ 501(c)(3) and 170(c)(2). The first of these provisions is the basis for federal tax-exempt status; the second is the basis for eligibility for donee status for purposes of the federal charitable contribution deduction. (Most organizations that engage in fundraising are able to offer their donors assurances that their gifts are deductible for federal and state income tax purposes because these organizations are described in IRC § 170(c)(2).) Organizations that are engaged in "testing for public safety" are referenced in IRC § 501(c)(3) but not IRC § 170(c)(2).

The charitable giving rules are summarized at § 5.14.

[7] Reg. § 1.501(c)(3)-1(d)(2). See *Law of Tax-Exempt Organizations,* § 6.1.

[8] Reg. § 1.501(c)(3)-1(d)(2). See *Law of Tax-Exempt Organizations,* § 6.4.

education or science,[9] lessening of the burdens of government,[10] community beautification and maintenance,[11] promotion of health,[12] promotion of social welfare,[13] promotion of environmental conservancy,[14] advancement of patriotism,[15] care of orphans,[16] maintenance of public confidence in the legal system,[17] facilitating student and cultural exchanges,[18] and promotion and advancement of amateur sports.[19]

The federal tax law also encompasses organizations defined as *charitable* in the broadest sense;[20] these include entities considered *educational, religious,* and *scientific*. Nonetheless, the term *charitable* as used in the federal tax context—including *education,*[21] *religion,*[22] and *science*[23]—is not as broad as the concept of tax exemption. Certainly the term is not as far-ranging as the concept of nonprofit organizations. Stated another way, nonprofit organizations are not necessarily tax-exempt, and tax-exempt organizations are not always charitable.

To be tax-exempt under federal law, a nonprofit organization must satisfy the rules pertaining to at least one of the categories of tax-exempt organizations set forth in the Internal Revenue Code.[24] In addition to those organizations that are recognized as charitable entities,[25] the realm of tax-exempt organizations under federal law embraces social welfare (including advocacy) organizations,[26] labor organizations,[27] trade and professional associations,[28] social clubs,[29]

---

[9] Reg. § 1.501(c)(3)-1(d)(2). See *Law of Tax-Exempt Organizations,* § 6.5.

[10] Reg. § 1.501(c)(3)-1(d)(2). See *Law of Tax-Exempt Organizations,* § 6.3.

[11] Rev. Rul. 78-85, 1978-1 C.B. 150. See *Law of Tax-Exempt Organizations,* § 6.6.

[12] Rev. Rul. 69-545, 1969-2 C.B. 117. See *Law of Tax-Exempt Organizations,* § 6.2.

[13] Reg. § 1.501(c)(3)-1(d)(2). See *Law of Tax-Exempt Organizations,* § 6.6.

[14] Rev. Rul. 76-204, 1976-1 C.B. 152. See *Law of Tax-Exempt Organizations,* § 6.10(a).

[15] Rev. Rul. 78-84, 1978-1 C.B. 150. See *Law of Tax-Exempt Organizations,* § 6.10(b).

[16] Rev. Rul. 80-200, 1980-2 C.B. 173. See *Law of Tax-Exempt Organizations,* § 6.10(f).

[17] *Kentucky Bar Foundation, Inc.* v. *Commissioner,* 78 T.C. 921 (1982). See *Law of Tax-Exempt Organizations,* § 6.10(f).

[18] Rev. Rul. 80-286, 1980-2 C.B. 179. See *Law of Tax-Exempt Organizations,* § 6.10(f).

[19] *Hutchinson Baseball Enterprises, Inc.* v. *Commissioner,* 73 T.C. 144 (1979), *aff'd,* 696 F.2d 757 (10th Cir. 1982). See *Law of Tax-Exempt Organizations,* § 6.10(c). Also IRC § 501(j). See *Law of Tax-Exempt Organizations,* § 10.2.

[20] The U.S. Supreme Court held that all organizations, encompassed by IRC § 501(c)(3), including those that are "educational" and "religious," are "charitable" in nature for federal tax law purposes (*Bob Jones University* v. *United States,* 461 U.S. 574 (1983)).

[21] See *Law of Tax-Exempt Organizations,* Chapter 7.

[22] *Id.* Chapter 8.

[23] *Id.* Chapter 9.

[24] The Internal Revenue Code provides for tax-exempt status under IRC § 501(a) for those nonprofit organizations, that are listed in IRC § 501(c). See *Law of Tax-Exempt Organizations,* Chapters 12–18. Other categories of tax-exempt organizations are described in IRC §§ 521, 526, 527, and 528. See *Law of Tax-Exempt Organizations,* Chapters 17, 18. Governmental entities are also tax-exempt. See *Law of Tax-Exempt Organizations,* §§ 6.9, 18.7.

[25] That is, organizations described in IRC § 501(c)(3).

[26] Organizations described in IRC § 501(c)(4). See *Law of Tax-Exempt Organizations,* Chapter 12. Social welfare organizations are the type of noncharitable organizations that are most likely to be subject to the state charitable solicitation acts.

[27] Organizations described in IRC § 501(c)(5). See *Law of Tax-Exempt Organizations,* § 15.1.

[28] IRC § 501(c)(6). See *Law of Tax-Exempt Organizations,* Chapter 13.

[29] IRC § 501(c)(7). See *Law of Tax-Exempt Organizations,* Chapter 14.

fraternal organizations,[30] veterans' organizations,[31] and political organizations.[32] Generally, with the exception of veterans' organizations,[33] contributions to these organizations are not deductible as charitable gifts.[34]

In general, the sweep of the states' charitable solicitation acts is not so
broad as to encompass all nonprofit organizations, nor is it so broad as to encompass all tax-exempt organizations. For example, these laws do not normally
embrace trade and professional associations[35] that are financially supported
largely by dues (payments for services), rather than by contributions. Likewise,
they do not normally cover private foundations,[36] which, while charitable in
nature, do not usually solicit contributions. By contrast, these laws are likely to
be attributable to organizations (other than purely charitable ones) that are
tax-exempt but cannot attract deductible contributions,[37] or are eligible to receive deductible contributions but are not usually regarded as charitable organizations, such as veterans' groups.[38]

Generally, the organizations that need to be concerned with the state
charitable solicitation laws are the following:

- Churches and other membership and nonmembership religious
  organizations[39]

- Educational institutions, including schools, colleges, and universities[40]

- Hospitals and other forms of health care providers[41]

- Publicly supported charitable organizations[42]

- Social welfare organizations[43]

Consequently, an organization that is recognized as a charitable entity
under federal tax law, and that engages in fundraising, is (unless specifically exempted)[44] assuredly subject to the state charitable solicitation laws. These laws
may, however, also encompass other types of tax-exempt organizations that solicit contributions.[45]

---

[30] Organizations described in IRC § 501(c)(8), (10). See *Law of Tax-Exempt Organizations*, § 18.4.

[31] IRC § 501(c)(4) or § 501(c)(19). See *Law of Tax-Exempt Organizations*, Chapter 12, § 18.10.

[32] IRC § 527. See *Law of Tax-Exempt Organizations*, Chapter 17.

[33] Contributions to veterans' organizations are deductible by reason of IRC § 170(c)(3).

[34] Only organizations described in IRC § 170(c) are eligible charitable donees. See *supra* note 6.

[35] See *supra* note 28.

[36] See Hopkins and Blazek, *Private Foundations: Tax Law and Compliance* (John Wiley & Sons, 1997);
Hopkins and Blazek, *The Legal Answer Book for Private Foundations* (John Wiley & Sons, 2001).

[37] E.g., organizations described in IRC § 501(c)(4). See *supra* notes 26 and 34.

[38] IRC § 501(c)(19). See *supra* note 31.

[39] IRC § 170(b)(1)(A)(i). See *Law of Tax-Exempt Organizations*, Chapter 8.

[40] IRC § 170(b)(1)(A)(ii). See *Law of Tax-Exempt Organizations*, Chapter 7.

[41] IRC § 170(b)(1)(A)(iii). See *Law of Tax-Exempt Organizations*, § 6.2.

[42] IRC §§ 170(b)(1)(A)(vi) (IRC § 509(a)(1) and 509(a)(2)). See *supra* note 36, Chapters 15 and
___, respectively.

[43] See *supra* notes 26 and 34.

[44] See § 3.5.

[45] See § 3.2(a).

§ 2.2 METHODS OF FUNDRAISING

Critical to an understanding of government regulation of charitable fundraising is an understanding of *fundraising* itself.[46]

Every charitable organization is entitled to receive and, indeed, welcomes support in the form of contributions. Contributed funds can be used only to support the goals and objectives that are consistent with the organization's stated mission—usually, to provide a benefit to others. When goals, mission, and public benefits are communicated to the public as institutional needs, they can stimulate gift support. Replies are acts of philanthropy that are motivated by numerous factors, including a sincere concern and a willingness to help others, to improve quality of service, or to advance knowledge. Such voluntary responses, whether of time, talent, or treasure, uplift the human spirit because they are directed to a charitable organization.

Requests for contributions are conducted by one or more fundraising methods. Fundraising is, in itself, a unique form of communication that "promotes" and "sells" the product (cause) and "asks for the order" at the same time. There is a common perception that there is a single type of activity called fundraising and that all gifts are made in cash. Most regulatory approaches seem founded on this perception, as are public attitudes—both positive and negative—toward charitable solicitations. In fact, charitable organizations employ several methods and techniques to solicit contributions. Gifts can be in several forms (such as cash, securities, personal property, and real estate), all of which are embraced within the term *fundraising*. The one feature shared equally is the objective—to ask for a gift that benefits someone else.

Asking is simple. There are only three ways: by mail, by telephone, or in person.[47] Mail solicitation is 16 times less effective than personal contact, but most fundraising uses this most impersonal of approaches. Organizing institutions and agencies to perform fundraising is much more complex and requires the careful, and sometimes simultaneous, application of many individual methods of solicitation by volunteers and employees working together. Each individual method of fundraising has its own characteristics regarding suitability for use, public acceptance, potential or capacity for success (gift revenue), and cost-effectiveness. Likewise, the reporting and enforcement aspects of regulatory systems—to be fair—should distinguish between the varieties of fundraising technique and their performance.[48]

---

[46] This analysis, and the one in § 2.3, was prepared by James M. Greenfield, FAHP, CFRE, author of *Fund-Raising: Evaluating and Managing the Fund Development Process, Second Edition* (New York: John Wiley & Sons, 1999), and *Fund-Raising Fundamentals: A Guide to Annual Giving for Professionals and Volunteers* (New York: John Wiley & Sons, 1994). His contribution is gratefully acknowledged by the author. The footnotes to §§ 2.2 and 2.3 were added by the author.

[47] This statement, in the modern era, seems quaint. This comment is not intended to be critical, but rather to illustrate how dramatically fundraising (and other) communications have changed in recent years. Thus, other ways a charitable organization can ask for a gift are by means of a Website, by e-mail, or by facsimile.

[48] See § 4.1.

The methods of asking are best understood by dividing them into three program areas: annual giving, special-purpose, and estate planning. The "pyramid of giving" (see page 33) illustrates how each area functions to perform individual tasks and to aid the progression of donor interest and involvement leading to increased gift results for each chosen charitable organization. Fifteen methods of fundraising are encompassed within the three program areas.

(a) Annual Giving Programs

The basic concept of annual giving programs is to recruit new donors and renew prior donors, whose gifts provide for annual operating needs. Some programs require only a staff professional to manage, but most require both staff and a volume of volunteer leaders and workers. Charities frequently conduct two or more forms of annual solicitation within a 12-month period; the net effect is to contact the same audience with multiple requests within the year. Churches make appeals weekly through the collection plate; United Way uses payroll deductions to ensure frequent payments. Such gift support is basic to the financial success of these organizations; their needs are urgent, and the funds are consumed immediately upon receipt.

The design behind the choice of any of these several methods offered during any one year is always the same—to recruit new donors and to renew (and upgrade) the gifts of the prior year's donors. Some donors prefer one method of giving over all others because they are most comfortable with that style. For example, benefit events are popular because they include attendance at social activities. Multiple-gift requests to present donors will increase net revenues faster than efforts to acquire new donors, because present donors are the best prospects for added gifts. No organization will be able to use every fundraising method (chiefly because of donor resistance or saturation), so rational selections are required.

A brief explanation of each method and its special value to the annual giving process is presented as follows, arranged in the order of least productive to most efficient.

1. *Direct Mail/Donor Acquisition.* Direct mail/donor acquisition fundraising uses direct mail response advertising (usually third class, bulk rate) in the form of letters to individuals who are not present donors, inviting them to participate at modest levels. One of the best methods to find and recruit new contributors, this program is perhaps best known to the public because people receive so many mail requests. Usually a charity can expect only a 1 to 2 percent rate of return on "bulk mail requests," but this is considered satisfactory. Successful "customer development" may require an investment of from $1.25 to $1.50 to raise $1.00, a formula well accepted in for-profit business circles but often criticized within charitable organizations. The value of new donors is not their first gift, however, but their potential for repeat gifts. Such first-time donors, with care and attention, can become future leaders, volunteer workers, and even benefactors.

§ 2.2   METHODS OF FUNDRAISING

The mail process includes (a) selecting audiences likely to respond to this organization;[49] (b) buying, renting, or leasing up-to-date mailing lists of audiences selected; (c) preparing a package containing a letter signed by someone whose name is recognized by most people, a response form with gift amounts suggested, a reply envelope, and a brochure or other information about the charity or the program offered for gift support; (d) scheduling the "mail drop" during the most productive times in the year for mail solicitation (October through December, March through June); and (e) preparing for replies, including gift processing, setting up donor records, and sending "thank you" messages.

2.   *Direct Mail/Donor Renewal.*   Direct mail/donor renewal fundraising is used to ask previous donors, who are the best prospects for annual giving, to give again. If some contact has occurred since the first gift, such as a report on the use of their gifts to render services to others, it is likely that 50 percent of prior donors will give again—at a minimum cost to the organization of a renewal letter. A feature called "upgrading," a request asking donors to consider a gift slightly above their last gift, works 15 percent of the time, and has the added value of helping preserve the current giving level. Prior donor support is predictable income for organizations that can estimate their ability to meet current needs because of committed levels of proven donor support.

3.   *Telephone and Television.*   Telephone calls to prospects and donors permit dialogue and are more successful than direct mail. Public response is not high (around 5 to 8 percent), perhaps because of the intrusive nature of phone calls and their frequent use by for-profit organizations. Television solicitation is more distant but is the best visual medium to convey the message (televangelists already have perfected this technique[50]). Both methods are expensive to initiate and require the instant response of donors (only 80 percent of pledge collections may be realized).

4.   *Special and Benefit Events.*   Special and benefit events are social occasions that use ticket sales and underwriting to generate revenue but incur direct costs for production. While popular, especially with volunteers, these events are typically among the most expensive and least profitable methods of fundraising in practice today. Events include everything from a bake sale and car wash to golf tournaments and formal balls. If well-managed, they should produce a 50 percent net profit. While most fundraising staff deplore the energy and hours required to support events, their greater value is in public relations visibility, both for the charity and its volunteers.

5.   *Support Group Organizations.*   Support groups are used to organize donors in a quasi-independent association around the charitable organization. Membership dues and sponsorship of events are used as revenue sources as well as "friend-raising" opportunities. Support groups are like civic organizations,

---

[49] The increasing sophistication of database companies is allowing them to target mailings more specifically to Americans identified by their racial or ethnic backgrounds; this practice is raising a host of ethical concerns (see, e.g., "The Ethics of 'Ethnicated' Mailing Lists," *Wash. Post*, Nov. 14, 1992, at A1).

[50] But see "Evangelists' Electronic Collection Plates Making Fewer Rounds," *Wash. Post*, Dec. 20, 1992, at A3.

with a board of directors and active committees, except that their purposes are committed to one charity (e.g., an alumni association). Valuable for their ability to develop committed annual donors, to organize and train volunteers, and to promote the charity in the community, support groups also require professional staff management. Smaller charities should consider support groups to secure annual gifts as well as the volunteers needed to produce benefit events and to aid the organization in other ways when needed.

6. *Donor Clubs and Associations.* Donor clubs and associations are donor-relations vehicles, similar to support groups, that are designed to enhance the link between donor and charity, thereby helping preserve annual gift support. Most organizations use higher gift levels (say, $1,000 and up) and prestigious names (e.g., President's Club) to separate these donors from all others. The clubs' selectivity and privileges help justify the higher gift required, which is rewarded by access to top officials and other benefits. Donor club members also represent a concentration of major gift prospects, whom charitable organizations treat as benefactors, and whose cultivation will pay dividends in the future.

7. *Annual Giving Campaign Committees.* Campaign committees are volunteer committees of peers using in-person solicitation methods to recruit the largest and most important annual gifts. The performance of such a committee will be the most lucrative of all the aforementioned annual giving methods. The committee is structured as a true campaign, with a general chairperson and division leaders for individual, business, and corporate prospects. After making their own contributions, each volunteer may be assigned from three to five prospects to visit and with whom to discuss an annual gift decision. Donors are receptive because someone they respect has taken the time to call on them on behalf of an organization. The volunteers also can report that they have made their own personal contributions.

8. *Other Annual Giving Methods.* Several other methods can also develop gift support on an annual basis:

(a) *Commemorative Giving.* A commemorative gift to a charity has the dual effect of honoring the recipient and aiding the donor's favorite charity at the same time. Most often, these gifts are memorials following the death of a family member, friend, or business colleague, and are directed by the family to their favorite organization. Commemorative gifts can also be given to mark a birthday, anniversary, promotion, graduation, or other important occasion, or to honor a friend, physician, or teacher.

(b) *Gifts in Kind.* Instead of cash, donors can make gifts of goods and services that can be used by the recipient organizations (such as Goodwill Industries, Salvation Army, St. Vincent de Paul Society) in their program activities. Businesses often donate products or excess merchandise, either for direct use (food or equipment) or for use as a benefit door prize or auction or raffle item.

(c) *Advertisements in Newspapers/Magazines.* Advertising, while the least likely solicitation method to stimulate a response, can promote an organization, a special campaign, a form of giving, or other purpose. Usually, direct mail or telephone follow-up is required to maximize the gift response from such multimedia techniques.

(d) *Door-to-Door and On-Street Solicitation.*   While on-street solicitation is less common today because of limited volunteer time, some organizations benefit from "cold calls" during neighborhood drives because the public recognizes the organization's name (e.g., the American Cancer Society's "Women's Walk") or has come to trust the organization's purposes (e.g., the Salvation Army's bellringers, chimney box, and red pot for collections at Christmastime). The difficulty in recent years has been abuse of public trust by a few organizations or individuals who "hustle" the public too hard or who run afoul of local regulations restricting solicitation, such as in airports and other public areas.

(e) *Sweepstakes and Lotteries.*   Where legal, charities can benefit from such forms of public solicitation as sweepstakes and lotteries. Most charities, however, prefer to avoid areas of questionable practice, which too often are viewed by the public as forms of gambling. Bingo remains the exception, but it too is carefully regulated and supervised.

(f) *Las Vegas and Monte Carlo Nights.*   Again, where legal, Las Vegas and Monte Carlo nights can develop gift revenues for a charity. State and local regulations for conduct of these events are strict, and may include a 5 to 10 percent fee taken from net proceeds. Like other special and benefit events, "casino" nights are hard to manage profitably because of high direct costs and overhead expenses.[51]

(g) *Mailings of Unsolicited Merchandise.*   The theory behind the practice of mailing unsolicited merchandise is that it engenders guilt in the recipients—presumably, recipients would feel guilty keeping something of value sent to them and thus would be more likely to respond with gift support. This type of method is less popular today because postage and material costs, along with public resistance (lack of response), are rising.

(h) *In-Plant Solicitations.*   Public solicitation in the workplace is usually controlled by the employer. Where in-plant solicitations are permitted, some employees resist being "cornered" and "pressured" to give. Usually, only United Way or other federated campaigns have been allowed into the workplace for this type of solicitation.

---

[51] In addition, local governments are increasing their regulation of this form of gambling. In general, "Charity Gambling: Who Gets the Take?," *Metro. Times*, Aug. 22, 1994, at C4 *(The Washington Times)*; Gattuso, "What's Ahead for Charity Gambling?," 24 *Fund Raising Mgmt.* (No. 7) 19 (1993); "Md. Slot Machines Raise Money—and Questions," *Wash. Post*, Sept. 27, 1993, at D1; "Charity Casinos Parlayed into Big Business," *Wash. Post*, Sept. 26, 1993, at B1; "Charities' Big Gamble" (subtitled "Games of chance raise millions for good works, but questions of fraud could tar non-profits' image, prompt more regulation"), V *Chron. of Phil.* (No. 15) 1 (May 18, 1993); "States Say Abuse Is Widespread in Charity Gains," II *Chron. of Phil.* (No. 10) 1 (Mar. 6, 1990). One newspaper account stated that "charitable fund-raising [by this method] has lost its innocence. The church basement roulette games that long have been a staple of charitable fundraising in . . . [a county near Washington, D.C.] have grown in recent years into a multi-million-dollar industry that is siphoning money from the people who are supposed to benefit into the pockets of professional gamblers . . ." ("P.G. Plays Weak Hand against Charity Casinos," *Wash. Post*, Feb. 20, 1993, at D1).

(i) *Federated Campaigns.*   Federated campaigns are communitywide solicitations organized to support a large number of civic, social, and welfare organizations in the community with a single, once-a-year fund drive. Public acceptance is high, management and fundraising costs are low (under 20 percent), and a "campaign period" is observed. Federated campaigns, such as those of the United Way and the Combined Federal Campaign, are usually directed to local corporations for annual gifts and to their employees (or to government employees), who are allowed to use payroll deduction. These campaigns require cooperation from those charitable organizations being supported, who must refrain from their own solicitations during the campaign period.

(b) Special-Purpose Programs

A successful base of annual giving support permits the charitable organization to conduct more selective programs of fundraising that will secure major gifts, grants, and capital campaigns toward larger and more significant projects. A request for large gifts differs from annual gift solicitation because the request is for a "one-time" gift, allows a multiyear pledge, and is directed toward one specific project or urgent need. Likely donors are skillful "investors" who will respond to a major gift request only after researching the organization and determining whether the project justifies their commitment. If the request fails their examination, it is likely to receive only token (or no) support.

Following is a brief explanation of how the three forms of special-purpose fundraising are employed.

1. *Major Gifts from Individuals.*   It takes courage to ask someone for $1 million. Current and committed donors are the best prospects. Before the request is made, careful research should ascertain the prospect's financial capability, enthusiasm for the organization, preparedness to accept this special project, and likely response to the "team" assembled to make the call. Also important is an early resolution of the donor recognition to be offered (election to the board, name on a building, or both). The project must be a "big idea," worthy of the level of investment required, perceived as absolutely essential, and a unique opportunity offered only once. In short, major gift solicitations should be performed as though they are a request for the largest and most significant gift decisions from these donors at this point in their lives.

2. *Grants from Government Agencies, Foundations, and Corporations.*   Separate skills and tools are required to succeed at grant-seeking. Grants are institutional decisions to provide support based on published policy and guidelines that demand careful observance of application procedures and deadlines. The decision is made by a group of people and, because of limited dollars, only one grant may be given for every 25 to 50 requests received. Usually, for a grant proposal to be accepted, the organization and its project must match perfectly the goals of the grantor.

3. *Capital Campaigns.*   A capital campaign is clearly the most successful, cost-effective, and enjoyable method of fundraising yet invented. Why? Because

■   28   ■

everyone is working together toward the same goal, the objective is significant to the future of the organization, major gifts are required (all through personal solicitation), start and end dates are goal markers, activities and excitement exist, and more. A capital campaign is the culmination of years of effort, both in design and consensus surrounding the organization's master plan for its future, which depends on experienced volunteers and enthusiastic donors. When everything comes together in a capital campaign, the result is success.

(c) Estate Planning Programs

An increasingly active area of fundraising involves gifts made by a donor now, to be realized by the charitable organization in the future. The term *gift planning* best describes this concept. These gifts either transfer assets to the charity now, in exchange for the donor's retaining an income for life, or transfer the remaining assets at the donor's death. This planning allows donors to remember their favorite charities in their estate and to plan gifts of their assets, now or at death. These gift decisions are usually made by donors who have some history of involvement and participation with the charities named in their estate and speak loudly of the donors' trust and confidence in the organizations and their future.

The four broad areas of planned giving are guided by income tax, gift tax, and estate tax law, plus layers of changing regulations. Estate planning is perhaps the single area of fundraising in which the tax consequences of giving are most prominent.

1. *Wills and Bequests.* The easiest way for donors to leave a gift is to specify in their will or living trust that "ten percent (10%) of the residue of my estate is to go to XYZ Charity." Organizations should provide donors with suitable but simple bequest language, to encourage them to include the organization in their will. These gifts may be outright transfers from the estate or may involve funding by means of a charitable trust created by a will.

2. *Pooled Income Funds.* A "starter gift" to show donors how gift planning works can be made by means of a pooled income fund. Individuals may join a "pool" of other donors whose funds are commingled, with interest earnings paid out according to a pro rata shares distribution based on the annual value of the invested funds. Similar to mutual funds, pooled income funds require donors to execute a simple trust agreement and transfer cash or securities to the charity, which adds their gift to the pooled income fund. Upon a donor's death, the value of his or her shares is removed from the fund and transferred to the charity for its use.

3. *Charitable Remainder Gifts.* Major gifts of property with appreciated value make excellent assets to transfer to a charitable organization in exchange for a retained life income based on the value of the gift at the time of transfer. These gifts are especially valuable to donors planning their retirement income and distribution of their assets. The structure of the trust agreement may be as a unitrust, annuity trust, or gift annuity. While the legal

structure of the three agreements is slightly different, the charity in each case assumes responsibility to manage the asset or its cash value and to pay the donor an income of 5 percent at least annually.

4. *Life Insurance/Wealth Replacement Trust.* Any individual may name his or her favorite charity as a beneficiary, in whole or in part, to a life insurance policy. This decision qualifies the value as a charitable contribution deduction. Some charitable organizations offer their own life insurance product, and premiums paid to the charity represent annual gifts for tax-deduction purposes. The charity uses the funds to pay premiums on a policy it owns, which names the charity as the sole beneficiary. The advantage to the donor is that the charity recognizes the death benefit value as the amount "credited" as a gift by the donor. The wealth replacement trust concept is linked to a charitable remainder trust; the donor uses the annual income to purchase a life insurance policy, usually for the value of the asset placed in trust, and names his or her heirs as beneficiaries, thus transferring to heirs the same value upon the donor's death.

(d) Reasonable Costs of Fundraising

Few charitable organizations are able to make use of every fundraising technique. Usually, only mature fund development programs in established charities have the necessary numbers of volunteers, donors, and prospective donors as well as an adequate professional and support staff, budgets, and operating systems to coordinate such a massive effort with efficiency.

Most organizations begin with the need to define the audiences who will support their mission and to seek their first gifts. Thereafter, attention is focused on securing annual operating revenues to stay in business, which requires constant attention to the annual giving solicitation methods. The choice of method(s) depends on several factors, including the scope of the organization's mission and the cost of fundraising. If the cause is national, the broadest solicitation outreach will be needed through direct mail, which is most expensive. If the purpose is local, concentration can expand audience selection to everyone in the area—again, expensive. In time, major gifts, grant requests, capital campaigns, and estate planning may be included to balance overall program productivity and cost-effectiveness.

By contrast, several types of organizations have the ability to engage in multiple fundraising methods simultaneously and with high profitability. Colleges pursue alumni constantly (annual gift, class gift, reunion gift, capital campaign, estate planning, plus requests for time and talent in leadership roles and as volunteers and workers). Private colleges do not approach the general public, but they often expand their solicitations to "anyone who walked across the campus one day." Other organizations must appeal to the general public because their cause, as well as their needs, requires them to reach out. Thus, advocacy groups combine fundraising with a call to action; churches, with the offer of a way to salvation; hospitals, with wellness education and provision of direct care; and so on.

Whatever the organization, its choice of fundraising method carries with it a differing cost-effectiveness performance. "Charities are not the same in how they perform fundraising nor does fundraising perform the same for every charity. Equally, efficient fundraising is not the measure of the importance or value of the cause."[52]

Choice of method requires attention to cost-effectiveness measurement. It costs money to raise money, but what are the reasonable cost levels? Studies by the American Association of Fund-Raising Counsel, the National Society of Fund-Raising Executives (now the AFP), and the Association for Healthcare Philanthropy reveal that, on average, it costs 20 cents to raise one dollar after a solicitation program has been in operation for a minimum of three years. Reasonable cost levels for various methods of fundraising are given as follows.

(i) Direct-Mail Acquisition.   To make the first sale, whether in for-profit sales or nonprofit fundraising, is expensive. Direct-response advertising is a popular and effective form of direct-mail acquisition used by both private and nonprofit enterprises. Reasonable cost levels for a nonprofit organization should not exceed $1.50 per dollar raised, with a corresponding 1 percent or higher level of participation (rate of return).

(ii) Direct-Mail Renewal.   Once a donor is acquired, the effort to renew this gift, either in a few months or next year, will be more cost-effective. Renewal costs should be within 20 cents per dollar raised, with a 50 percent renewal rate among prior donors.

(iii) Special Events and Benefits.   While highly popular with volunteers, benefits are expensive to conduct and usually are valuable for reasons other than raising money. A net goal of 50 cents per dollar raised against direct costs is the recommended guideline.

(iv) Corporations and Foundations.   Solicitation of corporate and foundation support is a highly selective and competitive method of fundraising. Expenses should not exceed 20 cents per dollar raised.

(v) Planned Giving.   Planned gifts, being complex and individually designed, require time to prepare and plenty of patience to mature. An average of 25 cents per dollar raised is the recommended guideline.[53]

(vi) Capital Campaigns.   The most profitable, cost-effective, and productive fundraising method available is capital campaigns. These campaigns focus on big ideas and solicit big gifts, require personal leadership and solicitation by volunteers, have professional staff direction, and usually yield good results. Capital campaign costs should not exceed 5 to 10 cents per dollar raised.

---

[52] Greenfield, "Fund-Raising Costs and Credibility: What the Public Needs to Know," *NSFRE J.,* Autumn 1988, at 49.

[53] Fink and Metzler, *The Costs and Benefits of Deferred Giving* (New York: Columbia University Press, 1982).

Regulations that focus on costs compared with gift revenues treat unfairly the realities of fundraising performances by charitable organizations, whether old or new. Simple bottom-line analysis is inadequate, can be misleading, and seriously fails to understand the nature of individual organizations, their unique environment, and their separate capacity for raising charitable contributions.

New, startup efforts (even for established charities) to begin a fundraising program are not likely to meet these "reasonable cost" guidelines for at least three years. Charities representing new causes or previously unknown or unpopular needs will be even less successful. The critical factors inherent in success—environment and capacity—also must reflect the realities surrounding the organization. A realistic analysis of local conditions will help set reasonable expectations based on factors such as availability of prospects, access to wealth, competition, local regulations, geography, style, public image, access to volunteers (including leadership), fundraising history, prior fiscal performance, volume and variety of fundraising methods offered, use of professional staff or consultants, existing donors for renewal and upgrading, established fund development office procedures, and more.[54]

§ 2.3 ROLE OF FUNDRAISING PROFESSIONAL

Fundraising executives refer to the development process as their guide. This process includes (1) acquiring donors, (2) renewing and upgrading donors, and (3) maximizing donors. Each phase represents an increased capacity to support charitable organizations. The process starts at the bottom of the pyramid of giving (Exhibit 2.1). Identification of prospects from those publics available to each charity is accomplished through the several annual giving methods. Each individual donor's progression up the pyramid requires time for communication of information and development of interests and of a level of personal involvement with the organization (the "friend-raising" phase). Major gift opportunities, while less frequent, are usually centered in capital campaigns and represent a continuing investment in response to a rising commitment and enthusiasm for the programs and services of the organization. The ultimate investment decision is usually made last, is frequently the largest gift, and may even come as part of the donor's estate.

Fundraising professionals are like symphony orchestra conductors. Before fine music can be produced, they need competent musicians, all the right instruments, the correct sheet music for each player, a concert hall, rehearsals, and an audience. Any one of the 15 fundraising methods can more easily be accomplished alone; to activate many methods simultaneously takes skill in managing the process of moving everyone forward together, in the same direction, toward the same objective, and at the same time.

---

[54] For more details about the environmental audit, see Greenfield, "The Fund-Raising Environmental Audit," 22 *Fund Raising Mgmt.* (No. 3) 28 (1991).

Exhibit 2.1. Pyramid of Giving

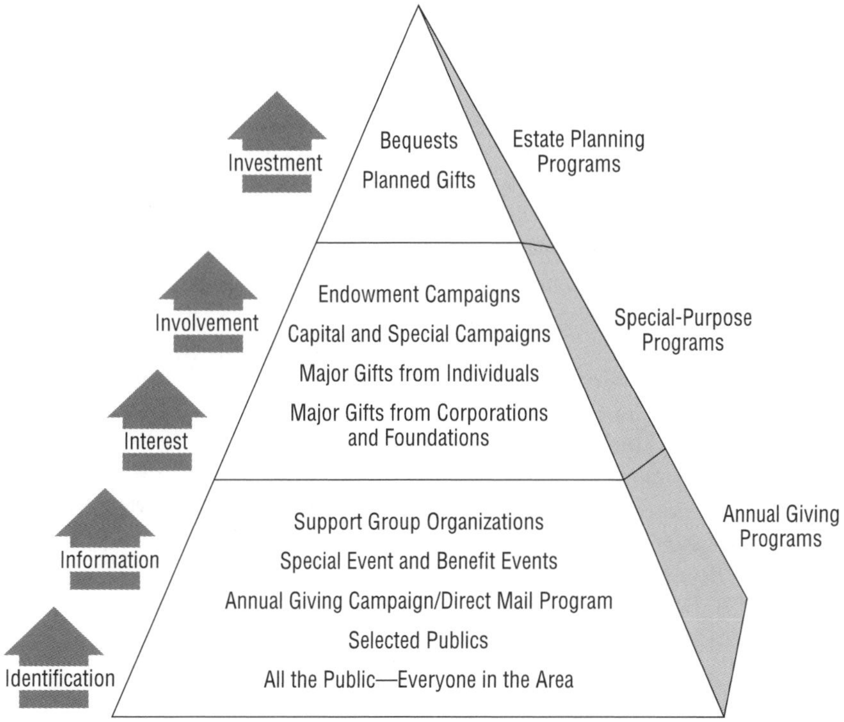

Investment

Involvement

Interest

Information

Identification

Bequests
Planned Gifts

Estate Planning
Programs

Endowment Campaigns
Capital and Special Campaigns
Major Gifts from Individuals
Major Gifts from Corporations
and Foundations

Special-Purpose
Programs

Support Group Organizations
Special Event and Benefit Events
Annual Giving Campaign/Direct Mail Program
Selected Publics
All the Public—Everyone in the Area

Annual Giving
Programs

The desired net effect is to stimulate multiple forms of asking for multiple gift decisions from donors and prospects each year, while at the same time selectively soliciting larger gifts from a few who have demonstrated greater potential from previous gift performance. All of this should be timed to meet institutional needs with funds delivered on schedule.

(a) Types of Professional Fundraisers

Three types of professional fundraising executives work for and with charitable organizations to direct and manage fundraising programs. Legislation and regulation provide guidelines for the relationship between organizations and those who perform fundraising on their behalf, and distinguish among the three types.

1. *Fund Development Officer.* A fund development officer is a full-time salaried employee of the organization and receives the same standard employment benefits of all other employees. Most regulations are silent about employees who perform fundraising, choosing rather to regulate the organization itself. The fund development officer designs the fundraising program in keeping with the organization's priority needs; selects the fundraising methods

required to produce the income needed; and supervises operations on a daily basis. To make the development process work, the development officer must also set and meet goals and objectives; identify committees; assign functions and manage them successfully; recruit and train leaders and volunteers; hire and train staff; write policies and procedures, have them approved, and see that they are followed; prepare budgets and supervise expenses; perform and report results and analyses; keep confidential records accurately and discreetly; design and implement a donor recognition system; and more.

2. *Fundraising Consultant.* A fundraising consultant is an individual or firm hired for a fee to provide services of advice and counsel to charitable organizations on the design, conduct, and evaluation of their fundraising enterprises. Most regulations require consultants to register with state authorities, file a copy of contracts for service, and be bonded when the handling of gift dollars will occur. Consultants are available to guide staff and volunteers on specific fundraising methods (direct mail, telephone, planned giving, capital campaigns, and the like), to perform objective studies and analysis of the design and conduct of comprehensive fundraising programs, and to provide executive search, marketing, public relations, and other services. Consultants do not usually conduct solicitations directly, nor do they handle gift money, but they can and do assist these efforts. Consulting staff can be retained to perform all of the duties of the fund development officer, usually for a specified period until full-time employees can be hired and trained.

3. *Professional Solicitor.* A professional solicitor is an individual (or firm) who is hired, for a fee or on a commission or percentage basis, to perform a fundraising program or special event directly in the name of the organization, to solicit and receive all gifts, to deposit funds and pay expenses, and to deliver net proceeds to the charity. Legislation and regulation of professional solicitors are the most intense because of past conduct by those whose fees and expenses have been high and who have delivered net proceeds in the area of only 20 percent or less of gross revenues. Solicitor firms are more likely to attract smaller and newer organizations (or "noncharities" for whom the gift deduction is no longer allowed) who believe they lack the ability to mount their own fundraising programs and thus are easy prey to the sales pitch that promises gift revenue with no effort on the organization's part.

In making a choice among fundraising professionals, charitable organizations should compare their cost-effectiveness. Fund development officers and professional consultants perform similarly and produce net returns of from 75 to 80 percent of net income. Professional solicitors return 20 percent or less of net income.

Several other features that relate to the separate role of fundraising professionals are discussed as follows.

(b) Growth toward a Profession

Fundraisers may call themselves professionals and engage in professional practices, but their field has not yet achieved accepted professional status. To do so requires a commonly accepted body of knowledge, a common standard of conduct (ethics), published literature, a theoretical base from established methods of research, and an accreditation process. Progress continues on all fronts but, in the view of some, remains incomplete at present.

(c) Professional Associations

National and local organizations have expanded to meet the needs of fundraisers, one of the fastest-growing new service areas of employment available in the United States. As of mid-2001, membership in the Association of Fundraising Professionals (AFP), formerly the National Society of Fund Raising Executives, which was founded in 1962, numbered more than 25,000 individuals in 149 chapters across the United States, 11 chapters in Canada, and 3 chapters in Mexico, plus 2 other chapters for members at large. The Council for the Advancement and Support of Education (CASE) and the Association for Healthcare Philanthropy (AHP) provide similar trade association services to their members. The American Association of Fund Raising Counsel (AAFRC) represents many of the larger national firms whose members practice as consultants. Hundreds of others who practice fundraising as staff or consultants are not members of any society. New professional associations, such as the National Council on Planned Giving, have emerged to meet the needs of specialists, and the Direct Mail Marketing Association includes members who service both for-profit and not-for-profit clients.

The primary purpose of these trade associations is to serve the members, usually by providing training in the profession through conferences, seminars, monthly meetings, workshops, journals, and newsletters. Efforts have begun to define a common curriculum of information organized along knowledge and experience levels to support career development. College curricula and degrees have been slow to develop, perhaps because of a lack of literature and a research base. Professional training, when linked to certification, can yield verification to members of their comprehension of basic principles plus a validation to employers of a level of competency.

(d) Accreditation and Certification

Licensure of fundraising professionals is not yet a serious consideration and could be unwieldy to implement, considering the more than one million tax-exempt charitable organizations doing business in the United States. Fundraising staff and consultants do benefit from participation in accreditation programs because they reflect a level of personal commitment to the craft and demonstrate levels of competency attained. Presently, the accepted certification programs are offered by the AHP and AFP.

(e) Standards of Conduct and Professional Practice

As with any emerging profession, common standards require time for development. Fundraising standards originated as codes of ethics but have since matured into standards of conduct and professional practice. While AAFRC,

AHP, CASE, and AFP have their own written texts in this area, they have not yet achieved a common standard to govern what is, in essence, the same form of activity.[55]

§ 2.4 ROLE OF ACCOUNTANT

An accountant serving a charitable organization that engages in fundraising also has a variety of responsibilities, as discussed in the following analysis.[56]

Accounting for fundraising costs is one of the most sensitive areas of financial accounting, reporting, and management for organizations that solicit funds from the public. The level of fundraising expenses with respect to contributions is generally perceived as an index of management performance. Amounts reported as fundraising expenses, accordingly, are carefully examined by organization constituents and directors, contributors, and regulatory agencies.

An accountant in an organization that solicits funds from the public has several important responsibilities, including accounting for fundraising costs in a manner that (1) is consistent with "generally accepted accounting principles"; (2) is consistent with the financial reporting requirements of state and other regulatory agencies; and (3) facilitates sound financial management of the organization.

(a) Generally Accepted Accounting Principles

Professional accounting literature applicable to not-for-profit organizations requires that organizations report fundraising expenses *separately* from other supporting expenses and program expenses.

Fundraising expenses generally include all costs involved in inducing others to contribute resources without receipt of economic benefits in return. Fundraising costs usually consist of the direct costs of solicitation (such as the cost of personnel, printing, postage, occupancy, and so on) and a fair allocation of overhead.

One aspect of accounting for fundraising costs is subject to considerable judgment—accounting for the joint costs (such as postage) of multiple-purpose materials, such as educational literature that also includes a request for funds. Formerly, accounting literature (and industry practice) was inconsistent on this issue. Some organizations allocated joint costs between

---

[55] For a summary of the role of, compensation of, and demand for the fundraising professional, see "Fund-Raisers' Own Funds Are Rising" (*Wall Street J.*, Mar. 2, 1993, at B1).

[56] This analysis was prepared by Richard Larkin, CPA, for use as part of this chapter. His contribution is gratefully acknowledged by the author. Additional information concerning financial management in this context is available in Gross, Jr., Larkin, and McCarthy, *Financial and Accounting Guide for Not-for-Profit Organizations* (6th ed. 2000; New York: John Wiley & Sons, Inc.).

respective functions. Other organizations did not allocate joint costs and reported joint fundraising and educational costs exclusively as fundraising expenses.

Functional allocation of multiple-purpose expenses is now required by the accounting profession in its most recent pronouncement on the subject, if certain criteria are met. Recommended bases of allocation include the content of the materials, the use made of materials, and costs associated with different functions.

(b) Financial Reporting Requirements

Nonprofit organizations that solicit funds in several states are confronted with a web of financial reporting requirements. Regulation of charities in different states is the responsibility of different agencies with different reporting requirements and different filing deadlines. In addition, charities are often subject to the registration and reporting requirements of local units of government.

Fundraising expenses frequently are a focus of state and local regulators. Different jurisdictions require different detail in reporting fundraising costs. Some states and municipalities have attempted to restrict the right of solicitation to organizations whose fundraising costs do not exceed a fixed percentage of contributions, but the federal courts have ruled this to be unconstitutional.

State and local regulation of charities is fluid and subject to unanticipated changes. Accountants, therefore, must closely monitor the reporting requirements of all jurisdictions in which their organization solicits funds from the public.

Accountants must also be alert to guidelines established by private "watchdog" agencies. These agencies, notably the Philanthropic Advisory Service of the Council of Better Business Bureaus, establish "standards" for nonprofit organizations. Deviation from these standards may result in public censure and in sanctions, in the form of reduced or withheld contributions from corporations and other grant-making organizations that judge potential donees and grantees on the basis of these standards.

(c) Financial Management

In addition to conforming with generally accepted accounting principles and with reporting requirements of various regulatory bodies, accounting for fundraising expenses should provide information that facilitates sound financial management.

Creation of information of this type usually requires a system of cost identification and cost allocation. Effective analysis of fundraising costs requires an accurate identification of fundraising cost components and an objective allocation of joint costs and overhead.

By relating the cost of various fundraising activities with the amount of contributions received—that is, identifying the cost of each dollar raised—fundraising policy may be enhanced and the results of fundraising activities may be improved.

§ 2.5 ROLE OF LAWYER

The legal counsel who represents or otherwise works for a charitable organization that is ensnarled in regulation of its fundraising likewise has a multitude of responsibilities. In addition to all other tasks that must be undertaken in serving the organization, he or she should:

- Review the law of each jurisdiction in which the organization solicits contributions and advise on compliance responsibilities.

- See that all applications, forms, reports, and the like are properly prepared and timely filed.

- Assist the organization where it is having difficulties with enforcement authorities, such as by helping prepare a statement in explanation of its fundraising costs or by arguing its case before administrative staff(s), state commission(s), or court(s).

- Review and advise as to agreements between the organization and professional fundraisers and/or professional solicitors.

- Assist the organization in the preparation of annual reports and other materials by which it presents its programs, sources of support, and expenses to the general public.

- Keep abreast of recent developments bearing on government regulation of fundraising by charitable organizations.

One problem facing lawyers who represent charitable organizations in the fundraising setting warrants particular mention. It is common knowledge that some states regulate charitable fundraising more stringently than others. It is also common knowledge that the states will not proceed against charitable organizations that are not in compliance with their law without first contacting organizations and requesting their compliance. Thus, many charitable organizations decide to not register and otherwise comply with the law of one or more states until they receive a formal request from each state to do so. Consequently, the lawyer is often asked this question: Which states *should* the organization register in and which state's law can the organization "safely ignore" until or unless contacted by the regulatory authorities? The problem for the lawyer is that he or she ought not to counsel flouting or breaking the law. Thus, the lawyer should advise the charitable organization client that it must adhere to the law of every state in which it is soliciting contributions and not wait for some informal notice or otherwise wait "until caught." The lawyer ought not advise the charitable organization client to comply with the law in the "rigorous regulatory" states and "wait to see what happens" in the others.

There is one subject about which the law is nearly nonexistent: the extent to which a charitable organization must register and otherwise comply with state (and local) law when it is soliciting contributions by means of its

Website.[57] Lawyers and others must await future developments for definitive answers on this point.

Occasionally, the argument will arise—either from charitable organizations or professional fundraisers, or both—that the states' charitable solicitation laws are inapplicable, either because the enforcement of them obstructs interstate commerce and/or that the law concerning use of the mails overrides state regulatory law. These contentions have been tried in the courts, have failed, and are not likely to have any currency in the future.

The lawyer's role in relation to fundraising regulation should not be performed in isolation but should be carefully coordinated, not only with the charitable organization's staff, officers, and governing board, but with other consultants, principally the accountant and the professional fundraiser.

§ 2.6   VIEWPOINT OF REGULATORS

(a) 1990 Commentary

As is attested to throughout the book, the methods and extent of government regulation of fundraising are controversial. This section provides the viewpoints of two seasoned regulators, including a perspective on the future of this aspect of the law.[58]

The latter half of the 1980s brought fundamental change to the regulation, by states, of charitable solicitation. The changes were precipitated by U.S. Supreme Court decisions that gave broad First Amendment protection to charities and by a major restructuring of accounting standards that charities follow in the preparation of financial statements. These events have influenced contemporary state regulation in different ways. On the one hand, it is more difficult to prosecute the burgeoning number of organizations that annually take in a huge number of tax-exempt dollars from a trusting citizenry but provide little or no public benefit in return. On the other hand, regulation has the potential for being more effective because states are focusing on alternative regulatory options that could, in the years ahead, prove to be better at controlling practices inimical to true philanthropy.

Before the U.S. Supreme Court decisions in 1980[59] and 1984,[60] the states' efforts to protect the public from those using the guise of charity for personal enrichment focused almost exclusively on the fundraising cost ratio. It was a simplistic approach that was not always fair. To be sure, the amount an organization spends on fundraising and management as a percentage of revenue is often a reliable indicator of whether the organization exists to serve the public

---

[57] See § 4.13.

[58] The 1990 and 1992 commentaries were prepared by David E. Ormstedt, Esq., Assistant Attorney General of the State of Connecticut. His contribution is gratefully acknowledged by the author. The 2000 commentary is based on an article written by Karl E. Emerson, Director, Bureau of Charitable Organizations, Department of State, of the Commonwealth of Pennsylvania.

[59] *Village of Schaumburg* v. *Citizens for a Better Environment*, 444 U.S. 618 (1980).

[60] *Maryland Secretary of State* v. *Joseph H. Munson Co.*, 467 U.S. 947 (1984).

or as a vehicle for private gain. Yet, as the Supreme Court correctly pointed out, that is not necessarily the case. There is sometimes good reason why a charity must incur seemingly high fundraising costs. While government regulation, not only of charity but of any industry, is rarely free from some unfairness, the Supreme Court's opinion that charitable solicitation is among the types of speech deserving fullest protection makes all but the most benign unfairness intolerable under the law. Thus, states had to abandon enforcing laws that made a low fundraising percentage the litmus test for legitimacy.

In the years immediately following 1984, the states tried a new approach. Under legislation adopted by several key states, a professional fundraiser hired by a charity had to disclose to the person being solicited the minimum percentage of the gross contributions the charity would receive from the fundraising campaign. From years of experience, the states knew that telephone soliciting conducted by professional fundraising firms was enormously expensive for the charities that were supposed to benefit. Whether this was because of high (or inflated) expenses, or because of the generous profits reaped by the fundraising firms, the bottom line for donors was the same—their contributions were not going very far. Yet donors had no reason to suspect that this was the case and, if they did suspect it, had no practical way to determine in any specific case whether their donation would benefit charity or some commercial operation. Thus, it seemed a reasonable regulatory objective to provide the potential donor with this information at the point of solicitation, when the donor is most in need of it. The Supreme Court ended this short-lived approach by its decision in a 1988 case, in which the Court held that it is unconstitutional to compel those raising money in the name of charity to say something they do not want to say.[61] Certainly, few charities or fundraisers want to talk about fundraising costs with a prospective donor.

The second event that helped determine the contemporary environment for state regulation was a change in the accounting standards that govern financial reporting by charities. The primary purpose rule, established in the 1960s in response to widely publicized scandals, required, with a limited exception, that the entire cost associated with making a fundraising appeal had to be reported as fundraising costs in a charity's financial statements.[62] Thus, if the primary purpose of a particular activity was to solicit contributions, virtually all costs of that activity were considered fundraising even if the appeal contained material that could be construed as having an educational value.

With the advent of state percentage limits on fundraising costs and the growth in the number of nontraditional charities whose programs were to advocate causes and affect public opinion, often using the same direct mail vehicle that contained their fundraising appeal, some charities sought a rescue from what they perceived as an overly restrictive accounting rule. In response, the American Institute of Certified Public Accountants (AICPA) changed the rule so that much of what used to be a fundraising cost could not be credited as

---

[61] *Riley* v. *National Federation of the Blind of North Carolina, Inc.,* 487 U.S. 781 (1988).
[62] *Standards of Accounting and Financial Reporting for Voluntary Health and Welfare Organizations* (New York: National Health Council, National Assembly of Voluntary Health and Welfare Organizations, and United Way of America, 1964).

a program cost.[63] The new rule contains purported criteria to determine whether there is a bona fide program component to an activity that also contains a request for money and, if there is, then the basis on which an allocation of costs should be made. The criteria, however, are vague and subject to wide variations in interpretation. In practice, the criteria serve only to discourage the most absurd allocation—not the merely bizarre.

The confluence of the line of court cases with the destabilizing of the accounting standards has created fertile ground for those who are more interested in personal gain than in serving society. One or more individuals (including a professional fundraiser in need of a client) can now establish a purported charity, obtain tax exemption by claiming it will engage in public education and advocacy on any one of myriad health and social welfare problems, prepare and mail annually millions of appeals that contain heart-wrenching stories about the extent of the problem, emphasize how contributions are desperately needed to solve it, and then use most of the revenue generated to pay the fundraiser to send out more of the same mailings and the rest to pay themselves a salary. The process is then repeated every few months. This scenario also works for telephone solicitation.

To a state regulator who may challenge this conduct, the organization points to the Supreme Court decisions to excuse its payment of virtually all of the contributions to the fundraiser. Moreover, the charity points to the heart-wrenching stories as evidence that the payments were not just for fundraising but also for implementing the organization's public education program. Any citizen who wants to examine the organization's financial statement before deciding whether to give will find that the organization reports having spent a significant portion of its revenue on program services. What the prospective donor will not know is that the program service was the mailing he or she received requesting a contribution and that the donation will be used to produce more talk about the problem. If the donor is lucky, a token amount will be used to actually help victims.

Another outgrowth of the court decisions is the phenomenal rise in the amount of telephone soliciting by paid soliciting firms on behalf of small to midsize charities and, most notably, police- and firefighter-related groups. In Connecticut, the number of registered soliciting firms nearly tripled in the years following the 1984 Supreme Court opinion. In 1989, Connecticut residents and businesses contributed $10.7 million in response to telephone solicitations offering tickets to a show or advertising space in a publication, a 24 percent increase over 1987. Only $2.8 million, or 26 percent, ever reached the intended beneficiaries.[64] The victims are not the groups that hire the solicitors; the victims are the donors. The telephone pitch is structured to lead the call

---

[63] Statement of Position 87-2, Accounting for Joint Costs of Informational Materials and Activities of Not-for-Profit Organizations that Include a Fundraising Appeal (New York: American Institute of Certified Public Accountants, 1987).

[64] Paid Telephone Soliciting in Connecticut During 1989 for Charitable, Civic, Police and Firefighter Organizations (a report to Clarine Nardi Riddle, Attorney General, and Mary M. Heslin, Commissioner of Consumer Protection; prepared by The Public Charities Unit, a joint program of the Dept. of Consumer Protection and the Office of the Attorney General) (Apr. 9, 1990).

recipients to believe that they are speaking to a volunteer member of the group. In the fast-paced sales pitch, little useful information is imparted, and the solicitor either avoids any discussion or lies about how much of the donation the group will actually see.

A standard defense to criticism by legislators, regulators, and the media is that fundraising costs of new, or small, or unpopular charities will necessarily be high, especially in the first few years of operation as they work to build a donor base. While this may be true, it is too often just a convenient excuse that conceals self-dealing and profiteering. It buys about five years of protection, which is plenty of time in which to do considerable damage. Before enough time has passed to prove that the organization's managers never had any intention of developing a bona fide charity, or that the professional fundraiser was merely milking the organization for all it could get, they have moved on to a new cause and started the cycle all over again. For those that have enjoyed enough success and remain in business after the "startup phase," a liberal allocation of fundraising costs to the program function keeps the organization competitive in the marketplace.

To be sure, the number of organizations engaging in these practices does not constitute the majority of all organizations soliciting for charitable purposes. Beyond question, most charities adhere to high fundraising standards and provide valuable, indispensable services; however, organizations engaged in these practices are also not the exception. The numbers are significant enough to cause great concern not only for the protection of the gifts of well-intentioned donors, but also for the deleterious effect the practices are having on the credibility of the nonprofit sector as a whole.

For state regulators, who are probably in the best position to observe the fundraising and financial reporting practices of charities across the board, and who daily receive complaints and inquiries from the public, the question is how to meet these challenges and maintain accountability by all charities without interfering with the ability of bona fide charities to raise funds and carry out their programs. The answer is not readily apparent, as evidenced by the spate of widely different legislative proposals across the country, including in the U.S. Congress, in the wake of the 1988 Supreme Court decision.

It would be ideal if state regulators and responsible leaders of the independent sector could work together to create a healthier climate for charitable giving. They could cooperate on legislation (although additional laws are not always needed or wise) or on programs to educate the public on the realities of fundraising and how to distinguish the wheat from the chaff. Unfortunately, real cooperation is unlikely to emerge as long as the independent sector is unwilling to acknowledge that there are problems in the sector that call for remedial action. The usual reactions of sector leaders to regulators' concerns are disbelief, denial, and charges that regulators are, either out of ignorance or on purpose, creating a destructive regulatory environment. In public, at least, they say that the problems are aberrations, perpetrated by a few fly-by-night operators. The solution, they often say, lies in sector self-policing and less government interference. To regulators, who know that the problems are well entrenched and too widespread to tolerate, and who have over the years heard a lot of talk about self-regulation but seen little evidence that the self-policers are willing to tackle the hard issues, the reaction of the sector appears perplexing and disingenuous. No doubt, some regulators do overreact and could benefit from the advice of the sector, but until regulators and the sector achieve a common frame of reference, productive cooperation will be difficult.

In the meantime, states are refining existing regulatory programs and exploring new ones. In the foreseeable future, state regulation will be characterized by the systematic dissemination of financial and programmatic information about soliciting charities, together with stepped-up enforcement and stiffer penalties for charities and professional fundraisers that engage in misrepresentation and self-dealing or that fail to file timely and accurate financial reports. To achieve those ends, states will be concentrating on several key areas.

Registration and financial reporting form the bedrock of any regulatory scheme. Despite their inadequacies, financial reports provide a good overview of individual charities as well as aggregate data on the sector. They are a valuable source of information to the public and for the detection of abuses. States must be vigilant to ensure the accuracy and timeliness of these reports. The public is not well served when states do not devote sufficient resources to monitor compliance with periodic reporting requirements.

Financial reporting requirements place considerable burden on national charities that must file reports with up to 40 states. Most states accept a copy of IRS Form 990 as the basic financial document, which at least partially addresses this issue. Many states, however, still require their own separate registration forms and supplemental financial schedules. This is one area in which an atmosphere of cooperation between the independent sector and the states could pay dividends in the nature of greater uniformity. Absent that, states should examine their requirements to determine whether they are asking for more than what they can reasonably expect to use in their regulatory programs.

In 1988, the Supreme Court suggested to the states that they could achieve their interest of informing donors how their contributions are spent by publicizing the information obtained from charities. Some states have taken this suggestion seriously, and more can be expected to do so. The systematic and timely release of accurate and comprehensive financial and programmatic information on charities and/or professional fundraisers is an extremely useful regulatory tool. The public is hungry for this information, which is not readily available from any other source. When done properly, it is a powerful form of disclosure that is far more effective than the difficult-to-enforce disclosure provision declared unconstitutional in 1988. Minnesota and Connecticut, for example, have published reports about paid telephone soliciting. New York has published key financial data on charities registered there. Maryland has by statute mandated a state public information program. Sophisticated data processing techniques will enable more states to institutionalize a public education program.

To protect the public from misleading and fraudulent solicitations, states are increasingly relying on statutory and common law authority in addition to that granted under traditional solicitation statutes. Consumer protection laws, patterned after but not identical to the Federal Trade Commission (FTC) Act, are well suited to combat deceptive practices of for-profit fundraisers. Although the FTC Act does not generally apply to nonprofit organizations, court decisions in Connecticut and Pennsylvania have upheld the use of similar state laws against charity defendants, relying on crucial differences between those state laws and the FTC Act with respect to the definition of trade and commerce.[65] These statutes often offer a broader range of remedies than do solicitation laws and, importantly, there is usually extensive reported case law interpreting them.

Statutes requiring the disclosure of specific financial information by charities and professional fundraisers at the point of solicitation are highly suspect after the 1988 Supreme Court opinion. The Court made it clear, however, that not all mandated disclosures are unconstitutional per se. For example, the Court observed that states could require professional fundraisers to clearly identify themselves as such during a solicitation. Seizing on this, legislation has been proposed in some states to require a charity to disclose in its solicitations if the primary purpose of the solicitation or the primary program of the charity is to conduct public education.

Whether these new regulatory approaches will be effective remains to be seen. What is certain is that the states feel compelled to try. In this period of regulatory transition, the opportunity exists for the independent sector to recognize the legitimate concerns of the states and to take steps to meet them. Whether that will happen also remains to be seen.

(b) 1992 Commentary

There are two dominant areas of concern to contemporary state charity regulators: (1) a continuing deterioration in the quality and reliability of financial reporting by charities, and (2) the ineffectiveness of legal standards in controlling misconduct by directors of charities. These concerns are reflected in litigation directed at alleged false financial reports, new regulatory initiatives, and growing media attention to charitable solicitation issues.

The problem described previously with respect to the AICPA statement of position concerning joint costs[66] continues. New problems with financial reporting, however, have been identified. Two states, Connecticut and Pennsylvania, have sued several national charities for filing financial reports that falsely value and identify in-kind contributions and expenses. According to those states, the reports, which were certified by auditors, grossly inflate the amounts the charities spent on program services. The states also charge that the charities falsely identified the purposes for which they distributed the commodities. One charity claimed that it spent several million dollars on "financial and in-kind aid to patients and their families having emergency and immediate needs associated with cancer." In reality, the states say, the "aid" was old vegetable seeds and books, with little or no market value.

[65] *Connecticut* v. *Cancer Fund of America,* Conn. L. Trib., Mar. 5, 1990, at 27 (Conn. Super. Ct., Feb. 22, 1990) (order denying motion to strike); *Pennsylvania* v. *Watson & Hughey Company,* No. 44 Misc. Docket (Pa. Commw. Ct., June 9, 1989) (order overruling demurrer).
[66] See *supra* note 63.

The effect of this accounting sleight-of-hand has been to make donors and other readers of the reports (IRS annual information return (Form 990)[67] and/or audited financial statements) believe that the charity is delivering a high level of program services at a low cost. It also has enabled the charities to report that their combined fundraising and administrative costs were less than 25 percent of revenue, which is the standard for participation in the Combined Federal Campaign.

States are also concerned that legal standards governing the conduct and liability of charity board members is ineffective in deterring abusive conduct. The trend in the law is to apply the corporate standard of care to directors, rather than the more exacting trustee standard.[68] The Revised Model Nonprofit Corporation Act takes this approach as well.[69] Statutes have been enacted immunizing volunteer board members from liability, except for "reckless, wilful or wanton misconduct."[70] The effect of this trend is to reduce the risk to board members who fail to exercise their duties of care and loyalty to their beneficiaries and the public, by making it more difficult for states to prosecute a charity director for self-dealing and other conflicts of interest.

Attempts to remedy these and other problems have contributed to a spate of legislation in the states. From Florida to Wisconsin to Alaska, states are enacting new or revamping existing legislation. Forty-four states now have some form of fundraising regulation—an increase of six states in just the past few years. States are also taking a tougher stance on accounting practices, particularly expense allocations.

In September 1992, the National Association of State Charity Officials adopted a statement on financial reporting by charities, which included recommendations for action. Among the recommendations are (1) state and federal regulators should more aggressively scrutinize and challenge financial information provided by charities; (2) government and private agencies providing financial information to the public should take every opportunity to educate the public on the true nature of the programs to which their donations are being applied; and (3) state regulators should report to licensing and disciplinary boards those CPA practitioners who abuse audit and accounting rules.[71]

The inability of states to adequately control abusive conduct by those acting in the name of charity, and the failure of authentic charities to realize that it is in their interest to deal with the underlying problems, particularly the accounting and reporting issues, have exposed the independent sector to damaging publicity. The following excerpt from a magazine article is an example of criticism charities are receiving in the popular press:

[67] See § 5.9.
[68] See *Stern* v. *Lucy Webb Hayes National Training School for Deaconesses and Missionaries*, 381 F. Supp. 1003 (D.D.C. 1974).
[69] *Revised Model Nonprofit Corporation Act*, Michael C. Hone, Reporter (Englewood Cliffs, NJ: Prentice-Hall, 1988).
[70] E.g., Conn. Gen. Stat. § 52-557m.
[71] The full text of the statement is printed in "Charity Regulators Vow to Get Tough," *Chron. Philanthropy*, Oct. 6, 1992, at 33.

> . . . unlike for-profit companies, which must adhere to fairly strict account-
> ing rules, charities are subject only to the vaguest of rules. As a result,
> donors often can't tell if a charity is efficient at collecting and disbursing
> money for worthy causes or just good at cooking its books.[72]

Criticism like this, much of it justified, cannot help but erode public confidence
in the sector. Yet sector leaders, in whose interest it is to have fraud and unethical
behavior minimized and who are in a position to help the public distinguish the
wheat from the chaff, too often continue to act as if no problem exists.[73]

(c) 2000 Commentary

Although the charitable sector makes significant contributions to society and
has been experiencing astonishing growth, it is no different from any other
sector of the economy in that it has its share of unscrupulous individuals who
seek to profit by defrauding innocent donors out of their hard-earned income
and, in some cases, their lifetime savings. These fraudulent schemes harm not
only contributors, who respond in the mistaken belief they are helping charitable causes, but also the charitable community, in that each new scandal
hurts legitimate charitable organizations by increasing skepticism in the giving public.

The states have the difficult, but essential, tasks of protecting their citizens from charlatans who prey on their charitable natures while challenging
them to recognize that all are benefited when worthy charitable organizations
are generously supported. The role of the states becomes even more critical
when major governmental cutbacks shift the responsibility for relieving many
of society's burdens to the charitable sector. The purpose of the states' charitable solicitation acts is to protect the states' residents and legitimate charitable
organizations.

The state charitable solicitation acts generally serve two important purposes: (1) they allow the public to get basic information about organizations
asking for contributions so donors can make better, more informed charitable
giving decisions; and (2) they help protect state residents from charitable solicitation fraud and misrepresentation.

§ 2.7 VIEWPOINT OF A REGULATED PROFESSIONAL

Most fundraising professionals do not believe that their practices in assisting
charities to acquire charitable gifts are in any way abusive to potential donors
or other citizens. It is no surprise, then, that they find government regulation

---

[72] Khalaf, "The Accounting Game Charities Play," *Forbes*, Oct. 26, 1992, at 252.
[73] See remarks of Suzanne Feurt, program officer at the Charles Stewart Mott Foundation, in
"Charities Must Prepare to Confront Greater Scrutiny of Their Affairs, Leaders Say," *Chron.
Philanthropy*, Nov. 3, 1992, at 8.

of philanthropy to be unduly restricting and a misdirection of resources. What follows is the view of one of these regulated professionals.[74]

The nonprofit organizations that collectively constitute the "third sector" of the U.S. economy are a loose and unorganized delivery system for services that are generally not profitable, are too cumbersome, or are too partisan for business or government to support. Our societal response is to fund these endeavors through private financial support of philanthropy. The impetus to modern philanthropy is the still rather vague and developing discipline of fundraising (also called development and/or financial resource development).

For the most part, the third sector is populated by well-intentioned, hard-working individuals whose dedication to a particular cause or goal takes precedence over personal gains and rewards. This description also includes the majority of fundraisers, particularly those whose careers are encompassed by employment solely as staff of nonprofit organizations.

The thinking of most practitioners is that the regulation of fundraising practices is similar to "preaching to the choir." Although no precise sources of data are available concerning the verifiable amount of fraud or other abuse in fundraising, it can safely be said that the actual level is far lower than the general perception holds, and quite laudable when compared with other forms of activity in our society. By and large, the fundraising activities engaged in to benefit nonprofit organizations are conducted with an exceptionally high degree of honesty and professionalism.

Regardless of their intent or reason for being enacted, regulations are perceived by practitioners of fundraising as a breach of the public's trust in the operation of nonprofit organizations or, at the very least, regulations are a nuisance. The members of the third sector generally believe that well-run, well-intentioned nonprofit organizations do not abuse the public's trust. Existing accounting and audit procedures, along with other routine guards against fraud and the like, are seen as adequate to protect fundraising activities, by and large. To be regulated is to be insulted by the "public," which the nonprofit organization and the fundraiser are working to assist. The real abuses are performed by "those other guys," the unprofessionals who will do anything for a buck.

That perception of selfless service does not exempt fundraisers from scrutiny, nor should it; however, such a perception, coupled with the decentralized and diverse nature of the third sector, creates a perfect environment for miscommunication, misunderstanding, and distrust with regard to fundraising regulation.

Although the regulated and the regulators have the same goal—the protection of the public from fraud and deception—the reality is that practitioners are generally unsupportive of regulation, and regulators are generally unaware of the third sector's nature and operations (concerning resource development) and of the impact that regulation has on delivery of services. In

[74] This analysis was prepared by Delmar R. Straecker, CFRE. His contribution is gratefully acknowledged by the author.

general, there is considerable confusion and too little action based on consistent dialogue and the understanding built by mutual respect.

Both extremes of regulation—too much and too little—are regrettable; however, to engage in any level of regulation with so little dialogue between concerned and affected parties is like running in the dark. Rather than spend precious resources and valuable time highlighting specific shortcomings and failures of regulation from either perspective, those who perceive a need for regulation and those who are to be regulated should develop simple and consistent communication. This communication could take several forms, such as annual or biannual meetings of representatives from fundraising professional associations and legislators and/or enforcement entities; testimony or position papers delivered during the regulatory development process; meetings, conferences, and symposia sponsored by philanthropic foundations interested in the health and well-being of the third sector; and the like.

The specific means of communications are not important if they are effective in stimulating and maintaining the much-needed dialogue. The real value lies in their ability to produce outcomes that answer some rather simple questions, such as:

- Are donors protected and is philanthropy nurtured?
- Are funds used to support those purposes for which they are solicited?
- Are the regulations fair to all nonprofit organizations?
- Can the regulations be evaluated for effectiveness?

Often, regulations are a reaction to a perceived form and level of abuse. The perception may be correct or incorrect; that is not the issue. The issue is that the enacted regulation rarely benefits from the type of exchanges described previously. Less or more regulation is not important; better regulation is.

§ 2.8 COPING WITH REGULATION: A SYSTEM FOR THE FUNDRAISING CHARITY

(a) Monitoring of Compliance Requirements

An organization that is subject to a substantial number of the charitable solicitation laws—and that undertakes to register and report under them—should design a system by which it can remain abreast of its varied compliance responsibilities.

The state charitable solicitation laws are published as part of each state's code of statutes. County, city, and town ordinances are similarly published. Other "law" with respect to these statutes and ordinances will appear as administrative regulations and rules, administrative and court decisions, and instructions with regard to applications and report forms.

Therefore, the first step is to ascertain which of the 51 jurisdictions (50 states and the District of Columbia) do not (as yet) have some form of a charitable solicitation act. At the present, there are three of these jurisdictions: Delaware, Montana, and Wyoming.

The second step is to identify the municipal ordinances that are applicable. No one has identified them all, but assuredly there are several in each state.[75] (Probably the most well-known and stringently enforced of these ordinances is the one in effect in the city of Los Angeles.)

The third step is to identify the jurisdictions in which, for one reason or another, the organization *voluntarily* refrains from conducting a solicitation.

The fourth step is to identify the status of the organization's compliance with the applicable solicitation laws. A typical evaluation would utilize this analysis of jurisdictions:

1. States in which the organization is registered.

2. States in which the organization is exempt from one or more requirements.

3. States in which the organization is pursuing initial registration.

4. States in which the organization does not know its status but is investigating its status.

5. States in which the organization is registered but where one or more questions are being raised that may lead to revocation or modification of the registration.

6. States in which the organization is registered but is operating under some type of conditional, temporary, or probationary status.

The fifth step is to identify any jurisdictions in which the organization has been prohibited from soliciting contributions.

The sixth step is to make an inventory of due dates for filing renewals of registration and reports.

The seventh step (an ongoing one) is to persist in all reasonable endeavors to remedy the organization's difficulties as reflected in the fourth (items 5 and 6) and fifth steps.

Any professional fundraiser or professional solicitor retained by a charitable organization has independent registration and reporting responsibilities. Therefore, the organization's compliance efforts should be carefully coordinated with those of its fundraiser(s), solicitor(s), or both.

(b) Public Relations

To responsibly, accurately, and promptly respond to inquiries from the general public, an organization should be prepared to disseminate an annual report upon request. (This may also be sent to others, without waiting for a request,

---

[75] The balance of this analysis is confined to state laws, but it is equally applicable to a system of local law compliance.

such as members, donors, community leaders, and other organizations.) A form letter from the organization's president or executive director may be effectively used to transmit the report.

With today's heavy emphasis on the issue of fundraising costs, the annual report or like document should discuss the organization's fundraising program and costs.

(c) Record Keeping and Financial Data

A principal focus of this field of government regulation is fundraising costs. Therefore, management should make a substantial effort to accurately ascertain and record both direct and indirect fundraising costs. This process will require careful analysis of individuals' activities (so as to isolate the portion of their compensation and related expenses that is attributable to fundraising) and careful allocation of expenditures (where an outlay is partially for fundraising and partially for something else, such as program).

Fundraising costs must be reflected in the annual information return filed by tax-exempt organizations with the IRS.[76] Although percentage limitations on fundraising costs are unconstitutional,[77] some state laws require disclosure of these costs in a variety of ways.[78]

In any event, most organizations wish to be able to consider their fundraising costs "reasonable," particularly in response to inquiries from donors or the media. Therefore, a fundraising organization should be prepared to demonstrate the reasonableness of its fundraising costs.[79]

[76] See § 5.9.
[77] See §§ 3.9, 4.1, 4.3.
[78] See § 3.15.
[79] For the principles an organization may utilize in explanation of the reasonableness of its fundraising costs, see § 4.1.

CHAPTER THREE

States' Charitable Solicitation Acts

§ 3.1 Summary
§ 3.2 Definitions
  (a) Charitable
  (b) Charitable Organizations
  (c) Solicitation
  (d) Sale
  (e) Contribution
  (f) Membership
  (g) Professional Fundraiser
  (h) Professional Solicitor
  (i) Commercial Co-Venturer
  (j) Administrative Agency
§ 3.3 Preapproval
§ 3.4 Annual Reporting
§ 3.5 Exemptions
  (a) Churches
  (b) Other Religious Organizations
  (c) Educational Institutions
  (d) Libraries
  (e) Museums
  (f) Health Care Institutions
  (g) Other Health Care Provider Organizations
  (h) Membership Organizations
  (i) Small Solicitations
  (j) Solicitations for Specified Individuals
  (k) Political Organizations
  (l) Veterans' Organizations
  (m) Named Organizations
  (n) Other Categories of Exempted Organizations
§ 3.6 Regulation of Professional Fundraisers
§ 3.7 Regulation of Professional Solicitors
§ 3.8 Regulation of Commercial Co-Venturers
§ 3.9 Limitations on Fundraising Costs
§ 3.10 Availability of Records
§ 3.11 Contracts
§ 3.12 Registered Agent Requirements
§ 3.13 Prohibited Acts
§ 3.14 Regulatory Prohibitions
§ 3.15 Disclosure Statements and Legends
§ 3.16 Reciprocal Agreements
§ 3.17 Solicitation Notice Requirements
§ 3.18 Fiduciary Relationships
§ 3.19 Powers of Attorney General
§ 3.20 Miscellaneous Provisions
§ 3.21 Sanctions
§ 3.22 Other Laws

Fundraising for charitable purposes in the United States is a heavily regulated activity. This regulation comes in many forms and is manifested at the federal, state, and local levels. Nearly all of the states regulate charitable fundraising—although the extent and intensity of enforcement varies greatly—and do so principally by means of statutes termed *charitable solicitation acts*.

These laws are often intricate. In addition to their complexity, there is a considerable absence of uniformity, although the states are making some progress toward uniform reporting. This combination of intricacy and non-conformity makes this a body of law with which it is difficult to comply—a problem aggravated by a disparity in regulations, rules, and forms. There are, nonetheless, some relatively common features of these laws.

§ 3.1 SUMMARY

More than 30 states have adopted what may be termed *comprehensive* charitable solicitation acts. A few states have not enacted a charitable solicitation statute. The remaining states (including the District of Columbia) have elected to regulate fundraising for charitable purposes by means of differing approaches.

The various state charitable solicitation acts are, to substantially understate the situation, diverse. The content of these laws is so disparate that any implication that it is possible to neatly generalize about their assorted terms, requirements, limitations, exceptions, and prohibitions would be misleading. Of even greater variance are the requirements imposed by the many regulations, rules, and forms promulgated to accompany and amplify the state statutes. Nonetheless, some basic commonalities can be found in the comprehensive charitable solicitation acts.

The fundamental features of many of these fundraising regulation laws are a series of definitions, registration or similar requirements for charitable organizations, annual reporting requirements for charitable organizations, exemption of certain charitable organizations from all or a portion of the statutory requirements, registration and reporting requirements for professional fundraisers, registration and reporting requirements for professional solicitors, requirements with respect to the conduct of charitable sales promotions, record-keeping and public information requirements, requirements regarding the contents of contracts involving fundraising charitable organizations, disclosure requirements, a range of prohibited acts, registered agent requirements, rules pertaining to reciprocal agreements, investigatory and injunctive authority vested in enforcement officials, civil and criminal penalties, and other sanctions.

§ 3.2 DEFINITIONS

Many of the states' charitable solicitation acts contain a glossary of the important terms used in these laws.

(a) Charitable

The function of the states' solicitation statutes is to regulate the process of fundraising for charitable purposes. Thus, the definition of the word *charitable* is a major factor in establishing the parameters of these laws.[1] The meaning of *charitable* in this context is usually considerably broader than the meaning used in the federal tax setting.[2]

In general, the law of charity emanates from the English common-law treatment of the term, derived largely from the law pertaining to trusts and property. The meaning of the term *charitable* under the law of the United States has been—and continues to be—developed largely through interpretations, by the courts and the IRS, of the meaning of the term for purposes of the federal tax exemption and the federal income, estate, and gift tax deductions. State law evolves in a similar fashion, although the term *charitable* is, as noted, more expansive when used for purposes of the states' charitable solicitation acts.

The word *charitable,* as employed in the state charitable solicitation act context, is broad and sufficiently encompassing to embrace all categories of organizations that are regarded as charitable entities for federal tax exemption and deduction purposes.[3] Therefore, the range of the term encompasses churches, and conventions, associations, integrated auxiliaries, and similar organizations of churches; other religious organizations; schools, colleges, universities, libraries, and museums; other educational organizations; hospitals, hospital systems, clinics, homes for the aged, other health care providers, and medical research organizations; other health care organizations; publicly supported organizations of all types; and certain organizations that are supportive of public charities.[4]

The states, however, in defining the term *charitable* for purposes of regulating charitable fundraising, often additionally sweep within the ambit of these laws some or all of the following purposes: philanthropic, benevolent, eleemosynary, public interest, social service, social advocacy, humane, voluntary, cultural, environmental, artistic, welfare, patriotic, and recreational. Thus, for example, some states' charitable solicitation acts reach fundraising by organizations that are classified as social welfare organizations for federal tax purposes.[5]

Some states' laws expressly incorporate within the reach of a charitable solicitation statute one or more purposes that otherwise would not be covered under the most expansive definition of *charitable.* Thus, a statute may include within its purview solicitations for *police, law enforcement, legal defense,* or *labor* purposes. This phenomenon may also be reflected in a statute's exemptions, such as a law exempting unions from the registration requirement imposed on charitable organizations.

Some solicitations by nonprofit organizations for contributions lie outside the range of a state's charitable solicitation act because the gifts are not to be used for charitable purposes. An illustration of this is solicitations of contributions by

---

[1] To a lesser extent, the boundaries of these laws are also somewhat set by the scope of the terms *solicit* (*infra* § (c)) and *contribution* (§ (e)).

[2] See § 2.1.

[3] See *The Law of Tax-Exempt Organizations,* Part Two; Hopkins, *The Tax Law of Charitable Giving,* 2d ed. (John Wiley & Sons, 2000), § 3.2.

[4] IRC §§ 501(c)(3), 509(a)(1) (IRC § 170(b)(1)(A)(i)-(vi)), and 509(a)(2)-(4).

[5] IRC § 501(c)(4). See Hopkins, *supra* note 3, Chapter 12.

political organizations or for political campaign purposes.[6] For the most part, these unreached solicitations are implicit in a reading of the statute on its face. Sometimes, however, a statute expressly recognizes this fact by means of an exclusion;[7] about 10 of these laws are expressly not applicable to solicitations for political purposes.

Some fundraising is undertaken for the benefit of a named individual. It is common for this type of solicitation to be excluded from one or more aspects of regulation. Also, although state regulators disagree on the point, a respectable argument can be made that fundraising for the benefit of one individual is not fundraising for a charitable objective because of the private benefit inherent in the effort. (For federal income tax purposes, an organization benefiting only one individual cannot be a charitable entity.[8])

No court opinion generally delineates the ultimate scope of these laws, from the standpoint of the boundaries of the term *charitable.*[9] In general, the government officials interpreting these statutes accord the concept of *charitable* great latitude when determining their jurisdiction over fundraising regulation matters.

(b) Charitable Organization

A *charitable organization* usually is defined for these purposes as any person organized and operated for a charitable[10] purpose. The word *person* is then broadly defined, employing terms such as individual, organization, trust, foundation, association, partnership, corporation, firm, company, society, league, or other group or combination acting as a unit.

Often, the term *charitable organization* also includes a person that "holds itself out" as a charitable entity or one that solicits or obtains contributions solicited from the public.[11]

These laws usually operate even in the absence of a soliciting charitable organization. That is, anyone soliciting for a charitable purpose generally is required to be in compliance with one or more of these statutes.

(c) Solicitation

Another key term usually defined in a charitable solicitation act is the word *solicitation. Solicitation* generally is broadly defined. This fact is evidenced not only by the express language of the definition but also by application of these acts to charitable solicitations conducted, in common terminology, "by any

---

[6] *Id.,* Chapter 17.

[7] A problem with this type of statutory exclusion is that it invites the argument that the excluded solicitations would be embraced by the statute absent the special exception.

[8] E.g., *Wendy L. Parker Rehabilitation Foundation, Inc.* v. *Commissioner,* 52 T.C.M. 51 (1986).

[9] For a discussion as to whether an organization that exists solely for the benefit of its membership can qualify as a charitable organization, see *Commonwealth* v. *Association of Community Organizations for Reform Now (ACORN),* 463 A.2d 406 (Pa. 1983). Also *Packel* v. *Frantz Advertising, Inc.,* 353 A.2d 492 (Pa. 1976).

[10] See § (a).

[11] A discussion of these points appears in *Packel* v. *Frantz Advertising, Inc., supra* note 9.

means whatsoever." A solicitation can be oral or written. It can take place by means of an in-person request, mail, facsimile, advertisement, other publication, television, radio, telephone, or other medium. Contemporary debate over the legal consequences of charitable solicitation over the Internet highlights the importance and scope of the word *solicitation.*

A most encompassing, yet typical, definition of the term reads as follows: the term *solicit* means any request, directly or indirectly, for money, credit, property, financial assistance, or other thing of any kind or value on the plea or representation that such money, credit, property, financial assistance, or other thing of any kind or value is to be used for a charitable purpose[12] or benefit a charitable organization.[13]

Usually, the word *solicitation* is used in tandem with the word *contribution.* The term may, however, encompass the pursuit of a grant from a private foundation, other nonprofit organization, or government department or agency. About a dozen states exclude the process of applying for a governmental grant from the term *solicitation.* Occasionally, state law will provide that the word *contribution* includes a grant from a governmental agency or will exclude the pursuit of a grant from a private foundation. Thus, a charitable organization seeking this type of financial assistance should explore the need to register pursuant to one or more charitable solicitation acts before submitting the grant proposal.

It is clear, although few solicitation acts expressly address the point, that the definition of *solicitation* entails seeking a charitable gift. There is no requirement that the solicitation be successful; that is, that the request actually results in the making of a gift.

One court created its own definition of the term *solicit* in this setting, writing that the "theme running through all the cases is that to solicit means 'to appeal for something,' 'to ask earnestly,' 'to make petition to,' 'to plead for,' 'to endeavor to obtain by asking,' and other similar expressions."[14] This court held that a state's charitable solicitation act did not apply to gambling activities held to generate funds destined for charitable purposes.[15]

(d) Sale

A few charitable solicitation acts include a definition of the term *sale* (or *sell* or *sold*). A statute may provide that a *sale* means the transfer of any property or the rendition of any service to any person in exchange for consideration. This may be said to include any purported contribution without which the property would not have been transferred or the services would not have been rendered.

The term *consideration* is the critical component of this definition, inasmuch as it represents the principal dividing line between a sale and a contribution.[16] *Consideration* is the core component of a bona fide contract: both parties

---

[12] See § (a).
[13] See § (b).
[14] *State* v. *Blakney,* 361 N.E. 2d 567, 568 (Ohio 1975).
[15] *Id.* Likewise *Brown* v. *Marine Club, Inc.,* 365 N.E. 2d 1277 (Ohio 1976).
[16] As to the latter, see *infra* § (e).

to the bargain must receive approximately equal value in exchange for the participation of the other. Consideration is the reason one person enters into a contract with another; the contracting party is motivated or impelled by the benefit to be derived from the contract (for goods or services), while the compensation to be received by the other contracting person is that person's inducement to the contract. A transaction that is not supported by consideration cannot be a sale.

Likewise, a transaction that is completely supported by consideration cannot be a gift. Some transactions partake of both elements, where the consideration is less than the amount gifted, in which case only the excess portion transferred is a gift. The two most common types of these transactions are the quid pro quo contribution[17] and the bargain sale.[18]

In those states that define a *commercial co-venture* as a *charitable sales promotion*,[19] the term *sale* usually is defined in that setting.

(e) Contribution

A *contribution* basically is a transfer of money or property in the absence of consideration—it is to be contrasted with a *sale*.[20] The term may be defined in a charitable solicitation act as a gift, contribution, bequest, devise, or other grant of any money, credit, financial assistance, or property of any kind or value. The statutory definition may embrace promises to contribute (pledges).

The law on this point is the most developed in, not surprisingly, the federal income tax charitable giving setting. Years ago, the U.S. Supreme Court observed that a contribution is a transfer motivated by "detached or disinterested generosity."[21] Another observation from the Court was that a "payment of money [or transfer of other property] generally cannot constitute a charitable contribution if the contributor expects a substantial benefit in return."[22] Earlier, the Court referred to a contribution as a transfer made "out of affection, respect, admiration, charity or like impulses."[23]

The Court has adopted use of the reference to consideration in determining what is a contribution. Thus, it wrote: "The *sine qua non* of a charitable contribution is a transfer of money or property without adequate consideration. The taxpayer, therefore, must at a minimum demonstrate that he [or she] purposefully contributed money or property in excess of the value of any benefit he [or she] received in return."[24] Essentially the same rule was subsequently articulated by the Court, when it ruled that an exchange having an "inherently

---

[17] See § 5.4.
[18] See *The Tax Law of Charitable Giving, supra* note 3 § 9.16.
[19] See § (i), § 4.7.
[20] See § (d).
[21] *Commissioner* v. *Duberstein*, 363 U.S. 278, 285 (1960), quoting from *Commissioner* v. *LoBue*, 351 U.S. 243, 246 (1956).
[22] *United States* v. *American Bar Endowment*, 477 U.S. 105, 116–117 (1986).
[23] *Robertson* v. *United States*, 343 U.S. 711, 714 (1952).
[24] *United States* v. *American Bar Endowment, supra* note 22 at 118.

reciprocal nature" is not a contribution and thus cannot be a charitable contribution where the recipient is a charitable organization.[25]

Dues, being payments for services, are not contributions. The term *dues* embraces payments by members of an organization in the form of membership dues, fees, assessments, or fines, as well as fees for services rendered to individual members.

A loan is not a contribution, including a loan to a charitable organization. If a person makes a loan to a charity, with the intent to subsequently forgive it, and the amount of the loan, or a portion of it, is subsequently forgiven, the amount forgiven becomes a contribution as of the date of forgiveness. As noted, a single transaction can embrace both the elements of a contribution and a sale.[26]

Essentially, the concept in this context is that a contribution is a payment to a charitable organization where the donor receives nothing of material value in return.[27] Thus, a court ruled that a state's charitable solicitation act did not apply to the solicitation of corporate sponsors for a marathon, stating that the transaction was a "commercial" one, "[i]t is not a gift," "[i]t is a corporate opportunity," and "[i]t has nothing to do with philanthropy."[28]

The amount or value of a charitable contribution may be pertinent in the application of a state's charitable solicitation act. Certain *small* solicitations are often exempted from these acts. These determinations are made on the basis of the monetary value of the gifts in the aggregate.[29] In most instances, these calculations are made on the basis of (i.e., are confined to) the payments, or portions of payments, that are in fact contributions.

(f) Membership

The states' charitable solicitation acts often define the word *membership* or *member.* The principal purpose, when this definition is given, is to define the term in relation to the exclusion for solicitations that are confined to the membership of the soliciting organization.[30]

The statute may define the term *membership* to mean those persons to whom, for payment of dues, fees, assessments, and the like, an organization provides services and confers a bona fide right, privilege, professional standing, honor, or other direct benefit, in addition to the right to vote, elect officers, or hold offices.

This type of statute is likely to add the point that the concept of *membership* does not extend to those persons who are granted a membership upon making a contribution as the result of a solicitation.

---

[25] *Hernandez* v. *Commissioner,* 490 U.S. 680, 692 (1989).

[26] *Id.*

[27] See *The Tax Law of Charitable Giving, supra* note 3 § 3.1.

[28] *Attorney General* v. *International Marathons, Inc.,* 467 N.E. 2d 51 (Mass. 1984).

[29] See § 3.5(i).

[30] See §§ 3.5, 4.8.

(g) Professional Fundraiser

There is considerable confusion about the meaning of the term *professional fundraiser*. The dilemma arises from the fact that the term, and its nemesis *professional solicitor,* was developed in an era when the roles of the parties were discrete and thus much easier to identify. Basically and historically, a professional fundraiser was a consultant—an individual or firm that did not directly participate in the solicitation process but rather who worked with the charity in designing the fundraising plan. In most cases, the charitable organization was the person that undertook the actual fundraising, using volunteers. By contrast, a *professional solicitor* was a person who was paid to solicit gifts in the name of the charity.

During this era, the roles were separate and distinct. The fundraiser planned and did not solicit. The solicitor pursued gifts and was not involved in planning the campaign. In many instances today, that formal dichotomy is followed. Increasingly, however, the roles are being blurred, usually because the professional fundraiser is undertaking one or more roles in the area of solicitation.

Most states adhere to a definition such as this: a *professional fundraiser* is any person who, for a flat fixed fee under a written agreement, plans, conducts, manages, carries on, advises or acts as a consultant, whether directly or indirectly, in connection with the solicitation of contributions for or on behalf of a charitable organization. This type of definition usually is followed by the admonition that a professional fundraiser may not actually solicit contributions as a part of the services.

Often excluded from the ambit of the term *professional fundraiser* are the officers and employees of a registered[31] or exempt[32] charitable organization. Also usually excluded from the term are lawyers, investment counselors, and bankers, even if they advise a client or customer to contribute to a charitable organization.

Some states use a definition of the term *professional fundraiser* in a different manner, with some, as discussed as follows, having a definition of the term that also encompasses most categories of professional solicitors. About a dozen of the states' laws lack any definition of this term.

Part of the reason for the confusion in this area is the variation in terminology among the states. In about one-fifth of the states, the person usually generically referenced as a *professional fundraiser* is identified by means of that term. Other states, however, intending the same meaning, use the term *professional fundraising counsel.* Still other states prefer *fundraising counsel.* Other terms used in various state laws are *fundraising consultant, professional fundraiser consultant, professional fundraising consultant, professional fundraising consultant,* and *professional fundraising counsel.*

Presently, the state laws regarding fundraising regulation reflect considerable misunderstanding of the meaning of the term *professional fundraiser* in

---

[31] See § 3.3.
[32] See § 3.5.

relation to the term *professional solicitor.*[33] As noted, some state laws so broadly define *professional fundraiser* (or equivalent term) that the term includes what is normally meant by *professional solicitor.* Terms used to describe a *professional solicitor* include phrases such as *professional fundraising firm, professional commercial fundraiser,* and *commercial fundraiser for charitable purposes.* A few states use the term *professional fundraiser* to describe what is generically meant by the term *professional solicitor.*

(h) Professional Solicitor

The discussion[34] about the traditional and contemporary roles of professional fundraisers and professional solicitors is to be recalled, in understanding the confusion between the two terms as seen from the perspective of the term *professional solicitor.*

The term *professional solicitor* is generally defined in a state charitable solicitation act in one of two ways.

Most states define the term *professional solicitor* to encompass one of three types of persons or relationships. One is a person who, for a financial or other consideration, (1) solicits contributions for or on behalf of a charitable organization, where the solicitation is performed personally or through agents or employees; or (2) the person solicits through agents or employees specially employed by or for a charitable organization, who are under the direction of such a person. The other is a person who, for a financial or other consideration, plans, conducts, manages, carries on, advises, or acts as a consultant to a charitable organization in connection with the solicitation of contributions but does not qualify as a professional fundraiser (or equivalent term).

When this definition (or something comparable to it) is used, about one-half of the states employ the term *professional solicitor.* A few use the term *paid solicitor.* Other phrases used are *professional commercial fundraiser, professional fundraising firm, paid fundraiser,* and *commercial fundraiser.*

This definitional approach is usually accompanied by exclusions for officers, employees, lawyers, investment counselors, and bankers. On rare occasions, there will be other exclusions, such as for persons whose sole responsibility is mailing fundraising literature.

Some states define the term *professional solicitor* to mean any person who is employed or retained for compensation by a professional fundraiser to solicit contributions for charitable purposes. With this definition, the terms used are *professional solicitor, paid solicitor,* or *professional fundraiser.*

The confusion in the law in this area, regarding the appropriate line of demarcation between the terms *professional fundraiser* and *professional solicitor,* is seen in use of the prevailing definition of the term *professional solicitor* in defining the term *professional fundraiser.* One law defines a professional solicitor as a *commercial fundraiser for charitable purposes,* while another law terms what is generally known as a professional solicitor as a *paid fundraiser.* The law in a

---

[33] See *infra* § (h).
[34] *Id.*

state dubs what is usually defined as a *professional solicitor* a *professional fundraiser* and separately defines the term *professional solicitor*.

(i) Commercial Co-Venturer

Commercial co-venturing occurs when a for-profit, commercial business enterprise announces to the general public that a portion (a specific amount or a specific percentage) of the purchase price of a product or service will, during a stated period, be paid to one or more named charitable organizations. This arrangement usually results in a charitable contribution by the business enterprise, the amount of which is determined by and depends on consumer response to the promotion. (There is no charitable deduction for participating consumers.) This venture produces gift revenue to the beneficiary charity or charities and positive community awareness for the business sponsor.

A traditional definition of the term *commercial co-venturer* (the for-profit business enterprise) is any person who for profit is regularly and primarily engaged in trade or commerce, other than in connection with the raising of funds or any other thing of value for a charitable organization, and who advertises that the purchase or use of goods, services, entertainment, or any other thing of value will benefit a charitable organization.

It has become more common to define a commercial co-venture as a *charitable sales promotion*. This approach defines the promotion as an advertising or sales campaign, conducted by a commercial co-venturer, which represents that the purchase or use of goods or services offered by the commercial co-venturer shall benefit, in whole or in part, a charitable organization or charitable purpose. In this setting, the term *commercial co-venturer* is defined as a person who for profit is regularly and primarily engaged in trade or commerce, other than in connection with soliciting for charitable organizations or purposes, and who conducts a charitable sales promotion. These definitions, or versions closely akin to them, are used in about a dozen states.

The term *commercial co-venture* is, in several respects, unfortunate. The word *co-venture* suggests that the charitable organization involved is engaged in some form of a joint venture with the participating business enterprise. Also, the term implies that the beneficiary charitable organization is embroiled in some undertaking that is *commercial*. Both connotations have potential adverse consequences in law, in the tax-exemption setting, and in the unrelated business income setting.

(j) Administrative Agency

The enumeration of definitions in a charitable solicitation act often includes reference to the state agency, department, or official with the responsibility for administration and enforcement of the statute. Predominantly, the administrative and enforcement authority is in the office of the state's attorney general. In many states, however, the authority is in the department of state.

Otherwise, there is little commonality regarding the location of the regulatory authority in this area. In several states, the emphasis is on consumer protection; thus, the authority is in a department of consumer protection, department of agriculture and consumer services, department of commerce and consumer affairs, a division of consumer protection within the department of commerce, and the like. In a few states, the orientation is regulation of business activity; in this case, the authority is in a department of economic development, department of business regulation, a department of regulation and licensing, and the like.

In some states, the authority to enforce the charitable solicitation act is vested in the attorney general, with the administrative or regulatory authority lodged in another department or agency of the government.

§ 3.3   PREAPPROVAL

A fundamental requirement of nearly every state charitable solicitation act is that a charitable organization (as defined in that law[35] and not exempted from the obligation[36]) that intends to solicit—by any means—contributions from persons in that state must first apply for and acquire permission to undertake the solicitation. This permission, which must be secured by both domestic (in-state) and foreign (out-of-state) charitable organizations, is characterized as a registration in most states. In other states, it is cast as an application for a license, a filing of a statement, a filing for a certificate, a filing for a permit, or a filing of a solicitation notice. Some states with a form of statutory law on this point do not have any registration or similar requirement for charitable entities.

Typical wording of a provision of this nature is that every charitable organization that intends to solicit contributions within the jurisdiction, or have funds solicited on its behalf, must, prior to any solicitation, file a registration statement.

If the application for this permission is successful, the result is authorization to conduct the solicitation. Application for the registration, license, or other permit is most frequently made to the office of the attorney general or the secretary of state.

Generally, the law requires a principal officer of the charitable organization to certify the accuracy of and to execute the registration statement, license, application, or the like.

The statute usually enumerates the categories of information, about the charitable organization and the solicitation, that must be in the registration statement or other application. These categories of information most frequently are some or all of the following:

- The name of the organization

- The name in which the organization intends to solicit contributions

- The principal address of the organization and the address of any office in the state or, in the absence of an office, the name and address of the person having custody of the organization's financial records

---

[35] See *supra* § 2(a).
[36] See *infra* § 5.

- The names and addresses of any chapters, branches, or affiliates to be located in the state

- The names and addresses of the organization's trustees, directors, officers, executive staff, and registered agent

- The place where and the date when the organization was legally established

- The form of the organization (corporation, trust, or unincorporated entity)

- A statement about the organization's classification as a tax-exempt organization under federal law[37]

- The purpose or purposes for which the organization was founded

- An income and expense statement, and an asset and liability statement, for the organization's immediately preceding tax year (perhaps audited), showing, among other items, the type and amount of funds raised, expenses for fundraising, and expenditures of the funds raised

- The methods by which solicitations will be made, including use of a professional fundraiser and/or professional solicitor[38]

- The purpose or purposes for which the contributions to be solicited will be used

- The names of the individuals who will have final responsibility for the custody of the contributions

- The names of the individuals responsible for the final distribution of the contributions

- A statement indicating whether the organization is or has ever been enjoined by one or more states from soliciting contributions

- Copies of contracts between the charitable organization and professional fundraisers and/or professional solicitors

It is common for the statute to authorize the state's regulatory agency to require, by regulations or otherwise, the submission of information in addition to that required by the statute.

The states' laws either expressly provide or contemplate that the regulatory authorities will examine the application and, where the application is legally sufficient, issue the permit or other authorization to proceed with the fundraising effort. The review authority at this stage of the process is exceedingly broad. At a minimum, the governmental authorities have the power to determine whether the application conforms with all of the legal requirements.

---

[37] In most instances, this classification will be as an organization that is tax-exempt under IRC § 501(a) because it is described in IRC § 501(c)(3). In general, see *supra* § 3.2(b).
[38] See *supra* § 2(g), (h).

At the same time, the discretion these officials have is not unlimited; legally, they are not empowered to make subjective judgments about the worthiness or similar attributes of applicant organizations.[39]

An investigation can ensue at this stage (as well as at any time thereafter). Most states' laws vest plenary investigative capacity in the regulatory and enforcement authorities, particularly the attorney general.[40]

Sometimes a chapter, branch, or other affiliate (other than an independent member agency of a federated fundraising organization) has the option of separately reporting the relevant information to the state. Alternatively, it reports to the parent organization, which is then required to furnish the information in a consolidated form to the state.

Permission to engage in fundraising for charitable purposes will not be issued where the regulatory authorities conclude that the charitable organization has omitted or materially misrepresented required information or would be acting in violation of one or more provisions of the state's charitable solicitation law. The law may provide that a permit to solicit will not be issued where a person violated the law, attempted to obtain the fundraising authorization by misrepresentation, or materially misrepresented the purposes and the manner in which contributions would be used.

Usually, the state levies a registration fee, which is either a fixed amount or an amount correlated with the level of contributions received, administrative or fundraising outlays, or the like.[41] Most of these statutes provide for a stated fixed fee; some states levy a fee the amount of which depends on the level of annual receipts. A state may allow the regulatory authorities to set the fee. Other states, however, allow a charitable organization to register its fundraising program without charge.

State laws differ as to the duration of the registration or other authorization to engage in charitable fundraising. In most states, the permit or license expires by law one year after the date of its issuance, at the close of the calendar year, or at the close of the organization's fiscal year. Renewal of the registration or other authorization is made by filing an updated application within a certain period before the expiration date of the existing registration. These statutes usually also require a supplemental filing during the time a registration is in effect, where there is a material change in the information submitted with the application.

In some states, the registration or other authorization remains in effect until withdrawn by the charitable organization or suspended or revoked by the state.

The statutory law in the other jurisdictions does not address the subject of duration of the authorization to engage in charitable fundraising.

These laws usually provide that, where the charitable organization has violated a provision of the applicable charitable solicitation act, the enforcement authorities are to suspend or revoke the registration or other authorization.

---

[39] See § 4.6.
[40] See § 4.19.
[41] See § 4.12 for a discussion of the constitutionality of this type of fee arrangement. Also see § 7.12.

The statute usually provides for some form of due process, including a hearing, in this type of circumstance.[42]

There often are separate registration requirements for professional fund-raisers and professional solicitors.[43]

The burdens of registration imposed on charitable organizations engaging in multistate charitable solicitations appear to be moderating, as the consequence of development of a unified registration statement. More than 30 states and the District of Columbia agreed to use the form. Some states, however, require supplemental information. This form is optional for use by participating charitable organizations.[44]

§ 3.4 ANNUAL REPORTING

Most state charitable solicitation acts require a soliciting charitable organization (unless exempt from the requirement[45]) to annually file information with the appropriate governmental agency. This is accomplished by filing a report, usually annually, which is the requirement in most states or an annual updating of the registration, as is the case in many states. Other states mandate the filing of an annual disclosure statement, the filing of an annual statement, a filing for an annual license, or the filing of a copy of the federal annual information return. There are states with some form of statutory law on this point that do not have any annual reporting or similar requirement for charitable entities. A few states mandate both annual registration and annual reports.

The categories of charitable organizations exempted from the annual reporting requirement usually are those also exempted from the preapproval requirement.

The charitable solicitation statute frequently mandates the contents of the annual reports. The information most often requested is the following:

- The gross amount of contributions pledged to and collected by the charitable organization—not just in the particular state but in all jurisdictions in which fundraising took place

- The amount from the solicitation that was or is to be devoted to charitable purposes, as well as the amounts paid or to be paid for fundraising (including the fees of professional fundraisers) and for administration

- Identification of any professional fundraisers and/or professional solicitors utilized

- The net receipts disbursed or dedicated for disbursement within the particular state, by category of expenditure

---

[42] See § 4.4.
[43] See § 6.7.
[44] The development of this unified registration statement is a welcome one. This advance toward simplicity and uniformity is somewhat marred by the additional supplemental statements and varying annual reports.
[45] See *infra* § 5.

In addition, a reporting charitable organization usually must file a financial statement covering the preceding accounting period, prepared in conformance with appropriate accounting standards. A few states require, by statute, that the reports be based on the accounting standards and reporting procedures promulgated by the Financial Accounting Standards Board and/or the American Institute of Certified Public Accountants (AICPA), while a state may mandate by statute use of the standards and procedures set forth in the standards for *Uniform Financial Reporting by Voluntary Health and Welfare Organizations.* Presumably, the regulatory officials in other states have the discretion to select the accounting principles with which charitable organizations must comply or to develop their own. Thus, the law may provide that each reporting charitable organization must report its expenditures in accordance with standards and classifications of accounts as prescribed by the attorney general, or a comparable official, to effect uniform reporting by organizations having similar activities and programs. These reports may have to be accompanied by an opinion of a certified public accountant.

The annual report is due at varying times as required by the states' charitable solicitation statutes. The filing may have to be made within 30 days after the close of the accounting period, within 60 days of that period, within 75 days of the period, within 90 days of the period, within five months of the period, or within six months of the period. The regulators in a few states are authorized by statute to require the filing of a report, in some instances in addition to an annual report, by a charitable organization with respect to some other period.

In some states, the annual report filing requirement, or the extent of it, depends on the level of annual contributions received and/or use of a professional fundraiser and/or professional solicitor. In a few states, a registration or other authorization may be cancelled or not renewed until the required annual report is filed.

The annual report of a parent charitable organization must include information with respect to all of its fundraising affiliated groups.

A few states provide, by statute, the fee to be paid with the filing of an annual report. In other states, any fees of this nature are set administratively.

Occasionally, a charitable organization soliciting contributions in a state is required to file financial reports on a quarterly basis during its first year of existence.

There often are separate reporting requirements for professional fundraisers and professional solicitors.[46]

§ 3.5   EXEMPTIONS

Most of the states' charitable solicitation acts provide some form of exemption from their requirements; however, these laws vary widely with respect to the exemptions available for organizations and solicitations. As noted, the basic

---

[46] See § 6.7.

definition of the term *charitable* is sufficiently broad to initially encompass all categories of charitable and other organizations.[47] Therefore, these laws are applicable to soliciting religious, educational, health care, and other charitable organizations, unless an exemption is expressly available to them.

These statutory exemptions may be available for an organization because of the nature of the entity or for an organization to the extent it engages in a particular type of solicitation. The exemption may be from the entirety of the statute or merely a portion of it. In some states, an exemption is not effective until the organization applies for it and is recognized by the state to have it.

(a) Churches

Churches and their closely related entities are often exempted from the entirety of the states' charitable solicitation acts.[48] A typical state's statute accords total exemption to any church or convention or association of churches, primarily operated for nonsecular purposes and no part of the net income of which inures to the direct benefit of any individual.

In many of these states this exemption is not found within the portion of the statute providing for exemptions but instead is located in the definition of charitable entities.

Some states' charitable solicitation laws grant this exemption only to churches and like organizations that have been classified as such by the IRS. These organizations, however, are not required to obtain recognition of tax-exempt status[49] and thus some of them do not have this type of classification; technically, then, these organizations are not eligible for the exemption.

(b) Other Religious Organizations

Many states provide an exemption for religious organizations in general from the totality of their charitable solicitation acts. A state law may exclude a corporation sole or other religious corporation, trust or organization incorporated or established for a religious purpose, any agency or organization incorporated or established for charitable, hospital, or educational purposes and engaging in effectuating one or more of such purposes, that is affiliated with, operated by, or supervised or controlled by a corporation sole or other religious corporation, trust or organization incorporated or established for religious purposes, and other religious agencies or organizations which serve religion by the preservation of religious rights and freedom from persecution or prejudice or fostering religion, including the moral and ethical aspects of a particular religious faith.

---

[47] See *supra* § 2(a).

[48] Because of constitutional law constraints and as a practical matter, the law does not normally attempt a definition of the term *church*. See *Law of Tax-Exempt Organizations* at 220–229. If an organization is regarded as a church or closely related organization for federal income tax purposes (IRC § 170(b)(1)(A)(i)), it presumably is treated the same for state fundraising regulation purposes.

[49] IRC § 508(c)(1)(A), which also applies with respect to integrated auxiliaries of churches, and conventions or associations of churches.

§ 3.5 EXEMPTIONS

It is less common for an exemption for religious organizations to be confined to the registration or other requirements as to preapproval. Some states provide religious organizations with exemption from their registration (and sometimes reporting) or like requirements.

(c) Educational Institutions

Some states exempt at least certain types of educational institutions (often with emphasis on higher education) from the entirety of their charitable solicitation acts. Usually, this exemption applies only where the institution is accredited. The more common practice is to exempt educational institutions from only the registration or other preapproval (and sometimes reporting) requirements.

States may, either as an alternative to or in addition to the foregoing approach, exempt from the registration and reporting requirements educational institutions that confine their solicitations to their "constituency." Thus, a state's law may provide an exemption from registration for any other educational institution confining its solicitation of contributions to its student body, alumni, faculty and trustees, and their families.

On occasion, a state may exempt solicitations by educational institutions of their constituency from the entirety of their charitable solicitation laws.

Many schools, colleges, and universities undertake their fundraising by means of related "foundations."[50] Several states expressly provide exemption, in tandem with whatever exemption their laws extend to educational institutions, to these supporting foundations. Some states exempt, from the registration requirements, parent–teacher associations affiliated with an educational institution, alumni organizations, and student groups.

(d) Libraries

Some states exempt nonprofit libraries from the registration and reporting requirements of their charitable solicitation acts.

Where a state charitable solicitation act fails to make an express provision for exemption for libraries, these institutions may be able to secure an exemption as educational institutions.

(e) Museums

Rarely does a state exempt nonprofit museums from the registration requirements of their charitable solicitation act.

---

[50] Foundations functioning on behalf of educational institutions that are operated by state governments are expressly recognized by the federal tax law, as concerns public charity and charitable donee classifications (IRC § 170(b)(1)(A)(iv)). See *Law of Tax-Exempt Organizations* at 368. Foundations functioning on behalf of other educational institutions are also public charities, often publicly supported ones (IRC §§ 170(b)(1)(A)(vi) (IRC § 509(a)(1)) and 509(a)(2)). See *Law of Tax-Exempt Organizations* at 387–402. Some of these foundations in the second category are supporting organizations (IRC § 509(a)(3)), although they may meet a test as to public support. See *Law of Tax-Exempt Organizations* at 368.

A museum may be able to acquire exemption from a state's charitable solicitation act as an educational institution, where express provision has not been made for it in the exemption clauses.

(f) Health Care Institutions

Some states exempt nonprofit hospitals from the registration or reporting requirements of their charitable solicitation acts. A state may similarly exempt foundations that are related to and supportive of hospitals.

A few states exempt nonprofit hospitals from the entirety of their charitable solicitation acts. A state may similarly exempt hospital-related foundations.

(g) Other Health Care Provider Organizations

A few state laws provide exemption from registration for volunteer rescue associations. A state charitable solicitation act may exempt volunteer ambulance organizations from its registration requirements.

A rare exemption from the registration requirements is for licensed medical care facilities, mental health organizations, and mental retardation centers. A charitable solicitation act may exempt from its registration and reporting requirements any nonprofit organization that operates facilities for the aged and chronically ill or nursing care facilities. Other exemptions are for volunteer health organizations and licensed healthcare service plans.

(h) Membership Organizations

Charitable solicitation acts are designed to apply to solicitations of the general public to protect its members from fundraising fraud and other misuses of charitable dollars. This body of law is intended to ward off misrepresentation in charitable giving by ensuring an appropriate flow of information to prospective and actual donors, thus preventing their being duped into giving in circumstances where the contributions are diverted to noncharitable ends.

Consequently, when a charitable organization solicits its own "constituency" (such as a college soliciting its alumni), it is appropriate to regard the solicitation as a *private* one and thus exempt from the regulatory requirements.[51] This exemption is based on the proposition that the regulatory protections are unnecessary because the donor's relationship with the donee charitable organization, by means of the membership status, is such that he, she, or it can easily obtain the requisite information without the need for intervention by the law.[52]

---

[51] As to this point, an analogy may be made to the federal securities laws, which differentiate between regulated sales of securities to the public and somewhat unregulated private offerings of securities.

[52] One court held that a state's charitable solicitation act was inapplicable to private foundations, for the reason that the "obvious intent" of the statute is "to regulate those charitable organizations, who solicit or accept contributions from persons or corporations *outside the charitable entity*" (*Estate of Campbell* v. *Lepley*, 532 P.2d 1374, 1375 (Okla. 1975)) (emphasis added).

§ 3.5 EXEMPTIONS

In reflection of this rationale, many states exempt organizations (or, in some instances, only certain categories of organizations)—but only from the registration or like requirements—that confine their solicitation to their membership. As noted, the scope of this exemption is confined by the definition accorded the term *member* or *membership*.

A few jurisdictions exempt organizations soliciting only their membership from the entirety of their charitable solicitation act.

These exemptions often are limited, such as where the solicitation is conducted only by members or where the conduct of the solicitation is solely by volunteers.

(i) Small Solicitations

For administrative convenience and to alleviate the burdens of regulation that would otherwise be imposed, many of the state charitable solicitation acts exempt small solicitation efforts from the registration or similar requirements. The definition as to what is *small*, however, varies considerably from state to state.

A provision in a solicitation act typically exempts from registration charitable organizations which do not intend to solicit and receive and do not actually solicit or receive contributions from the public in excess of $10,000 during a calendar year or do not receive contributions from more than 10 persons during a calendar year. While there are variations in the phrasing of these provisions, some states provide for this exemption with the threshold set at $25,000, a few states have this type of provision with a threshold of $10,000; other limitations are $8,000, $5,000, $4,000, $3,000, and $1,500. Often, this exemption is accompanied by a provision that triggers applicability of the registration requirement should contributions exceed the threshold amount. Thus, the state statute may add a rule that, if a charitable organization that does not intend to solicit or receive contributions from the public in excess of $10,000 during a calendar year does actually solicit or receive contributions in excess of such amount, whether or not all such contributions are received during a calendar year, the charitable organization shall, within 30 days after the date the contributions reach $10,000, register with and report to the appropriate agency.

This exemption may be confined to organizations in which fundraising is conducted wholly by volunteers.[53]

A few states provide for this exemption from the entirety of their charitable solicitation act.

As another approach to excluding small solicitations, some states exempt organizations that do not intend to annually receive contributions from more than 10 persons. On a rare occasion, a solicitation by a charitable organization is exempt where up to as many as 100 persons were solicited. There may be an exemption for these solicitations when conducted by a private foundation.

---

[53] This type of provision has been applied in the courts (e.g., *Salvation Mission Army Workers Holy Orthodox Christian Church* v. *Commonwealth*, 383 A.2d 995 (Pa. 1978); *Blenski* v. *State*, 245 N.W.2d 906 (Wis. 1976)).

(j) Solicitations for Specified Individuals

Many states exempt from the registration and reporting requirements of their charitable solicitation acts solicitations that are solely for the benefit of specified individuals.

Thus, a charitable solicitation statute may make this exemption available for persons requesting contributions for the relief of any individual specified by name at the time of the solicitation when all of the contributions collected without any deductions whatsoever are turned over to the named beneficiary for his or her use. As this phrasing indicates, this exemption is usually voided where professional fundraising assistance is used.

As discussed, this type of exemption is often in conflict with the concept of solicitations for charitable purposes.

Rarely will these solicitations be exempt from the totality of the charitable solicitation act.

(k) Political Organizations

Some states exempt political organizations from the entirety of their charitable solicitation acts. Others exempt political organizations from the registration and reporting requirements of their acts. This is one of those exemptions that need not be stated, in that fundraising for political organizations is always outside the ambit of a state's charitable solicitation act.

(l) Veterans' Organizations

Several states exempt veterans' organizations from the registration and reporting requirements of their charitable solicitation acts.

(m) Named Organizations

Some state charitable solicitation acts provide exemption—usually only from the registration requirements—for organizations identified by name.[54]

This practice is evidenced in provisions granting this type of exemption to the American Red Cross, boys' clubs, named educational institutions, Boy Scouts and Girl Scouts organizations, girls' clubs, the Junior League, Young Men's and Young Women's Christian Associations, and a children's trust fund.

(n) Other Categories of Exempted Organizations

The state charitable solicitation acts contain exemptions—usually from the registration requirements—for a variety of other categories of charitable organizations. The scope of these exemptions is vast: some expressly mandate a filing requirement for the exemption, solicitations only by volunteers, no private inurement, solicitations only of members, and other limitations.

---

[54] These provisions are of dubious legality (see § 4.5).

§ 3.5 EXEMPTIONS

This type of exemption, albeit with some restrictions in some states, may be extended to include firefighting organizations; fraternal organizations; social groups; patriotic organizations; historical societies; civic organizations; nonprofit nurseries or other children's groups; certain organizations receiving an allocation from community chests, united funds, and the like; federally chartered organizations; law enforcement groups; community service organizations; youth organizations; labor unions; business and professional associations; senior citizen centers; grange organizations; civil defense organizations; civil rights organizations; fraternities and sororities associated with a variety of organizations; debt counseling agencies; state-based charitable trusts; persons seeking contributions and grants only from corporations and private foundations; and persons seeking grants only from private foundations.

The law in a few states provides that a noncommercial radio or television station is exempt from the state's charitable solicitation act's registration requirements. There is the occasional exemption from registration requirements for organizations that do not have an office within the jurisdiction; that solicit in the state solely by means of telephone, telegraph, direct mail, or advertising in national media; and that have a chapter or affiliate that itself has registered in the state. A rare exemption from registration requirements is available for any charitable organization located outside the state, if the organization filed the registration documents required under the charitable solicitation laws of the state in which it is located, the registration documents required under the laws of other states, and such federal forms[55] as may be required by rule.

Other exemptions from the registration and/or reporting requirements may encompass any publicly supported community foundation or publicly supported community trust, state-based charitable trusts, civil defense organizations, noncommercial newspapers, or debt counseling agencies.

In a rare exemption, organizations of hunters, fishermen, and target shooters are exempt from the entirety of the charitable solicitation act.

An unusual provision may exempt from the registration and reporting requirements of a charitable solicitation act all charitable organizations that are tax-exempt under federal law.[56] A state may have a similar exemption (albeit only from registration), although many categories of tax-exempt charitable organizations must file proof of their tax-exempt status with the state. In several states, solicitations for federal, state, and/or local governments are exempt.

A wide range of nonprofit, tax-exempt organizations are exempt from the states' charitable solicitation acts because these entities are not *charitable* as that term is defined in the applicable statutes.[57]

The foregoing exemptions are not necessarily absolute or automatic. That is, in some states, a charitable organization (but not necessarily all categories of such organizations) must first secure a determination from the state regulatory authorities as to its status as an organization exempt from some or all of the charitable solicitation act's requirements; in some states, some or all of the

---

[55] Principally, the federal annual information return (Form 990). In general, see § 5.9.
[56] This exemption, which of course exempts all or nearly all charitable entities, is available for all organizations that are tax-exempt by reason of IRC § 501(c)(3).
[57] See *supra* § 2(a).

exemptions are precluded or revoked where a charitable organization uses the services of a professional fundraiser; and, in some states, the exemption is precluded or revoked where a charitable organization uses the services of a professional solicitor.

§ 3.6 REGULATION OF PROFESSIONAL FUNDRAISERS

The state charitable solicitation statutes often require a professional fundraiser, acting on behalf of a charitable organization that is subject to the particular statute, to register with the appropriate state agency and otherwise be in conformity with the statute. This registration must be completed before the professional fundraiser commences to act in that capacity for a charitable organization soliciting funds in the state.

The scope of this registration and of other regulatory requirements is largely governed by the reach of the definition, under a state's charitable solicitation law, of the term *professional fundraiser*.[58]

This registration is usually effective for a period of one year, with expiration of the registration set to occur on a stated date, and is renewable.

Often, these laws also impose reporting requirements for professional fundraisers. A few state charitable solicitation acts mandate annual reports. The far more common practice is annual registration.

An applicant for this registration is usually required to file with and have approved by the appropriate state officials a bond in a statutorily set sum. These bond amounts are as follows: $25,000, $20,000, $15,000, $10,000, $5,000, or $2,500. These bonds inure to the benefit of the state in reimbursement for any losses resulting from malfeasance, nonfeasance, or misfeasance in the conduct of a professional fundraiser in connection with charitable solicitation activities.[59]

Most of these statutes require professional fundraisers to maintain accurate books and records, and to do so for a stated period (generally, three years).

§ 3.7 REGULATION OF PROFESSIONAL SOLICITORS

Usually, the states' charitable solicitation acts require professional solicitors to register in accordance with and otherwise comply with the statute. These laws often also impose a variety of reporting, disclosure, and other requirements. Thus, many states require annual (or sometimes other) reports from professional solicitors; the more common practice is annual registration. Some states require both.

The statutory bonding requirements for professional solicitors are as follows: $50,000, $25,000, $20,000, $15,000, $10,000, or $5,000.

---

[58] See § 4.2(g).

[59] A state may have an alternative to the use of bonds, in that a certificate of deposit, letter of credit, or U.S. obligation can be filed in lieu of a bond. This approach allows investment assets to be pledged while not disturbing the underlying investment. It eliminates the expense of premiums, and reduces the time and expense associated with renewals of bonds.

The scope of these regulatory requirements is largely governed by the reach of the definition, under a state's charitable solicitations law, of the term *professional solicitor*.[60] The wide variation in these definitions is frequently confusing.

§ 3.8   REGULATION OF COMMERCIAL CO-VENTURERS

Several states have some form of law relating to the regulation of commercial co-venturing; many of these states use the concept of the *charitable sales promotion*. These forms of regulation emphasize disclosure of information about the promotion to the public; other requirements are registration of commercial co-venturers, a contract with the charitable organization and commercial co-venturer, formal consent from the charity, and/or a report from the commercial co-venturer.

A bond for commercial co-venturers may be required; the bond amount is likely to be set at $10,000.

§ 3.9   LIMITATIONS ON FUNDRAISING COSTS

One of the most controversial issues in the field of fundraising for charitable purposes is the matter of fundraising costs. While there is general agreement that charitable fundraising costs should be *reasonable,* there is much disagreement and misunderstanding as to what in fact is a reasonable fundraising expense. There also is disagreement about how to determine the reasonableness of fundraising costs. Ascertainment of the reasonableness of a fundraising cost depends on a variety of facts and circumstances.[61]

Many of the states long tried to prevent charitable organizations with (allegedly) "high," "unreasonable," or "excessive" fundraising costs from soliciting contributions within their jurisdictions. The traditional mechanism for doing this was denial of permission to solicit in the state if a charity's fundraising costs exceeded a particular percentage of total contributions or revenues received. This percentage ceiling came in two forms: (1) an *absolute limitation* (i.e., one without a means of proving reasonableness, irrespective of a particular percentage) and (2) a *rebuttable limitation* (where the prohibition on fundraising could be overcome by a showing that the fundraising expenses were in fact reasonable, notwithstanding the percentage that may have been produced). It is now settled, however, that this mechanism is unconstitutional as a violation of the rights of free speech of soliciting charitable organizations.[62]

Consequently, the states have been forced to repeal these percentage limitations, although the practice is dying hard. As an illustration, until a few years ago, the law of a state prohibited registration by a charitable organization, professional fundraiser, or professional solicitor where the charity would

---

[60] See *supra* § 2(h).
[61] See § 4.1.
[62] See § 4.3.

receive less than 90 percent of the receipts of a solicitation. According to a representative of the state's tax commission, which at that time administered the state's charitable solicitation act, the provision had not yet been removed from the statute by the state legislature, and was therefore still being enforced. This was the case even though the state attorney general's office had written an opinion stating that the provision was unconstitutional. Another state had a provision that a fundraising cost of a charitable organization that is in excess of 30 percent of total revenue was presumed to be unreasonable; a charitable organization with an unreasonable fundraising cost could not register in the state. That rule was repealed.

The law of another state provided that a charitable organization registered under its solicitation statute could not expend an "unreasonable" amount of its gross contributions for fundraising. An amount in excess of 25 percent of total contributions was presumed to be unreasonable, and the secretary of state was empowered to—using unstated criteria—approve higher costs. This provision was subsequently removed from the state's charitable solicitation statute.

An unsuccessful attempt involved shifting the limitation away from the charitable organization and placing it on the amount of compensation received by the professional solicitor. Thus, one state had a provision prohibiting a professional solicitor from receiving more than 25 percent of the total amount received in a solicitation. This rule has since been removed from the solicitation act; during the time it was part of the statute, the state regulators conceded that the law was unconstitutional and not being enforced. The law of another state provided that a charitable organization could not pay a professional solicitor an amount in excess of 15 percent of the contributions received. This law also asserted a rebuttable presumption in connection with the fundraising costs of charitable organizations, which placed a general limitation on fundraising costs of 35 percent, albeit with an opportunity for higher expenses in the event of "special facts and circumstances." This provision was not enforced and has since been eliminated.

The law of another state provided that a charitable organization may not pay a professional solicitor more than 25 percent of contributions received and that a charitable organization may not have fundraising expenses in excess of 50 percent of contributions received, again with an opportunity for the allowance of higher expenses in the case of special circumstances. During the time before the provision was removed, the state regulators were uncertain as to whether or how to enforce it. The law of another state provided that a charitable organization could not pay a professional solicitor for services in connection with the solicitation of contributions in excess of a "reasonable per cent" of gifts raised. This law also authorized the state's secretary of state to pass judgment on the contract between a charitable organization and a professional solicitor, and to force renegotiation of the agreement or perhaps disallow it where the contract would "involve an excessively high fundraising cost." These rules are no longer in the law, and the state regulators evinced little interest in enforcing them while they were.

Rules aimed at imposing ceilings on the compensation paid to professional solicitors are not proving easy to eradicate. One of them was struck down as unconstitutional in 1994[63] and another was rendered ineffectual in 1995.[64] Yet, as discussed next, provisions in the states' charitable solicitation acts involving percentages remain plentiful.

Many states require a statement about any percentage compensation in the contract between the charitable organization and the professional fundraiser and/or professional solicitor. One rule in this regard provides that the contract must state the "guaranteed minimum percentage of the gross receipts from contributions which will be remitted to the charitable organization" and the "percentage of the gross revenue for which the solicitor shall be compensated." One state requires that a contract between a charitable organization and a professional fundraiser be filed with the state where there is percentage-based compensation.

Some states utilize the percentage approach in setting disclosure. Of these, a few require that the solicitor disclose, at the point of solicitation, the funds that the charity will receive, stated as a percentage, and a state will occasionally require this type of disclosure following a request by the prospective donor for the information. A state may require a disclosure of this nature upon the request of anyone or require a charitable organization's fundraising cost percentage to be stated in its registration statement. In a few states, solicitation literature used by a charitable organization must include a statement that, upon request, financial and other information about the soliciting charity may be obtained directly from the state.[65]

A rare rule prohibits a professional fundraiser from receiving compensation from a charitable organization if the compensation depends wholly or partly on the number or value of charitable contributions that result from the effort of the fundraiser.

§ 3.10   AVAILABILITY OF RECORDS

The information filed in accordance with a state's charitable solicitation act, whether contained in an application for registration, annual report, contract, or other document, is a matter of public record. This requirement encompasses information filed by charitable organizations, professional fundraisers, professional solicitors, and commercial co-venturers. The fact that these records are public is usually stated in the statute.

For example, the law may provide that statements, reports, professional fundraising counsel contracts or professional solicitor contracts, and all other documents and information required to be filed shall become government records in the department or agency and be open to the general public for inspection at such times and under such conditions as may be prescribed.

This type of provision is frequently buttressed by a record-keeping requirement. In almost all instances, this record-keeping obligation is imposed

---

[63] *Kentucky State Police Professional Association* v. *Gorman,* 870 F. Supp. 166 (E.D. Ky. 1994).
[64] *National Federation of Nonprofits* v. *Lungren* (N.D. Cal., order issued Mar. 29, 1995).
[65] See § 4.15.

on the soliciting charitable organization; however, in some states, the require-ment is confined to professional fundraisers, professional solicitors, and/or commercial co-venturers.

Many of these laws require that the information be maintained, by the reg-ulators and/or the regulated, for a stated period, usually three years. Where the records must be maintained by a regulated entity (such as the soliciting charitable organization or professional fundraiser), the law often requires that the information be open to inspection at all reasonable times by the appropriate officials of the state. Most of these laws require a charitable organization, and/or related professional fundraisers, professional solicitors, and commercial co-venturers, to keep "true and complete" records to ensure compliance with the laws requiring disclosure of information and the availability of records.

§ 3.11 CONTRACTS

Many of the state charitable solicitation acts require that the relationship be-tween a charitable organization and a professional fundraiser, and/or between a charitable organization and a professional solicitor, be evidenced in a written agreement. This contract must be filed with the state soon after the document is executed.

A few of the states with laws pertaining to commercial co-venturers have a like requirement with respect to contracts entered into between chari-table organizations and business enterprises.

The states that make these requirements applicable to charitable organi-zations and professional fundraisers, but not to charitable organizations and professional solicitors, are often the states that define a professional solicitor as one who is an employee of a professional fundraiser.[66]

Several state charitable solicitation acts contain rules that mandate cer-tain provisions in a contract between a charitable organization and a profes-sional fundraiser, professional solicitor, and/or commercial co-venturer.[67] The law may require that any one of these three types of contracts must con-tain (1) a concise and accurate statement of the charitable organization's right to cancel; (2) a concise and accurate statement of the period during which the contract may be cancelled; (3) the address to which the notice of cancellation is to be sent; (4) the address of the secretary of state, to whom a duplicate of the notice of cancellation is to be sent; and (5) a statement of the financial arrangement between the parties.

§ 3.12 REGISTERED AGENT REQUIREMENTS

A state charitable solicitation act often contemplates that a charitable organiza-tion, professional fundraiser, and/or professional solicitor will appoint a regis-tered agent in the state where contributions are being solicited. A *registered*

---

[66] See *supra* § 2(h).
[67] These requirements are discussed in § 7.7.

agent is a person who, as agent for the entity, is the formal point of contact for anyone who is required to or desires to communicate with the entity. In general, organizations (particularly corporations) are required by law to maintain a registered agent in the state or states in which they are formed and headquartered, and in any other state in which they are doing business. A registered agent can be an individual who is a resident of the state, a corporation that is authorized by the state to function as a registered agent for corporations, or (in some states) a lawyer who is a member of the bar of that state.

Thus, where a charitable organization, professional fundraiser, or professional solicitor is incorporated under the law of a state or has its principal place of activity or business in a particular state (a *domestic* state), it is required to appoint a registered agent in conformity with the requirements of that state.

Where a charitable organization, professional fundraiser, or professional solicitor has its principal place of activity or business in a state other than that in which the charitable solicitation is being conducted (a *foreign* state), however, it likely will not have appointed a registered agent in that state.[68] In this situation, the charitable solicitation act in several states provides that, where the foreign charitable organization, professional fundraiser, and/or professional solicitor participates in a charitable solicitation in the state, the administrator of the act is deemed, by virtue of the solicitation activity, to have been irrevocably appointed as its agent for purposes of service of process and similar functions.

Occasionally, rules of this nature are applicable with respect to commercial co-venturing.

§ 3.13   PROHIBITED ACTS

Nearly all of the state charitable solicitation acts contain a list of one or more types of conduct—often termed *prohibited acts*—that may not be lawfully engaged in by a charitable organization (and perhaps a professional fundraiser, professional solicitor, and/or commercial co-venturer).

These prohibited acts may entail some or all of the following:

- A person may not, for the purpose of soliciting charitable contributions, use the name of another person (except that of an officer, director, or trustee of the charitable organization by or for which contributions are solicited) without the consent of the other person.[69] This prohibition extends to the use of an individual's name on

---

[68] This is because this type of charitable solicitation is not usually regarded as *doing business* within a state (see *infra* note 77).

[69] This type of rule has been upheld in the courts (e.g., *Lewis* v. *Congress of Racial Equality,* 274 S.E.2d 287 (S.C. 1981); *Blenski* v. *State, supra* note 53; *People* v. *Caldwell,* 290 N.E.2d 279 (Ill. 1982)). In *Blenski,* the court stated that the "crime of unauthorized use of names is directed at protecting the public against being misled and not protecting the person whose name is used. This purpose does not require that liability for this crime be imposed for each individual person whose name is used, particularly where . . . the unauthorized uses are simultaneously committed" (at 911).

stationery or in an advertisement or brochure, or as one who has contributed to, sponsored, or endorsed the organization.

- A person may not, for the purpose of soliciting contributions, use a name, symbol, or statement so closely related or similar to that used by another charitable organization or government agency that it would tend to confuse or mislead the public.[70]

- A person may not use or exploit the fact of registration with the state to lead the public to believe that the registration in any manner constitutes an endorsement or approval by the state.

- A person may not misrepresent to or mislead anyone, by any manner, means, practice, or device, to believe that the organization on behalf of which the solicitation is being conducted is a charitable organization or that the proceeds of the solicitation will be used for charitable purposes, where that is not the case.

- A person may not represent that the solicitation is for or on behalf of a charitable organization or otherwise induce contributions from the public without proper authorization from the charitable organization.[71]

Some states prohibit a professional solicitor from soliciting for a charitable organization unless the solicitor has a written and otherwise valid authorization from the organization, has the authorization in his or her possession when making solicitations, and displays the authorization upon request to the person being solicited, police officers, or agents of the state.

§ 3.14 REGULATORY PROHIBITIONS

Some states have provisions in their charitable solicitation acts that go beyond the usual regulation of the process of raising funds for charitable purposes.

In many states, it is expressly unlawful for a charitable organization to solicit and/or expend funds raised for purposes that are not charitable or for purposes not referenced in the application submitted as part of the registration process.

Most of the states have disclosure rules as part of their charitable solicitation acts, as a condition to a lawful fundraising effort. A few states have point-of-solicitation disclosure requirements imposed on charitable organizations, and several states have such requirements with respect to solicitations by professional solicitors.

---

[70] This type of provision has been upheld in the courts (e.g., *American Gold Star Mothers, Inc.* v. *Gold Star Mothers, Inc.*, 191 F.2d 488 (D.C. Cir. 1951); *People ex rel. Brown* v. *Illinois State Troopers Lodge No. 41*, 286 N.E.2d 524 (Ill. 1972)). An illustration of the misapplication of this type of rule by regulatory authorities appears in *City of Evanston* v. *Evanston Fire Fighters Association, Local 742, International Association of Fire Fighters, AFL-CIO-CLC*, 545 N.E.2d 252, 262–266 (Ill. 1989).
[71] In general, see § 7.5.

Many states have rules concerning the solicitation of tickets to be used at promotional or fundraising events.

In some states, the law imposes specific requirements on the boards of directors of soliciting charitable organizations. Directors of charitable entities may be expressly obligated to supervise the organizations' fundraising activities. A charitable solicitation law may prohibit certain conflicts of interest at the board level in the fundraising setting. One of these laws requires a charity to "substantiate a valid governing structure." A state law has directions to the board as to investment management activities, another places limitations on the ability of a charitable organization to indemnify its directors, and under one law, a charitable organization cannot solicit funds in the state if its directors have been convicted of certain crimes.

§ 3.15   DISCLOSURE STATEMENTS AND LEGENDS

Some states' charitable solicitation laws require a charitable organization engaged in fundraising in the jurisdiction to, in furtherance of a consumer protection objective, disclose the availability of certain information to prospective contributors.

For example, in several states, a prospective donor must be given a *disclosure statement,* which includes the name of the charitable organization, the address and telephone number where a request for a copy of the organization's financial statement should be directed, and a statement that relevant documents and information filed under the state's law are available from the state's regulatory office.

Some of these state laws require a *legend* that must be utilized in a charitable solicitation. As an illustration, one of these laws requires the following on all written solicitations and on written confirmations, receipts, or reminders subsequent to an oral solicitation:

> A copy of the official registration and financial information may be obtained from the Pennsylvania Department of State by calling toll-free, within Pennsylvania, 1 (800) 732-0999. Registration does not imply endorsement.

One state requires charitable organizations to print their state registration number on solicitation materials.

These requirements impose burdens on charitable organizations that solicit contributions on a multistate basis. One organization has devised an all-purpose legend that reads as follows:

> You may obtain a copy of _____'s [the organization's name] financial report by writing to it at _____ [organization's address]. For your information, _____ registers with agencies in many states. Some of them will supply you with the financial and registration information they have on file.
>
> Residents of the following states may request information from the offices indicated (the toll-free numbers are for use only within the respective

states: Florida—Div. of Consumer Services, Charitable Solicitations, The Capitol, Tallahassee, FL 32339; Maryland—Office of the Secretary of State, Statehouse, Annapolis, MD 21401, 1-800-825-4510; New York—Office of Charities Registration, 162 Washington St., Albany, NY 12231; Pennsylvania—Department of State, Bureau of Charitable Organizations, Harrisburg, PA 17120, 1-800-732-0999; Virginia—Division of Consumer Affairs, P.O. Box 1163, Richmond, VA 23209, 1-800-552-9963; Washington—Office of the Secretary of State, Charitable Solicitation Division, Olympia, WA 98504, 1-800-332-4483; West Virginia—Secretary of State, State Capitol, Charleston, WV 25305. Registration with a state agency does not imply the state's endorsement. MICS _____.[72]

§ 3.16   RECIPROCAL AGREEMENTS

As the foregoing indicates, the requirements of the state charitable solicitation acts can vary widely, as can the regulations, rules, and forms promulgated to accompany and expand these laws, and the enforcement activities with respect to them. This makes it difficult and expensive for a charitable organization soliciting contributions on a nationwide basis to lawfully comply with all of the varying requirements. Some states have attempted to remedy this situation by pursuing methods to bring their laws, and interpretations and enforcement of them, into some conformity with other states' requirements.

For the most part, state regulators have the inherent authority (where revision of the statutory law is not necessary) to promulgate regulations, rules, forms, and enforcement policies that are comparable to similar requirements in other states. Nonetheless, some states' charitable solicitation acts contain a provision that, if earnestly followed, could somewhat alleviate this lack of uniformity. This provision authorizes the appropriate state official to enter into reciprocal agreements with his or her counterparts in other states to exchange information about charitable organizations, professional fundraisers, and professional solicitors; accept filings made by these persons in the other states where the information required is substantially similar; and grant exemptions to organizations that are granted exemption under the other state's statute where the laws are substantially similar.

§ 3.17   SOLICITATION NOTICE REQUIREMENTS

One of the contemporary trends in the development of state charitable solicitation acts is the growing number and stringency of requirements applicable to professional solicitors. The emphasis has been on increased reporting and other forms of disclosure to a governmental agency, to the charitable

---

[72] This proposed multistate legend was prepared by Robert S. Tigner, General Counsel, Association of Direct Response Fundraising Counsel. His contribution is gratefully acknowledged.

organization involved, and/or to the solicited public, particularly by means of a *solicitation notice.*

A typical requirement obligates a professional solicitor to file a solicitation notice with the regulatory body within 20 days prior to the commencement of a solicitation. This solicitation notice, which must be under oath, must include a description of the solicitation event or campaign, the location and telephone number from which the solicitation is to be conducted, the names and residence addresses of all employees, agents, or other persons who are to solicit during the campaign, and the account number and location of all bank accounts where receipts from the campaign are to be deposited. Copies of campaign solicitation literature, including the text of solicitations to be made orally, must be attached to the solicitation notice. The charitable organization on whose behalf the solicitor is acting must certify that the solicitation notice and accompanying material are "true and complete."

In other states, the solicitation notice may require additional items of information, such as whether the solicitor will at any time have custody of the contributions received, a "full and fair" description of the charitable program for which the solicitation is being conducted, the fundraising methods to be used, the dates when the solicitation will commence and terminate, and information concerning any investigation or litigation regarding the professional solicitor's solicitation activities within the previous six years. Some states also require that a copy of the contract between the charitable organization and the professional solicitor be attached to the solicitation notice.

Using a somewhat similar approach, a few states require a professional solicitor to provide the charitable organization involved with an accounting after the conclusion of a solicitation.

Some states require a solicitor to carry a solicitation card that contains certain information and to display the card to prospective donors.

§ 3.18 FIDUCIARY RELATIONSHIPS

Another relatively recent category of provision to emerge in state charitable solicitation acts is the one adopted by a few states, which statutorily (as opposed to by means of the common law) makes professional fundraisers and/or professional solicitors fiduciaries with respect to the charitable organization involved.[73] This designation, among other outcomes, increases the legal liability of these persons. A typical provision of this nature states that every person soliciting, collecting, or expending contributions for charitable purposes, and every officer, director, trustee, and employee of any such person concerned with the solicitation, collection, or expenditure of such contributions, is deemed to be a fiduciary and acting in a fiduciary capacity.

---

[73] A *fiduciary* is a person who has special responsibilities in connection with the administration, investment, and distribution of property that belongs to someone else; this range of duties is termed *fiduciary responsibility.*

§ 3.19 POWERS OF ATTORNEY GENERAL

Frequently, a state charitable solicitation statute invests the state's attorney general (or, occasionally, some other official) with specific powers in connection with administration and enforcement of the statute.[74] Usually, the attorney general is authorized to investigate the operations or conduct of charitable organizations, professional fundraisers, and professional solicitors who are subject to the statute, and to issue orders having the same force and effect as a subpoena. The attorney general is often expressly empowered to initiate an action in court to enjoin, preliminarily or permanently, a charitable organization, professional fundraiser, professional solicitor, or other person who engages in a method, act, or practice in violation of the statute or a rule or regulation promulgated in connection with the statute; or employs or uses in a solicitation of charitable contributions a device, scheme, or artifice to defraud, or to obtain money or property by means of any false pretense, deception, representation, or promise.

Occasionally, the attorney general is collaterally granted some or all of this authority with respect to individuals or organizations masquerading as charitable organizations or as charitable organizations entitled to an exemption from the statutory requirements. Thus, the statute may empower the state's attorney general to institute legal action against a charitable organization or person which or who operates under the guise or pretense of being an organization or person exempted by the act and is not in fact an organization or person entitled to such an exemption.

These state statutes usually include the obligatory provision that they may not be construed to limit or restrict the exercise of powers or performance of duties of the attorney general that he or she otherwise is authorized to exercise or perform under any other provision of law. The charitable solicitation act is likely to explicate this principle, by providing that the attorney general must enforce the due application of funds given or appropriated to public charities within the state and prevent breaches of trust in the administration thereof.

§ 3.20 MISCELLANEOUS PROVISIONS

In several states, a solicitor is required to place contributions in an account at a financial institution; in most of these states, the account must be solely in the name of the charitable organizations involved.

In some states, charitable organizations and/or professional solicitors are required to timely send confirmations or receipts of contributions to the donors. The law may provide an opportunity for a donor to subsequently cancel a contribution. In a few states, the solicitation of contributions in the state is deemed to be *doing business* in the state.

---

[74] An excellent discussion of the role of an attorney general in overseeing charitable organizations appears in *City of Evanston* v. *Evanston Fire Fighters Association, Local 742, International Association of Fire Fighters, AFL-CIO-CLC, supra* note 70, at 256–262.

The laws in some states mandate a public education program as to charitable giving and fundraising abuses.

In most states, the regulatory officials are expressly granted the authority to promulgate rules and regulations to accompany the particular state's charitable solicitation act.

In some states, the law provides that county or municipal units of government may adopt other and/or more stringent requirements regarding the solicitation of charitable contributions and, expressly or impliedly, that these requirements will not be preempted by the state law. This rule is sometimes referred to as the *municipal option.*

In a few states, a provision makes it clear that the charitable solicitation law may not be construed to restrict the exercise of authority generally accorded to the state's attorney general.

Occasionally, the regulators must make an annual report to the governor and the legislature on the activities with respect to charitable solicitations in the state. In a few states, the regulators must maintain a registry of charitable organizations or professional solicitors.

The law may authorize a commission or council to serve, in an advisory capacity and/or otherwise, as part of the administration of the state's charitable solicitation act.

In a few states, there are limitations as to use of the telephone for charitable solicitation purposes, particularly where the callers are compensated. One jurisdiction flatly prohibits the practice.[75] Others state the hours during which the calls may be made, either by a charitable organization, a professional fundraiser, or a professional solicitor. The law may prohibit a gift solicitation by telephone where there is harassment, intimidation, or torment.

§ 3.21 SANCTIONS

The means of enforcing a state charitable solicitation act are plentiful. The principal enforcement mechanisms, which come into play upon the occurrence of one or more violations of the act, are the following: authorization of the revocation, cancellation, or denial of a registration; authorization of an investigation by the appropriate governmental officials; authorization of injunctive proceedings; authorization of the levying of fines and other penalties; and authorization of the imposition of criminal penalties (including imprisonment). Many states characterize violations of these statutes as misdemeanors, with specific penalties referenced elsewhere in the state's code of laws. One state mandates loss of tax-exempt status as a sanction, while some states affirmatively recognize private actions.

In some states, a violation of the state's charitable solicitation act simultaneously constitutes a violation of the state's unfair trade practices or deceptive practices law.

---

[75] This type of restriction, however, is unconstitutional (see § 4.3).

In all of the jurisdictions, a person may be found to have committed a fraud against the public, in the setting of the solicitation of charitable gifts.[76]

§ 3.22 OTHER LAWS

In addition to the panoply of state charitable solicitation acts, charitable organizations soliciting gift support from the public may have to face other state statutory or other regulatory requirements. These include:

- A state's nonprofit corporation act, which has registration and annual reporting requirements for foreign (out-of-state) corporations that are *doing business* within the state. It is not clear whether, as a matter of general law, the solicitation of charitable contributions in a foreign state constitutes doing business in the state.[77] Some states provide, by statute, that fundraising is the conduct of business activities in their jurisdictions. If the solicitation of charitable contributions were declared, as a matter of general law, a business transaction in the states, the compliance consequences would be enormous, considering the fact that nearly every state has a nonprofit corporation act. This type of a requirement would cause a charitable organization that is soliciting contributions in every state to register and report more than 90 times each year, not taking into account federal and local law requirements!

- A state insurance law, which may embody a requirement that a charitable organization writing charitable gift annuity contracts obtain a permit to do so and subsequently file annual statements.

---

[76] E.g., *Commonwealth* v. *Events International, Inc.*, 585 A.2d 1146 (Pa. 1991); *People ex rel. Scott* v. *Gorman*, 421 N.E.2d 228 (Ill. 1981); *People ex rel. Scott* v. *Police Hall of Fame, Inc.*, 376 N.E.2d 665 (Ill. 1978). In general, Suhrke, "What Can Be Done About Fund Raising 'Fraud'?," XXVI *Phil. Monthly* (No. 6) 5 (1993).

[77] One court observed that "[i]t is doubtful . . . whether the solicitation of funds for a charitable purpose is, to use the statutory words, the 'carrying on, conducting or transaction of business'" (*Lefkowitz* v. *Burden*, 254 N.Y.S.2d 943, 944–945 (1964). A subsequent court opinion, however, suggested that the solicitation of funds constitutes doing business in a state (*Commonwealth* v. *Events International, Inc., supra* note 76, at 1151).

Clearly, a charitable organization organized in one state and maintaining an office or similar physical presence in another state is doing business in the latter state. The general rule is that merely mailing charitable solicitation material into a state is not doing business in that state, although a contrary approach can be established by statute or regulation. In many states, the determination as to whether an organization is doing business in a state is under the jurisdiction of the secretary of state, whereas the registration and reporting requirements of a charitable solicitation act are administered by the attorney general. In some states (such as California), a determination that a charitable organization is doing business in the state leads to a requirement that the organization file for and receive a ruling as to its tax-exempt status in the state (or else be subject to state taxation). Thus, fundraising in a state can entail an obligation on the part of the charitable organization to file with three separate agencies in the state.

- A state's *blue sky statute* regulating securities offerings, which may be applicable to offers to sell and to sales of interests in, and the operation of, pooled income funds. These laws may also apply with respect to charitable remainder annuity trusts and unitrusts.[78]

- A state's law prohibiting fraudulent advertising or other fraudulent or deceptive practices.[79]

- A state's version of the Uniform Supervision of Trustees for Charitable Purposes Act, which requires a charitable trust to file with the state attorney general a copy of its governing instrument, an inventory of the charitable assets, and an annual report. Of similar scope and effect are the state laws that invest the state attorney general with plenary investigative power over charitable organizations.

- State law concerning charitable contribution deductions and eligibility for tax-exempt status as a charitable entity.[80]

As this chapter indicates, the states' charitable solicitation acts—despite some overall common features—are rather disparate. The breadth and depth of these laws testify to the failure of efforts during many years to make them more uniform, for the purpose of easing compliance with and administrating them. State law regulation of charitable soliciting continues to expand, and indications are rather clear that the states will continue to go their separate ways in this arena, rebuffing the attempts of those who would integrate and streamline this regulatory scheme.

---

[78] E.g., Horner and Makens, "Securities Regulation of Fundraising Activities of Religious and Other Nonprofit Organizations," XXVII *Stetson L. Rev.* (No. 2) 473 (Fall 1997).

[79] E.g., *People* v. *Gellard,* 68 N.E.2d 600 (N.Y. 1946). A challenge to a state's use of an unfair trade practices act and state sweepstakes law to regulate charitable fundraising failed, with the court finding that the plaintiffs lacked standing to bring the suit (*American Charities for Reasonable Fundraising Regulation, Inc.* v. *Shiffrin,* 46 F. Supp. 2d 143 (D. Conn. 1999)).

The state of Minnesota, in mid-1999, charged a charity located in Louisiana and its fundraising company with the use of deceptive tactics in raising money, by telephone, for terminally ill children (Williams, "Minn. Sues Charity, Solicitors Over Telephone Appeals," XI *Chron. of Phil.* (No. 14) 29 (May 6, 1999)).

[80] In addition to these state requirements, there are hundreds of county and city ordinances, as noted *supra* note 1. The constitutionality of these ordinances is a subject that is attracting increasing attention. Two of these ordinances, portions of which were struck down as being unconstitutional, are discussed in Chapter 5 (see the analyses of the *Gospel Missions of America* case).

One of the obvious aspects of these ordinances is the enormous administrative and financial burden they place on charities that raise funds statewide, regionally, and certainly nationally. A court has, however, rejected the argument that the costs of compliance with these ordinances is an unconstitutional form of direct or indirect regulation of interstate commerce; it also held that the substantial benefit to the county involved outweighs any compliance difficulties. Further, a free speech argument (see § 5.3) failed; the court myopically wrote: "The County also correctly points out that localities are well within their power to regulate charitable solicitation within their territorial boundaries" (*American Charities for Reasonable Fundraising Regulation, Inc.* v. *Pinellas County,* 32 F. Supp. 2d 1308, 1325 (M.D. Fla. 1998)).

CHAPTER FOUR

State Regulation of Fundraising: Legal Issues

§ 4.1 **Regulation of Fundraising Costs**
  (a) The Disclosure Dilemma
  (b) The Fundraising Cost Percentage Approach
  (c) Fundraising Cost Line Item Approach
  (d) Floating Average Approach
  (e) Pluralization Approach
  (f) Average Gift Size Factor
  (g) Regulated Disclosure Approach
  (h) Contemporary Perspective
    (i) Period of Existence
    (ii) Programs and Purposes
    (iii) Constituency
    (iv) Methods of Fundraising
    (v) Average Gift Size
    (vi) Unforeseen Circumstances
    (vii) Other Factors
§ 4.2 **Police Power**
§ 4.3 **Fundraising as Free Speech**
  (a) State of Law Before 1980 Supreme Court Decision
  (b) Free Speech Principles in Fundraising Context
    (i) The *Schaumburg* Case
    (ii) The *Munson* Case
    (iii) The *Riley* Case
    (iv) The Dissents
    (v) Subsequent Litigation

  (c) State of Law Subsequent to Supreme Court Decisions
  (d) Airport Terminal Solicitations
  (e) Outer Boundaries of Doctrine
§ 4.4 **Due Process Rights**
§ 4.5 **Equal Protection Rights**
§ 4.6 **Delegation of Legislative Authority**
§ 4.7 **Treatment of Religious Organizations**
  (a) Basic Concepts
  (b) Constitutionality of Exemption
§ 4.8 **Other Constitutional Law Issues**
§ 4.9 **Exemption for Membership Groups**
§ 4.10 **Defining *Professional Fundraiser* and *Professional Solicitor***
§ 4.11 **Direct Mail Fundraising Guidelines**
§ 4.12 **Registration Fees**
§ 4.13 **Fund-Raising Over Internet and State Law Restrictions**
  (a) Internet Fundraising in General
  (b) Charleston Principles
§ 4.14 **Conclusions**

Several issues of law arise concerning the application of state charitable solicitation acts. These issues stand in stark contrast to the general administration of the state charitable solicitation acts. They are reflective of what one court described as the "direct conflict [between] the power of a government to license and regulate those who wish to pursue a professional calling [that is, professional fundraisers] with the rights of free speech protected by the First

Amendment."[1] Another court stated the dilemma more broadly: "It is no easy task to draft a facially neutral and neutral-content ordinance consistent with the first and fourteenth amendments that will protect the public from fraud and harassment in [the] solicitation of funds."[2]

§ 4.1   REGULATION OF FUNDRAISING COSTS

State regulation of charitable solicitations has been on the rise for years, and all indications are that this trend will continue. One of the most important issues arising out of this regulation, and an intense focus of the regulatory attention, is the matter of fundraising costs incurred by charities—internal expenses and fees paid to professional fundraisers, professional solicitors, or both.

There have been well-publicized abuses—and more may be anticipated—of "charitable" entities with excessive fundraising costs, and this exposure has tainted the thinking of many on the subject: the general public, state legislators, and state and local regulators.

Several research projects have been undertaken over the years to examine the matter of fundraising costs experienced by charitable organizations, including the issue of the elements that should be taken into account in assessing the reasonableness of fundraising costs and how to appropriately report these costs.[3] Presumably, all agree that the fundraising costs of every charitable institution and organization should be reasonable, yet there is not much of a consensus as to how to evaluate the reasonableness of fundraising costs.

In the meantime, however, the thought of many state legislators and regulators is hardening—to the detriment of charitable organizations that have what some may regard as "above average" fundraising costs. State regulatory patterns are becoming fixed, and some legislatures in states with charitable solicitation acts presently in place are beginning to rewrite their laws in more stringent fashion. A solution is clearly called for, and some proposals are discussed as follows. But first, consideration must be given to the fundamental elements underlying the issue.

(a) The Disclosure Dilemma

One of the essential functions of most of the state charitable solicitation acts is to promote disclosure of information to the public. A matter of principal concern among charitable groups, and thoughtful legislators and regulators, is the appropriate mode by which to effect public disclosure by organizations soliciting support for philanthropic purposes. This issue basically has revolved around two conflicting positions, represented by the catch phrases *point-of-solicitation disclosure* and *disclosure-on-demand.*

---

[1] *Heritage Publishing Company* v. *Fishman*, 634 F. Supp. 1489, 1499 (D. Minn. 1986).
[2] *International Society for Krishna Consciousness of Houston, Inc.* v. *City of Houston, Texas*, 689 F.2d 541, 543 (5th Cir. 1982).
[3] E.g., "Fund Raising Costs—A Progress Report," XII *Phil. Monthly* (No. 10) 19 (1979).

Under the point-of-solicitation disclosure concept, certain information must be stated as part of the solicitation materials. The solicitation-on-demand approach generally requires that a soliciting charitable organization provide information to the public upon request; in some instances, the solicitation materials must bear notice of the availability of this information.

Proponents of the point-of-solicitation disclosure approach insist that it is the only effective way to ensure that the general public has at least minimal information about a charitable organization at the time the decision as to whether to contribute is made. They assert that most people will not bother to seek information from charities, with the result being little, if any, authentic disclosure. (This view, of course, is becoming anachronistic because considerable information about charitable organizations and fundraising by them is becoming readily available over the Internet.) These advocates view the matter as one akin to consumer protection, with analogy made to existing labeling requirements on containers of food, medicine, and the like.

Opponents of the point-of-solicitation disclosure approach (including proponents of the disclosure-on-demand approach) insist that meaningful and balanced information about a charitable organization (particularly financial data) cannot be presented as part of the solicitation process. They note that the purpose of a solicitation is to raise funds, and they contend that cluttering a solicitation mailing or broadcast with statistical and other information makes the solicitation more confusing and less appealing and, hence, generates fewer dollars, while at the same time making the solicitation more costly to undertake. They also assert that true disclosure cannot be effected by the mere provision of snippets of data and that this type of a requirement would be counterproductive to the law by enhancing the likelihood that misleading information will be transmitted.

At any rate, this line of reasoning continues, authentic public disclosure is not derived as the result of one-on-one correspondence between a charitable organization and a potential donor but rather from access to and publication of the pertinent information by independent watch-dog agencies, government agencies, the media, and other interested groups. Finally, this reasoning rejects the analogy to federal packaging disclosure requirements on the ground that making a charitable contribution is a voluntary act, which affords ample time to secure information if it is wanted, while buying and ingesting food and medicine are done out of necessity and without a reasonable opportunity to write the producer or manufacturer for data about the contents of a foodstuff, drug, or similar item that will likely be consumed before any response is forthcoming.

Thus, in designing or evaluating a charitable solicitation law, the mode of disclosure is a threshold issue. In part, the dispute between the two basic disclosure approaches can be resolved or mitigated by the outcome of the decision as to the items of information to be disclosed at the point of solicitation. For example, even the most vehement opponents of general point-of-solicitation disclosure do not object to a requirement that the solicitation literature include a statement about the purpose of the soliciting charitable organization and the intended use of the contributions solicited. Presumably, most solicitation materials contain this information in any case and, therefore, this type of a requirement, by itself, should pose scant cause for concern (other than the fact that it is mandated by law). By contrast, any requirement that the solicitation materials state the organization's fundraising costs, and perhaps require that these costs be expressed as a percentage of contributions or other receipts, generates considerable controversy and opposition.

(b) The Fundraising Cost Percentage Approach

One observer stated that "in the field today, there is no agreed-upon base for determining fundraising cost percentages."[4] Although that statement was made over 25 years ago, it remains correct today. Irrespective of the context (governmental or nongovernmental), however, the most common practice is to express a charitable organization's fundraising costs in terms of a single percentage. These costs are usually expressed as a function of total receipts or of charitable contributions, using the prior year's financial data.

This approach is popular because of the ease of ascertaining a percentage and using it as a base of comparison of charitable groups. For example, a person researching financial data might see one organization's annual gifts of $100,000 and fundraising costs of $15,000, and another organization's annual gifts of $100,000 and fundraising costs of $20,000, and conclude that the organization with fundraising costs of 15 percent is more *efficient* or *well-managed,* or even *better* (and thus more deserving of charitable support) than the organization with fundraising costs of 20 percent. Moreover, this use of a percentage readily lends itself to the disclosure-at-point-of-solicitation approach, since a simple percentage can be easily displayed on the solicitation literature and, as noted, used by potential donors to evaluate and compare the various soliciting groups.

The percentage approach is roundly attacked on two fundamental bases: (1) because there is no universal standard for computing fundraising costs, meaningful comparisons of organizations are precluded, and (2) a single percentage is a misleading factor to use in evaluating an organization's fundraising practices and overall eligibility for charitable dollars. For example, in the previous illustration, the organization showing fundraising costs of 15 percent may not be including some outlays (perhaps allocable shares of indirect costs) in the calculation, while the organization with fundraising costs of 20 percent is including these outlays. In fact, both organizations' fundraising expenses may be identical (or, perhaps, were the same reporting system being used, the 15-percent organization may show higher fundraising costs than the 20-percent organization). This is not a matter of fraud or cheating but rather one of lack of uniformity and understanding about the expense elements to take into account in constructing the ratio. Also, there may be quite valid reasons, even assuming identical means of determining the percentages, as to why one organization's fundraising costs exceed another's—reasons that have nothing to do with efficiency, cost effectiveness, or program merit. In fact, the 20-percent organization may be better managed than the 15-percent organization.

---

[4] Grimes, "The Fund-Raising Percent as a Quantitative Standard for Regulation of Public Charities," Report to Commission on Private Philanthropy and Public Needs (1975).

Another difficulty with the fundraising cost percentage approach is that it gives undue emphasis and prominence to fundraising costs, by the starkness of a percentage and by stating it in isolation from other financial information. Thus, an organization with annual fundraising expenditures of 10 percent, general administrative and management expenses of 10 percent, charitable outlays of 5 percent, with the remaining 75 percent of its funds expended for speculative land investments, would appear under this approach just as qualified for public support as an organization with the same fundraising and administrative costs but with the remaining 80 percent of its outlays devoted to charitable ends.

Still another concern relates to the fact that fundraising practices are diverse and unique to various types of tax-exempt organizations. Therefore, fundraising costs stated as a single percentage may not be a meaningful indicator of anything or—worse yet—may be so misleading as to be counterproductive to the disclosure motive and unfair to certain categories of charitable groups.

An institution such as a school, college, university, or hospital is likely to have an established donor base and a wide range of fundraising (in this context, termed *development* or *advancement*) methods, including annual giving, planned giving, and charitable bequest programs. This type of an institution is therefore likely to have a relatively low fundraising cost percentage, as may an organization enjoying extensive volunteer assistance. By contrast, another type of organization competing for charitable dollars may be spending most of its money to acquire a donor base, such as a new organization just commencing a direct mail fundraising effort, or may be required to rely heavily on costly fundraising techniques, such as special events. This latter type of organization is therefore likely to have a very high fundraising cost percentage, such as 80 or 90 percent, or even in excess of 100 percent.

The relative merit of these varying categories of organizations cannot be measured by their respective fundraising cost percentages. As noted, a high fundraising cost percentage is by no means indicative of inefficient operation or lack of a worthy purpose. Conversely, it can be shown that an organization that is poorly managed and/or expending excessive sums on fundraising can nonetheless have a low fundraising cost percentage, perhaps attributable to one or more large charitable bequests or unexpected lifetime gifts, or low fundraising costs in one area to offset excessive fundraising costs in another. Also, the fundraising costs for a multiyear capital campaign, which are normally incurred in the initial months of the campaign, or in relation to the establishment of a planned giving program, will introduce additional distortions relative to a single fundraising cost percentage based on a lone year's experience.

As discussed,[5] a once-employed device appearing in state and municipal charitable solicitation laws was the fundraising cost percentage used as a ceiling on permissible outlays. In some instances, the ceiling was an absolute one, barring the solicitation where the maximum was exceeded; it may have been imposed on total fundraising expenses, on fees paid to professional fundraisers, and/or on fees paid to professional solicitors. In other cases, the percentage was used to create a presumption as to whether a fundraising cost was reasonable; an organization could rebut a presumption of unreasonable fundraising

[5] See § 3.9.

costs by demonstrating special facts and circumstances. Percentage-based limitations have, however, been declared unconstitutional, as being violations of free speech.[6]

The realities of the costs of fundraising for charitable purposes are poorly understood by the general public, and in some instances by government regulators and legislators. The maxim that "it takes money to raise money" is frequently incompatible with the typical individual's view of how a charitable dollar should be spent. Many groups understandably fear that the fundraising cost percentage approach will be used by the public as a ranking system by which to evaluate charities for giving purposes. Those holding this view insist that, at least until a uniform and equitable method for calculating the fundraising cost percentage is in place, such a "batting average" approach is an inappropriate way to assess the relative worth of charitable groups. Many are convinced that heavy utilization of this basis of comparison will touch off a "price war" among charitable organizations, igniting unnecessary and unproductive competition among philanthropic entities as to which organizations' fundraising costs are the "lowest."[7]

(c) Fundraising Cost Line Item Approach

Opponents of the fundraising cost percentage approach generally contend that the only suitable manner in which to present a charitable organization's fundraising costs is as part of its financial statements. This approach thus envisions an income and expense statement that displays fundraising costs as a line item, treated no differently from any other category of expenses.

Proponents of line item treatment of fundraising costs assert that mere fairness dictates this approach: (1) it enables an organization to present its fundraising costs in the context of its overall range of costs, and thus does not place undue emphasis on fundraising expenses by causing them to be evaluated in isolation, as is the case with the percentage approach, and (2) it avoids the unfair and misleading aspects, as discussed previously, of the percentage approach.

Again, this matter of the proper method of fundraising costs disclosure becomes inextricably entwined with the point-of-solicitation disclosure versus disclosure-on-demand conflict. It is much more difficult to convey graphically the amount of an organization's fundraising costs using the line item approach rather than the percentage approach, even if a meaningful financial statement is provided at the point of solicitation (which itself may prove impractical). It is also more difficult to make easy comparisons of organizations' fundraising costs when readers have only aggregate sums to consider (although readers can, of course, construct their own fractions and percentages).

Advocates of the line item approach say that this is as it should be, because fundraising cost computations are a complex and intricate matter, that fast and easy fundraising expense calculations are not appropriate, and that

---

[6] See § 4.3.
[7] Analyses of the impact of percentage limitations on charities' fundraising costs appear in Boyle & Jacobs, "Fund-Raising Costs," XII *Phil. Monthly* (No. 4) 5 (1979); Gross, "Fund-Raising and Program Cost Ratios," VIII *Phil. Monthly* (No. 5) 28 (1975).

fundraising cost disclosure cannot meaningfully be achieved at the point of solicitation.

(d) Floating Average Approach

Those who are aware of the deficiencies of the fundraising cost percentage approach, yet believe its virtues (principally, its usage in conjunction with point-of-solicitation disclosure) outweigh those of the fundraising cost line item approach, often seek a means to mitigate the excesses of the percentage approach by proposing a floating or moving average in lieu of a percentage based on only one year's experience. This average would reflect fundraising expense performance over a three- or four-year period. Thus, for example, an organization that raised $100,000 in contributions in each of four consecutive years and incurred fundraising costs of $70,000 in the first year, $50,000 in the second year, $30,000 in the third year, and $10,000 in the fourth year, could, while disclosing its costs during its fifth year, report that its fundraising costs during its previous four years averaged 40 percent rather than having to disclose in year two that its fundraising costs for the prior year were 70 percent; in year three, its prior year's costs were 50 percent; and so forth.

In this fashion, the same essential facts would be disclosed but in a manner that would eliminate the adverse consequences (such as a shortfall in giving) of disclosing only the initial months' costs. This approach would iron out the distortions that appear in a year-by-year evaluation, such as high start-up costs, unexpected and/or large gifts, and unanticipated gains or failures in the solicitation unique to a single year.

There is ample precedent for this approach in the law at the federal level. Congress at present requires the utilization of such a computation in assessing a charitable organization's eligibility for nonprivate foundation status[8] and for compliance with the annual information return (Form 990) filing requirements[9] and the elective legislative activities rules for charitable, educational, religious, and similar categories of organizations.[10]

A fundamental deficiency, however, separates the moving average idea from actual usage: a rule that did not require an organization to report fundraising costs until after two or three years of existence would be an open invitation for abuse by those who would simply create a new soliciting organization every few months and thus never report actual fundraising performance. Moreover, a rule that required annual percentage reporting until a moving average period was achieved (i.e., after three or four years of existence) would defeat its purpose, particularly for new organizations.

(e) Pluralization Approach

Much contemporary thinking has been devoted to this question of the proper method of measuring and reporting fundraising costs. Among the more im-

---

[8] IRC §§ 509(a)(1) and 170(b)(1)(A)(vi), and 509(a)(2).
[9] IRC § 6033(a)(2)(A)(ii).
[10] IRC § 501(h)(1).

pressive of the concepts to emerge is the idea that fundraising costs must be *pluralized* to be meaningful.[11] This approach does not find fault so much with the idea of utilizing a percentage to display fundraising costs as it does with the idea that a true measure of fundraising costs can be captured in a single percentage. According to those who support this concept, the "only way to fairly and productively understand the fundraising costs of an organization that utilizes more than one . . . [fundraising method] is not to look at the total of such costs for a particular period but to look at the total of such costs for each fundraising activity over a period of several years."[12]

In truth, there is no such thing as a single expense for something called *fundraising*, because there is no lone activity that represents *fundraising*. There are many types of fundraising efforts and, while research has yet to document the precise parameters, each effort carries with it a range of costs expressed as a percentage that may be termed reasonable. Also, a fundraising cost that is considered reasonable for one fundraising method is not necessarily reasonable for another. The pluralization doctrine calls for a fundraising cost percentage to be assigned to each of the fundraising methods and for abandonment of reliance on the bottom-line ratio or percentage.

The pluralization approach is predicated on the fundamental fact that there are at least six categories of fundraising methods: donor acquisition by direct mail, donor renewal by direct mail, capital campaigns, special events, planned giving and bequest programs, and indirect campaigns.[13]

The pluralization approach postulates that these fundraising methods may involve associated costs in the following maximum but reasonable amounts: donor acquisition, about 120 percent; donor renewal, about 10 percent; special events, about 20 percent; capital programs, about 15 percent; planned gifts and bequests programs, about 15 percent; and indirect campaigns, about 5 percent.[14] An organization's fundraising costs, where all are reasonable, might be pluralized as shown in Exhibit 4.1.

As noted, one of the great distortions perpetuated by the use of a single percentage to reflect fundraising costs is the fact that the bottom-line percentage can easily camouflage "high" or "inefficient" fundraising costs, which is the very element that this approach is designed to highlight. An organization with fundraising costs expressed on a pluralized basis, as in Exhibit 4.2, illustrates the point.

The deficiency in the bottom-line percentage approach is that it can shelter unreasonable fundraising costs. By any known measurement technique, a total fundraising cost percentage of 12.3 percent is certainly reasonable, yet the

---

[11] E.g., Smallwood and Levis, "The Realities of Fund-Raising Costs and Accountability." X *Phil. Monthly* (No. 9), 3 (1977). Also Smallwood, "Measuring Fund-Raising Costs," V *Case Currents* 18 (Jan. 1979).

[12] Smallwood and Levis, *supra* note 11, at 5.

[13] See *supra* § 2.2.

[14] It must be stressed, as it was by Smallwood and Levis, that these fundraising activities and figures are not based on actual data; thus the percentage figures should not be construed to represent industry standards or norms for reasonable fundraising costs. The charts reproduced herein originally appeared in the article cited *supra* note 11.

Exhibit 4.1. ABC Institution Fundraising Cost-Effectiveness Analysis for the Year Ended December 31, 200X

	Revenue	Expenses	Net	Percentage of Expenses to Revenue
New donor acquisition	$ 116,000	$135,000	$ (19,000)	116.4%
Donor renewal	3,650,000	359,000	3,291,000	10.0
Special events	104,000	18,000	86,000	17.3
Capital programs	692,000	78,000	614,000	11.3
Planned gifts and bequests	481,000	56,000	425,000	11.6
Indirect campaigns	275,000	8,000	267,000	2.9
Total/Overall ratio	$5,318,000	$654,000	$4,664,000	12.3%

fact of unreasonably high donor acquisition costs is hidden in Exhibit 4.2 by offsetting savings in other fundraising outlay areas.

Another deficiency of the single fundraising cost percentage is its unworkability with respect to a new fundraising organization or an organization newly commencing a fundraising effort. This type of an organization lacks a constituency of donors, and its efforts must be concentrated on acquiring that constituency (*donor acquisition*), a much more expensive undertaking than acquiring contributions from those constituting an established donor base (*donor renewal*). Exhibit 4.3 shows how an organization in this position might show its fundraising costs, all of which are reasonable, on a pluralized basis. Without question, many in the general public, in legislative bodies, and in regulatory agencies would regard fundraising costs of 90 percent to be excessive or unreasonable.

The pluralization approach also exposes costs of one method of fundraising, other than direct mail, that are high, even though the bottom-line percentage denotes total fundraising costs that would be generally recognized as reasonable. For example, the costs of an institution's capital

Exhibit 4.2. ABC Institution Fundraising Cost-Effectiveness Analysis for the Year Ended December 31, 200X

	Revenue	Expenses	Net	Percentage of Expense to Revenue
New donor acquisition (direct mail)	$ 116,000	$245,000	$ (129,000)	211.2%
Donor renewal (direct mail)	3,650,000	249,000	3,401,000	6.9
Special events	104,000	18,000	86,000	17.3
Capital programs	692,000	78,000	614,000	11.3
Planned gifts and bequests	481,000	56,000	425,000	11.6
Indirect campaigns	275,000	8,000	267,000	2.9
Total/Overall ratio	$5,318,000	$654,000	$4,664,000	12.3%

Exhibit 4.3. ABC Institution Fundraising Cost-Effectiveness Analysis for the Year Ended December 31, 200X

	Revenue	Expenses	Net	Percentage of Expense to Revenue
New donor acquisition (direct mail)	$250,000	$245,000	$ 5,000	98.0%
Donor renewal (direct mail)	47,000	9,000	38,000	19.2
Special events	18,000	13,000	5,000	72.2
Capital programs	—	—	—	—
Planned gifts and bequests	—	15,000	(15,000)	NA
Indirect campaigns	—	—	—	
Total/Overall ratio	$315,000	$282,000	$33,000	90.0%

programs may be high, yet be offset by other, reasonable fundraising costs, as Exhibit 4.4 illustrates.

Charitable institutions that rely heavily on large gifts of property, where the size and timing of receipt of the contribution bear little relationship to the associated fundraising cost outlays and the timing of the expenditures, can show total fundraising costs at a level of reasonableness, notwithstanding excessive costs with respect to other fundraising methods. This point is illustrated by Exhibit 4.5. In this instance, the hypothetical institution was fortunate to receive, in the year involved, substantial planned gifts and charitable bequests, which sheltered high costs being expended in its other fundraising efforts. Thus, although three categories of fundraising costs were excessive, the institution's total fundraising costs appear reasonable when expressed as a single percentage.

Consequently, the singular contribution of the pluralization method of stating fundraising costs is that it exposes the fallacy of the bottom-line ratio. That is, the single percentage approach, while regarded by many as an essential element of complete disclosure, can make the fundraising costs of certain

Exhibit 4.4. ABC Institution Fundraising Cost-Effectiveness Analysis for the Year Ended December 31, 200X

	Revenue	Expenses	Net	Percentage of Expense to Revenue
New donor acquisition (direct mail)	$ 150,000	$ 160,000	$ (10,000)	106.7%
Donor renewal (direct mail)	1,678,000	178,000	1,500,000	10.6
Special events	85,000	22,000	63,000	25.9
Capital programs	12,350,000	1,791,000	10,559,000	14.5
Planned gifts and bequests	780,000	32,000	748,000	4.1
Indirect campaigns	—	—	—	—
Total/Overall ratio	$15,043,000	$2,183,000	$12,860,000	15.0%

Exhibit 4.5. ABC Institution Fundraising Cost-Effectiveness Analysis for the Year Ended December 31, 200X

	Revenue	Expenses	Net	Percentage of Expense to Revenue
New donor acquisition (direct mail)	$ 115,000	$230,000	$ (115,000)	200.0%
Donor renewal (direct mail)	650,000	195,000	455,000	30.0
Special events	225,000	135,000	90,000	60.0
Capital programs	—	—	—	—
Planned gifts and bequests	1,850,000	6,400	1,843,000	0.3
Indirect campaign	—	—	—	—
Total/Overall ratio	$2,840,000	$566,400	$2,273,000	19.94%

organizations appear "unreasonable" when in fact they are reasonable and—in an outcome perversely counterproductive to the objective of disclosure—can make the fundraising costs of some organizations appear reasonable when in fact they are unreasonable. As has been stated: "Where more than one fundraising technique is being practiced, the bottom-line ratio measurement device can be misleading, manipulated, and counterproductive to and defeating of the principal purposes of the focus on fundraising costs: meaningful and informative disclosure and accurate measurement of fundraising effectiveness."[15]

To date, the pluralization approach of reporting fundraising costs, while a major contribution to the theory of the matter, has not been widely adopted in practice. The pluralization approach has, however, facilitated greater understanding of the complexities of measuring and evaluating the fundraising costs of charitable organizations. It is a useful technique by which an organization can make an internal assessment of its fundraising performance. Perhaps of greatest importance, as discussed later, is the availability of this approach as a method for demonstrating to those concerned about the matter why a charitable organization's fundraising costs are reasonable in the face of a seemingly high single fundraising percentage.

(f) Average Gift Size Factor

The problem of fairly measuring the reasonableness of charitable organizations' fundraising costs is, of course, a particularly acute one for those organizations that, for one reason or another, have relatively high fundraising cost bottom-line ratios. These organizations are all too frequently perceived by regulators, legislators, standards enforcers, donors, media representatives, and others as being ill-intentioned, poorly managed, or both.

---

[15] Smallwood and Levis, *supra* note 11, at 8.

One study has shown that a well-intentioned and well-managed charitable organization that is adversely and unfairly affected by application of set percentage limitations on fundraising costs is likely to have very low cost-per-gift and cost-per-solicitation factors.[16] This type of organization, however, is also likely to depend on comparatively small contributions. Thus, an unfair comparison results when the fundraising cost ratios of this type of organization are compared with those of another charitable organization whose average gift size is much higher but whose cost ratios are relatively smaller when measured by the overall percentage of fundraising costs in relation to contributions. Thus, the former organization appears to have "high" costs of fundraising, while in fact the latter organization has higher costs per gift.

In illustration of this point, envision two charitable organizations, Charity A and Charity B, both of which received $1 million in contributions in the year under comparison. While A's total fundraising costs were $450,000, B's were only $150,000. Thus, B's single percentage fundraising outlay would be 15 percent, and A's would be 45 percent, perhaps putting it in considerable difficulty with prospective donors, the media, and independent watch-dog agencies. But, this comparison is lacking because it fails to reveal one additional and essential factor: the number of gifts, from which can be determined the average gift size and the cost per gift. For Charity A and Charity B, this information is hypothesized as follows:

Charity	Number of Gifts	Average Gift Size	Cost per Gift
A	200,000	$ 5.00	$2.25
B	30,000	33.33	5.00

This example shows that it is inappropriate to compare Charity A with Charity B. That is, using the fundraising cost percentage factor as the basis of comparison, B appears more cost-effective than A, but this conclusion is misleading and unfair to A because it has a lower average gift. Conversely, a comparison on the basis of the cost-per-gift factor shows A as being more cost-effective, but this result is unfair to B because it has a higher average gift. Thus, it can be contended that disclosure of a charitable organization's number of gifts—by category—is essential for a complete and fair evaluation of fundraising costs, and that any comparisons of fundraising performance should occur only between organizations with similar constituencies, based on a number of factors, particularly average gift size.

This approach could lead to a form of point-of-solicitation disclosure that would be an incentive to donors to make larger (more cost-effective) gifts to the disclosing organization. For example, an organization with a fundraising cost percentage of 45 percent and an average gift size of $5 could utilize the following statement in its solicitation literature:

---

[16] Unpublished paper by Wilson C. Levis (Nov. 28, 1979).

We believe an educated donor is our best donor. Because fundraising costs are a major point of discussion in the press and elsewhere, we want you to know exactly how much of your gift will be used for fundraising.

In 2002, we spent an average of $2.25 per gift on fundraising overhead.

The following gift table is provided for your information. Please review it when considering your gift.

| | | | Fundraising Expense | |
| | | | --- | --- |
Check One	Gift Categories	Amount of Your Gift	Cost of Your Gift	Percent of Your Gift
—	Average gift	$ 5.00	$ 2.25	45%
—	General gift	10.00	3.00	30
—	Special gift	25.00	5.00	20
—	Advanced gift	50.00	7.50	15
—	Major gift	100.00	10.00	10
—	Leadership gift	250.00	12.50	5
		or more	more than	less than
		$ _____	$12.50	5%

This approach does not necessarily supplant the need for reporting fundraising costs on a pluralized basis and highlights the unsuitability of the bottom-line percentage as a measurement of fundraising performance. Indeed, the two approaches can be merged so that an organization exceeding the applicable administrative percentage would be required to report on a pluralized basis and display supplemental data concerning its fundraising activity in a manner that might resemble Exhibit 4.6.

Internal management guidelines to determine reasonable fundraising cost percentages are being developed, building on the average gift size concept.[17] These guidelines will vary in relation to the category of fundraising activity, in keeping with the pluralization approach. One of the basic principles underlying the development of these guidelines is the separation of what may be termed "capacity-building" activities from other activities that produce gift revenue. Capacity-building activities essentially are donor acquisition (list-building) programs and special events (of the public relations and marketing type).

Some believe that it is appropriate to take these costs out of the usual computation of fundraising costs because these activities are not primarily fundraising activities. Instead, as noted, they are list-building and public relations activities. These activities tend also to yield little or no net receipts, reflecting the substantial expense associated with them. These expenses, when

[17] "Nonprofit Management Guidelines for Reasonable Fund-Raising Cost Percentages." Nonprofit Management Group. Baruch College. New York (discussion draft, Nov. 1992). A newer version of this proposal was published by the same source on May 10, 1993, with the title "Evaluating Fund Raising ROI [Return On Investment] By Category of Campaign Activity and Average Gift Size Range."

Exhibit 4.6. Illustrative Fundraising Cost-Effectiveness Comparison by Type of Fundraising Activity

Type of Fund-raising Activity	Number of Volunteers	Number of Prospects	Budget or Cost	Cost per Prospect	Number of Gifts	Revenue	Fund-raising Ratio	Average Gift	Cost per Gift
Direct mail—acquisition	1	100,000	$ 15,000	$ 0.15	3,000	$ 15,000	100%	$ 5.00	$ 5.00
Direct mail—renewal	1	50,000	25,000	0.50	20,000	100,000	25	5.00	1.25
Volunteer solicited	2,000	20,000	40,000	2.00	10,000	100,000	40	10.00	4.00
Volunteer solicited—general gifts	250	2,500	15,000	6.00	2,000	100,000	15	50.00	7.50
Volunteer solicited—special gifts	100	1,000	20,000	20.00	800	200,000	10	250.00	25.00
Special event—general	30	3,000	3,750	1.25	300	7,500	50	25.00	12.50
Special event—major	200	10,000	30,000	3.00	1,000	100,000	30	100.00	30.00
Capital project	200	2,000	400,000	200.00	500	5,000,000	8	10,000.00	800.00
Corporation and foundation solicitation	10	300	60,000	200.00	50	600,000	10	12,000.00	1,200.00
Government agency solicitation	10	30	60,000	2,000.00	15	750,000	8	50,000.00	4,000.00
Bequests and trusts	—	400	40,000	100.00	50	500,000	8	10,000.00	500.00
Federated allocations	—	1	5,000	5,000.00	1	200,000	3	200,000.00	6,000.00

considered as part of a fundraising cost as a single number (or percentage), usually unfairly distort the fundraising expense amount.

Thus, these guidelines of reasonableness would have the cost associated with a public relations type of special event as 100 percent of receipts. The cost of a donor acquisition program would be around 150 percent of receipts. Thus, this pluralization approach starkly shows the unfairness inherent in (1) determining a fundraising cost of a charity as a single number and (2) including the costs of capacity-building activities with the fundraising expenses.

The standards for the true fundraising activities are based on the type of fundraising activity and the average gift size. The seven categories of fundraising that are used in these standards are (1) donor renewal programs (the solicitation of prior donors of gifts less than $1,000), (2) special events (that are not primarily public relations or marketing activities), (3) major individual gifts solicitations (from prior donors), (4) seeking of planned gifts, (5) capital and endowment campaigns, (6) corporate gift- and foundation grant-seeking, and (7) seeking of government grants. The average gift size is divided into six categories: (1) $1 to $10, (2) $10 to $24, (3) $25 to $100, (4) $100 to $1,000, (5) $1,000 to $10,000, and (6) $10,000 and above.

The standard of reasonable fundraising cost is thus determined by blending the two sets of factors. For example, according to these guidelines, it would be reasonable to have a fundraising cost percentage of 75 percent for gifts in the $1 to $10 range, but not for the $100 to $1,000 range, where the standard of reasonableness would be 25 percent. Likewise, a fundraising cost of 25 percent would be reasonable for a capital campaign in connection with seeking gifts in the $100 to $1,000 range, while the percentage for gifts of $10,000 and above in the same campaign would be 12 percent.

A fundraising cost percentage that exceeds the appropriate guideline may, according to this approach, indicate "unreasonable levels of performance" requiring an explanation to document why the costs occurred and to determine the conclusions to be drawn from the experience. In a sense, these guidelines are a management tool, in that they force resolution of the question as to whether to continue the fundraising activity as it is presently designed and conducted or to redesign it for a more productive outcome before it is used again.[18]

(g) Regulated Disclosure Approach

For many, the existing manner of the state statutory approaches for regulating fundraising for charity has proven to be unsatisfactory and perhaps even counterproductive. The varying state laws are, pursuant to this view, encumbered with arbitrary requirements, needlessly penalize (in terms of cost of compliance and other burdens on the right to solicit) well-intentioned charitable organizations, and improperly substitute the judgment of the state for the judgment of the giving public. This view perceives a desperate need for a new and enlightened approach to government regulation of fundraising for charity in the face of the ever-expanding scope of governmental involvement in this

---

[18] These guidelines are gaining acceptance in the public media, e.g., Khalaf and Heuslein, "Evaluating Fundraising Efficiency," *Forbes*, Oct. 26, 1992, at 256.

area. (This approach was expounded before developments in the law that found fundraising cost percentage limitations to be unconstitutional.) Advocates of this approach argue that the states should not under any circumstances deny charities the right to solicit contributions, that both rebuttable percentage limitations and tests of what fundraising performances are reasonable are arbitrary because of the variation in interpretation from regulator to regulator, and that even a mandated set of factors to be utilized in assessing the reasonableness of an organization's fundraising costs is an arbitrary approach because of the possibility that different regulators may interpret the same factors to arrive at different conclusions. In an effort to establish the proper regulatory role of the states in this area, and to preserve an effective level of charitable giving, a model charitable solicitation act has been devised.[19]

This proposal contains many of the provisions common to most charitable solicitation statutes: a listing of definitions, a registration requirement for charitable organizations (with no exemptions), a registration and bonding requirement for professional fundraisers, record-retention and contract-filing requirements, an annual reporting obligation imposed on fundraisers, a reciprocal agreement clause, and an enumeration of penalties. The core of this proposal, however, lies in the reporting requirement that would be imposed on soliciting charitable organizations, the frequency of which, unlike any existing approach, would vary in inverse proportion to the level of the organization's fundraising costs.

Under the proposal, a charitable organization with relatively low fundraising costs would be "rewarded" by having to report less often than a charitable organization with relatively high fundraising costs. This entails reporting according to a tripartite timetable, as follows:

1. An organization whose fundraising costs are less than 35 percent of its total gross income for the preceding fiscal year would report biennially.

2. An organization whose fundraising costs are between 35 and 50 percent of gross income would report annually.

3. An organization whose fundraising costs are in excess of 50 percent of gross income would report semiannually, once following the close of its fiscal year and again following the close of the first six months of its subsequent fiscal year.

All reports would have to be prepared in conformance with the accounting principles and reporting procedures established by the American Institute of Certified Public Accountants (AICPA).

The regulator in each state would be required to prepare and publish biennially a "Donor's Directory of Financial Information," made available to the general public at cost. This directory would include an enumeration of registered charities, the total amount of contributions received by each, the amounts of outlays for program and fundraising experienced by each, and an enumeration of registered fundraisers and their compensation.

---

[19] Stevenson, "Regulation in the 80's: A New Approach," XIII *Phil. Monthly* (No. 1) 34 (1980).

This proposal would, it is thought, benefit each state's charities and donors by "(1) elimination of the state's unpopular role as judge and jury in deciding the worthiness of a particular charitable cause; (2) adoption of the concept of a self-supporting regulatory program, thereby lessening the financial burden on the general tax-paying public; (3) staggered financial reporting, which rewards a charitable organization with low fundraising costs by lessening its administrative burden; [and] (4) readily available and easily understood financial information on which to evaluate the performance of charitable organizations and professional fundraisers."[20]

(h) Contemporary Perspective

Along with recent developments in the law that have made percentage restrictions on fundraising costs unconstitutional[21] has come an easing of pressure to develop law and/or regulatory practice that mandates a system for fairly ascertaining fundraising costs. Nonetheless, the fundamental problem persists, inasmuch as some of the state laws force disclosure of fundraising costs;[22] the IRS is displaying renewed interest in the subject;[23] and prospective donors and the media consistently focus on the matter, particularly because annual information returns of tax-exempt organizations, which contain fundraising costs, are public documents.[24]

Despite these visible storm clouds, charitable organizations adversely affected by the focus of government regulators and the general public on levels of annual fundraising costs have yet to undertake a coordinated effort to obtain fair and effective rules concerning determination of the expenses of fundraising for charitable purposes. Yet these groups, and others sympathetic to their plight, are positioned to support an endeavor that could achieve an appropriate resolution to this plaguing regulatory dilemma. Because of the constitutional law aspects, this matter is less of a regulatory problem and more of an educational effort. Everyone from the media to judges needs help in understanding the realities of costs of fundraising.

The ideal would be to develop some consensus between the well-intentioned regulated and the regulators concerning the most effective means for determining fundraising costs and parameters for the reasonableness of these costs.

[20] *Id.* at 40.
[21] See *infra* § 3.
[22] See § 3.15.
[23] See § 5.1.
[24] See § 5.6. Despite the constitutional law aspects of the matter, judges as human beings often have a visceral reaction to "high" fundraising costs, believing that "high" fundraising cost percentages are patently inconsistent with charitable ends. For example:

> The amount expended for charitable purposes is approximately nine percent of the receipts. It is not to be considered that when only nine percent of the total proceeds of activities conducted solely for charity goes to a charity, the operator is in accordance with either the [state] Constitution or the statutes.
> The court does find that the amount of money applied by the defendants to charitable purposes is, per se, unreasonable (*Brown* v. *Marine Club, Inc.*, 365 N.E.2d 1277, 1283 (Ohio 1976)).

The law is filled with requirements that something be reasonable. How the term is defined in practice depends on the particular facts and circumstances. With respect to fundraising, there is no general agreement on the circumstances and factors to be evaluated in ascertaining reasonableness. (In the past, before these percentage limitations were found unconstitutional, this ambiguity caused situations in which charities were denied the authority to solicit contributions in some states because regulators found the fundraising costs to be "too high."[25]) From the charities' point of view, it is difficult to frame a presentation that fundraising costs are reasonable where the organization lacks knowledge of the factors to be used in assessing the costs—or where there is no agreement about the factors.

The factors to be considered in determining the reasonableness of the annual fundraising expenses of a charitable organization include the following.

(i) Period of Existence. The period of time a charitable organization has been in existence should be taken into consideration in determining the reasonableness of its fundraising expenses. A new organization, or an organization newly undertaking a solicitation, may incur fundraising expenses in the initial years of the solicitation that are higher, in relation to total annual receipts, than the costs incurred in subsequent years. Part of this aspect of the matter pertains to the development of an organization's donor base or constituency.

(ii) Programs and Purposes. The nature of a charitable organization's programs and purposes should be taken into consideration in this regard, with particular emphasis on whether the organization advocates one or more causes and disseminates substantive information to the general public as part of the same process by which the organization solicits contributions. Consideration should also be given to whether a charitable organization's programs and purposes involve a subject matter with general public appeal or are sufficiently controversial or unpopular that public support may not readily be forthcoming.

(iii) Constituency. The nature of and extent to which a charitable organization has an established constituency of donors should be taken into account in determining the reasonableness of its fundraising expenses. This factor looks to whether the organization has established a broad base of support

---

[25] Traditionally, the courts have been quite strict in the evaluation of percentage levels of fundraising for charity, guided perhaps by the philosophy expressed by one state court: "[P]hilanthropy should be as free as possible from the hard and sometimes avaricious bargains of the market place" (*People* v. *Stone*, 197 N.Y.S. 2d 380, 383 (1959)). In that case, the court concluded that, "absent special circumstances to justify it, . . . the [fee] charge made by the defendant [a fundraiser], of 45 cents for every dollar collected, is grossly excessive and . . . his failure to inform the contributing public of this percentage arrangement is a fraud upon that public" (*id.*). Also *Lefkowitz* v. *Burden*, 254 N.Y.S. 2d 943 (1964) ($34,651 collected from solicitations and $1,495 expended for charitable purposes). A federal court refused to exempt a fundraising effort (sale of bonds by a nonprofit hospital) from the securities laws, in part because a "substantial purpose" of the bond offering "is to enrich the promoters by providing them with large profits from the enterprise;" the "promoters" were to receive as compensation 10 percent of the proceeds (*Securities and Exchange Commission* v. *Children's Hospital*, 214 F. Supp. 883, 889 (D. Ariz. 1963)).

throughout the general public or whether the organization must create such a base as part of its solicitation process.

(iv) Methods of Fundraising. The methods selected by a charitable organization or available to it to implement its fundraising program should be evaluated in this regard. Consideration should be given to those organizations that, for one or more reasons, must conduct their fundraising by means of only one method of solicitation (such as direct mail).

(v) Average Gift Size. The size of the average annual contribution received by a charitable organization should be taken into consideration in determining the reasonableness of its fundraising expenses. The object of this factor is to ascertain the dependency of the organization on small contributions and whether it is nonetheless cost-effective in the management and expenditure of its receipts.

(vi) Unforeseen Circumstances. The extent to which the expenses of the solicitation effort or efforts of a charitable organization depend on or are otherwise materially affected by unforeseen circumstances should be taken into consideration in this regard.

(vii) Other Factors. The estimate by a charitable organization of its fundraising expenses, and money and property to be raised or received during the immediately succeeding 12-month period, and its reasons for the estimate, including any program for reducing its annual fundraising expenses, should be acknowledged as factors. Also of relevance is the extent to which an organization is organized and operated to attract new and additional public or governmental support on a continuous basis.[26]

These concepts and these factors are beginning to receive greater appreciation in the courts. For example, one court, in finding unconstitutional a disclosure statute triggered when a charitable organization's program outlays were less than 70 percent of funds collected, observed:

> [M]any charities operate below the 70 percent threshold during the early years when they are engaged in building a substantial donor base. Their financial allocations to "program services" may be low simply because they are just getting operations under way and attempting to fulfill a need that is unmet by other organizations. Charities or non-profit groups may also expend more on fundraising or management costs relative to program services because they serve unpopular causes. In either case, it cannot be said that the organization is either fraudulent or less "efficient" in meeting charitable purposes than others with relatively low fundraising or management costs and consequently higher percentage allocations to program services. . . .

---

[26] Also Solomon, "12 Factors in Determining 'Reasonable' Fund-Raising Costs," XII *Phil. Monthly* (No. 11) 30 (1979). Some argue that charitable organizations' fundraising costs should increase (e.g., Levis, "Increased Giving By Investing More Money in Fund Raising—Wisely," XXIII *Phil. Monthly* (Nos. 4 and 5) 51 (1990)).

> More importantly, however, the very organizations most deserving of First Amendment protections—those involved in the dissemination of information, discussion, and advocacy of public issues . . . are likely to have relatively high solicitation or fundraising costs (and therefore lower percentages of donations allocated to program services), not because they are fraudulent or any less efficient in furthering their causes than other nonprofit or charitable organizations, but because the very nature of their activities cause these costs to be high.[27]

The court wrote that, "[g]iven these fundamental flaws in the design and operation" of this provision, "it is only fortuitous that, in some of its applications, this statute might accomplish the State's goals of preventing fraud and providing information to prospective donors about the effectiveness of their contributions in furthering charitable purposes."[28]

A related subject warrants mention, if only because of the proposal for point-of-solicitation disclosure of fundraising costs. This subject is the accounting standards and reporting procedures used to determine these costs. At present, there is substantial variation throughout the philanthropic community about the accounting principles that are followed. Some state laws prescribe use of the *Standards of Accounting and Financial Reporting for Voluntary Health and Welfare Organization* rules, some follow the AICPA Audit Guide rules, some authorize the regulators to develop their own rules, and some fail to address the subject. These variations can have significant consequences on the fundraising cost figure that is ascertained, as evidenced, for example, by the conflict over the extent to which certain costs can be allocated to program and fundraising.[29]

---

[27] *State* v. *Events International, Inc.*, 528 A.2d 458, 462 (Me. 1987).

[28] *Id.*

[29] Among the most controversial issues in the accounting field relating to fundraising is whether or to what extent certain costs can be allocated in part to program and in part to fundraising. For example, many charities understandably consider the costs of mailings or other information activities as being allocable partly to educational efforts and partly to solicitation efforts. This matter is not resolved in the accounting profession, as illustrated by the fact that where the allocation is "reasonable" it is countenanced by the AICPA Statement of Position and the federal standards as embodied in the revised Form 990 requirements, while the *Standards of Accounting and Financial Reporting for Voluntary Health and Welfare Organizations* (the "Black Book") requires the costs to be treated largely as fundraising expenses.

This matter came to the fore in 1979 when the New York Department of State, Office of Charities Registration, restated a rule concerning "multiple purpose information activities," a code phrase for direct mail endeavors whereby charities regard (or would like to regard) the effort as part program and part fundraising. The State of New York opted to continue with the Black Book standards. Thus, the New York rule remains that where an appeal for funds is included as an "essential element" of the activity, nearly all of the costs must be regarded as fundraising expenses. The only exception—other than cases of "non-essential elements"—is that direct costs of educational material included in a multipurpose activity (such as drafting, design, and printing costs) may be charged to program. But all other costs (such as postage and consultants' fees) must be allocated wholly to fundraising. Expenses for multipurpose information activities, other than fundraising costs, however, may be "appropriately allocated and reported."

On occasion, it is difficult to determine just when and how an expenditure may be allocated part to program and part to fundraising (e.g., *Rehabilitation Center and Workshop, Inc.* v. *Commonwealth*, 405 A.2d 980, 983 (Pa. 1979) (where an issue was whether some of the compensation of

§ 4.2 POLICE POWER

Each state and municipality inherently possesses the *police power*.[30] This power enables a state or similar political subdivision to regulate—within the bounds of constitutional and other law principles—the conduct of its citizens and others, so as to protect the safety, health, or welfare of its people. At the same time, there is tension in this area of the law, in that the states may not unduly burden or discriminate in the context of interstate commerce.[31]

Generally, it is clear that a state can enact and enforce, in the exercise of its police power, a charitable solicitation act that requires a charity planning on fundraising in the jurisdiction first to register with (or secure a license or permit from) the appropriate regulatory authorities and subsequently to render periodic reports about the results of the solicitation.[32] There is nothing inherently unlawful about such a law that also requires professional fundraisers and professional solicitors similarly to register and report, that empowers the regulatory authorities to investigate the activities of these organizations and persons in the presence of reasonable cause to do so, and that imposes injunctive remedies, fines, and imprisonment for violation of the statute.[33] It appears

disabled or handicapped individuals, who worked in a direct mail fundraising program, could be treated as expenditures for rehabilitation (program), in that evidence showed that the mailing program "was an aid in the development of social attitudes, eye–hand coordination, and gross and fine manipulation")).

The annual information return filed by most tax-exempt organizations (Form 990) requires that, if the organization reported as program services any joint costs from a "combined educational campaign and fundraising solicitation," the organization must identify the aggregate amount of the joint costs and the specific amounts allocated to program services, fundraising, and management and general (Part II).

[30] E.g., *Thomas* v. *Collins,* 323 U.S. 516 (1945).

[31] The Supreme Court ruled that a state having a property tax exemption for charitable organizations cannot deny that exemption to charitable entities solely because they principally serve nonresidents. The Court reasoned that this type of discriminatory tax exemption is a violation of the commerce clause and thus cannot stand, notwithstanding the states' general authority to legislate on subjects relating to the health, life, and safety of their citizens (*Camps Newfound/ Owatonna, Inc.* v. *Town of Harrison, Maine,* 117 S. Ct. 1590 (1997)). In general, Brody, "Hocking the Halo: Implications of the Charities' Winning Briefs in *Camps Newfound/Owatonna, Inc.,*" XXVII *Stetson L. Rev.* (No. 2) 433 (Fall 1997).

[32] See § 3.3. For example, *Church of Scientology Flag Services Org., Inc.* v. *City of Clearwater,* 756 F. Supp. 1498 (M.D. Fla. 1991) (where the court upheld the constitutionality of a municipal ordinance regulating charitable fundraising by means of features such as the filing of a registration statement, maintenance of records, annual reports, and prohibited acts; the challenges to the ordinance were based on freedom of religion, freedom of speech, freedom of association, overbreadth, privacy, vagueness, and delegation of legislative authority claims). Likewise, *Gospel Missions of America* v. *Bennett,* 951 F. Supp. 1429 (C.D. Fla. 1997) (court found that it was constitutional for a city ordinance to require charity to supply an "information card" before soliciting charitable contributions, mandate disclosure of information relating solely to the solicitation, require that a system of accounting be maintained according to customary accounting principles, and authorize the city to investigate the books and records underlying charitable organizations' financial statements; comparable provisions in a county ordinance were also upheld).

[33] For example, *Indiana Voluntary Firemen's Association, Inc.* v. *Pearson,* 700 F. Supp. 421 (S.D. Ind. 1988) (where the court ruled that the state can constitutionally require solicitors to disclose that they are professional solicitors at the time of solicitation and a subsequent written affirmation of the disclosure).

clear that a state can regulate charitable fundraising notwithstanding the fact that the solicitation occurs in interstate commerce, utilizes the federal postal system, or does both.

In a typical instance, a state's charitable solicitation act was found to "not unduly interfere with interstate commerce, and the commerce clause [of the U.S. Constitution] does not prevent this Court from assuming jurisdiction over the subject matter of this litigation."[34] The court added that the postal clause of the Constitution does "not . . . deny the several states the power to regulate activities whose performance may be effectuated through the use of the mails" [footnote omitted].[35] The characterization of the postal clause to the contrary would, wrote the court, "effectively strip the states of any regulatory power over the importation of products, where such importation is accomplished via the mails, and would thus provide a ready vehicle for the perpetration of fraud and other evils."[36] Another court subsequently stated that, while compliance with a state charitable solicitation act "may burden interstate commerce to some degree, that burden is outweighed by this State's interest in protecting its citizens from the fraud and deceit of unscrupulous 'charitable' organizations."[37]

The rationale is that charitable solicitations may be reasonably regulated to protect the public from deceit, fraud, unreasonable annoyance, or the unscrupulous obtaining of money under a pretense that the money is being collected for a charitable purpose.[38]

One court stated this rationale as follows:

> And the utmost limit of reasonable regulation in the matter is reached by acts protecting the public from charlatans and imposters, insuring knowledge on the part of the donors of the purposes to which their contributions may be put, coupled with adequate safeguards against malversation as to the funds received.[39]

In like vein, one commentator observed:

> The occupation of soliciting for charities is subject to the police power so far as relates to a reasonable supervision over the persons so engaged and for the application and use of the contributions received to the purposes intended, in order to prevent unscrupulous persons from obtaining money or other things under the pretense that they are to be applied to charity,

[34] *Commonwealth* v. *National Federation of the Blind*, 335 A.2d 832, 837 (Pa. 1975).
[35] *Id.*
[36] *Id.*
[37] *Commonwealth* v. *National Federation of the Blind*, 370 A.2d 732, 737 (Pa. 1977).
[38] *Village of Schaumburg* v. *Citizens for a Better Environment* ("*Schaumburg*"), 444 U.S. 620 (1980); *American Cancer Society* v. *City of Dayton* ("*American Cancer Society*"), 114 N.E.2d 219, 224 (1953). The federal postal laws have been interpreted as restricting regulation of charitable fundraising at the local level, however, as evidenced by the text of a decision by the Controller's Office in the city of Indianapolis on March 17, 1980: "Please be advised that it is held that where a charitable solicitation is conducted solely through the use of the U.S. Mail and such charity has no agents or employees operating or transacting business within the City of Indianapolis, the County of Marion or the State of Indiana, that no jurisdiction or authority to require licensure exists."
[39] *In re Dart*, 155 P. 63, 66 (1916).

and to prevent the wrongful diversion of such funds to other uses, or to secure them from waste. Measures reasonably tending to these ends are unquestionably valid.[40]

A state supreme court characterized a city's authority to regulate charitable solicitations as follows:

> The city has the power to enact an ordinance to protect itself from charlatans and imposters and insuring knowledge on the part of donors to charities of the purposes to which their contributions may be put, coupled with adequate safeguards against the misuse or diversion of the funds raised by the charities. The city may by general and nondiscriminatory legislation regulate the time, place, and the manner of soliciting, and may protect its citizens from fraudulent solicitation by requiring a stranger in the community, before permitting him publicly to solicit funds for any purpose, to establish his identity and his authority to act for the cause which he purports to represent, and may require information which will insure that the purposes of the solicitation will be free from any element of deceit and fraud.[41]

Still another court held:

> A city has the right to regulate the use of its streets and may protect its citizens from the fraud and abuse to which charitable solicitations are susceptible when in the hands of unscrupulous persons seeking personal and selfish profit.[42]

And another court wrote:

> The state can protect its citizens from fraudulent solicitation and insure that funds raised actually find their way to the organization for which the solicitation was given by requiring a stranger in the community to establish his identity and his authority to act for the cause he purports to represent before permitting him to publicly solicit funds for any purpose.[43]

As noted, counties, cities, and like jurisdictions also possess the police power. One court broadly stated that "localities are well within their power to regulate charitable solicitation within their territorial boundaries."[44] These ordinances may be authorized by state statute and often permit the governmental jurisdiction to enact rules that are more stringent than those imposed by state law.

Despite the inherent police power lodged in the states and municipalities (to regulate the charitable solicitation process and otherwise), and the general

---

[40] *McQuillin on Municipal Corporations* (3d ed.) § 19.32.

[41] *American Cancer Society, supra* note 38, at 224.

[42] *National Foundation* v. *City of Fort Worth, Texas ("National Foundation")*, 307 F. Supp. 177, 186 (N.D. Tex. 1967), *aff'd*, 415 F.2d 41 (5th Cir. 1969), *cert. denied*, 396 U.S. 1040 (1970). Also *Seattle* v. *Rogers*, 106 P.2d 598 (1940).

[43] *Church of Scientology Flag Services Org., Inc.* v. *City of Clearwater, supra* note 32, at 1515.

[44] *American Charities for Reasonable Fundraising Regulation, Inc.* v. *Pinellas County*, 32 F. Supp. 2d 1308, 1325 (M.D. Fla. 1998).

scope of the power, principles of law operate to confine its reach. Most of these principles are based on constitutional law precepts, such as freedom of speech, procedural and substantive due process, and equal protection of the laws, as well as the standards usually imposed by statutory law, which bars the exercise of the police power in a manner that is whimsical, indiscriminate, or arbitrary.[45]

Courts usually indulge a strong presumption in favor of the constitutionality of legislation. Thus, a court generally will not pass on the constitutionality of a statute or ordinance unless or until it becomes necessary to do so to dispose of the case before it. This means that one challenging a law on constitutional grounds has the substantial burden of convincing a court that constitutional law principles are to govern the outcome of the case.[46]

The Fourteenth Amendment to the U.S. Constitution provides that a state may not "deprive any person of life, liberty, or property, without due process of law; nor deny to any person within its jurisdiction the equal protection of the laws." Most state constitutions contain comparable provisions. The term *liberty*, as used in the Fourteenth Amendment, includes the liberties of freedom of speech and of the press, as well as the general right of liberty of action, as guaranteed by the First Amendment and similar state constitution provisions.[47]

In addition to these fundamental constitutional law protections, there is at least one other pertinent precept of law. This is that the basic regulatory policy must be established by the legislature, including the general standards to be adhered to by the enforcement agency in the performance of its functions, and that the administrative agency, in its rule-making or fact-finding role, must function within the boundaries of the legislatively devised policy and in conformance with it.

In many instances, a solicitation by a charity for contributions is part fundraising and part dissemination of information, the latter being an educational activity. It is indisputable that such a charitable solicitation is action that is sheltered by the constitutional law guarantees and protections as previously discussed, particularly as respects the rights of free speech.[48]

An example of the interplay between the police power of the states and the prohibition on the burdening of interstate commerce is provided in the area of taxation. A state may not enact a tax that provides a competitive advantage to local businesses, because that would be a form of impermissible discrimination against interstate commerce. To pass constitutional muster, a state tax on interstate commerce must be applied to an activity with a substantial nexus with the taxing state, fairly apportioned, nondiscriminatory against interstate commerce, and fairly related to the services provided by the state.

This standard does not apply, however, when the imposition qualifies as a *user fee*. This is a fee collected by a government as reimbursement for use of government-owned or government-provided facilities or services. For example, a charitable organization that wants the IRS to recognize it as a tax-exempt entity

---

[45] E.g., *Hornsby* v. *Allen*, 326 F.2d 605 (5th Cir. 1964).

[46] Once that burden is met, however, these laws can be a fertile field for the finding of constitutional law violations (e.g., *Gospel Missions of America* v. *Bennett, supra* note 32).

[47] *Cantwell* v. *Connecticut*, 310 U.S. 296 (1940).

[48] See *infra* § 3.

must pay a user fee for that service.[49] The registration fees levied pursuant to states' charitable solicitation acts are seen as user fees.[50] The rationale for the distinction between general revenue taxes and user fees is that, where a "tax" is narrowly drawn to reimburse a government for its actual expenses, the possibility that the tax will discriminate against interstate commerce is sharply diminished.

Consequently, the laws that regulate charitable solicitations are by no means constitutionally deficient per se. They are, instead, legitimate utilizations of the states' police power, and those who vociferously complain about the states' regulation in this field must face this basic fact. At the same time, these laws must, like all legislation, conform to certain basic legal standards or face challenges in the courts. As one court observed, while the "government may regulate solicitation in order to protect the community from fraud, . . . [a]ny action impinging upon the freedom of expression and discussion . . . must be minimal, and intimately related to an articulated, substantial government interest."[51] The Supreme Court stated that, while government has "legitimate interests" in this field, it must serve these interests "by narrowly drawn regulations" that do not unnecessarily interfere with First Amendment freedoms.[52] Another court characterized this right of "freedom of action" to fundraise for authentic charity as follows:

> [S]ince every person has the right to solicit contributions for charity if he acts in good faith and makes an honest application of the funds so obtained, regulations of this character which are arbitrary and which assume to say what person or what institution may or may not engage in charitable work are objectionable, as a denial of a common right. The police power cannot be used in such an arbitrary, unreasonable and oppressive manner.[53]

The lawsuits against enforcement of these laws that are currently prevailing are not those that confront the statutes broadside but those that focus on one or more aspects of specific applicability, such as these laws' impact on the practice of religious beliefs, alleged violations of free speech rights caused by refusals to allow solicitations by organizations with fundraising costs in excess of a set percentage, or alleged violations of equal protection rights stemming from exemptions or preferences shown to certain organizations.

§ 4.3 FUNDRAISING AS FREE SPEECH

As a result of significant action by the U.S. Supreme Court throughout the 1980s, in the form of three major opinions, it is amply clear that fundraising for

---

[49] See § 5.7.
[50] See §§ 4.11 and 7.11.
[51] *Citizens for a Better Environment* v. *Village of Schaumburg* (N.D. Ill. 1979).
[52] *Schaumburg, supra* note 38. In this case, the Supreme Court suggested the type of laws that would be suitable: proscription on fraud by solicitors, disclosure of finances of charities to the public, registration and reporting pursuant to state charitable acts, and antitrespass ordinances.
[53] *American Cancer Society, supra* note 38, at 224. Also *City of Fort Worth* v. *Craik*, 411 S.W.3d 541, 542 (1967).

charitable purposes is an exercise of the right of free speech, under both federal and state law principles. This application of the First and Fourteenth Amendments to the U.S. Constitution stands as the single most important bar to more stringent government regulation of the process of soliciting charitable contributions.

Government has, as discussed, the police power to regulate the process of soliciting contributions for charitable purposes.[54] It cannot exercise this power, however, in a manner that unduly intrudes on the rights of free speech of the soliciting charities and their consultants and solicitors.

The most significant clash between a government's police power to regulate for the benefit of its citizens and the free speech rights associated with charitable solicitations involves the application of percentage limitations on fundraising costs as a basis for determining whether a charity may lawfully solicit funds in a jurisdiction.[55] These percentage limitations are, by application of contemporary Supreme Court pronouncements, blatantly violative of charities' free speech rights or, more formally stated, are unconstitutionally overbroad in violation of the First and Fourteenth Amendments to the U.S. Constitution.

The First Amendment to the Constitution states that "Congress shall make no law . . . abridging the freedom of speech. . . ." This prohibition is made applicable to the states through application of the Fourteenth Amendment.

The law makes a distinction between protected speech and "commercial" speech. The latter is treated as the subject of economic regulation, the scope of which must be tested only for rationality.[56] Laws regulating protected speech, however, must be narrowly tailored to an appropriate governmental interest. In the three Supreme Court decisions in this field in the 1980s, the dissenters argued that the fundraising regulation statutes are only limiting commercial speech and that they do so in a reasonable manner.

(a) State of Law Before 1980 Supreme Court Decision

As noted, three Supreme Court decisions during the 1980s spoke directly to the matter of the status of charitable fundraising in relation to free speech rights. The first of these decisions, concerning a town ordinance enacted to regulate the activities of "peddlers and solicitors," was handed down in 1980.

Before 1980, however, the law on the point was not nearly as settled as it is today. It is true that the Supreme Court observed in 1977 that "our cases long have protected speech even though it is in the form of . . . a solicitation to pay or contribute money."[57] In 1980, the Supreme Court embellished this conclusion: "Prior authorities . . . clearly establish that charitable appeals for funds, on the street or door to door, involve a variety of speech interests—communication of

---

[54] See *supra* § 2.

[55] See *supra* § 1.

[56] E.g., *State* v. *O'Neill Investigators, Inc.*, 609 P.2d 520 (Alaska 1980).

[57] *Bates* v. *State Bar of Arizona*, 433 U.S. 350, 363 (1977), citing *New York Times Co.* v. *Sullivan*, 376 U.S. 254 (1964).

information, the dissemination and propagation of views and ideas, and the advocacy of causes—that are within the protection of the First Amendment."[58]

There was authority for the proposition that the states, through the exercise of their police power, cannot exercise this power in such a manner as to unduly intrude on the rights of free speech.[59] An impressive line of Supreme Court cases relevant to canvassing and soliciting by charitable organizations buttresses this conclusion.

For example, one of the early opinions from the Supreme Court in this area held that a state statute, requiring labor organizers to register with and procure an organizer's card from a designated state official before soliciting memberships in labor unions, imposed a previous restraint on the organizers' rights of free speech and free assembly, in violation of the First and Fourteenth Amendments to the U.S. Constitution.[60]

Another early opinion from the Court held that a city ordinance, forbidding as a nuisance the distribution, by hand or otherwise, of literature of any kind without first obtaining written permission from the city manager, violated the Fourteenth Amendment by subjecting freedom of the press to license and censorship.[61]

In another illustration, the Court held that a municipal ordinance, prohibiting solicitation and distribution of circulars by house-to-house canvassing, unless licensed by the police following an inquiry and decision amounting to censorship, was void as applied to those who delivered literature and solicited contributions house to house in the name of religion.[62]

Likewise, a state statute that forbids any person to solicit contributions for a religious cause, unless a certificate for the solicitation is first procured from a designated official, who is required to determine whether the cause is in fact a religious one and who may withhold approval if it is determined that it is not, was held unconstitutional by the Court as a prior restraint on the free exercise of religion and a deprivation of liberty without due process of law in violation of the Fourteenth Amendment.[63]

Thereafter, the Court held that the streets are proper places for the exercise of the freedom of communicating information and disseminating opinion, and that, though the states and municipalities may appropriately regulate the privilege in the public interest, they may not unduly burden or proscribe its employment in these public thoroughfares.[64]

The Court held that a state may not, consistent with the Fourteenth Amendment, prohibit the distribution of handbills in the pursuit of a clearly religious activity merely because the handbills invite the purchase of books for the improved understanding of the religion or because they seek to promote the raising of funds for religious purposes.[65]

---

[58] *Schaumburg, supra* note 38, at 632.

[59] E.g., *Hynes v. Mayor of Oradell,* 425 U.S. 610 (1976).

[60] *Thomas v. Collins, supra* note 30.

[61] *Lovell v. Griffin,* 303 U.S. 444 (1938).

[62] *Schneider v. Irvington,* 308 U.S. 147 (1939).

[63] *Cantwell v. Connecticut, supra* note 47.

[64] *Valentine v. Chrestensen,* 316 U.S. 52 (1942). Cf. *Breard v. Alexandria,* 341 U.S. 622 (1951).

[65] *Jamison v. Texas,* 318 U.S. 413 (1942). Also *Largent v. Texas,* 318 U.S. 418 (1942).

The Court also held that a municipal ordinance that, as construed and applied, required religious corporations to pay a license tax as a condition to the pursuit of their activities was invalid under the U.S. Constitution as a denial of freedom of speech, press, and religion.[66]

To the extent that the constitutionality of percentage limitations in the fundraising context was analyzed by the courts, it was thought that the rebuttable percentage limitation[67] passed constitutional law muster.[68] The Court upheld a law by which regulators can determine the reasonableness of fundraising costs by use of this type of limitation. Nonetheless, future developments in this area of the law were somewhat anticipated in this opinion, with the Court observing that a "fixed percentage limitation on the costs of solicitation might be undesirable and inapplicable if applied to all types of charitable organizations."[69] But the Court added: "The ordinance before us . . . permits a determination of the reasonableness of the ratio between the cost of solicitation and the amount collected."[70]

Despite the foregoing body of law, it was not until the series of decisions in the 1980s that the Supreme Court so starkly laid down the pertinent legal principles that govern today and so forcefully applied them to void fundraising regulation laws as being unconstitutionally overbroad in transgression of free speech principles.

(b) Free Speech Principles in Fundraising Context

The three Supreme Court opinions in this area in the 1980s laid down these fundamental constitutional law precepts:

- The solicitation of charitable contributions is not commercial speech but protected speech.

- Any restrictions on charitable fundraising must be narrowly tailored to advance a legitimate governmental interest.

- . Where the issue is the constitutionality of the use of percentages to assess the legality or other consequences in law of fundraising expenses and the state's interest is the prevention of fraud, the use of percentages will be voided because such a use is unconstitutionally overbroad.

- Where a state has a sufficient interest to regulate charitable fundraising, the nexus between the mode of regulation and the furtherance of that interest must be substantial.

---

[66] *Murdock* v. *Pennsylvania*, 319 U.S. 105 (1943).

[67] See *supra* § 1.

[68] *National Foundation, supra* note 42.

[69] *National Foundation*, 415 F.2d, *supra* note 42, at 46.

[70] *Id.* Some state courts were heading in the other direction, however (e.g., *People ex rel. Scott* v. *Police Hall of Fame*, 376 N.E.2d 665 (Ill. 1978)) (holding that a state statute requiring that at least 75 percent of funds raised be devoted to charitable purposes is constitutional; "[t]hat statutory formula was devised to secure protection for the donations given charities by the public and we do not perceive that it unconstitutionally limits the charities in the exercise of their first amendment rights" (*id.* at 673)).

- A fundraising regulation law cannot constitutionally burden a charitable speaker or a speaker for a charity with unwanted speech during the course of a solicitation.

- A state can constitutionally regulate charitable fundraising by means of antifraud laws, antitrespass laws, and disclosure laws.

- Overregulation of charitable solicitations leads to the chilling of speech in direct contravention of free speech principles.

A summary and analysis of each of these three opinions from the U.S. Supreme Court follows.

(i) **Schaumburg** *Case.* The first of these three Supreme Court opinions emanated from its consideration of a municipal ordinance that prohibited door-to-door or on-street solicitations by charitable organizations that expend more than 25 percent of their receipts for fundraising and administration. Thus, that law forced the requirement that, for a lawful charitable solicitation to occur, the fundraising charity devote at least 75 percent of receipts for charitable program purposes. This percentage limitation was absolute, in that it did not permit a charitable organization to demonstrate the reasonableness of its nonprogram expenses, notwithstanding the fact that the costs exceed the limitation.

The ordinance was that of the village of Schaumburg, Illinois. The village denied a fundraising permit to the Citizens for a Better Environment (CBE) because the CBE could not demonstrate that 75 percent of its receipts would be used for charitable purposes. The CBE was a nonprofit, environmental protection organization, characterized by the Supreme Court as one of a category of organizations that were "advocacy-oriented."[71] It employed "canvassers" who traveled door to door distributing literature and answering questions on environmental topics, soliciting contributions, and receiving complaints about environmental matters for which the CBE might afford assistance.

Unable to secure a permit to solicit in the village, the CBE sued, alleging that the ordinance violated free speech principles, specifically, the First and Fourteenth Amendments to the U.S. Constitution. The CBE prevailed in the trial court, in the federal court of appeals, and in the U.S. Supreme Court, with all three courts finding the ordinance to be unconstitutionally overbroad as an unwarranted transgression of free speech rights.

The village claimed that it was merely exercising its police powers in an attempt to prevent fraud and protect public safety and residential privacy. The Supreme Court agreed that the village had a substantial governmental interest in so protecting the public but concluded that this interest was "only peripherally promoted by the 75-percent requirement and could be sufficiently served by measures less destructive of First Amendment interests."[72] Thus, in this conflict between the police power and free speech rights, the latter predominated. As the Court stated the matter, "The Village may serve its legitimate interests, but it must do so by narrowly drawn regulations

[71] *Schaumburg, supra* note 38, at 627.
[72] *Id.* at 636.

■ 114 ■

designed to serve those interests without unnecessarily interfering with First Amendment freedoms."[73]

The Supreme Court wrote that "charitable appeals for funds, on the street or door to door, involve a variety of speech interests—communication of information, the dissemination and propagation of views and ideas, and the advocacy of causes—that are within the protection of the First Amendment."[74] Thus, the Court in this opinion did not expressly hold that all types of charitable solicitations are forms of protected speech; rather, this constitutional law shelter was provided only for the form of solicitation that is "characteristically intertwined with informative and perhaps persuasive speech seeking support for particular causes or for particular views on economic, political, or social issues."[75] Consequently, this opinion left open the question as to whether protected solicitations are only those that are intermixed with program functions, as opposed to fundraising efforts, such as annual giving appeals and planned gift solicitations, where little or no "advocacy" is present.

Also, just as there was lack of clarity as to whether every charitable solicitation is an act involving free speech, the Court's opinion could have been interpreted to mean that its holding was not applicable to every type of charitable organization. The Court cited, but did not discuss, the appellate court's observation that the 75 percent limitation might be enforceable against the "more traditional charitable organizations" or "where solicitors represent themselves as mere conduits for contributions."[76] Rather, the Court said that the 75 percent rule cannot constitutionally be applied to "advocacy" groups, defined as "organizations whose primary purpose is not to provide money or services for the poor, the needy or other worthy objects of charity, but to gather and disseminate information about and advocate positions on matters of public concern."[77] Quoting from the appellate court's discussion of this point, the Court added that these groups characteristically use paid solicitors who "necessarily combine" the solicitation of financial support with the "functions of information dissemination, discussion, and advocacy of public issues."[78]

Having defined this class of charities, the Court recognized that, even though the salaries they pay were reasonable, they would necessarily expend more than 25 percent of their receipts on salaries and administrative expenses.[79] Then, as observed, the Court proceeded to conclude that a bar on charitable solicitations, applied to these types of charitable organizations by means of the 75-percent limitation, is an unjustified infringement of the First and Fourteenth Amendments to the U.S. Constitution.

One of the principal consequences of this case was the Court's rejection of the absolute percentage limitation on fundraising and administrative costs as a basis for prohibiting charitable solicitations. The Court observed that the "submission [by the village] is that any organization using more than 25% of its

[73] *Id.* at 637.
[74] *Id.* at 632.
[75] *Id.*
[76] *Id.* at 620.
[77] *Id.*
[78] *Id.*
[79] *Id.*

receipts on fundraising, salaries and overhead is not a charitable, but a commercial, for-profit enterprise and that to permit it to represent itself as a charity is fraudulent."[80] The Court wrote that this is not the proper conclusion to be drawn and that "this cannot be true of those organizations that are primarily engaged in research, advocacy or public education and that use their own paid staff to carry out these functions as well as to solicit financial support."[81] Likewise, the Court could not find a substantial relationship between the 75-percent limitation and the protection of public safety or of residential privacy.

The opinion concerning the village of Schaumburg ordinance clearly stated that an *absolute* percentage limitation on fundraising costs as applied to *advocacy* organizations that solicit *door to door* is unconstitutional. This opinion, however, left open these significant questions: (1) Is a *rebuttable* percentage limitation on fundraising costs likewise a violation of free speech rights?[82] (2) Are these protections available to charitable organizations *other than* advocacy groups? (3) Are these protections available to types of fundraising *other than* door-to-door (or on-street) appeals? and (4) What is the validity of percentage limitations that apply, not directly to a charity, but to the compensation of a professional fundraiser or professional solicitor? As discussed next, these questions (and others) were resolved in subsequent Supreme Court pronouncements.

(ii) **Munson** *Case.* Four years later, the U.S. Supreme Court again considered a charitable solicitation law—a statute enacted as part of the law of the state of Maryland.[83] The law generally prohibited, within the state, the solicitation of contributions for a charitable organization that has paid or will pay as expenses more than 25 percent of the amount raised. This law, however, unlike the rigid ordinance of the village of Schaumburg, contained a provision authorizing a waiver, pursuant to rules to be developed by the secretary of state, of the percentage limitation "in those instances where the 25% limitation would effectively prevent a charitable organization from raising contributions." Because of this challenge of the law by Joseph H. Munson Co., Inc., a professional fundraiser, this was the first time that the Court considered the so-called rebuttable percentage limitation in the fundraising context.

Before reviewing the Maryland statute, the Court revisited its rationale for striking down the Schaumburg ordinance. The Court noted its earlier pronouncement that the absolute percentage limitation was a "direct and substantial" limitation on protected activity that could not be upheld because it was not a "precisely tailored means of accommodating" the legitimate interests of the village in protecting the public from fraud, crime, and undue annoyance.[84]

---

[80] *Id.* at 636.

[81] *Id.* at 636–637.

[82] An opinion, written in the immediate aftermath of *Schaumburg* and straining to uphold a fundraising cost limitation featuring a rebuttable presumption (using reasoning that would later be rejected (see *infra* text accompanying notes 84–96), appears as *Holloway* v. *Brown*, 403 N.E.2d 191 (Ohio 1980)).

[83] *Secretary of State of Maryland* v. *Joseph H. Munson Co., Inc.* ("*Munson*"), 467 U.S. 947 (1984), *aff'g* 448 A.2d 935 (Md. 1982), *rev'g* 426 A.2d 985 (Md. 1981), *aff'g* decision of Circuit Court for Anne Arundel County, Maryland.

[84] *Munson,* 467 U.S. at 961.

The Court again noted that the fundamental flaw underlying the municipal ordinance was the assumption that a charity with fundraising expenses in excess of a fixed percentage was operating in a commercial manner; the Court observed that "there is no necessary connection between fraud and high solicitation and administrative costs."[85]

In answer to the question as to "whether the constitutional deficiencies in a percentage limitation on funds expended in [charitable] solicitation are remedied by the possibility of an administrative waiver of the limitation for a charity that can demonstrate financial necessity," the U.S. Supreme Court concluded that the "waiver provision does not save the statute."[86] Once again, the law deploying a percentage limitation was found inherently defective because "it operates on a fundamentally mistaken premise that high solicitation costs are an accurate measure of fraud."[87]

The Court seemed to concede that the Maryland statute may be somewhat more effective at repelling fraud than the Schaumburg ordinance, due to the waiver provision. But it added that the fact that "the statute in some of its applications actually prevents the misdirection of funds from the organization's purported charitable goal is little more than fortuitous."[88] The Court posited these examples: the statute may well restrict free speech that "results in high costs but is itself a part of the charity's goal or that is simply attributable to the fact that the charity's cause proves to be unpopular," yet "if an organization indulges in fraud, there is nothing in the percentage limitation that prevents it from misdirecting funds."[89] "In either event," the Court concluded, "the percentage limitation, though restricting solicitation costs, will have done nothing to prevent fraud."[90]

"[I]n all its applications," wrote the Court, "the [Maryland] statute creates an unnecessary risk of chilling free speech."[91] The Court reasserted its theme in these contexts: "The possibility of a waiver may decrease the number of impermissible applications of the statute, but it does nothing to remedy the statute's fundamental defect."[92]

The state offered reasons in the nature of characteristics of its law, other than the waiver provision, as to why its statute should be salvaged in contradistinction with the Schaumburg ordinance. The Court was unmoved by these features: (1) a charity's ability to solicit funds without having to first prove compliance with the percentage limitation, (2) the limitation applies only to fundraising expenses and not to a variety of other noncharitable expenditures (such as postage), (3) a charity's ability to elect to apply the percentage limitation on a campaign-by-campaign basis, and (4) the applicability of the statute to all forms of fundraising for charitable purposes, not just door-to-door solicitation.

[85] Id.
[86] Id. at 962.
[87] Id. at 966.
[88] Id. at 967.
[89] Id.
[90] Id.
[91] Id. at 968.
[92] Id.

As to the first of these propositions, the Court found elements of a "before-the-fact" prohibition on solicitation, such as the requirement that a contract between a charity and a professional fundraiser must be filed with the state in advance of a solicitation and the fact that the registration of a professional fundraiser will be approved by the state only where the application is in conformity with the statute. But more importantly, the Court decided that this distinction about restraint before or after the commencement of fundraising makes little difference, in that "[w]hether the charity is prevented from engaging in First Amendment activity by the lack of a solicitation permit or by the knowledge that its fundraising activity is illegal if it cannot satisfy the percentage limitation, the chill on the protected activity is the same."[93]

As to the second and third points, the Court dismissed the distinctions as meaning "only that the statute will not apply to as many charities as did the [Schaumburg] ordinance . . ." and added that they "do nothing to alter the fact that significant fundraising activity protected by the First Amendment is barred by the percentage limitation."[94]

The fourth point was rejected on the ground that the broader scope of the statute "does not remedy the fact that the statute promotes the State's interest only peripherally."[95] Dryly, the Court wrote that the "statute's aim [in attempting to attack fraud] is not improved by the fact that it fires at a number of targets."[96]

Thus, the percentage limitation enacted in the state of Maryland was voided by the U.S. Supreme Court on the same ground as that of the Schaumburg ordinance: it was unconstitutionally overbroad in transgression of free speech rights.

Regarding the four questions left unanswered by the Supreme Court in 1980 when considering the municipal ordinance, the Court in 1984 clearly answered the first question in the affirmative: a rebuttable percentage limitation is just as constitutionally deficient as an absolute one.

The second and third questions basically went unaddressed in this second opinion. Yet there is nothing in the opinion concerning the Maryland statute that suggests that free speech rights are extended only to advocacy groups. Indeed, throughout most of the opinion, reference is only to charities, with the Court observing that advocacy groups are the "organizations that were of primary concern to the Court" in its prior opinion.[97] The only instance of an attempt by the Court in 1984 to bifurcate the charitable world in these regards came when it made reference to "organizations that have high fundraising costs not due to protected First Amendment activity"; this distinction was dismissed with the observation that "this statute cannot distinguish those organizations from charities that have high costs due to protected First Amendment activities."[98] Consequently, there should be little doubt that free speech

[93] *Id.* at 969.
[94] *Id.*
[95] *Id.*
[96] *Id.* at 970.
[97] *Id.* at 963.
[98] *Id.* at 966.

rights in these regards are extended to all charities, either because the law treats all charitable organizations as protected when fundraising or because the law has yet to contemplate a statute that can constitutionally distinguish between the two categories of charitable entities.

Moreover, there is nothing in the opinion concerning the Maryland statute that suggests that free speech protections are available only for fundraising that occurs door to door. Indeed, the opinion specifically notes, without comment as to the distinction, that the statute "regulates all charitable fundraising, and not just door-to-door solicitation."[99] Again, there should be little doubt that free speech rights in these regards are extended to all forms of fundraising for charitable purposes.

The fourth question was not fully answered in the opinion concerning the Maryland statute. Yet the ultimate outcome was subtly hinted at in the 1984 opinion. In the case construing the Maryland statute, the plaintiff was not a charitable organization but a professional fundraiser. This generated a number of legal problems, principally the question of standing, but the merits of the opinion implicitly stated that free speech rights in the charitable fundraising context extended beyond rights asserted directly by or on behalf of charitable organizations.

(iii) **Riley Case.** Surprisingly, during the 1980s, the U.S. Supreme Court elected to revisit the charitable fundraising/free speech issue a third time. By this time, Justice William H. Rehnquist, the principal author of the dissents in the previous two cases had become the Chief Justice of the Supreme Court, and it is fairly obvious that he orchestrated the taking of the case in one last attempt to trim the reach of the prior two opinions. But this failed.

In 1988, the U.S. Supreme Court rendered still another opinion addressing the constitutionality of a charitable fundraising regulation law.[100] At issue in this instance were provisions of the North Carolina charitable solicitation act. Just as the Maryland statute attempted to sidestep constitutional law infirmities by being more sophisticated than the Schaumburg ordinance, the North Carolina statute tried to be constitutional by being more sophisticated than the Maryland law. Part of the problem with the North Carolina statute was that it was worded as a near parody of the previous Supreme Court rulings and as a too-obvious attempt to stay within the boundaries of fundraising regulation circumscribed by the law of free speech rights.

The North Carolina charitable solicitation law did not place a limitation on fundraising expenses by charitable organizations. Rather, it endeavored to constitutionally place a limitation on the amount or extent of fees paid by a charitable organization to professional fundraisers or professional solicitors. The general rule as articulated by this law was that a professional fundraiser or solicitor could not lawfully charge a charitable organization an "excessive and unreasonable" fee. This law established a three-tiered schedule, using percentage-based mechanical presumptions, for determining whether a particular fee was in fact excessive and unreasonable.

---

[99] *Id.* at 969.
[100] *Riley* v. *National Federation of the Blind of North Carolina, Inc.* ("*Riley*"), 487 U.S. 781 (1988), *aff'g* 817 F.2d 102 (4th Cir. 1987), *aff'g* 635 F. Supp. 256 (E.D.N.Car. 1986).

Under the North Carolina statute, a fee that was not in excess of 20 percent of the gross receipts collected was deemed "reasonable and nonexcessive." Where a fee was between 20 and 35 percent of gross receipts collected, the law deemed the fee to be excessive and unreasonable upon a showing that the solicitation at issue "did not involve the dissemination of information, discussion, or advocacy relating to public issues as directed by the . . . [charitable organization] which is to benefit from the solicitation." A fee in excess of 35 percent was presumed to be excessive and unreasonable, although the fundraiser or solicitor could rebut the presumption by showing that the amount of the fee was necessary because (1) the solicitation involved the dissemination of information or advocacy on public issues directed by the charity, or (2) otherwise the ability of the charity to raise money or communicate its ideas and positions to the public would be seriously diminished. The Court went on to describe an additional feature of the North Carolina statute, in that "even where a prima facie showing of unreasonableness has been rebutted, the fact-finder must still make an ultimate determination, on a case-by-case basis, as to whether the fee was reasonable—a showing that the solicitation involved the advocacy or dissemination of information does not alone establish that the total fee was reasonable."[101]

The U.S. Supreme Court concluded that the three-tiered, percentage-based definition of a "reasonable" fundraising fee in the North Carolina law failed to pass constitutional muster, as being unduly burdensome of free speech. It rejected the rationale that the statute is constitutional because it was designed to ensure that the maximum amount of funds reaches the charity on the ground that the law is overbroad and in violation of the "First Amendment's command that government regulation of speech must be measured in minimums, not maximums."[102] The Court likewise dismissed the thought that the North Carolina law's flexibility more narrowly tailors it to the state's asserted interests than was the case with the Maryland statute or the Schaumburg ordinance, noting that "[p]ermitting rebuttal cannot supply the missing nexus between the percentages and the State's interest."[103]

The Court considered other justifications offered by the state of North Carolina for regulating the reasonableness of fundraisers' fees, portraying them as resting on one or both of two premises: "(1) that charitable organizations are economically unable to negotiate fair or reasonable contracts without governmental assistance; or (2) that charities are incapable of deciding for themselves the most effective way to exercise their First Amendment rights."[104] Rejecting both premises, the Court wrote that there is no constitutional law basis for the claim by the state of "the power to establish a single transcendent criterion by which it can bind the charities' speaking decisions," finding the state's position "paternalistic."[105]

The Court observed that the "First Amendment mandates that we presume that speakers, not the government, know best both what they want to say

[101] *Riley*, 487 U.S. at 786.
[102] *Id.* at 790.
[103] *Id.* at 793.
[104] *Id.* at 790.
[105] *Id.*

and how to say it."[106] "To this end," continued the Court, the "government, even with the purest of motives, may not substitute its judgment as to how best to speak for that of speakers and listeners; free and robust debate cannot thrive if directed by the government."[107] On this point, the Court then administered this coup de grace: "We perceive no reason to engraft an exception to this settled rule for charities."[108]

The Court in this case also attacked the general concept of forcing fundraising charities to prove "reasonableness" of fees on the basis of the size of the fundraiser's fee. That fee, wrote the Court, may be one of many factors affecting fundraising expenses; others include the type of fundraising involved and the integration of a non-fundraising event with a fundraising effort.[109] Moreover, added the Court, the law is "impermissibly insensitive to the realities faced by small or unpopular charities, which must often pay more than 35% of the gross receipts collected to the fundraiser due to the difficulty of attracting donors" and thus its "scheme must necessarily chill speech in direct contravention of the First Amendment's dictates."[110]

In this case invalidating this aspect of the North Carolina statute, the Court returned to a theme articulated in its opinion concerning the Maryland law: the ability of the states to combat fundraising fraud by means of antifraud statutes and general disclosure requirements. The Court acknowledged that these laws may not be the most efficient methods of preventing fraud, but added that "the First Amendment does not permit the State to sacrifice speech for efficiency."[111]

Having dispensed with this aspect of the North Carolina law (by voiding it), the Court turned to a somewhat comparable feature: another provision requiring that professional fundraisers disclose to potential donors, before an appeal for funds, the percentage of charitable contributions collected during the previous 12 months that were expended for charitable purposes. While the state contended that this was a limitation only on commercial speech, in that it relates merely to the fundraiser's profits from a solicitation, the Court wrote that, even if that is true, "we do not believe that the speech retains its commercial character when it is inextricably intertwined with otherwise fully protected speech."[112] Deciding that "we cannot parcel out the speech, applying one test to one phrase and another test to another phrase,"[113] the Court held that this "prophylactic, imprecise, and unduly burdensome rule" is unconstitutional.[114]

These three U.S. Supreme Court opinions set the stage for more litigation over the permissible reach of state charitable solicitation laws. The essence of these opinions appears at the outset of this section. Aside from the specific rules to be gleaned from these three decisions, the one basic principle of law

---

[106] *Id.* at 790–791.
[107] *Id.* at 791.
[108] *Id.*
[109] *Id.* at 791–792.
[110] *Id.* at 793–794.
[111] *Id.* at 795.
[112] *Id.* at 796.
[113] *Id.*
[114] *Id.* at 800.

that is most important is that these fundraising regulation laws "may not burden a speaker [be it a charity or a fundraising professional] with unwanted
speech during the course of a solicitation."[115]

(iv) Dissents. Each of these three U.S. Supreme Court opinions was accompanied by a dissenting opinion. The fundamental theme of the dissents was
that charitable fundraising is a type of commercial speech and that the provisions limiting fundraising expenses are merely forms of economic regulation
with no First Amendment implication. The corollary to this view is that the percentage ceilings are permissible as being "reasonable" approaches to regulation.

The essence of the dissent in the opinion concerning the ordinance of
the village of Schaumburg was that "a simple request for money lies far from
the core protections of the First Amendment. . . ."[116] In this context, the dissenting view was that "the community's interest in insuring that the collecting organization meet some objective financial criteria is indisputably valid,"
so that the community can insulate itself "against panhandlers, profiteers,
and peddlers."[117]

The dissents distinguished the pre-1980 state of law in this area by stating that the statutes were struck down because of the amount of discretion
vested in the regulators to grant or deny permits on the basis of vague or nonexistent criteria, or because the matter involved the distribution of information
(as opposed to requests for contributions). The view embodied in the dissents
is that the law should be different when the rule "deals not with the dissemination of ideas, but rather with the solicitation of money."[118]

The dissent in the 1980 case summarized its position with the view that
the ordinance, "while perhaps too strict to suit some tastes, affects only door-
to-door solicitation for financial contributions, leaves little or no discretion in
the hands of municipal authorities to 'censor' unpopular speech, and is rationally related to the community's collective desire to bestow its largess upon
organizations that are truly 'charitable.'"[119]

The dissent in the case involving the Maryland statute added an argument as a result of the nature of the particular facts of the case. This was the
contention that constitutional rights cannot be "asserted vicariously,"[120]
namely (in the case), by a professional fundraiser rather than a charitable organization, leading to the thought that the overbreadth doctrine is inapplicable in
the case. This approach was then used to lead into the argument that, again,
the speech is commercial speech. Yet, in this latter setting, the underlying

---

[115] *Id.* See "State Governments Revise Fundraising Laws," XXII *Phil. Monthly* (No. 7) 5 (1989);
Copilevitz, "After The Life of Riley," XXI *Phil. Monthly* (No. 5) 20 (1988); Suhrke, "North Carolina
Loses At The Supreme Court," XXI *Phil. Monthly* (No. 4) 5 (1988); Copilevitz, "Protected Speech
and Commerce," XXI *Phil. Monthly* (No. 2) 11 (1988); "A Major Fund Raising Case At The Supreme
Court," XXI *Phil. Monthly* (No. 1) 4 (1988).
[116] *Schaumburg, supra* note 38, at 644.
[117] *Id.*
[118] *Id.* at 641.
[119] *Id.* at 645.
[120] *Munson,* 467 U.S., *supra* note 83, at 977.

premise of the argument reflected a slight shift of view by observing that the "challenged Maryland statute functions primarily as an economic regulation setting a limit on the fees charged by professional fundraisers."[121] This observation seems to indicate an abandonment of the view, for purposes of dissent writing, that fundraising by charities is commercial speech and to focus instead on the argument that the statute, when applied to fundraisers, involves commercial speech. Any impact on fundraising by charities was considered "incidental and indirect,"[122] so that there is no need to subject the law to strict First Amendment scrutiny. The dissent in the case involving the Maryland statute reinvoked the point that the limitations on the fees charged by professional fundraisers served several legitimate and substantial governmental interests. And, finally, the dissent in the case tried to distinguish the Maryland law from the Schaumburg ordinance on the ground of the various flexibilities inherent in the percentage limitation contained in the latter provision.

The dissent in the case concerning the North Carolina law expectedly repeated the arguments in the prior two dissents. This dissent, however, argued that, even if the other two cases were rightfully decided, this one was not because the fee limitations "put no direct burden on the charities themselves."[123] Once again, the contention was advanced that the matter is one of economic regulation only, with the Court majority accused of stretching for applicability of free speech principles: "As far as I know, this Court has never held that an economic regulation with some impact on protected speech, no matter how small or indirect, must be subjected to strict scrutiny under the First Amendment."[124] This dissent also found that the approach of the statute in ascertaining the reasonableness of fundraisers' fees "protects against the vices of the fixed-percentage scheme struck down in 1984," and that the "fee provisions of the statute thus satisfy the constitutional requirement that it be narrowly tailored to serve the State's compelling interests."[125]

As to the professional fundraisers' disclosure requirement, the dissent contended that the rule survives free speech analysis in that the "required disclosure of true facts in the course of what is at least in part a 'commercial' transaction—the solicitation of money by a professional fundraiser—does not necessarily create such a burden on core protected speech as to require that strict scrutiny be applied."[126]

(v) Subsequent Litigation.   The tenor of the second and third of the previous opinions emanating from the U.S. Supreme Court indicated that the free speech principles extended to fundraising for charitable purposes are not necessarily dependent on the type of charitable entity involved nor on the type of fundraising involved. Subsequent pronouncements indicate that the lower

---

[121] *Id.* at 978.
[122] *Id.* at 947.
[123] *Riley*, 487 U.S., *supra* note 100, at 806.
[124] *Id.* at 807.
[125] *Id.* at 809–810.
[126] *Id.* at 811.

courts are embracing these principles in settings other than considerations of the limitations on fundraising expenses.[127]

(c) State of Law Subsequent to Supreme Court Decisions

A significant case that developed in the aftermath of these three Supreme Court pronouncements concerned application of the Virginia charitable solicitation act.[128] The opinion involved did not create any new law but reinforced legal principles so articulately promulgated by the Supreme Court during the 1980s.

The litigation was initiated by a corporation that was in the business of providing fundraising services to police organizations and firefighter unions. The organization contracted with local police fraternal organizations in Virginia to solicit advertising for publications used in a fundraising campaign.

The opinion pertained to four aspects of the Virginia statute. One of these provisions required professional solicitors to submit the script of an oral solicitation to the state at least 10 days before the commencement of solicitation. The state argued that this section promoted the state's interest in the prevention of fraud and misrepresentation in solicitation, and that it was the only effective regulation of fundraising by telephone.

The appellate court found, however, that the section was an unconstitutional prior restraint on speech. It held that, while the state has a legitimate interest in preventing fraud and misrepresentation, there "is a thin line between reviewing a script for misrepresentations and reviewing it for content."[129] The court wrote that state officials were able to "recast solicitation scripts so as to reflect their judgment as to how a solicitation can be made."[130] The state attempted to convince the court that its officials properly utilized this section, but the court held that none of the state's assurances persuaded it that "bureaucratic review of solicitation scripts is not rife with potential for abuse."[131]

As to the thought that this section may be the most effective means of monitoring telephone solicitations, the court quoted Supreme Court pronouncements in observing that the "First Amendment does not permit the State to sacrifice speech for efficiency."[132]

Another provision of the Virginia law requires professional solicitors to disclose in writing that financial statements for the most recent fiscal year are available from the state. The state contended that this section promotes its interest in public education regarding charitable organizations and prevents

---

[127] See "State Regulators Are Still (1989) Coming To Terms With . . . *Schaumburg* (1980), *Munson* (1984), and *Riley* (1988)," XXII *Phil. Monthly* (No. 8) 20 (1989). A brief history of the case law in this area is the subject of Copilevitz, "The Historical Role of the First Amendment in Charitable Appeals," XXVII *Stetson L. Rev.* (No. 2) 457 (Fall 1997).

[128] *Telco Communications, Inc.* v. *Carbaugh*, 885 F.2d 1225 (4th Cir. 1989), *aff'g in part and rev'g in part*, 700 F. Supp. 294 (E.D. Va. 1988).

[129] *Id.*, 885 F.2d at 1233.

[130] *Id.*

[131] *Id.*

[132] *Id.*

fraud and harassment, and also that the requirement is narrowly tailored to further these interests. The court responded: "We agree."[133]

The agreement was based on the thought that informing the public and preventing fraud are substantial state interests, which are fostered by the provision. The court ruled that the state's interest in "adding to the public knowledge of professional solicitations" is not one that is inherently incompatible with free speech rights.[134] The provision was characterized as one that "educates the public generally about the availability of financial information on solicitors."[135]

The information contained in the financial statements was held to be "invaluable," in that a donor can use the information "to learn further about a solicitor's operations," and the provision was held to assist in preventing fraud.[136] The requirement was found to be narrowly tailored and thus a permissible exercise of state authority.

Also at issue was the Virginia rule that a professional solicitor must disclose to potential donors the percentage of their contribution that will be received by the charitable organization for its use. The challenge to the constitutionality of this provision was held moot, on the ground that the state had conceded the fatal flaw of the statute, under free speech law analysis, and that there was no "reasonable expectation" that the state would seek to enforce the requirement.[137] This change of heart on the part of the state was occasioned by the most recent of the three Supreme Court opinions,[138] and the court "decline[d] to indulge any presumption with respect to their conduct other than one of good faith."[139]

The final provision at issue concerned the ability of the state to suspend or revoke the registration of a solicitor if certain provisions of the statute were violated. This aspect of the complaint was dismissed because the pleadings and records underlying the complaint were found to be inadequate.

The doctrine laid down by the U.S. Supreme Court, starting in 1980, holding, as noted, that the regulation of the process of fundraising for charitable purposes must be undertaken only by the most restrictive of means because the solicitation of gifts is a free speech right of the charities, has spawned subsequent applications of that principle.

The rule has been applied many times in a variety of settings. In 1989 alone, there were seven applications of the doctrine, including the decision just discussed, which construed portions of the Virginia charitable solicitation act.

Thus, the Supreme Court struck down a provision of the amended Federal Communications Act, which attempted to impose an outright ban on indecent interstate commercial telephone messages ("dial-a-porn").[140] The government wanted the ban as a way to prevent minors from gaining access to the messages.

---

[133] *Id.* at 1231.
[134] *Id.*
[135] *Id.*
[136] *Id.*
[137] *Id.*
[138] *Riley,* 487 U.S., *supra* note 100.
[139] *Telco Communications, Inc.* v. *Carbaugh,* 885 F.2d, *supra* note 128, at 1231.
[140] *Sable Communications of California, Inc.* v. *Federal Communications Commission,* 492 U.S. 115 (1989).

But the Court found that, notwithstanding the compelling interest in protecting the physical and psychological well-being of minors, the prohibition "far exceeds that which is necessary to limit the access of minors to such messages," and thus the "ban does not survive constitutional scrutiny."[141] That is, the statute was found to be overbroad in relation to the problem to be solved and thus unconstitutional, since free speech is involved. (A similar prohibition involving obscene dial-a-porn recordings was upheld, because the protection of the free speech right does not extend to obscene speech.)

The Supreme Court declined to undertake an overbreadth analysis in another case, but only because the statute in question was amended before the Court's review. At issue was a law prohibiting adults from posing or exhibiting minors "in a state of nudity" for purposes of visual presentation in a publication or photograph. The Massachusetts Supreme Judicial Court reversed the conviction of a man who took photographs of his partially nude and physically mature 14-year-old stepdaughter.[142] There is little doubt that the Supreme Court would have reversed this conviction as well, given the opportunity—the Massachusetts court found the posing to be an act of free speech.

The U.S. Court of Appeals for the Eighth Circuit construed the provisions of the Hatch Act, which is the law forbidding partisan political activity by federal employees.[143] The case concerned the solicitation of funds from governmental employees, which is illegal to the extent used for partisan political campaigns; the appellate court ruled, however, that the act cannot constitutionally prohibit solicitations for lobbying because that is protected speech. The court of appeals observed: "Solicitations necessarily involve advocacy and deserve the full protection of the First Amendment."[144]

The U.S. Court of Appeals for the Fourth Circuit found unconstitutional the federal regulation prohibiting solicitations on property of the U.S. Postal Service.[145] The sidewalk in front of the post office involved was held to be a public forum, with the prohibition found to be neither a reasonable manner restriction nor narrowly drawn to accomplish a significant governmental interest. The court observed that the speech at issue was political, not commercial, and endorsed the precept that gift solicitation and substantive, informative speech can be intertwined.[146] Dismissing postal service assertions of obstructions of customers, the court wrote: "Outright prohibition of a medium of expression will always prove the easier and more efficient course. Yet liberty itself is no efficient concept, and the rights of citizens and interests of government are best reconciled not by total bans but through finespun accommodations."[147]

This opinion was reversed by the Supreme Court, however, when a majority concluded that in-person solicitation of money on the post office sidewalk could be prohibited without violating free speech rights.[148] A plurality of the

---

[141] *Id.* at 131.
[142] *Massachusetts* v. *Oakes*, 518 N.E.2d 836 (Mass. 1989), *vac'd and rem'd*, 491 U.S. 576 (1989).
[143] *Bauers* v. *Cornett*, 865 F.2d 1517 (8th Cir. 1989).
[144] *Id.* at 1520, note 2.
[145] *United States* v. *Kokinda*, 866 F.2d 699 (4th Cir. 1989).
[146] *Id.* at 703.
[147] *Id.* at 704.
[148] *United States* v. *Kokinda*, 497 U.S. 720 (1990).

court found that the sidewalk was a nonpublic forum, being intended "solely to assist postal patrons" to obtain access to postal services.[149] The in-person solicitation of funds was held to be "inherently disruptive of the postal service's business" in that it "impedes the normal flow of traffic."[150] This decision enabled the Court to use a reasonableness test, which permits restrictions on speech in nonpublic forums as long as they are viewpoint-neutral.[151]

The U.S. Court of Appeals for the Fifth Circuit had occasion to discuss both of these elements—the presence of a compelling governmental interest and the narrowness of a restriction on free speech—in finding that a city's fire department rule was unconstitutionally applied to a firefighter, who, to the unhappiness of his employer, spoke to the media about the department's shortcomings in fighting a fire, in violation of his free speech rights.[152] This rule was found to support governmental interests but held to violate the second test, in that it was too sweeping in its application.

The U.S. District Court for the District of Columbia struck down the record-keeping requirements and certain other provisions of the Child Protection and Obscenity Enforcement Act (enacted in 1988) as violating free speech principles.[153] The record-keeping requirements were to be imposed on categories of material broader than obscene material and, thus, on material protected by free speech rights. Noting that "[l]aws that burden material protected by the First Amendment must be approached from a skeptical point of view and must be given strict scrutiny,"[154] the court concluded that, notwithstanding a legitimate governmental interest—i.e., efforts to eliminate child pornography—the record-keeping requirements burden too heavily the right to produce protected material and were not narrowly tailored to fit the government's interest.

Other applications of the free speech doctrine have been made in the context of fundraising for charity.

A challenge to a city ordinance regulating charitable fundraising was unsuccessful, with a federal appellate court holding that the regulatory framework was constitutional.[155] The ordinance had been amended, however, just before the court's consideration of the case; the regulatory scheme was substantially simplified and various provisions excised that would have been rendered unconstitutional as being in violation of free speech rights.[156] One of the provisions that was timely removed accorded the government the authority to disqualify an applicant charitable organization when more than 25 percent of the funds to be collected were to be used for noncharitable purposes.

The Supreme Court of Tennessee found unconstitutional a provision in the state's charitable solicitation act forbidding telemarketing for charitable

---

[149] *Id.* at 728.

[150] *Id.* at 732–734.

[151] E.g., *Cornelius* v. *NAACP Legal Defense and Educational Fund*, 473 U.S. 788 (1985); *Perry Education Association* v. *Perry Local Educators' Association*, 460 U.S. 37 (1983).

[152] *Moore* v. *City of Kilgore, Texas*, 877 F.2d 364 (5th Cir. 1989).

[153] *American Library Association* v. *Thornburgh*, 713 F. Supp. 469 (D.D.C. 1989).

[154] *Id.* at 476.

[155] *International Society for Krishna Consciousness of Houston, Inc.* v. *City of Houston, supra* note 2.

[156] *Id.* at 546–47.

purposes and thus voided the provision.[157] The statute banned telephone solicitations for gifts by professional solicitors, and defined the term *telephone solicitations* sufficiently broad to embrace the activities of many professional fundraisers. The court held that an outright ban on telephone solicitations is impermissible as violative of charities' rights of free speech. It noted that the state must use the least restrictive means to protect its citizens from charitable fundraising fraud and observed that the state failed to show that the ban on telephone fundraising provides any deterrence to fraud.[158] The Tennessee court also found unconstitutional a limitation on the fees paid to professional solicitors (15 percent of contributions solicited).

A federal district court found that the provision of a Massachusetts law that limited a professional solicitor's compensation to 25 percent of moneys raised for charity is unconstitutional because it impermissibly intruded on the free speech rights of charitable organizations.[159] Concluding (as is clearly now the law) that "[p]ercentage limitations on charities' fundraising expenditures are too imprecise a tool to protect the public from fraud,"[160] the court held that the statute was more than merely an allowable economic regulation of professional solicitors, in that it unduly burdened charitable free speech, and that there are less restrictive means available to accomplish the state's interest in protecting public confidence in charitable solicitations.[161] On appeal, this opinion was affirmed, with the appellate court dismissing the argument differentiating between percentage limitations on charitable organizations and professional solicitors as being a "distinction without a difference."[162]

A similar opinion was issued by another federal district court holding that a percentage limitation on the compensation of professional solicitors serving charitable organizations constitutes a direct and substantial limitation on the free speech interests of solicitors and charities.[163] The same refrain was echoed: "Whether the statute limits what a charity may pay or what a professional fundraiser may receive simply does not affect the impact that the limitation has on the free speech rights of the charity."[164] Again, the potential of a waiver from the limitation was held to not remedy its fundamental defect, and

---

[157] *WRG Enterprises, Inc.* v. *Crowell*, 758 S.W.2d 214 (Tenn. 1988).

[158] Also *Planned Parenthood League* v. *Attorney General*, 464 N.E.2d 55, *cert. denied*, 469 U.S. 858 (1984); *Optimist Club of North Raleigh* v. *Riley*, 563 F. Supp. 847 (E.D.N.Car. 1982).

[159] *Bellotti* v. *Telco Communications, Inc.*, 650 F. Supp. 149 (D. Mass. 1986).

[160] *Id.* at 153.

[161] This opinion reflected *Munson* and anticipated *Riley*, in holding that a percentage limit on a professional solicitor unduly burdens fundraising for charity to the same extent as such a limit imposed directly on a charity's fundraising costs. The court observed that the percentage limitation in this case "is, in effect, the other side of the same coin that was invalidated in *Munson*" (*id.* at 152). Cf. *Streich* v. *Pennsylvania Commission On Charitable Organizations*, 579 F. Supp. 172 (M.D. Pa. 1984), upholding the constitutionality of a statute imposing a 15-percent compensation limit on professional solicitors (but decided prior to *Munson* and *Riley*). Yet another court found that the identical percentage compensation limit was unconstitutional (in an opinion prepared prior to *Munson* and *Riley*) (*State* v. *W.R.G. Enterprises, Inc.*, 314 N.W.2d 842 (N. Dak. 1982)).

[162] *Shannon* v. *Telco Communication, Inc.*, 824 F.2d 150, 152 (1st Cir. 1987).

[163] *Heritage Publishing Company* v. *Fishman, supra* note 1.

[164] *Id.* at 1504.

the means utilized to accomplish the state's objective of preventing fraud were held to be too imprecise.[165]

Still another federal court concluded that, although a law requiring disclosure to prospective donors of a person's status as a solicitor was constitutional, requirements of disclosure of the percentage of contributions to be received by a charity that will be devoted to charitable purposes and sending of confirmation containing this percentage amount were unconstitutional, as violations of the doctrine of free speech.[166]

A state court held constitutional a statute requiring a professional solicitor for charitable organizations to register, report, pay an annual fee, and procure a bond.[167] The statute was characterized as "designed to protect a charitably minded public from being improperly solicited, abused and even defrauded."[168] The court wrote that the law "bears a rational relationship to the valid state objective," which is the protection and advancement of the "public's health, safety, morals, and general welfare."[169]

A state court held unconstitutional a statute requiring an organization that plans, promotes, and operates fundraising events for charitable organizations to disclose to prospective donors the amount to be expended for fundraising, management, and program, where the program amount is less than 70 percent of the total received.[170] The court said that implicit in this percentage "triggering device" for the disclosures "is an assumption, on the part of the Legislature, that when less than 70 percent of a charitable contribution is allocated to the 'program services' of a recipient charitable organization, the organization's 'efficiency' and its purported charitable purpose are both suspect, and it should therefore be required to disclose its financial innerworkings to prospective contributors."[171] The court concluded that these premises are "untenable" and thus that the statute has "fundamental flaws in . . . [its] design and operation."[172]

A state court held unconstitutional a charitable solicitation act provision that compelled a fundraiser who charged a fee in excess of 50 percent of the adjusted gross proceeds to disclose to the person solicited that the charity received less than one-half of the adjusted gross proceeds.[173] The court wrote

---

[165] The *Heritage* case involved a challenge to basically the entire Minnesota charitable solicitation act. The court found the main features of the act constitutional, such as the ability of the regulators to deny a registration or license, the procedures for obtaining a license, the investigatory provisions, the cease-and-desist order procedure, the bond requirements, the requirement that a professional fundraiser have a written authorization from the charity involved, and the rulemaking authority. Also *City of Angels Mission Church* v. *City of Houston*, 716 F. Supp. 982 (S.D. Tex. 1989). Cf. *Holy Spirit Association for Unification of World Christianity* v. *Hodge*, 582 F. Supp. 592 (N.D. Tex. 1984), where a challenge to a fundraising ordinance in Amarillo, Texas, was partially successful.

[166] *Indiana Voluntary Firemen's Association, Inc.* v. *Pearson*, 700 F. Supp. 421 (S.D. Ind. 1988).

[167] *Wickman* v. *Firestone*, 500 So.2d 740 (Fla. 1987).

[168] *Id.* at 741.

[169] *Id.* at 741–742.

[170] *State* v. *Events International, Inc.*, 528 A.2d 458 (Me. 1987).

[171] *Id.* at 461.

[172] *Id.* at 461, 462.

[173] *People* v. *French*, 762 P.2d 1369 (Colo. 1988).

that "more narrowly tailored means of preventing fraud are available than compelling the fundraiser to disclose to the person solicited the percentage of funds that the charity receives."[174] The court suggested that the fundraiser can be compelled to file financial information with the state for public dissemination or the state can vigorously enforce its antifraud laws.[175]

A state court upheld the constitutionality of an ordinance that required charitable organizations to, as a prerequisite for obtaining a solicitation permit, disclose the percentage of funds received as gifts that was used for fundraising.[176] The court wrote that "at least this ordinance makes no discriminatory regulation at some set percentage of costs to total contributions and provides a way for each resident of the city to know the costs of the campaign and then decide whether that cost is reasonable or excessive according to standards which each giver may choose to use."[177] Added the court: "The ordinance places no limitation on Freedom of Speech and permits each solicitor to say whatever is considered necessary to try to obtain contributions for whatever charity is involved."[178]

A federal court ruled that the following provisions of a state charitable solicitation act do not violate the charitable organization's free speech rights: (1) require a charitable organization to disclose, upon request of the person solicited, the estimated percentages of the funds collected that will be applied to program and fundraising, and (2) require the contract or other written statement between a charitable organization and a professional fundraiser and/or professional solicitor to provide the amount, percentage, or other method of compensation to be received by the fundraiser or solicitor.[179] This court also held that a "state can require charities soliciting funds within its borders to accurately describe their mission and how the donations will be used" and "can also require oversight of fundraising activities and prohibit undisclosed conflicts of interest that might affect the operations of the charity."[180] In response to the state's assertion that it examines fundraising percentages "only as one signal that further inquiry into possible fraudulent conduct might be necessary," however, the court cautioned the state regulators that "any denial of a charity's registration based, even in part, upon the charity's percentage of expenditures for administrative or fundraising expenses would violate the first amendment."[181]

A section of a county[182] ordinance regulating charitable solicitations was found unconstitutional because it enabled the agency involved to deny or revoke a required information card if the agency found that the percentage of contributions raised that would be available for charitable programs is "unreasonably small," based on various criteria including "inefficient operation" or

---

[174] Id. at 1375.
[175] See supra text accompanying note 111.
[176] City of El Paso v. El Paso Jaycees, 758 S.W.2d 789 (Tex. 1988).
[177] Id. at 792.
[178] Id.
[179] Famine Relief Fund v. State of West Virginia, 905 F.2d 747 (4th Cir. 1990).
[180] Id. at 752.
[181] Id. at 753.
[182] Los Angeles.

the payment of unreasonable compensation. The court observed that although the provision did not constitute a "fixed percentage limitation" on the costs of solicitation, it nonetheless imposed an unwarranted "cost-effectiveness" requirement.[183] This provision, said the court, "impermissibly conditions the exercise of First Amendment rights on business efficiency," including allowing the government to arbitrarily determine the value of services.[184]

One state's law made it a prohibited act to represent, when a professional solicitor is soliciting funds, that a charitable organization will be the recipient of the funds when the solicitor pursuant to a contract is allowed to or will receive more than 50 percent of the gross receipts as compensation. Echoing what has become a line of solidly established case law, a court held that this provision was "unduly burdensome and not narrowly tailored to the state's interest in preventing fraud."[185] A similar law enacted in another state was likewise thereafter struck down.[186]

Thus, legislators and regulators—despite clear direction from the Supreme Court over 20 years ago—are persisting in attempts to fashion laws prohibiting fundraising for charity using rules based on percentages, and failing each time. The regulators' ongoing disdain for free speech principles in this context was reflected in a report from a state's department of law and public safety, which opened with this lament: "United States Supreme Court decisions have prohibited states from enacting laws which utilized percentages to prescribe the money a charity must use for charitable purposes or to limit the amount spent on fund raising."[187] It is unseemly at the least for lawyers for the states to use public funds to complain about constraints imposed by the First Amendment.

Another aspect of the interrelationship between the principles of free speech and charitable fundraising involves burgeoning disclosure requirements.[188] A court stated that the "potential chilling effect [of certain disclosure requirements] on the exercise of [protected] First Amendment rights . . . is manifest, together with the invasion of privacy."[189] Two provisions of a city[190] ordinance were struck down on this basis: one that required

---

[183] *Gospel Missions of America* v. *Bennett, supra* note 32, at 1451.

[184] *Id.*

[185] *Kentucky State Police Professional Association* v. *Gorman,* 870 F. Supp. 166, 169 (E.D. Ky. 1994).

[186] *National Federation of Nonprofits* v. *Lungren,* (N.D. Cal., order issued Mar. 29, 1995).

[187] "Interim Report to the Governor and Legislature on the Charitable Registration and Investigation Act of 1994," New Jersey Department of Law & Public Safety, Division of Consumer Affairs 3 (1995) (bearing the slogan "Take Advantage of Us So No One Takes Advantage of You"). In connection with the matter referenced *supra* note 186, in a letter dated September 7, 1994, the attorney general of California wrote to the state's governor, requesting a veto of the measure on the ground that the Supreme Court has repeatedly held that "using percentages to determine the legality of the fundraiser's fee is an unwarranted limitation on protected speech as reflected in charitable fundraising activities, and is not narrowly tailored to the state's interest in preventing fraud"; however, the attorney general also observed that the unconstitutional provision was nonetheless "laudable as public policy."

[188] See, e.g., §§ 3.15 and 3.17. The recent emphasis on forms of disclosure requirements by governments is a response to the fact that they can no longer regulate fundraising on the basis of percentages of funds devoted to program or to solicitation costs.

[189] *Holy Spirit Association for Unification of World Christianity* v. *Hodge, supra* note 165, at 601.

[190] Los Angeles.

a "detailed financial statement" for the most recent year and one that required disclosure of the name, address, and telephone number of each trustee, director, and officer. These disclosures were said to "directly expose the applicant's internal operations to public scrutiny and are unrelated to any legitimate governmental interest, including the [c]ity's stated interest in preventing fraudulent solicitations."[191]

On this basis, this court struck down two provisions of a county[192] ordinance. One, part of a registration requirement, mandated that applicants file a "specific statement of all contributions collected or received" within the year preceding the filing, including the "expenditures or use made of such contributions, together with the names and addresses of all persons or associations receiving . . . compensation . . . from such contributions and the respective amounts thereof." This law was deemed facially invalid because it is "unduly burdensome, unnecessarily compels applicants to disclose their internal operations, and fails to materially advance the [c]ounty's substantial and legitimate interest in preventing fraudulent solicitations."[193] The other required disclosure of the names and addresses of an applicant's directors and officers, and submission of a copy of the applicant's board resolution authorizing the solicitation. Said the court: "These requirements similarly chill the exercise of free speech rights by compelling publication of the applicant's private and internal operations and are not intimately related to the [c]ounty's legitimate interest in preventing fraud."[194]

It is nonetheless clear that the basic features of a state's charitable solicitation act will pass constitutional law muster. This was illustrated by a federal court decision in 1998, upholding one of these laws[195]—principally against a free speech challenge. The features of this law that were found to be lawful are the registration and disclosure requirements, the registration fee, a bond or letter of credit requirement, and the authority in the state to deny or revoke a fundraising license in certain circumstances.[196]

Likewise, a county charitable solicitation ordinance[197] was upheld in the face of a broad challenge, including one based on free speech principles. The ordinance contains a typical array of registration, reporting, and disclosure

---

[191] *Gospel Missions of America* v. *Bennett, supra* note 32, at 1443.

[192] Los Angeles.

[193] *Gospel Missions of America* v. *Bennett, supra* note 32, at 1450.

[194] *Id.*

[195] The Utah Charitable Solicitations Act.

[196] *American Target Advertising, Inc.* v. *Giani*, 23 F. Supp. 2d 1303 (D. Utah 1998). Registration fees and a bond requirement were upheld in *Dayton Area Visually Impaired Persons, Inc.* v. *Fisher*, 70 F.3d 1474 (6th Cir. 1995).

A provision in a state's constitution, barring advertising of bingo games by charitable (and certain other nonprofit) organizations, was struck down by a federal district court as being a violation of commercial speech guaranteed under the First Amendment. The advertising restrictions were found to be unnecessarily extensive and the state was found to have available other, nonspeech restrictions that would adequately protect its interests. This case was ruled not to involve the higher level of free speech associated with charitable fundraising (see *supra* § 5.3(b)(iv)) (*Association of Charitable Games of Missouri* v. *Missouri Gaming Commission*, 1998 U.S. Dist. LEXIS 14433 (W.D. Mo. 1998)).

[197] An ordinance of Pinellas County, Florida.

requirements, imposed on charitable organizations and professional solicitors. The court observed that the purpose of the ordinance, which is to prevent fraud and other forms of deception in charitable solicitations, amounted to a substantial county interest. The court found that the various provisions of the ordinance that were challenged are sufficiently narrowly tailored to satisfy First Amendment scrutiny.[198]

The last few years have not witnessed litigation of this nature. Perhaps, finally, the regulatory community has accepted these restraints on them accorded by free speech principles. It is to be hoped that this illegal approach to regulating the fundraising activities of the nation's charitable organizations has been eradicated.

(d) Airport Terminal Solicitations

The courts have devoted considerable attention to the constitutionality of regulations governing the raising of funds and the distribution of literature for charitable purposes in government-owned and -operated airport terminals. They have held that these airport terminals are public forums, with the result that restrictions on charitable fundraising in these facilities are subject to the restrictions, discussed earlier, under the free speech doctrine, which void laws that are overbroad in relation to the furtherance of legitimate governmental interests.[199]

The law in this area classifies government-owned property as being one of three types: the traditional public forum, the public forum created by government designation, and the nonpublic forum. Examples of traditional public forums are public streets, sidewalks, and parks. A speaker (including a solicitor of charitable gifts) may be excluded from a traditional public forum only when the exclusion is necessary to serve a compelling state interest and the exclusion is narrowly drawn to achieve that interest.

Designated public forums are areas that are not traditionally open to assembly and debate but have been intentionally opened, by government authorities, for public discourse. As one appellate court stated, "[n]onpublic fora lack the characteristics of traditional public fora and have not been acknowledged by the pertinent governmental authority as consistent with expressive activity."[200] The test for exclusion, however, is the same with respect to traditional public forums; that is, the government may impose only reasonable time, place, and manner restrictions, unless there is a compelling state interest.

In contrast, restrictions on speech are permissible in nonpublic forums as long as they are reasonable and viewpoint-neutral.

This court of appeals chose a new perspective on these situations involving charitable solicitations on government-owned property. Despite the

---

[198] *American Charities for Reasonable Fundraising Regulation, Inc.* v. *Pinellas County, supra* note 44.
[199] E.g., *Jamison* v. *City of St. Louis*, 828 F.2d 1280 (8th Cir. 1987), *cert. denied*, 485 U.S. 987 (1988); *Jews for Jesus, Inc.* v. *Board of Airport Commissioners*, 785 F.2d 791 (9th Cir. 1986), *aff'd on other grounds*, 482 U.S. 569 (1987); *Fernandes* v. *Limmer*, 663 F.2d 619 (5th Cir. 1981) *cert. dismissed*, 458 U.S. 1124 (1982); *International Society for Krishna Consciousness, Inc.* v. *Rochford*, 585 F.2d 263 (7th Cir. 1978).
[200] *International Society for Krishna Consciousness, Inc.* v. *Lee*, 925 F.2d 576, 580 (2d Cir. 1991).

"considerable weight of unanimous authority," the appellate court found that the Supreme Court in 1990 "altered public forum analysis."[201]

The plaintiff in the case, the International Society for Krishna Consciousness ("ISKCON"), is a religious organization. Its members perform a ritual known as *sankirtan*, which consists of "going into public places, disseminating religious literature, and soliciting funds to support the religion."[202] The court found that the "primary purpose" of sankirtan is fundraising.[203]

The government authority with control over the portions of airports not leased to airlines (terminals) promulgated a regulation forbidding the solicitation of money and the repetitive distribution of literature within terminals. The public has access to the terminals, which contain a variety of commercial establishments (restaurants, bars, bookstores, gift shops, and the like).

The court observed that the airports involved (Kennedy International, LaGuardia, and Newark International) are among the "busiest and most heavily used metropolitan airport complexes in the world."[204] The court noted that, "[a]lthough these areas are open to the public, virtually everyone who enters the terminal does so for a purpose related to air travel."[205] Wrote the court: "These include travelers, persons meeting or seeing off passengers, members of flight crews, and employees of the terminal, an airline or a business in the terminal."[206]

There was no dispute that ISKCON's practice of sankirtan is protected speech for First Amendment/free speech purposes. The issue was whether the terminals are "traditional public fora" for ISKCON's protected activities. The trial court, taking its cue from various circuits,[207] found that the terminals are open to the public, heavily traveled, and contain a wide array of commercial establishments, and thus are akin to public sidewalks, so that the regulation should be struck down.[208]

This appellate court found the airport terminals comparable to the post office's sidewalk. Wrote the court, the terminals are "remote from pedestrian thoroughfares and are intended solely to facilitate a particular type of transaction—air travel—unrelated to protected expression."[209] The court continued: "Persons using the passageways in terminals are not there primarily to meet a friend for lunch, windowshop, take the air, or engage in any of the multitude of other purposes for which typical downtown streets are used. They are there solely as air travelers, persons connected with air travelers, or employees or businesses serving air travelers."[210]

[201] *Id.* (The reference to the Supreme Court action in 1990 is to *United States* v. *Kokinda, supra* note 148.)
[202] *Id.* at 577.
[203] *Id.*
[204] *Id.* at 578.
[205] *Id.*
[206] *Id.*
[207] See *supra* note 199.
[208] *International Society for Krishna Consciousness, Inc.* v. *Lee,* 721 F. Supp. 572 (S.D.N.Y. 1989).
[209] *International Society for Krishna Consciousness, Inc.* v. *Lee, supra* note 200, at 581.
[210] *Id.*

The court reasoned that, just as the Postal Service has a significant interest in protecting users of the type of branch office that was considered by the Supreme Court in 1990 from the in-person solicitation of funds, the government has an "interest in protecting its airport patrons from the identical disruption of in-person solicitation."[211]

The court read the 1990 Supreme Court opinion to distinguish between "passageways or other facilities that exist solely to facilitate the public's carrying on of a particular endeavor—subway or air travel, for example—and passageways that enable the public to carry out the multitude of purposes persons pursue in their daily life—the typical Main Street."[212] Said the court: "The former are nonpublic fora, and government may prohibit the in-person solicitation of funds at least where those using the passageway or facility might be disrupted by such solicitation."[213]

The court observed that "[a]ir travelers, who are often weighted down by cumbersome baggage and may be hurrying to catch a plane or to arrange ground transportation, will find in-person solicitation even more disruptive than did the postal patrons" in the 1990 Supreme Court case.[214] The objective of preventing disruption of the public in passageways or facilities that are "among society's chokepoints" was thus found to be a legitimate time, place, and manner restriction.[215]

By contrast, the court upheld the trial court in concluding that the airport authority must provide reasonable access to the terminals for the distribution of literature.

The chief judge of the appellate court dissented, concluding that the airport terminals are traditional public forums. The dissent found that the physical characteristics of a forum do not necessarily determine traditional public forum status, nor do the purposes for which a forum is designed and to which it is put. Calling for a "balancing test," the dissent characterized the court majority's conclusion as "simplistic."[216]

Subsequently, the U.S. Supreme Court decided that an airport terminal operated by a public authority is not a "public forum" and thus that a ban on charitable solicitations in the terminal is permissible, on the ground that that form of regulation need satisfy only a standard of reasonableness.[217] In so holding, the Court affirmed the conclusions of the appellate court.[218]

In a companion case, the Court held that a general ban on distribution of literature in an airport terminal is invalid under the First Amendment.[219] There was no dispute that the organization's practice of sankirtan is protected speech for purposes of free speech analysis. The issue was whether the airline terminals are "traditional public fora." The trial court had held they were,

---

[211] Id.

[212] Id.

[213] Id. at 581–582.

[214] Id. at 582.

[215] Id.

[216] Id. at 583–584.

[217] International Society for Krishna Consciousness, Inc. v. Lee, 505 U.S. 672 (1992).

[218] Id., supra note 181.

[219] Lee v. International Society for Krishna Consciousness, 505 U.S. 830 (1992).

while the appellate court, influenced by an intervening court opinion,[220] held they were not.

The Court majority concluded that an airport terminal operated by a public authority is a nonpublic forum. This meant that the ban on solicitation on these premises had to satisfy only a reasonableness standard. (By contrast, if the premises were found to be a public forum, the regulation would have to be narrowly drawn to achieve a compelling state interest—a test the regulation could not meet.)

The Court majority wrote that neither by tradition nor purpose can airport terminals be described as public forums. The Court observed that airports have not historically been made available for speech activity. Nor do airports—given the lateness with which the modern air terminal has made its appearance—qualify as property that has "immemorially," "time out of mind," been held in the public trust and used for the purposes of expressive activity—a test for public forum treatment.

The ban on solicitation was found to be reasonable. Solicitation was held to have a disruptive effect on business by slowing the path of both those who must decide whether to contribute and those who must alter their paths to avoid the solicitation. In addition, the Court majority was concerned that a solicitor may cause duress by targeting the most vulnerable persons or commit fraud by concealing his or her affiliation or shortchanging donors. The Court felt that this problem is compounded by the fact that many of the "targets" would be on short schedule, and thus would be unlikely to stop and complain to authorities.[221]

The airport authority was found to have determined that it can best achieve its legitimate interest in monitoring solicitation activity, to ensure that travelers are not unduly interfered with, by limiting solicitation to the sidewalk areas outside the terminals. The airport authority was found to have reasonable cause to worry that the incremental effects of having one group and then another seek access to the premises would prove quite disruptive.

It was uncontested that the solicitation at issue in this case was a form of speech protected by the First Amendment. The Court wrote, however, it is "well settled that the government need not permit all forms of speech on property that it owns and controls."[222] The issue thus became the standard of review of the regulation prohibiting the solicitation.

The Court majority found that the "tradition of airport activity does not demonstrate that airports have historically been made available for speech activity."[223] It relied heavily on an earlier opinion in which the Court held that public property, such as streets and parks, have "immemorially been held in trust for the use of the public and, time out of mind, have been used for purposes of assembly, communicating thoughts between citizens, and discussing public questions."[224] The Court cited the "lateness with which the modern air

[220] *United States* v. *Kokinda, supra* note 148.
[221] *International Society for Krishna Consciousness, Inc.* v. *Lee, supra* note 217, at 2708.
[222] *Id.* at 2705.
[223] *Id.* at 2706.
[224] *Hague* v. *Committee for Industrial Organization,* 307 U.S. 496, 516 (1939).

terminal has made its appearance" as evidence that the standard articulated earlier could not be met.[225]

The Court majority also rejected the thought that airport terminals "have been intentionally opened by their operators to such activity."[226] This it proved by reference to the litigation on the subject. The purpose of air terminals, wrote the Court, is the "facilitation of passenger air travel, not the promotion of expression."[227]

A concurring opinion viewed the property involved somewhat differently, finding that the airport authority is operating a "multipurpose environment"—part airport and part "shopping mall."[228] But this difference in viewpoint did not alter the view of the reasonableness of the regulations.

The authors of another concurring opinion saw the facts in a substantially different manner. It was argued that the airport corridors and shopping areas outside of the passenger security zones are public forums. The authority's rule disallowing "in-person solicitation of money for immediate payment" was said to be a "narrow and valid regulation of the time, place, and manner of protected speech in this forum, or else is a valid regulation of the nonspeech element of expressive conduct."[229] Thus, the majority's ban was interpreted as permitting solicitation of funds where payment would be made later (usually, by mail).

In the second of these concurring opinions, it was said that the Court majority's analysis of what makes a forum "public" was "flawed at the very beginning." It continued: "It leaves the government with almost unlimited authority to restrict speech on its property by doing nothing more than articulating a non-speech-related purpose for the area, and it leaves almost no scope for the development of new public forums absent the rare approval of the government. The Court's error lies in its conclusion that the public-forum status of public property depends on the government's defined purpose for the property, or on an explicit decision by the government to dedicate the property to expressive activity. In my view, the inquiry must be an objective one, based on the actual, physical characteristics and uses of the property."[230]

It was said that the Court should "recognize that open, public spaces and thoroughfares which are suitable for discourse may be public forums, whatever their historical pedigree and without concern for a precise classification of the property." It added: "Without this recognition our forum doctrine retains no relevance in times of fast-changing technology and increasing insularity."[231] It was found "critical" that metropolitan airports be regarded as "areas for protected speech." This opinion concluded: "If the objective, physical characteristics of the property at issue and the actual public access and uses which have been permitted by the government indicate that

---

[225] *International Society for Krishna Consciousness, Inc.* v. *Lee, supra* note 217, at 2706.
[226] *Id.* at 2706–2707.
[227] *Id.* at 2707.
[228] *Id.* at 2713.
[229] *Id.* at 2715.
[230] *Id.* at 2716.
[231] *Id.* at 2717.

expressive activity would be appropriate and compatible with those uses, the property is a public forum."[232]

Having found that only a test of reasonableness is necessary, the Court majority had little difficulty finding the regulation to be reasonable. The Court wrote of the "disruptive effect that solicitation may have on business," thereby slowing the normal flow of traffic. "Delays may be particularly costly in this setting," said the Court, "as a flight missed by only a few minutes can result in hours' worth of subsequent inconvenience."[233]

The Court majority was also concerned about "face-to-face solicitation [which] presents risks of duress that are an appropriate target of regulation." It wrote of the "skillful, and unprincipled, solicitor [that] can target the most vulnerable, including those accompanying children or those suffering physical impairment and who cannot easily avoid the solicitation." The majority also wrote of the "unsavory solicitor [who] can also commit fraud through concealment of his affiliation or through deliberate efforts to shortchange those who agree to purchase." The Court added: "Compounding this problem is the fact that, in an airport, the targets of such activity frequently are on tight schedules. . . . As a result, the airport faces considerable difficulty in achieving its legitimate interest in monitoring solicitation activity to assure that travelers are not interfered with unduly."[234]

The Court majority approvingly noted that the airport authority "has concluded that its interest in monitoring the activities can best be accomplished by limiting solicitation and distribution to the sidewalk areas outside the terminals." It wrote that "[t]hus the resulting access of those who would solicit the general public is quite complete."[235]

In the first of these concurring opinions, it was observed that, while airports are not public forums, that "does not mean that the government can restrict speech in whatever way it likes." It was said: "The determination that airports are not public fora thus only begins our inquiry."[236]

The nature of the property was viewed quite differently than it was in the majority opinion. It was written that the airport authority "has created a huge complex open to travelers and nontravelers alike"; the authority "is operating a shopping mall as well as an airport."[237] The test was said to be whether the regulations are "reasonably related to maintaining the multipurpose environment that the . . . [a]uthority has deliberately created."[238] The conclusion was that they are.

As to the second of these concurring opinions, the authors were not overly impressed with the airport authority's argument about congestion in the airports' corridors, which "makes expressive activity inconsistent with the airports' primary purpose, which is to facilitate air travel."[239] These thoughts

[232] *Id.* at 2718.
[233] *Id.* at 2708.
[234] *Id.*
[235] *Id.* at 2709.
[236] *Id.* at 2712.
[237] *Id.*
[238] *Id.* at 2713.
[239] *Id.* at 2719.

were offered: "The First Amendment is often inconsistent. But that is beside the point. Inconvenience does not absolve the government of its obligation to tolerate speech."[240]

(e) Outer Boundaries of Doctrine

Thus, since 1980, as a consequence of opinions from the U.S. Supreme Court and other courts, there has been an impressive array of opinions holding that a charitable organization, when fundraising, is engaging in one of the highest forms of free speech. The consequence of this is that state regulation of the fundraising process for charities must be by only the narrowest of means, rather than by a regulatory approach that is merely reasonable. Thus, when a state overregulates in this field, the offensive law is struck down as being unconstitutional because of violation of the First and Fourteenth Amendments to the U.S. Constitution.

There is a limit, however, to the reach of a constitutional right. This is the case in the realm of fundraising regulation. According to the U.S. Court of Appeals for the Seventh Circuit, at least one of the limits pertains to gambling events.[241] The case concerned the law in Indiana, which was amended in 1992 to add restrictions to the conduct of bingo games by charitable organizations. A charitable organization that violated several of these restrictions was directed by the state to cease conducting the games. The charity refused to comply and the matter ended up in court. The charity's principal argument was that the state acted in violation of free speech rights in curtailing the bingo operation, because it was one of the charity's ways of espousing its program and soliciting contributions. The court of appeals rejected that argument, saying that wagering money is an activity that can be regulated without transgressing free speech principles. The court wrote that the state's charitable gaming act did not curtail expression (speech). Rather, it said, the law is neutral with respect to the content and viewpoint of expression; therefore, the law was found to be constitutional.[242]

The playing of bingo was found to not be speech. The court wrote that the process "employ[s] vocal chords" (such as the shouting of "BINGO!") but is not "expression."[243] Thus, the court rejected the premise that simply terming an activity *fundraising* automatically brings into play constitutional law protections. The appellate court opined that a "regulation that serves purposes unrelated to the content of expression is deemed neutral, even if it has an incidental effect on some speakers or messages but not others."[244] The Indiana statute

---

[240] *Id.*

[241] *There to Care, Inc.*, v. *Commissioner of Indiana Department of Revenue*, 19 F.3d 1165 (7th Cir. 1994).

[242] The lawyer for the organization, during oral argument, pushed that premise to the maximum, arguing that it could "stage a bullfight in the Hoosier Dome" without regulation, "if in its view that contest would raise money for its endeavors and be a good forum for the dissemination of its views" (*id.* at 1168).

[243] *Id.* at 1167.

[244] *Id.* at 1168.

was found to be "indifferent" to the content and viewpoint of expression by charitable organizations.[245]

The organization represented to the court that it used bingo games to disseminate information about its activities: "Posters on the walls proclaim its mission; during the games organizers recruit volunteers; net proceeds of the games support charitable endeavors that may include speech."[246] But the court pointed out that "persons who seek to engage in speech cannot avoid the application of state laws that are neutral with regard to the content and viewpoint of their expression."[247] The court gave as an illustration of its point the imposition of sales and use taxes on religious articles in common with other merchandise.[248]

This court found the gambling limitation statute to be no different than zoning and rent control laws, which can "disable" charities, because of their neutrality. It concluded, in effect, that government can regulate expressive activity as long as the regulation is justified without reference to the content of the regulated speech. The statute "regulates the process of wagering," the court wrote, "rather than expression that may accompany gambling."[249]

This emphasis on *neutral* legislation, then, seemingly marks the outer boundary of the ambit of protected fundraising speech. Events may be regulated; expression may not be. This demarcation raises interesting questions. For example, a growing number of state charitable solicitation acts mandate the contents of contracts between charities and fundraisers.[250] These provisions, however, are unique to charitable fundraising; the state does not try to dictate the provisions of all contracts. Are these requirements now suspect under the Seventh Circuit's reasoning?

It has been thought that a ban on charitable fundraising by telephone would be unconstitutional; but suppose a state banned all forms of solicitation by telephone during certain hours. The placing of a telephone call is an activity; an across-the-board ban on its use would be neutral with respect to the content of the expression. Would that type of law be constitutional?

The court explicitly noted that "[g]ambling has traditionally been closely regulated or even forbidden, without anyone suspecting that these restrictions violate the first amendment."[251] Thus, this was an "easy" case—but easy cases often make bad law. The Seventh Circuit's broad activity/expression dichotomy undoubtedly will undergo refinement in the months and years ahead.

What has happened here is that the law of free speech and charitable fundraising has been extended to a point where it has bumped up against another doctrine of law, concerning the rules that serve purposes unrelated to the content of expression. These rules are considered, from a constitutional law viewpoint, to be neutral; this is the case even though the law may have an incidental effect on some speakers or messages. Thus, as the Supreme Court has

---

[245] *Id.* at 1169.
[246] *Id.* at 1168.
[247] *Id.*
[248] *Jimmy Swaggart Ministries* v. *California Board of Equalization*, 493 U.S. 378 (1990).
[249] *There to Care, Inc.* v. *Commissioner of Indiana Department of Revenue, supra* note 241, at 1168.
[250] See § 3.11.
[251] *There to Care, Inc.* v. *Commissioner of Indiana Department of Revenue, supra* note 241, at 1167.

held, government regulation of expressive activity is content-neutral as long as it is "justified without reference to the content of the regulated speech."[252]

§ 4.4 DUE PROCESS RIGHTS

Laws regulating the fundraising activities of charitable organizations and those who assist them in this regard must afford these persons their due process rights as prescribed by the Fifth and Fourteenth Amendments to the U.S. Constitution. The Fifth Amendment provides that a person may not be "deprived of life, liberty, or property, without due process of law." This principle is made applicable to the states by means of the Fourteenth Amendment.

In the context of the state charitable solicitation acts, the principal due process arguments came with respect to limitations on fundraising costs. As discussed,[253] these limitations are unconstitutional, as violations of the right of free speech. The free speech transgressions occur irrespective of whether the percentage limitation is *absolute* (that is, where a charitable organization is not afforded the opportunity to demonstrate to the regulators that its fundraising costs are reasonable, notwithstanding the fact that the percentage ceiling is exceeded) or *rebuttable* (where there is no flexible standard but instead a presumption that expenses in excess of a percentage are unreasonable).

Nonetheless, in the due process setting, the absolute percentage limitation probably amounted to a violation of due process rights. The rebuttable percentage limitation may well have been in compliance with due process requirements because the charities were afforded the opportunity to demonstrate the reasonableness of their fundraising costs—and thus become or remain registered in the jurisdiction—notwithstanding the fact that fundraising costs exceed the rebuttable percentage limitation.

Still, these laws contain ample opportunities for due process rights to be recognized or violated. For example, some states provide for review of contracts between charitable organizations and professional fundraisers and/or professional solicitors. Thus, the secretary of state may be empowered to undertake this review of contracts between charities and professional solicitors; if the secretary is not satisfied that the agreement does not "involve an excessively high fundraising cost," he or she can "disapprove" the contract. Yet the statute does not state guidelines or procedures to be followed by the secretary in making that determination.

As an example, the law in one state had the following statutory structure: (1) where the regulatory office denies a charity's registration statement, the charity cannot solicit funds in the state unless the denial is reversed; (2) within 15 days of the denial, the charity can request a hearing, which must be held within 15 days from the date of the request; (3) if the hearing is unfavorable to

---

[252] *Ward* v. *Rock Against Racism*, 491 U.S. 781, 791 (1989), quoting from *Clark* v. *Community for Creative Non-Violence*, 468 U.S. 288, 293 (1984). Other cases that bear on this point are *Federal Trade Commission* v. *Superior Court Trial Lawyers Association*, 493 U.S. 411, 430 (1990); *United States* v. *Albertini*, 472 U.S. 675 (1985); *United States* v. *O'Brien*, 391 U.S. 367 (1968).
[253] See § 5.3.

the charity, it may seek judicial review of the decision; and (4) during the period the charity is awaiting a judicial determination of the correctness of the administrative denial of the registration, the charity may not solicit contributions in the state. This statutory scheme was held to be a denial of due process rights as a prior restraint on the charity's speech.[254] The Supreme Court wrote that "whether the [charitable solicitation licensing requirement] regulates before- or after-the-fact makes little difference," because the "chill on the protected activity is the same."[255]

The Supreme Court enunciated three due process protections required for any prior restraint on speech.[256] First, the state must initiate judicial action to restrict a person's First Amendment right and the state must have the burden of proof in the action. Second, any regulatory act must provide assurance that the free exercise of protected speech will not be delayed while the state seeks judicial review. Third, judicial review must be prompt. The above statutory scheme fell because (1) the state can (and did) prohibit the charity's solicitation activities without first bringing any judicial action; (2) it is the charity that must seek an administrative hearing and judicial review after its registration is denied; (3) the statute does not specify who bears the burden of proof in these proceedings; and (4) the charity remains unable to solicit funds while judicial review is pending.

Another example is a provision embodied in one of these laws, which enables the regulators to withhold the issuance of a fundraising permit to a charity until it submits a "satisfactory" statement of the factual basis for the projected percentage of contributions that will be devoted to charitable purposes. This type of rule is unconstitutional inasmuch as there is an absence of procedural and substantive criteria for making that determination.[257] In a comparable setting, this type of law was struck down because of the lack of appropriate procedural safeguards, because there were no time limits within which the government had to act.[258]

Still another illustration: city and county ordinances were found to be facially invalid because, having mandated the use of an "information card," the governments were authorized to void the card on the basis of information received by the governments and there were no time constraints as to issuance of a replacement card.[259] Another provision of the county ordinance was invalidated because it required the charitable organization to return the solicitation card following the close of a solicitation, with no opportunity to obtain an extension of the solicitation period.

Some other statutory provisions that are potential due process violations are these: a rule that a charitable organization cannot expend an "unreasonable" amount for management expenses, a rule that a registration can be suspended

---

[254] *Famine Relief Fund* v. *State of West Virginia, supra* note 179.

[255] *Munson,* 467 U.S., *supra* note 83, at 969.

[256] *Freedman* v. *Maryland,* 380 U.S. 51 (1965) (invalidating a requirement of a state license prior to public screening of motion pictures).

[257] Rules of this nature are also unconstitutional because of the discretion vested in government officials (see § 4.6) and because of vagueness (see § 4.8).

[258] *Gospel Missions of America* v. *Bennett, supra* note 32.

[259] *Id.*

or revoked where the applicant has engaged in a "dishonest" practice, and a rule that a license can be revoked where the contributions solicited are not being applied for the purposes stated in the application for the license.

Any time a fundraising regulation statute contains requirements that are buttressed by subjective findings by the regulators, a potential for a due process abuse exists.[260]

§ 4.5 EQUAL PROTECTION RIGHTS

A charitable solicitation act must conform with the guarantee of equal protection of the laws as provided by the Fourteenth Amendment to the U.S. Constitution. This means that such an act may not contain a discriminatory classification of organizations.

An equal protection argument is most frequently raised in connection with the exceptions from coverage provided for in a charitable solicitation act. For example, many of these laws exempt from the registration and/or reporting requirements organizations (such as churches and fraternal organizations) that solicit funds solely from their members.[261]

The conventional wisdom has been that there is nothing unreasonable or arbitrary in exempting from these requirements organizations that solicit only from their memberships, in that the considerations in such solicitations, compared to solicitations from the general public,[262] are different. This approach has been seen to be in conformance with the general rule that states have the power, as part of the police authority, to exercise wide discretion in classifying organizations in the adoption of laws, as long as the basis for doing so is not arbitrary.[263] In the charitable solicitations field, the traditional rule has been that the "high standard of the organizations released from the license [or registration] requirement, their known capacity for effective labor in the realms of benevolence, clearly justifies the exemption accorded them."[264]

Subsequent decisions, however, are raising questions as to the constitutionality of these exemptions.[265] Nonetheless, organizations already accountable to government (such as colleges, universities, and hospitals) or to their membership may validly be granted exemption, if only as a matter of administrative convenience because a state may lack the resources to monitor solicitations by every charitable entity. On occasion, the classification conflict is between the solicitation activities of charitable and commercial organizations; the test is whether

---

[260] In general, *Fernandes* v. *Limmer, supra* note 199.

[261] See § 4.9.

[262] See *National Foundation, supra* note 42.

[263] E.g., *Lindsley* v. *Natural Carbonic Gas Co.*, 220 U.S. 61 (1911). See § 2.

[264] *Commonwealth* v. *McDermott*, 145 A. 858, 860 (1929). In one instance, a court upheld the constitutionality of a statute that generally prohibited the solicitation of rides and business on public highways but made an exception for charitable organizations soliciting contributions (*People* v. *Tosch*, 501 N.E.2d 1253 (Ill. 1986).

[265] E.g., *Heritage Village Church and Missionary Fellowship, Inc.* v. *North Carolina*, 40 N.C. App. 429 (1979), *aff'd*, 263 S.E.2d 726 (1980).

there is adequate justification for a denial of the right to solicit funds for charitable purposes while simultaneously allowing purely commercial solicitation activities.[266] As one court stated: "Sufficient regulatory interests may justify selective exclusions from a public forum because conflicting demands on the same place may compel the state to choose from among several potential users and uses, but such justifications will be carefully scrutinized."[267]

A 1991 court opinion illustrated the vagaries of application of the equal protection doctrine in this setting. A federal district court approved the findings of a U.S. magistrate, which were that a state statute, prohibiting the solicitation of contributions from the public where the gifts will be for the benefit of law enforcement groups, is unconstitutional.[268] The case concerned a section of the state's Solicitation by Law Enforcement Officers Act ("Act"), which prohibits the solicitation of property from the general public "when the property, or any part of it, in any way benefits, is intended to benefit, or is represented to be for the benefit of any law enforcement officer, law enforcement agency, or law enforcement association." Violation of this law is punishable as an unfair trade practice.

As to this case, various police organizations and individuals wished to solicit advertising from the general public for inclusion in publications. An individual wanted to advertise in and receive copies of police publications. Another individual, a professional fundraiser and publisher, sought to solicit advertisements for publications on behalf of police unions and officers. The Act barred these activities. The plaintiffs thus alleged that the Act violated the First and Fourteenth Amendments to the U.S. Constitution in that it served as an unconstitutional prior restraint on their freedom of speech, was unconstitutionally vague, was unconstitutionally overbroad, and denied them equal protection of the laws. The state contended that the issue of the unconstitutionality of the Act was resolved, and rejected, in 1985, when a challenge to the constitutionality of the Act failed.[269] The court, however, placed emphasis on the fact that the Act was amended in 1989 to create an exception for the Department of the Attorney General and enacted special, private legislation to allow solicitation for a memorial to slain police officers. The special law waived this prohibition of the Act for one year to allow gift solicitation for the memorial. In 1990, a further extension of this waiver was approved.

The plaintiffs in this case argued to the court that the 1985 case turned on the premise that all charitable solicitation by police officers and law enforcement organizations is "inherently coercive." The court said that the enactment of these private laws "calls that premise into question," undermining the "binding force" of the 1985 opinion.[270] The court in 1985 held that the state could burden types of charitable solicitation, where the state could demonstrate that the

---

[266] E.g., *City of Angels Mission Church* v. *City of Houston, supra* note 165; *Houston Chronicle* v. *City of Houston,* 620 S.W.2d 833 (Tex. 1981).

[267] *City of Angels Mission Church* v. *City of Houston, Texas, supra* note 165, citing *Police Department of City of Chicago* v. *Mosley,* 408 U.S. 92 (1972).

[268] *Auburn Police Union* v. *Tierney,* 756 F. Supp. 610 (D. Me. 1991), 762 F. Supp. 3 (D. Me. 1991).

[269] *State* v. *Maine State Troopers Associations,* 491 A.2d 538 (Me. 1985), *appeal dismissed,* 474 U.S. 802 (1985).

[270] *Auburn Police Union* v. *Tierney, supra* note 268, at 616.

challenged law served a compelling governmental interest and was narrowly tailored to be the least restrictive means of furthering that interest. The 1985 opinion concluded that the requisite state interest was present. It stated that the "State's interest in protecting the reputation of its law enforcement bodies is undeniably substantial."[271] This court added: "Indeed, we would be hard pressed to suggest a weightier interest."[272]

The three subsequent revisions of this law, however, were held in the present case to crack the foundation on which the 1985 court judged the Act to be narrowly tailored: that the appearance of coercion inheres in every solicitation for the benefit of law enforcement personnel.[273] The court concluded that, by its adjustment of the law in this area, the state legislature admitted that "its complete ban sweeps too broadly insofar as it encompasses the activities of a different kind of law enforcer—the Attorney General's office."[274]

The court added that "[e]ven more damaging, the Legislature has revealed its interest to be less than absolute by determining that it must selectively yield for causes such as the memorial."[275] Thus, it concluded that a "complete prohibition on police solicitation is not narrowly tailored to . . . [the state's] evident interest in banning some, but not all, such solicitation."[276] With that, the court pronounced the offending provision of the Act to be "unconstitutionally overbroad and invalid on its face."[277]

"To resurrect its statute," wrote the court, the "State must isolate the elements of police solicitation that produce coercion and then tailor its statute to root them out evenhandedly."[278] It added: "Provisions of the private law allowing solicitation for the memorial suggest, for example, that the State is particularly concerned that officers not solicit in uniform and that a single overseer approve and track all solicitors."[279]

Still another equal protection argument stems from the fact that some state charitable solicitation acts provide one or more forms of exemption from them for organizations identified by name. While this is a relatively common practice,[280] it technically is repugnant to the Fourteenth Amendment. In one case, a city ordinance prohibited charitable solicitations unless the charity first obtained the consent of the city council. One charity, however, was identified by name and exempted from this requirement. During a review of the ordinance for constitutional law qualification, a federal appellate court held that "it is obvious that the exemption of the . . . [named charity] constitutes a deprivation of the equal protection of the laws."[281]

---

[271] *State* v. *Maine State Troopers Association, supra* note 269, at 542.
[272] *Id.*
[273] *Auburn Police Union* v. *Tierney, supra* note 268, at 618.
[274] *Id.*
[275] *Id.*
[276] *Id.*
[277] *Id.*
[278] *Id.*
[279] *Id.*
[280] See § 3.5.
[281] *Adams* v. *City of Park Ridge*, 293 F.2d 585 (7th Cir. 1961), citing *Morey* v. *Doud*, 354 U.S. 457 (1957); *Niemotko* v. *State of Maryland*, 340 U.S. 268 (1951); *City of Seattle* v. *Rogers*, 106 P.2d 598 (1940).

An application of the equal protection argument as applied in the fundraising context was seen in a case challenging the constitutionality of the imposition of a registration fee on professional solicitors in the employ of professional fundraisers.[282] The issue in the case was whether the levying of this fee, while excluding officers, volunteers, employees of charitable organizations, and fundraising counsel from the payment of it, violated the equal protection clause of the Fourteenth Amendment. The court ruled that there was no constitutional law impairment with respect to this distinction.

Rejected was the contention that solicitors were being discriminated against on the basis of the content of their speech; the court observed that "all professional solicitors not working in-house for a charitable organization are charged the $80 fee, without regard to their viewpoints."[283] The court noted that the equal protection doctrine requires only that a distinction of this nature "have some relevance to the purposes for which the classification is made."[284] Citing the fact that the statute sets forth comprehensive registration and fee payment requirements for charitable organizations, professional fundraisers, and professional solicitors, the challenged provision was characterized as merely ensuring that regulation is extended to "independent professional solicitors who are not otherwise regulated."[285]

Another equal protection argument—as yet unadvanced in the courts—is that these laws that treat an organization differently (such as with respect to registration or the consequences of fundraising costs), depending on whether it is using a professional fundraiser, are constitutionally deficient in relation to the equal protection clause.

§ 4.6 DELEGATION OF LEGISLATIVE AUTHORITY

It is a cardinal principle of administrative law that an administrative agency may find facts and issue regulations but must do so in the context of a policy established by a legislative body, which has fixed standards for the guidance of the agency in the performance of its functions. Administrative enforcement of charitable solicitation acts is subject to this principle.

Thus, the Supreme Court observed that a "narrowly drawn ordinance, that does not vest in [governmental] officials the undefined power to determine what messages residents will hear may serve [the government's] important interests without running afoul of the First Amendment."[286] However, "[i]n the area of free expression, a licensing statute placing unbridled discretion

---

[282] *National Awareness Foundation* v. *Abrams*, 50 F.3d 1159 (2d Cir. 1995).

[283] *Id.* at 1167–1168.

[284] *Baxstrom* v. *Herold*, 383 U.S. 107, 111 (1966).

[285] *National Awareness Foundation* v. *Abrams*, *supra* note 282, at 1168. In a case involving the principles of commercial speech, a court found an equal protection violation, in that a provision in a state's constitution precluded charitable organizations from advertising their bingo games, while riverboat casinos in the state were not prohibited from advertising casino gambling. (*Association of Charitable Games of Missouri* v. *Missouri Gaming Commission*, *supra* note 196)

[286] *Hynes* v. *Mayor of Oradell*, *supra* note 59, at 617.

in the hands of a government official or agency constitutes a prior restraint and may result in censorship."[287]

This principle of law was employed by the Supreme Court of Ohio to void a charitable solicitation ordinance adopted by the city of Dayton. The ordinance empowered a board with the authority to deny to a charity the right to solicit funds in that city, upon a finding that the objective of the charity is "adequately covered" by another charity previously issued a solicitation permit. Pursuant to this ordinance, the board rejected an application to solicit funds in the city that was submitted by a unit of the American Cancer Society, on the ground that a hospital with an existing permit and the local community chest were adequately covering the objective of the unit's proposed solicitation, namely, a drive to generate funds to combat cancer. The board also concluded that the solicitation by the unit would be an unwarranted burden on the persons to be solicited, that it would hinder the activity of other organizations to which a permit had been granted, and that the solicitation would be incompatible with the public welfare.

In invalidating the Dayton charitable solicitation ordinance, the state supreme court observed:

> The law which separates the lawful vesting of power for administrative purposes and the delegation of legislative, discretionary, and unreasonable power is frequently a thin one obscured in a twilight zone, but a legislative body cannot vest powers in a commission which restrict persons or organizations unless in the legislation there is set up some standards of action which relate to legitimate objects for the exercise of the police power and which operate equally upon all persons and organizations. A law which operates arbitrarily and with discrimination upon those engaged in the same enterprises cannot be valid, nor can one which gives arbitrary powers to a commission which are in no way related to the public health, safety, or welfare.

> Although the board and the commission doubtless acted in good faith, it is obvious from what we have said that [the laws at issue] are invalid as not reasonably related to the public welfare and grant powers to a commission giving it a right to restrict privileges of organizations and persons, without standards, properly within the police power, to guide it, thus enabling it to exercise arbitrary powers in conflict with constitutional guaranties.[288]

Thus, the state supreme court upheld the findings of the lower courts and the issuance of an injunction prohibiting the city from enforcing the ordinance against the American Cancer Society unit.

In the charitable solicitation act context, then, the regulators do not have unfettered authority to determine which charities may solicit funds within the jurisdiction.[289] The flaw of the Dayton ordinance was the arbitrary power vested in the enforcement authorities to make such judgments as whether the

---

[287] *City of Lakewood* v. *Plain Dealer Publishing Co.*, 486 U.S. 750, 757 (1988).

[288] *American Cancer Society, supra* note 38, at 225.

[289] E.g., *Ex Parte Williams*, 139 S.W.2d 485 (1940), *cert. denied sub nom. Williams* v. *Golden*, 311 U.S. 675 (1940); *Ex Parte White*, 41 P.2d 488 (1935); *Commonwealth* v. *Everett*, 170 A. 720 (1934).

applicant for a permit proposes to serve an object, purpose, or movement in a field not adequately covered. Even where it is permissible for the regulators to make a determination involving an appraisal of facts, an exercise of judgment, and the formation of an opinion, the process must occur in reference to legislatively derived standards that are properly within the police power. The following observation of the court remains applicable today:

> We know of no law which authorizes reasonable regulation to include the power to determine which of two equally charitable organizations may be permitted to solicit in a particular field or which gives a legislative body the authority to give the power to decide, without standards or rules properly within the police power, whether one worthy charity shall have an opportunity to present its case to the public and another shall not be entitled so to do.[290]

A similar case involved a statute in Connecticut that provided that no person shall solicit money for any alleged religious, charitable, or philanthropic cause unless such cause was first approved by the secretary of the state's Public Welfare Council. The conviction of some of the members of Jehovah's Witnesses under the statute was reversed, with the reversal upheld by the U.S. Supreme Court, because the statute was held to be in violation of the First and Fourteenth Amendments to the U.S. Constitution. The Supreme Court there stated that, while the state generally may regulate charitable solicitations in the interest of public safety, peace, or convenience, it cannot condition the solicitation upon a license, the granting of which rests on the determination by a state authority as to what is a religious cause.[291] The Court characterized the secretary's role and its conclusion as follows:

> He is not to issue a certificate as a matter of course. His decision to issue or refuse it involves appraisal of facts, the exercise of judgment, and the formation of an opinion. He is authorized to withhold his approval if he determines that the cause is not a religious one. Such a censorship of religion as the means of determining its right to survive is a denial of liberty protected by the First Amendment and included in the liberty which is within the protection of the Fourteenth.[292]

One court upheld a city ordinance in the face of an assertion that the regulatory official involved was delegated an "arbitrary power to determine what constitutes a charitable, religious, etc., organization and purpose and to grant or withhold permits or licenses for charitable organizations without prescribing any guidelines for the exercise of the officer's discretion."[293] The court found that the ordinance contained "sufficient guidelines" and "detailed provisions," so that the regulatory official was not bestowed "unbridled discretion to make broad determinations without guidelines."[294]

---

[290] *American Cancer Society, supra* note 38, at 226–227.
[291] *Cantwell* v. *Connecticut, supra* note 47. Also *Jones* v. *City of Opelika*, 316 U.S. 584 (1942).
[292] *Cantwell* v. *Connecticut, supra* note 47, at 305.
[293] *League of Mercy Association, Inc.* v. *Walt*, 376 So.2d 892, 893 (Fla. 1979).
[294] *Id.* at 893.

Some state statutes continue to authorize the regulators to act with a breadth of discretion that raises questions about the arbitrariness of their actions and whether legislative power has been unconstitutionally delegated. For example, a charitable solicitation act once granted "full discretion" to the secretary of state in allowing a solicitation, and the secretary had the authority to decide whether a charitable organization was "reputable" and whether the purposes involved were "legitimate and worthy." Another act authorizes the state to permit solicitations by "bona fide" charitable groups.

Portions of a city ordinance regulating charitable solicitations were found unconstitutional because the provisions involved improperly placed "unbridled discretion" in the hands of city officials, "constituting a prior restraint on protected speech lacking procedural safeguards to guard against potential censorship."[295] One of these provisions accorded the department that regulates charitable fundraising the power to make a "judgment" as to whether a charitable organization's registration statement disclosed "sufficient information" to the public; that agency was empowered to seek additional information if it wished. Another defective provision, as part of the ability of the department to issue information cards in connection with a charitable solicitation, empowered the agency to include "any additional information which in the opinion of the [d]epartment will be of assistance to the public in determining the nature and worthiness of the solicitation." Still another provision found constitutionally infirm was a requirement that the department verify that an applicant professional fundraiser is of "good character." In addition, the ordinance failed constitutional law muster on this ground because the applicant charity must demonstrate "sufficient financial resources" to "successfully fulfill" its obligations; certain procedures in the law were deemed to be utter failures in obviating the dangers of a censorship system.

Provisions of a county ordinance regulating charitable fundraising were found unconstitutional for the same reason: unbridled discretion in governmental officials. One provision found facially invalid enabled the governing commission, when "in its opinion" the application for an information card did not disclose "sufficient information," to require the applicant to file "such additional information as the commission may require." The information card may be denied or revoked if the commission determines that the applicant is "unfit to be trusted . . . or has a bad moral character, intemperate habits, or a bad reputation for truth, honesty, or integrity"; that provision was held "blatantly unconstitutional."[296] Still another defective provision enabled the commission to deny or revoke an information card if it found that the percentage of contributions raised for charitable activities is "unreasonably small" because of "inefficient operation, the payment of one or more salaries in amounts substantially greater than the reasonable value of the services performed, or for other similar reasons."[297]

---

[295] *Gospel Missions of America* v. *Bennett, supra* note 32, at 1443.
[296] *Id.* at 1451.
[297] This last provision was also deemed unconstitutional on the ground that the percentage-of-contributions concept is contrary to free speech rights (see § 4.3).

Sometimes, the *retention* of legislative authority is a constitutional law violation, such as where the legislative body is able to withhold or grant a permit for charitable fundraising in the absence of objective standards. For example, this type of law was voided, as being a violation of due process requirements, where the fundraising permit could be issued in the "uncontrolled discretion" of the legislative branch.[298] This can be another form of prior restraint on First Amendment freedoms that the law will not tolerate.[299]

§ 4.7 TREATMENT OF RELIGIOUS ORGANIZATIONS

(a) Basic Concepts

The First Amendment provides, in the religion clauses, that "Congress shall make no law respecting an establishment of religion, or prohibiting the free exercise thereof. . . ." While most First Amendment cases involve either the establishment clause or the free exercise clause, both of these religion clauses are directed toward the same goal: the maintenance of government neutrality with regard to affairs of religion. Thus, the Supreme Court observed that "the First Amendment rests upon the premise that both religion and government can best work to achieve their lofty aims if each is left free from the other within its respective sphere."[300]

Free exercise clause cases generally arise out of conflict between secular laws and individual religious beliefs. The free exercise clause has been characterized by the Supreme Court as follows:

> The door of the Free Exercise Clause stands tightly closed against any governmental regulation of religious beliefs as such. [citations omitted] Government may neither compel affirmation of a repugnant belief, [citation omitted] nor penalize or discriminate against individuals or groups because they hold religious views abhorrent to the authorities. . . . On the other hand, the Court has rejected the challenges under the Free Exercise Clause to governmental regulations of certain overt acts prompted by religious beliefs or principles, for "even when the action is in accord with one's religious convictions, [it] is not totally free from legislative restrictions."[301]

The Court added that "in this highly sensitive constitutional area, '[o]nly the gravest abuses, endangering paramount interest, give occasion for permissible limitation.'"[302]

---

[298] *Adams* v. *City of Park Ridge,* 293 F.2d 585 (7th Cir. 1961).
[299] E.g., *Staub* v. *City of Baxley,* 355 U.S. 313 (1958); *Morey* v. *Doud, supra* note 263; *Breard* v. *City of Alexandria, supra* note 64; *Martin* v. *City of Struthers,* 319 U.S. 141 (1943); *Schneider* v. *State,* 308 U.S. 147 (1939).
[300] *Illinois ex rel. McCollum* v. *Board of Education,* 333 U.S. 203, 212 (1948).
[301] *Sherbert* v. *Verner,* 374 U.S. 398, 402–403 (1963).
[302] *Id.* at 406, quoting from *Thomas* v. *Collins, supra* note 30, at 530.

The more significant free exercise cases include the clash between the secular law prohibiting polygamy and the precepts of the Mormon religion,[303] military service requirements and conscientious objectors' principles,[304] state unemployment compensation laws requiring Saturday work and the dictates of the Seventh Day Adventists' religion,[305] compulsory school attendance laws and the doctrines of the Amish religion,[306] and a license tax on canvassing and the missionary evangelism objectives of Jehovah's Witnesses.[307] Where there is to be government regulation, notwithstanding free exercise claims, there must be a showing by the government of "some substantial threat to public safety, place, or order."[308] Thus, courts have upheld a compulsory vaccination requirement,[309] prosecution of faith healers practicing medicine without a license,[310] and a prohibition of snake handling as part of religious ceremonies.[311]

Short of this type of a "substantial threat," however, the government may not investigate or review matters of ecclesiastical cognizance. This principle frequently manifests itself in the realm of alleged employment discrimination in violation of the Civil Rights Act of 1964.[312] Thus, there must be a compelling governmental interest in regulation before an organization's free exercise rights may be infringed.[313]

While the free exercise clause cases usually involve alleged unwarranted intrusions of government into the sphere of individuals' religious beliefs, the establishment clause cases usually involve governmental regulation of religious institutions. These cases frequently arise as attacks on the propriety of state aid (often to religious schools) or special treatment (such as tax exemption) to religious organizations.[314] This clause is designed to prohibit the government from establishing a religion, or aiding a religion, or preferring one religion over another. Thus, the Supreme Court has observed that the establishment clause is intended to avoid "sponsorship, financial support, and active involvement of the sovereign in religious activity."[315]

The Supreme Court has repeatedly held that the First Amendment is intended to avoid substantial entangling church–state relationships. In one case, where state aid to religious schools, conditioned on pervasive restrictions, was held to be excessive entanglement, the Court stated:

---

[303] *Reynolds* v. *United States*, 98 U.S. 145 (1878).

[304] *Gillette* v. *United States*, 401 U.S. 437 (1971).

[305] *Sherbert* v. *Verner*, *supra* note 301.

[306] *Wisconsin* v. *Yoder*, 406 U.S. 205 (1972).

[307] *Murdock* v. *Pennsylvania*, 319 U.S. 105 (1943).

[308] *Sherbert* v. *Verner*, *supra* note 301, at 403.

[309] *Jacobson* v. *Massachusetts*, 197 U.S. 11 (1905).

[310] *People* v. *Handzik*, 102 N.E.2d 340 (1964).

[311] *Kirk* v. *Commonwealth*, 44 S.E.2d 409 (1947).

[312] E.g., *McClure* v. *Salvation Army*, 460 F.2d 553 (5th Cir. 1972); *Catholic Bishop of Chicago* v. *NLRB*, 559 F.2d 1112 (7th Cir. 1977), *aff'd*, 440 U.S. 490 (1979).

[313] In general, see Clark, "Guidelines for the Free Exercise Clause," 83 *Harv. L. Rev.* 327 (1969).

[314] E.g., *Committee for Public Education* v. *Nyquist*, 413 U.S. 756 (1973); *Lemon* v. *Kurtzman*, 403 U.S. 602 (1971); *Walz* v. *Tax Commission*, 397 U.S. 664 (1970); *Eagle* v. *Vitale*, 370 U.S. 421 (1962); *Abington School District* v. *Schempp*, 374 U.S. 203 (1953); *Zorach* v. *Clausen*, 343 U.S. 306 (1952); *Ilinois ex rel. McCollum* v. *Board of Education*, *supra* note 300; *Everson* v. *Board of Education*, 330 U.S. 1 (1946).

[315] *Lemon* v. *Kurtzman*, *supra* note 314, at 612.

> . . . [a] comprehensive, discriminating, and continuing state surveillance will inevitably be required to ensure that these restrictions are obeyed and the First Amendment otherwise respected. . . . This kind of state inspection and evaluation of religious content of a religious organization is fraught with the sort of entanglement that the Constitution forbids. It is a relationship pregnant with dangers of excessive government direction of church schools and hence of churches . . . and we cannot ignore here the danger that pervasive modern governmental power will ultimately intrude on religion and thus conflict with the Religion Clauses.[316]

Thus, where there is significant government investigation and/or surveillance, particularly analysis of the sincerity or application of religious beliefs, or a religious institution, there is likely to be a violation of the establishment clause.[317]

Subsequently, the Supreme Court further articulated the applicable law on this point:

> It is part of our settled jurisprudence that the "Establishment Clause prohibits government from abandoning secular purposes in order to put an imprimatur on one religion, or on religion as such, or to favor the adherents of any sect or religious organization." The core notion animating the requirement that a statute possess "a secular legislative purpose" and that "its principal or primary effect . . . be one that neither advances nor inhibits religion," is not only that government may not be overly hostile to religion but also that it may not place its prestige, coercive authority, or resources behind a single religious faith or behind religious belief in general, compelling nonadherents to support the practices or proselytizing of favored religious organizations and conveying the message that those who do not contribute gladly are less than full members of the community.[318]

Thus, an exemption for religious organizations can provide unjustifiable assistance to religious solicitors and, in some instances, "cannot but 'convey a message of endorsement' to the slighted members of the community."[319]

In a posture of particular significance to the law of tax-exempt organizations, the Supreme Court articulated the possibility of permissible government involvement with religious organizations, but in a manner that furthers neutrality. Thus, the Court, in a case concerning an attack on tax exemption for religious properties as being violative of the establishment clause, said that the government may become involved in matters relating to religious organizations so as "to mark boundaries to avoid excessive entanglement" and to adhere to the "policy of neutrality that derives from an accommodation of the Establishment and Free Exercise Clauses that has prevented that kind of involvement that would tip the balance toward government control of Church or government restraint on religious practice. . . ."[320] Consequently, the current stance of the law as articulated by the Supreme Court is that tax exemption for

[316] *Id.* at 619–620.
[317] E.g. *Presbyterian Church* v. *Hull Church,* 393 U.S. 440 (1969); *Caulfield* v. *Hirsh,* 95 L.R.R.M. 3164 (E.D. Pa. 1977).
[318] *Texas Monthly, Inc.* v. *Bullock,* 489 U.S. 1, 8–9 (1989) (citations omitted).
[319] *Id.* at 15 (citations omitted).
[320] *Walz* v. *Tax Commission, supra* note 314, at 669–670.

religious organizations does not violate the First Amendment since it promotes neutrality, inasmuch as the alternative of nonexemption would necessarily lead to prohibited excessive entanglements (such as valuation of property, imposition of tax liens, and foreclosures).

As regards nonprofit organizations seeking tax exemption as religious entities, it is difficult to mark the boundary between proper government regulation and unconstitutional entanglement. Not infrequently, for example, a religious organization will claim a violation of its constitutional rights when the IRS probes too extensively in seeking information about it in the context of evaluation of an application for recognition of exemption. The courts appear agreed, however, that the IRS is obligated, when processing an application for recognition of tax exemption, to make inquiries and gather information to determine whether the organization's purposes and activities conform with the statutory requirements, and that such an investigation is beyond the pale of the First Amendment's guarantee of freedom of religion.[321]

The Supreme Court has summed up its approach to establishment clause and free exercise clause cases succinctly: "In short, when we are presented with a state law granting a denominational preference, our precedents demand that we treat the law as suspect and that we apply strict scrutiny in adjudging its constitutionality."[322]

It is against this constitutional law backdrop that the efforts by government to regulate the fundraising practices of religious entities may be viewed.

(b) Constitutionality of Exemption

Many of the state charitable solicitation acts provide some form of exemption for religious organizations.[323] Presumably, this traditional exemption derives from the belief that the First and Fourteenth Amendments to the U.S. Constitution (and comparable provisions of state constitutions) prohibit such regulation of religious groups. Nonetheless, in the face of some fundraising abuses committed in the name of religion, some states have attempted to expand applicability of their charitable solicitation acts to religious organizations. In response, some organizations are challenging these new requirements, claiming that they are laws respecting an establishment of religion and a prohibition on the free exercise of religion. Successful challenges would, of course, stem any tide toward greater regulation of fundraising by religious groups, while a general upholding of this form of regulation of religious entities could prompt other states' legislatures to repeal the exemptions for religious organizations in their charitable solicitation acts.

A line of Supreme Court cases extending back to the 1940s bears on the matter of state and local regulation of solicitations by religious organizations.[324] In one case, three members of a religious group were convicted, under

---

[321] *United States et al.* v. *Toy National Bank et al.*, 79-1 U.S.T.C. ¶ 9344 (N.D. Ia. 1979); *General Conference of the Free Church of America* v. *Commissioner*, 71 T.C. 920, 930–932 (1979); *Coomes* v. *Commissioner*, 572 F.2d 554 (6th Cir. 1978).

[322] *Larson* v. *Valente*, 456 U.S. 228, 246 (1982).

[323] See § 3.5.

[324] A fuller analysis of this subject appears at 76 A.L.R. 3d 924 (1977).

a state statute that forbade the solicitation of contributions by religious or other philanthropic causes without obtaining government approval, for selling books, distributing pamphlets, and soliciting donations. The state courts upheld the law on the ground that it was valid as an attempt to protect the public from fraud, but the Supreme Court set aside the convictions.[325] The Court held that a "general regulation, in the public interest, of solicitation, which does not involve any religious test and does not unreasonably obstruct or delay the collection of funds is not open to any constitutional objection."[326] The Court went on, however, to state that to condition the solicitation of aid for the perpetuation of religious views or systems upon a license, the grant of which rests in the exercise of a determination by state authority as to what is a "religious cause" is an invalid prior restraint on the free exercise of religion.[327]

Subsequently, the Court struck down a tax on the sale of religious literature, holding that the sale of this literature by itinerant evangelists in the course of spreading their doctrine was not a commercial enterprise beyond the protection of the First Amendment.[328] Likewise, a license tax applied against an evangelist or preacher who sold religious books door to door for his livelihood was declared unconstitutional, because the activity, although commercial to some degree, was primarily religious.[329]

Another grouping of cases, however, injects a different perspective. Representative of these cases is the upholding by the Supreme Court of California of a Los Angeles municipal code provision that requires all solicitors for charitable purposes to register with the city and to comply with other general regulation.[330] The court observed that "many activities prompted by religious motives can hardly be differentiated from secular activities."[331] In the case, the funds contributed were used by the organization to "carry on their religious home missionary and evangelical work among the poor and underprivileged," which the court found to be a secular activity.[332] Therefore, the court ruled that the organization's activities were subject to regulation, notwithstanding the fact that the ordinance exempted "solicitation made solely for evangelical, missionary, or religious purposes."[333]

A recent case involving members of ISKCON who solicited contributions, disseminated religious tracts, and sold religious material at Chicago's O'Hare Airport had echoed the early Supreme Court opinions in striking city airport regulations.[334] The regulations at issue required persons to register with airport authorities each day before soliciting or distributing literature, with no exemption for religious groups. The court said that, although conduct cannot

---

[325] *Cantwell* v. *Connecticut, supra* note 47.

[326] *Id.* at 305.

[327] *Id.* at 307.

[328] *Murdock* v. *Pennsylvania, supra* note 307.

[329] *Follett* v. *Town of McCormick,* 321 U.S. 573 (1944).

[330] *Gospel Army* v. *City of Los Angeles,* 163 P.2d 704 (1945).

[331] *Id.* at 711.

[332] *Id.* at 706.

[333] The rationales of this and similar opinions, however, are today to be questioned, in that they antedate the Supreme Court trilogy of cases (see text accompanied by *supra* notes 71–115).

[334] *International Society for Krishna Consciousness, Inc.* v. *Rochford,* 425 F. Supp. 734 (M.D. Ill. 1977), *aff'd and rev'd,* 585 F.2d 263 (7th Cir. 1978).

be made religious by the zeal of the practitioners, the "mere fact that religious literature is sold, or contributions solicited, does not put this form of evangelism outside the pale of constitutional protection."[335] Because the activity was protected by the First Amendment, the discretionary power granted to municipal officials, which allowed them to deny permits, was too broad to be upheld.

A summary of the current state of the law on this subject may be as follows. First, where the purpose of the solicitation pursued by a religious organization is primarily religious, regulation of the activity must pass a test of strict scrutiny, showing that (1) the state has a compelling interest in undertaking the regulation; (2) the statute has a secular purpose; (3) the primary effect of the law neither advances nor inhibits religion; and (4) the law does not foster excessive government entanglement with religion.[336] Second, if the state's interest is sufficiently compelling, then, although the law inhibits religion to some degree, it may validly outweigh the religious interest.[337] Third—and this is the element that is the most difficult of certainty—it *may* be that, where the funds solicited are to be used for a secular purpose, the state can regulate—in exercise of its police power—the fundraising of a religious group to the same degree as a secular group.[338] The Supreme Court indicated this type of an approach when it upheld the constitutionality of tax exemptions for religious organizations for properties used solely for religious worship, with the exemption viewed as merely sparing the exercise of religion from the burden of property taxation as is done for a broad class of charitable organizations.[339] Similarly, in cases of public aid to church-related schools, where the establishment clause is the chief concern, the Supreme Court has found no excessive entanglement even where there is state supervision of these schools, including annual review of expenditures.[340]

One of the most important recent cases raising these issues occurred in North Carolina, where a church successfully alleged that application of that state's charitable solicitation act to it would violate the federal and state constitutions in that the statute purports to establish, and deny to it the free exercise of, religion, and otherwise constitute an unreasonable intrusion by the state into the constitutionally protected area of religion.[341]

The church won its case at the trial, appellate, and supreme court levels. The courts found the North Carolina charitable solicitation act as applied to religious groups unconstitutional in a variety of ways, as being violative of both the U.S. and North Carolina constitutions.

Before 1977, the North Carolina law, like nearly all of these laws, provided a blanket exemption for religious organizations. The North Carolina statute was amended, however, effective July 1, 1977, to require the filing of an application for a license to solicit contributions in the state by a religious organization "if its financial support is derived primarily from contributions

[335] *Id.*, 425 F. Supp.
[336] See *Lemon* v. *Kurtzman, supra* note 314.
[337] See *Wisconsin* v. *Yoder, supra* note 306.
[338] See *Gospel Army* v. *City of Los Angeles, supra* note 330.
[339] *Walz* v. *Tax Commission, supra* note 314.
[340] *Roemer* v. *Maryland Public Works Board*, 426 U.S. 736 (1976).
[341] *Heritage Village Church and Missionary Fellowship, Inc.* v. *North Carolina, supra* note 265.

solicited from persons other than its own members." This law change caused the plaintiff organization to lose its exemption, and the same fate befell another group that intervened in the case, the Holy Spirit Association for the Unification of World Christianity. Thus, the lawsuit ensued.

The trial court found that the general exemption for religious organizations in the North Carolina law was unconstitutional, in relation to the membership provision, because it "creates an establishment of religion."[342] (The statute defined "religious purposes" in terms of practices carried on "according to the rights of a particular denomination.") Moreover, the court held, without explanation, that this provision denied the plaintiff(s) the equal protection of the laws.

The court struck down as unconstitutional the 1977 provision narrowing the exemption on these grounds: (1) it arbitrarily discriminates between religious organizations primarily supported by contributions solicited from nonmembers and nonreligious organizations so supported; (2) it arbitrarily discriminates between religious organizations supported primarily by members and religious organizations supported primarily by nonmembers; and (3) the distinction between the two types of organizations created by the law is not reasonably related to the purposes of the act.[343] The first of these grounds is puzzling, because the effect of the statute is to treat these organizations alike, not discriminate between them.

The court, however, did not stop there. The act was found to be unconstitutionally vague, depriving the organization of due process,[344] because the term *members* was not defined. Portions of the act were ruled unconstitutional because they are "arbitrary and irrational," overbroad in their regulation, and delegate excessive authority to the state regulators.[345]

The statute was found unconstitutional as respects its applicability to religious organizations on still other grounds. The regulation of fundraising by religious groups was held to be a "prior restraint" upon the exercise of religious functions. The requirement that religious organizations have to secure a license "with respect to their secular activities" was determined to be an interference with the free exercise of religion. The discretion in the state to determine what is a "religious purpose" was ruled unconstitutional.[346]

For these and still other reasons, the trial court permanently enjoined and restrained the state regulators from requiring either plaintiff organization to apply for or obtain a license to solicit contributions.

The state of North Carolina tendered the appropriate arguments to the court. It contended that the regulation of charitable solicitations is a reasonable exercise of the police power of the state. It asserted that the regulation imposes no burdens on the free exercise of religion. Rather, it argued, the state legislature sought merely to subject religious organizations that solicit beyond their membership to the same disclosure provisions and fraud-prevention regulations as are applicable to secular charitable organizations. The general rationale

[342] *Id.*, 40 N.C. App. at 445.
[343] *Id.* at 448.
[344] See § 4.4.
[345] *Heritage Village Church and Missionary Fellowship, Inc.* v. *North Carolina, supra* note 265, 40 N.C. App. at 448.
[346] *Id.* at 454.

for charitable solicitation acts was repeatedly asserted: the public has the right to know how and where their contributions are spent and to be protected from unscrupulous promoters and fraudulent schemes.

The state thus contended that the act did not violate either the free exercise or establishment clauses. It also took the position that freedom of speech and of press rights was not being abridged, nor was the equal protection clause.

The church asserted that the North Carolina charitable solicitation statute, as applicable to it, went beyond the police power of the state and into areas protected by the federal and state constitutions. The principal argument was that the statute unconstitutionally prefers one mode of worship over another, namely, the traditional denominational church with an established congregation, as opposed to (in the words of the church's brief) the "modern evangelical mode of worship . . . which makes use of electronic communications media on a vast scale" and which is a nondenominational ministry. The solicitation of funds by a religious group was characterized as a religious function in itself.

While not all of the conclusions of law expressed by the trial court in the North Carolina case were fully treated by the higher courts, the three opinions taken together form a clear holding that:

1. The solicitation of funds from the general public by a religious organization is, in and of itself, a religious activity, particularly where the organization practices evangelism.

2. The religion clauses of the First Amendment dictate a policy of neutrality that prevents undue governmental involvement in religious affairs, and this fundamental principle is fully applicable to state charitable solicitation acts.

3. A total exemption for religious organizations from such an act avoids First Amendment problems because its effect is one of benevolent neutrality, partaking of neither sponsorship of nor hostility toward religious affairs.

4. A distinction in such an act between religious organizations on the basis of whether they solicit the general public is an impermissible establishment of, and entanglement with, religion.

5. The foregoing does not necessarily mean that the state is powerless to prevent fraud in charitable solicitations by religious organizations.

These principles were applied in connection with a case involving city and county ordinances that, although they provided an exemption for solicitations made "solely for evangelical, missionary, or religious purposes," authorized the government involved, when this type of solicitation was made "in a manner which, in the opinion of [the government], is calculated to give, or may give, the impression . . . that the purpose of such solicitation is either in whole or in part charitable," to investigate the matter and publicize its findings "as it deems best to advise the public of the facts of the case." These ordinances were found to violate the establishment clause, in that they were in contravention of the criteria laid down by the Supreme Court in this area.[347] The city and county failed to articulate a secular legislative purpose that would justify their preference for solicitations solely for religious purposes. By exclusively exempting solicitations for religious purposes, the ordinances were held to be impermissibly advancing religion. The ordinances were said to create excessive entanglement between church and state by requiring the city and county governments to examine and monitor religious solicitations, to determine whether a solicitation "has been, is being, or is intended to be" for religious purposes, to review the true purpose of the solicitation (in the government's opinion) and whether any element of the fundraising is "charitable," and, depending on its findings, take certain action. The court wrote that this "government involvement in religious activity is excessive and is a 'continuing one calling for official and continuing surveillance leading to an impermissible degree of entanglement.' "[348]

Another approach that some of the states have taken in this context is to exclude religious organizations from the blanket exemption where the funds received from sources other than their constituency exceed a certain percentage. (This is a rather obvious attempt to leave the "mainline" churches and other religious organizations exempt from fundraising regulation, while subjecting the "newer" or "unorthodox" religions to regulation.) An illustration of this point is the charitable solicitation law in Minnesota, which until 1978, exempted all religious organizations from the requirements of the statute. In that year, however, the law was amended to provide that only those religious organizations that received more than one-half of their total contributions from members or affiliated organizations would remain eligible for the exemption (the "50-percent rule").

This 50-percent rule was challenged in the courts, with the trial court and the appellate court[349] concluding that the "inexplicable religious classification"[350] embodied in the 50-percent rule violated the establishment clause. The case reached the Supreme Court, which held that the 50-percent rule "clearly grants denominational preferences of the sort consistently and firmly deprecated in our precedents" and thus "that rule must be invalidated unless it is justified by a compelling governmental interest."[351] The Court acknowledged that the state "has a significant interest in protecting its citizens from abusive practices in the solicitation of funds for charity, and that this interest retains importance when the solicitation is conducted by a religious organization."[352] The Court found, however, that the 50-percent rule itself is not closely fitted to furtherance of a compelling governmental interest and that it therefore violated the establishment clause.[353] In so doing, the Court rejected, as having no substantial support in the case's record, the premises underlying the state's arguments that (1) members of a religious organization "can and will exercise

---

[347] See the text *supra* accompanied by note 326.
[348] *Gospel Missions of America* v. *Bennett, supra* note 32, at 1449, 1452 (citation omitted).
[349] *Valente* v. *Larson*, 637 F.2d 562 (8th Cir. 1981).
[350] *Id.* at 565–570.
[351] *Larson* v. *Valente, supra* note 322, at 246–247.
[352] *Id.* at 248.
[353] *Id.* at 255.

supervision and control over the organization's solicitation activities when membership contributions exceed 50 percent," (2) "membership control, assuming its existence, is an adequate safeguard against abusive solicitations of the public by the organization," and (3) "the need for public disclosure rises in proportion with the *percentage* of nonmember contributions."[354] The Court wrote that the 50-percent rule "effects the *selective* legislative imposition of burdens and advantages upon particular denominations,"[355] which is "precisely the sort of official denominational preference that the Framers of the First Amendment forbade."[356]

There may be one exception to the general fact that there is little advocacy for a substantial increase in government regulation of fundraising, and the outcome of government's response to this exceptional situation may say much about its treatment of all charitable institutions over the coming years. The exception is that group of charitable entities the media have tagged as religious *cults*.

The word *cult* does not have what could properly be termed a precise legal meaning, but it captures the public's (and some of the regulators') anger, dismay, confusion, and/or misgivings about religious cults, sects, communal groups, unorthodox churches, and the like. Whatever wording may be employed, these organizations can be safely encompassed by the term *nontraditional* religious groups.

Religious organizations, including "conventional" churches, have a multicentury, Western world tradition of immunity from entanglement with governmental regulatory authority. This is manifested in English common law and has always been reflected in a host of U.S. statutory laws, including the Internal Revenue Code. As noted, the U.S. and state constitutions afford organized religion with explicit protections against interference by the state.

With this background and battery of legal shields, it is ironic that religious groups are triggering the clamor for their regulation (and prosecution) by the state. The record in recent years is starkly dramatic. The nation has watched attempts to shelter drug usage as a religious practice; mail-order ministries springing up as income and real estate tax dodges; and churches and other religious organizations amassing great wealth, tax-free.

The affairs of the Unification Church, the Worldwide Church of God, the Church of Scientology, and Hare Krishna sects are given heavy coverage in the media. The public reads of federal and state probes into religious groups' activities and operations, and FBI raids on their premises. Other disparate events further darken public suspicions.

---

[354] *Id.* at 249 (emphasis in original).

[355] *Id.* at 254 (emphasis in original).

[356] *Id.* at 255. Indeed, the Court cited the debates on the legislation, where one state senator explained that the 50-percent rule was "an attempt to deal with the religious organizations which are soliciting on the street and soliciting by direct mail, but who are not substantial religious organizations in . . . our state" and where another senator said that "what you're trying to get at here is [sic] the people that are running around airports and running around streets and soliciting people and you're trying to remove them from the exemption that normally applies to religious organizations" (*id.* at 254).

All of these and other doubts about this type of organization surfaced after the revelations about the Peoples Temple and the Jonestown tragedy. In addition to what Jim Jones was doing in Guyana, there is great concern about children in cults, the rising deprogramming industry, and the spread of new consciousness movements. State and local investigations have resulted, and a much-publicized, but largely counterproductive, U.S. Senate hearing was held in February 1979. This phenomenon continues into the present day, as illustrated by the activities of the sect led by David Koresh within the Branch Davidian compound in Waco, Texas; congressional hearings on the appropriateness of a federal raid on the compound were held in 1993 and 1995.

Then, of course, there have been the fundraising exposés. The chief one of current times was the direct-mail fundraising abuses conducted in the name of the Pallottine Fathers. Subsequently, it was reported that Pope John Paul II prevented an investigation of the expenditures and investment practices of another order, the Pauline Fathers.

Religious groups have become more active in lobbying activities in recent years, in the face of their inability to elect coverage under the 1976 liberalized legislative efforts rules.[357]

The answer to this dilemma—if in fact there is one—is not readily at hand. Even assuming an absence of any constitutional law impediments, the range of options open to Congress is not great. For example, federal law might:

- Regulate investment practices,

- Seek to prevent self-dealing, including unreasonable salaries and benefits,

- Constrict program efforts,

- More tightly control lobbying practices,

- Regulate fundraising activities,

- Mandate minimal spending on exempt function activities,

- Direct the composition of boards of directors,

- Restrict forms of business activity and involvement.

As noted, it is by no means clear whether constitutional law precepts would tolerate such regulation. At a minimum, the current state of the law seems to be that, to the extent that government regulation of religious groups is permissible, it must be undertaken equally with respect to all components of the charitable spectrum.[358]

For example, a federal district court upheld the constitutionality of a municipal ordinance, as applicable to a religious organization, requiring charitable

---

[357] See § 5.9.

[358] E.g., *Taylor* v. *City of Knoxville,* 566 F. Supp. 925 (E.D. Tenn. 1983), and *Sylte* v. *The Metropolitan Government of Nashville and Davidson County,* 493 F. Supp. 313 (M.D. Tenn. 1980) (where ordinances were struck down because the investigators had extensive authority to inquire into the practices and beliefs of fundraising religious organizations).

organizations to file registration statements or to make available to their members private disclosure statements, on the ground that the ordinance is directed at conduct, rather than belief, with a secular purpose and effect, and is justified by the governmental interest in public safety.[359] At any rate, to mark the outer boundaries, the compelling governmental interest test is not required when the government action involves a religion-neutral *criminal* law.[360] Even as to the civil laws, "[r]outine regulatory interaction which involves no inquiries into religious doctrine, . . . no delegation of state power to a religious body, . . . and no 'detailed monitoring and close administrative contact' between secular and religious bodies, . . . does not itself violate the nonentanglement command."[361]

Thus, whatever government does with respect to the cults, it presumably must do to all charitable groups. If the publicity about these entities subsides, so may the lawmakers' desire—such as it may be—to regulate them. But, if regulation is to be forthcoming, chances are it will not be confined to nontraditional religious organizations.

Notwithstanding the developments in constitutional law, the fact remains that some abusive fundraising is being perpetrated in the name of religion. Some argue strenuously that the need to protect the public and reputable religious organizations dictates the applicability of disclosure laws to all types of charitable, including religious, groups and that this can be done constitutionally.[362] Others contend that First Amendment (and other constitutional) protections shield religious groups from fundraising regulation. At the present, it must be conceded that it is an open question whether this regulation as applied to religious organizations involves unconstitutional infringements on the free exercise of religion and/or an unconstitutional entanglement of church and state.[363]

§ 4.8 OTHER CONSTITUTIONAL LAW ISSUES

Other principles of constitutional law can operate to void a charitable fundraising statute. These are usually variants of free speech considerations[364] but warrant special emphasis.

---

[359] *Church of Scientology Flag Services Org., Inc.* v. *City of Clearwater, supra* note 32. Also *Church of the Lukumi Babalu Aye, Inc.* v. *City of Hialeah*, 723 F. Supp. 1467 (S.D. Fla. 1989) (holding that a municipal ordinance regulating ritual sacrifices of animals was not unconstitutional as applied to religious organizations).

[360] *Employment Division, Department of Human Resources of Oregon* v. *Smith*, 494 U.S. 872 (1990).

[361] *Hernandez* v. *Commissioner*, 490 U.S. 680, 696–697 (1989), quoted in *Jimmy Swaggart Ministries* v. *Board of Equalization*, 493 U.S. 378, 395 (1990).

[362] E.g., Rakay and Sugarman, "A Reconsideration of the Religious Exemption: The Need for Financial Disclosure of Religious Fund-Raising and Solicitation Practices," 9 *Loyola U. L. J.* 863 (1978).

[363] A "standard" municipal ordinance regulating fundraising for charitable purposes was upheld in the face of a challenge as to its constitutionality under the free exercise and establishment clauses in *Church of Scientology Flag Services Org., Inc.* v. *City of Clearwater, supra* note 32.

[364] In general, see § 4.3.

A statute can be unconstitutionally vague. Laws of this nature are found to be contrary to constitutional precepts when they are so vague that persons "of common intelligence must necessarily guess at [their] meaning and differ as to [their] application."[365] The Supreme Court stated: "The general test of vagueness applies with particular force in review of laws dealing with speech. 'Stricter standards of permissible statutory vagueness may be applied to a statute having a potentially inhibiting effect on speech; a man may the less be required to act at his peril here, because the free dissemination of ideas may be the loser.' "[366] One court struck down a registration requirement because the law, in addition to specifying certain information that had to be provided, also allowed the government involved to require, in its discretion, additional information (a common provision). Inasmuch as, "[f]rom reading the statute, it is impossible to discern with precision what information must be provided" as part of the registration process, the vagueness caused the law to be found facially invalid.[367]

A government cannot mandate or regulate the content of protected speech. This has particular relevance to the increasing tendency of states to require a soliciting charitable organization to make certain statements to prospective donors. In one instance, city and county ordinances that required the use of an "information card" were held unconstitutional because the ordinances mandated the inclusion of information, which the city and county viewed as being of "assistance to the public in determining the nature and worthiness of the solicitation."[368]

§ 4.9 EXEMPTION FOR MEMBERSHIP GROUPS

Several states provide an exemption, in whole or in part, from the requirements of their charitable solicitation act with respect to solicitations by organizations of their members. This is done because these laws are usually designed to apply to solicitations of the general public and because an organization's members are deemed to have a sufficiently intimate relationship with the organization so as not to require the protection afforded by a charitable solicitation act.

Because of the obvious potential breadth of this exemption, the definition of the term *member* becomes crucial in evaluating the availability of the exemption. Many of these state laws contain a provision designed to avert the most transparent abuse of the exemption, which states that a member does not include one who is designated a member upon the making of a solicited contribution.[369]

---

[365] *Connally* v. *General Construction Co.*, 269 U.S. 385, 391 (1926).

[366] *Hynes* v. *Mayor of Oradell, supra* note 59, at 620 (quoting *Smith* v. *California*, 361 U.S. 147, 151 (1959)).

[367] *Gospel Missions of America* v. *Bennett, supra* note 32, at 1443.

[368] *Id.* at 1445.

[369] E.g., *Blenski* v. *State*, 245 N.W.2d 906 (Wis. 1976).

The concept of a member in this context appears to carry with it three essential elements: (1) the member must pay dues, fees, assessments, or the like; (2) in return, the member receives a right, privilege, standing, honor, services, or other benefit; and (3) the member acquires the right to vote, elect officers, or hold office. Where these elements are present, the person is said to be a "bona fide" member.

Thus, the charitable solicitation act definition of *member* rules out application of the term to *associate* or *affiliate* or any other form of nonvoting member. Otherwise, the general rule pursuant to state nonprofit corporation laws is that a member of this type of a corporation is one who possesses whatever rights or privileges of membership are stated in the organization's articles of organization (such as articles of incorporation or constitution) or bylaws.[370] But the typical state charitable solicitation act concept of *bona fide member* is likely to be narrower than the definition accorded the term by the organization in its own governing instruments.

Two of the aforementioned criteria may be relatively easy to satisfy. That is, the facts may readily demonstrate that the member bears the responsibility of financially supporting the organization by means of the payment to it of dues, assessments, or the like (as distinguished from contributions) and that the member has the right to receive one or more tangible benefits of membership, such as a magazine or newsletter, or the ability to attend an annual convention or similar meeting.

In designing a membership with the charitable solicitation act exemptions in mind, however, an organization should consider that the regulators will likely look beyond the agreement of the parties as expressed in the governing instruments in search of evidence of some participation by the members in the planning, activities, or programs of the organization, such as attendance at meetings in a voting capacity, performance of some of the work of the organization, or service as officers and/or directors.[371]

For some groups, satisfaction of all of these tests may not be feasible. For example, an authentic national convention of voting members may be impractical, as may direct participation in the organization's work or election of an organization's board of directors and/or officers, in whole or in part, by authentic members. Also, those who support the organization may wish to do so in the form of gifts, which are deductible, rather than dues, which (unless they qualify as business expenses) are not.

Thus, at a minimum, the bona fides of membership, in this context at least, require more than merely denominating the maker of every solicited gift a *member*. How much more will be required to evidence an authentic membership will

---

[370] "Membership is based on the regulations of the association and constitutes a contract between the organization and the individual" (*Rachford* v. *Indemnity Insurance Co. of North America,* 183 F. Supp. 875, 879 (S.D. Cal. 1960)). "[T]he test for determining whether a given person is a member of an organization is internal to that organization" (*United Nuclear Corporation* v. *NLRB,* 340 F.2d 133, 137 (1st Cir. 1965)). Also *Estate of Freshour,* 345 P.2d 689 (1959).

[371] For a discussion of the elements of a membership relationship, see *Fisher* v. *United States,* 231 F.2d 99 (9th Cir. 1956).

depend on how many of the foregoing factors a state's regulators will demand be present.

§ 4.10 DEFINING *PROFESSIONAL FUNDRAISER* AND *PROFESSIONAL SOLICITOR*

The typical state charitable solicitation act defines the terms *professional fundraiser* (or like term) and *professional solicitor*.[372] There is confusion, however, as to the application of these terms in actual practice. The distinctions are of more than passing consequence; for example, a professional fundraiser may not care to be regarded as a professional solicitor, and a professional solicitor is likely to be subjected to more stringent forms of regulation than is the case with a professional fundraiser.

The term *professional fundraiser* is often defined as a person who "plans, conducts, manages, carries on, advises or acts as a consultant, whether directly or indirectly, in connection with soliciting contributions for, or on behalf of any charitable organization but who actually solicits no contributions as a part of such services." By contrast, a "professional solicitor" is one who "solicits contributions for, or on behalf of, a charitable organization," either personally or through agents or employees, and who does not qualify as a professional fundraiser.

As a general proposition, a professional fundraiser is a consultant who plans and advises with respect to a charitable solicitation. In nearly all instances involving a professional fundraiser, the charitable organization is itself the solicitor of charitable contributions. The professional fundraiser, functioning in an advisory capacity, does not become involved in the actual pursuit of gifts.

A professional solicitor, however, directly participates in the solicitation process. Generally, these persons are those who engage in house-to-house or building-to-building canvassing, placement of and collection from receptacles in public places, and charitable solicitations by means of the telephone.[373]

The distinction between the terms—and, unfortunately, a growing tendency to blur the distinction—can be seen in cases involving professional fundraisers who provide counsel in the field of charitable solicitations by direct mail. Typically, the services provided by such a person (either directly or by subcontract) are threefold: (1) the writing, design, and production of literature; (2) the securing of suitable mailing lists; and (3) supervision of the mailing of the solicitation literature. Usually, these services are not provided by the firm acting independently but by working in tandem with the charitable organization at each stage of the solicitation process.

There is a growing tendency by state regulators to regard a firm providing these services as a professional solicitor—largely because of its direct

---

[372] See § 3.2.

[373] E.g., 60 Am. Jur. 2d, Peddlers, Solicitors, and Transient Dealers §§ 29, 32, and 35; *Derby* v. *Hiegart*, 325 P.2d 35 (1958); *City of Shreveport* v. *Teague*, 8 So.2d 640 (1942); *State* v. *Mauer*, 182 A.2d 175 (1962).

participation in the mailing process.[374] (There is no question that the act of mailing an appeal for contributions is a solicitation.) As a general proposition, however, classification of such a firm, which is in fact a fundraiser, as a professional solicitor is not reasonable. Where the mailing is done pursuant to the charity's postal permit, the charity's name, logo, signature, and the like are utilized, and there is no use of the firm's name or other identification in the mailing, the charitable organization is the solicitor.

When such a firm places the prepared literature into the postal system—an act of "mailing"—it is acting as agent for the charity. Were this not the case, the charity's preferential postage rates could not be used. The prosecution of this agency function by such a firm should not convert the firm into a professional solicitor. It would make more sense to characterize the persons who actually deliver the charity's mail as solicitors than to treat the firm as such. But, in point of fact and law, both the firm and its employees, and the U.S. Postal Service employees involved, are agents of the charitable organization, which is the solicitor.[375]

The artificiality of treating such a firm as a professional solicitor can be seen in the consequence in law of a change in the facts. That is, the firm can avoid classification as a professional solicitor by ceasing to supervise the mailing. This can happen by having the firm design and produce the mailing pieces, affix the addressee labels, and then ship the millions of pieces (at great cost and inconvenience to the charity) to the charitable organization, so that it in turn could physically insert the literature into the postal system. Surely the drafters of the state charitable solicitation acts intended no such result when they defined the two terms.

One of the flaws of this line of thinking is that it assumes that there must be a professional solicitor in the picture. In the direct mail context, with rare exception,[376] only the charity itself can be the solicitor; there is no professional solicitor in this setting. By analogy, a solicitation by means of a television program is that of the persons involved in organizing and producing the solicitation; neither the owners of the theater or studio where the program was presented nor the owners of the television network that carries the appeal are thereby converted into professional solicitors.[377]

Finally, as to the matter of treating a fundraising firm as a professional solicitor, this position would convert into a professional solicitor every fundraiser serving a charitable organization, where the services involve supervision of the organization's mailings. To avoid this result, mammoth shipments of prepared mailings from fundraiser to charity would be required, at enormous

[374] See Opinion and Order of the Commission on Charitable Organizations, Commonwealth of Pennsylvania, dated Aug. 14, 1979, holding that a firm that provides direct mail services and that conceives of itself as a professional fundraiser "is a professional solicitor because it supervises the mailing."

[375] The U.S. Postal Service functions as agent of those who use the mails (e.g., 17 Am. Jur. 2d, Contracts §§ 49, 51).

[376] For example, a charity could compensate a person for soliciting gifts for it on that person's own stationery, and the person would contact prospective donors of that person's sole choosing; such a person would presumably be a professional solicitor.

[377] So held in *People v. Framer*, 139 N.Y.S. 2d 331 (1954).

cost and inconvenience, so that the charity rather than the fundraiser could physically commence the mailing.

Worse, the states have altered their charitable solicitation acts in recent years to strenuously regulate the activities of individuals and companies termed *professional solicitors.* Depending on the breadth of the definition of the term, many fundraising professionals, believing themselves to be professional fundraisers (consultants), could be regarded, with unpleasant results, as solicitors.

§ 4.11 DIRECT-MAIL FUNDRAISING GUIDELINES

Ten states, seven tax-exempt organizations, and a professional fundraising firm reached, on January 10, 1991, an out-of-court settlement, ending two years of litigation. The total settlement amount was $2.1 million. Part of the settlement is a consent decree that contains standards agreed to by the states that attempt to guide charitable organizations in the design of sweepstakes.

The states involved were Connecticut, Illinois, Massachusetts, Minnesota, New Jersey, New York, Oregon, Pennsylvania, Virginia, and Washington. The professional fundraising firm was the Watson & Hughey Company of Alexandria, Virginia ("W & H").

The litigation arose in early 1989 as a result of certain fundraising appeals of a "sweepstakes" format, which were designed by W & H. All of the tax-exempt organizations involved in this litigation were clients of W & H. The states charged that certain types of sweepstakes were deceptive. These included certain "instant cash" sweepstakes and an "attorney notification" sweepstakes.

A lawyer who represented the charitable organizations said in a prepared statement that the "settlement does not involve any admission of wrongdoing or any violation of any law. Moreover, no civil penalties were involved. Our clients will discharge their obligations under the settlement by making grants, over a period of five years, to qualified recipients located in the states involved in the settlement."[378]

An outcome of this settlement is 20-plus pages of rules for fundraising using sweepstakes promotions. This lawyer said: "We developed precise and exacting standards which will guide not only our clients, but all exempt organizations and fundraising counsel which are contemplating solicitations of the 'sweepstakes' format."[379]

W & H, the exempt organizations, and others were enjoined from the solicitation of charitable contributions or of memberships in connection with any fundraising by any medium in these states in connection with a sweepstakes or contest unless the solicitation is in conformity with the new rules. These standards emphasize disclosure of the rules of the contest, the prizes won, and the odds of winning. They also impose rules on the fundraising firm, mandating at least quarterly reporting to the charity involved.

The states involved (and others) are using these standards with other fundraising organizations. The standards are extensive and include the following:

---

[378] VIII *Nonprofit Counsel* (No. 2) 1 (Feb. 1991).
[379] *Id.*

- Any such solicitation must clearly and conspicuously disclose, in connection with a sweepstakes or contest, the complete rules in at least ten-point typeface or eight-point bold and on a paper or surface with a contrasting background which the recipient is not asked to return for any reason. In instances of television or radio solicitations, the rules must be referred to by audio or video disclosure. In the case of television, the standards dictate the type and background to be used, and the length of time text must appear on the screen.

- The solicitation must clearly and conspicuously contain, in the body of the solicitation, a reference to the rules of the sweepstakes in print the same size as the predominant type size used in the main text of the solicitation.

- If the solicitation states or implies that the recipient has won a prize, it must clearly and conspicuously state in the body of the solicitation, in print the same size as the predominant type size used in the main text of the solicitation, the prize the recipient has won or the range of prizes.

- The solicitation must clearly and conspicuously state in the rules the value of each prize; the actual number of each prize to be awarded; for a sweepstakes, the odds of receiving each prize; and the method of determining winning entries.

- The solicitation must clearly and conspicuously state in Arabic numerals, written in a clear and conspicuous manner, all dollar amounts, numbers of prizes, and odds of winning.

- Where the sweepstakes or contest is being conducted with multiple sponsors, the odds statement must disclose the odds based on the total maximum number of participants.

- The solicitation must clearly and conspicuously state in the text of the solicitation and the rules that no contribution or other consideration is required as a condition of entering or winning.

The fundraiser and the charities were enjoined from engaging in a wide range of charitable solicitation activities in the states involved, including those which:

- State or imply that the recipient has entered a sweepstakes or contest without disclosing what affirmative act, if any, the recipient must take to remain eligible in the sweepstakes or contest.

- State or imply that the recipient has already entered or been in a second or other successive round of a sweepstakes or contest unless the recipient has in fact agreed to enter that round by consenting in writing or knowingly taking some other affirmative step.

- Conduct a sweepstakes or contest in which solicitations are disseminated to recipients later than 10 days preceding the deadline for entering the sweepstakes or contest or for claiming a prize.

- State or imply that the recipient has already won or may have won a sweepstakes or contest without clearly and conspicuously disclosing what affirmative act, if any, the recipient must take in order to claim a prize.

- State or imply that the recipient has won or will win a sweepstakes or contest unless the recipient has already entered and has been selected on the basis of chance from among a pool of persons significantly larger than the group selected to receive a prize or award.

- State or imply that the recipient has won or will win a prize in a sweepstakes, if the value of the prize is less than $10, unless the prize won is clearly and conspicuously disclosed in the main body of the solicitation.

- State or imply that the recipient is eligible to receive a premium unless a description of the premium or its value is clearly and conspicuously disclosed in either the main body of the solicitation or the rules.

- State or imply that the recipient will receive in a sweepstakes or contest anything of a value greater than its actual value.

- State or imply that the largest prize to be awarded in a sweepstakes or contest is larger than the largest prize that will actually be awarded.

- Falsely state or imply that the recipient is guaranteed to win anything of value in a sweepstakes or contest.

- State or imply that a sweepstakes participant's chances of winning are greater than the true odds.

- Falsely state or imply that the recipient is a "finalist."

- Contain a document resembling a check, or state or imply in the solicitation material that it contains a check unless certain requirements are satisfied.

- Contain a document resembling a bill unless the document is clearly and conspicuously marked "This is not a bill," "Voluntary contribution," "Optional contribution," or words of like import, and where other requirements are satisfied.

- State or imply that the failure to contribute or pay money, enter a sweepstakes, return a claim certificate or coupon, or otherwise respond to a solicitation may, could, or will result in a penalty or forfeiture (other than a loss of a prize or eligibility to win a prize as set forth in the sweepstakes rules).

- Include in a solicitation for a sweepstakes or contest any rules about another sweepstakes or contest, which is not offered in the solicitation.

- Falsely state or imply that any charity involved in this matter has supported, funded, conducted, or otherwise participated in any program, service, or other activity to any greater extent than is, in fact, accurate.

- State or imply that any charity involved in this matter has planned or projected any activity unless the organization has a good-faith plan and reasonably believes that it will be able to carry out the activity.

- Falsely state or imply that any charity involved in this matter has already conducted or completed any activity.

- Falsely state or imply, in the case of activities not conducted solely by a charity involved in this matter, the extent of the charity's support of or participation in the activity.

- Misrepresent in the disclosure statement the amount of money expended on charitable activities, including public education expenses.

- Misrepresent the amount or percentage of funds raised through the solicitation, which will be used in the future for purposes other than fundraising, or the amount or percentage of funds raised through the solicitation, which will be used for a particular purpose.

- Request a donor to send any charity involved in this matter a void or cancelled check or a duplicate or copy of a check in order to enter or claim a prize in a sweepstakes.

- Mislead the recipient of any solicitation as to the source, sponsorship, or affiliation of any charity involved in this matter by the use of trademarks, symbols, emblems, or the like, which are owned exclusively by another organization and as a result are likely to cause confusion between the charity involved and the other organization.

Moreover, the fundraiser and the charities involved were permanently barred from mailing or otherwise communicating with residents of the states involved with any solicitation in connection with a sweepstakes, contest, or other charitable solicitation or request for membership fees that represents or implies that the solicitation is a legal notification or is from a governmental agency when it is not. Likewise barred were communications with residents as to a sweepstakes or contest that has the letterhead, signature, or other indicia of representation or approval by a lawyer.

The consent decree also addressed the content of contracts between W & H and charitable organizations, prohibited the filing of false or misleading financial reports with any state, mandated that the charities involved "have a lawful governing structure in which an independent board shall direct and control the activities and conduct of the organization," and prohibited the charities from entering into contracts for fundraising services unless the terms of the agreement are "fair and reasonable" and are in conformity with the consent decree.

§ 4.12   REGISTRATION FEES

It is a common practice for a state's charitable solicitation law to embody a registration fee. These fees must be tested against principles protecting free speech, in that freedom of expression must be "available to all, not merely to those who can pay their own way."[380] The courts have held that a "licensing fee to be used in defraying administrative costs is permissible, but only to the extent that the fees are necessary."[381] The constitutionality of this type of fee in the charitable solicitation setting was the subject of federal appellate court opinions issued in 1994 and 1995.

In one, the legality of a sliding-scale fee was challenged. The court held that the fee system, which requires a charitable organization seeking to solicit in the state to pay a sliding-scale registration fee based on its nationwide level of public contributions in the prior year, was constitutional.[382]

Before the challenged registration fee was part of the law, the state's charitable solicitation act provided for a one-time registration fee of $50, with annual renewals at no additional charge. The secretary of state decided that the funds generated by means of this one-time fee fell short of the costs incurred in administering the law and monitoring charitable organizations soliciting in the state. Thus, the secretary successfully persuaded the state legislature to reinstate an annual fee—a sliding-scale fee that would yield funds approximate to the costs of administering and enforcing this charitable solicitation act.

The fee structure is: $50 where the total gifts were at least $25,000 but less than $50,001; $75 where the gifts were at least $50,001 but less than $75,001; $100 where the gifts were at least $75,001 but less than $100,001; and $200 where the gifts were at least $100,001. A charitable organization raised money principally as membership dues and contributions in response to direct mail solicitations to nonmembers. Based in another jurisdiction, it annually sent out 200,000 to 250,000 mailings around the country, including about 15,000 to residents of the state with the sliding-scale fee. Receiving annual gifts in excess of $100,001, it was required to pay an annual registration fee in the state in the amount of $200.

The organization refused to pay this fee and filed a lawsuit, challenging the legality of the fee system. The claim was that the statutory fee violated the organization's rights of free speech[383] and of due process,[384] and was an undue or discriminatory burden on interstate commerce.[385] A district court ruled in favor of the state, and an appeal followed.

Integral to resolution of this issue was a determination as to whether this registration fee system is a general revenue tax or a user fee assessed to defray the costs of state-provided services.[386] The appellate court held that the state's registration fee structure failed to qualify as a lawful general revenue tax when reviewed against the rules prohibiting undue burdening of interstate commerce. The court, however, also concluded that the state's sliding-scale registration fee is a user fee and that it is "constitutionally sound."[387] The fee

---

[380] *Murdock v. Pennsylvania, supra* note 307, at 111.

[381] *Fernandes v. Limmer, supra* note 260, at 633 (citations omitted). Also *Holy Spirit Association for Unification of World Christianity v. Hodge, supra* note 165, at 604.

[382] *Center for Auto Safety, Incorporated v. Athey,* 37 F.3d 139 (4th Cir. 1994).

[383] See § 4.3.

[384] See § 4.4.

[385] See § 4.2.

[386] *Id.,* text accompanied by notes 49 and 50.

[387] *Center for Auto Safety, Incorporated v. Athey, supra* note 382, at 143.

structure was said to represent a "fair, if imperfect, approximation of the cost of using . . . [the state's] facilities and services for the charity's benefit."[388] The facts were said to show that the state's costs of "monitoring charities increase with larger charities."[389] This cost increase, the court observed, "arises because larger charities generally generate more registration and renewal documents to review, require more research relating to administrative, management, and membership activities, and give rise to more public inquiries, more paperwork requiring data entry, and more investigative effort."[390] Thus, "because a charity's fee is directly related to the workload the charity is expected to create for the Secretary, the sliding scale fee is a fair, if imperfect, approximation of . . . [the state's] costs."[391] Also, the court wrote, this sliding-scale fee does not discriminate against interstate commerce, inasmuch as it does not differentiate between state-based and out-of-state charitable organizations. Further, the court found that the registration fees are not excessive in relation to the costs incurred by the state.

The charitable organization involved contended that this registration fee cannot be a user fee, in that the state does not provide it with the requisite *service*. The organization relied on prior law for the assertion that the user fee analysis is applicable only where the government is seeking to recoup the costs of operating a facility or providing a service. It argued that the state does not provide any services to soliciting charitable organizations and that, because it solicits only by mail, it does not use any of the state's facilities.

Conceding that the state's fee, "although not the typical user fee, nonetheless fits comfortably within the user fee category," the court held that "charities seeking to solicit in . . . [the state] use the state's apparatus for regulating charities."[392] This, the court ascertained, is a "benefit," in the form of the "privilege of soliciting in . . . [the state] where donor confidence is enhanced owing to the state's regulation of charities."[393]

The solicitation of contributions by charitable organizations is a form of free speech; thus, while the solicitation can be regulated, this can only occur where the regulation is narrowly tailored to achieve a legitimate governmental interest, is content-neutral in terms and effect, and does not unduly burden free speech.[394]

This sliding-scale fee arrangement was held by the court of appeals to "represent a narrowly tailored governmental regulation of speech."[395] The state's officials are not afforded any discretion in the imposition of a

---

[388] *Id.*

[389] *Id.*

[390] *Id.*

[391] *Id.*

[392] *Id.*

[393] *Id.* at 143–144. This astonishing analysis is explored in § 7.12. A similar sliding-scale fee structure in a county ordinance was upheld in *American Charities for Reasonable Fundraising Regulation, Inc.* v. *Pinellas County, supra* note 44.

[394] See § 4.3.

[395] *Center for Auto Safety, Incorporated* v. *Athey, supra* note 382, at 145.

registration fee because the rates are set by statute.[396] The fee package was also held to be content-neutral: the fee was the same irrespective of the cause espoused or the opinion of the government of the cause. For these reasons, the state's registration fee requirement was ruled to not violate principles of free speech.[397]

The other case involved a challenge to the constitutionality of a state statute that imposes an $80 registration fee on professional solicitors. The parties agreed that the state may levy this type of a fee where it is nominal and set to defray the administration of the law; at issue was whether the costs to the attorney general's office of enforcing the law may be considered. The costs incurred by the state exceed the fees received only if administrative and enforcement costs are regarded. The appellate court ruled that both elements of expense to the state may be taken into account in establishing the fee.[398]

The court wrote that "fees that serve not as revenue taxes, but rather as a means to meet the expenses incident to the administration of a regulation and to the maintenance of public order in the matter regulated are constitutionally permissible."[399] To the argument that "penal/quasi-criminal enforcement actions" concerning fraud and misappropriation of funds should not be taken into account, the court ruled that both costs are necessary in the supervision of charitable organizations. At the same time, the court said that enforcement costs may not be so included *simply because* they are in some manner related to the enforcement of" the statute, but that the "propriety of inclusion of particular enforcement costs should be determined case-by-case."[400] Then, the court found that both sets of costs may be included in the case, making the fee a "legitimate" one that merely defrays them, in that there is a "sufficient link" between the attorney general's enforcement activities with respect to the law and the revenues collected pursuant to it.[401]

---

[396] A registration fee would be unconstitutional if the amount of it was set on the basis of the content of the speech. In an analogous circumstance, a county ordinance permitting a government administrator to vary the fee for assembling or parading to reflect the estimated cost of maintaining public order was held facially unconstitutional due to the absence of narrowly drawn, reasonable, and definite standards to guide the determination (*Forsyth County, Georgia* v. *Nationalist Movement,* 112 S. Ct. 2395 (1992)). The U.S. Supreme Court faulted this ordinance, in that the decision as to how much to charge or whether to charge at all for police protection and administrative time was left to the "whim" of the administrator, in that he or she was "not required to rely on any objective factors" (*id.* at 2403). The Court added: "Nothing in the law or its application prevents the official from encouraging some views and discouraging others through the arbitrary application of fees" (*id.*).

[397] The due process claim apparently was not pursued on appeal; the appellate court did not write on the point.

[398] *National Awareness Foundation* v. *Abrams, supra* note 282.

[399] *Id.* at 1165.

[400] *Id.* at 1166 (emphasis in original).

[401] *Id.* at 1167. Subsequently, the requirements that a professional fundraiser pay a $55 fee (and post a $5,000 bond) were found to directly restrain protected speech and thus were pronounced facially unconstitutional, because the government did not demonstrate a "link between the fee and the bond and the costs of the licensing process" (*Gospel Missions of America* v. *Bennett, supra* note 32, at 1447).

§ 4.13   FUNDRAISING OVER INTERNET AND STATE LAW RESTRICTIONS

The Internet has greatly expanded the number of charitable organizations capable of carrying out multistate solicitation activities. Essentially, to reach potential donors in all of the states, an organization needs nothing more than a personal computer and an account with an Internet provider. Once established, the organization's charitable appeal can instantly be made available to the entire Internet community. The large national and international charities with the resources necessary to assure compliance with the various state regulatory regimes are thus no longer the only ones affected by state charitable solicitation laws. Instead, even the smallest organizations, operating on shoestring budgets, are beginning to tap the national contributions market. Thus, the new technology does indeed alter the nature of communication in the charitable solicitations context—it renders it inexpensive.

(a)   Internet Fundraising in General[402]

One of the most difficult of contemporary issues is whether fundraising by charitable organizations by means of the Internet constitutes fundraising in every state—or, for that matter, in every locality. Current thinking generally is that, technically, it does. If those states asserting jurisdiction over Internet fundraising are justified in doing so, the result will be that even the smallest organizations—too small to afford multistate solicitation efforts over the telephone or through the mail—will be required to register under numerous state charitable solicitation laws simply by virtue of utilizing the new communications technology to solicit contributions. If they do not (or cannot) assure state-law compliance, they will be forced to decide between risking legal action in several foreign states or refraining from speaking altogether. The question is whether, under this new mix of facts, those state laws impermissibly restrict speech protected under the First Amendment.

But there is another, more interesting, question that must first be addressed: From a legal perspective, should Internet fundraising appeals be treated any differently solely because they take place on the Internet? That is, should communication over this new medium be treated as anything other than communication, for which there already is a rich regulatory scheme?

To determine whether the various state charitable solicitation regimes unduly intrude on the protected speech interest in such solicitation, the existing regulatory framework must be applied to the new set of facts. The first step in this analysis is to ascertain whether the act of placing an appeal for funds in a document on a computer in one state can subject the organization to the jurisdiction of a foreign state. There is as yet no law directly on this subject.

---

[402] This subsection is a summary of a paper by Paul E. Monaghan, Jr., Esq., Tyler Cooper & Alcorn, New Haven, Connecticut, titled "Charitable Solicitation Over the Internet and State Law Restrictions," prepared under the direction of Professor John Simon, Yale Law School (1996), and adopted with permission.

Although not entirely on point, however, one court opinion may shed some light on the matter.

A federal court of appeals, in 1996, had the opportunity to discuss the legal status of computer-borne communications in the First Amendment context. Two individuals ran an adult-oriented bulletin board service from their home in California. The site was accessible to others around the nation via modems and telephone lines.

Working with the local U.S. Attorney's office in Tennessee, a postal inspector purchased a membership in this bulletin board service and succeeded in downloading allegedly obscene images from the bulletin board. The U.S. Attorney's office filed criminal charges against these individuals for, among other things, transmitting obscenity over interstate telephone lines from their computer. By relatively conservative Memphis community standards, the images involved were found by a jury in fact to constitute obscenity; the couple was convicted.

On appeal, this federal appellate court affirmed the convictions, holding inter alia that the crime of "knowingly us[ing] a facility or means of interstate commerce for the purpose of distributing obscene materials" did not require proof that the defendants had specific knowledge of the destination of each transmittal at the time it occurred.[403] Of interest in the Internet context, in determining that the crime occurred in Tennessee, rather than in California, the court placed considerable weight on its finding that "substantial evidence introduced at trial demonstrated that the . . . [bulletin board service] was set up so members located in other jurisdictions could access and order [obscene] files which would then be instantaneously transmitted in interstate commerce."[404]

If the reasoning of this appellate court is followed by the state courts, it appears that communication via computer constitutes sufficient contact with the foreign state to subject the communicator to local law. Applied in the charitable solicitation context, then, the import of this court decision is clear: Soliciting funds over the Internet, where users download Web pages residing in foreign jurisdictions, in all likelihood will constitute sufficient contact to subject the organization to the jurisdiction of the foreign state, and therefore to the foreign charitable solicitation regime.

It must next be determined whether such interstate communication constitutes *solicitation* encompassed by the laws of the states. Though no definite answer can be divined from the language of any one statute, a brief survey of some state statutes strongly indicates that Internet solicitation will be held in many jurisdictions to be subject to regulation.[405] For example, in one state, solicitation covered by the charitable solicitation act is defined as the making of a fundraising request "through any medium," regardless of whether any contribution is received. In another state, the charitable solicitation law applies to all "request[s] of any kind for a contribution." In another state, the law embraces "each request for a contribution." The statutory scheme in another state applies to "any request, plea, entreaty, demand or invitation, or attempt thereof, to

---

[403] *United States* v. *Thomas*, 74 F.3d 701 (6th Cir. 1996).
[404] *Id.* at 709.
[405] See § 3.2.

give money or property, in connection with which . . . any appeal is made for charitable purposes." In still another state, the law applies to organizations "soliciting or collecting by agents or solicitors, upon ways or in any other public places within the commonwealth to which the public have a right of access."

Certainly, it is difficult to see how Internet fundraising is not caught by any of these strikingly broad provisions. As currently written, then, the statutes of at least five states can easily be construed to reach Internet charitable fundraising.

Indeed, it is likely that most, if not all, of the state charitable fundraising regulation regimes may be so construed, and that those statutes that fail as currently written can be appropriately amended without much trouble.

(b) Charleston Principles

If the assumption is that the solicitation of funds by charitable organizations by means of the Internet constitutes fundraising in every state, then the charitable community is facing an enormous burden. Many in the regulatory sector realize that, if this technically is the law, some form of relief for soliciting charities is warranted.

To this end, the National Association of State Charity Officials (NASCO) issued guidelines to assist charitable organizations that solicit contributions, and their fundraisers, in deciding whether it is necessary to register fundraising efforts in the states when the solicitations are made by e-mail or on their Websites. The guidelines are a product of discussion that was initiated at NASCO's 1999 annual conference in Charleston, South Carolina. Hence, the guidelines are termed the "Charleston Principles" (Principles). The Principles are not law but rather nonbinding guidance to NASCO members.

The Principles are rested on a fundamental proposition (which probably is true): "Existing registration statutes generally, of their own terms, encompass and apply to Internet solicitations." Although the Principles do not say so in so many words, another fundamental proposition is that requiring registration of all charities soliciting gifts by means of the Internet and their fundraisers in all states with registration requirements is untenable. Thus, the scope of potential registration must be narrowed or, as the Principles put it, state charity officials must "address the issue of who has to register where."

(i) General Principles. The Principles differentiate between entities that are domiciled in a state and those that are domiciled outside the state. (An entity is domiciled in a state if its principal place of business is in that state.)

An entity that is domiciled in a state and uses the Internet to conduct charitable solicitations in that state must, the Principles provide, register in that state. This reflects the prevailing view that the Internet is a form of communication, and the law does not make a distinction between that form of communication and another (such as use of the mails). The rule applies "without regard to whether the Internet solicitation methods it uses are passive or interactive, maintained by itself or another entity with which it contracts, or whether it conducts solicitations in any other manner."

Matters become more complex in an instance where an entity is fundraising in a state in which it is not domiciled. Registration in the state is nonetheless required if:

- The organization's non-Internet activities alone are sufficient to require registration;

- It solicits contributions through an interactive Website; and

- Either the entity—
  - Specifically targets persons physically located in the state for solicitation, or
  - Receives contributions from donors in the state on a repeated and ongoing basis or a substantial basis through its Website; or

- The entity solicits contributions through a site that is not interactive but either specifically invites further offline activity to complete a contribution, or establishes other contacts with that state, such as sending e-mail messages or other communications that promote the Website, and the entity engages in one of the foregoing (sub-bulleted) two activities.

Obviously, considerable line-drawing often will be required in the actual application of these rules. The matter becomes even more interesting when some definitions are factored in.

(ii) **Definitions.** An *interactive Website* is a site that "permits a contributor to make a contribution, or purchase a product in connection with a charitable solicitation, by electronically completing the transaction, such as by submitting credit card information or authorizing an electronic funds transfer." These sites include those through which a donor "may complete a transaction online through any online mechanism processing a financial transaction even if completion requires the use of linked or redirected sites." A Website is considered *interactive* if it has this capacity, irrespective of whether donors actually use it.

The phrase *specifically target persons physically located in the state for solicitation* means to engage in one of two practices:

- Include on the Website an express or implied reference to soliciting contributions from persons in that state; or

- Otherwise affirmatively appeal to residents of the state, such as by advertising or sending messages to persons located in the state (electronically or otherwise) when the entity knows, or reasonably should know, that the recipient is physically located in the state.

Charities operating on a "purely local basis," or within a "limited geographic area," do not target states outside their operating area if their Website makes clear in context that their fundraising focus is limited to that area, even if they receive contributions from outside that area on less than a repeated and ongoing basis or on a substantial basis.

To receive contributions from a state on a *repeated and ongoing basis* or a *substantial basis* means "receiving contributions within the entity's fiscal year, or relevant portion of a fiscal year, that are of sufficient volume to establish the regular or significant (as opposed to rare, isolated, or insubstantial) nature of these contributions."

States are encouraged to set, and communicate to the regulated entities, "numerical [sic] levels at which it [sic] will regard this criterion as satisfied." These levels should, the Principles say, define *repeated and ongoing* in terms of a number of contributions and *substantial* in terms of a total dollar amount of contributions or percentage of total contributions received by or on behalf of the charity. The meeting of one of these thresholds would give rise to a registration requirement but would not limit an enforcement action for deceptive solicitations.

(iii)   Other Principles.   Another Principle is that an entity that solicits via e-mail in a particular state is to be treated the same as one that solicits by means of telephone or direct mail, if the soliciting party knew or reasonably should have known that the recipient was a resident of or was physically located in that state.

The Principles address the circumstance as to whether a charity is required to register in a particular state when the operator of a Website, through which contributions for that charity are solicited or received, is required to register but the charity does not independently satisfy the registration criteria. If the law of the state does not universally require the registration of all charities on whose behalf contributions are solicited or received through a commercial fundraiser, commercial co-venturer, or fundraising counsel who is required to register, then the state should independently apply the criteria to each charity and only require registration by charities that independently meet the tests. If, however, the law of the state universally requires registration of all charities under these circumstances, the state should consider whether, as a matter of "prosecutorial discretion, public policy, and the prioritized use of limited resources," it would take action to enforce registration requirements as to charities that do not independently meet the criteria.

Still another Principle is that solicitations for the sale of a product or service, that include a representation that some portion of the price shall be devoted to a charitable organization or charitable purpose (*commercial co-venturing, charitable sales promotion*, or *cause-related marketing*) shall be governed by the same standards as otherwise set out in the Principles governing charitable solicitations.

(iv)   "Exclusions."   There are two exclusions from the registration requirements (although they really are not "exclusions" at all). One is that maintaining or operating a Website that does not contain a solicitation of contributions but merely provides program services by means of the Internet does not, by itself, invoke a requirement to register. This is the case even if unsolicited contributions are received.

The other "exclusion" is for entities that solely provide administrative, supportive, or technical services to charities without providing substantive content, or advice concerning substantive content; they are not required to register. These entities include Internet service providers and organizations that do no more than process online transactions for a separate firm that operates a Website or provides similar services. This exclusion does not, of course, encompass professional fundraisers, fundraising counsel, or commercial co-venturers.

(v) Responsibilities for Multi-State Filers. The Principles provide that state charity officials "recognize that the burden of compliance by charitable organizations and their agents, professional fundraisers, commercial co-venturers and/or professional fundraising counsel should be kept reasonable in relation to the benefits to the public achieved by registration." Projects to create "common forms," such as the unified registration statement, are "strongly encouraged."

State charity offices are "strongly encouraged" to publish their registration and reporting forms, their laws and regulations, and other related information on the Internet to facilitate registration and reporting by charitable organizations and their agents.

The Principles encourage development of information technology infrastructure to facilitate electronic registration and reporting. Also encouraged is Internet posting by charitable organizations of their application for recognition of exempt status, the IRS ruling, the most recent annual information returns, and their state registration statement(s). (This latter practice, of course, is also encouraged by the federal tax law, which obviates the need to provide hard copies of these federal documents to requestors when they are made available on the Internet.)

§ 4.14 CONCLUSIONS

The foregoing is a survey of the principal legal issues involved in the state regulation of the process of raising contributions for charitable purposes. There are, of course, still other issues of law that impact on charitable fundraising.

As the legislation in this field mounts and the states attempt to regulate the fundraising process in ingenious ways (and without use of percentage limitations), more challenges in the form of litigation can be anticipated. As noted at the outset, there is substantial tension between the general right of the states to legislate in this area and the free speech and other rights of charitable organizations and their fundraising professionals.[406] This tension is not abating, and thus these and other legal issues associated with the application of state charitable solicitation acts continue to ferment and fester.[407]

---

[406] See *supra* notes 1 and 2.

[407] State regulation of fundraising (using that term in a broad sense) can occur in contexts not involving charitable solicitation acts. For example, at present, some state attorneys general are developing guidelines by which to regulate *marketing partnerships* between charitable organizations and for-profit businesses. A summary of this report is at XI *Chron. of Phil.* (No. 13) 48 (April 22, 1999). These arrangements entail charity endorsements or advertising that suggest that a charity is endorsing or warranting a product or service. A hearing was held in New York at the end of May on the proposal. In general, Giorgianni, "Charities Criticize Proposals to Regulate Marketing Deals," XI *Chron. of Phil.* (No. 16) 37 (June 3, 1999).

CHAPTER FIVE

Federal Regulation of Fundraising

§ 5.1 **IRS Audit Guidelines**
(a) History
(b) Special Emphasis Program
(c) Checksheet
(d) Audit Guidance
(e) Conclusion

§ 5.2 **Fundraising Disclosure by Charitable Organizations**

§ 5.3 **Charitable Gift Substantiation Requirements**

§ 5.4 **Quid Pro Quo Contribution Rules**

§ 5.5 **Fundraising Disclosure by Noncharitable Organizations**

§ 5.6 **Intermediate Sanctions**
(a) Basic Concepts of Intermediate Sanctions
    (i) Exempt Organizations Involved
    (ii) Excess Benefit Transactions
    (iii) Revenue-Sharing Transactions
    (iv) Rebuttable Presumption of Reasonableness
    (v) Disqualified Persons
    (vi) Initial Contract Exception
    (vii) Tax Structure
    (viii) Correction
    (ix) Reporting of Excess Benefit Transactions
    (x) Scope of Sanctions
(b) Intermediate Sanctions Rules as Applied to Fundraising
    (i) Tax-Exempt Organizations Involved
    (ii) Disqualified Persons in Fundraising Context
    (iii) Excess Benefit Transactions in Fundraising Context

    (iv) Initial Contract Exception
    (v) Rebuttable Presumption of Reasonableness
    (vi) Reporting of Excess Benefit Transactions
    (vii) Tax Penalties

§ 5.7 **Unrelated Business Rules**
(a) Basic Concepts of Unrelated Income Taxation
    (i) Introduction
    (ii) Deduction Rules
    (iii) Trade or Business
    (iv) Regularly Carried On
    (v) Substantially Related
    (vi) Exceptions
    (vii) Modifications
    (viii) Partnership Rule
(b) Unrelated Income Rules as Applied to Fundraising
    (i) Fundraising as Business
    (ii) Regularly Carried-on Test
    (iii) Private Benefit
    (iv) Fundraising and Program Activities
    (v) Principal–Agent Relationships
    (vi) Royalty Exception
    (vii) Commercial Co-Ventures
    (viii) Cause-Related Marketing
    (ix) Corporate Services

§ 5.8 **Exemption Application Process**
(a) Recognition of Tax-Exempt Status
(b) Application Procedure
(c) Application
    (i) Part I
    (ii) Part II

    (iii)   Part III
    (iv)   Summary

§ 5.9   **Reporting Requirements**
    (a) Filing Categories
    (b) Income-Producing Activities
    (c) Reporting
    (d) Functional Accounting
    (e) Other Information
    (f) Other Fundraising Aspects
    (g) Related Organizations
    (h) Inspection Requirements
    (i) Disclosure Requirements
    (j) Penalties

§ 5.10 **Lobbying Restrictions**

§ 5.11 **Public Charity Classifications**

§ 5.12 **School Record-Retention Requirements**

§ 5.13 **Fundraising Compensation Arrangements**

§ 5.14 **Charitable Deduction Rules**
    (a) Meaning of Gift
    (b) Qualified Donees
    (c) Gift Properties
    (d) Percentage Limitations
    (e) Deduction Reduction Rules
    (f) Twice Basis Deductions
    (g) Partial Interest Gifts
    (h) Appraisal Requirements
    (i) Receipt, Record-Keeping, and Reporting Rules
    (j) Receipt and Record-Keeping Requirements for Small Gifts
    (k) Reporting Requirements

§ 5.15 **Commensurate Test**
    (a) Facts
    (b) Law and Analysis
        (i)   Allocations
        (ii) Commensurate Test
        (iii) Private Benefit Standard
        (iv) Substantial Nonexempt Purpose Test
    (c) Perspective

§ 5.16 **Special Events and Corporate Sponsorships**
    (a) Special Events
    (b) Donor Recognition Programs
        (i)   Introduction
        (ii) Qualified Sponsorship Payments

§ 5.17 **IRS College and University Examination Guidelines**

§ 5.18 **Postal Laws**
    (a) Introduction
    (b) Qualifying Organizations
        (i)   Religious Organizations
        (ii) Educational Organizations
        (iii) Philanthropic Organizations
        (iv) Other Categories
    (c) Application for Authorization
    (d) Eligible and Ineligible Matter
    (e) Postage Statement

§ 5.19 **Antitrust Laws**

§ 5.20 **Securities Laws**

§ 5.21 **FTC Telemarketing Rule**

§ 5.22 **Internet Communications**
    (a) Introduction
    (b) IRS Request for Comments
    (c) Internet Communications Issues
        (i)   Unrelated Business Rules in General
        (ii) Links
        (iii) Corporate Sponsorships
        (iv) Periodicals
        (v)   Auctions
        (vi) Co-Venture Programs
        (vii) Online Storefronts
        (viii) Virtual Trade Shows

§ 5.23 **Health Insurance Portability and Accountability Act Regulations**

There is not, today, a federal charitable solicitations law,[1] nor is there any immediate prospect of one. Nonetheless, the federal government aggressively regulates the process of raising funds for charitable purposes. Indeed, in a

---

[1] See Chapter 6 for a summary of efforts over the years to enact a federal charitable fundraising regulation law.

dramatic change of policy,[2] regulation of this type is a high priority at the IRS. Other components of the federal government play roles in this regard, including the Department of the Treasury, the U.S. Postal Service, and the Federal Trade Commission.

§ 5.1   IRS AUDIT GUIDELINES

The IRS is using its inherent authority, in conjunction with its task of administering the federal tax laws, to regulate in the field of fundraising for charitable purposes. In part, this is the result of mandates to the IRS, from Congress, to step up its review of charitable fundraising.[3]

The impetus for regulation in this area stemmed from a phenomenon that is sweeping and, in some instances, swamping the charitable—and other tax-exempt organizations—field: *disclosure*. At the beginning, the push was for disclosure of transfers of money or property to charity that were not contributions. Other aspects of disclosure followed. This force has yet to play itself out.

A segment of the legislative history of one of these laws,[4] contained in a report of the Committee on the Budget of the House of Representatives, accompanying what was to become the Omnibus Budget Reconciliation Act of 1987,[5] is meaningful for charitable organizations. While recognizing that this law is inapplicable to charitable organizations, the committee expressed its concern that "some charities may not make sufficient disclosure, in soliciting donations, membership dues, payments for admissions or merchandise, or other support, of the extent (if any) to which the payors may be entitled to charitable deductions for such payments."[6] The committee reviewed situations where charities may "suggest or imply" the deductibility of payments where that is not the case, contrasting them with "other charities [that] carefully and correctly advise their supporters of the long-standing tax rules governing the deductibility of payments made to a charitable organization in return for, or with expectation of, a financial or economic benefit to the payor."[7]

The House Committee on the Budget launched this aspect of the IRS regulation of charitable fundraising with its expression of its "anticipat[ion] that the Internal Revenue Service will monitor the extent to which taxpayers are

---

[2] Prior to the 1980s, the IRS was reticent about its involvement in the field of regulation of fundraising by charitable organizations. For example, in 1974, the then-Commissioner of Internal Revenue stated: "The IRS has little power to do much about the few charitable organizations which seem to be forever skating on thin ice in their fund-raising activities" (remarks by Donald Alexander, National Association of Attorneys General Committee on the Office of Attorney General, *Regulation of Charitable Trust and Solicitations Summary of the Special Meeting of the Subcommittee on Charitable Trusts and Solicitations* 60 (1974)). Since then, however, the IRS amassed considerable power in the area, some of it accorded by Congress, and now uses it with unusual exuberance. In general, Hopkins, "IRS Now Regulating Fundraising for Charity," 2 *J. Tax'n Exempt Org.* 4 (Summer 1990).

[3] This law is discussed *infra* at §§ 2–4.

[4] See *infra* § 5.

[5] H.R. Rep. No. 100-391, 100th Cong., 1st Sess. 1607–1608 (1988).

[6] *Id.* at 1607.

[7] *Id.* at 1607–1608.

being furnished accurate and sufficient information by charitable organizations as to the nondeductibility of payments to such organizations where benefits or privileges are received in return, so that such taxpayers can correctly compute their Federal income tax liability."[8] As will be seen, however, the IRS has considerably expanded this mandate beyond the bounds of "monitoring."

The IRS includes analysis of fundraising programs of charitable organizations in its examinations and other reviews of these entities. This process started in earnest in early 1990, as manifested by documentation developed by the National Office of the IRS and issued to its agents in the field, including a remarkable *checksheet*. Although this checksheet is no longer formally being used, it set the stage for the IRS's scrutiny of charitable fundraising and reflects a certain attitude or mindset toward the subject.

(a) History

Before engaging in a discussion of this checksheet and its implications, some background is appropriate. Today's fundraising regulation initiatives by the IRS can only be fully appreciated in light of this history.

The fundraising community long dreaded the inevitable day the IRS began to actively regulate the process of raising funds for charitable purposes. This new activism directly affects not only the charities that raise funds but also the fundraising professionals who assist them.

This occasion did not materialize as most observers had expected. That is, no great exposé of fundraising fraud by a particular organization was uncovered by the media; no IRS audit led the IRS to act. There was no development of new regulations on the subject at the Department of the Treasury, no enactment of a far-reaching statute by Congress.

Instead, fundraising regulation through the tax system arrived because the IRS decided to act with respect to a long-standing problem—some characterize it as an *abuse*. The problem is the casting of a payment to a charitable organization as a deductible gift when in fact the transaction does not involve a gift at all or is only partially a gift.

The IRS position or, for that matter, the law in this regard is not new: a payment to a charitable organization is not a gift where the donor receives something of approximately equal value in return. That position was made explicit in 1967, when the IRS published an extensive revenue ruling on the point.[9] At that time, and since, it has been the view of the IRS that charities have an obligation to notify their patrons when payments to them are not gifts, or are only partially gifts, particularly in the context of a special fundraising event.[10]

There were, over the years, a few instances of deliberate and blatant wrongdoing in this area. Undoubtedly, there were individuals who wrote a check, for example, to a school for something acquired at the school's annual

---

[8] *Id.* at 1608.
[9] Rev. Rul. 67-246, 1967-2 C.B. 104.
[10] As discussed *infra* §§ 2 and 3, this position is now largely memorialized in statutory law.

auction and who could not resist the temptation to report the payment as a deductible gift on their tax return. The same may be said of raffles, sweepstakes, book sales, sports tournaments, dinner and theater events, dues payments, and the like. But there was no evidence of abuse sufficient to justify a massive IRS regulatory response.[11]

Matters changed somewhat when some charities began explicitly or implicitly telling "donors" that their payments to the organizations were deductible as gifts, when in fact they were not or were only partially deductible. This practice became so overt and pervasive that the IRS decided that the time had come to act.

It needs to be said, however, that most charitable organizations that advertised gift deductibility, when this deductibility was not available, acted in good faith. They simply lacked an understanding of the rules. Most fundraising professionals did not contemplate the meaning of the word *gift* and were unaware of the 1967 pronouncement from the IRS or, if they were aware of it, did not fully understand its import.[12] (From a legal standpoint, of course, these are not adequate defenses for wrongdoing.)

The distinction between deductible and nondeductible payments to charity is not always clear. Murky questions can and do arise where the payor receives admissions or merchandise, or other benefits or privileges, in return for the payment. Indeed, in 1986, the U.S. Supreme Court wrote: "A payment of money [or transfer of property] *generally* cannot constitute a charitable contribution if the contributor expects a substantial benefit in return."[13] Essentially the same rule was articulated by the Court in 1989, when it ruled that an exchange having an "inherently reciprocal nature" is not a gift and thus cannot be a charitable gift, where the recipient is a charity.[14]

The seriousness of the IRS's intensity on this subject was revealed at the final meeting of the IRS Exempt Organization Advisory Group, on January 10, 1989. Then-Commissioner Lawrence B. Gibbs opened the session with the charge that charities and their fundraisers are engaged in "questionable" and "egregious" fundraising practices, notably suggestions that certain payments are deductible gifts when in fact they are not. Then-Assistant Commissioner for Employee Plans and Exempt Organizations Robert I. Brauer made clear the IRS view that these abuses are not isolated but are "widespread practices that involve quite legitimate charities." Gibbs stated that charities must "clean up their act in this regard" or face stiff regulation from the IRS.[15]

---

[11] It is impossible to know how widespread this practice was and, for that matter, is. The most pleasant and optimistic view of all of this is that this treatment of payments as gifts was done in ignorance and out of naivete. An example of the problem, however, is provided *infra* note 61. Irrespective of the scope of these misdeeds, it is remarkable that it spawned the rules discussed *infra* §§ 3, 4.

[12] The law as to what is a *gift* in this setting is summarized in Hopkins, *The Tax Law of Charitable Giving, Second Ed.* (New York: John Wiley & Sons, Inc., 2000) ("*Tax Law of Charitable Giving*"), § 3.1.

[13] *United States* v. *American Bar Endowment*, 477 U.S. 105, 116–117 (1986) (emphasis added).

[14] *Hernandez* v. *Commissioner*, 490 U.S. 680, 692 (1989).

[15] See VI *Nonprofit Couns.* (No. 2) 7 (1989).

(b) Special Emphasis Program

The IRS launched its attack on these forms of fundraising misperformance by inaugurating a Special Emphasis Program. This program came to have two parts: an educational phase and an audit phase.[16]

The first phase of the Special Emphasis Program took place throughout 1989: the IRS engaged in educational efforts to explain the rules to charities. This aspect of the program consisted of speeches by representatives of the IRS, workshops with charitable groups, and the encouragement of educational efforts by national charitable organizations. (Certain aspects of this educational phase are continuing.)

During this phase, the IRS began reviewing charities' annual information returns (principally, Form 990) for 1988.[17] Special emphasis was placed on the returns filed by organizations that were engaged in gift solicitation. Charitable organizations that were not in compliance with the disclosure rules received letters from the IRS requesting immediate conformance with the requirements. There was also talk of more audits of charities and donors, review of donor lists, and the imposition of various tax penalties.

The regulation by the IRS of fundraising for charity became much more serious when the second phase of the Special Emphasis Program was initiated, in early 1990. This aspect of the IRS's involvement and scrutiny was evidenced in the aforementioned extraordinary checksheet sent by the IRS National Office to its agents in the field, to enable them to review the fundraising practices of charitable organizations.

(c) Checksheet

The checksheet, bearing the title "Exempt Organizations Charitable Solicitations Compliance Improvement Program Study Checksheet," reflected the beginning of the second phase of the IRS's Special Emphasis Program concerning solicitation practices of charitable organizations.[18] As noted, the first phase consisted of programs designed to educate charities and their fundraising professionals about the law governing the extent of deductibility of contributions.

This checksheet required the auditing agent to review, in conjunction with examinations of annual information returns, the fundraising practices of charities, including the solicitation of gifts where the donor is provided a benefit, the use of special events, the conduct of bingo and other games of chance, travel tours, thrift stores, and the receipt of noncash contributions. A special section inquired about the use of professional fundraisers. The checksheet consisted of 82 questions, plus requests for financial information.

Regarding the use of fundraising professionals, the checksheet required the agent to obtain the name and address of the fundraiser, details about direct

---

[16] "IRS' Hard Look At 'Special Event' Fundraising," XXI *Phil. Monthly,* (No. 9) 5 (1988).
[17] See *infra* § 8.
[18] In general, "IRS Is Going to 'Evaluate the Overall State of Fund Raising'," XXIII *Phil. Monthly* (No. 1) 10 (1990).

mail fundraising (including the cost of the mailings, the number of donor responses, and the amount of gifts generated from the mailings), a copy of any written agreement between the fundraiser and the charity, the nature of the fundraiser's compensation (flat fee or commission), and information about whether the fundraiser had check-writing or check-cashing authority.

One question asked the agent to determine whether the charity met the *commensurate test*. This test, established by the IRS in 1964,[19] basically looks to see whether a charitable organization is carrying on charitable works commensurate in scope with its financial resources. In the particular facts underlying the ruling, the charity derived most of its income as rent, yet preserved its tax exemption because it satisfied the commensurate test. Until 1990, the commensurate test was not applied in the fundraising context; in applying the test in this setting, the examining agent is supposed to ascertain whether the charitable organization involved is engaging in sufficient charitable activity in relation to its available resources (including gifts received through fundraising efforts), as compared to the time and expense of fundraising.[20]

Other questions were asked about the use of fundraising professionals. One of them was: "Was the charity created by an owner, officer, director, trustee, or employee of the professional fundraiser?" Another was: "Is any officer, director, trustee, or employee of the charity employed by or connected with the professional fundraiser in any ownership of business, investment venture, or family relationship?"

The checksheet focused on the nature of benefits, goods, or services provided to donors. These items included retail merchandise, new and donated merchandise received at an auction, tickets for a game of chance, tuition at an educational institution, travel, tickets to an athletic or other event, discounts, free subscriptions, and preferential seating at a college or university athletic event. The document asked whether the charity made any reference to deductibility of the payment in its solicitation or promotional literature or in any thank-you letter, receipt ticket, or other written receipt.

As to gifts of property, a list of all noncash gifts whose fair market value exceeds $500 during the year under examination must be provided to the IRS. The IRS asked who valued the gift property, whether a proper receipt was provided, whether there was an agreement between the donor and donee as to disposition of the property, and whether the requisite forms were properly completed and filed.[21]

The questions concerning travel tours spotlighted IRS concerns in this area. Questions included: "Did the promotional travel literature and/or other written documentation indicate that the tours were educational? Did the promotional travel literature and/or other written documentation contain discussions of any social or recreational aspects of the tour? Did the charity have a

---

[19] Rev. Rul. 64-182, 1964-1 C.B. (Pt. 1) 186.
[20] See *infra* § 15.
[21] See *infra* § 14.

contract or do business with a for-profit travel agency? If yes, did the charity receive any fee from the travel agency?"[22]

The inquiry into the conduct of bingo and other games of chance illustrated the degree of complexity this field of law can stimulate. The first question concerned whether the bingo activity satisfies the tests by which it can be exempted from the definition of unrelated business.[23] If not, the agent was expected to determine whether an income tax return[24] was filed and, if not, to secure the delinquent return. A set of questions pertained to the conduct of games of chance. Another question asked whether the game of chance or income from it was embraced by one of the statutory exceptions (such as a business substantially conducted by volunteers). The checksheet required the agent to find out whether the charity timely filed the proper information returns[25] and withholding returns[26] for the winners of the games. Finally, the IRS wanted to know whether the charity hired outside contractors to specifically operate bingo and other games of chance.

The agent was requested to report on any penalties he or she assessed against the charity. These included failure to file a tax return,[27] failure to pay a tax,[28] failure to file a complete or accurate exempt organization information return,[29] substantial understatement of liability,[30] promotion of abusive tax shelters,[31] aiding and abetting understatements of tax liability,[32] failure to file certain information returns,[33] failure to file certain payee statements,[34] and failure to include correct information on an information return or payee statement.[35]

(d) Audit Guidance

In directions sent to the field in February 1990, concerning the phase II examinations, the IRS headquarters wrote that "it is essential that the examinations be thorough." It continued: "The EO [Exempt Organizations] examiner must pursue the examination to a point where he/she can conclude that all areas and data concerning fundraising activities have been considered."[36]

---

[22]This matter of charitable organizations conducting travel tours became such a major issue that it evolved into a regulation project, with final regulations issued (T.D. 8874) in 2000 (Reg. § 1.513-7).

[23] IRC § 513(f). See *infra* § 7(a)(vi).

[24] Form 990-T.

[25] Form 1099-MISC.

[26] Form W2-G.

[27] IRC § 6651(a)(1).

[28] IRC § 6651(a)(2).

[29] IRC § 6652(c)(1)(A)(ii).

[30] IRC § 6661.

[31] IRC § 6700.

[32] IRC § 6701.

[33] IRC § 6721.

[34] IRC § 6722.

[35] IRC § 6723.

[36] Internal Revenue Manual Transmittal 7(10)00–164 (Feb. 23, 1990), transmitting Manual Supplement 7(10) G-59, § 11.02.

This guidance stated that the second phase of the program will "focus on all aspects of fundraising and charitable solicitations."[37] Some of the practices the IRS was looking for were the following:

- Misleading statements in solicitations literature that "imply deductibility of contributions, where none probably exists."

- Contracts with professional fundraisers, where they use "questionable" fundraising methods to solicit contributions from the general public.

- Solicitations that mislead donors into thinking that their donations will be used for charitable purposes, when in fact the donations may be used for noncharitable purposes (such as administrative and fundraising costs that constitute a significant portion of the solicited funds or property).

- Fundraising activities that result in other tax consequences (such as the generation of taxable income).

These directions continued: "The scope and depth of the examination should be sufficient to fully disclose the nature of abusive situations involving fundraising activities that mislead donors to claim the incorrect charitable contribution deduction; misrepresent the use of the solicited funds; engage in questionable fundraising practices or techniques, etc."[38] There was such an insistence on thoroughness because the results of this study were "to be used in a report that will be submitted to Congress."[39] As far as can be ascertained, however, a formal report on this subject was never prepared by the IRS.

Thus, what started out in 1967 as concern with overdeductibility in the setting of payments to charities evolved and blossomed into an examination by the IRS of all "questionable fundraising practices or techniques."

(e) Conclusion

The launching of this Special Emphasis Program, particularly the preparation and dissemination of the checksheet, was one of several significant developments, illustrating the fact that the federal government, particularly the IRS, is monitoring and regulating the charitable fundraising process. This checksheet represents an extraordinary use of the IRS's resources to investigate charitable fundraising. One particularly striking aspect of this matter is that some of the information requested, particularly that pertaining to the use of professional fundraisers, had little or no correlation with any requirements of law—at least at that time.

In a sense, the Special Emphasis Program did not work. That is, it was unsuccessful to the extent it was intended to preclude the enactment of statutory law on the subject.

[37] *Id.* § 11.09.
[38] *Id.* § 11.03.
[39] *Id.* § 11.02.

The Special Emphasis Program is part of a larger message: The federal government is now firmly entrenched in the regulation of charitable fundraising. This regulation is an important component of government oversight and intervention in the philanthropic process.[40]

§ 5.2 FUNDRAISING DISCLOSURE BY CHARITABLE ORGANIZATIONS

It has long been the position of the IRS that a payment to a charitable organization, where the payor receives something of equivalent value in return, is not a *gift* for charitable deduction purposes. The long-standing position of the IRS in this regard has also been that a payment to a charity, where the payor receives value in return, is deductible as a charitable gift only to the extent that the amount transferred exceeds the value received by the donor. Further, it has long been the position of the IRS that it is the responsibility of charitable organizations to inform their patrons of this distinction between deductible and nondeductible payments.[41] The latter includes dues, payments for admissions or merchandise, and other material benefits and privileges received in return for the payment.

These rules have, on occasion, been honored in their breach. As a consequence, in mid-1988, the Commissioner of Internal Revenue sent this message to the nation's charities: "I . . . ask your help in more accurately informing taxpayers as to the deductibility of payments by patrons of your fundraising events."[42] This message from the IRS announced the aforementioned Special Emphasis Program, whereby the IRS was seeking to "ascertain the extent to which taxpayers are furnished accurate and sufficient information concerning the deductibility of their contributions."[43]

The Commissioner's message focused on fundraising events, where part or all of a payment to a charitable organization is attributable to the purchase of admission or some other privilege. In this context, the law presumes that the total amount paid is equivalent to the benefits received in return. That presumption can be rebutted in appropriate instances, where there is a true gift element in the payment.

This matter has several manifestations. One is the fundraising event, where something of value is provided to the patron, such as a dinner or entertainment. The charity is expected to determine the fair market value of the

---

[40]The IRS's Fiscal Year 2002 Exempt Organizations Implementing Guidelines, issued in October 2001, reflect and continue the agency's emphasis on regulation of charitable fundraising. One of the unique aspects of these Guidelines is the IRS's view of the tax-exempt sector as a cluster of *market segments* (preliminarily, 35 of them), to be studied and then perhaps audited. Six market segment studies are underway (with respect to social clubs, labor organizations, membership associations, community foundations, social service organizations, and religious organizations), all of which involve fundraising issues. Also launched is an initiative to examine certain donor-advised funds.

[41] Rev. Rul. 67-246, *supra* note 9.

[42] IRS Publication 1391.

[43] *Id.*

event and to notify the patron that only the amount of the payment that is in excess of that value (if any) is deductible as a charitable gift. For example, a fundraising event may center around a dinner; the ticket is $70 and the dinner is worth $50. In compliance with the IRS position, the patron should be told that only $20 of the $70 is deductible as a charitable gift. (The portion of the total amount paid that reflects the purchase of the dinner may, in certain circumstances, be deductible as an ordinary and necessary business expense.[44])

In determining fair value, a charity must look to comparable circumstances. The cost of the event to the charity is largely irrelevant.[45] Thus, a charity may have a dinner provided to it without cost (such as a donation from a caterer), yet the dinner still has a value to the recipient.

Another manifestation of this problem occurs when a donor makes a contribution and receives something of value in return. A payment of $20 that results in a T-shirt or tote bag worth $10 is a gift of $10, not $20. This distinction is sometimes difficult to ascertain; often, it is relative. Is the donor of $1 million supposed to reduce the gift deduction by $10 because he or she is sent a T-shirt? The answer is no, yet it is hard to draw the line in this regard between a $20 donor and a $1 million donor. This is the dilemma, for example, with respect to college and university athletic scholarship programs[46] and the distribution of greeting cards by veterans' organizations.[47]

A third aspect is a payment to a charitable organization that is not deductible at all. Obvious examples include payments of tuition to tax-exempt schools and payments for health care services to tax-exempt hospitals. Other payments of this nature are dues, subscriptions, purchases made at auctions,[48] and purchases of raffle and sweepstakes tickets.

Thus, the IRS expects charities, before solicitation, to determine the nondeductible portion of a payment and to clearly state the separate amounts on a ticket or other evidence of payment furnished to the contributor.

The IRS privately ruled that there are no sanctions for violation of these disclosure rules.[49] There has been discussion, however, of application of the aiding and abetting, and other penalties,[50] and of potential litigation in this area. There has also been discussion of the use of the unrelated income rules in this setting,[51] as well as of theories by which an organization's tax exemption could be revoked for failure to comport with these rules.

---

[44] IRC § 162.

[45] Cost is a factor when making the calculation as to what is a *token item* (see *infra* text accompanied by note 56).

[46] Where, however, an individual makes a payment to or for the benefit of a college or university, and that payment would be deductible as a charitable contribution but for the fact that the individual receives the right to purchase seating at an athletic event in the institution's athletic stadium, 80 percent of the payment is treated as a charitable contribution (IRS § 170(l)).

[47] E.g., *Veterans of Foreign Wars, Department of Michigan* v. *Commissioner*, 89 T.C. 7 (1987); *Veterans of Foreign Wars of the United States, Department of Missouri, Inc.* v. *United States*, 85-2 U.S.T.C. ¶ 9605 (W.D. Mo. 1984).

[48] See § 7.11.

[49] IRS Priv. Ltr. Rul. 8832003.

[50] See *supra* notes 27–35.

[51] See *infra* § 7.

The IRS also is reviewing tax returns, looking for situations where a charitable deduction is being claimed, when in fact only a portion or perhaps none of the payment is properly deductible as a gift.

In 1990, the IRS issued guidelines to enable charitable organizations to properly advise their patrons as to the deductibility, if any, of payments made to them where the patrons are receiving something in return for their payments.[52] These guidelines were issued as part of a program at the IRS to require charitable organizations to disclose to donors and other payors the extent to which the payments are deductible, where a benefit or service is provided by the payor. These guidelines are also being used by reviewing IRS agents.

One of the many problems facing charitable organizations because of the disclosure requirement is what to do about small items or other benefits that are of token value in relation to the amount contributed. These guidelines contain rules whereby a benefit can be regarded as inconsequential or insubstantial, so that the full amount of a payment to a charity becomes deductible as a charitable gift.

Under these guidelines, benefits received in connection with a payment to a charitable organization will be considered to have insubstantial fair market value (so that the payment is fully deductible as a gift) for purposes of advising donors, where two requirements are met:

1. The payment occurs in the context of a fundraising campaign in which the charity informs patrons as to how much of their payment is a deductible contribution, and

2. Either—

   a. The fair market value of all of the benefits received in connection with the payment is not more than the lesser of 2 percent of the payment or $50 (adjusted for inflation[53]), or

   b. The payment is $25 (adjusted for inflation[54]) or more, and the only benefits received in connection with the payment are token items bearing the organization's name or logo.

For these purposes, *token items* include items such as bookmarks, calendars, key chains, mugs, posters, and T-shirts. Also, the costs of all of the benefits received by a donor must, in the aggregate, be within the statutory limits established for a *low-cost article*; this is an article with a cost not in excess of $5 (indexed for inflation[55]), that is distributed incidental to a charitable solicitation.[56]

With respect to the first of these two requirements, where a charitable organization is providing only insubstantial benefits in return for a payment,

---

[52] Rev. Proc. 90-12, 1990-1 C.B. 471, as amplified by Rev. Proc. 92-49, 1992-1 C.B. 987, and modified by Rev. Proc. 92-102, 1992-2 C.B. 579.
[53] See Appendix D.
[54] See Appendix E.
[55] See Appendix F.
[56] IRC § 513(h)(2).

disclosure of the fair market value of the benefits is not required. Fundraising materials should, however, include a statement to this effect:

> Under Internal Revenue Service guidelines, the estimated value of [the benefits received] is not substantial; therefore, the full amount of your payment is a deductible contribution.

In a situation where it is impractical to state in every solicitation how much of a payment is deductible, the charitable organization can, under these guidelines, seek a ruling from the IRS concerning an alternative procedure. This circumstance can arise, for example, in connection with the offering of a number of premiums in an on-air fundraising announcement by an educational organization.

Resolving what was a difficult problem for many organizations, these guidelines state that newsletters or program guides (other than commercial quality publications) are treated as not having measurable value or cost if their primary purpose is to inform members about the activities of an organization and if they are not available to nonmembers by paid subscription or through newsstand sales.

The charitable community was unable to achieve a level of compliance with these IRS disclosure guidelines that was satisfactory to Congress. Consequently, efforts commenced to write statutory law on the subject, which came to be known as *substantiation requirements*[57] and *quid pro quo contribution rules*.[58] Legislation to this end was nearly enacted as part of the Revenue Act of 1992 and was enacted as part of the Omnibus Budget Reconciliation Act of 1993.

The legislative history of the 1992 proposal contained the following, which is indicative of the attitude of Congress as to the need for these rules:

> Difficult problems of tax administration arise with respect to fundraising techniques in which an organization that is eligible to receive deductible contributions provides goods or services in consideration for payments from donors. Organizations that engage in such fundraising practices often do not inform their donors that all or a portion of the amount paid by the donor may not be deductible as a charitable contribution. Consequently, the [Senate Finance] [C]ommittee believes . . . it appropriate that, in all cases where a charity receives a *quid pro quo* contribution (i.e., a payment made partly as a contribution and partly in consideration for goods or services furnished to the payor by the donee organization) the charity should inform the donor that the [federal income tax charitable contribution] deduction . . . is limited to the amount by which the payment exceeds the value of the goods or services furnished, and provide a good-faith estimate of the value of such goods or services.[59]

---

[57] See *infra* § 3.

[58] See *infra* § 4.

[59] "Technical Explanation of the Finance Committee Amendment" (Technical Explanation), at 586. The Technical Explanation was not formally printed; it was, however, reproduced in the Congressional Record (138 Cong. Rec. (No. 112) S11246 (Aug. 3, 1992)).

§ 5.3 CHARITABLE GIFT SUBSTANTIATION REQUIREMENTS

In 1993, a significant dimension was added to the federal law of charitable fundraising regulation when Congress enacted charitable gift substantiation requirements. These rules, applicable to both individual and corporate donors, took effect on January 1, 1994.[60]

Under these rules, donors who make a separate charitable contribution of $250 or more in a year, for which they claim a charitable contribution deduction, must obtain written substantiation from the donee charitable organization.

More specifically, the charitable deduction is not allowed for a *separate contribution* of $250 or more unless the donor has written substantiation from the charitable donee of the contribution in the form of a *contemporaneous written acknowledgment*.[61] Thus, for contributions made in 1994 and thereafter, donors cannot rely solely on a cancelled check as substantiation for a gift of $250 or more. (A cancelled check will suffice as substantiation for gifts of less than $250.[62])

An acknowledgment meets this requirement if it includes the following information: (1) the amount of money and a description (but not value) of any property other than money that was contributed; (2) whether the donee organization provided any goods or services in consideration, in whole or in part, for any money or property contributed; and (3) a description and good-faith estimate of the value of any goods or services involved or, if the goods or services consist solely of intangible religious benefits, a statement to that effect.[63]

The phrase *intangible religious benefit* means "any intangible religious benefit which is provided by an organization organized exclusively for religious purposes and which generally is not sold in a commercial transaction outside the donative context."[64] An *acknowledgment* is considered to be *contemporaneous* if the contributor obtains the acknowledgment on or before the earlier of (1) the date on which the donor filed a tax return for the taxable year in which the contribution was made or (2) the due date (including extensions) for filing the return.[65] Even when no good or service is provided to a donor, a statement to that effect must appear in the acknowledgment.

As noted, this substantiation rule applies with respect to *separate payments*. Separate payments generally are treated as separate contributions and

---

[60] This substantiation procedure is in addition to the rules that require the provision of certain information if the amount of the claimed charitable deduction for all noncash contributions is in excess of $500.

[61] IRC § 170(f)(8)(A). Also Reg. § 1.170A-13(f)(1). The following is an excellent example of the type of practice Congress hoped will be eradicated by these substantiation rules: A taxpayer had "canceled checks showing $500 to $1,000 weekly payments to his church. During an audit, an IRS agent checked with the minister to verify that the money had actually been given to the church. Indeed it had, but the minister added a critical piece of information: The taxpayer was a coin collector who bought the change that worshippers dropped in the collection plate each week" (48 *Kiplinger's Personal Finance Magazine* (No. 5) 140 (May 1994)).

[62] See *supra* § 2.

[63] IRC § 170(f)(8)(B); Reg. § 1.170A-13(f)(2).

[64] IRC § 170(f)(8)(B), last sentence. Various forms of intangible religious benefits were enumerated in the dissenting opinion of Justice Sandra Day O'Connor in *Hernandez v. United States*, 490 U.S. 680, 707-711 (1989).

[65] IRC § 170(f)(8)(C); Reg. § 1.170A-13(f)(3).

are not aggregated for the purpose of applying the $250 threshold. Where contributions are paid by withholding from wages, the deduction from each paycheck is treated as a separate payment.[66]

The written acknowledgment of a separate gift is not required to take any particular form. Thus, acknowledgments may be made by letter, postcard, or computer-generated form. A donee charitable organization may prepare a separate acknowledgment for each contribution or may provide donors with periodic (such as annual) acknowledgments that set forth the required information for each contribution of $250 or more made by the donor during the period.[67]

For the substantiation to be contemporaneous, it must be obtained no later than the date the donor filed a tax return for the year in which the contribution was made. If the return is filed after the due date or extended due date, the substantiation must have been obtained by the due date or extended due date.

It is the responsibility of a donor to obtain the substantiation and maintain it in his or her records. (Again, the charitable contribution deduction depends on compliance with these rules.)

The substantiation rules do not impose on charitable organizations any requirement as to the reporting of gift information to the IRS. Charitable organizations potentially have the option to avoid these rules by filing an information return with the IRS, reporting information sufficient to substantiate the amount of the deductible contribution.[68]

This substantiation procedure is in addition to:

- The rules that require the provision of certain information if the amount of the claimed charitable deduction for all noncash contributions exceeds $500,[69] and

- The rules that apply to noncash gifts exceeding $5,000 per item or group of similar items (other than certain publicly traded securities), where the services of a qualified appraiser are required and the charitable donee must acknowledge receipt of the gift and provide certain other information.[70]

Tax regulations pertain to contributions made by means of withholding from individuals' wages and payment by individuals' employers to donee charitable

---

[66] H. Rep. 103-213, 103d Cong., 1st Sess. 565, note 29 (1993). In the case of credit card rebate plans (the details of which are the subject of § 3.1(h)), in an instance of a lump-sum payment of $250 or more by the sponsoring company to a charitable organization, the cardholder must obtain the requisite substantiation of the gift from the charity for the gift to be deductible (Priv. Ltr. Rul. 9623035). The company thus must supply donee organizations with the amounts of cardholders' contributions, as well as the names and addresses of the cardholders, to enable the charities to provide the required contemporaneous written acknowledgment.

[67] Id. at 565, note 32. A charitable organization that knowingly provides a false written substantiation to a donor may be subject to the penalty for aiding and abetting an understatement of tax liability (IRC § 6701).

[68] IRC § 170(f)(8)(D). This approach has not, however, been implemented by regulations and currently is not available. Earlier versions of this requirement would have caused donee charitable organizations to file information returns with the IRS reflecting contributions made to them.

[69] Reg. § 1.170A-13(b)(3). See § 14(j).

[70] Reg. § 1.170A-13(c). See § 14(h).

organizations. (The problems in this setting include the fact that the donee charity often does not know the identities of the donors/employees nor the amounts contributed by each.) These regulations state that gifts of this nature may be substantiated by both:

- A pay receipt or other document (such as Form W-2) furnished by the donor's employer that sets forth the amount withheld by the employer for the purpose of payment to a donee charity, and

- A pledge card or other document prepared by or at the direction of the donee organization that includes a statement to the effect that the organization does not provide goods or services in whole or partial consideration for any contributions made to the organization by payroll deduction.[71]

For purposes of the $250 threshold in relation to contributions made by payroll deduction, the amount withheld from each payment is treated as a separate contribution.[72] Thus, the substantiation requirement does not apply to contributions made by means of payroll deduction unless the employer deducts $250 or more from a single paycheck for the purposes of making a charitable gift. The preamble to these regulations contains a discussion of this question: Can a Form W-2 that reflects the total amount contributed by payroll deduction, but does not separately list each contribution of $250 or more, be used as evidence of the amount withheld from the employee's wages to be paid to the donee charitable organization? The IRS noted that the statute provides that an acknowledgment must reflect the amount of cash and a description of property other than cash contributed to a charitable organization. When a person makes multiple contributions to a charitable organization, the law does not require the acknowledgment to list each contribution separately. Consequently, an acknowledgment may substantiate multiple contributions with a statement of the total amount contributed by a person during the year, rather than an itemized list of separate contributions. Therefore, said the IRS, a Form W-2 reflecting an employee's total annual contribution, without separately listing the amount of each contribution, can be used as evidence of the amount withheld from the employee's wages. (The IRS determined that the regulations need not address this point.)

A charitable organization, or a Principal Combined Fund Organization for purposes of the Combined Federal Campaign and acting in that capacity, that receives a payment made as a contribution is treated as a donee organization for purposes of the substantiation requirements, even if the organization (pursuant to the donor's instructions or otherwise) distributes the amount received to one or more charitable organizations.[73]

This preamble also contains a discussion of a problem, the answer to which from the IRS was: Stop engaging in the practice. This concerns the making of lump-sum contributions by employees through their employers other than by payroll deduction. Employees may make contributions in the form of

[71] Reg. § 1.170A-13(f)(11)(i).
[72] Reg. § 1.170A-13(f)(11)(ii).
[73] Reg. § 1.170A-13(f)(12).

checks payable to their employer, who then deposits the checks in an employer account and sends the donee charity a single check drawn on the employer account. When employees' payments are transferred to a donee organization in this manner, it is difficult for the charitable organization to identify the persons who made the contributions, and thus the employees may be unable to obtain the requisite substantiation. These difficulties, the IRS advised, can be eliminated if the employees' contribution checks are made payable to the donee organization and the employer forwards the employees' checks to the charitable organization. (In the context of political fundraising, this is known as "bundling.") The donee organization then is in a position to provide the necessary substantiation as it otherwise would. (The regulations remain silent on the subject.) This rule is inapplicable, however, in a case where the distributee organization provides goods or services as part of a transaction "structured with a view to avoid taking the goods or services into account in determining the amount of the [charitable] deduction."[74]

The regulations define a *good-faith* estimate as meaning the donee charitable organization's estimate of the fair market value of any goods or services, "without regard to the manner in which the organization in fact made that estimate."[75]

These regulations also define the phrase *in consideration for.* A charitable organization is considered as providing goods or services in consideration for a person's payment if, at the time the person makes the payment, the person receives or expects to receive goods or services in exchange for the payment.[76] Goods or services a donee charity provides in consideration for a payment by a person would include goods or services provided in a year other than the year in which the payment is made.[77]

---

[74] *Id.* During the course of hearings on July 11–12, 1995, the House Ways and Means Committee considered a proposal to repeal this charitable gift substantiation rule (see II *Fund-Raising Regulation Report* (No. 5) 2 (Sept./Oct. 1995). Subsequently, the Department of the Treasury expressed its opposition to the proposal on two grounds: (1) these rules are intended to "stop known abuse" of the charitable deduction by those who seek to deduct payments to charity that are actually not contributions; and (2) the requirements provide the IRS with an "effective mechanism" for verifying that a payment to a charitable organization "genuinely" represents a charitable contribution (see II *Fund-Raising Regulation Report* (No. 6) 9 (Nov./Dec. 1995).

[75] Reg. § 1.170A-13(f)(7). The phrase *goods or services* means money, property, services, benefits, and privileges (Reg. § 1.170A-13(f)(5)).

[76] Reg. § 1.170A-13(f)(6).

[77] This rule relates to a subject that torments the fundraising professional: What to do about the situation in which a charitable organization decides, months after contributions have been made, to honor a class of donors by providing them a tangible benefit, such as a thank-you dinner? The event or other benefit may be provided in a subsequent year. Does the fair market value of this benefit have to be subtracted from the amount of the gift for deduction purposes? The answer generally is no. This is affirmed by these regulations, which require that the goods or services be provided "at the time" the payment is made, when the donor receives or expects to receive a benefit. In this instance, the donors did not receive or expect to receive a dinner or anything else at the time of their gifts. But suppose a charitable organization develops a regular pattern of providing these after-the-fact benefits. At what point do expectations arise? This is probably not something the regulations can further address; it may have to be left to a facts-and-circumstances analysis. The regulations observe, however, that the benefit can arise in a year other than (usually, subsequent to) the year of the gift.

Certain goods or services may be disregarded when applying these substantiation rules:

- Those that have an insubstantial value, in that the fair market value of all the benefits received is not more than 2 percent of the contribution or $50 (indexed for inflation), whichever is less.[78]

- Those that have an insubstantial value, in that the contribution is $25 or more (indexed for inflation) and the only benefits received by the donor in return have an aggregate cost of not more than a low-cost article, which generally is one with a cost not in excess of $5 (indexed for inflation).[79]

- Annual membership benefits offered to an individual for a payment of no more than $75 per year that consist of rights or privileges that the individual can exercise frequently during the membership period.[80] This exception is not available with respect to payments made in exchange for the opportunity for preferred seating at athletic events of educational institutions, for which there are special rules.[81] Examples of these rights and privileges include free or discounted admission to the organization's facilities or events, free or discounted parking, preferred access to goods or services, and discounts on the purchase of goods or services.

- Annual membership benefits offered to an individual for a payment of no more than $75 per year that consist of admission to events during the membership period that are open only to members of the donee organization.[82] For this rule to apply, the organization must reasonably project that the cost per person (excluding any allocable overhead) for each event is within the limits established for low-cost articles.[83] The projected cost to the donee organization is determined at the time the organization first offers its membership package for the year.

- Goods or services provided by a charitable organization to an entity's employees in return for a payment to the organization, to the extent the goods or services provided to each employee are the same as those covered by the previous two exceptions.[84] When one or more of these goods or services are provided to the donor, the contemporaneous

---

[78] Reg. § 1.170A-13(f)(8)(i)(A). See Appendix D.

[79] IRC § 513(h)(2); Reg. § 1.170A-13(f)(8)(i)(A). See Appendixes E and F.

[80] Reg. § 1.170A-13(f)(8)(i)(B)(1).

[81] IRC § 170(l); Reg. § 1.170A-13(f)(14).

[82] Reg. § 1.170A-13(f)(8)(i)(B)(2).

[83] IRC § 513(h)(2).

[84] Reg. § 1.170A-13(f)(9)(i). An acknowledgment in a program at a charity-sponsored event identifying a person as a donor to the charity also is an inconsequential benefit with no significant value; "[s]uch privileges as being associated with or being known as a benefactor of the [charitable] organization are not significant return benefits that have monetary value" (Rev. Rul. 68-432, 1968-2 C.B. 104).

written acknowledgment may indicate that no goods or services were provided in exchange for the donor's payment.

These regulations illustrate the rules pertaining to membership benefits, rights, and privileges. An example is offered concerning a charitable organization operating a performing arts center.[85] In return for a payment of $75, the center offers a package of basic membership benefits, which includes the right to purchase tickets to performances one week before they go on sale to the general public; free parking in its garage during evening and weekend performances; and a 10 percent discount on merchandise sold in its gift shop. In exchange for a $150 payment, the center offers a package of preferred membership benefits, which includes all of the benefits in the $75 package as well as a poster that is sold in the center's gift shop for $20. The basic membership and the preferred membership are each valid for 12 months and there are approximately 50 performances of various productions at the center during a 12-month period. The gift shop is open for several hours each week and at performance times. An individual is solicited by the center to make a contribution, being offered the preferred membership option. This individual makes a payment of $300. This individual can satisfy the substantiation requirement by obtaining a contemporaneous written acknowledgment from the center that includes a description of the poster and a good-faith estimate of its fair market value ($20), and disregards the remaining membership benefits.

There is another example.[86] A charitable organization operating a community theater organization performs four plays every summer; each is performed twice. In return for a membership fee of $60, the organization offers its members free admission to any of its performances. Nonmembers may purchase tickets on a performance-by-performance basis for $15 a ticket. An individual, being solicited by the organization to make a contribution, is advised that the membership benefit will be provided for a payment of $60 or more. This individual chooses to make a payment of $350 to the organization and receives in exchange the membership benefit. This membership benefit does not qualify for the exclusion because it is not a privilege that can be exercised frequently (due to the limited number of performances offered). Therefore, to meet the substantiation requirements, a contemporaneous written acknowledgment of the $350 payment would have to include a description of the free admission benefit and a good-faith estimate of its value. (The example does not continue to state that that value is $60 and the charitable deduction thus is $290.)

If a person makes a contribution of $250 or more to a charitable organization and, in return, the charity offers the person's employees goods or services (other than those that may be disregarded), the contemporaneous written acknowledgment of the person's contribution does not have to include a good-faith estimate of the value of the goods or services, but must include a description of those goods or services.[87]

---

[85] Reg. § 1.170A-13(f)(8)(ii), Example 1.
[86] *Id.*, Example 3.
[87] Reg. § 1.170A-13(f)(9)(ii).

An individual who incurred unreimbursed expenditures incident to the rendition of services is treated as having obtained a contemporaneous written acknowledgment of the expenditures if the individual:

- Has adequate records to substantiate the amount of the expenditures, and

- Timely obtains a statement prepared by the donee charity containing (1) a description of the services provided, (2) a statement as to whether the donee provides any goods or services in consideration, in whole or in part, for the unreimbursed expenditures, and (3) the information summarized in the third and fourth of these items that must be reflected in the written acknowledgment.[88]

The substantiation rules do not apply to a transfer of property to a charitable remainder trust or a charitable lead trust.[89] They do, however, apply with respect to transfers by means of pooled income funds. The reason for this distinction is grounded in the fact that the grantor of a remainder trust or lead trust is not required to designate a specific organization as the charitable beneficiary at the time property is transferred to the trust, so in these instances there is no designated charity available to provide a contemporaneous written acknowledgment to a donor. Also, even when a specific beneficiary is designated, the identification of the charity can be revocable. By contrast, a pooled income fund must be created and maintained by the charitable organization to which the remainder interests are contributed.

If a partnership or S corporation makes a charitable contribution of $250 or more, the partnership or corporation is treated as the taxpayer for gift substantiation purposes.[90] Therefore, the partnership or corporation must substantiate the contribution with a contemporaneous written acknowledgment from the donee charity before reporting the contribution on its income tax return for the appropriate year, and must maintain the contemporaneous written acknowledgment in its records. A partner of a partnership or a shareholder of an S corporation is not required to obtain any additional substantiation for his or her share of the partnership's or S corporation's charitable contribution.

If a person's payment to a charitable organization is matched, in whole or in part, by another payor, and the person receives goods or services in consideration for the payment and some or all of the matched payment, the goods or services are treated as provided in consideration for the person's payment and not in consideration for the matching payment.[91]

---

[88] Reg. § 1.170A-13(f)(10).

[89] Reg. § 1.170A-13(f)(13).

[90] Reg. § 1.170A-13(f)(15). If a person purchases an annuity from a charitable organization and claims a charitable contribution deduction of $250 or more for the excess of the amount paid over the value of the annuity, the contemporaneous written acknowledgment must state whether any goods or services in addition to the annuity were provided to the person (Reg. § 1.170A-13(f)(16)). The contemporaneous written acknowledgment need not include a good-faith estimate of the value of the annuity (*id.*).

[91] Reg. § 1.170A-13(f)(17). An idea for simplified compliance by donors and donees with the charitable gift substantiation rules is the subject of discussion in the charitable community (e.g., 69

§ 5.4 QUID PRO QUO CONTRIBUTION RULES

Congress appreciably added to the federal law of charitable fundraising regulation in 1993 when it enacted certain *quid pro quo* requirements. These rules, applicable to both individual and corporate donors, took effect on January 1, 1994.

A *quid pro quo contribution* is a payment "made partly as a contribution and partly in consideration for goods or services provided to the payor by the donee organization."[92] The term does not include a payment made to an organization, operated exclusively for religious purposes, in return for which the donor receives solely an intangible religious benefit that generally is not sold in a commercial transaction outside the donative context.[93]

Specifically, if a charitable organization (other than a state, a possession of the United States, a political subdivision of a state or possession, the United States, and the District of Columbia[94]) receives a quid pro quo contribution in excess of $75, the organization must, in connection with the solicitation or receipt of the contribution, provide a written statement that (1) informs the donor that the amount of the contribution that is deductible for federal income tax purposes is limited to the excess of the amount of any money and the value of any property other than money contributed by the donor over the value of the goods or services provided by the organization and (2) provides the donor with a good-faith estimate of the value of the goods or services.[95]

It is intended that this disclosure be made in a manner that is reasonably likely to come to the attention of the donor. Therefore, immersing the disclosure in fine print in a larger document is inadequate.[96]

For purposes of the $75 threshold, separate payments made at different times of the year with respect to separate fundraising events generally will not be aggregated.

These rules do not apply where only de minimis, token goods or services (such as key chains and bumper stickers) are provided to the donor. In defining these terms, prior IRS pronouncements are followed.[97] Also, these rules do not apply to transactions that do not have a donative element (such as the charging of tuition by a school, the charging of health care fees by a hospital, or the sale of items by a museum).[98]

Tax Notes 793 (Nov. 6, 1995)). The thought advanced is that the contributor has a rubber stamp made, by which the following is printed on the back of the contribution check: "The negotiation of this check constitutes an acknowledgment that the amount thereof was received by the payee as a charitable contribution and that no goods or services were provided in consideration thereof." The Department of the Treasury has never addressed the efficacy of this approach.

[92] IRC § 6115(b).

[93] *Id.* See *supra* § 3, text accompanied by note 64.

[94] IRC §§ 6115(a), 170(c)(1).

[95] IRC § 6115(a). For contributions that have a value of $75 or less, the body of law described in *supra* § 2 continues to apply.

[96] H. Rep. 103-213, 103d Cong., 1st Sess. 566, note 35 (1993).

[97] See text accompanied by *supra* notes 78–79.

[98] H. Rep. 103-213, *supra* note 96, at 566. The IRS issued temporary regulations (T.D. 8544) and proposed regulations (IA-74-93) to accompany these rules. A hearing on them was held on November 10, 1995, at which time witnesses from the charitable sector expressed dismay at the prospect of having to value benefits, particularly intangible ones, provided in exchange for charitable

A nearly identical disclosure provision was part of the Revenue Act of 1992, which was vetoed. The report of the Senate Finance Committee, which accompanied the proposal, however, contained the following explanation of the need for these rules:

> Difficult problems of tax administration arise with respect to fundraising techniques in which an organization that is eligible to receive deductible contributions provides goods or services in consideration for payments from donors. Organizations that engage in such fundraising practices often do not inform their donors that all or a portion of the amount paid by the donor may not be deductible as a charitable contribution. Consequently, the [Senate Finance] [C]ommittee believes . . . it is appropriate that, in all cases where a charity receives a *quid pro quo* contribution . . . the charity should inform the donor that the [federal income tax charitable contribution] deduction . . . is limited to the amount by which the payment exceeds the value of goods or services furnished, and provide a good faith estimate of the value of such goods or services.[99]

There is a penalty for violation of these requirements.[100]

Under final regulations issued in 1996, a charitable organization is able to use "any reasonable methodology in making a good faith estimate, provided it applies the methodology in good faith."[101] A good-faith estimate of the value of goods or services that are not generally available in a commercial transaction may, under these regulations, be determined by reference to the fair market value of similar or comparable goods or services. Goods or services may be similar or comparable even though they do not have the "unique qualities of the goods or services that are being valued."[102]

Two examples are offered. One concerns a charitable organization operating a museum.[103] In return for a payment of $50,000 or more, the museum allows a donor to hold a private event in one of its rooms; in the room is a display of a unique collection of art. No other private events are permitted to be held in the museum. In the community, there are four hotels with ballrooms having the same capacity as the room in the museum. Two of these hotels have ballrooms that offer amenities and atmosphere that are similar to the amenities and atmosphere of the room in the museum; none of them have any art collections. Because the capacity, amenities, and atmosphere of the ballrooms in these two hotels are comparable to the capacity, amenities, and atmosphere of the room in the museum, a good-faith estimate of the benefits received from

---

contributions. A summary of this hearing is at 2 *Fund-Raising Regulation Report* (No. 1) 1 (Jan./Feb. 1995). There is little in the final regulations to assuage their concerns.

[99] "Technical Explanation of the Finance Committee Amendment" ("Technical Explanation"), at 586. The Technical Explanation was not formally printed; it is, however, reproduced in the *Congressional Record* (138 *Cong. Rec.* (No. 112) S11246 (Aug. 3, 1992)).

[100] IRC § 6714. This requirement is separate from the substantiality rules (see *supra* § 3). An organization may be able to meet both sets of requirements with the same written document. An organization in this position, however, should be careful to satisfy the quid pro quo contribution rules in a timely manner because of this penalty.

[101] Reg. § 1.6115-1(a)(1).

[102] Reg. § 1.6115-1(a)(2).

[103] Reg. § 1.6115-1(a)(3), Example 1.

the museum may be determined by reference to the cost of renting either of the two hotel ballrooms. The cost of renting one of these ballrooms is $2,500. Thus, a good-faith estimate of the fair market value of the right to host a private event in the room in the museum is $2,500. Here, the ballrooms in the two hotels are considered similar and comparable facilities in relation to the museum's room for valuation purposes, notwithstanding the fact that the room in the museum displays a unique collection of art.

In another example, a charitable organization offers to provide a one-hour tennis lesson with a tennis professional in return for the first payment of $500 or more it receives.[104] The professional provides tennis lessons on a commercial basis at the rate of $100 per hour. An individual pays the charity $500 and in return receives the tennis lesson. A good-faith estimate of the fair market value of the tennis lesson provided in exchange for the payment is $100.

In this context, the regulations somewhat address the matter of the involvement of celebrities. This is another of the problems plaguing the fundraising community, as was articulated so well at an IRS hearing in November 1994.[105] This subject is not addressed by a separate regulation but rather by an example.[106] A charity holds a promotion in which it states that, in return for the first payment of $1,000 or more it receives, it will provide a dinner for two followed by an evening tour of a museum conducted by an artist whose most recent works are on display there. The artist does not provide tours of the museum on a commercial basis. Typically, tours of the museum are free to the public. An individual pays $1,000 to the charity and in exchange receives a dinner valued at $100 and the museum tour. Because the tours are typically free to the public, a good-faith estimate of the value of the tour conducted by the artist is $0. The fact that the tour is conducted by the artist rather than one of the museum's regular tour guides does not render the tours dissimilar or incomparable for valuation purposes.[107]

Five types of goods or services are disregarded for purposes of the quid pro quo contribution rules.[108] A comparable rule as to goods or services provided to employees of donors is applicable in this context.[109]

No part of this type of a payment can be considered a deductible charitable gift unless two elements exist: (1) the patron makes a payment in an amount that is in fact in excess of the fair market value of the goods or services received, and (2) the patron intends to make a payment in an amount that exceeds that fair market value.[110] This requirement of the element of *intent* may

---

[104] Reg. § 1.6115-1(a)(3), Example 2.

[105] See *supra* note 74.

[106] Reg. § 1.6115-1(a)(3), Example 3.

[107] This rule as to celebrity presence is more important for what it does not say than what it says. Basically, the regulation states that if the celebrity does something from what he or she is known for (e.g., a painter conducting a tour), the fact that he or she is part of the event can be ignored for valuation purposes. The regulation suggests, however, that if the celebrity does what he or she is celebrated for (e.g., a singer or a comedian who performs as such), the value of that performance—being a service available on a commercial basis—should be taken into account in valuing the event.

[108] See § 3, text accompanied by notes 78–84.

[109] *Id.*, text accompanied by note 87.

[110] Reg. § 1.170A-1(h)(1).

prove to be relatively harmless, as the patron is likely to know the charity's good-faith estimate figure in advance of the payment and thus cannot help but have this intent. Still, proving intent is not always easy. This development is unfortunate, inasmuch as the law has been evolving to a more mechanical (and thus less reliant on subjective proof) test: any payment to a charitable organization in excess of fair market value is regarded as a charitable gift.[111]

§ 5.5 FUNDRAISING DISCLOSURE BY NONCHARITABLE ORGANIZATIONS

Congress brought the IRS into the field of regulation of fundraising when it legislated certain fundraising disclosure rules.[112] These rules are not applicable to charitable organizations,[113] although the legislative history accompanying them strongly hinted that this type of statutory law would be extended to charities if they persisted in securing payments from individuals that are not gifts (such as dues, payments for raffle tickets, or bids at auctions) under circumstances where the payors think, sometimes because of explicit or implicit suggestions from the charity involved, that the payments are gifts and try to deduct them as charitable contributions.[114]

These fundraising disclosure rules, which are thus applicable to all types of tax-exempt organizations, principally social welfare organizations,[115] other than charitable ones, are designed to prevent these noncharitable organizations from engaging in fundraising activities under circumstances in which donors will assume that the contributions are tax-deductible, when in fact they are not. These rules do not, however, apply to an organization that has annual gross receipts that are normally no more than $100,000.[116] Also, where all of the parties being solicited are tax-exempt organizations, the solicitation need

[111] A payment made to a charitable organization in excess of an item's fair market value is not necessarily the consequence of donative intent. In the case of an auction, for example, the patron (successful bidder) may just intensely want the item, or be motivated by peer pressure or extensive access to an open bar; charity may be the farthest thing from the patron's mind.
[112] IRC § 6113. The IRS published rules to accompany this law in 1988, as IRS Notice 88-120, 1988-2 C.B. 454.
[113] That is, this law does not apply to organizations described in IRC § 501(c)(3).
[114] Extension of this type of law in fact occurred (see *supra* §§ 3 and 4).
[115] That is, organizations that are described in IRC § 501(c)(4) and that are tax-exempt under IRC § 501(a).
[116] IRC § 6113(b)(2)(A). In determining this threshold, the same principles that obtain in ascertaining the annual information return (Form 990) $25,000 filing threshold apply (Rev. Proc. 82-23, 1983-1 C.B. 687). In general, these rules utilize a three-year average. The organization must include the required disclosure statement on all solicitations made more than 30 days after reaching $300,000 in gross receipts for the three-year period of the calculation (IRS Notice 88-120, *supra* note 112).
A local, regional, or state chapter of an organization with gross receipts under $100,000 must include the disclosure statement in its solicitations if at least 25 percent of the money solicited will go to the national, or other, unit of the organization that has annual gross receipts over $100,000, because the solicitation is considered as being, in part, on behalf of the unit. Also, if a trade association or labor union with over $100,000 in annual gross receipts solicits funds that will pass through to a political action committee with less than $100,000 in annual gross receipts, the solicitation must include the required disclosure statement.

not include the disclosure statement (inasmuch as these grantors have no need for a charitable deduction).[117]

Technically, in general, this law applies to any organization to which contributions are not deductible as charitable gifts and which (1) is tax-exempt,[118] (2) is a political organization,[119] (3) was either type of organization at any time during the five-year period ending on the date of the fundraising solicitation, or (4) is a successor to one of these organizations at any time during this five-year period.[120] The IRS is accorded the authority to treat any group of two or more organizations as one organization for these purposes where "necessary or appropriate" to prevent the avoidance of these rules through the use of multiple organizations.[121]

Under these rules, each fundraising solicitation by or on behalf of a tax-exempt noncharitable organization must contain an express statement, in a "conspicuous and easily recognizable format," that gifts to it are not deductible as charitable contributions for federal income tax purposes.[122] (The IRS has promulgated rules as to this statement; these rules are discussed as follows.) A *fundraising solicitation* is any solicitation of gifts made in written or printed form, by television, radio, or telephone (although there is an exclusion for letters or calls not part of a coordinated fundraising campaign soliciting no more than 10 persons during a calendar year).[123] Despite the reference in the statute to "contributions and gifts," the IRS interprets this rule to mandate the disclosure when any tax-exempt organization (other than a charity) seeks funds, such as dues from members.

Failure to satisfy this disclosure requirement can result in imposition of penalties.[124] The penalty is $1,000 per day (maximum of $10,000 per year), albeit with a reasonable cause exception. In an instance of an intentional disregard of these rules, however, the penalty for the day on which the offense occurred is the greater of $1,000 or 50 percent of the aggregate cost of the solicitations that took place on that day, and the $10,000 limitation is inapplicable. For these purposes, the days involved are those on which the solicitation was telecast, broadcast, mailed, otherwise distributed, or telephoned.

The IRS promulgated rules in amplification of this law, particularly the requirement of a disclosure statement.[125] The rules, which include guidance in the form of "safe-harbor" provisions, address the format of the disclosure statement in instances of use of print media, telephone, television, and radio. They provide examples of acceptable disclosure language and methods (which, when

---

[117] IRS Notice 88-120, *supra* note 112.

[118] That is, is described in IRC § 501(a) and IRC § 501(c) (other than, as noted *supra* note 113, IRC § 501(c)(3)).

[119] That is, is described in IRC § 527.

[120] IRC § 6113(b)(1). For this purpose, a fraternal organization (one described in IRC § 170(c)(4)) is treated as a charitable organization only with respect to solicitations for contributions that are to be used exclusively for purposes referred to in IRC § 170(c)(4) (IRC § 6113(b)(3)).

[121] IRC § 6113(b)(2)(B).

[122] IRC § 6113(a).

[123] IRC § 6113(c).

[124] IRC § 6710.

[125] IRS Notice 88-120, *supra* note 112.

followed, amount to the safe-harbor guidelines), and of included and excluded solicitations. They also contain guidelines for determining the $100,000 threshold.

The safe-harbor guideline for print media (including solicitations by mail and in newspapers) is fourfold: (1) the solicitation includes language such as the following: "Contributions or gifts to [name of organization] are not deductible as charitable contributions for federal income tax purposes"; (2) the statement is in at least the same type size as the primary message stated in the body of the letter, leaflet, or advertisement; (3) the statement is included on the message side of any card or tear-off section that the contributor returns with the contribution; and (4) the statement is either the first sentence in a paragraph or itself constitutes a paragraph.

The safe-harbor guideline for telephone solicitations includes the first of the above elements. In addition, the guideline requires that (1) the statement be made in close proximity to the request for contributions, during the same telephone call, by the telephone solicitor, and (2) any written confirmation or billing sent to a person pledging to contribute during the telephone solicitation be in compliance with the requirements for print media solicitations.

Solicitation by television must, to conform with this guideline, include a solicitation statement that complies with the first of the print medium requirements. Also, if the statement is spoken, it must be in close proximity to the request for contributions. If the statement appears on the television screen, it must be in large, easily readable type appearing on the screen for at least five seconds.

In the case of a solicitation by radio, the statement must, to meet the safe-harbor test, comply with the first of the print medium requirements. Also, the statement must be made in close proximity to the request for contributions during the same radio solicitation announcement.

Where the soliciting organization is a membership entity, classified as a trade or business association or other form of business league,[126] or a labor or agricultural organization,[127] the following statement conforms to the safe-harbor guideline: "Contributions or gifts to [name of organization] are not tax-deductible as charitable contributions. They may be tax-deductible, however, as ordinary and necessary business expenses."

If an organization makes a solicitation to which these rules apply and the solicitation does not comply with the applicable safe-harbor guideline, the IRS is authorized to evaluate all of the facts and circumstances to determine whether the solicitation meets the disclosure rule. A "good-faith effort" to comply with these requirements is an important factor in the evaluation of the facts and circumstances. Nonetheless, disclosure statements made in "fine print" do not comply with the statutory requirement.[128]

This disclosure requirement applies to solicitations for voluntary contributions as well as solicitations for attendance at testimonials and similar

---

[126] That is, is an organization described in IRC § 501(c)(6) and is tax-exempt under IRC § 501(a).
[127] That is, is an organization described in IRC § 501(c)(5) and is tax-exempt under IRC § 501(a).
[128] In one instance, a political organization that conducted fundraising by means of telemarketing and direct mail was found to be in violation of these rules: a notice of nondeductibility of contributions was not included in its telephone solicitations or pledge statements, and the print used in some of its written notices was too small (Priv. Ltr. Rul. 9315001).

fundraising events. The disclosure must be made in the case of solicitations for contributions to political action committees.

Exempt from this disclosure rule are the billing of those who advertise in an organization's publications, billing by social clubs for food and beverages, billing of attendees of a conference, billing for insurance premiums of an insurance program operated or sponsored by an organization, billing of members of a community association for mandatory payments for police and fire (and similar) protection, and billing for payments to a voluntary employees' beneficiary association as well as similar payments to a trust for pension and/or health benefits.

General material discussing the benefits of membership in a tax-exempt organization, such as a trade association or labor union, does not have to include the required disclosure statement. The statement is required, however, where the material both requests payment and specifies the amount requested as membership dues. If a person responds to the general material discussing the benefits of membership, the follow-up material requesting the payment of a specific amount in membership dues (such as a union checkoff card or a trade association billing statement for a new member) must include the disclosure statement. General material discussing a political candidacy and requesting persons to vote for the candidate or "support" the candidate need not include the disclosure statement, unless the material specifically requests either a financial contribution or a contribution of volunteer services in support of the candidate.

§ 5.6   INTERMEDIATE SANCTIONS

The *intermediate sanctions* rules, added to the federal tax law in 1996,[129] constitute the most dramatic body of statutory law, affecting public charities and those who engage in fundraising for them, enacted since creation of the fundamental tax rules for charities in 1969.[130] The most significant aspect of these rules is the emphasis on the sanctioning (taxation) of those persons who engaged in impermissible private transactions with public charities, rather than revocation of the organizations' tax-exempt status.[131]

These sanctions are termed *intermediate*, because they generally are posited between what was, before their enactment, two extremes: when the

---

[129] IRC § 4958, which was made retroactively effective as of September 14, 1995. The report of the House Committee on Ways and Means (H. Rep. 104-506, 104th Cong., 2d Sess. (1996)) (for purposes of this § 5.6, "House Report"), constitutes the totality of the legislative history of the intermediate sanctions rules.

The IRS proposed regulations to accompany these rules in 1998 (REG-246256-96). In January, 2001, the IRS issued these regulations in temporary form (T.D. 8920) and again in proposed form. The temporary regulations were set to expire on January 9, 2004. Final regulations were issued, however, on January 21, 2002 (T.D. 8978).

[130] This reference is to the Tax Reform Act of 1969, which enacted law defining public charities and private foundations (see *infra* § 11), expanded the charitable giving rules (see *infra* § 14), and codified the law as to planned giving (*id.*).

[131] See *infra* § 13.

IRS found an act of private inurement, its formal choices were to terminate the organization's tax-exempt status or do nothing.

(a) Basic Concepts of Intermediate Sanctions

Pursuant to the intermediate sanctions rules, tax sanctions—structured as penalty excise taxes—may be imposed on the disqualified persons (discussed later) who improperly benefited from the transaction and on the organization managers (discussed later) who participated in the transaction knowing that it was improper. These rules do not prohibit a transaction between an applicable tax-exempt organization and disqualified persons with respect to it. Rather, the rules require that the terms and conditions of the transaction be reasonable.

(i) Exempt Organizations Involved.   The sanctions apply with respect to tax-exempt public charities[132] and tax-exempt social welfare organizations. These organizations are termed *applicable tax-exempt organizations.*[133] Organizations of this nature include any organization described in either of these two categories of exempt organizations at any time during the five-year period ending on the date of the transaction.[134]

There are no exemptions from these rules. That is, all tax-exempt public charities and all tax-exempt social welfare organizations are applicable tax-exempt organizations.

(ii) Excess Benefit Transactions.   This tax regime has as its heart the excess benefit transaction. Essentially, an excess benefit transaction is the same as a private inurement transaction. In an instance of one of these transactions, tax sanctions can be imposed on the disqualified person or persons who improperly benefited from the transaction and perhaps on any organization managers who participated in the transaction knowing that it was improper.

The term *excess benefit transaction* is based on the contract law concept of *consideration,* which means the approximately equal benefits that parties to a contract must receive from the arrangement; consideration is required for the agreement to be enforceable. An excess benefit transaction is any transaction in which an economic benefit is provided by an applicable tax-exempt organization directly or indirectly to or for the use of any disqualified person, if the value of the economic benefit provided by the exempt organization exceeds the value of the consideration (including the performance of services) received for providing the benefit.[135] This type of benefit is known as an *excess benefit.*[136]

The principal focus is on *compensation,* which generally is all economic benefits provided by an applicable tax-exempt organization in exchange for performance of services. Compensation generally includes all forms of cash and noncash compensation (including salary, fees, bonuses, severance payments,

---

[132] See *infra* § 11.
[133] IRC § 4958(e)(1).
[134] IRC § 4958(e)(2).
[135] IRC § 4958(c)(1)(A); Reg. § 53.4958-4(a)(1).
[136] IRC § 4958(c)(1)(B).

and deferred compensation), payment of liability insurance premiums, payments to welfare benefit plans (such as medical, dental, life insurance, severance pay, and disability benefits plans), and fringe benefits.[137]

An economic benefit may not be treated as consideration for performance of services unless the organization clearly intended and made the payments as compensation for services.[138] In determining whether payments or transactions of this nature are forms of compensation, the relevant factors include whether the appropriate decision-making body approved the transfer as compensation in accordance with established procedures and whether the organization and the recipient reported the transfer (other than in the case of nontaxable fringe benefits) as compensation on relevant returns or other forms.[139]

The phrasing *directly* or *indirectly* means the provision of an economic benefit directly by the organization or indirectly by means of a controlled entity. Thus, an applicable tax-exempt organization cannot avoid involvement in an excess benefit transaction by causing a controlled entity to engage in the transaction.[140]

Existing law standards, including those established under the law concerning ordinary and necessary business expenses,[141] apply in determining reasonableness of compensation and fair market value.[142] In this regard, an individual need not necessarily accept reduced compensation merely because he or she renders services to a tax-exempt, as opposed to a taxable, organization.[143] If there are comparable institutions in the for-profit sector (such as hospitals), compensation paid to their executives may be taken into account in determining reasonableness.

There is no requirement, generally, that a disqualified person *know* that a transaction is an excess benefit transaction. An individual can act in good faith and nonetheless be penalized for engaging in what turns out to be an excess benefit transaction.

(iii) Revenue-Sharing Transactions. To the extent provided in tax regulations, the term *excess benefit transaction* includes any transaction in which the amount of any economic benefit provided to or for the use of a disqualified person is determined in whole or in part by the revenues of one or more activities of the organization but only if the transaction results in impermissible private inurement.[144] In this context, the excess benefit is the amount of impermissible private inurement.

This type of compensation structure is a *revenue-sharing arrangement.* These rules, technically, are not in force because accompanying tax regulations

---

[137] Reg. § 53.4958-4(b)(1)(ii)(B).

[138] IRC § 4958(c)(1)(A).

[139] House Report at 57.

[140] *Id.* at 56, note 3; Reg. § 53.4958-4(a)(2).

[141] IRC § 162.

[142] These standards traditionally have been a battery of factors looked to by the courts and the IRS; this approach is known as the *multifactor test.* In the for-profit setting, however, some courts use an alternative standard, known as the *independent investor test.*

[143] House Report at 56, note 5.

[144] IRC § 4958(c)(2).

have not been promulgated.[145] Nonetheless, the IRS is applying the general rules to revenue-sharing arrangements.

A revenue-sharing arrangement may be an excess benefit transaction if it permits a disqualified person to receive additional compensation without providing proportional benefits that contribute to the charitable organization's accomplishment of its exempt purpose.[146]

(iv) Rebuttable Presumption of Reasonableness. There is a *rebuttable presumption of reasonableness* with respect to compensation and other arrangements with disqualified persons. Where the criteria of the presumption are satisfied, the burden of proving an excess benefit transaction shifts to the IRS. The presumption arises where the arrangement was approved by a board of directors or trustees (or committee of the board) that was composed entirely of individuals unrelated to and not subject to the control of the disqualified persons involved in the arrangement, obtained and relied upon appropriate data as to comparability, and adequately documented the basis for its determination.[147]

(v) Disqualified Persons. In this context, the term *disqualified person* means any person who was, at any time during the five-year period ending on the date of the transaction involved, in a position to exercise substantial influence over the affairs of the organization.[148] The term also means a member of the family of an individual who meets this definition and an entity in which persons described in either of these two categories own more than a 35 percent interest.[149]

The following persons are deemed—automatically—to be disqualified persons (i.e., to have substantial influence): voting members of the governing body; presidents, chief executive officers, and chief operating officers; and treasurers and chief financial officers.[150] Persons deemed to not have substantial influence include other tax-exempt charitable organizations and employees who are not highly compensated employees for employee benefit purposes.[151]

Certain facts and circumstances are considered in determining whether a person is a disqualified person. Facts and circumstances that tend to show substantial influence include the fact that the person founded the organization; the person is a substantial contributor to the organization; the person's compensation is primarily based on revenues derived from activities of the organization that the person controls; the person has or shares authority to control or determine a substantial portion of the organization's capital expenditures, operating budget, or compensation for employees; or the person manages a discrete segment or activity of the organization that represents a

---

[145] As to the final regulations, the matter was reserved (Reg. § 53.4958-5).
[146] This was the standard under the proposed regulations (Prop. Reg. § 53.4958-6(d)(1)(iii)).
[147] This rebuttable presumption was created, not by statute, but by language in the House Report. It is reflected in the final regulations (Reg. § 53.4958-6).
[148] IRC § 4958(f)(1)(A); Reg. § 53.4958-3(a)(1).
[149] IRC § 4958(f)(1)(B), (C).
[150] Reg. § 53.4958-3(c).
[151] Reg. § 53.4958-3(d).

substantial portion of the activities, assets, income, or expenses of the organization, as compared with the organization as a whole.[152]

Facts and circumstances that tend to show no substantial influence over the affairs of an organization include the fact that the person has taken a vow of poverty on behalf of a religious organization; the person functioned as a lawyer, accountant, or investment manager or adviser; or the person does not participate in any management decisions affecting the organization as a whole or a discrete segment or activity of the organization that represents a substantial portion of the organization's activities, assets, income, or expenses.[153]

Disqualified persons include *organization managers.* These are individuals who are trustees, directors, or officers of an applicable tax-exempt organization, as well as those having powers or responsibilities similar to those of trustees, directors, or officers of the organization.[154] The term *member of the family* is defined as (1) spouses, ancestors, children, grandchildren, great grandchildren, and the spouses of children, grandchildren, and great grandchildren, and (2) the brothers and sisters (whether by the whole or half-blood) of the individual and their spouses.[155]

(vi) Initial Contract Exception.   The intermediate sanctions rules do not apply to a fixed payment made to a person pursuant to an initial contract. A *fixed payment* is an amount of money or other property specified in the contract, or determined by a fixed formula specified in the contract, which is to be paid or transferred in exchange for the provision of specified services or property.[156] A *fixed formula* may incorporate an amount that depends on future events (such as an increase in the Consumer Price Index) or contingencies, provided that no person exercises discretion when calculating the amount of a payment or deciding whether to make a payment (such as a bonus). A specified event or contingency may include the amount of revenues generated by (or other objective measure of) one or more activities of the charitable organization.

A fixed payment does not include any amount paid to a person under a reimbursement or similar arrangement where discretion is exercised by any person with respect to the amount of expenses incurred or reimbursed.

An *initial contract* is a binding written contract between an applicable tax-exempt organization and a person who was not a disqualified person immediately before entering into the contract. This exception, however, does not apply to any fixed payment made pursuant to an initial contract during any tax year of the person contracting with the organization, if the person fails to perform substantially the person's obligations under the contract during that year.

A written binding contract that provides that the contract is terminable or subject to cancellation by the applicable tax-exempt organization (other than as a result of a lack of substantial performance by the disqualified person) without the other party's consent and without substantial penalty to the

---

[152] Reg. § 53.4958-3(e)(2).
[153] Reg. § 53.4953-3(a)(3).
[154] IRC § 4958(f)(2).
[155] IRC § 4958(f)(4).
[156] Reg. § 53.4958-4(3)(ii).

organization is treated as a new contract as of the earliest date that any such termination or cancellation, if made, would be effective.

A compensation package can be partially sheltered by these rules. For example, a person can have a base salary that is a fixed payment pursuant to an initial contract and also have an annual performance-based bonus.

(vii) Tax Structure. The intermediate sanctions penalties are structured as excise taxes. A disqualified person who benefited from an excess benefit transaction is subject to an initial excise tax equal to 25 percent of the amount of the excess benefit.[157] An additional tax, in an amount equal to 200 percent of the amount involved, may be imposed on a disqualified person where the initial tax was imposed and if there was no correction (defined below) of the excess benefit transaction within a specified period.[158]

An organization manager who participated in an excess benefit transaction, knowing that it was this type of a transaction, is subject to an initial excise tax of 10 percent of the excess benefit where an initial tax is imposed on a disqualified person.[159]

Taxes on excess benefit transactions that are corrected (see following discussion) within the correction period may be eligible for abatement.[160]

(viii) Correction. In addition to payment of the tax penalties, the transaction must be corrected. The term *correction* means undoing the excess benefit to the extent possible and taking any additional measures necessary to place the organization in a financial position not worse than that in which it would be if the disqualified person were dealing under the highest fiduciary standards.[161]

The correction amount with respect to an excess benefit transaction is the sum of the excess benefit and interest on the excess benefit.[162] The amount of the interest charge is determined by multiplying the amount of the excess benefit by an interest rate, compounded annually, for the period from the date the excess benefit transaction occurred to the date of correction.

Caution should be exercised when correcting an excess benefit transaction. If not undertaken properly, the attempted undoing of the arrangement can cause another excess benefit transaction.

(ix) Reporting of Excess Benefit Transactions. Disqualified persons and organization managers liable for payment of excise taxes as the result of excess benefit transactions are required to file Form 4720 as the return by which these taxes are paid. An excess benefit transaction must also be reported on the annual information return of the applicable tax-exempt organization.[163]

---

[157] IRC § 4958(a)(1).
[158] IRC § 4958(b).
[159] IRC § 4958(a)(2).
[160] IRC §§ 4961, 4962.
[161] IRC § 4958(f)(6).
[162] Reg. § 53.4958-7(c).
[163] Form 990, Part VI, line 89a-c.

(x) Scope of Sanctions.   These intermediate sanctions may be imposed by the IRS in lieu of or in addition to revocation of an organization's tax-exempt status.[164] The sanctions are, in general, to be the sole sanction imposed in those cases in which the excess benefit does not rise to such a level as to call into question whether, on the whole, the organization functions as a charitable or social welfare organization.

In practice, the revocation of tax-exempt status, with or without the imposition of these excise taxes, is to occur only when the organization no longer operates as a charitable or social welfare organization.[165] Preexisting law principles apply in determining whether an organization no longer operates as a tax-exempt organization. The loss of tax-exempt status could occur in a year, or as of a year, the organization was involved in a transaction constituting a substantial amount of private inurement.

(b) Intermediate Sanctions Rules as Applied to Fundraising

In the fundraising setting, the issues basically involve the circumstances when a person involved in the fundraising process is a disqualified person and when a transaction in the fundraising context is an impermissible transaction (i.e., one giving rise to taxation).

(i) Tax-Exempt Organizations Involved.   These intermediate sanctions apply with respect to all charitable organizations, other than private foundations. That is, the sanctions apply with respect to all public charities. Therefore, from the standpoint of charitable fundraising, the charity involved is almost certain to be an applicable tax-exempt organization.

(ii) Disqualified Persons in Fundraising Context.   Generally, a fundraising executive is not a disqualified person with respect to the charitable organization being served. He or she is not normally in a position to exercise substantial influence over the affairs of the organization. This is usually the case when the fundraiser is an employee (such as a director of development) or a consultant (independent contractor).

There are, nonetheless, situations where the fundraising professional is a disqualified person. The fundraiser may be an organization manager. If the fundraising function is in a related entity, such as a foundation[166] directly affiliated with a university or hospital, and the fundraiser is the chief executive officer of that foundation, he or she would be a disqualified person with respect to the foundation under the general rule. Occasionally, a fundraiser will be a disqualified person by virtue of being a member of the family.

An independent fundraising person may be considered a disqualified person. This is particularly the case where the person has control over a fundraising program of a charitable organization that is a meaningful source of

---

[164] House Report at 59.

[165] *Id.,* note 15.

[166] This use of the term *foundation* means an entity that is a public charity, rather than a private foundation (see *infra* § 11), and thus is an applicable tax-exempt organization.

the organization's revenue. It is noted that the fact that a person manages a discrete segment or activity of an organization, that represents a substantial portion of the activities, assets, income, or expenses of the organization, tends to lead to the conclusion that the person is a disqualified person.

This is an area where charities and their fundraising professionals need to proceed with caution. The IRS is of the view that a person who manages a discrete, meaningful segment or activity of a charitable organization *is* a disqualified person. The IRS tried, by means of proposed regulations, to make that the absolute rule.[167] Because that would be overreaching in relation to the statutory definition, however, the IRS was relegated to placement of this factor as an element in a facts-and-circumstances test.

As an example, a charitable organization decided to use bingo games as a method of generating revenue. The charity entered into a contract with a company that operates these games. This company managed the promotion and operation of the bingo activity; provided all necessary staff, equipment, and services; and paid the charity a percentage of the revenue from the bingo activity. The company retained the balance of the proceeds. The charity provided no goods or services in connection with the bingo operation other than the use of its hall for the bingo games. The annual gross revenue earned from the games represented more than one-half of the charity's total annual revenue. The company's compensation is primarily based on revenues from an activity that it controls. Because the company managed a discrete activity of the charitable organization that represented a substantial portion of the charity's income, the IRS is of the view that the company is a disqualified person with respect to the charitable organization.[168]

(iii) Excess Benefit Transactions in Fundraising Context. The most obvious instance of the existence of an excess benefit transaction in the fundraising context is the payment of excessive compensation to the fundraising executive, as employee or consultant, assuming the fundraiser is a disqualified person.

Some fundraisers are compensated, in whole or in part, on the basis of the revenue flow of the charitable organization involved. This arrangement may be structured as a commission or some other form of percentage-based compensation. In any event, it is likely to be a revenue-sharing arrangement.

At the present, as noted, the specific provision concerning revenue-sharing arrangements is not in force. Nonetheless, the IRS is reviewing these compensation structures, using the general definition of the term *excess benefit transaction*. It may be advisable to limit the amount of this type of compensation, irrespective of how it is ascertained. The fact that a revenue-sharing arrangement is subject to a cap is a relevant factor in determining the reasonableness of compensation.[169]

As noted, the fact that a person's compensation is primarily based on revenues derived from activities of the organization that the person controls is a factor leading toward a decision that the person is a disqualified person.

---

[167] Prop. Reg. § 53.4958-3(e)(1).
[168] Reg. § 53.4958-3(g), Example 5.
[169] Reg. § 53.4958-4(b)(ii).

One of the greatest concerns in this setting pertains to arrangements involving special events, where the events are coordinated, if not entirely conducted, by for-profit companies. As discussed, a company of this nature can be regarded as a disqualified person. In that event, the fees paid to the company would be tested against a standard of reasonableness.

(iv) Initial Contract Exception.   The initial contract exception can be of considerable utility in the fundraising setting. It is available when a charitable organization hires a fundraising professional, whether as an employee or independent contractor, where the person was not a disqualified person immediately before entering into the contract.[170] Where the parameters of the exception are satisfied, the compensation arrangement is totally exempted from the intermediate sanctions penalties.

It is clear, then, that the charitable organization and/or fundraising professional who believes there may be liability associated with a transaction with a charitable organization should endeavor to satisfy the criteria of the initial contract exception.

(v) Rebuttable Presumption of Reasonableness.   The rebuttable presumption of reasonableness can also be useful for the fundraising professional, particularly in circumstances where the initial contract exception cannot apply. The fundraiser should endeavor to be certain that the various elements of the presumption are satisfied, to shift the burden of proof to the IRS in the event of a challenge to the reasonableness of compensation.

(vi) Reporting of Excess Benefit Transactions.   It is sometimes said that the intermediate sanctions rules are a concern only to disqualified persons and not to the charitable organization involved or other persons who are not disqualified persons; however, this often is not the case. From a fundraising perspective, a charitable organization embroiled in an excess benefit transaction is expected to report that transaction on its annual information return, which is a public document.[171] The result, at a minimum, can be adverse

---

[170] The initial contract exception—known informally as the *first bite rule*—has a curious genesis. It originated in the realm of the law of fundraising. The exception was stimulated by a controversial decision by a federal court of appeals, which held that a fundraising company was not an insider (see *infra* § 13) with respect to a public charity, even though the trial court found that the company had taken control of the charity and manipulated its assets for the company's private ends (*United Cancer Council, Inc.* v. *Commissioner*, 165 F.3d 1173 (7th Cir. 1999), *reversing and remanding* 109 T.C. 326 (1997). In its preamble to the temporary regulations, the IRS wrote that this appellate court held that private inurement "cannot result from a contractual relationship negotiated at arm's length with a party having no prior relationship with the organization, regardless of the relative bargaining strength of the parties or resultant control over the tax-exempt organization created by the terms of the contract." One will search the pages of the *United Cancer Council* opinion in vain for such a holding; it is not there. The court said nothing on the matter of "no prior relationship" and found that "the party" did not control the charity to begin with. Although the initial contract exception can be inferred from the court's holding, it is at best a shaky foundation on which to build this rule of law.

[171] See *infra* § 9(i).

publicity, which can harm the work of the fundraising professional, even if the fundraiser is not the disqualified person involved.

(vii) Tax Penalties. If a fundraising professional, hired by a charitable organization (e.g., as an employee), is paid excessive compensation, the arrangement would be a taxable excess benefit transaction, assuming absence of the rebuttable presumption of reasonableness and the initial contract exception.

Assume, as an illustration, that this fundraising professional was paid a compensation package of $200,000, for a three-year period. Following audit, the IRS concluded that this individual's services were worth only $100,000. This fundraising executive would then owe initial excise taxes totaling $75,000 (a $25,000 tax per year on the excess benefit of $100,000). Also, this compensation arrangement would have to be corrected by the fundraiser, by means of payment of $300,000 to the charity, plus suitable interest. If these steps were not timely taken, the fundraiser may have additional excise taxes imposed, totaling $600,000. The total obligation of the fundraiser would be $975,000, not including penalties, interest, and legal fees. A board member who approved this compensation package, knowing it to be excessive, would be liable for $10,000 in taxes and perhaps the taxes of one or more other board members.

§ 5.7 UNRELATED BUSINESS RULES

One of the ways in which the IRS is regulating fundraising for charitable purposes is by means of the unrelated business rules. Before an analysis of the application of these rules to charitable fundraising, however, an overview of the rules is appropriate.[172]

(a) Basic Concepts of Unrelated Income Taxation

The law of tax-exempt organizations divides the activities of charitable and other tax-exempt organizations into two categories: those that are related to the performance of tax-exempt functions and those that are not. The net income derived from the latter group of activities, termed *unrelated activities,* is subject to tax. That is, the revenues associated with unrelated activities are taxable, taking into account the deductible expenses generated by or allocable to these activities.

Therefore, even though a charitable organization generally achieves federal income tax exemption, it nonetheless remains potentially taxable on any unrelated business income.[173] This tax is levied on nonprofit corporations and unincorporated associations[174] at the corporate rates[175] or on charitable trusts[176] at the individual rates.[177]

---

[172] In general, see *Law of Tax-Exempt Organizations* at 850–961.
[173] IRC § 501(b).
[174] IRC § 511(a)(1).
[175] IRC § 11.
[176] IRC § 511(b).
[177] IRC § 1(d).

(i) Introduction.   The taxation of unrelated income, a feature of the federal tax laws since 1950, is based on the concept that tax-exempt organizations should not compete with for-profit organizations. Also, the unrelated income rules are believed to be a more effective and workable sanction for authentic enforcement of the law of tax-exempt organizations than denial or revocation of tax-exempt status.

The unrelated income rules are based on a simple concept: The unrelated business income tax applies only to active business income that arises from activities that are *unrelated* to the organization's exempt purposes. Yet, despite the simplicity of the tax structure, it is not always easy to determine which activities of a tax-exempt organization are related to exempt purposes and which are unrelated businesses.

If a substantial portion of an organization's income is from unrelated sources, the organization will not qualify for tax exemption. That is, to be tax-exempt, a nonprofit organization must be organized and operated primarily for exempt purposes. An organization may satisfy the requirements for tax exemption as a charitable organization, however, even though it operates a business as a substantial part of its activities, where the operation of the business is in furtherance of the organization's exempt purposes and where the organization is not organized and operated for the primary purpose of carrying on an unrelated business (technically termed a *trade or business*). In determining the existence or nonexistence of this primary purpose, all of the circumstances must be considered, including the size and extent of the business and of the activities that are in furtherance of one or more exempt purposes.[178]

At the other end of the spectrum, incidental business activity will not alone cause a charitable or other type of tax-exempt organization to lose or be denied tax exemption, although the income derived from the activity may be taxable.[179] That is, the federal tax law allows a tax-exempt organization to engage in a certain amount of income-producing activity that is unrelated to exempt purposes.

Business activities may preclude initial qualification of an otherwise tax-exempt organization as a charitable or other entity. This can occur through failure to satisfy the operational test that determines whether the organization is being operated principally for exempt purposes.[180] Likewise, an organization will not meet the organizational test if its articles of organization (the document by which it was established) empower it, as more than an insubstantial part of its functions, to carry on activities that do not further its exempt purpose.[181]

---

[178] Reg. § 1.501(c)(3)-1(e)(1). There is, however, authority for the proposition that a charitable organization can operate a significant extent of unrelated business and not thereby endanger its tax-exempt status when the purpose for engaging in the unrelated activity is furtherance of exempt purposes (Tech. Adv. Mem. 200021056).

[179] E.g., Rev. Rul. 66-221, 1966-2 C.B. 220.

[180] See *Law of Tax-Exempt Organizations* § 4.5.

[181] See *id.* at 109–117.

The unrelated business income tax applies with respect to all charitable and nearly all other types of tax-exempt organizations.[182] They include religious organizations (including churches), educational organizations (including universities, colleges, and schools), health care organizations (including hospitals), and scientific organizations (including research entities).[183] This tax also applies with respect to any college or university that is an agency or instrumentality of any government or political subdivision of a government, or that is owned or operated by a government or political subdivision, or by any agency or instrumentality of one or more governments or political subdivisions, and further applies to any corporation wholly owned by one or more of these colleges or universities.[184]

Beyond the realm of charitable entities, the rules are applicable with respect to social welfare organizations (including advocacy groups),[185] labor organizations (including unions),[186] trade and professional associations,[187] fraternal organizations,[188] and veterans' organizations.[189] Special rules[190] tax all income not related to exempt functions (including investment income) of social clubs,[191] homeowners' associations,[192] and political organizations.[193]

The few tax-exempt organizations that are excepted from the tax are instrumentalities of the federal government,[194] certain religious and apostolic organizations,[195] farmers' cooperatives,[196] and shipowners' protection and indemnity associations.[197]

Certain organizations are not generally subject to the unrelated business rules simply because they are not allowed to engage in any active business endeavors. This is the case, for example, with respect to private foundations (within limitations) and title-holding organizations.[198] As to the former, the operation of an active business (externally or internally) by a private foundation would likely trigger application of the excess business holdings restrictions.[199] As to the latter, tax-exempt title-holding corporations are allowed to engage in unrelated business activities to the extent the income derived is from the holding of real property and generally as long as the unrelated income is not in excess of 10 percent of annual gross income.[200]

---

[182] IRC § 511(a)(2)(A).
[183] These organizations are encompassed by IRC § 501(c)(3).
[184] IRC § 511(a)(2)(B).
[185] IRC § 501(c)(4) organizations. See *Law of Tax-Exempt Organizations,* Chapter 12.
[186] IRC § 501(c)(5) organizations. See *Law of Tax-Exempt Organizations* § 15.1.
[187] IRC § 501(c)(6) organizations. See *Law of Tax-Exempt Organizations,* Chapter 13.
[188] IRC §§ 501(c)(8) and (10) organizations. See *Law of Tax-Exempt Organizations* § 18.4.
[189] IRC § 501(c)(19) organizations. See *Law of Tax-Exempt Organizations* § 18.10.
[190] See *Law of Tax-Exempt Organizations* §§ 14.13, 28.3.
[191] IRC § 501(c)(7) organizations. See *Law of Tax-Exempt Organizations,* Chapter 14.
[192] IRC § 528 organizations. See *Law of Tax-Exempt Organizations* § 18.3.
[193] IRC § 527 organizations. See *Law of Tax-Exempt Organizations,* Chapter 17.
[194] IRC § 501(c)(1) organizations. See *Law of Tax-Exempt Organizations* § 18.1.
[195] IRC § 501(d) organizations. See *Law of Tax-Exempt Organizations* § 8.7.
[196] IRC § 521 organizations. See *Law of Tax-Exempt Organizations* § 18.11.
[197] IRC § 526. See *Law of Tax-Exempt Organizations* § 18.12.
[198] IRC §§ 501(c)(2) and 501(c)(25) organizations. See *Law of Tax-Exempt Organizations* § 18.2.
[199] See *Law of Tax-Exempt Organizations* § 11.4(c).
[200] IRC § 501(c)(2) (last sentence) and (c)(25)(G).

§ 5.7 UNRELATED BUSINESS RULES

The original concept underlying these rules was that of the *outside* business owned and perhaps operated by a tax-exempt organization. In 1969, however, Congress significantly expanded the reach of these rules by authorizing the IRS to evaluate activities conducted by exempt organizations internally—so-called *inside* activities.

The primary objective of the unrelated business income tax is to eliminate a source of unfair competition for for-profit businesses by placing the unrelated business activities of tax-exempt organizations on the same tax basis as the nonexempt business endeavors with which they compete.[201] Thus, the report of the House of Representatives Committee on Ways and Means that accompanied the 1950 legislation states that the "problem at which the tax on unrelated business income is directed here is primarily that of unfair competition" and the "tax-free status of . . . [nonprofit] organizations enables them to use their profits tax-free to expand operations, while their competitors can expand only with the profits remaining after taxes."[202] The Senate Finance Committee reaffirmed this position in 1976 when it noted that one "major purpose" of the unrelated income tax "is to make certain that an exempt organization does not commercially exploit its exempt status for the purpose of unfairly competing with taxpaying organizations."[203]

The absence or presence of unfair competition, however, is not among the criteria generally used to assess whether the revenue from a particular activity is subject to the unrelated income tax. Thus, it is possible for an exempt organization's activity to be wholly noncompetitive with an activity of a for-profit organization and nonetheless be treated as an unrelated business. For example, in a case finding that the operation of a bingo game by an exempt organization creates unrelated business income, a court observed that the "tax on unrelated business income is not limited to income earned by a trade or business that operates in competition with taxpaying entities."[204] Yet, the IRS and courts increasingly take the concept of unfair competition into account in application of the unrelated income rules.

The term *unrelated trade or business* is defined to mean any trade or business that is regularly carried on, the conduct of which is not substantially related to the exercise or performance by the exempt organization of its exempt purpose or function.[205] The conduct of a business is not substantially related to an organization's exempt purpose solely because the organization may need the income or because of the use the organization makes of the profits derived from the business.

Therefore, absent an exception, gross income of a charitable or other tax-exempt organization is subject to the tax on unrelated business income where three factors are present: it is income from a trade or business, the business is regularly carried on by the organization, and the conduct of the trade or

[201] Reg. § 1.513-1(b).
[202] H.R. Rep. No. 2319, 81st Cong., 2d Sess. (1950) at 36–37. Also S. Rep. No. 2375, 81st Cong., 2d Sess. (1950) at 28–29.
[203] S. Rep. No. 94-938, 94th Cong., 2d Sess. (1976) at 601.
[204] *Clarence LaBelle Post No. 217* v. *United States*, 580 F.2d 270 (8th Cir. 1978), *cert. dismissed*, 439 U.S. 1040 (1978). Cf. IRC § 513(f) (see text accompanied by *infra* note 255).
[205] IRC § 513(a).

business is not substantially related to the organization's performance of its exempt functions.[206]

Thus, in adopting these rules in 1950 and in amplifying them in 1969, Congress has not prohibited commercial ventures by nonprofit organizations nor has it levied taxes only on the receipts of businesses that bear no relation at all to the tax-exempt purposes of nonprofit organizations. Instead, it struck a balance between, as the U.S. Supreme Court phrased it, "its two objectives of encouraging benevolent enterprise and restraining unfair competition."[207]

The unrelated business rules are in a peculiar state of affairs these days. Despite the statutory scheme, the courts are simultaneously developing additional and sometimes different criteria for assessing the presence of unrelated business. It is out of this context that the doctrine of *commerciality* is emerging.[208] The result is considerable confusion about the law in this area and the extensive judgmental leeway on the part of the courts and the IRS in applying it.

A large part of the impetus for revision of the law of unrelated income taxation was the charge by the small business community of unfair competition. The difference between the circumstances in the 1950s and 50 years later is that the competing activities of nonprofit organizations in the 1950s were of the unrelated variety, while as of the turn of the 21st century many of the competing activities are, under existing law, related to exempt functions. Moreover, increasingly, activities that were once thought to be fundraising (nontaxable) functions are being considered unrelated businesses, with the net income subject to taxation.

(ii) Deduction Rules. Generally, the term *unrelated business taxable income* means the gross income derived by an organization from an unrelated trade or business, regularly carried on by the organization, less business deductions that are directly connected with the carrying on of the trade or business.[209] For purposes of computing unrelated business taxable income, both such gross income and business deductions are computed with certain modifications, as discussed as follows.

To be *directly connected with* the conduct of unrelated business, an item of deduction generally must have a proximate and primary relationship to the carrying on of that business. In the case of an organization that derives gross income from the regular conduct of two or more unrelated business activities, unrelated business taxable income is the aggregate of gross income from all such unrelated business activities less the aggregate of the deductions allowed with respect to all these unrelated business activities.[210] Expenses, depreciation, and similar items attributable solely to the conduct of unrelated business are proximately and primarily related to that business and therefore qualify

---

[206] Reg. § 1.513-1(a).

[207] *United States* v. *American College of Physicians*, 475 U.S. 834, 838 (1986).

[208] This doctrine emerged in the Internal Revenue Code when Congress developed the concept of *commercial-type insurance* (IRC § 501(m)). See *Law of Tax-Exempt Organizations* § 22.1.

[209] IRC § 512(a)(1).

[210] Reg. § 1.512(a)-1(a).

for deduction to the extent that they meet the requirements of relevant provisions of the federal tax law.[211]

Where facilities or personnel are used both to carry on exempt functions and to conduct unrelated trade or business, the expenses, depreciation, and similar items attributable to the facilities or personnel (as, for example, items of overhead) must be allocated between the two uses on a reasonable basis. The portion of any such item so allocated to the unrelated trade or business must be proximately and primarily related to that business, and is allowable as a deduction in computing unrelated business income in the manner and to the extent permitted by the federal tax law.[212] In certain cases, gross income is derived from unrelated trade or business that exploits an exempt function. Generally, in these cases, expenses, depreciation, and similar items attributable to the conduct of the exempt function are not deductible in computing unrelated business taxable income. Because these items are incident to a function of the type, which is the chief purpose of the organization to conduct, they do not possess proximate and primary relationship to the unrelated trade or business. Therefore, they do not qualify as being directly connected with that business.[213]

(iii) Trade or Business. The term *trade or business* includes any activity that is carried on for the production of income from the sale of goods or the performance of services.[214] Moreover, an "activity does not lose identity as trade or business merely because it is carried on within a larger aggregate of similar activities or within a larger complex of other endeavors which may, or may not, be related to the exempt purposes of the organization."[215] Additionally, "[w]here an activity carried on for profit constitutes an unrelated trade or business, no part of such trade or business shall be excluded from such classification merely because it does not result in profit."[216]

By enactment of these rules in 1969, Congress confirmed the government's contention that income for a particular activity can be taxed as unrelated business income even where the activity is an integral part of a larger activity that is in furtherance of an exempt purpose. This provision is directed at, but is not confined to, activities of soliciting, selling, and publishing commercial advertising, even where the advertising is published in an exempt organization publication that contains editorial matter related to the exempt purposes of the organization. With this authority, the IRS is empowered to fragment an exempt organization's operation, run as an integrated whole, into its component parts in search of an unrelated trade or business.

This expansive definition of the term *trade or business* embraces nearly every activity of a tax-exempt organization. In this sense, every tax-exempt

---

[211] E.g., IRC §§ 162, 167; Reg. § 1.512(a)-1(b).
[212] Reg. § 1.512(a)-1(c). In *Rensselaer Polytechnic Institute* v. *Commissioner*, 732 F.2d 1058 (2d Cir. 1984), *aff'g* 79 T.C. 967 (1982), the court approved a more liberal test based on the reasonableness of expenses.
[213] Reg. § 1.512(a)-1(d).
[214] IRC § 513(c); Reg. § 1.513-1(b).
[215] *Id.*
[216] *Id.*

organization is viewed as a bundle of activities, each of which is a trade or business. (This definition has nothing to do with whether a particular activity is related or unrelated; there are related businesses and unrelated businesses.) Thus, the IRS is authorized to examine each of the activities in the bundle of activities constituting an exempt organization, in search of unrelated business. Each activity in the bundle can be examined as though it existed wholly independently of the others; an unrelated activity cannot, as a matter of law, be hidden from scrutiny by tucking it in among a host of related activities. This rule is known as the *fragmentation rule.*

Nothing in the statutory definition of the term *trade or business* requires the tax-exempt organization to engage in the activity with a profit motive. The courts, however, increasingly are engrafting the profit motive requirement onto the definition, as the result of a 1987 Supreme Court decision.[217] Thus, for example, the U.S. Tax Court held, in a case involving an activity of a trade association that consistently produced losses, that the ongoing losses are evidence that the activity was not engaged in with the requisite profit motive and therefore is not a business.[218]

Not every activity of an exempt organization that generates a financial return is a trade or business for purposes of the unrelated income tax rules. As the U.S. Supreme Court observed: the "narrow category of trade or business" is a "concept which falls far short of reaching every income or profit-making activity."[219]

Likewise, it is clear that the management of an investment portfolio composed wholly of the manager's own securities does not constitute the carrying on of a trade or business. For example, the Supreme Court held that the mere keeping of records and collection of interest and dividends from securities through managerial attention to the investments is not the operation of a business.[220] On that occasion, the Court sustained the government's position that "mere personal investment activities never constitute carrying on a trade or business."[221] Subsequently, the Supreme Court stated that "investing is not a trade or business."[222] Likewise, the Ninth Circuit Court of Appeals observed

---

[217] *Commissioner of Internal Revenue* v. *Groetzinger,* 480 U.S. 23 (1987).

[218] *National Water Well Association, Inc.* v. *Commissioner,* 92 T.C. 75 (1989).

[219] *Whipple* v. *Commissioner,* 373 U.S. 193, 197, 201 (1963). Also *Blake Construction Co., Inc.* v. *United States,* 572 F.2d 820 (Ct. Cl. 1978); *Monfore* v. *United States,* 77-2 U.S.T.C. ¶ 9528 (Ct. Cl. 1977); *McDowell* v. *Ribicoff,* 292 F.2d 174 (3d Cir. 1961), *cert. denied,* 368 U.S. 919 (1961).

There are three recent cases holding that an activity conducted by a tax-exempt organization does not rise to the level of a *business: American Academy of Family Physicians* v. *United States,* 91 F.3d 1155 (8th Cir. 1996)) (activity not sufficiently extensive over a substantial period of time to be considered a business); *Laborer's International Union of North America* v. *Commissioner,* 82 T.C.M. 158 (2001)) (activity in question did not compete with taxable entities); *Vigilant Hose Company of Emmitsburg* v. *United States,* 2001 U.S.T.C. ¶ 50,458 (D. Md. 2001)) (gambling held an economic activity not rising to the level of a business).

[220] *Higgins* v. *Commissioner,* 312 U.S. 212, 218 (1941).

[221] *Id.* at 215.

[222] *Whipple* v. *Commissioner, supra* note 219, at 202.

that "the mere management of investments . . . is insufficient to constitute the carrying on of a trade or business."[223]

It is also clear that investment activities do not constitute the carrying on of a trade or business in this context. Thus, the IRS ruled that the receipt of income by an exempt employee's trust from installment notes purchased from the employer-settlor is not income derived from the operation of an unrelated trade or business.[224] The IRS noted that the trust "merely keeps the records and receives the periodic payments of principal and interest collected for it by the employer." Consequently, it is clear that mere record keeping and income collection for a person's own investments do not constitute the carrying on of a trade or business.

Therefore, income that is *passive* income is generally not taxed, on the ground that it is not income derived from the active conduct of a trade or business. This exception, contained in the modifications discussed below, generally extends to forms of income such as dividends, interest, annuities, royalties, rents, and capital gain. Also, as discussed as follows, certain other items of income and activities are specifically exempted from the unrelated income tax.

(iv) Regularly Carried On. In determining whether a trade or business from which a particular amount of gross income is derived is *regularly carried on,* within the meaning of the unrelated trade or business rules, regard must be given to the frequency and continuity with which the activities productive of the income are conducted and the manner in which they are pursued. (It is in this context that the statutory law comes the closest to using a general doctrine of commerciality.) This requirement must be applied in light of the purpose of the unrelated business income tax, which is to place exempt organization business activities on the same tax basis as the nonexempt business endeavors with which they compete. Hence, for example, specific business activities of an exempt organization will ordinarily be deemed to be regularly carried on if they manifest a frequency and continuity, and are pursued in a manner, generally similar to comparable commercial activities of nonexempt organizations.[225]

Where income-producing activities are of a kind normally conducted by nonexempt commercial organizations on a year-round basis, the conduct of the activities by an exempt organization over a period of only a few weeks does not constitute the regular carrying on of a trade or business. For example, the operation of a sandwich stand by a hospital auxiliary for only two weeks at a state fair would not be the regular conduct of a trade or business. Similarly, if a charitable organization holds an occasional dance to which the public is admitted for a charge, hiring an orchestra and entertainers for the purpose, such an

---

[223] *Continental Trading, Inc.* v. *Commissioner,* 265 F.2d 40, 43 (9th Cir. 1959), *cert denied,* 361 U.S. 827 (1959). Also *Van Wart* v. *Commissioner,* 295 U.S. 112, 115 (1935); *Deputy* v. *duPont,* 308 U.S. 488, 499 (1940) (concurring opinion); *Commissioner* v. *Burnett,* 118 F.2d 659, 660–661 (5th Cir. 1941); Rev. Rul. 56-511, 1956-2 C.B. 170.
[224] Rev. Rul. 69-574, 1969-2 C.B. 130.
[225] Reg. § 1.513-1(c)(1).

activity would not be a trade or business regularly carried on.[226] The conduct of year-round business activities for one day each week, however, would constitute the regular carrying on of a trade or business. Thus, the operation of a commercial parking lot on one day of each week would be the regular conduct of a trade or business. Where income-producing activities are of a kind normally undertaken by nonexempt commercial organizations only on a seasonal basis, the conduct of such activities by an exempt organization during a significant portion of the season ordinarily constitutes the regular conduct of a trade or business. For example, the operation of a track for horse racing for several weeks of a year would be considered the regular conduct of a trade or business because it is usual to carry on this type of trade or business only during a particular season.[227]

In determining whether intermittently conducted activities are regularly carried on, the manner of conduct of the activities must be compared with the manner in which commercial activities are normally pursued by nonexempt organizations. In general, exempt organization business activities that are engaged in only discontinuously or periodically will not be considered regularly carried on if they are conducted without the competitive and promotional efforts typical of commercial endeavors. For example, the publication of advertising in programs for sports events or music or drama performances will not ordinarily be deemed to be the regular carrying on of business; however, where the nonqualifying sales are not merely casual but are systematically and consistently promoted and carried on by the organization, they meet the requirement of regularity.[228]

Certain intermittent income-producing activities occur so infrequently that neither their recurrence nor the manner of their conduct will cause them to be regarded as trade or business regularly carried on. For example, income-producing or fundraising activities lasting only a short period will not ordinarily be treated as regularly carried on if they recur only occasionally or sporadically. Furthermore, these activities will not be regarded as regularly carried on merely because they are conducted on an annually recurrent basis. Accordingly, income derived from the conduct of an annual dance or similar fundraising event for charity would not be income from a trade or business regularly carried on.[229]

(v) Substantially Related. Gross income derives from *unrelated trade or business* within the meaning of these rules if the conduct of the trade or business that produces the income is not substantially related (other than through the production of funds) to the purposes for which exemption is granted. The presence of this requirement necessitates an examination of the relationship between the business activities that generate the particular income in question—the activities, that is, of producing or distributing the

[226] S. Rep. No. 2375, *supra* note 202, at 106–107.
[227] Reg. § 1.513-1(c)(2)(i).
[228] Reg. § 1.513-1(c)(2)(ii).
[229] Reg. § 1.513-1(c)(2)(iii). E.g., *Orange County Builders Association, Inc. v. United States*, 65-2 U.S.T.C. ¶ 9679 (S.D. Cal. 1965).

goods or performing the services involved—and the accomplishment of the organization's exempt purposes.[230]

Trade or business is *related* to exempt purposes in the relevant sense only where the conduct of the business activity has a causal relationship to the achievement of an exempt purpose (other than through the production of income) and it is *substantially related* only if the causal relationship is a substantial one. Thus, for the conduct of trade or business from which a particular amount of gross income is derived to be substantially related to the purposes for which exemption is granted, the production or distribution of the goods or the performance of the services from which the gross income is derived must contribute importantly to the accomplishment of those purposes.[231] Where the production or distribution of the goods or the performance of the services does not contribute importantly to the accomplishment of the exempt purposes of an organization, the income from the sale of the goods or the performance of the service does not derive from the conduct of related trade or business. Whether activities productive of gross income contribute importantly to the accomplishment of any purpose for which an organization is granted exemption depends in each case on the facts and circumstances involved.[232]

In determining whether activities contribute importantly to the accomplishment of an exempt purpose, the size and extent of the activities involved must be considered in relation to the nature and extent of the exempt function that they purport to serve. Thus, where income is realized by an exempt organization from activities that are in part related to the performance of its exempt functions, but which are conducted on a larger scale than is reasonably necessary for performance of these functions, the gross income attributable to that portion of the activities in excess of the needs of exempt functions constitutes gross income from the conduct of unrelated trade or business.[233]

Gross income derived from charges for the performance of exempt functions does not constitute gross income from the conduct of unrelated trade or business. This principle encompasses income generated by functions such as performances by students enrolled in a school for training children in the performing arts, the conduct of refresher courses to improve the trade skills of members of a trade union, and the presentation of a trade show (at which sales do not occur) for exhibiting industry products by a trade association to stimulate demand for the products.[234]

Ordinarily, gross income from the sale of products that result from the performance of exempt functions does not constitute gross income from the conduct of unrelated trade or business if the products are sold in substantially the same state they are in upon completion of the exempt functions. Thus, in the case of a tax-exempt organization engaged in a program of rehabilitation of handicapped persons, income from sales of articles made by these persons as a part of their rehabilitation training would not be gross income from conduct of unrelated trade

---

[230] Reg. § 1.513-1(d)(1).
[231] E.g., Rev. Rul. 75-472, 1975-2 C.B. 208.
[232] Reg. § 1.513-1(d)(2). E.g., *Huron Clinic Foundation* v. *United States,* 212 F. Supp. 847 (D.S. Dak. 1962).
[233] Reg. § 1.513-1(d)(3).
[234] Reg. § 1.513-1(d)(4)(i).

or business. The income in this case would be from the sale of products whose production contributed importantly to the accomplishment of purposes for which exemption is granted the organization—namely, rehabilitation of the handicapped. Conversely, if a product resulting from an exempt function is utilized or exploited in further business endeavors beyond those reasonably appropriate or necessary for disposition in the state it is in upon completion of exempt functions, the gross income derived therefrom would be from the conduct of unrelated trade or business. Thus, in the case of an experimental dairy herd maintained for scientific purposes by a tax-exempt organization, income from sale of milk and cream produced in the ordinary course of operation of the project would not be gross income from conduct of unrelated trade or business. If the organization were to utilize the milk and cream in the further manufacture of food items such as ice cream and pastries, however, the gross income from the sale of the products would be from the conduct of unrelated trade or business unless the manufacturing activities themselves contribute importantly to the accomplishment of an exempt purpose of the organization.[235]

An asset or facility necessary to the conduct of exempt functions may also be employed in a commercial endeavor. In these cases, the mere fact of the use of the asset or facility in exempt functions does not, by itself, make the income from the commercial endeavor gross income from related trade or business. The test, instead, is whether the activities productive of the income in question contribute importantly to the accomplishment of exempt purposes. Assume, for example, that a tax-exempt museum has a theater auditorium that is specially designed and equipped for showing educational films in connection with its program of public education in the arts and sciences. The theater is a principal feature of the museum and is in continuous operation during the hours the museum is open to the public. If the organization were to operate the theater as an ordinary motion picture theater for public entertainment during the evening hours when the museum was closed, gross income from the operation would be gross income from conduct of unrelated trade or business.[236]

Activities carried on by an organization in the performance of exempt functions may generate goodwill or other intangibles that are capable of being exploited in commercial endeavors. Where an organization exploits such an intangible in commercial activities, the mere fact that the resultant income depends in part on an exempt function of the organization does not make it gross income from related trade or business. In these cases, unless the commercial activities themselves contribute importantly to accomplishing an exempt purpose, the income they produce is gross income from the conduct of unrelated trade or business.[237]

---

[235] Reg. § 1.513-1(d)(4)(ii). As another example, a charitable organization that operated a salmon hatchery as an exempt function was advised by the IRS that it could sell a portion of its harvested salmon stock in an unprocessed condition to fish processors in an untaxed business, although conversion of the fish into and sale of them as salmon nuggets (fish that was seasoned, formed into nugget shape, breaded, and fried) would create unrelated business (Priv. Ltr. Rul. 9320042).
[236] Reg. § 1.513-1(d)(4)(iii).
[237] Reg. § 1.513-1(d)(4)(iv).

The law is replete with court cases and IRS rulings providing illustrations of related and unrelated activities. Colleges and universities can operate dormitories, cafeterias, and bookstores as related activities but can be taxable on travel tours and sports camps. Hospitals may operate gift shops, snack bars, and parking lots as related activities but may be taxable on sales of pharmaceuticals to the general public and on the sale of laboratory testing services to physicians. Museums may, without taxation, sell items reflective of their collections but be taxable on the sale of souvenirs. Trade associations may find themselves taxable on sales of items and particular services to members, while dues and subscription revenue are nontaxable. Fundraising events may be characterized as unrelated activities, particularly when compensation is paid or when the activity is regularly carried on.

(vi) Exceptions. Exempt from the scope of unrelated trade or business is a business in which substantially all of the work in carrying on the business is performed for the organization without compensation.[238] An example involving this exception is an exempt orphanage operating a secondhand clothing store and selling to the general public, where substantially all of the work in running the store is performed by volunteers.[239] As to the scope of this exception, Congress intended to provide an exclusion from the definition of unrelated trade or business only for those unrelated business activities in which the performance of services is a material income-producing factor in carrying on the business, and substantially all such services are performed without compensation.[240]

Also excluded is a business, in the case of a charitable organization or a state college or university, which is carried on by the organization primarily for the convenience of its members, students, patients, officers, or employees.[241] An example involving this exception is a laundry operated by a college for the purpose of laundering dormitory linens and the clothing of students.[242] Further, unrelated trade or business does not include a business that is the selling of merchandise, substantially all of which has been received by the organization as gifts or contributions.[243] This last exception is available for thrift shops that sell donated clothes and books to the general public.[244]

Payments to a tax-exempt organization for lending securities to a broker and the return of identical securities are not items of unrelated business taxable income.[245] For this nontaxation treatment to apply, the security loans must be fully collateralized and must be terminable on five business days' notice by the lending organization. Further, an agreement between the parties must provide for reasonable procedures to implement the obligation of the borrower to

---

[238] IRC § 513(a)(1).

[239] S. Rep. No. 2375, *supra* note 202, at 108. Also *Greene County Medical Society Foundation* v. *United States*, 345 F. Supp. 900 (W.D. Mo. 1972); Rev. Rul. 56-152, 1956-1 C.B. 56.

[240] H.R. Rep. No. 2319, *supra* note 202, at 37, and S. Rep. No. 2375, *supra* note 202, at 107–108. E.g., Rev. Rul. 78-144, 1978-1 C.B. 168.

[241] IRC § 513(a)(2). E.g., Rev. Rul. 69-268, 1969-1 C.B. 160; Rev. Rul. 55-676, 1955-2 C.B. 266.

[242] S. Rep. No. 2375, *supra* note 202, at 108.

[243] IRC § 513(a)(3). E.g., *Disabled Veterans Service Foundation* v. *Commissioner*, 29 T.C.M. 202 (1970).

[244] Rev. Rul. 71-581, 1971-2 C.B. 236.

[245] IRC § 512(a)(5).

furnish collateral to the lender with a fair market value on each business day the loan is outstanding, in an amount at least equal to the fair market value of the security at the close of business on the preceding day.

There are additional exceptions, including the conduct of entertainment at fairs and expositions and of trade shows by exempt organizations, the performance of certain services by hospitals for small hospitals, the conduct of certain bingo games, the sale of low-cost articles, and the rental of mailing lists under certain circumstances. Each of these exceptions is discussed next.

The rule with respect to entertainment at fairs and expositions[246] applies to charitable, social welfare, labor, agricultural, and horticultural organizations that regularly conduct, as a substantial exempt purpose, an agricultural and educational fair or exposition.[247]

The term *unrelated trade or business* does not include qualified *public entertainment activities* of an eligible organization.[248] This term is defined to mean "any entertainment or recreational activity of a kind traditionally conducted at fairs or expositions promoting agricultural and educational purposes, including but not limited to, an activity one of the purposes of which is to attract the public to fairs or expositions or to promote the breeding of animals or the development of products or equipment."[249]

No unrelated income taxation is to occur with respect to the operation of a *qualified public entertainment activity* that meets one of the following conditions: the public entertainment activity is conducted (1) in conjunction with an international, national, state, regional, or local fair or exposition, (2) in accordance with state law, which permits that activity to be conducted solely by an eligible type of exempt organization or by a governmental entity, or (3) in accordance with state law, which permits that activity to be conducted under license for not more than 20 days in any year and which permits the organization to pay a lower percentage of the revenue from this activity than the state requires from other organizations.[250]

The rule with respect to trade show activities[251] applies to labor, agricultural and horticultural organizations, and business leagues, which regularly conduct, as a substantial exempt purpose, shows that stimulate interest in and demand for the products of a particular industry or segment of it.

As respects the third of these items, the IRS maintains that income derived by a tax-exempt hospital from providing services to other exempt hospitals constitutes unrelated business income to the hospital providing the services, on the theory that the providing of services to other hospitals is not an activity that is substantially related to the tax-exempt purpose of the hospital providing the services.[252] Congress acted to reverse this position in the case of small hospitals.

---

[246] IRC § 513(d)(1) and (2).
[247] IRC § 513(d)(2)(C).
[248] IRC § 513(d)(1).
[249] IRC § 513(d)(2)(A).
[250] IRC § 513(d)(2)(B).
[251] IRC § 513(d)(1) and (3).
[252] Rev. Rul. 69-633, 1969-2 C.B. 121.

Where a tax-exempt hospital provides certain services[253] only to other tax-exempt hospitals, there will not be an unrelated business as long as each of the recipient hospitals has facilities to serve not more than 100 inpatients and the services would be consistent with the recipient hospitals' exempt purposes if performed by them on their own behalf.[254]

Bingo game income realized by most tax-exempt organizations is not subject to the unrelated business income tax.[255] This exclusion applies where the bingo game is not conducted on a commercial basis and where the games do not violate state or local laws.

For a charitable, veterans', or other organization, to which contributions are deductible, the term *unrelated business* does not include activities relating to the distribution of low-cost articles if the distribution of the articles is incidental to the solicitation of charitable contributions.[256] A *low-cost article* is one that has a cost, not in excess of $5 (indexed for inflation[257]), to the organization that distributes the item or has the item distributed for it.[258] A *distribution* qualifies under this rule if it is not made at the request of the distributee, it is made without the express consent of the distributee, and the articles that are distributed are accompanied by a request for a charitable contribution from the distributee to the organization and a statement that the distributee may retain the article whether or not a contribution is made.[259]

Also, for a charitable, veterans', or other organization, to which contributions are deductible, the concept of a business does not include exchanging with another similar organization the names and addresses of donors to or members of the organization, or the renting of these lists to another similar organization.[260]

(vii) Modifications. In determining unrelated business taxable income, both gross income derived from an unrelated trade or business and business deductions are computed by taking into account certain *modifications.*[261]

Passive income—namely dividends, interest, payments with respect to securities loans, annuities, royalties, certain rents (generally of real estate), and gain from the disposition of property—is generally excluded from unrelated business taxable income, along with directly connected deductions.[262]

The legislative history of these provisions indicates that Congress believed that *passive* income should not be taxed under these rules "where it is used for exempt purposes because investments producing incomes of these

---

[253] Those described in IRC § 501(e)(1)(A).

[254] IRC § 513(e).

[255] IRC § 513(f).

[256] IRC § 513(h)(1)(A).

[257] See *supra* note 79.

[258] IRC § 513(h)(2).

[259] IRC § 513(h)(3). The IRS is of the view that this exception is not available where the solicitation is in competition with for-profit vendors or where the solicitation is illegal (Tech. Adv. Mem. 9652004).

[260] IRC § 513(h)(1)(B).

[261] IRC § 512(b).

[262] IRC § 512(b)(1), (2), (3), and (5); Reg. § 1.512(b)-1(a)-(d).

types have long been recognized as proper for educational and charitable organizations."[263] The strict definitional classifications of the types of passive income are not dispositive of the question as to their treatment in relation to the modification rules. Rather, "[w]hether a particular item of income falls within any of the modifications . . . shall be determined by all of the facts and circumstances of each case."[264]

The legislative history of the unrelated business income tax provisions is amply clear on the point that Congress, in enacting these modifications, did not intend and has not authorized taxation of the passive receipt of income by exempt organizations, and that a technical satisfaction of the definitional requirements of the terms used in the statute is not required. Thus, the Senate Finance Committee observed in 1950 that the unrelated income tax was to apply to "so much of . . . [organizations'] income as rises from *active business enterprises* which are unrelated to the exempt purposes of the organizations."[265] The Committee added: "The problem at which the tax on unrelated business income is directed is primarily that of unfair competition."[266] Speaking of the exclusion for passive sources of income, the Committee stated:

> Dividends, interest, royalties, most rents, capital gains and losses and *similar items* are excluded from the base of the tax on unrelated income because your committee believes that they are "passive" in character and are not likely to result in serious competition for taxable business having similar income. Moreover, investment-producing incomes of these types have long been recognized as a proper source of revenue for educational and charitable organizations and trusts.[267]

It seems unmistakable that passive income, regardless of type, is properly includable within the exclusions provided by the modifications.[268] (As discussed below, however, there is a recent line of thinking that asserts, at least as to the exclusion for royalties, that the exclusion may be available irrespective of whether the income is passive in nature.[269])

The exclusion relating to gains and losses from the disposition of property does not extend to dispositions of inventory or property held primarily for sale to customers in the ordinary course of business.[270]

There are, however, important exceptions to this general exemption for passive income: (1) income in the form of rent, royalties, and the like from an active business is taxable; that is, merely labeling an item of income as rent, royalty, or the like does not make it tax-free;[271] (2) the unrelated debt-financed

---

[263] H.R. Rep. No. 2319, *supra* note 202, at 38. Also S. Rep. No. 2375, *supra* note 202, at 30–31.
[264] Reg. § 1.512(b)-1.
[265] S. Rep. No. 2375, *supra* note 202, at 27 (emphasis supplied).
[266] *Id.* at 28.
[267] *Id.* at 30–31 (emphasis supplied).
[268] Also see H.R. Rep. No. 2319, *supra* note 202, at 36–38.
[269] See *infra* § (b)(vi).
[270] IRC § 512(b)(5); Reg. § 1.512(b)-1(d).
[271] For the exclusion for rental income to apply, it is necessary that the underlying document be a *lease* rather than a *license* (Priv. Ltr. Rul. 9740032).

income rules[272] override the general exemption for passive income; and (3) interest, annuities, rents, and royalties (but not dividends) from a controlled corporation may be taxable.[273]

Income derived from research for government is excluded, as is income derived from research for anyone in the case of a college, university, or hospital and of fundamental research units.[274] According to the legislative history, *research* includes "not only fundamental research but also applied research such as testing and experimental construction and production."[275] As respects the separate exemption for college, university, or hospital research, it is clear that "funds received for research by other institutions [do not] necessarily represent unrelated business income," such as a grant by a corporation to a foundation to finance scientific research if the results of the research were to be made freely available to the public.[276]

A specific deduction of $1,000[277] makes the first $1,000 of unrelated business income automatically nontaxable. The purpose of this deduction is to eliminate the need for payments of small amounts of tax.

(viii) Partnership Rule.   Generally, a trade or business regularly carried on by a partnership of which an exempt organization is a member is an unrelated trade or business with respect to the organization. In computing its unrelated business taxable income, the organization must (subject to the modifications rules) include its share (whether or not distributed) of the gross income of the partnership from the unrelated trade or business and its share of the partnership deductions directly connected with this gross income.[278]

(b) Unrelated Income Rules as Applied to Fundraising

It is a substantial understatement to say that charitable organizations do not normally regard their fundraising activities as unrelated business endeavors. Yet, unknown to many in the philanthropic community, fundraising practices and the unrelated business rules have been enduring a precarious relationship for years.

Historically, the IRS refrained from applying the unrelated income rules to charitable gift solicitation efforts. In recent years, however, this restraint has been abandoned, with the IRS utilizing the unrelated income rules to characterize the receipts from certain fundraising activities as taxable income. As noted, this use of these rules is one of the means by which the IRS is embarking on regulation of fundraising for charity.

(i) Fundraising as Business.   Many fundraising practices possess the technical characteristics of an unrelated trade or business. Reviewing the criteria for

[272] IRC § 514.
[273] IRC § 512(b)(13).
[274] IRC § 512(b)(7), (8), and (9); Reg. § 1.512(b)-1(f).
[275] H.R. Rep. No. 2319, *supra* note 202, at 37.
[276] S. Rep. No. 2375, *supra* note 202, at 30.
[277] IRC § 512(b)(12).
[278] IRC § 512(c)(1); Reg. § 1.512(c)-1.

unrelated income taxation summarized earlier, some fundraising activities are trades or businesses, regularly carried on, and not efforts that are substantially related to the performance of tax-exempt functions. Further, applying the tests often used by the IRS and the courts, some fundraising endeavors have a commercial counterpart and are being conducted in competition with that counterpart, and are being undertaken with the objective of realizing a profit.[279] Treatment of a fundraising effort as an unrelated business may appear to be a rather strained result, and certainly is not consistent with the intent of Congress when it enacted the unrelated income rules in 1950, but nonetheless can be a logical and technically accurate application of the rules.

Until recently, the IRS avoided application of the unrelated income rules to charitable organizations' fundraising endeavors. Even if the matter was given much thought, the rationale seems to have been that either the fundraising activity was not a trade or business or was not regularly carried on.

The rationale that fundraising activities are not *businesses* was expressed by the Senate Committee on Finance in 1969, when it stated that "where an activity does not possess the characteristics of a trade or business within the meaning of IRC [§] 162, such as when an organization sends out low-cost articles incidental to the solicitation of charitable contributions, the unrelated business income tax does not apply since the organization is not in competition with taxable organizations."[280] An examination of this rationale, however, reveals two elements that substantially undermine its widespread application: the funds received by the organization were in the form of gifts, not payments for the articles or services provided, and the activity was not in competition with commercial endeavors. Either or both of these two elements may be absent in a charitable fundraising endeavor.

Thus, a tax-exempt organization may engage in fundraising efforts that have their commercial counterparts. Some of these activities are sheltered by law from consideration as businesses, such as a business (1) in which substantially all of the work is performed for the organization by volunteers,[281] (2) carried on primarily for the convenience of the organization's members, students, patients, officers, or employees,[282] or (3) which consists of the sale of merchandise, substantially all of which has been received by the organization as gifts.[283] Also, a statute exempts from unrelated business income taxation the receipts from certain types of bingo games.[284]

Perhaps the beginning of serious regard of fundraising activities as businesses can be traced to the enactment of the Tax Reform Act of 1969, where

---

[279] The fact that the "profits" of an activity are destined for use in furtherance of exempt functions cannot be considered in assessing whether an activity is an unrelated one (IRC § 513(a)). One court, addressing an analogous circumstance (application of the "feeder organization" rules of IRC § 502), said of an organization: "That it gave all its profits to an educational institution availeth it nothing in the mundane field of taxation, however much the children in our schools have profited from its beneficence" (*SICO Foundation* v. *United States*, 295 F.2d 924, 925 (Ct. Cl. 1961), *reh'g denied*, 297 F.2d 557 (Ct. Cl. 1962)).

[280] S. Rep. No. 91-522, 91st Cong., 1st Sess. 71 (1969); Reg. § 1.513-1(b).

[281] IRC § 513(a)(1).

[282] IRC § 513(a)(2).

[283] IRC § 513(a)(3). E.g., Rev. Rul. 71-581, 1971-2 C.B. 236.

[284] IRC § 513(f).

Congress authorized the taxation of revenue from the acquisition and publication of advertising in the magazines of tax-exempt organizations. To accomplish this result, Congress codified two rules previously contained in the income tax regulations: it enacted laws that state: (1) the term *trade or business* includes any activity carried on for the production of income from the sale of goods or the performance of services, and (2) an activity of producing or distributing goods or performing services from which gross income is derived does not lose identity as a trade or business merely because it is carried on within a larger aggregate of similar activities or within a larger complex of other endeavors that may or may not be related to the exempt purposes of the organization.[285]

Needless to say, this definition of the term *trade or business* is encompassing. The IRS, for example, observed that the definition of the term "is not limited to integrated aggregates of assets, activities, and good will which comprise businesses" for purposes of other tax rules.[286] In addition to the breadth of this definition, the IRS is, as noted, authorized by statute to examine an exempt organization's activities one by one (rather than as a single bundle of activities) and fragment its operations in search of unrelated business endeavors.[287] As the result of both of these rules, the fundraising practices of charitable organizations are now, more than ever, exposed and thus more vulnerable to the charge that they are unrelated businesses.

The IRS has not been reticent, in recent years, to apply these rules in an expansionist manner. For example, the IRS sought (unsuccessfully) to characterize as an unrelated business the selling by universities of the televising and broadcasting rights in connection with the institutions' athletic events.[288] Also, the IRS attempted (again unsuccessfully, because of overriding action by Congress) to narrowly interpret the rules (discussed previously) portraying certain forms of income as *passive* income to contend that income from the writing of options[289] and from the lending of securities[290] by exempt organizations is taxable as unrelated business income.

More directly, the IRS held that the regular sales of membership mailing lists by an exempt educational organization to colleges and business firms for the production of income is an unrelated trade or business.[291] Furthermore, the IRS[292] and the courts[293] have regarded the regular conduct of bingo games by exempt organizations to be unrelated activities. As noted, Congress subsequently developed partial exemptions for these types of activities,[294] but the point is that the IRS advanced the positions. Other illustrations of fundraising

---

[285] IRC § 513(c); Reg. § 1.513-1 (b).
[286] *Exempt Organizations Handbook* (IRM 7751), at (36)21(1).
[287] See *supra* text accompanied by note 215.
[288] See *Law of Tax-Exempt Organizations* § 26.5(a)(ii).
[289] See *id.* at 937.
[290] See *id.* at 937–942, 955, 969.
[291] Rev. Rul. 72-431, 1972-2 C.B. 281.
[292] Rev. Rul. 59-330, 1959-2 C.B. 153.
[293] *Clarence La Belle Post No. 217* v. *United States, supra* note 204.
[294] See *supra* text accompanied by notes 255 and 260.

that have been considered by the IRS to be unrelated business are special events such as concerts,[295] and golf tournaments and charity balls.[296]

A federal court of appeals held that a solicitation of charitable contributions by means of the mailing of greeting cards to potential contributors did not constitute the conduct of an unrelated trade or business.[297] The case concerned a school that unsuccessfully attempted to raise funds from private foundations and other organizations, so it turned to a program of mailing packages of greeting cards to prospective donors, with information about the school and a request for contributions. An outside firm printed, packaged, and mailed the greeting cards and the accompanying solicitation letter. The court rejected the government's contention that the solicitation was a trade or business, finding that the greeting cards were not being sold but were distributed incidentally to the solicitation of charitable contributions. As noted, the income tax regulations provide that an "activity does not possess the characteristics of a trade or business . . . when an organization sends out low-cost articles incidental to the solicitation of charitable contributions."[298] The government argued that this rule was inapplicable in this case because the funds involved were not gifts, but the court said that to read the law in that narrow manner would "completely emasculate" the exception.[299] The court held that the case turned on the fact that the unrelated income rules were designed to prevent nonprofit organizations from unfairly competing with for-profit companies, and that the school's fundraising program did not give it an "unfair competitive advantage over taxpaying greeting card businesses."[300]

While the decision is undoubtedly a correct one, three troublesome facts should be considered: the IRS pursued the issue in the first instance, even into litigation; the trial court agreed with the IRS position; and the IRS at trial secured a verdict by jury.

The U.S. Court of Claims (now the U.S. Court of Federal Claims) subsequently examined application of the unrelated business rules as they relate to certain fundraising efforts of a national veterans' organization.[301] The case focused on two fundraising practices of the organization. The first was its practice of offering items (premiums) to potential donors as part of its semiannual direct mail solicitation. The premiums, offered in exchange for contributions of $2.00, $3.00, or $5.00, were maps, charts, calendars, and books. The rationale for this use of premiums was that it gained the attention of the recipients so that more initial responses were obtained or, in instances involving prior donors, the level of contributions was upgraded. The second practice was the rental of names on the organization's mailing list to both tax-exempt and

---

[295] Priv. Ltr. Rul. 9712001.

[296] Priv. Ltr. Rul. 200128059.

[297] *The Hope School* v. *United States*, 612 F.2d 298 (7th Cir. 1980).

[298] See *supra* text accompanied by note 280.

[299] *The Hope School* v. *United States, supra* note 297, at 302.

[300] *Id.* at 304. Also *Veterans of Foreign Wars, Department of Missouri, Inc.* v. *United States, supra* note 46. An appeal of this decision was not authorized, with the IRS believing a preferential vehicle on the issue was *Veterans of Foreign Wars, Department of Michigan* v. *Commissioner, supra* note 47, which turned out to be accurate.

[301] *Disabled American Veterans* v. *United States*, 80-2 U.S.T.C. ¶ 9568 (Ct. Cl. 1980).

commercial organizations. The court found that certain of the organization's solicitation activities using premiums constituted a trade or business because they were conducted in a competitive and commercial manner. In making the differentiation, the court ruled that "if the contribution required for any one premium was set at an amount greatly in excess of the retail value of the premiums concerned, a competitive situation would not be present."[302] Because the $2.00 premium items were valued at $0.85 to $1.00 and the $3.00 items were valued at $1.50, the court concluded that there was not any unrelated business activity. But, because the $5.00 premium items were valued at $2.95 to $5.45, the court found the requisite trade or business, noting that the sending of a $5.00 contribution "may well have formed a contract binding . . . [the organization] to furnish the premium item."[303] Also finding that the solicitation was regularly carried on, because of "sufficient similarity to a commercial endeavor,"[304] and was not an activity related to the organization's tax-exempt purposes (notwithstanding the utility of the premiums as attention-getting devices), the court declared the presence of an unrelated business. The court also determined that the rental of the organization's donor list is a trade or business that is regularly carried on and that is not substantially related to the accomplishment of its tax-exempt purposes.[305]

It is clear from these two court cases that the use of premiums as part of a fundraising activity is much less likely to be considered an unrelated trade or business if the items are mailed with the solicitation. That is, where the recipients are informed that the premiums can be retained without any obligation to make a contribution, the activity is not conducted in a competitive manner and hence presumably is not a trade or business. But, as the Court of Claims observed, "[w]hen premiums are advertised and offered only in exchange for prior contributions in stated amounts, the activity takes on much more of a commercial nature."[306]

Subsequently, the full Court of Claims adopted the trial judge's report, with some modifications but none concerning the substantive unrelated business issues. Thus, the position of the entire court in the case was that the amounts received by the veterans' organization from a semiannual solicitations program utilizing premium items constituted unrelated business income and that the amounts received by the organization from the rental of its mailing list also constituted unrelated business income. Consequently, the emerging law appears to be that "when premiums are advertised and offered only in exchange for prior contributions in stated amounts,"[307] the activity becomes a commercial one. If the organization, however "had mailed the premiums with its solicitations and had informed the recipients that the premiums could be

---

[302] *Id.* at 84,855.
[303] *Id.*
[304] *Id.* at 84,856.
[305] This determination upholds the IRS position on the point as stated in Rev. Rul. 72-431, *supra* note 291.
[306] *Disabled American Veterans* v. *United States, supra* note 301, at 84,855.
[307] *Disabled American Veterans* v. *United States*, 650 F.2d 1178, 1187 (Ct. Cl. 1981).

retained without any obligation arising to make a contribution,"[308] the activity would not be a business because it is not a competitive practice.[309]

Armed with this victory out of the Court of Claims, the IRS is applying the rule concerning premium items to situations where organizations distribute greeting cards for the purpose of raising funds. Some charitable groups have engrafted onto their greeting card distribution program some elements that go beyond the mere sending of cards in the hope that a contribution will result. Some of these factors include "suggesting" a minimum contribution, which is equivalent to the retail value of the cards, and invoicing the recipient of the cards for the amount requested. In one instance, an organization entered into a contract with an independent card distributor, which distributed cards to the organization's members. A minimum contribution was requested per box of cards, and follow-up notices were sent to nonresponsive recipients requesting either payment for the cards or their return. The distributor was paid a fixed amount for each box of cards mailed. In another instance, an organization solicited orders for cards at the time it mailed its newsletter. In some years, a commercial supplier processed the orders; in other years, the organization fulfilled the requests. In all instances, a "minimum price" was suggested. Individuals who returned money that was less than the suggested price were invoiced for the difference.

In the first instance, the IRS held that the program involved sale of the cards.[310] The IRS noted that commercial practices were being employed, namely, payment for or return of the cards, and the sending of follow-up notices. Because of these practices, the IRS concluded that the payments were not *gifts* because they were not "voluntary" and because the amount paid exceeded the fair market value of the cards. The receipts were thus characterized as a sale of the cards at their fair market value in a competitive manner. In the second instance, the IRS stressed the same factors. Again, the program was said to be "indistinguishable from normal commercial operations."[311] Therefore, it is clear that the IRS will treat a greeting card distribution program as an unrelated business where there is a "suggested" price equivalent to the retail value of the cards and where the recipients are invoiced for the payment. Where the cards are distributed without any obligation to the recipient and where there is no subsequent invoicing, however, the better view is that the activity is not an unrelated business and any support provided in response to the appeal is a deductible charitable contribution.[312]

---

[308] *Id.* at 1186.

[309] Also *The Hope School* v. *United States, supra* note 297.

[310] Priv. Ltr. Rul. 8203134.

[311] Priv. Ltr. Rul. 8232011.

[312] For an unrelated business to create taxable income, the business must, as noted, be regularly carried on. In both of the two instances discussed, the cards distributed were Christmas cards; the IRS determined that the period within which to measure regularity is the "Christmas season" rather than the full year. Also, in both instances, the organization attempted to cast the greeting card program as a related activity. One organization placed its logo on the cards; the other mailed literature about its programs with the cards. The IRS was not persuaded that either exercise made the card-distribution program a related activity.

This matter developed further when the IRS embarked on litigation characterizing card distribution programs of tax-exempt veterans' organizations as unrelated businesses, in the face of the contention that the programs constitute forms of fundraising. Although the government lost the first case in this series,[313] the U.S. Tax Court subsequently ruled that the revenue derived by a veterans' organization from the distribution of Christmas cards to its members constitutes unrelated business income.[314] While recipients of the boxes of cards were not under any legal obligation to pay for them, the literature was written to convey the impression that the cards cannot be considered unsolicited. This card program involved the organization for about one week of time per month from September through February of each year. The program produced substantial profits, being the second largest revenue source for the organization (behind dues). The veterans' organization contended that the boxes of cards were gifts to its members (in the nature of premiums) and that the monies sent to it from the members also were gifts. It rejected the thought that it was *selling* the cards and thus that a *business* was involved. The organization also contended that the activity was not regularly carried on (and therefore not taxable) and that the card dissemination was a related activity in that it promoted comradeship among its members. In finding the activity to be a business, the court concluded that the organization had a profit motive and that the card program constituted the "sale of goods," noting that 85 to 90 percent of those who paid for the cards paid precisely the amount requested ($2.00 or $3.00, depending on the year involved). It further found that the exception in the tax regulations for *low-cost articles*[315] was inapplicable, in part because of its rejection of the thought that there was any solicitation of contributions. The card program was held to be regularly carried on because of its extent on a seasonal basis and taxable because it was not related to the advancement of the organization's purposes.

Thus, since the raising of funds by a charitable organization is not in itself an exempt function, many types of fundraising activities are vulnerable to the claim that they are unrelated trades or businesses.

(ii) Regularly Carried-on Test.   In many instances, the only rationale that precludes taxation of the net income derived from a fundraising effort is the fact that the fundraising is not regularly carried on.

The rationale that fundraising activities are not taxable businesses because they are not regularly carried on finds support in the early IRS literature. The basic position of the IRS is that "exempt organization business activities which are engaged in only discontinuously or periodically will not be considered regularly carried on if they are conducted without the competitive and promotional efforts typical of commercial endeavors."[316] As noted earlier, the operation of a sandwich stand by a hospital auxiliary for two weeks at

---

[313] *Veterans of Foreign Wars, Department of Missouri, Inc. v. United States, supra* note 47.
[314] *Veterans of Foreign Wars, Department of Michigan* v. *Commissioner, supra* note 47.
[315] See *supra* text accompanied by note 258.
[316] *Exempt Organizations Handbook, supra* note 286, at (36)30(2)(d).

a state fair is not the regular conduct of a trade or business,[317] while the operation of a parking lot for commercial purposes one day each week on a year-round basis is the regular conduct of a trade or business.[318] Thus, the IRS observed that an "annually recurrent dance or similar fundraising event for charity would not be regular since it occurs so infrequently."[319]

In one case, the U.S. Tax Court concluded that the annual fundraising activity of a charitable organization, consisting of the presentation and sponsoring of a professional vaudeville show one weekend per year, was not regularly carried on.[320] The court observed: "The fact that an organization seeks to insure the success of its fundraising venture by beginning to plan and prepare for it earlier should not adversely affect the tax treatment of the income derived from the venture."[321] Indeed, the court went on to note that the IRS "apparently believes that all fundraisers of exempt organizations are conducted by amateurs in an amateurish manner. We do not believe that this is, nor should be, the case. It is entirely reasonable for an exempt organization to hire professionals in an effort to insure the success of a fundraiser. . . ."[322]

Just as many fundraising practices are technically trades or businesses, however, so are many regularly carried on. Inasmuch as the other rationales for avoiding unrelated income taxation (principally, the contention that the activity is substantially related or that the income is passive) are unlikely to apply in the fundraising context, it is today quite possible for a fundraising activity to be deemed a trade or business that is regularly carried on and an undertaking that is not substantially related to the exercise of a charitable organization's exempt purposes.

There are several instances of the assumption by the IRS of this position, and they are multiplying. One is a 1979 private letter ruling, concerning a case involving a religious organization that conducted, as its principal fundraising activity, bingo games and related concessions.[323] Players were charged a fixed amount for the use of bingo cards, the games were held on three nights each week, and the receipts from and expenses of the games were substantial. The IRS concluded that the "bingo games constitute a trade or business with the general public, the conduct of which is not substantially related to the exercise or the performance by the organization of the purpose for which it was organized other than the use it makes of the profits derived from the games."[324]

[317] Id. at (36)30(2)(a).
[318] Id. at (36)30(2)(b).
[319] Id. at (36)30(2)(f). A charity may be found to be engaged in an unrelated business for conducting this type of fundraising event, however, where it is done for the benefit of another charity (Rev. Rul. 75-201, 1975-1 C.B. 164).
[320] Suffolk County Patrolmen's Benevolent Association, Inc. v. Commissioner, 77 T.C. 1314 (1981).
[321] Id. at 1324.
[322] Id. at 1323.
[323] Priv. Ltr. Rul. 7946001. Also, KJ's Fund Raisers, Inc. v. Commissioner, 74 T.C.M. 669 (1997); P.L.L. Scholarship Fund v. Commissioner, 82 T.C. 196 (1984); Piety, Inc. v. Commissioner, 82 T.C. 193 (1984).
[324] The organization was unable to utilize the exemption from unrelated income taxation afforded by IRC § 513(f) because, under the law of the state in which it is organized (Texas), the bingo games constituted, at that time, an illegal lottery. This quote does not include the finding of the IRS that this gambling activity was also regularly carried on. In a subsequent case, on similar facts, the IRS and the charitable organization stipulated that the gambling operations,

The IRS is giving an expansive reading to the rules concerning activities that are regularly carried on, no longer confining the analysis to the period of time the event actually took place. The IRS also takes into account the amount of time the organization prepared for the activity (*preparatory time*) and the time following the activity and still associated with it (*winding-down time*). An activity may be found to be regularly carried on when preparatory time and winding-down time are considered, but not when only the time of the event is evaluated. One court has rejected the view that preparatory time is to be regarded for this purpose.[325] The IRS remains in disagreement with these holdings and is continuing to litigate the issue.[326]

(iii) Private Benefit. It is common for a charitable organization to provide to prospective donors information about the tax and other financial implications of a contribution. This is particularly the case in the context of planned giving.[327] Yet, case law suggests that the provision of services of this nature rises to the level of impermissible private benefit, which would endanger the tax-exempt status of the organization.

A fundamental precept of the federal tax law concerning charitable organizations is that they may not, without imperiling their tax-exempt status, be operated in a manner that causes persons to derive a private benefit from their operations.[328] Yet the provision of services that amount to personal financial and tax planning—an essential element of the appreciated property and planned gift techniques—may not be considered exempt activities but rather the provision of private benefit. While it would seem nearly inconceivable to contend that, when a charitable organization works with a donor to effect a major gift that will generate significant tax savings for the donor by reason of a charitable contribution deduction, the organization is jeopardizing its tax-exempt status because it is providing a *private benefit*, this conclusion was the import of this case.

The case concerned the tax status of an organization that engaged in financial counseling by providing tax planning services (including charitable giving considerations) to wealthy individuals referred to it by subscribing religious organizations. The counseling given by the organization consisted of advice on how a contributor might increase current or planned gifts to religious organizations, including the development of a financial plan that, among other objectives, resulted in a reduction of federal income and estate taxes.

conducted in the name of fundraising, were regularly carried on for purposes of unrelated income taxation (*Executive Network Club* v. *Commissioner,* 69 T.C.M. 1680 (1995)).

[325] *National Collegiate Athletic Association* v. *Commissioner,* 914 F.2d 1417 (10th Cir. 1990). The view was also dismissed in *Suffolk County Patrolmen's Benevolent Association, Inc.* v. *Commissioner, supra* note 320.

[326] Action on Decision No. 1991-015; Tech. Adv. Mem. 9509002 and 9147007. In one of these instances, a tax-exempt organization sponsored a concert series open to the public occupying two weekends each year, one in the spring and one in the fall. The preparation and ticket solicitation for each of the concerts usually occupies up to six months. Taking into account the preparatory time involved, the IRS concluded that the concerts were unrelated business activities that were regularly carried on (Tech. Adv. Mem. 9712001).

[327] The concepts of these and other aspects of planned giving are discussed in Hopkins, *supra* note 12, particularly Chapters 3, 8, and 11–17.

[328] Reg. §§ 1.501(a)-1(c) and 1.501(c) (3)-1(c)(2).

The position of the IRS was that this organization could not qualify for federal income tax exemption because it served the private interests of individuals by enabling them to reduce their tax burden. The organization's position was that it was merely engaging in activities that tax-exempt organizations may themselves undertake without loss of their tax exemption. The court agreed with the government, finding that the organization's "sole financial planning activity, albeit an exempt purpose furthering . . . [exempt] fundraising efforts, has a nonexempt purpose of offering advice to individuals on tax matters that reduces an individual's personal and estate tax liabilities."[329] As the court dryly stated, "We do not find within the scope of the word charity that the financial planning for wealthy individuals described in this case is a charitable purpose."[330]

In this opinion, the court singled out the planned giving techniques for portrayal as methods that give rise to unwarranted private benefit. Thus, the court observed:

> For example, when petitioner advises a contributor to establish a charitable unitrust gift, the contributor ultimately forfeits the remainder. Nevertheless, this loss is voluntarily exchanged for considerable lifetime advantages. Unitrusts generate substantial income and estate and gift tax benefits, such as retained income for life, reduced capital gains tax, if any, on the exchange of appreciated investments, favorable tax rates for part or all of the income payments on certain investments, and lower probate costs. Consequently, there are real and substantial benefits inuring to the contributors by the petitioner's activities.[331]

Concluded the court: "We think the tax benefits inuring to the contributors are . . . substantial enough to deny exemption."[332]

Subsequently, the Tax Court again evinced a lack of understanding of fundraising for charity and thus issued an opinion that raised anew questions about the imposition of the unrelated income tax in the fundraising context.[333] At issue was the tax status of a membership organization for citizens' band radio operators that used insurance, travel, and discount plans to attract new members. The organization contended that it was only doing what many tax-exempt organizations do to raise contributions, analogizing these activities to fundraising events such as rallies and dinners. The court rejected this argument, defining a "fundraising event" as a "single occurrence that may occur on limited occasions during a given year and its purpose is to further the exempt activities of the organization."[334] These events were contrasted with activities that "are continuous or continual activities which are certainly more pervasive a part of the organization than a sporadic event and [that are] . . . an end in

---

[329] *Christian Stewardship Assistance, Inc.* v. *Commissioner,* 70 T.C. 1037, 1940 (1978).
[330] *Id.* at 1043.
[331] *Id.* at 1044.
[332] *Id.*
[333] *U.S. CB Radio Association, No. 1, Inc.* v. *Commissioner,* 42 T.C. M. 1441 (1981).
[334] *Id.* at 1444.

themselves."[335] A wide variety of fundraising methods other than special events are "continuous" and "pervasive," and are intended "to further the exempt activities of the organization." Also, no legitimate fundraising activity is an end in itself, yet many tax-exempt organizations and institutions have major, ongoing fundraising and development programs that are permanent fixtures among the totality of the entities' activities. This decision, then, is another in a series of cases that is forming the foundation for the contention that certain types of fundraising endeavors are unrelated businesses.

In a 1983 case, the Tax Court concluded that a novel "fundraising" scheme was an unrelated trade or business. A nonprofit school consulted with a tax-shelter investments firm in search of fundraising methods, with the result being a program in which individuals purchased various real properties from the school, which the school simultaneously purchased from third parties; both the sellers and the buyers were clients of the investments firm. There were about 22 of these transactions during the years at issue, from which the school received income reflecting the difference between the sales prices and the purchase prices. Finding the "simultaneous purchase and sale of real estate . . . not substantially related to the exercise or performance of [the school's] . . . exempt function," the court held that the net income from the transactions was unrelated taxable income.[336]

In another case that same year, the Tax Court held that an admittedly religious organization was not tax-exempt because it engaged in a substantial nonexempt purpose, which was the counseling of individuals on the purported tax benefits accruing to those who become ministers of the organization.[337] The court found the organization, which went by the name of The Ecclesiastical Order of the Ism of Am, akin to a "commercial tax service, albeit within a narrower field (i.e., tax benefits to ministers and churches) and a narrower class of customers (i.e., petitioner's ministers)," and thus said that it served private purposes.[338] The many detailed discussions in the organization's literature of ways to maximize tax benefits led the court to observe that "although petitioner may well advocate belief in the God of Am, it also advocates belief in the God of Tax Avoidance."[339] In words that have considerable implications for fundraising for charitable purposes generally, the court wrote that a "substantial nonexempt purpose does not become an exempt purpose simply because it promotes the organization in some way."[340] The court somewhat recognized the larger meaning of its opinion and attempted to narrow its scope by noting that "[w]e are not holding today that any group which discusses the tax consequences of donations to and/or expenditures of its organization is in danger of losing or not acquiring tax-exempt status."[341]

---

[335] *Id.*

[336] *Parklane Residential School, Inc.* v. *Commissioner*, 45 T.C.M. 988 (1983).

[337] *The Ecclesiastical Order of Ism of Am, Inc.* v. *Commissioner*, 80 T.C. 833 (1983), *aff'd*, 740 F.2d 967 (6th Cir. 1984), *cert. denied*, 471 U.S. 1015 (1985).

[338] *Id.* 80 T.C. at 839. (See also *Universal Life Church, Inc.* v. *United States*, 87-2 U.S.T.C. ¶ 9617 (Ct. Cl. 1987).)

[339] *Id.* at 840.

[340] *Id.* at 841.

[341] *Id.* at 842.

The Tax Court revisited this theme early in 1984, holding that an organization, the membership of which is religious missions, was not entitled to tax-exempt status as a religious organization because it engaged in the substantial nonexempt purpose of providing financial and tax advice.[342] Once again, the court was heavily influenced by the recent rush of cases before it, concerning, in the words of the court, "efforts of taxpayers to hide behind the cover of purported tax-exempt religious organizations for significant tax avoidance purposes."[343] As the court saw the facts of the case, each member "mission" was the result of individuals attempting to create churches involving only their families to "convert after-tax personal and family expenses into tax deductible charitable contributions";[344] the central organization provided sample incorporation papers, tax seminars, and other forms of tax advice and assistance to those creating the missions. Consequently, the court was persuaded that the "pattern of tax avoidance activities which appears to be present at the membership level, combined with . . . [the organization's] admitted role as a tax advisor to its members," justified the conclusion that the organization was ineligible for tax exemption.[345]

(iv) Fundraising and Program Activities. Part of the dilemma in this area stems from *functional accounting,* a process adopted by the IRS several years ago and imposed on charitable organizations as part of the annual information return preparation and filing process. This method of accounting separates a charitable organization's functions into three categories: program, administration, and fundraising.[346] The dilemma exists because many individuals—including some in law and fundraising—continue to regard fundraising as part of program because its purpose is to promote the organization's activities in some fashion. This misunderstanding is in part fueled by the distinctions in law—accounting notwithstanding—simply between exempt functions and nonexempt functions. Because it is inconceivable that fundraising is a nonexempt function, it must be an exempt function—so the reasoning goes. From that position, it is an easy jump in logic to the conclusion that fundraising is the same as program (as neither is a nonexempt function), but such a conclusion is erroneous.

From this perspective, the tax consequences where a small charity holds an annual car wash, a symphony hosts an annual theater party, a hospital sponsors an annual ball, or a university maintains a planned-giving program are unclear. In each of these cases, functional accounting dictates that the expenses associated with those activities be allocated to *fundraising.* But do these activities constitute *program* or are they *nonexempt functions?* In the four illustrations, the activities are not programs. They are nonexempt functions, and as to the latter they are insubstantial activities. In many cases, then, the tax aspects of fundraising come down to this: Is the fundraising activity substantial

---

[342] *National Association of American Churches* v. *Commissioner,* 82 T.C. 18 (1984).
[343] *Id.* at 29–30.
[344] *Id.* at 31.
[345] *Id.* at 32.
[346] This three-part classification of functions of charitable organizations is reflected on the annual information return nearly all of them must file (see *infra* § 9(d)).

(in relation to the organization's other and overall activities) or is it a business? Special-event fundraising is likely to be the prime candidate for classification as a business, particularly where the event has a commercial counterpart. Some examples of this include car washes, bake sales, games, theater parties, dinner parties, and dances. As noted, it is the fact that these events are not regularly carried on that usually spares them taxation.[347]

Consequently, most fundraising efforts by charitable organizations will escape unrelated income taxation. Those that are taxed are held frequently, are operated in a commercial manner, and utilize paid assistance. Nonetheless, this still leaves the fact that fundraising is not *program* and is a *nonexempt function*. Two other principles of tax law apply in this setting. One is that the existence of a single nonexempt purpose, if substantial in nature, will destroy a tax exemption regardless of the number or importance of truly exempt purposes.[348] The other is that a tax-exempt organization must serve public purposes and will lose its exemption if it serves private purposes.[349] An illustration of the latter principle in the fundraising context is discussed above.[350]

Thus, the IRS has been embarking on a new approach for regulating charitable fundraising, by characterizing it as unrelated business,[351] and the courts are trending toward a line of thinking that equates charitable giving and associated tax planning with private benefit, thereby causing denial or loss of tax exemption. Either way, the basic rules governing federal income tax exemption and unrelated business activity are being applied in relation to fundraising endeavors, so that fundraising charitable groups are facing a new wave of regulation, with their exempt status or unrelated income taxation as the government's leverage.

The foregoing analysis notwithstanding, the U.S. Claims Court became the first court to squarely face and analyze the difference, for tax purposes, between a fundraising activity and a business activity. The specific issue before this court was whether income, received by a charitable organization as the result of assignments to it of dividends paid in connection with insurance coverages purchased by members of a related professional association at group rates, was to be taxed as unrelated income. The court ruled that the program constituted fundraising, not a commercial venture.[352] While, as discussed,[353] this holding was subsequently overturned, the opportunity was presented to develop a contrast between fundraising efforts and business undertakings.

At the outset, the court wrote that, where the tax-exempt organization involved in an unrelated income tax case is a charitable one, the "court must distinguish between those activities that constitute a trade or business and those that are merely fundraising."[354] Admittedly, said the court, this distinction is

---

[347] See *supra* § (b)(ii).

[348] See *Law of Tax-Exempt Organizations* § 4.6.

[349] *Id.,* Chapter 19.

[350] See *supra* text accompanied by note 329.

[351] The Internal Revenue Manual § 331(2), as amended in 1982, directs Internal Revenue Service agents to, as part of their examination of public charities, "[c]onsider the [charities'] method of raising funds and whether such income is subject to unrelated business income tax."

[352] *American Bar Endowment* v. *United States,* 84-1 U.S.T.C. ¶ 9204 (Cl. Ct. 1984).

[353] See *infra* text accompanying notes 360–365.

[354] *American Bar Endowment* v. *United States, supra* note 352 at 83,350.

not always readily apparent, as "[c]haritable activities are sometimes so similar to commercial transactions that it becomes very difficult to determine whether the organization is raising money 'from the sale of goods or the performance of services' [the statutory definition of a *business* activity[355]] or whether the goods or services are provided merely as an incident to a fundraising activity."[356] Nonetheless, the court held that the test is whether the activity in question is "operated in a competitive, commercial manner," which is a "question of fact and turns upon the circumstances of each case."[357] "At bottom," the court wrote, "the inquiry is whether the actions of the participants conform with normal assumptions about how people behave in a commercial context" and "[i]f they do not, it may be because the participants are engaged in a charitable fundraising activity."[358]

In the specific case and in application of these rules, the court stressed five elements: (1) the activity under examination was a pioneering idea at its inception, (2) the activity was originally devised as a fundraising effort and has been so presented since then, (3) the "staggering amount of money" and "astounding profitability" that are generated by the activity,[359] (4) the degree of the organization's candor toward its members and the public concerning the operation and revenue of the program, and (5) the fact that the activity is operated with the consent and approval of the association's membership. Concerning the third element, substantial profits and consistently high profit margins are usually cited as reasons for determining that the activity involved is a business. In this case, however, the amounts of money involved were so great that they could not be rationalized in conventional business analysis terms; the only explanation that was suitable to the court was that the funds were the result of successful charitable fundraising.

Despite the findings of the lower courts, the U.S. Supreme Court held that the provision of group insurance policies, underwritten by major insurance companies, by the American Bar Endowment (ABE), a charitable organization, to its members constituted the carrying on of an unrelated trade or business.[360] The Court noted that the organization negotiated premium rates with insurers, selected the insurers that provided the coverage, solicited its membership, collected the premiums, transmitted the premiums to the insurer, maintained files on each policyholder, answered members' questions concerning insurance policies, and screened claims for benefits. In finding the activity to be a business, the Court observed that the ABE "prices its insurance to remain competitive with the rest of the market," the Court "can easily view this case as a standard example of monopoly pricing," and the case "presents an example of precisely the sort of unfair competition that Congress intended to prevent."[361] The Court

---

[355] IRC § 513(c).

[356] *American Bar Endowment* v. *United States, supra* note 352 at 83,350. Indeed, the court observed that, "[o]ver the years, charities have adopted fund-raising schemes that are increasingly complex and sophisticated, relying on many business techniques" (*id.*).

[357] *Id.* at 83,351. Also *Disabled American Veterans* v. *United States, supra* note 301.

[358] *Id.*

[359] *Id.* at 83,351–83,352.

[360] *United States* v. *American Bar Endowment, supra* note 13.

[361] *Id.* at 112–114.

concluded that the "only valid argument in ABE's favor, therefore, is that the insurance program is billed as a fundraising effort."[362] But the Court summarily rejected this contention with a rather peculiar observation: "That fact, standing alone, cannot be determinative, or any exempt organization could engage in a tax-free business by 'giving away' its product in return for a 'contribution' equal to the market value of the product."[363] That, however, is not the state of the law.[364] The dissent concluded that the provision of insurance to the ABE members was not competitive with commercial enterprises and that the program was "operated as a charitable fundraising endeavor."[365]

As contemporary fundraising techniques have become more intricate and creative, so too have applications of the unrelated business income rules in this setting. This has been in part due to the increasing activism of the IRS in the charitable fundraising context, as illustrated by the intense scrutiny now being accorded by the IRS to the field of special events and corporate sponsorships.[366] This field, however, is only one of many in the realm of charitable fundraising concerning the IRS and the courts.

(v) Principal–Agent Relationships. Some charitable organizations, in an attempt to minimize their exposure to the unrelated business income tax, contract with independent companies for services pertaining to fundraising that might be considered unrelated activities if the organizations were to conduct the activities themselves. Often, this approach is successful, but it can backfire if the company is regarded as an agent of the charity. (The functions of an agent are regarded in the law as those of the principal.) In this instance, the activities of the agent are attributed to the charitable organization (the principal) for the purpose of calculating the extent of the total activities to, in turn, determine whether the bundle of activities constitutes a business that has been regularly carried on. One court adopted this position of the IRS, concluding that a publishing company operated as an agent of a charitable organization, so that the agent's advertising solicitation services were deemed to be activities of the charity.[367]

(vi) Royalty Exception. Another current creative undertaking by fundraising charitable organizations is to attempt to structure an activity so that the income generated by the activity can be considered a tax-free royalty.[368] Because the term *royalty* is not defined in the Internal Revenue Code or the tax regulations, the scope of the term has been the subject of considerable litigation. There are essentially three ways to define the boundaries of what is a royalty,

---

[362] *Id.* at 115.

[363] *Id.*

[364] *Disabled American Veterans* v. *United States, supra* note 301.

[365] *United States* v. *American Bar Endowment, supra* note 13 at 125. Subsequent revisions in this program led the IRS to conclude that it was no longer an unrelated business (Priv. Ltr. Rul. 8725056).

[366] See *infra* § 16.

[367] *National Collegiate Athletic Association* v. *Commissioner,* 92 T.C. 456 (1989), *aff'd, supra* note 325.

[368] See *supra* text accompanied by notes 262–269.

which basically is a payment for the right to use an item of intangible property: (1) as only a payment that is a form of investment income, when no services may be provided by the royalty recipient; (2) as only a payment that is a form of passive income, when an insubstantial amount of services may be provided by the royalty recipient; or (3) as any payment that constitutes a royalty irrespective of the extent of services the recipient of the royalty may provide.

The position of the IRS was, for some time, that a royalty is excluded from unrelated business income taxation only when it satisfies the first of these definitions, that is, is investment income. Thus, the IRS asserted that if a charitable or other type of tax-exempt organization is actively participating in the undertaking that generates the income (such as promoting a product or service to its membership or making public endorsements), the organization is part of a joint venture and the exclusion for royalties is unavailable. This view has been dramatically rejected by the U.S. Tax Court, which has held that, to be excludable from taxation, the income need only be a payment for the use of one or more valuable intangible property rights.[369] In one instance, that court held that revenue from the rental of mailing lists (where the statutory exception[370] was unavailable) was properly treated as a royalty.[371] In another, that court extended this analysis to income received from an affinity card program.[372]

The core of this interpretation of the royalty exception by the Tax Court is that, although Congress may have believed that royalties and similar types of excluded income are passive,[373] that does not necessarily mean that they must always, in fact, be passive.[374] Stated in the reverse, this view holds that a statutorily classified item of income excludable from tax remains excludable irrespective of whether the income is derived from an investment, is passive, or is generated from the active conduct of a trade or business.

As the consequence of an appeal of the Tax Court's findings, an opinion issued by the U.S. Court of Appeals for the Ninth Circuit in mid-1996 represents the most authoritative court analysis of this issue. Reviewing dictionary definitions of the term *royalty*, this appellate court concluded that a royalty is a payment for the right to use intangible property. In a sharp departure from the Tax Court approach, however, the court added that a royalty "cannot include

---

[369] *Disabled American Veterans* v. *Commissioner*, 94 T.C. 60 (1990), *rev'd on other grounds*, 942 F.2d 309 (6th Cir. 1991).

[370] See *supra* text accompanied by notes 255 and 260.

[371] *Sierra Club, Inc.* v. *Commissioner*, 65 T.C.M. 2582 (1993) ("*Sierra Club I*").

[372] *Sierra Club, Inc.* v. *Commissioner*, 103 T.C. 307 (1994) ("*Sierra Club II*"). Also *Oregon State University Alumni Ass'n, Inc.* v. *Commissioner*, 71 T.C.M. 1935 (1996); *Alumni Ass'n of the University of Oregon, Inc.* v. *Commissioner*, 71 T.C.M. 2093 (1996); *Mississippi State University Alumni, Inc.* v. *Commissioner*, 71 T.C.M. 458 (1997) (appeal not taken). The initial view of the IRS was that affinity card program revenues are not taxable because they are passive royalty income (Priv. Ltr. Rul. 8747066), but that determination was withdrawn (Priv. Ltr. Rul. 8823109).

[373] See *supra* quotation accompanied by note 267.

[374] This view is based on additional language in the committee reports indicating that the exception for dividends, interest, annuities, royalties, and the like "applies not only to investment income [a concept broader than passive income], but also to such items as business interest on overdue open accounts receivable" (S. Rep. No. 2375, *supra* note 202, at 108; H.R. Rep. No. 2139, *supra* note 202, at 110).

compensation for services rendered by the owner of the property."[375] Thus, the Ninth Circuit adopted the second of the definitions as to the scope of the royalty exception.[376]

This definition is a compromise between the position taken by tax-exempt organizations and that of the IRS. The court of appeals wrote that, to the extent the Service "claims that a tax-exempt organization can do *nothing* to acquire such fees," the agency is "incorrect."[377] Yet, "to the extent that . . . [an exempt organization] appears to argue that a 'royalty' is any payment for the use of a property right—such as a copyright—regardless of any additional services that are performed in addition to the owner simply permitting another to use the right at issue, we disagree."[378]

The Ninth Circuit's reading of the facts concerning the mailing list rentals favored the exempt organization in the litigation, which had contracted out many of the services involved in marketing and renting its lists. The court found that the organization "did nothing more than collect a fee" for these rentals.[379] The income received by the organization from the list rentals was held to be royalty income and not payment for services.[380] The circumstances concerning the affinity card program were afforded far different treatment. The appellate court disapproved of the way in which the Tax Court had resolved certain factual issues, namely, in favor of the exempt organization involved. This court also strongly suggested that the affinity card program fees were not excludable royalties, because of the extent of services provided.[381]

The Tax Court decided the affinity card program case in mid-1999.[382] This case, therefore, turned on whether the exempt organization involved was rendering services in connection with the program. The organization, of course, had argued that its name, logo, and mailing list are intangible assets, and that pursuant to the agreement with the card services company it had licensed those properties to the company in exchange for payments that constitute royalties. The IRS asserted that the organization, in this connection, was in a business involving "marketing," "sponsoring," "promoting," and/or "endorsing" the credit card program. The government contended that the contracts entered into by the exempt organization were for services only and that the resulting income was not royalty income because the organization was being paid for these services.

---

[375] *Sierra Club, Inc.* v. *Commissioner*, 86 F.3d 1526, 1532 (9th Cir. 1996) ("*Sierra Club III*"). This element of the definition of a royalty is consistent with the long-time stance of the IRS that "royalties do not include payments for personal services" (Rev. Rul. 81-178, 1981-2 C.B. 135).

[376] There is precedent for this approach (*Disabled American Veterans* v. *United States, supra* note 307; *Fraternal Order of Police, Illinois State Troopers Lodge No. 41* v. *Commissioner*, 833 F.2d 717 (7th Cir. 1987); *Disabled American Veterans* v. *Commissioner, supra* note 369 (6th Cir.); *Texas Farm Bureau* v. *United States*, 53 F.3d 120 (5th Cir. 1995).

[377] *Sierra Club III, supra* note 375, at 1535 (emphasis in original).

[378] *Id.*

[379] *Id.* at 1536.

[380] Consequently, *Sierra Club I, supra* note 371, was affirmed by *Sierra Club III, supra* note 375.

[381] Consequently, *Sierra Club III, supra* note 372, was reversed by *Sierra Club III, supra* note 375, and the case remanded so that the Tax Court could once again make findings of fact and conclusions of law, this time following a trial rather than by grant of summary judgment.

[382] *Sierra Club, Inc.* v. *Commissioner*, 77 T.C.M. 1569 (1999) ("*Sierra Club IV*").

The Tax Court focused on the agreement between the organization and the card company. The provisions regulating the company's use of the exempt organization's name and marks were seen as being in the contract to preserve the organization's property interests in those items. The right to advise and consent with regard to the marketing material prepared by the company was viewed as a right intended to safeguard the organization's name, marks, logo, and other intangibles used in the marketing. Thus, the financial consideration the organization received under this agreement was held to be, at least in part, consideration for the use of valuable intangible property, and as such constituted royalties.

The government asserted that the exempt organization provided seven types of services, all as part of the contention that it was in the business of marketing the credit card program to its members. None of these assertions was successful. One of these sets of asserted services was the organization's control over the marketing materials by way of its power to negate. Also, the organization was provided monthly accountings by the card company. Nonetheless, the court was moved by the fact that the organization did not receive a fee for any marketing activities and did not share in any economics realized by the company in its expenditures made in carrying out its marketing responsibilities.

The court expressly held that the exempt organization's rights in this regard were not inconsistent with a royalty arrangement. These rights were characterized as only evidencing the organization's concern with "protecting the worth of its property interest in its good name and marks."[383] It was held not to be an indirect method of putting the organization in the business of marketing.

The court rejected the idea that the credit card was being offered by the organization as a member service. The bank involved was the financial institution that extended credit to the members, and it was the card company's marketing efforts that brought the possibility of the credit card and certain other services to the attention of the members. Mere endorsement of the program was held not to be a service provided by the organization.

Although the card company advertised in the exempt organization's publications, it was not given any financial preferences. The company used the organization's nonprofit mail permit on one occasion but the court was convinced that that was a mistake. The license agreement, requiring the organization to "cooperate" with the company, was found by the court to "not [be] an agreement to endorse or promote the credit card program beyond the endorsement that necessarily results from [the organization's] license of its logo, name, and the other intangibles here in question."[384]

In short, none of the receipts of this exempt organization were in consideration for services provided by the organization as part of the credit card program. All of the receipts were found to be in consideration for the use of the organization's valuable intangible property and, as such, constituted tax-excludable royalties.

There is a vagary in the Ninth Circuit's opinion as to the range of the gap between merely collecting a fee (with no activities) and the amount of tolerable

[383] Id. at 1577.
[384] Id. at 1578.

activity the court seemingly contemplates within the boundaries as to what constitutes an excludable royalty. In the context of mailing list rentals, two examples were offered: provision of a rate sheet listing the fee charged for use of each copyrighted design, and retention of the right to approve how the design is used and marketed. Activities that are problematic in this area in general are endorsements, use of the tax-exempt organization's postal permit to send solicitation materials, publishing of paid advertising, the right of the exempt organization to advise with respect to marketing materials, sorting mailing lists, provision of list information on magnetic tape or labels, and provision of other clerical, telephone, and administrative services.[385]

During the pendency of this litigation, the IRS held to its views in its rulings. For example, the IRS ruled that payments by a commercial enterprise for use of the name and logo of a charitable organization are taxable as unrelated business income (and are not excludable royalties) because the charity also provided endorsements of the business's services.[386]

The denouement of the government's stance came when two other appellate court cases on the subject of the exclusion for royalty income were decided in favor of the tax-exempt organizations.[387] By this point, the IRS realized that this series of defeats was insurmountable—that the courts were not accepting its interpretation of the scope of the tax-excludible royalty. The IRS National Office, late in 1999, communicated with its exempt organizations specialists in the field, essentially capitulating on the point; a memorandum distributed to them stated bluntly that "[c]ases should be resolved in a manner consistent with the existing court cases."[388] This memorandum added that "it is now clear that courts will continue to find the income [generated by activities such as mailing list rentals and affinity card programs] to be excluded royalty income unless the factual record clearly reflects more than unsubstantial services being provided." Two factors were highlighted by the IRS as establishing non-taxable royalty income: where the involvement of the exempt organization is

---

[385] In the aftermath of the Ninth Circuit's decision, the Tax Court ruled that payments received by a tax-exempt organization for the use of its mailing list are not subject to unrelated business income taxation because they constitute royalties (*Common Cause* v. *Commissioner*, 112 T.C. 332 (1999)). The rental lists are stored at a computer service business and the exempt organization retains the services of a list manager and list broker. Payments from mailers are remitted by the list manager to the organization, less the manager's and broker's commissions and payments to the computer house. With one exception, all of the activities of the parties were deemed to be *royalty-related*, that is, designed to exploit or protect the exempt organization's intangible property. Certain activities provided solely to mailers by list brokers were found not to be royalty-related. The court also concluded that none of these parties were functioning as agents of the exempt organization, so none of the activities and payments were attributable to the exempt organization. Also *Planned Parenthood Federation of America, Inc.* v. *Commissioner*, 77 T.C.M. 2227 (1999); *Mississippi State University Alumni, Inc.* v. *Commissioner*, 74 T.C.M. 458 (1999).

[386] Priv. Ltr. Rul. 9450028. In subsequent rulings, the IRS has found a royalty to be present (Priv. Ltr. Ruls. 9816027, 9709029, and 9703025) and not present (Tech. Adv. Mem. 9723001; Priv. Ltr. Rul. 9810030).

[387] *Oregon State University Alumni Association, Inc.* v. *Commissioner; Alumni Association of the University of Oregon, Inc.* v. *Commissioner*, 193 F.3d 1098 (9th Cir. 1999), *aff'g*, 71 T.C.M. 1935 (1996), 71 T.C.M. 2093 (1996).

[388] Memorandum from Jay H. Rotz, IRS Exempt Organizations Division, National Office, dated December 16, 1999.

"relatively minimal" and where the exempt organization "hired outside contractors to perform most services associated with the exploitation of the use of intangible property."[389]

The matter of income from the exchange of mailing lists continues to fester. The statutory exception for this type of exchange is only applicable when the parties to the exchange are charitable entities.[390] The position of the IRS has consistently been that the exchange of mailing lists by a tax-exempt organization with similar exempt organizations does not create unrelated business income (namely, barter income of an amount equal to the value of the lists received).[391] The rationale is that the activity is not a business because it is not carried on for profit but rather to obtain the names of potential donors. The IRS is also of the view that this type of exchange is a business that is substantially related to the organization's exempt function as being a "generally accepted method used by publicly supported organizations to assist them in maintaining and enhancing their active donor files."[392] Where a tax-exempt organization exchanges mailing lists to produce income, however, it is the view of the IRS that the transaction is economically the same as a rental and thus is an unrelated trade or business.[393] The IRS rejects the argument that an exchange of mailing lists creates capital gain that is excluded from taxation.[394] It also does not accept the contention that the exchange is a tax-free like-kind exchange of property[395] because title to the property does not pass and the exchange is only a one-time (rather than permanent) transaction. The IRS, however, will not rule on how this form of income is to be calculated, including the deductions that may be available, stating that this is to be ascertained on a case-by-case basis.[396]

One of the arguments persistently advanced by the IRS is that the statutory exception protecting certain mailing list transactions from taxation is to be read as permitting (perhaps requiring) taxation of these transactions in situations where the exception is not available. This contention is equally persistently rejected in the courts.[397] The legislative history of the provision is to the contrary of the IRS position. One element of this history states as follows: "No inference is intended as to whether or not revenues from mailing list activities other than those described in the provision, or from mailing list activities described in the provision, but occurring prior to the effective date, constitute unrelated business income."[398] This point was also reflected in the House debate on the legislation, in remarks offered by the then-Chairman of the House Committee on Ways and Means: this provision "carries no inference whatever

---

[389] An issue under consideration at the IRS is whether there should be an allocation of a single payment between compensation for the use of intangible property and compensation for more than insubstantial services.

[390] IRC § 513(h)(1)(B)(i).

[391] E.g., Priv. Ltr. Rul. 8127019.

[392] Id.

[393] E.g., Tech. Adv. Mem. 9502009; Priv. Ltr. Ruls. 9250001 and 8127019.

[394] See supra text accompanied by note 262.

[395] IRC § 1031(a).

[396] Tech. Adv. Mem. 9502009.

[397] E.g., Common Cause v. Commissioner, supra note 385.

[398] Staff of Joint Comm. on Taxation, General Explanation of the Tax Reform Act of 1986 1325 (J. Comm. Print 1987).

that mailing list revenues beyond its scope or prior to its effective date should be considered taxable to an exempt organization."[399]

(vii) Commercial Co-Ventures.   The IRS has assumed a generous stance concerning *charitable sales promotions* or *commercial co-ventures,* where a charitable organization consents to be a donee under circumstances in which a commercial business agrees to make a gift to the charity, with that agreement advertised to the public, and where the amount of the gift is predicated on the extent of products sold or services provided by the business to the public during a particular time period.[400] The IRS agrees with the charitable community that these payments are contributions, deductible as such; in practice, these payments are often deducted as business expenses.

(viii) Cause-Related Marketing.   The position of the IRS as to *cause-related marketing* is different. In these circumstances, the charitable organization is marketing a product or service to the public, or similarly using its resources. These efforts are analyzed by the IRS, applying traditional unrelated business income analysis. Often, the activity is considered a business that is regularly carried on, albeit a related (and thus nontaxable) one. The activity can also be regarded as an unrelated business, however, particularly where the marketing is considered to be commercial in nature.

(ix) Corporate Services.   It has become increasingly common for a charitable or other tax-exempt organization to provide services to another charitable or other tax-exempt organization, in circumstances where the services are not inherently exempt functions. These services are management, other administrative, or fundraising services; they have come to be known as *corporate services.*

Traditionally, the provision of corporate services was considered by the IRS to be the conduct of unrelated business. In recent years, however, the IRS reviewed the tax aspects of joint operating agreements, which are contracts by which a number of health care providers and associated entities function on an interrelated basis, resulting in health care provider networks.[401] Within these networks is the provision of corporate services by some of these organizations, for compensation.

Were this compensation taxable as unrelated business income, these networks would not be workable. Resolving this issue, the IRS, on the basis of law developed in another context,[402] concluded that the income flows arising from the provision of these corporate services should be regarded as a *matter of accounting,* which means that the income is disregarded for unrelated business income purposes. To have this result, however, the IRS ruled that the relationship between the organizations must either be that of parent and subsidiary or be analogous to that of parent and subsidiary.

---

[399] 132 *Cong. Rec.* 26208 (Sept. 25, 1986).
[400] See §§ 3.8 and 7.4.
[401] See Hyatt and Hopkins, *The Law of Tax-Exempt Healthcare Organizations, Second Edition* (John Wiley & Sons: New York, 2001) §§ 21.5, 24.14.
[402] Rev. Rul. 77-72, 1977-1 C.B. 157.

This development was transformative for many other types of tax-exempt organizations because the tax law rationale underlying these agreements could not be confined to the context of joint operating agreements. It meant that any situation in which one tax-exempt organization has a parent–subsidiary relationship with another exempt organization (such as an exempt organization with a related fundraising foundation) could be protected by this rationale. It also meant that the matter-of-accounting rationale could be extended to any arrangement where the relationship between two tax-exempt organizations is analogous to that of parent and subsidiary.

Some time passed before this rationale was extended outside the realm of joint operating agreements. The first occasion where this happened involved a tax-exempt social welfare organization, which provided corporate services to its related foundation.[403] There, a parent–subsidiary relationship was found. Thereafter, the IRS began issuing rulings on the matter of what it means to have a relationship that is analogous to that of parent and subsidiary.[404]

These developments make it clear that a tax-exempt organization can provide corporate services to another tax-exempt organization, without engaging in unrelated business activity, as long as the relationship is at least analogous to that of parent and subsidiary. These activities may include fundraising services.

§ 5.8 EXEMPTION APPLICATION PROCESS

Under the federal income tax system, every element of gross income received by a person—whether a corporate entity or a human being—is subject to taxation, unless there is an express statutory provision that exempts from tax either that form of income or that type of person.[405]

Many types of nonprofit organizations are eligible for exemption from the federal income tax.[406] The exemption, however, is not forthcoming merely because an organization is not organized and operated for profit. Organizations are tax-exempt where they meet the requirements of the particular statutory provision that authorizes the tax-exempt status.

(a) Recognition of Tax-Exempt Status

Whether a nonprofit organization is entitled to tax exemption, on an initial or continuing basis, is a matter of law. The U.S. Congress—not the IRS—defines the categories of organizations that are eligible for tax exemption, and it is up to Congress to determine whether an exemption from tax should be continued, in whole or in part. Except for state and local governmental entities, there is no constitutional right to a tax exemption.

Despite what is often thought, the IRS does not *grant* tax-exempt status. Congress, by means of sections of the Internal Revenue Code that it has

---

[403] Priv. Ltr. Rul. 200022056.
[404] The first of these appears to be Priv. Ltr. Rul. 200108045.
[405] IRC § 61.
[406] See § 2.1.

enacted, performs that role. Rather, the function of the IRS in this regard is to *recognize* tax exemptions that Congress has created.

Consequently, when an organization applies to the IRS for a ruling or determination as to tax-exempt status, it is requesting the IRS to recognize a tax exemption that already exists (assuming the organization qualifies). Similarly, the IRS may determine that an organization is no longer entitled to tax-exempt status and revoke its prior recognition of exempt status.

For many nonprofit organizations that are eligible for tax exemption, it is not required that the exemption be recognized by the IRS. Whether a nonprofit organization seeks an IRS determination on the point is a management decision, which usually takes into account the degree of confidence the individuals involved have in the eligibility for the exemption and the costs associated with the application process. Most organizations in this position elect to pursue recognition of tax-exempt status.

Charitable organizations (and certain employee benefit organizations) must, however, to be tax-exempt and to be charitable donees, file (successfully) with the IRS an application for recognition of the exemption.[407] Thus, by contrast, entities such as social welfare organizations, labor organizations, trade and professional associations, social clubs, and veterans' organizations need not (but may) file an application for recognition of tax-exempt status.[408]

Unlike most requests for a ruling from the IRS (which are commenced by a letter to the IRS), a request for recognition of tax exemption is initiated by filing a form, entitled "Application for Recognition of Exemption." Charitable organizations file Form 1023; most other organizations file Form 1024.

Subject only to the authority in the IRS to revoke recognition of exemption for good cause (such as a change in the law), an organization that has been recognized by the IRS as being tax-exempt can rely on the determination as long as there are no substantial changes in its character, purposes, or methods of operation.[409] Should material changes occur, the organization should notify the IRS and may have to obtain a reevaluation of its exempt status.

(b) Application Procedure

The IRS has promulgated rules by which a ruling or determination letter may be issued to an organization in response to the filing of an application for recognition of its tax-exempt status.[410] An organization seeking recognition of exemption should file the application with the IRS Service Center in Cincinnati, Ohio. Usually, the determination of exemption will be made at that level. If the application presents a matter of some controversy or an unresolved or novel point of law, however, the application will be sent on to the headquarters of the IRS in Washington, D.C., for resolution at that level.

This application process requires the organization to reveal some information about its fundraising program.

---

[407] IRC § 508(a). The rules for the employee benefit organizations appear in IRC § 505(c)(1).
[408] E.g., Rev. Rul. 80-108, 1980-1 C.B. 119.
[409] Reg. § 1.501(a)-1(a)(2).
[410] Rev. Proc. 90-27, 1990-1 C.B. 514. See *Law of Tax-Exempt Organizations* § 23.2.

A ruling or determination will be issued to an organization, as long as the application and supporting documents establish that it meets the particular statutory requirements. The application must include a statement describing the organization's purposes, copies of its governing instruments (such as, in the case of a corporation, its articles of incorporation and bylaws) and either a financial statement or a proposed multiyear budget.

The application filed by a charitable organization must also include a summary of the sources of its financial support, its fundraising program, the composition of its governing body (usually board of directors), its relationship with other organizations (if any), the nature of its services or products and the basis for any charges for them, and its membership (if any).

An application for recognition of exemption should be regarded as an important legal document and prepared accordingly. Throughout an organization's existence, it will likely be called on to provide its application for recognition of exemption to others for review. Indeed, a nonprofit organization is required by federal law to keep a copy of this application available for scrutiny or retention by anyone during regular business hours.[411]

(c) Application

The application for recognition of tax exemption filed by charitable organizations (Form 1023) comes in a packet.[412] This packet includes instructions for preparation of the form, the form itself (in duplicate), and the Form 872-C (discussed later). Only one copy of Form 1023 need be filed with the IRS; the other copy may be used in drafting the application.

(i) Part I. Part I of Form 1023 requests certain basic information about the applicant organization, such as its name, location address, Website address, and date of formation. Every nonprofit organization must have an *employer identification number* (even if there are no employees); this is obtained by filing a Form SS-4. The Form SS-4 may be filed as soon as the organization is formed and organized, or it may be filed with the Form 1023.

The contact person (question 3) may be either someone directly involved with the organization, such as an officer or director, or an independent representative of the organization, such as a lawyer or accountant. If this type of a representative is being used, he or she must be granted a power of attorney, which is filed with the application, on Form 2848.

The organization must state the month in which its annual accounting period ends (question 4). The determination of a fiscal year should be given some thought; most organizations use the calendar year (in which case the answer is "December"). Whatever period is selected, the organization should be certain that the same period is stated on Form SS-4 and used when compiling its multiyear budget (see below).

---

[411] IRC § 6104(d).

[412] This analysis is based on Form 1023 dated September 1998, pages 1–9 of which appear in Appendix B.

The date of formation is to be provided (question 5). If incorporated, for example, this date will be the date the state agency received the articles of incorporation. This date is significant in relation to the *15-month rule* (see following discussion).

Question 10 of Form 1023 requires an applicant organization to identify its *type*. The organization must be one of three types: nonprofit corporation, trust, or unincorporated association.[413]

If a corporation, the attachments will be the articles of incorporation and bylaws, any amendments to these documents, and the certificates of incorporation and amendment (if any) issued by the state. If a trust, the attachments will be the trust document(s). If an unincorporated association, the attachments will be the constitution and bylaws.

(ii) Part II. The applicant charitable organization must identify, in order of size, its sources of financial support (question 2). The answers are typically contributions from the general public, other contributions, grants, dues, other exempt function (fee-for-service) revenue, and/or investment income. Whatever sources of support are identified here, the organization should be careful to be consistent when preparing the multiyear budget and selecting the non-private foundation status, if any (see following discussion).

The organization must describe its actual and planned fundraising program (question 3). The organization should summarize its use of, or plans to use, selective mailings, fundraising committees, volunteers, professional fundraisers, and the like. Again, the organization should be certain to conform its discussion of financial support with that of its fundraising plans. The organization can describe a detailed fundraising program or it can state that it has yet to develop a semblance of a fundraising program.

The organization must provide a narrative description of its activities (question 1). Usually, this is an essay that describes the organization's programs and should be carefully written. Good practice is to open with a description of the organization's purposes, followed by one or more paragraphs summarizing its program activities. This response should be as full as is reasonable and may well occupy more space than is provided, in which case the response can be in the form of a separate exhibit.

The names and addresses of the organization's officers and directors must be provided, along with the amount (if any) of their annual compensation (question 4). As to compensation, this includes all compensation, not just that for serving as an officer or director (or trustee).

Question 5, concerning relationships with other organizations, can be important for some organizations. As a general rule, it does not matter whether the charitable organization has a special relationship with, or is controlled by, another organization. For example, some charitable organizations are controlled by other types of tax-exempt organizations, such as social welfare organizations or trade associations, or are controlled by for-profit corporations (such as corporation-related foundations).

---

[413] See *Law of Tax-Exempt Organizations* § 4.1.

Question 11, concerning membership groups, is basically self-explanatory. It relates to organizations that have a true membership, however, not merely arrangements where the concept of a *membership* is used as a fundraising technique.

(iii) Part III. Question 5 of Part I, concerning the date of formation of an organization, can be of no particular importance or it can be of extreme importance, depending on the circumstances. The basic rule, reflected in question 1, is that the recognition of exemption will be retroactive to the date of formation of the charitable organization where the application is filed with the IRS within 15 months from the end of the month in which the organization was established.[414] For example, if the organization is created on January 15, 2002, and the application for recognition of exemption is filed on or before April 30, 2003, the recognition of exemption (if granted) will be retroactive to January 15, 2002, irrespective of when the determination is made by the IRS. To continue with this example, however, if the application is filed on or after May 1, 2003, the recognition of exemption generally would, under the 15-month rule, be effective only as of the date the application was received by the IRS. (Nonetheless, as discussed later, the emergence of a 27-month rule has somewhat alleviated the time pressures in this context.)

As to the matter of tax-exempt status, the 15-month rule may not be of any particular importance, in that the charitable organization can qualify as a tax-exempt social welfare organization (which does not require recognition of tax-exempt status) until the date of its classification as a charitable organization.[415] This alleviation of the tax-exemption problem, as reflected in question 6, however, is of no assistance with respect to the posture of the organization as a charitable donee or as a nonprivate foundation (if the latter is applicable). Donors making gifts during the interim period will, upon audit, find their charitable deductions disallowed. Private foundations making grants during the interim period may be subject to taxation for failure to exercise *expenditure responsibility*.[416] Thus, an organization desiring to be recognized as a charitable organization from its date of formation should make an effort to file a completed application for recognition of tax exemption before the expiration of the 15-month period.

There are, nonetheless, some exceptions to the 15-month rule. One is an automatic 12-month extension of time within which to file the application (question 3);[417] this has essentially converted the standard to a 27-month rule. In some instances, the IRS can accord relief in this area (question 4). Certain small organizations, churches, conventions or associations of churches, integrated auxiliaries of churches, and other organizations are exempted from this application requirement (question 2).[418]

---

[414] IRC § 508(a). See *Law of Tax-Exempt Organizations* § 23.3.

[415] Rev. Rul. 80-108, *supra* note 408.

[416] See Hopkins and Blazek, *Private Foundations: Tax Law and Compliance* (John Wiley & Sons, 1997) ("*Private Foundations*") § 9.6.

[417] Rev. Proc. 92-85, 1992-2 C.B. 490.

[418] IRC § 508(c).

Questions 7 through 9 can be of significant consequence. This is where the public charity/private foundation rules come into play.[419] If the applicant charitable organization is a private foundation, the answer to question 7 is yes. If the organization is seeking classification as a private operating foundation, it should so indicate in response to question 8 and complete Schedule E.

If the organization believes it can avoid private foundation status by reason of being one of the entities listed in question 9, however, it must select either a *definitive* ruling or an *advance* ruling. For new charitable organizations (i.e., those with a tax year of less than eight months) that are seeking to be classified as publicly supported entities, an advance ruling (selected by responding to question 10) is the correct choice. This is because they lack the financial history to demonstrate actual public support, which is required before a publicly supported organization can receive a definitive ruling. If the applicant believes it will be supported principally by gifts and grants, it should check the box correlating with question 9(h). The box of question 9(i) is for organizations that are expecting support in the form of a blend of gifts, grants, and exempt function income.

Either type of putative publicly supported organization must demonstrate its initial qualification for nonprivate foundation status by convincing the IRS that it will receive the requisite extent of public support. This is done by submitting a proposed budget. This budget summarizes contemplated types of revenue (such as gifts, grants, exempt function revenue, and investment income) and types of expenses (such as expenditures for program, compensation, occupancy, telephone, travel, postage, and fundraising), for each of five years. For this purpose, a year is a period consisting of at least eight months. (For new organizations, this budget is submitted in lieu of the financial statements reflected in Part IV of Form 1023.) The five-year period is the *advance ruling period.* Thus, as question 10 reflects, an organization with a tax year of at least eight months, but that has a period of existence of less than five years, can obtain either an advance or definitive ruling.

In designing the budget, the five years involved are the fiscal years of the organization. The applicant organization should be certain that the fiscal year used to develop the budget is the same period referenced in the response to question 4 of Part I. Also in this process, the organization should be certain that the types of revenue stated in the budget correspond to the types of revenue summarized in the response to question 2 of Part III.

The advance ruling pertains only to the applicant organization's status as a publicly supported entity. That is, it is not an advance ruling as to tax-exempt status or charitable donee status. Thus, the advance ruling period is a probationary or conditional ruling, as to public charity status. Once the advance ruling period expires and the organization has in fact received adequate public support during the five-year period, that fact will be reported to the IRS, which will in turn issue a definitive ruling that it is a publicly supported charity. Just as the advance ruling is conditional, the definitive ruling is permanent (unless upset by a subsequent loss of qualification or change in the law).

---

[419] See *infra* § 11.

The publicly supported charitable organization must, during and after the expiration of the advance ruling period, continue to show that it qualifies as a publicly supported charity, assuming it wants to retain that status. This is done by reporting the financial support information as part of the annual information return.[420]

It does not matter which type of publicly supported organization the charitable entity is at any point in its existence; the principal objective is to qualify, at any one time, under one category or another. Thus, an organization can shift from one classification of publicly supported organization to another throughout its duration. Likewise, a charitable organization can, without concern, select one category of publicly supported organization when it completes Part III and only satisfy the requirements of the other category as of the close of the advance ruling period.

If an organization selects a category of publicly supported charitable organization when it prepares Part III, and finds at the close of the advance ruling period that it did not meet either set of requirements for publicly supported status, it will be categorized as a private foundation, unless it can demonstrate eligibility for otherwise avoiding private foundation status. This can be done if the organization qualifies as an entity such as a church, school, hospital, or supporting organization (see following discussion).

If the organization is classified as a private foundation after the close of its advance ruling period, it will have to pay the excise tax on its net investment income[421] for each of the years in the advance ruling period (and thereafter). For the IRS to be able to assess the tax retroactively, the taxpayer must agree to waive the running of the statute of limitations, which otherwise would preclude the IRS from reaching that far back. The waiver is granted by the execution of Form 872-C (in duplicate), which, as noted, is part of the Form 1023 package.

An applicant organization that qualifies as a church, school, hospital, supporting organization, or the like is eligible to receive a definitive ruling at the outset because its financial support is not the factor used in classifying it as a public entity. Instead, its public status derives from what it does programmatically.

An organization can receive a definitive ruling that it is publicly supported if it has been in existence for, as noted, a tax year of at least eight months and received the requisite public support during that period. The organization in this situation would submit a completed Part IV for each of these years.

Every organization that is requesting a definitive ruling must evidence its selection of nonprivate foundation status by answering question 12 or 13 of Part III. Question 10 is to be answered by organizations seeking an advance ruling. Certain organizations are required to submit a schedule (question 14); these organizations include churches (Schedule A), schools (Schedule B), supporting organizations (Schedule D), scholarship-granting organizations (Schedule H), and successors to for-profit entities (Schedule I).

---

[420] See *infra* § 9.
[421] See *Private Foundations,* Chapter 10.

(iv) Summary. This application for recognition of tax exemption as a charitable organization, if properly completed, amounts to a rather complete portrait of the programs, fundraising plans, and other aspects of the applicant organization. That is why it is important to devote some time and thinking to the preparation of the form. It is, as noted,[422] a public document and, during the course of the organization's existence, the organization probably will be called on from time to time to supply a copy of the application. Because those who request the document are likely to be prospective donors or grantors, or representatives of the media, it is particularly important that it be properly prepared.[423]

If a fundraising professional—either in-house executive or consultant—is serving an applicant organization at this stage, he or she should participate in the preparation of this application. Too frequently, however, that is not the case, which can cause the portions of the application that pertain to fundraising to be incomplete or inaccurate.

§ 5.9 REPORTING REQUIREMENTS

One of the most important aspects of federal regulation of the charitable solicitation process is accomplished by means of the annual reporting obligations imposed on most charitable and other tax-exempt organizations. That is, with some exceptions, a charitable organization must annually file an information return[424] with the IRS.[425] These returns are filed with the IRS Service Center in Ogden, Utah.

(a) Filing Categories

Organizations with gross receipts that are normally not in excess of $25,000 need not file annual information returns,[426] although it is the view of the IRS that these organizations should file the identification part of the form. In determining the $25,000 threshold, an organization takes into account (1) net rental income (gross rents less expenses); (2) net amounts received from the sale of assets other than inventory (gross amounts from the assets, less basis in assets and expenses of sale); (3) net receipts from special fundraising events and activities; and (4) gross profit or loss from other sales (gross sales, less returns, allowances, and cost of goods sold).

---

[422] See *supra* text accompanied by note 411.

[423] A more detailed analysis of the application for recognition of tax exemption (Form 1023), with sample responses, appears in Hopkins, *Starting and Managing a Nonprofit Organization: A Legal Guide* (John Wiley & Sons, 2001).

[424] Principally, Form 990. Private foundations, a form of charitable organization (see *infra* § 11) that rarely engages in fundraising, file Form 990-PF. Political organizations file Form 990-POL; black lung benefit trusts file Form 990-BL; religious or apostolic organizations file Form 1065.

[425] IRC § 6033(a)(1). See *Law of Tax-Exempt Organizations* at § 24.3. This analysis is based on the annual information return to be used by most tax-exempt organizations for calendar year 2000 or for fiscal years beginning in 2001. This form appears in Appendix C.

[426] IRC § 6033(a)(2)(A)(ii); Reg. § 1.6033-2(g)(1)(iii); Rev. Proc. 83-23, 1983-1 C.B. 687, § 3.01. This exception is not available, however, for private foundations.

Organizations with annual gross receipts that are normally in excess of $25,000 but less than $100,000, and that have end-of-year assets with a value below $250,000, may file a two-page annual information return.[427] Thus, tax-exempt organizations generally are classified as being in one of three filing categories: those that need not file at all, those that can file the short form, and those that must file the complete return.

Aside from the filing exemption accorded small organizations, other categories of tax-exempt entities are excused from the filing requirements. These include churches, interchurch organizations of local units of a church, conventions or associations of churches, certain integrated auxiliaries of churches, and certain internally supported, church-controlled organizations; schools below college level affiliated with a church or operated by a religious order; mission societies sponsored by or affiliated with one or more churches or church denominations, if more than one-half of the society's activities are conducted in or directed at persons in foreign countries; exclusively religious activities of a religious order; many types of state institutions and affiliated entities; and certain instrumentalities of the United States.[428]

(b) Income-Producing Activities

A principal component of Form 990 is Part VII, which consists of an extensive reporting of income-producing activities. The information sought is designed to provide Congress with data needed to assess the impact of current or future unrelated business income rules and to enable the IRS to better administer the unrelated income laws.[429]

Part VII of the form requires a tax-exempt organization to identify each income-producing activity. These activities include those that generate various forms of program service revenue, membership dues and assessments, and investment income, as well as sales of assets and special fundraising events. The revenue from each reported activity must be categorized as unrelated business income, exempt function (related) income, or income excluded from tax by a particular provision of the Internal Revenue Code. The IRS has devised a system of codes to use in classifying income excludable from taxation because of a particular section of the Internal Revenue Code (see following discussion).

When an exempt organization classifies an item of income as related, it must explain (in Part VIII) how the associated activity contributed importantly to the accomplishment of exempt purposes. (The fact that an activity generates funds that are used for tax-exempt purposes does not make that activity a related one.)

The instructions to the return include a chart of the *exclusion codes*. There is a code for each rationale for excluding otherwise unrelated income from taxation, such as for an activity that is not regularly carried on or one that is conducted substantially by volunteers. One exclusion code that is particularly noteworthy is number 40, which is to be used for an activity that is not considered a *business* to

---

[427] Form 990-EZ.
[428] Rev. Proc. 83-23, *supra* note 426 § 3.01.
[429] See *supra* § 7.

begin with because the activity is not carried on with a *profit motive,* since there have been losses. Where an activity is so classified, the losses from it cannot be offset against gain from other unrelated activities.

(c) Reporting

An organization is required to report (on line 1 of Part I) all amounts received as contributions and grants. The instructions state that *contributions* means "payments, or the part of any payment, for which the payer (donor) does not receive full consideration from the recipient (donee) organization." Organizations must attach a schedule listing contributors who, during the year, gave the organization, directly or indirectly, money or property worth at least $5,000. Gifts of less than $1,000 are not included for this purpose.

Separate reporting is required for program service revenue, membership dues and assessments, investment income, asset sales, revenue from special fundraising events, and other revenue.

Revenue from special fundraising activities (such as dinners, door-to-door sales of merchandise, carnivals, and bingo games) generally is, as noted, separately reported (on line 9). When the payment is part a purchase for the event or activity and part a contribution, however, the gift portion is reported separately (on line 1a) from the purchase portion. Direct expenses associated with special fundraising events are subtracted on the face of the return. A schedule that lists the three largest (in terms of gross receipts) special events conducted by the organization must be attached to the return.

Revenue, for these purposes, does not include the value of services donated to an organization or the free use of materials, equipment, or facilities. These items may be reported elsewhere (Part VI, line 82).

In general, expenses must be totaled and allocated, pursuant to principles of *functional accounting,* to three categories: program, management, and fundraising. In practice, however, far more detail about expense allocation is required. For example, as noted, there are allocations regarding special fundraising activities. Also, charitable organizations should keep records about legislative activities.

(d) Functional Accounting

The annual information return requires charitable organizations to use the functional method of accounting as the means to report their expenses (Part II). This approach to accounting for an organization's expenses requires not only the identification, line by line, of expenses, but also an allocation of expenses by function, namely, the categories of *program services, management and general,* and *fundraising.*

Proper compliance with the requirements of the functional method of accounting obligates organizations to maintain detailed records of their fundraising (and other) expenses; the fundraising component of each line-item expenditure must be separately identified and reported. This requirement that the fundraising elements of all expenditures be separately identified may reveal some indirect fundraising costs that, when combined with direct fundraising expenses, result in the reporting of considerably higher total outlays for fundraising. This, in turn, could have adverse repercussions with respect to the organization's status under state charitable solicitation acts, particularly those that seek to force disclosure of organizations' fundraising expenses.[430] This approach to the reporting of expenses raises other pertinent accounting issues, not the least of which is the basis to be used in making these allocations among functions[431] and whether the state regulators will accept reports containing the allocations as being in compliance with the states' reporting requirements.

The instructions accompanying the return define the term *fundraising expense* as "all expenses, including allocable overhead costs, incurred in: (*a*) publicizing and conducting fundraising campaigns; (*b*) soliciting bequests, grants from foundations or other organizations, or government grants . . . ; (*c*) participating in federated fundraising campaigns; (*d*) preparing and distributing fundraising manuals, instructions, and other materials; and (*e*) conducting special fundraising events that generate contributions. . . ." The IRS does not differentiate, when using the term *professional fundraiser*, between fundraising counsel and solicitors, in that it defines the phrase *professional fundraising fees* to mean the "organization's fees to outside fundraisers for solicitation campaigns they conducted, or for providing consulting services in connection with a solicitation of contributions by the organization itself."[432]

(e) Other Information

At least four other areas of disclosure pertaining to fundraising are mandated by the annual information return. First, the return requires organizations to separately identify their sources of *program service revenue* (Part II). Second, organizations have the option of distinguishing between the reporting of revenue that is restricted and revenue that is unrestricted (Part I). Third, organizations must report their receipts from and expenses of *special fundraising events and activities*, with information separately provided for each type of event. The regulations state that these events include dinners, dances, carnivals, raffles, bingo games, and door-to-door sales of merchandise. (As noted, an organization uses only the net receipts from these events in computing the $25,000 of receipts that may dictate the extent of the organization's reporting obligations.)

---

[430] See § 4.3.

[431] The instructions accompanying Form 990 state that "[o]rganizations should follow their normal method of accounting in reporting their total expenses paid or incurred," and "any reasonable method may be used to allocate expenses among the three categories," and "[f]igures should be reasonably accurate if precise figures cannot be determined."

[432] See §§ 3.2(g), (h), 7.2. The IRS's Fiscal Year 2002 Exempt Organizations Implementing Guidelines, issued in October 2001, as part of an outline of the agency's examination program for the period, stated that "[a]gents who examine Forms 990 of public charities will check to see whether fund raising income and expenses are being properly reported." After noting that media reports are indicating that some charitable organizations are reporting only net fundraising income, the Guidelines state that "[a]gents should check amounts reported on Form 990 against the organization's audited financial statements and/or other books and records to determine whether the fund raising income and expenses are properly reported."

As to special fundraising events, the IRS observes in the return's instructions that "[t]hese activities only incidentally accomplish an exempt purpose" and that "[t]heir sole or primary purpose is to raise funds (other than contributions) to finance the organization's exempt activities." "This is done," the instructions continue, "by offering goods or services of more than a nominal value (compared to the price charged) in return for a payment that is more than the direct cost of those goods or services." Thus, an activity that only generates contributions (such as a direct mail campaign) is not a special fundraising event. A special fundraising event, however, can generate both contributions and revenue, such as when a purchaser pays more than the value of the goods or services furnished.[433]

Some or all of the dollar limitations applicable with respect to the annual information return filing requirements may not apply when an organization is using the form in place of state or local report forms. Examples of federal-law dollar limitations that do not meet some state requirements are the $25,000 gross receipts minimum that creates the obligation to file with the IRS, the identification-only format for organizations that report revenue of $25,000 or less, and the $50,000 minimum for listing professional fees in Schedule A of Form 990.

The contents of the annual information return pertain to the relationship between the federal government and the state regulatory agencies with respect to the regulation of fundraising for charity. These levels of government are coordinating their respective roles. The IRS has taken a significant step toward implementation of this process by stating, in its summary of its adoption of the present return, that "[s]tates are encouraged to use this return as the basic form satisfying State reporting requirements" and adding that "[a]ny additional information needed by a particular State could be provided by that State's own supplemental schedules and by requiring every filer to complete all parts of the Form 990 to be filed with the State." Some states use the Form 990 as the form for providing financial information in compliance with the states' charitable solicitation acts; the IRS wants to know the states in which the return is filed and expects the organizations to report that information (in Part VII).

(f) Other Fundraising Aspects

The instructions to the return point out that some states and local government units will accept a copy of Form 990 (and, where applicable, Schedule A) in place of all or part of their own financial report forms. Usually, this aspect of the matter pertains to filing compliance under the states' charitable solicitation acts.

The instructions observe that *doing business* in a particular state may entail the filing of returns there. They gratuitously note that the concept of doing business may include the solicitation of contributions or grants. This is

---

[433] See *supra* § 4.

a matter largely of state law; some charitable solicitation laws expressly regard acts of charitable fundraising as the doing of business in the state.[434]

Charitable organizations must keep sample copies of their fundraising materials, such as dues statements, tickets, and receipts. Also to be retained are sample copies of advertising copy and scripts used in soliciting gifts by means of radio and television.

(g) Related Organizations

In their annual returns on Schedule A of Form 990, which is filed only by charitable organizations,[435] these organizations must disclose information with respect to their direct or indirect transfers to, and other direct or indirect relationships with, other tax-exempt organizations (not including other charitable organizations), including political organizations.[436]

(h) Inspection Requirements

These annual information returns must be made available for public inspection upon request.[437] (Approved applications for exemption from federal income tax also must be made available.[438]) Some information is not publicly accessible, however, such as an organization's list of contributors.

In general, all parts of the return, including all required schedules and attachments (again, other than a list of donors), must be made available for public inspection. Of particular note is the Schedule A required of most charitable organizations, which contains information about the compensation of organizations' employees. Inspection must be permitted during regular business hours at the organization's principal office and at each of its regional or district offices having three or more employees.

(i) Disclosure Requirements

The foregoing inspection requirements have been largely supplanted by document disclosure requirements. The general rule in this regard is that a charitable or other tax-exempt organization must provide a copy without charge, other than a reasonable fee for reproduction and actual postage costs, of all or any part of any return required to be made available for public inspection to any individual who makes a request for the copy in person or in writing.[439] Generally, the names and addresses of donors need not be disclosed.[440] Certain information can be withheld from public disclosure, such as trade secrets,

---

[434] See § 3.22.

[435] IRC § 6033(b).

[436] IRC § 6033(b)(9).

[437] IRC § 6104(d)(1)(A)(i).

[438] IRC § 6104(d)(1)(A)(ii).

[439] IRC § 6104(d)(1)(B). For most categories of tax-exempt organizations, including public charities, the effective date of these requirements is June 8, 1999 (Reg. § 301.6104(d)-3(h)). See *The Law of Tax-Exempt Organizations* § 24.4(b).

[440] IRC § 6104(d)(3)(A).

patents, and donors.[441] (These requirements also apply with respect to applications for recognition of tax exemption.)

A tax-exempt organization is not required to comply with requests for copies of the returns (or application) if the organization has made the documents widely available. (The rules as to inspection of the documents nonetheless continue to apply.) An exempt organization can make a document *widely available* by posting it on a World Wide Web page that the organization has established and maintains. It can also satisfy this exception if the document is posted as part of a database of similar documents of other exempt organizations on a World Wide Web page established and maintained by another entity.[442]

(j) Penalties

Failure of a tax-exempt organization to file the appropriate annual information return can result in penalties. In general, a penalty of $20 a day, not to exceed the lesser of $10,000 or 5 percent of the gross receipts of the organization for the year, may be imposed where a return is filed late, unless the organization can show that the late filing was due to reasonable cause.[443] If more than one individual is responsible, these persons are jointly and individually liable for the penalty.[444] In the case of an organization having gross receipts in excess of $1 million for a year, however, the penalty can be $100 per day, with the maximum penalty set at $50,000. These penalties may also be imposed if an incomplete return is filed or incorrect information is submitted.

Further, if a complete return is not filed or correct information is not furnished, and a period of correction has expired, the individual failing to comply will be charged a penalty of $10 per day, not to exceed $5,000, unless he or she is able to show that the noncompliance was due to reasonable cause.

A penalty applies with respect to a failure to comply with the public inspection and disclosure requirements.[445] This is $20 for each day that an inspection was not permitted, up to a maximum of $10,000 per return. A penalty will not be imposed if the failure is due to reasonable cause. A person who willfully fails to comply with the requirement is subject to an additional penalty of $5,000.[446] (Similar penalties apply for failure to make proper disclosure of an exemption application.[447])

Ideally, the fundraising professional serving a reporting organization should review the entity's annual information return before it is filed, to ensure accuracy as to the portions of it concerning fundraising. Actual practice, however, is far from this paragon; it is uncommon for management of a charitable organization to cause the return to be subject to this type of evaluation. This is regrettable; as the return becomes of greater utility at the federal and

---

[441] IRC § 6104(d)(3)(B), (a)(1)(D).
[442] Reg. § 301.6104(d)-4(b)(2)(i).
[443] IRC § 6652(c)(1)(A).
[444] IRC § 6652(c)(1)(B)(ii).
[445] IRC § 6652(c)(1)(C).
[446] IRC § 6685.
[447] IRC § 6652(c)(1)(D).

state level in the fundraising context, the perspective of a fundraiser should not be ignored.

§ 5.10 LOBBYING RESTRICTIONS

In 1990, the Treasury Department and the IRS issued regulations that define the term *fundraising costs* and spell out rules by which to distinguish these costs from (i.e., allocate between) the expenses of administration and program. These regulations were drawn as part of the effort to promulgate rules to implement requirements enacted in 1976, which govern lobbying by certain charitable organizations.

Normally, lobbying by charities and fundraising by charities are separate considerations. Thus, the intricacies of the lobbying tax rules enacted in 1976 would seem of dubious relevance, but, as it turns out, these rules are indeed quite pertinent.

A charitable organization is required by the federal tax laws to ensure that "no substantial part of the activities" of the organization constitutes "carrying on propaganda, or otherwise attempting to influence legislation." Years of considerable and continuing uncertainty regarding the meaning and scope of these rules[448] led Congress, in enacting the Tax Reform Act of 1976, to clarify and amplify the proscription. This was done by the enactment of laws that measure the substantiality of lobbying activities as a function of funds expended. A charitable organization, assuming it is eligible to do so,[449] must affirmatively elect to come under these rules.[450]

While these rules are extensive and complex, the pertinent provision is that which formulates the lobbying standards in terms of declining percentages of aggregate expenditures. For charitable organizations that elect to come within these rules,[451] the basic permitted annual level of expenditures for legislative efforts is 20 percent of the first $500,000 of an organization's expenditures for exempt purposes, plus 15 percent of the next $500,000, 10 percent of the next $500,000, and 5 percent of any remaining expenditures, with the total amount spent for legislative activities in any one year by an organization not to exceed $1,000,000. No more than one-fourth of these amounts may be expended for grass-roots lobbying.[452]

In computing the permissible lobbying amount, the percentages are applied to the organization's tax-exempt expenditures, which, however, do not include fundraising expenditures. Thus, it becomes necessary for an organization endeavoring to comply with these rules to distinguish between its fundraising costs and its other costs.

The expenditures against which these percentages are applied are termed *exempt purpose expenditures*, which means the amounts paid or incurred to

[448] See *Law of Tax-Exempt Organizations* § 20.3.
[449] Reg. § 1.501(h)-2(b), (e).
[450] IRC § 501(h)(3), (4), and (6). See *Law of Tax-Exempt Organizations* § 20.5.
[451] IRC § 501(h)(4).
[452] IRC § 4911(c)(2).

accomplish charitable, educational, religious, scientific, and like purposes. The law expressly allows, as exempt purpose expenditures, administrative expenses associated with exempt functions and expenses for legislative activities. Exempt purpose expenditures, however, do not include amounts paid to or incurred for:

1. A separate fundraising unit of the organization,[453] or

2. One or more other organizations, if the amounts are paid or incurred primarily for fundraising.[454]

Nonetheless, exempt purpose expenditures include all other types of fundraising expenditures.[455]

The legislative history of these rules provides scant guidance about the allocation and other accounting aspects. (The only mention of accounting precepts is that amounts properly chargeable to capital account are to be capitalized and that, when a capital item is depreciable, a reasonable allowance for depreciation, computed on a straight-line basis, is to be treated as an exempt-purpose expenditure.) Guided by the regulations, electing organizations must make a reasonable judgment as to the calculation of exempt purpose expenditures, lobbying expenditures (both direct and grass roots), and fundraising expenditures.

An organization's first task in computing fundraising costs must therefore be to determine its direct fundraising costs. These costs include such items as payments to fundraising consultants, salaries to employees principally involved in fundraising, travel, telephone, postage, and supplies. (These items must also be identified with respect to any lobbying expenses.) Even with respect to these so-called direct items, there may well have to be allocations, such as between the educational (program) aspects and the fundraising aspects, of the expenses of creating and delivering printed material.

Subsequently, an organization must ascertain its indirect costs, to be apportioned to fundraising, lobbying, and other factors. These costs include items such as salaries of supportive personnel, rent, and utilities. Here again, the basis by which these costs are allocated to the various components is crucial in computing permissible lobbying expenses accurately. The regulations indicate that the IRS will be demanding extensive cost allocations—thus, the IRS has promulgated standards by which these allocations are to be made.

Finally, there is the matter of defining the term *fundraising* which, of course, must be done before costs can be determined and apportioned. For the most part, these costs will be readily ascertainable. Many organizations, however, actively pursue grant support from foundations, corporations, and/or federal agencies. Using the term in its broadest sense, these activities may be termed *fundraising*, yet they bear little relationship to the solicitations of the general public that generally constitute acknowledged forms of fundraising. Other questions arise, such as the proper classification of costs of a feasibility

---

[453] IRC § 4911(e)(1)(C)(i).
[454] IRC § 4911(e)(1)(C)(ii). See, however, *infra* text accompanied by note 465.
[455] Reg. § 56.4911-4(b)(8).

study, particularly where the consultant recommends against a campaign or other fundraising effort.

Strict application of these requirements may be nearly impossible. As an illustration, assume an organization raises its financial support by means of direct mail. The organization takes the position that a portion of the mailings consists of educational material (and thus the costs related to that portion are program expenses) and that the remainder of the literature is an appeal for contributions (and thus the costs related to that portion are fundraising expenses). Also, as part of the mailings, the organization discusses the pendency of certain legislative proposals and the need for congressional action, and, as a separately identifiable part of the mailings, specifically asks the recipients to contact their representatives in Congress urging their support of the legislation. In such an instance, the costs of the mailings would have to be allocated to program, general lobbying, grass-roots lobbying, and fundraising. Needless to say, the internal record-keeping obligations and justifications can become extensive, as can the IRS audit exposure.

As noted, amounts paid to or incurred for a separate fundraising unit of an organization, and certain other fundraising outlays, are not exempt purpose expenditures and thus are not in the base of expenditures used to calculate permissible percentages of lobbying expenditures.[456] For this purpose, the term *fundraising* includes:

1. Soliciting dues or contributions from members of the organization, from persons whose dues are in arrears, or from the general public;

2. Soliciting grants from businesses or other organizations, including charitable entities; or

3. Soliciting grants from a governmental unit,[457] or any agency or instrumentality of a governmental unit.[458]

One of the two types of fundraising expenditures is the expenditures paid to or incurred for a separate fundraising unit of the organization or of an organization affiliated with it.[459] A *separate fundraising unit* is (1) two or more individuals, a majority of whose time is spent on fundraising for the organization or (2) any separate accounting unit that is devoted to fundraising.[460] (Thus, where one employee is spending all or some of his or her time on fundraising, all of the expenses of this individual are exempt-purpose expenditures.) For these purposes, amounts paid to or incurred for a separate fundraising unit include all amounts incurred for the creation, production, copying, and distribution of the fundraising portion of a separate fundraising unit's communication.[461] For example, a public charity that has elected to come within these rules,[462] and that has a

---

[456] See *supra* text accompanied by notes 453 and 454. Also Reg. § 56.4911-4(c)(3).
[457] IRC § 170(c)(1).
[458] Reg. § 56.4911-4(f)(1).
[459] See *supra* text accompanied by note 453.
[460] Reg. § 56.4911-4(f)(2).
[461] *Id.*
[462] See *supra* text accompanied by note 450.

separate fundraising unit, may not count the cost of postage for a separate fundraising unit's fundraising communications as an exempt-purpose expenditure even though, under the charity's accounting system, that cost is attributable to the mailroom rather than to the separate fundraising unit.[463]

Thus, in determining fundraising expenses, an organization need allocate to fundraising only those expenses of a communication that are attributable to gift solicitation and membership development. This is the case even though, under the laws of one or more states, all of the expenses of the communication would be considered fundraising expenses.

The other category of fundraising expense encompasses amounts paid to or incurred by an organization to one or more other organizations, where the amounts are paid or incurred primarily for fundraising.[464] The tax regulations, however, expand this category of excluded expenditure to embrace amounts paid to or incurred for any person not an employee, or any organization not an affiliated organization, if paid or incurred primarily for fundraising, but only where the person or organization engages in fundraising, fundraising counselling, or the provision of similar advice or services.[465] Thus, the regulation sweeps in payments to individual fundraising consultants, even if they are not providing their services through an organization. It is apparent that the regulation applies this law to both professional fundraisers and professional solicitors. The term *similar advice or services* is unclear, however.[466]

The regulations governing lobbying by charitable organizations are therefore of direct relevance to the fundraising community.[467] Among the

---

[463] Reg. § 56.4911-4(f)(2).

[464] See *supra* text accompanied by note 454.

[465] Reg. § 56.4911-4(c)(4).

[466] For a discussion of the underlying rationale for the exclusion of certain fundraising expenses from the base of exempt purpose expenditures, see "The Bruce and Jerry Show—Or How Fund-Raising Expenses Are Handled in the New Lobbying Regulations," 5 *Exempt Org. Tax Rev.* (No. 1) 3 (1992).

[467] A related issue can arise in characterizing a direct mail effort as being grass-roots lobbying rather than fundraising, with the IRS perhaps inclined to treat it as the former for purposes of regulation, particularly where the fundraising literature has a legislative theme. In a technical advice memorandum interpreting the IRC § 501(c)(3) limitation on attempts to influence legislation, the IRS has held that the facts and circumstances of the mail appeal for funds will determine whether it is merely a fundraising appeal or a disguised attempt at grass-roots lobbying. Some of the factors the IRS considered important in determining that a direct mail solicitation was not grass-roots lobbying included the use of an outside fundraising consultant; the consultant's preparation of the text of the letter, its graphics and design, and the type of postage used going out and coming in; the design of the involvement devices included in the mailing; the use of standard fundraising techniques such as the number of times paragraphs asking for more money were included in the text (usually 30 percent of total text); whether the consultant ever consulted with lobbyists or policy analysts of the soliciting organization to ensure uniformity or correctness in the discussion of the legislative topic or theme; whether there was any direct request in the letter that the solicitee do anything other than send money or return a poll card; if a poll card was used (involving an opinion on the legislative topic), whether the poll card was disregarded or not used in some legislative format by the soliciting organization; whether the soliciting organization had an institutional point of view, expressed through its publications or otherwise, which publicly favored or opposed pending or proposed legislation consistent with the theme of the solicitation letter; the type of mailing lists used by the fundraising consultant and whether the mailing lists had a political orientation; and finally, whether the fundraising appeal was a financial success.

other forms of regulatory authority plaguing charitable organizations and fundraising these days, then, is the evolving lobbying law, and the fundraising community is well advised to understand the scope of the regulations and submit comments on the rules where questions arise.

§ 5.11 PUBLIC CHARITY CLASSIFICATIONS

An organization that is a charitable organization must either be categorized as a *private foundation* or acquire recognition from the IRS that it qualifies as a *public charity*.[468] Inasmuch as every charitable organization is rebuttably presumed to be a private foundation,[469] an organization finds public charity classification (if it can) by being described in one or more of the exceptions to the statutory definition of the term private foundation.[470]

Many institutions are automatically exempted from classification as private foundations because of the nature of their exempt function (such as by being churches,[471] educational institutions,[472] or hospitals[473]) or of the nature of their relationship (a supportive one) to one or more other public charities.[474] The non–private-foundation status of other types of charitable entities, however, is predicated not on the nature of their operations or structure but on the type of their financial support. In this context, fundraising and IRS regulation once again entwine.

There are three categories of charitable organizations whose non–private-foundation status wholly depends on the type of their financial support. A discussion of each follows.

1.   One type of publicly supported organization is that which normally receives a substantial part of its financial support (other than income from an exempt function) from a governmental unit or from contributions from the general public.[475] An organization can achieve public charity status pursuant to these rules in one of two ways: (a) where the total amount of its support normally derived from governmental or public sources, or both, is at least one-third of the total amount normally received, or (b) where a *facts and circumstances test* is met, in which case the total amount of governmental and/or public support normally received by the organization may be as low as 10 percent of its total support normally received. The amount of requisite public support (the numerator of the support fraction) is composed of contributions from an individual, trust, corporation, or other organization but only to the extent that the total amount of the contributions by any person during the computation period does not exceed

---

[468] IRC § 508(b). Certain organizations are exempted from this requirement, however, by IRC § 508(c). In general, see *Law of Tax-Exempt Organizations* § 23.4.
[469] Rev. Rul. 73-504, 1973-2 C.B. 190.
[470] IRC § 509(a).
[471] IRC §§ 170(b)(1)(A)(i) and 509(a)(1).
[472] IRC §§ 170(b)(1)(A)(ii) and 509(a)(1).
[473] IRC §§ 170(b)(1)(A)(iii) and 509(a)(1).
[474] IRC § 509(a)(3).
[475] IRC §§ 170(b)(1)(A)(vi) and 509(a)(1).

2 percent of the charitable organization's total support for the period. This 2 percent limitation does not apply to support received from governmental units or to contributions from certain types of public charities, nor are unusual grants taken into account in computing the applicable percentage. The extent of requisite public support generally is measured over a four-year, floating period.

For example, one of the elements of the facts and circumstances test is the extent to which the organization is attracting public support. This element is satisfied where the organization can demonstrate an active and ongoing fundraising program, as described as follows:

> An organization must be so organized and operated as to attract new and additional public or governmental support on a continuous basis. An organization will be considered to meet this requirement if it maintains a continuous and bona fide program for solicitation of funds from the general public, community, or membership group involved, or if it carries on activities designed to attract support from governmental units or other organizations described in section 170(b)(1)(A)(i) through (vi). In determining whether an organization maintains a continuous and bona fide program for solicitation of funds from the general public or community, consideration will be given to whether the scope of its fundraising activities is reasonable in light of its charitable activities. Consideration will also be given to the fact that an organization may, in its early years of existence, limit the scope of its solicitation to persons deemed most likely to provide seed money in an amount sufficient to enable it to commence its charitable activities and expand its solicitation program.[476]

2. Another type of publicly supported organization is that which normally receives more than one-third of its support in each tax year from any combination of (a) gifts, grants, contributions, or membership fees, and (b) gross receipts from admissions, sales of merchandise, performance of services, or furnishing of facilities in activities related to the organization's tax-exempt functions.[477] This support must derive from governmental units, certain types of public charities, and persons other than those who have a close relationship with the organization. In computing the amount of support received from gross receipts that is allowable toward the one-third requirement, gross receipts from related activities received from any person or from any bureau or similar agency of a governmental unit are includable in any tax year only to the extent that these receipts do not exceed the greater of $5,000 or 1 percent of the organization's support in that year. The extent of requisite public support generally is measured over a four-year, floating period.[478]

3. The third category of charitable organization that predicates its non–private-foundation classification on the degree of its public support is the supporting foundation that provides financial assistance to public colleges and universities.[479] This type of organization must normally receive a substantial

---

[476] Reg. § 1.170A-9(e)(3)(ii). In general, see *Private Foundations* § 15.4.
[477] IRC § 509(a)(2).
[478] See *Private Foundations* § 15.7.
[479] IRC §§ 170(b)(1)(A)(iv) and 509(a)(1).

part of its support (exclusive of income received in the exercise or performance of its exempt activities) from the United States, one or more states, or political subdivisions thereof, or from direct or indirect contributions from the general public. As is the case with the other categories, the extent of requisite public support generally is measured over a four-year, floating period.[480]

A charitable organization that fails to meet one or more sets of these rules (and that cannot otherwise qualify as a type of public charity) is denominated a private foundation and thus becomes subjected to the complex and restrictive rules applicable only to foundations. These rules prohibit, in effect, self-dealing, large business holdings, and jeopardizing investments; mandate annual distributions for charitable ends and a range of requirements concerning program expenditures; and levy a tax on investment income.[481] A charitable organization that can do so is well advised to qualify as an entity other than a private foundation.

To so qualify, the organization's non–private-foundation status may well depend on the extent of its public support. Thus, unlike most forms of federal and state regulation of fundraising for charity, which inhibit or make more costly the fundraising function, the type of regulation embodied in the private foundation definitional rules often promotes charitable solicitations of the general public.

Consequently, the IRS may be monitoring the extent of a charitable organization's fundraising efforts, to ascertain whether the organization qualifies as an entity other than a private foundation.

§ 5.12 SCHOOL RECORD-RETENTION REQUIREMENTS

Private tax-exempt educational institutions may not have racially discriminatory policies. The Secretary of the Treasury and the Commissioner of Internal Revenue were enjoined from approving any application for exemption for, continuing any current exemption for, or approving charitable contribution deductions to any private school in Mississippi that does not show that it has a publicized policy of nondiscrimination.[482] The court found a "Federal public policy against support for racial segregation of schools, public or private" and held that the law "does not contemplate the granting of special Federal tax benefits to trusts or organizations . . . whose organization or operation contravene[s] Federal public policy."[483] Thus, this position is essentially founded on the principle that the statutes providing tax deductions and exemptions are not construed to be applicable to actions that are either illegal or contrary to public policy. The court concluded: "Under the conditions of today they [the tax exemption and charitable deduction provisions[484]] can no longer be

---

[480] See *Private Foundations* § 15.5.
[481] *Id.*, Chapters 5–10.
[482] *Green* v. *Connally*, 330 F. Supp. 1150 (D.D.C. 1971), *aff'd sub nom. Coit* v. *Green*, 404 U.S. 997 (1971).
[483] *Id.* 330 F. Supp. at 1163, 1162.
[484] IRC §§ 501(c)(3) and 170(c)(2).

construed as to provide to private schools operating on a racially discriminatory premise the support of the exemptions and deductions which Federal tax law affords to charitable organizations and their sponsors."[485]

The IRS in 1971 stated that it would deny tax-exempt status to any private school that otherwise meets the requirements of tax exemption but "does not have a racially nondiscriminatory policy as to students."[486] Subsequently, in several states, the IRS has identified private schools to which contributions can no longer be assured to be tax-deductible because the schools lack such a policy.

The IRS initially announced its position on the exempt status of private nonprofit schools in 1967, when it stated that exemption and deductibility of contributions would be denied if a school is operated on a segregated basis.[487] The position was basically reaffirmed early in 1970, and the IRS began announcing denials of exemption later that year, but a clamor began for stricter guidelines when the granting of exemptions to allegedly segregated schools resumed.

The IRS, in 1972, issued guidelines and record-keeping requirements for determining whether private schools that have exemption rulings or are applying for this exemption have racially nondiscriminatory policies toward enrolling students.[488] The definition of such a policy remained that of the 1971 ruling, namely, that the school "admits the students of any race to all the rights, privileges, programs, and activities generally accorded or made available to students at that school" and that the school "does not discriminate on the basis of race in administration of its educational policies, admissions policies, scholarship and loan programs, and athletic and other school-administered programs."

Late in 1975, the IRS promulgated guidelines that superseded the 1972 rules.[489] Under the 1975 rules, the racially nondiscriminatory policy of every private school must be stated in its governing instruments or governing body resolution, and in its brochures, catalogues, and similar publications. This policy must be publicized to all segments of the general community served by the school, either by notice in a newspaper or by use of broadcast media. All programs and facilities must be operated in a racially nondiscriminatory manner, and all scholarships or comparable benefits must be offered on such a basis. Each school must annually certify its racial nondiscrimination policy.

These guidelines state the information that every school filing an application for recognition of exempt status must provide. Also included are an assortment of record-keeping requirements mandating the retention, for at least three years, of records indicating the racial composition of the school's student body, faculty, and administrative staff; records documenting the award of financial assistance; copies of all brochures, catalogues, and advertising dealing with student admissions, programs, and scholarships; and copies of all materials used by or on behalf of the school to solicit contributions. Failure to maintain or to produce the required reports and information ostensibly creates a

---

[485] *Green* v. *Connally, supra* note 482, 330 F. Supp. at 1164.
[486] Rev. Rul. 71-477, 1971-2 C.B. 230.
[487] Rev. Rul. 67-325, 1967-2 C.B. 113.
[488] Rev. Proc. 72-54, 1972-2 C.B. 834.
[489] Rev. Proc. 75-50, 1975-2 C.B. 587.

presumption that the school has failed to comply with the guidelines and thus has a racially discriminatory policy toward students.

In general, a private school must be able to demonstrate affirmatively (such as upon audit) that it has adopted a racially nondiscriminatory policy toward its students, that the policy has been made known to the general public, and that, since the adoption of the policy, it has operated in a bona fide manner in accordance with it.[490]

The position of the IRS that a private educational institution that has racially discriminatory policies cannot qualify as a charitable organization was upheld by the U.S. Supreme Court in 1983.[491] The rationale underlying this conclusion was a *public policy rationale,* in that "entitlement to tax exemption depends on meeting certain common law standards of charity—namely, that an institution seeking tax-exempt status must serve a public purpose and not be contrary to established public policy."[492] The Court wrote that an institution that is to be tax-exempt because it is a charitable entity "must demonstrably serve and be in harmony with the public interest" and its "purpose must not be so at odds with the common community conscience as to undermine any public benefit that might otherwise be conferred."[493]

§ 5.13 FUNDRAISING COMPENSATION ARRANGEMENTS

Charitable organizations must, among other requirements, be operated so that they do not cause any inurement of their net earnings to certain individuals in their private capacity or otherwise cause impermissible private benefit.[494] Where either of these rules is violated, the organization involved can lose or be deprived of its tax-exempt status.

The private inurement doctrine is the principle of law that essentially separates nonprofit organizations from for-profit organizations.[495] An organization that is operated *for profit* is one where the profits are destined for those who are the owners of the business, such as shareholders of a corporation who receive the corporate profits (net earnings) by means of dividends (the concept does not relate to profits at the entity level). A nonprofit organization, by contrast, is expected to retain its profits at the entity level; to be tax-exempt, a nonprofit organization cannot allow its net earnings to be passed along (inure) to those who are the equivalent of its owners. The private inurement doctrine is basically applicable only with respect to a tax-exempt organization and those who have some special relationship to it (*insiders*).[496]

By contrast, the private benefit doctrine derives from the rule that a charitable organization must be primarily organized and operated for the advancement

---

[490] E.g., *Calhoun Academy* v. *Commissioner,* 94 T.C. 284 (1990).
[491] *Bob Jones University* v. *United States,* 461 U.S 574 (1983), *aff'g* 639 F.2d 147 (4th Cir. 1980), *rev'g* 468 F. Supp. 890 (D.S.C. 1978).
[492] *Id.,* 461 U.S. at 586.
[493] *Id.* at 592.
[494] See *Law of Tax-Exempt Organizations,* Chapter 19.
[495] See § 7.12.
[496] E.g., *Sound Health Association* v. *Commissioner,* 71 T.C. 158 (1978).

of charitable purposes.[497] Operations for unwarranted private benefit are not, of course, regarded as operations for tax-exempt ends.[498] This doctrine has greater breadth than the private inurement doctrine, and its application is not confined to those who are insiders with respect to an organization.[499]

There are two aspects of this matter, only one of which is directly related to this analysis. The first is the matter of the fundraising costs of a charitable organization.[500] The second is the matter of the payment of fees for fundraising to employees and/or consultants. In either instance, the organization needs to be certain that its fundraising does not unduly dominate in relation to its program activities, inasmuch as the IRS is empowered to assess whether a charitable organization is maintaining a program that is commensurate in scope with its financial resources.[501] Precisely how this *commensurate test* will be applied in the fundraising setting is unclear, but the IRS has shown interest in application of the doctrine.[502]

The private inurement doctrine and/or private benefit doctrine can be triggered when a charitable organization pays excessive or otherwise unreasonable compensation for services.[503] Therefore, a charitable organization may not, without endangering its tax-exempt status, pay a fundraising professional an amount that is excessive or unreasonable. To a large extent, the matter of excessiveness is one of fact. Whether a particular amount of compensation is excessive essentially depends on fees paid in the community for comparable services, the experience of the professional, the type of fundraising involved, the nature of the charitable cause, and the overall resources of the charitable organization. As noted, in many states, the compensation for fundraising services must be stated in a contract between the charitable organization and the fundraising professional, with the agreement filed with the regulatory authorities.[504]

Questions about the propriety of compensation of a fundraising professional may not have as much to do with the amount being paid as the manner in which it is determined. This is particularly true with respect to compensation that is ascertained on the basis of a commission or percentage.

Although the IRS tends to be suspicious of fundraising compensation that is based on percentages of contributions received,[505] the courts have been rather tolerant of the practice. In one instance, a compensation arrangement based on a

---

[497] Reg. § 1.501(c)(3)-1(c)(1).

[498] In one instance, an otherwise charitable organization was denied tax-exempt status because its method of fundraising (bingo games) attracted individuals to the cocktail lounge where the games were held, thereby privately benefiting the owners of the lounge (*P.L.L. Scholarship Fund* v. *Commissioner*, 82 T.C. 196 (1984)).

[499] E.g., *American Campaign Academy* v. *Commissioner*, 92 T.C. 1053 (1989).

[500] This aspect of the matter is explored at §§ 4.1 and 7.1.

[501] Rev. Rul. 64-182, *supra* note 19.

[502] A question in the fundraising audit checksheet (see *supra* § 1) concerns application of this commensurate test. Also § 7.12.

[503] E.g., *Church by Mail, Inc.* v. *Commissioner*, 765 F.2d 1387 (9th Cir. 1985) (where ministers of a church were found to be excessively compensated when their church salaries were aggregated with that from a direct mail company owned by them and hired by the church).

[504] See § 3.11.

[505] See *supra* § 1.

percentage of gross receipts was held by a court to constitute private inurement, where the facts were somewhat egregious in nature and there was no upper limit as to total compensation.[506] This opinion suggests that one way to avoid private inurement or private benefit when using percentage compensation arrangements is to place a ceiling on the total amount to be paid—assuming, of course, that the total amount is not excessive.

Nonetheless, the same court, in a subsequent opinion, restricted the reach of its earlier decision by holding that private inurement does not occur when a tax-exempt organization pays its president a commission determined by a percentage of contributions procured by him. The court held that the standard is whether the compensation is reasonable, not the manner in which it is ascertained. Fundraising commissions that "are directly contingent on success in procuring funds" were held to be an "incentive well-suited to the budget of a fledgling organization."[507] In reaching this conclusion, the court reviewed states' charitable solicitation acts governing payments to professional solicitors,[508] which the court characterized as "sanction[ing] such commissions and in many cases endorse[ing] percentage commissions higher than" the percentage commission paid by the organization involved in the case.[509]

Thereafter, another court found occasion to observe that "there is nothing insidious or evil about a commission-based compensation system."[510] An arrangement whereby those who successfully procure contributions to a charitable organization are paid a percentage of the gifts received was judged "reasonable," despite the absence of any limit as to an absolute amount of compensation.[511]

The advent of the intermediate sanctions rules[512] may bring a considerable change in the state of this law. In that context, these types of compensation are known as *revenue-sharing arrangements*. Although there is no imminent development, it is inevitable that a fundraising compensation arrangement will be tested under these rules, with the potential sanction not necessarily being revocation of the tax-exempt status of a charitable organization but the imposition of monetary penalties on a fundraising entity.

Attempts have been made from time to time by associations of fundraising professionals to maintain, in their codes of ethics, prohibitions against compensation based on percentages of funds raised. Although these restrictions have considerable merit,[513] they appear to be violations of the antitrust laws as illegal restraints of trade, and thus cannot lawfully be enforced.[514]

---

[506] *People of God Community* v. *Commissioner*, 75 T.C. 127 (1980).
[507] *World Family Corporation* v. *Commissioner*, 81 T.C. 958, 970 (1983).
[508] See § 3.7.
[509] *World Family Corporation* v. *Commissioner*, supra note 507, at 970.
[510] *National Foundation, Inc.* v. *United States*, 87-2 U.S.T.C. ¶ 9602 (Ct. Cl. 1987).
[511] *Id.* Percentage-based compensation may not be "insidious" or "evil" but some find it "unseemly" (e.g., *Kushnir* v. *American Medical Center at Denver*, 492 P.2d 906 (Colo. App. 1971) (suit by solicitor of funds seeking 50 percent of charitable bequest)).
[512] See *supra* § 6.
[513] E.g., Greenfield, "Professional Compensation," *The Journal* 35 (National Society of Fund-Raising Executives, Summer 1990).
[514] E.g., "American Institute of Certified Public Accountants; Proposed Consent Agreement With Analysis To Aid Public Comment," 54 *Fed. Reg.* 13,529 (Apr. 4, 1989).

Aside from the reasonableness of a compensation package, there is another fundamental consideration: a charitable or other category of tax-exempt organization may not, without transgressing the private inurement doctrine, pay compensation where services are not actually rendered. For example, an organization was denied tax-exempt status because it advanced funds to telephone solicitors, to be offset against earned commissions, where some of the solicitors resigned before they earned commissions equal to or exceeding their advances.[515]

Still other developments continue to inform this analysis, most notably additions to the law regarding permissible and impermissible joint ventures involving health care entities or other public charities and for-profit co-venturers. Among other outcomes, these developments are reshaping and expanding the private benefit doctrine, in ways of direct importance to relationships between charities and those who provide fundraising services for them.

A Tax Court opinion issued in 1999 and affirmed in 2001[516] is proving to be a momentous opinion; it is having a major impact on the operation of health care entities. From a larger perspective, however, this case means much for public charities in general. It is one in a series of cases (more assuredly will follow) where a variety of major law doctrines in the exempt organizations field swirl about: private inurement, private benefit, intermediate sanctions, involvement in partnerships and other joint ventures, and commerciality.

From a health law perspective, this case is seen as an example of the whole hospital joint venture, which it obviously is. The case provides judicial underpinning for the IRS's position regarding these ventures.[517] The fundamental principle is that when a public charity (in the case, a surgical center) cedes authority over its operations to a related for-profit organization, it will quite likely lose its tax-exempt status.

From the larger perspective, however, this case is a *private benefit* case; indeed, it is a significant private benefit case. In the past, some advisors would evaluate a set of facts involving a transaction between a public charity and a for-profit person (including a fundraiser) and determine if that person was an *insider* (for private benefit purposes) or a *disqualified person* (for excess benefit transaction purposes). If the answer to both questions was no, the analysis ended. Clearly, this can no longer be the practice because of the sudden emergence of the private benefit doctrine as a major force. This is because private benefit can occur even where the person being benefited is not an insider or disqualified person. In the case, the court wrote that impermissible private benefit can be conferred on "unrelated or disinterested" persons.[518]

Another reason the private benefit doctrine has not received much attention until recent years is that it is somewhat hidden. It is not to be found in the Internal Revenue Code, nor is it in the regulations. There have been, until recently, few court opinions on the subject. As the Tax Court stated in this joint

---

[515] *Senior Citizens of Missouri, Inc.* v. *Commissioner,* 56 T.C.M. 480 (1988).

[516] *Redlands Surgical Services* v. *Commissioner,* 113 T.C. 47 (1999), *aff'd,* 2001-1 U.S.T.C. ¶50, 271 (9th Cir. 2001).

[517] Rev. Rul. 98-15, 1998-1 C.B. 718.

[518] *Redlands Surgical Services* v. *Commissioner, supra* note 516, at 74.

venture case, the private benefit proscription "inheres in the requirement that an organization operate exclusively [primarily] for exempt purposes."[519]

Until recently, most of the private benefit cases concerned public charities' relationships with individuals. In the prime case in this regard, a school failed to gain exemption because it, according to the court, conferred private benefit (other than insubstantially) on individuals in their private capacity.[520] This joint venture case, however, is forcing public charities to face another application of the private benefit doctrine: their relationships with for-profit organizations.

The case teaches that a fundamental concept in this context is *control*. The opinion stands as a warning to all public charities to examine their relationships with for-profit entities to see if they have lost control of their resources to a for-profit entity. Examples are relationships as reflected in management agreements, leases, fundraising contracts, and, of course, partnership or other joint venture agreements. The horrific aspect of all of this is that it is irrelevant if the public charity is in fact engaging in exempt activities and if the fees paid by the exempt organization to the for-profit one are reasonable (traditional private inurement analysis). There still can be private benefit.

That rule of law is the essence of a case decided by the Tax Court in 1979.[521] The point has been made subsequently, however. Thus, in another case, a court wrote: "The critical inquiry is not whether particular contractual payments to a related for-profit organization are reasonable or excessive, but instead whether the entire enterprise is carried on in such a manner that the for-profit organization benefits substantially from the operation of [the nonprofit organization]."[522]

The case in this area that has been regarded as being on the outer reaches of all this is the 1979 decision. That case has almost been forgotten—until now. One of the underdiscussed aspects of the joint venture case is its resurrection of the law embodied in the 1979 case. The problem is that the 1979 case involved extreme facts, and the Tax Court took a hard line.

In the 1979 case, several for-profit organizations that did not have any formal structural control over the nonprofit entity in question nevertheless exerted "considerable control" over its activities. The for-profit entities set fees that the nonprofit organization charged the public for training sessions, required the nonprofit organization to carry on certain types of educational activities, and provided management personnel paid for and responsible to one of the for-profit organizations. Under a licensing agreement with the for-profit organizations, the nonprofit entity was allowed to use certain intellectual property for 10 years; at the end of the licensing period, all copyrighted material, including new material developed by the nonprofit organization, was required to be turned over to the for-profit organizations. The nonprofit organization was required to use its excess funds for the development of certain research. The for-profit organizations also required that trainers and local

---

[519] *Id.*

[520] *American Campaign Academy* v. *Commissioner, supra* note 499.

[521] *est of Hawaii* v. *Commissioner,* 71 T.C. 1067 (1979), *aff'd* 647 F.2d 170 (9th Cir. 1981).

[522] *Church by Mail, Inc.* v. *Commissioner, supra* note 503, at 1392.

organizations sign an agreement not to compete with "est" for two years after terminating their relationship with "est" organizations.

The Tax Court concluded in that case that the nonprofit organization was "part of a franchise system which is operated for private benefit and . . . its affiliation with this system taints it with a substantial commercial purpose."[523] The "ultimate beneficiaries" of the nonprofit organization's activities were found to be the for-profit corporations; the nonprofit organization was "simply the instrument to subsidize the for-profit corporations and not vice versa."[524] The nonprofit organization was held to not be operating exclusively for charitable purposes.

This 1979 case, then, has framed the borders (to date, anyway) of this analysis. Even without formal control over the ostensible tax-exempt organization by one or more for-profit entities, the ostensible exempt organization can be seen as merely the instrument to subsidize a for-profit organization. The nonprofit organization's "affiliation" with a for-profit entity or a "system" involving one or more for-profit entities can taint the nonprofit organization with a substantial commercial purpose. The result is private benefit that causes the nonprofit organization to lose or be denied tax-exempt status.

Matters worsen within these boundaries when there is actual control. This is the message sent by the joint venture decision. In that case, the public charity became a co-general partner with a for-profit organization in a partnership that owns and operates the surgery center. The arrangement was managed by a for-profit management company that is affiliated with the for-profit co-general partner. The participation in the partnership was the public charity's sole activity. (Hence the name *whole hospital joint venture.*) The court termed this "passive participation in a for-profit health-service enterprise."[525]

The Tax Court concluded in the joint venture case that it is "patently clear" that the partnership was not being operated in an exclusively charitable manner.[526] The income-producing activity of the partnership was characterized as "indivisible."[527] No "discrete part" of these activities was "severable from those activities that produce income to be applied to the other partners' profit."[528]

The heart of the joint venture case is that to the extent that a public charity "cedes control over its sole activity to for-profit parties [by, in this case, entering into the joint venture] having an independent economic interest in the same activity and having no obligation to put charitable purposes ahead of profit-making objectives," the charity cannot be assured that the partnership will in fact be operated in furtherance of charitable purposes.[529] The consequence is the conferring on the for-profit parties of "significant private benefits."[530]

---

[523] *est of Hawaii* v. *Commissioner, supra* note 521, 71 T.C. at 1080.
[524] *Id.* at 1081, 1082.
[525] *Redlands Surgical Services* v. *Commissioner, supra* note 516, 113 T.C. at 77.
[526] *Id.*
[527] *Id.*
[528] *Id.*
[529] *Id.* at 78.
[530] *Id.*

This matter of control is not always so stark as was the situation in the joint venture case. For example, the litigation involving the United Cancer Council[531] shows how courts can differ over whether a nonprofit organization is controlled by a for-profit one. This matter is also reflected in the definitions of *disqualified person* in the intermediate sanctions area.[532]

Further, it would be a mistake for a public charity to disregard the joint venture case on the basis that the charity is not involved in a partnership. There does not have to be a formal partnership agreement for the rules to apply. The law can characterize the relationship between two organizations as a *joint venture* even though neither organization has an intent or desire to be in a joint venture. In some of the cases that the IRS lost on the issue of whether revenue constitutes a royalty,[533] the IRS asserted that the exempt organizations involved were effectively participating in a joint venture.

What can a public charity do to protect itself against allegations of this type of private benefit? Obviously, the main factor is to not lose control over program activities. Another element is one of documentation; the agreements and other documents involved should stress the powers and functions of the nonprofit organization. Contracts should be negotiated at arm's length. Contracts for services should not have long terms. (The management agreement in the joint venture case had the partnership, and thus the charity, locked in for at least 15 years.) If a partnership is involved, the public charity should try to have assets and other resources apart from those invested in the partnership. The public charity should try to receive gifts and grants on an ongoing basis and not rely solely on exempt function revenue. (This factor is prompted by the commerciality doctrine.) Overall, the exempt organization should not be operated to provide to a for-profit entity a nonincidental "advantage; profit; fruit; privilege; gain; [or] interest."[534]

Future enforcement by the IRS of this aspect of this law is to be expected. Loss of tax-exempt status and/or adverse publicity may be in the offing for some charitable organizations. As one commentator observed: "Charitable organizations must be very careful in structuring commission arrangements with fundraisers and solicitors, lest they jeopardize their exempt status."[535]

Nonetheless, in this context, the focus is likely to be more on application of the intermediate sanctions rules.[536] That is, if unreasonable compensation is being paid, or some other excess benefit is being provided, to a disqualified person in the fundraising setting, it is more probable that the IRS will view the matter as an excess benefit transaction and impose one or more intermediate

---

[531] See § 7.12.

[532] See *supra* § 6.

[533] See *supra* § 7.

[534] *American Campaign Academy* v. *Commissioner*, *supra* note 499, at 1065.

[535] Henske, Jr., "Where the IRS Draws the Line on Payments to Professional Fundraisers," 1 *J. Tax'n Exempt Org.* (No. 2) 11, 15 (1989). Also Warner, "Why Charging Commissions Is a Bad Idea," VI *Chron. Phil.* (No. 3) 41 (Nov. 16, 1993); letters to editor in response at VI *Chron. Phil.* (No. 10) 54 (Mar. 8, 1994) and (No. 12) 44–46 (Apr. 5, 1994); "Point–Counterpoint: Commission-Based Compensation," *NSFRE D.C. Area Chapter News* (Greater Washington, D.C. Area Chapter, National Society of Fund-Raising Executives (Mar. 1992)).

[536] See *supra* § 6.

sanctions penalties (excise taxes) on the disqualified person, rather than utilize the private inurement doctrine and revoke the charitable organization's tax-exempt status. (Or, the IRS may do both.) If the transgression does not directly or indirectly involve a disqualified person, however, the IRS can only deploy the private benefit doctrine.[537]

§ 5.14 CHARITABLE DEDUCTION RULES

The process of raising funds for charitable organizations is further regulated by federal law by means of the rules pertaining to the allowability of deductions for charitable gifts.

The basic concept of the federal income tax charitable contribution deduction is that individual taxpayers who itemize deductions, and corporate taxpayers, can deduct, subject to a variety of limitations, an amount equivalent to the value of a contribution to a qualified donee.[538] A *charitable contribution* for income tax purposes is a gift to or for the use of one or more *qualified donees.*[539]

Charitable gifts are also the subject of gift tax and estate tax deductions.[540]

(a) Meaning of Gift

The federal tax law on the subject of the tax aspects of charitable giving is contained in the Internal Revenue Code and in the interpretations of that body of law found in court opinions, Treasury Department and IRS regulations, and IRS public and private rulings. This body of law is specific on such components of the law of charitable giving as qualification of charitable donees, percentage limitations on a year's deductibility, gifts of particular types of property (such as inventory and works of art), and eligibility of various planned giving vehicles.

Despite the extensive treatment of this aspect of the law, there is an omission in the developed rules concerning charitable giving. That is, the law is scarce on the meaning of the word *gift.* This is highly significant; obviously, there must be a gift before there can be a charitable gift.

Integral to the concept of the charitable contribution deduction, then, is the fundamental requirement that the cash or property transferred to a charitable donee be transferred pursuant to a transaction that is in fact a gift. Just because cash is paid, or property is transferred, to a charity does not necessarily mean that the payment or transfer is a gift. Consequently,

---

[537] In a matter involving a private foundation, the IRS concluded that the provision of an unwarranted benefit, that was more than insubstantial, to an individual would not be self-dealing (IRC § 4941) because the individual was not a disqualified person, yet the agency advised that the transaction would trigger the private benefit doctrine and thus endanger the foundation's tax-exempt status (Priv. Ltr. Rul. 200114040).

[538] IRC § 170. This body of law is explored in greater detail in *Tax Law of Charitable Giving.*

[539] IRC § 170(c).

[540] IRC §§ 2522 and 2055, respectively.

when a university's tuition, a hospital's health care fee, or an association's dues are paid, there is no gift, and thus no charitable deduction for the payment.

There is some law (mostly generated by the federal courts) as to what constitutes a gift. (The Internal Revenue Code and the tax regulations are essentially silent on the subject.) Basically, a gift has two elements: it is a transfer that is voluntary and it is motivated by something other than consideration (namely, something being received in return for a payment). (Where payments are made to receive something in exchange, the transaction is more in the nature of a contract.) The law places more emphasis on the second element than on the first. Thus, the income tax regulations state that a transfer is not a contribution when made "with a reasonable expectation of financial return commensurate with the amount of the donation."[541] Instead, this type of a payment is a purchase (of a product or a service). A corollary of this simple rule is that a single transaction can be partially a gift and partially a purchase, and only the gift portion is deductible when a charity is the payee.[542]

Decades ago, the U.S. Supreme Court observed that a gift is a transfer motivated by "detached or disinterested generosity."[543] (This is the factor frequently referred to as *donative intent*.) One federal court of appeals put the matter more starkly, succinctly observing that this is a "particularly confused issue of federal taxation."[544] Not content with that summation, the court went on to portray the existing Internal Revenue Code structure on this subject as "cryptic," and delivered the indictment that "neither Congress nor the courts have offered any very satisfactory definition" of the terms *gift* and *contribution*.[545]

These concepts have been visited many times. One manifestation has been the availability of a charitable deduction for the transfer of money to a college or university, where the transferor is granted preferential access to good seating at the institution's athletic events. Although the IRS refused to regard these payments as gifts, finding that the payment results in receipt of a "substantial benefit,"[546] Congress enacted a special rule to accommodate these payments for tax purposes.[547] The IRS has struggled with this issue for years (e.g., in the early 1980s, when it was popular for homes to be auctioned, with benefits accruing to a charitable organization); the IRS ruled that those who purchase tickets from a charity are not making gifts. Other recent manifestations of this phenomenon include the various "tax shelter" programs involving gifts of artwork and the use of premiums and other items of property to donors in response to their contributions.

The U.S. Supreme Court's 1989 ruling[548] regarding what constitutes a charitable gift comports precisely with the IRS position, which, for years, has

---

[541] Reg. § 1.162-15(b).

[542] See *supra* § 4.

[543] *Commissioner* v. *Duberstein*, 363 U.S. 278, 286 (1960). Also *United States* v. *American Bar Endowment*, *supra* note 13.

[544] *Miller* v. *Internal Revenue Service*, 829 F.2d 500, 502 (4th Cir. 1987).

[545] *Id.* at 502.

[546] Rev. Rul. 84-132, 1984-2 C.B. 55.

[547] IRC § 170(l), which provides that 80 percent of an amount provided to an educational institution, where the payor receives the right to purchase tickets for an athletic event at the institution, is deductible as a charitable contribution.

[548] *Hernandez* v. *Commissioner*, *supra* note 14.

been that, when a "donor" receives some benefit or privilege in return for a payment to charity, the payment may not, in whole or in part, constitute a deductible charitable gift.[549]

(b)   Qualified Donees

Qualified donees are charitable organizations (including educational, religious, and scientific entities),[550] certain fraternal organizations, most veterans' organizations, governmental entities, and certain cemetery companies.[551] Regarding charitable organizations, contributions to both private and public charities are deductible, although the law favors gifts to the latter.

Federal, state, and local governmental bodies are, under the tax law, charitable donees. Other law may, however, preclude a governmental entity from accepting charitable gifts. In many instances, a charitable organization can be established to solicit deductible contributions for and make grants to governmental bodies. This is a common technique for public schools, colleges, universities, and hospitals.[552]

In some instances, an otherwise nonqualifying organization may be the recipient of a deductible charitable gift, where the gift property is used for charitable purposes or received as agent for a charitable organization. An example of the former is a gift to a trade association that is earmarked for a charitable fund within the association.[553] An example of the latter is an additional amount paid by customers of a utility company, when paying their bills to the company, where the additional amounts are earmarked for a charitable organization that assists individuals with emergency energy-related needs.[554]

(c)   Gift Properties

Aside from the eligibility of the gift recipient, the other basic element in determining whether a charitable contribution is deductible is the nature of the property given. Basically, the distinctions are between outright giving and planned giving, and between gifts of cash and gifts of property. In many instances, the tax law of charitable giving differentiates between personal property and real property, and between tangible property and intangible property (the latter being stocks and bonds). The value of a qualified charitable contribution of an item of property often is its fair market value.

---

[549] According to the tax regulations, no part of a payment that an individual makes to or for the use of a charitable organization, that is in consideration for goods or services, is a gift for income tax deductibility purposes unless the individual intended to make a payment in an amount that exceeds the fair market value of the goods or services received (in which case only that excess amount can be a deductible gift) and the individual actually made that type of a payment (Reg. § 1.170A-1(h)(1), (2)). This places greater emphasis on donative intent than was previously the case.

[550] Organizations described in IRC § 501(c)(3), other than those that test for public safety.

[551] IRC § 170(c).

[552] IRC § 170(b)(1)(A)(iv).

[553] Rev. Rul. 54-243, 1954-1 C.B. 92.

[554] Rev. Rul. 85-184, 1985-2 C.B. 84.

The federal income tax treatment of gifts of property depends on whether the property is *capital gain property*. The tax law makes a distinction between long-term capital gain and short-term capital gain (although generally this net gain of either type is taxed as ordinary income). Property that is neither long-term capital gain property nor short-term capital gain property is *ordinary income property*. Short-term capital gain property is generally treated the same as ordinary income property. These terms are based on the tax classification of the type of revenue that would be generated upon sale of the property. In general, therefore, the operative distinction is between capital gain property (actually long-term capital gain property) and ordinary income property.

Capital gain property is property that is a capital asset, has appreciated in value, and if sold, would create long-term capital gain.[555] To result in long-term capital gain, property generally must be held for the long-term capital gain holding period, which is 12 months. Most forms of capital gain property are stocks, bonds, and real estate.

The charitable deduction for capital gain property is often equal to the fair market value of the property or at least is computed using that value. Gifts of ordinary income property generally produce a deduction equivalent to the donor's basis in the property. The law provides exceptions to the basis-only rule, such as in the instance of gifts by a corporation out of its inventory.[556]

(d) Percentage Limitations

The deductibility of charitable contributions for a particular tax year is confined by certain percentage limitations, which, in the case of individuals, are a function of the donor's *contribution base*. An individual's contribution base is essentially his or her adjusted gross income.[557] There are five of these percentage limitations. Again, the limitations depend on several factors—principally, the nature of the charitable recipient and the nature of the property donated. The examples in this section assume an individual donor ("Donor") with a contribution base (adjusted gross income) each year in the amount of $100,000.

First, there is a percentage limitation of 50 percent of a donor's contribution base for contributions of cash and ordinary income property to public charities and private operating foundations.[558] Thus, Donor may, in any one year, make deductible gifts of cash to public charities up to a total of $50,000. Where an individual makes a contribution or contributions to one or more public charities (or operating foundations) to the extent that the 50 percent limitation is exceeded, the excess generally may be carried forward and deducted in one or more (up to five) subsequent years.[559] Thus, if Donor gave $60,000 to public charities in year one (and made no other charitable gifts), he or she would be entitled to a deduction of $50,000 in year one and $10,000 in year two.

---

[555] IRC § 170(b)(1)(C)(iv).
[556] IRC § 170(e)(3).
[557] IRC § 170(b)(1)(F).
[558] IRC § 170(b)(1)(B).
[559] IRC § 170(b)(1)(B), last sentence, and (d)(1).

Another percentage limitation is 30 percent of contribution base for gifts of capital gain property to public charities and private operating foundations.[560] Thus, Donor may, in any one year, contribute up to $30,000 in qualifying stocks, bonds, real estate, and similar property to one or more public charities and enjoy a charitable deduction for that amount (assuming no other charitable gifts that year). Any excess is subject to the carryforward rule described earlier.[561] Thus, if Donor gave $50,000 in capital gain property to public charities in year one (and made no other charitable gifts that year), he or she would be entitled to a charitable contribution deduction of $30,000 in year one and $20,000 in year two.

A donor who makes gifts of cash and capital gain property to public charities (and/or private operating foundations) in any one year generally must use a blend of these percentage limitations.[562] For example, if Donor in year one gives $50,000 in cash and $30,000 in appreciated capital gain property to a public charity, his or her charitable deduction in year one consists of the $30,000 of capital gain property and $20,000 of cash (thereby capping the deduction with the overall 50 percent ceiling); the other $30,000 of cash is carried forward for deductibility (depending on Donor's other circumstances) in year two.

A donor of capital gain property to public charities and/or private operating foundations may use the 50 percent limitation, instead of the 30 percent limitation, where the amount of the contribution is reduced by all of the unrealized appreciation in the value of the property.[563] This election, which is irrevocable,[564] is usually made in situations where the donor wants a larger deduction in the year of the gift and the property has not appreciated in value to a great extent.

The fourth and fifth percentage limitations apply with respect to gifts to private foundations and certain other charitable donees (other than public charities and private operating foundations). These "other charitable donees" are generally veterans' and fraternal organizations. For contributions of cash and ordinary income property to private foundations and these other entities, the deduction may not exceed 30 percent of the individual donor's contribution base.[565] The carryover rules apply to this type of gift. Thus, if Donor gives $50,000 in cash to one or more private foundations in year one, his or her charitable deduction for that year (assuming no other charitable gifts) is $30,000, with the balance of $20,000 carried forward for potential deductibility in subsequent years.

These rules also blend with the percentage limitations applicable with respect to gifts to public charities. For example, if in year one Donor gave $65,000 to charity, of which $25,000 went to a public charity and $40,000 to a private foundation, his or her charitable deduction for that year would be $50,000, consisting of $30,000 of the gift to the private foundation and $20,000 of the gift to the public charity; the remaining $10,000 of the gift to the foundation and the

---

[560] IRC § 170(b)(1)(C)(i).
[561] IRC § 170(b)(1)(C)(ii).
[562] IRC § 170(b)(1)(B).
[563] IRC § 170(b)(1)(C)(iii).
[564] *Woodbury* v. *Commissioner*, 900 F.2d 1457 (10th Cir. 1990).
[565] IRC § 170(b)(1)(B)(i).

remaining $5,000 of the gift to the public charity would be carried forward and made available for deductibility in year two.

The fifth percentage limitation is 20 percent of contribution base in the case of gifts of capital gain property to private foundations and other charitable donees (other than public charities and private operating foundations).[566] There is a carryforward for any excess deduction in the case of these gifts.[567] For example, if Donor gives appreciated securities, having a value of $30,000, to a private foundation in year one, his or her charitable deduction for year one (assuming no other charitable gifts) is $20,000; the remaining $10,000 would never be deductible. To avoid this situation, Donor would contribute $20,000 of the securities in year one and postpone the gift of the remaining $10,000 in securities until year two. Or, if the value of the stock may substantially decline and an immediate charitable deduction is of prime concern, Donor could, in year one, donate $20,000 of the securities to the private foundation and donate $10,000 of the securities to a public charity.

Deductible charitable contributions by corporations in any tax year may not exceed 10 percent of pretax net income.[568] Excess amounts may be carried forward and deducted in subsequent years (up to five years).[569] For gifts by corporations, the federal tax laws do not differentiate between gifts to public charities and private foundations. As an illustration, a corporation that grosses $1 million in a year and incurs $900,000 in expenses in that year (not including charitable gifts) may generally contribute to charity and deduct in that year an amount up to $10,000 (10 percent of $100,000); in computing its taxes, this corporation would report taxable income of $90,000. If the corporation instead gave $20,000 in that year, the foregoing numbers would stay the same, except that the corporation would have a $10,000 charitable contribution carryforward.

A corporation on the accrual method of accounting can elect to treat a contribution as having been paid in a tax year if it is actually paid during the first 2½ months of the following year.[570] Corporate gifts of property are generally subject to the deduction reduction rules discussed as follows.

(e) Deduction Reduction Rules

A donor (individual or corporate) that makes a gift of ordinary income property to any charity (public or private) must confine the charitable deduction to the amount of the cost basis of the property.[571] That is, the deduction is not based on the fair market value of the property; it must be reduced by the amount that would, if sold, have been gain (ordinary income). As an example, if Donor gave to a charity an item of ordinary income property having a value of $1,000 for which he or she paid $600, the charitable deduction would be $600.

Any donor who makes a gift of capital gain property to a public charity generally can, as noted previously, compute the charitable deduction using the

---

[566] IRC § 170(b)(1)(D)(i).
[567] IRC § 170(b)(1)(D)(ii).
[568] IRC § 170(b)(2).
[569] IRC § 170(d)(2).
[570] IRC § 170(a)(2).
[571] IRC § 170(e)(1)(A).

property's fair market value at the time of the gift, irrespective of basis and with no taxation of the appreciation (the capital gain inherent in the property). A donor who makes a gift of capital gain tangible personal property (e.g., a work of art) to a public charity, however, must reduce the deduction by all of the long-term capital gain that would have been recognized had the donor sold the property at its fair market value as of the date of contribution, where the use by the donee is unrelated to its tax-exempt purposes.[572]

Generally, a donor who makes a gift of capital gain property to a private foundation must reduce the amount of the otherwise allowable deduction by all of the appreciation element in the gift property.[573] An individual is, however, allowed full fair market value for a contribution to a private foundation of certain publicly traded stock.[574]

(f) Twice-Basis Deductions

As a general rule, when a corporation makes a charitable gift of property from its inventory, the resulting charitable deduction is confined to an amount equal to the donor's basis in the donated property. In most instances, this basis amount is rather small, being equal to the cost of producing the property. Under certain circumstances, however, corporate donors can receive a greater charitable deduction for gifts out of their inventory. Where the tests are satisfied, the deduction can be equal to cost basis, plus one-half of the appreciated value of the property.[575] Nonetheless, this charitable deduction may not, in any event, exceed an amount equal to twice the property's cost basis.

Five requirements have to be met for this twice-basis charitable deduction to be available: (1) the donated property must be used by the charitable donee for a related use; (2) the donated property must be used solely for the care of the ill, the needy, or infants; (3) the property may not be transferred by the donee in exchange for money, other property, or services; (4) the donor must receive a written statement from the donee representing that the use and disposition of the donated property will be in conformance with these rules; and (5) where the donated property is subject to regulation under the Federal Food, Drug, and Cosmetic Act, the property must fully satisfy the applicable requirements of that statute on the date of transfer and for 180 days prior thereto.

Also, for these rules to apply, the donee must be a public charity; that is, it cannot be a private foundation, including a private operating foundation. Further, an "S corporation"—the tax status of many small businesses—cannot utilize these rules.

A similar rule applies with respect to contributions of scientific property used for research,[576] and contributions of computer technology and equipment for elementary and secondary school purposes.[577]

---

[572] IRC § 170(e)(1)(B)(i).
[573] IRC § 170(e)(1)(B)(ii).
[574] IRC § 170(e)(5).
[575] IRC § 170(e)(3).
[576] IRC § 170(e)(4).
[577] IRC § 170(e)(6).

(g) Partial Interest Gifts

Most charitable gifts are of all interests in property; that is, by giving, the donor parts with all right, title, and interest in the property. But a deductible gift may be made in the form of a contribution of less than a donor's entire interest in the property. This is termed a gift of a *partial interest.*

As a general rule, charitable deductions for gifts of partial interests in property, including the right to use property, are denied.[578] But, the exceptions, which are many, are gifts made in trust form (using a *split-interest trust*);[579] gifts of an outright remainder interest in a personal residence or farm;[580] gifts of an undivided portion of one's entire interest in a property;[581] and a remainder interest in real property that is granted to a public charity exclusively for conservation purposes.[582]

Contributions of income interests in property in trust are basically confined to the use of charitable lead trusts.[583] Aside from the charitable gift annuity and the above-described gifts of remainder interests, there is no charitable deduction for a contribution of a remainder interest in property unless it is in trust and is one of three types: a charitable remainder annuity trust, a charitable remainder unitrust, or a pooled income fund.[584]

Defective charitable split-interest trusts may be reformed to preserve the charitable deduction where certain requirements are satisfied.[585]

(h) Appraisal Requirements

The law contains requirements that apply to the substantiation of deductions claimed by an individual, a closely held corporation, a personal service corporation, a partnership, or a small business (S) corporation for charitable contributions of certain property.[586] Property to which these rules apply is termed *charitable deduction property.* If the contributed property is a partial interest in an item of property, the appraisal must be of the partial interest.[587] These substantiation requirements must be complied with if the charitable deduction is to be allowed.[588]

The requirements apply to contributions of property (other than money and publicly traded securities) if the aggregate claimed or reported value of the

---

[578] IRC § 170(f)(3)(A).
[579] IRC § 170(f)(2).
[580] IRC § 170(f)(3)(B)(i).
[581] IRC § 170(f)(3)(B)(ii).
[582] IRC §§ 170(f)(3)(B)(iii) and 170(h).
[583] IRC § 170(f)(2)(B).
[584] IRC § 170(f)(2)(A). The concept of partial interest gifts from the standpoint of planned gifts is discussed in *Tax Law of Charitable Giving* § 5.3. Charitable gift annuities are the subject of *id.,* Chapter 14; charitable lead trusts are the subject of Chapter 16; charitable remainder trusts are the subject of Chapter 12; pooled income funds are the subject of Chapter 13; and other forms of planned giving are the subject of Chapter 15.
[585] IRC § 170(f)(7).
[586] Reg. § 1.170A-13(c).
[587] Reg. § 1.170A-13(c)(1)(ii).
[588] Reg. § 1.170A-13(c)(2).

property (and all similar items of property for which deductions for charitable contributions are claimed or reported by the same donor for the same tax year, whether or not donated to the same charitable donee) is in excess of $5,000.[589]

The phrase *similar items of property* means "property of the same generic category or type," including stamp collections, coin collections, lithographs, paintings, photographs, books, nonpublicly traded stock, other nonpublicly traded securities, land, buildings, clothing, jewelry, furniture, electronic equipment, household appliances, toys, everyday kitchenware, china, crystal, or silver.[590] For example, if a donor claimed, in one year, deductions of $2,000 for books given to College A, $2,500 for books given to College B, and $900 for books given to College C, the $5,000 threshold would be exceeded. Therefore, this donor would have to obtain a qualified appraisal for the books and attach to the appropriate income tax return three appraisal summaries for the books donated to the three colleges.

For this type of gift, the donor must obtain a *qualified appraisal* and attach an *appraisal summary* to the return on which the deduction is claimed.[591] In the case of nonpublicly traded stock, however, the claimed value of which does not exceed $10,000 but is greater than $5,000, the donor does not have to obtain a qualified appraisal but must attach a partially completed appraisal summary form to the tax or information return on which the deduction is claimed.[592]

A qualified appraisal is an appraisal document that:

- Relates to an appraisal that is made not earlier than 60 days before the date of contribution of the appraisal property

- Is prepared, signed, and dated by a qualified appraiser (or appraisers)

- Contains the requisite information

- Does not involve a prohibited type of appraisal fee[593]

Certain information must be included in a qualified appraisal:

- A description of the property in sufficient detail for a person who is not generally familiar with the type of property to ascertain that the property that was appraised is the property being contributed

- The physical condition of the property (in the case of tangible property)

- The date of contribution of the property

- The terms of any agreement between the parties relating to any subsequent disposition of the property, including restrictions on the charity's use of the gift property

- The name, address, and tax identification number of the appraiser

---

[589] Reg. § 1.170A-13(c)(1)(i).
[590] Reg. § 1.170A-13(c)(7)(iii).
[591] Reg. § 1.170A-13(c)(2)(i)(A), (B).
[592] Reg. § 1.170A-13(c)(2)(ii).
[593] Reg. § 1.170A-13(c)(3)(i).

- The qualifications of the qualified appraiser (or appraisers)

- A statement that the appraisal was prepared for income tax purposes

- The date or dates on which the property was appraised

- The appraised fair market value of the property on the date of contribution

- The method of valuation used to determine the fair market value of the property

- The specific basis for the valuation[594]

The qualified appraisal must be received by the donor before the due date (including extensions) of the return on which the deduction for the contributed property is first claimed or, in the case of a deduction first claimed on an amended return, the date on which the return is filed.[595]

A separate qualified appraisal is required for each item of property that is not included in a group of similar items of property.[596] One qualified appraisal is required for a group of similar items of property contributed in the same tax year, as long as the appraisal includes all of the required information for each item.[597] The appraiser may, however, select any items the aggregate value of which is appraised at $100 or less, for which a group description—rather than a specific description of each item—is adequate.[598] The appraisal must be retained by the donor "for so long as it may be relevant in the administration of any internal revenue law."[599]

The appraisal summary must be submitted on a form prescribed by the IRS (Form 8283, Section B), signed and dated by the charitable donee and qualified appraiser (or appraisers), and attached to the donor's return on which a deduction with respect to the appraised property is first claimed or reported.[600] The signature by the donee does not represent concurrence in the appraised value of the contributed property.

The following information must be included in the appraisal summary:

- The name and taxpayer identification number of the donor (for example, the social security number of an individual)

- A description of the property in requisite detail

- A brief summary of the condition of the property at the time of the gift (in the case of tangible property)

- The manner and date of acquisition of the property by the donor

[594] Reg. § 1.170A-13(c)(3)(ii).
[595] Reg. § 1.170A-13(c)(3)(iv)(B).
[596] Reg. § 1.170A-13(c)(3)(iv)(A).
[597] Id.
[598] Id.
[599] Reg. § 1.170A-13(c)(3)(iv)(C).
[600] Reg. § 1.170A-13(c)(4).

- The cost basis of the property

- The name, address, and taxpayer identification number of the charitable donee

- The date the donee received the property

- A statement explaining whether the charitable contribution was made by means of a bargain sale,[601] and the amount of any consideration received from the donee for the contribution

- The name, address, and taxpayer identification number of the qualified appraiser (or appraisers)

- The appraised fair market value of the property on the date of contribution

- A declaration by the appraiser[602]

The rules pertaining to separate appraisals, noted earlier, also apply with respect to appraisal summaries.[603] A donor who contributed similar items of property to more than one charitable donee must, however, attach a separate appraisal summary for each donee.[604]

Every donor who presents an appraisal summary to a charitable organization for signature must furnish a copy of the appraisal summary to the charitable donee.[605] If the donor is a partnership or small business corporation, the donor must provide a copy of the appraisal summary to every partner or shareholder who receives an allocation of a deduction for a charitable contribution of property described in the appraisal summary.[606] The partner or shareholder must attach the appraisal summary to the partner's or shareholder's return.[607] If a donor (or partner or shareholder of a donor) fails to attach the appraisal summary to the return, a charitable deduction will not be disallowed if the donor (or partner or shareholder) submits an appraisal summary within 90 days of being requested to do so by the IRS, as long as the failure to attach the appraisal summary was a good-faith omission and certain other requirements are met (including timely completion of the appraisal).[608]

The appraisal summary form (Form 8283, Section A) must be filed by contributors where the total value of all noncash contributions exceeds $500 and is less than $5,000. This portion of the form must also be used to report contributions of publicly traded securities, even where the value of them is in excess of $5,000.

Special rules apply for the substantiation of charitable deductions for gifts of nonpublicly traded securities (such as Israeli bonds). When a five-part

---

[601] See *Tax Law of Charitable Giving* § 9.16.
[602] Reg. § 1.170A-13(c)(4)(ii).
[603] Reg. § 1.170A-13(c)(4)(iv)(A).
[604] Reg. § 1.170A-13(c)(4)(iv)(B).
[605] Reg. § 1.170A-13(c)(4)(iv)(E).
[606] Reg. § 1.170A-13(c)(4)(iv)(F).
[607] Reg. § 1.170A-13(c)(4)(iv)(G).
[608] Reg. § 1.170A-13(c)(4)(iv)(H).

test is satisfied, charitable deductions are permitted for securities that are not publicly exchanged and for which there are no published quotations.

The term *qualified appraiser* means an individual who includes on the appraisal summary a declaration that:

- He or she holds himself or herself out to the public as an appraiser or performs appraisals on a regular basis;

- Because of the appraiser's qualifications as described in the appraisal, he or she is qualified to make appraisals of the type of property being valued;

- The appraiser is not one of the persons excluded by these rules from being a qualified appraiser; and

- The appraiser understands that an intentionally false or fraudulent overstatement of the value of the property described in the qualified appraisal or appraisal summary may subject the appraiser to a civil penalty for aiding and abetting an understatement of tax liability,[609] and, consequently, the appraiser may have appraisals disregarded.[610]

Notwithstanding these requirements, an individual is not a qualified appraiser if the donor had knowledge of facts that would cause a reasonable person to expect the appraiser to falsely overstate the value of the donated property.[611] Also, the donor, donee, or certain other related persons cannot be qualified appraisers of the property involved in the gift transaction.[612]

More than one appraiser may appraise the donated property, as long as each appraiser complies with these requirements, including signing the qualified appraisal and appraisal summary.[613] If more than one appraiser appraises the property, the donor does not have to use each appraiser's appraisal for purposes of substantiating the charitable deduction.[614]

Generally, no part of the fee arrangement for a qualified appraisal can be based on a percentage of the appraised value of the property.[615] If a fee arrangement is based, in whole or in part, on the amount of the appraised value of the property, if any, that is allowed as a charitable deduction, after IRS examination or otherwise, it is treated as a fee based on a percentage of the appraised value of the property.[616] (This rule does not apply in certain circumstances to appraisal fees paid to a generally recognized association that regulates appraisers.[617])

---

[609] IRC § 6701.
[610] Reg. § 1.170A-13(c)(5)(i).
[611] Reg. § 1.170A-13(c)(5)(ii).
[612] Reg. § 1.170A-13(c)(5)(iv). In formulating these rules, the IRS rejected the thought of including in the criteria for qualified appraisers certain professional standards or the establishment of a registry of qualified appraisers.
[613] Reg. § 1.170A-13(c)(5)(iii).
[614] *Id.*
[615] Reg. § 1.170A-13(c)(6)(i).
[616] *Id.*
[617] Reg. § 1.170A-13(c)(6)(ii).

In any situation involving a gift of property, the charitable organization that receives the gift must value the property for purposes of its own record-keeping and reporting purposes. The charitable donee is not required (and, in some instances, may not be able[618]), however, to share that valuation with the donor.

Many of these requirements apply to the donor. Therefore, technically, compliance with them is the responsibility of the donor and not the charitable donee. As a matter of donor relations (if only because the charitable deduction usually depends on adherence to the rules), however, the charitable organization will want to be certain that its donors are made aware of the rules and probably assist them in assembling the necessary records and in otherwise complying with the requirements.

A separate set of rules applies appraisal requirements to regular corporations (corporations other than those referenced previously, termed C corporations). These rules, in general, require these corporations to obtain a qualified independent appraisal to validly claim a charitable contribution deduction for gifts of most non-money property having a value in excess of $5,000.[619]

These rules, when proposed, would have applied in instances when a regular corporation makes a charitable contribution of property that constitutes part of its inventory. Gifts of this nature are often the subject of a special deduction provision.[620] In response to complaints of burdens of overregulation by the corporate giving community, the IRS subsequently announced[621] a rule exempting certain corporations from the need to obtain appraisals for gifts of inventory.[622] These corporations, instead, are required to include summary information in their annual tax return, such as a description of the inventory contributed and the valuation method used (such as retail pricing). This information is embodied in a *partially completed appraisal summary.*

---

[618] See *supra* text accompanied by note 591.

[619] Reg. § 1.170A-13(c)(2)(ii).

[620] IRC § 170(e)(3). See *Tax Law of Charitable Giving* § 9.3.

[621] IR-88-137.

[622] The problem facing the charitable community in this regard was the fear that the more burdensome the regulatory process required in conjunction with gifts of inventory, the greater the likelihood that corporations would not make this type of gift. Also, the price set by these corporations for the items they manufacture is based on their assessment of what the market will accept. Partially, the price is determined by the cost of developing and marketing the items; the price is also partially a function of what the consuming public is willing to pay—the classic law definition of the fair market value of an item of property. An independent appraiser cannot provide any better determination of value than the contributing corporation. Further, an appraisal of inventory gifts is usually a pointless act. At best, the deduction will be an amount no greater than twice the corporation's cost basis in the property, so the fair market value of the property is likely to be irrelevant.

Section 6281 of the Technical and Miscellaneous Revenue Act of 1988 (102 Stat. 3342, P.L. 100-647) authorized the Department of the Treasury to promulgate regulations allowing regular corporations to provide, in the case of charitable gifts of inventory, less detailed substantiation than that required for other corporations. The Treasury Department had, however, already agreed to the above-described compromise by the time this legislation was finalized.

(i) Receipt, Record-Keeping, and Reporting Rules

There is a battery of rules to which a donor to a charitable organization and the donee charitable organization must adhere, as a condition of allowance of the otherwise allowable federal income tax charitable contribution deduction. That is, where there is noncompliance with these rules, the donor will not be entitled to the charitable deduction, notwithstanding the fact that all other applicable rules have been followed. These rules—some of which are termed *substantiation requirements*—embrace receipt, record-keeping, and reporting requirements.

An individual who itemizes deductions must separately state (on Schedule A of the federal income tax return, Form 1040) the aggregate amount of charitable contributions of money and the aggregate amount of charitable gifts of property.

There are two sets of these substantiation rules. One set is found in tax regulations that were promulgated in 1984; the other is in statutory law that was enacted in 1993.[623] The statutory rules apply with respect to charitable contributions of $250 or more. Thus, the preexisting regulations remain applicable with respect to gifts that are less than $250 in value. When the gift is of property that has a value in excess of $5,000, the appraisal rules[624] apply.

(j) Receipt and Record-Keeping Requirements for Small Gifts

In the case of contributions of money or property to charity, when the value of the gift in a year is less than $250, a donor—individual or corporate—must keep some record of the gift. This record must be maintained irrespective of the size of the gift. Preferably, the record will be a cancelled check or a receipt from the charitable donee.[625] Otherwise, the record must be *written* and *reliable*.[626] The record must show the name of the charitable donee, the date of the contribution, and the amount of the contribution.[627]

A letter or other communication from the charitable donee acknowledging receipt of the contribution, and showing the date and amount of the contribution, constitutes a *receipt*.[628] A donor has the burden of establishing reliability of a written record other than a check or receipt. The reliability of this type of written record is determined on the basis of all of the facts and circumstances of a particular case. Factors indicating that this other written evidence is reliable include:

- The contemporaneous nature of the writing that evidences the contribution

- The regularity of the donor's record-keeping procedures

---

[623] See *supra* § 3.
[624] See *supra* § (h).
[625] Reg. § 1.170A-13(a)(1)(i), (ii).
[626] Reg. § 1.170A-13(a)(1)(iii).
[627] *Id.*
[628] Reg. § 1.170A-13(a)(1)(ii).

- In the case of a contribution of a "small amount" (that term is not defined), any other written evidence from the recipient charitable organization evidencing the making of a gift that would not otherwise constitute a receipt[629]

As to the second of these factors, "a contemporaneous diary entry stating the amount and date of the donation and the name of the donee charitable organization made by a taxpayer who regularly makes such diary entries would generally be considered reliable."[630] As to the third of these factors, the evidence would include an "emblem, button, or other token traditionally associated with a charitable organization and regularly given by the organization to persons making cash donations."[631]

Concerning contributions of property (other than money) to a charitable organization, a corporate or individual donor must obtain a receipt from the recipient charitable organization and a reliable written record of specified information with respect to the donated property.[632]

This receipt must include the name of the donee, the date and location of the contribution, and a "description of the property in detail reasonably sufficient under the circumstances."[633] When these regulations were initially promulgated (in proposed form), they required that the charitable organization donee provide a statement as to the value of the property. In response to complaints about that requirement, the regulations were revised to state that "[a]lthough the fair market value of the property is one of the circumstances to be taken into account in determining the amount of detail to be included on the receipt, such value need not be stated on the receipt."[634]

For these purposes, a letter or other written communication from the donee acknowledging receipt of the contribution, showing the date of the contribution, and containing the required description of the property contributed constitutes a *receipt*.[635] A receipt is not required, however, in instances where the gift is made in circumstances "where it is impractical to obtain a receipt (e.g., by depositing property at a charity's unattended drop site)."[636] In these instances, the donor must "maintain reliable written records" with respect to each item of donated property.[637]

Also, the donor of appreciated property to charity must maintain a *reliable written record* of specified information with respect to each item of property.[638] This information must include the following:[639]

---

[629] Reg. § 1.170A-13(a)(2)(i).
[630] Reg. § 1.170A-13(a)(2)(i)(B).
[631] Reg. § 1.170A-13(a)(2)(i)(C).
[632] Reg. § 1.170A-13(b)(1).
[633] Reg. § 1.170A-13(b)(1)(i)–(iii).
[634] Reg. § 1.170A-13(b)(1)(iii).
[635] Reg. § 1.170A-13(b)(1).
[636] *Id.*
[637] *Id.*
[638] Reg. § 1.170A-13(b)(2)(i).
[639] Reg. § 1.170A-13(b)(2)(ii).

- The name and address of the charitable donee

- The date and location of the contribution

- A description of the property "in detail reasonable under the circumstances (including the value of the property)"[640]

- In the case of securities, the name of the issuing company, the type of security, and whether it is regularly traded on a stock exchange or in an over-the-counter market

- The fair market value of the property at the time of the gift, the method utilized in determining the value, and a copy of the signed report of the appraiser (if any)

- The cost or other basis of the property, and, if it is ordinary income property or other type of property where the deduction must be reduced by all or a portion of the gain, the reduction in the amount of the charitable contribution, and the manner in which the reduction was determined

- Where the gift is of a remainder interest or an income interest, the total amount claimed as a deduction for the year due to the gift and the amount claimed as a deduction in any prior year or years for gifts of other interests in the property, the name and address of each organization to which any such contribution was made, the place where any such property, which is tangible property, is located or kept, and the name of any person, other than the organization to which the property giving rise to the deduction was contributed, having actual possession of the property

- The terms of any agreement or understanding entered into by or on behalf of the donor "which relates to the use, sale, or other disposition of the property contributed,"[641] such as:

  a. Any restriction, temporary or permanent, on the charity's right to use or dispose of the property,

  b. A retention or conveyance of the right to the income from the donated property or to possession of the property, including the right to vote donated securities, to acquire the property by purchase or otherwise, or to designate the person having the income, possession, or right to acquire, or

  c. An earmarking of the property for a particular use.[642]

Additional rules apply with respect to gifts of property (other than money) for which the donor claims a federal income tax charitable contribution deduction

---

[640] Reg. § 1.170A-13(b)(2)(ii)(C).
[641] Reg. § 1.170A-13(b)(2)(ii)(G).
[642] Id.

in excess of $500.[643] Under these rules, however, the donor is required to maintain additional records, regarding:

- The manner of acquisition of the property, as, for example, by purchase, gift, bequest, inheritance, or exchange, and the approximate date of acquisition of the property by the donor or, if the property was created, produced, or manufactured by or for the donor, the approximate date the property was substantially completed;[644] and

- The cost or other basis of the property, other than publicly traded securities, held by the donor for a period less than the long-term capital gains holding period immediately preceding the date on which the contribution was made and, when the information is available, of property, other than publicly traded securities, held for the long-term capital gains holding period preceding the date on which the contribution was made.[645]

This information generally is to be provided as part of the donor's income tax return.[646] If the donor has reasonable cause for not being able to provide the information, the donor must attach an explanatory statement to the return.[647] If the donor can demonstrate this reasonable cause, the donor will not be disallowed a charitable contribution deduction for failure to comply with the rules pertaining to gifts of property having a value in excess of $500.[648]

(k) Reporting Requirements

Federal law requires the filing of an information return by certain charitable donees that make certain dispositions of contributed property (*charitable deduction property*).[649]

A charitable donee that sells, exchanges, consumes, or otherwise disposes of gift property within two years after the date of the donor's contribution of the property must file an information return (Form 8282) with the IRS. A copy of the donee information return must be provided to the donor and retained by the donee.

This information return must contain the following:

- The name, address, and taxpayer identification numbers of the donor and the donee

- A sufficient description of the property

---

[643] Reg. § 1.170A-13(b)(3).
[644] Reg. § 1.170A-13(b)(3)(i)(A).
[645] Reg. § 1.170A-13(b)(3)(i)(B).
[646] Reg. § 1.170A-13(b)(3)(ii).
[647] *Id.*
[648] *Id.*
[649] IRC § 6050L.

- The date of the contribution
- The amount received on the disposition
- The date of the disposition

This reporting obligation is not required with respect to an item of charitable deduction property disposed of by sale, if the appraisal summary signed by the donee with respect to the item contains, at the time of the donee's signature, a statement signed by the donor that the appraised value of the item does not exceed $500. For these purposes, items that form a set (e.g., a collection of books written by the same author, components of a stereo system, or a group of place settings of a pattern of silverware) are considered one item. Also, all nonpublicly traded stock is considered one item, as are all nonpublicly traded securities other than nonpublicly traded stock.

This exception is designed to embrace the situation where a donor contributes to a charity items of property that, taken together, are worth more than $5,000 (thereby triggering the appraisal and appraisal summary requirements) and where the charity (within the two-year period) sells one of these items which, at the time the charity signed the appraisal summary, had a value of no more than $500. For example, if an individual donated the entire contents of a house to a charity, an appraisal summary may be done with respect to all of the items as a group, and the charity may thereafter sell some of the items individually. To the extent that each item had a value that is less than $500, the charity would not have to file the information return with respect to the sale(s).

One of the vague aspects of this rule is the underlying assumption of application of the aggregation rule. For example, to build on the previous illustration, the contents of the house consisted of furniture valued at $5,000, jewelry valued at $5,000, clothing valued at $5,000, and art works valued at $5,000. While the safe approach may be to secure an appraisal for all of the $20,000 in property, an appraisal (and an appraisal summary) may not be required in the first instance because the properties are not *similar.* If that is the case, the property is not charitable deduction property to begin with.

This reporting obligation also does not apply to a situation where the charitable donee consumes or distributes, without consideration, the property in the course of performing an exempt function.

This donee information return must be filed within 125 days of the disposition of the charitable deduction property.

A successor donee may be required to file this information return if this donee disposes of charitable deduction property within two years after the date of the donor's contribution to the original donee. A *successor donee* is any donee of charitable contribution property other than the original donee.[650]

---

[650] Ann. 88-120, 1988-38 I.R.B. 27.

§ 5.15 COMMENSURATE TEST

The IRS, late in 1990, revoked the tax-exempt status of a charitable organization essentially on the ground that its fundraising costs were too high. The position of the IRS in this regard is contained in a technical advice memorandum (TAM).[651] The organization subsequently prevailed in litigation as to its tax-exempt status, although the litigation did not involve the fundraising cost issue.[652]

The IRS's lawyers initially based their conclusions on three grounds: (1) the organization failed to carry on a charitable program commensurate in scope with its financial resources; (2) the organization was operated for the private interest of the direct mail fundraiser involved rather than for a public interest; and (3) the organization was operated for the substantial nonexempt purpose of operating direct mail fundraising.

The IRS was also displeased with the charitable organization's method of allocating expenses between public education and fundraising. Finding the educational portion of the mailings to be insignificant, the IRS concluded that there should not be any allocation of expenses to program activities.

(a) Facts

The organization was established to combat cancer. It was formed to promote and encourage research, engage in public and professional education and direct service, and coordinate the efforts of member agencies. In the early 1980s, the organization concluded it could no longer subsist wholly on membership dues and, in 1984, contracted with a direct mail fundraising firm.

The fundraising firm charged the charity five cents per piece for donor acquisition mailings and ten cents per piece for donor renewal mailings. Additional fees were levied for postage, design and production of mailings, mailing and handling, receipt and accounting of donations, and the like. As these charges were to be paid from gross receipts of the mailings, the charity was able to launch this fundraising effort at no initial cost to itself.

The fundraising firm would create a mailing package and secure approval of it from the charity; a test mailing was then run. On the basis of the results, the mailing was printed. An independent list management firm prepared the mailings and delivered them to the postal service.

The principal method of fundraising was use of a variety of sweepstakes programs and similar prize offerings. The IRS found these fundraising offerings to be "often misleading." The IRS wrote of recipients who believed they had been "victimized"; the result was a battery of lawsuits by state attorneys general against the charity and the fundraiser. The IRS concluded that these activities were "neither necessary nor valuable in achieving . . . [the charity's] educational or health goals, except to obtain money." The IRS further observed that the charity and the fundraiser "selected the recipients of the letters based

---

[651] This TAM is reproduced at 4 *Exempt Org. Tax Review* (No. 5) 726 (July 1991).
[652] See *supra* note 170.

on sweepstakes/fundraising decisions rather than any need of the recipients for educational information."

According to the IRS, in 1986, the charity expended $315,577 for charitable purposes, out of $7.88 million (4.1%). The figures for 1987 were $398,557 out of $10.41 million (3.8%). (As discussed later, these figures do not include the amount spent for "public education" as asserted by the charity.) The organization expended about 2.5% on management expenses. The rest of the money was paid to the fundraiser.

When the charitable organization filed its annual information return (Form 990) with the IRS, it allocated expenses for numerous mailings to either public education or fundraising. It did not allocate expenses to what it regarded as "generic" information (such as language that described the organization, sweepstakes rules, and entry tickets, coupons, and envelopes). The allocation was based on a line count of the various mailings.

The charitable organization's ascertainment of its exempt and fundraising expenses was as follows. For 1986, its donor acquisition costs were 45 percent and its exempt function expenditures were 55 percent of total outlays. The comparables for 1987 were 43 percent for program and 57 percent for fundraising. For 1986 and 1987, the organization's donor renewal costs were 51 percent and its exempt function expenditures were 49 percent.

Much of the organization's "public education" content was basic information in very small print. Often, this information was located on the reverse side of sweepstakes tickets that had to be returned for entry; therefore, these items could not be kept for future information purposes by the recipient.

The IRS followed the charitable organization's allocation approach, except that it factored in the generic material as noneducational material. It concluded that less than 10 percent of the mailings' content was educational.

In the face of many lawsuits and negative publicity, the charity terminated its contract with the fundraiser. It contracted with another fundraiser that did not use these tactics; its gift receipts were insufficient. It filed for bankruptcy in mid-1990.

(b) Law and Analysis

(i) *Allocations.* The TAM stated that the "Service recognizes that many educational and religious organizations . . . carry out their exempt functions through directly mailing educational or religious material that also contain elements of fundraising." The IRS continued: "In fact fundraising letters are sometimes the principal means by which the general public is made aware of the exempt purposes and programs of an organization." Consequently, the IRS, in this TAM, concluded that "reasonable allocations of mixed programs are allowed."

But then the IRS's lawyers concluded that the "extent that an allocation may be taken between fundraising and program-related activities depends on the facts and circumstances of each particular case." In this case, the IRS concluded that the "vast bulk of . . . [the charity's] fundraising mail-outs had very little content that could be described as having educational value. . . ." The IRS concluded that the educational content in the fundraising material was thus "insubstantial."

The IRS found that the "thrust of . . . [the charity's] fundraising literature is the solicitation of readers to participate in a sweepstakes in an effort to raise funds rather than to educate the public." The IRS added that the "appeal to fund research and find a cure for . . . [the disease involved] is secondary in the letters to an appeal to acquire wealth through gambling."

Using both linear and square-inch methods, the IRS measured sample mailings and concluded that over 90 percent of the content of the mailings was not educational. In so doing, the IRS, as noted, included generic material.

(ii) Commensurate Test.   An important aspect of this TAM is its analysis of the *commensurate test.* This test, established by the IRS in 1964,[653] endeavors to determine whether a charitable organization is carrying on charitable works commensurate in scope with its financial resources. In the particular facts underlying the ruling, the charity derived most of its income from rents, yet preserved its tax exemption because it satisfied the commensurate test.

The test was applied in 1967,[654] then went unused until 1990, when the IRS launched the second phase of its Special Emphasis Program concerning charitable solicitations. The commensurate test was resurrected and made a part of federal fundraising regulation by its inclusion in the 82-question "Exempt Organizations Charitable Solicitations Compliance Improvement Program Study Checksheet."[655]

According to the TAM, the commensurate test, when applied in the fundraising context, means that an "organization whose principal activity consists of the raising of funds must carry on a charitable program commensurate in scope with its financial resources in order to qualify for section 501(c)(3) exemption."

Wrote the IRS:

> The "commensurate test" does not lend itself to a rigid numerical distribution formula—there is no fixed percentage of income that an organization must pay out for charitable purposes. The financial resources of any organization may be affected by such factors as start-up costs, overhead, scale of operations, whether labor is volunteer or salaried, phone or postal costs, etc. In each case, therefore, the particular facts and circumstances of the organization must be considered. Accordingly, a specific payout percentage does not automatically mandate the conclusion that the organization under consideration has a primary purpose that is not charitable. In each case, it should be ascertained whether the failure to make real and substantial contributions for charitable purposes is due to reasonable cause. . . .
>
> While there is no specified payout percentage, and while special facts and circumstances may control the conclusion, distribution levels that are low invite close scrutiny. The "commensurate test" requires that

---

[653] Rev. Rul. 64-182, 1964-1 C.B. (Pt. 1) 186.
[654] Rev. Rul. 67-4, 1967-1 C.B. 121.
[655] See *supra* § 1.

organizations have a charitable program that is both real and, taking the organization's circumstances and financial resources into account, substantial. Therefore, an organization that raises funds for charitable purposes but consistently uses virtually all its income for administrative and promotional expenses with little or no direct charitable accomplishments cannot reasonably argue that its charitable program is commensurate with its financial resources and capabilities.

The IRS found that, during the two years under review, the organization expended 3.9 percent of its revenues for charitable programs. The IRS's lawyers characterized that as a "truly insignificant figure compared to all the time and treasure involved." Under all of the facts and circumstances discovered, the IRS decided that the organization did not carry on a charitable program commensurate in scope with its financial resources. Consequently, it was recommended that the organization's exemption be revoked as of the date the organization entered into the contract with the fundraising firm.

(iii) Private Benefit Standard. The IRS also proposed revocation of this exemption on the ground that the charity had been operated for the private interest of the fundraiser rather than the public interest.

This is an application of the private benefit doctrine so dramatically expanded by the Tax Court in 1989.[656] The doctrine allows an exemption to be revoked where there is private benefit, even though there is no violation of the statutory prohibition on private inurement.

The private inurement doctrine requires an *insider;* the private benefit rule does not.[657] The IRS conceded that the fundraiser did not control the charity in this case, but it found the relationship to be "symbiotic."

(iv) Substantial Nonexempt Purpose Test. Another basis for revocation of the exemption was application of the substantial nonexempt purpose test. The IRS held that "engaging in wide-scale sweepstakes activities with often misleading contest representations [was] neither necessary nor valuable in achieving . . . [the organization's] educational or health goals, except to obtain money." The IRS found that the organization's "gambling devices" were essentially indistinguishable from devices used by commercial entities such as Reader's Digest and Publishers Clearinghouse. The organization's fundraising activities were characterized by the IRS as being "indistinguishable from ordinary commercial activities."

(c) Perspective

This TAM is an extraordinary document. It represents one of the most recent efforts by the IRS to step up overall regulation of the charitable fundraising process. The law has evolved considerably from the days when the IRS was

[656] *American Campaign Academy* v. *Commissioner, supra* note 499.
[657] See § 7.12. Also *Law of Tax-Exempt Organizations,* Chapter 19, particularly §§ 9.3, 9.4, and 9.10.

concerned only about disclosure to donors of transfers, or portions of transfers, that are not gifts.[658] The two phases of the Special Emphasis Program, followed by the checksheet, were the next steps.[659] Increased audit activity and self-audit through expanded annual information returns (Forms 990) followed.[660] Then came this application of the commensurate test, which reflects a belief within the IRS that the agency has the authority to cause an organization's tax exemption to depend solely on the extent of its fundraising costs.

This doctrine has been invented by individuals other than legislators. There is no specific statutory authority for the commensurate test. Indeed, there is precious little judicial authority either. The IRS cited one case in support of its position.[661] In that case, the U.S. Tax Court held that an organization that had made "almost imperceptible progress toward achieving its charitable goals" did not qualify for tax-exempt status.[662] The court did not use the words *commensurate test*, but the IRS claims that is the test that the court applied. The commensurate test now has new life, and it is certain to be an audit issue for the future.

The IRS position on allocations is also important. The IRS in this TAM said that it is "sensitive" to external allocation guidelines such as those promulgated by the American Institute of Certified Public Accountants (AICPA). Nonetheless, the IRS will not be allowing allocations at all where there is "very little" program activity or content.

By injecting application of the private benefit doctrine into the fundraising context, this TAM appears to signal extensive government use of the private benefit doctrine. Finally, the IRS used the commerciality doctrine.

Thus, with one document, the IRS took another giant step into the realm of charitable fundraising regulation. Now, in addition to all of the other regulation burdening the fundraising community, it must be concerned with future applications of the commensurate test, the private benefit standard, and the commerciality doctrine.[663]

§ 5.16 SPECIAL EVENTS AND CORPORATE SPONSORSHIPS

(a) Special Events

Special events (or benefit events) are social occasions that use ticket sales and underwriting to generate revenue. These events are typically the most expensive and least profitable method of charitable fundraising. Nonetheless, they

---

[658] See *supra* § 2.

[659] *Id.*

[660] See *supra* § 1.

[661] *Make A Joyful Noise, Inc.* v. *Commissioner*, 56 T.C.M. 1003 (1989).

[662] *Id.* at 1006.

[663] In general, Suhrke, "Important, New Fund Raising Law Is Being Made—in Tax Court," XXVI *Phil. Monthly* (No. 7) 5 (1993); Lehrfeld, "Challenging Deviant Fund Raising: Commentary on the Commensurate Expenditure Test for Retaining 501(c)(3) Status," NYU Twentieth Conf. on Tax Planning for 501(c)(3) Organizations, *Proceedings*, Chap. 7 (New York: Matthew Bender & Co., Inc., 1992); Murdich, "Fundraising Expenses and the UCC," 3 *J. Tax'n Exempt Org.* 31 (Fall 1992).)

have a great value in public relations visibility, both for the charitable organization involved and for its volunteers.[664]

Examples of these special events include annual balls, auctions, bake sales, car washes, dinners, fairs and festivals, games of chance (such as bingo, raffles, and sweepstakes), luncheons, sports tournaments (particularly golf and tennis), and theater outings.

There is some confusion in the law as to exactly what a special event, in the charitable fundraising context, is. For instance, one court defined a *fundraising event* as a "single occurrence that may occur on limited occasions during a given year and its purpose is to further the exempt activities of the organization."[665] These events were contrasted with activities that "are continuous or continual activities which are certainly more pervasive a part of the organization than a sporadic event and [that are] . . . an end in themselves."[666] A wide variety of fundraising methods, other than special events, however, are "continuous" and "pervasive." Moreover, the purpose of special events is rarely to "further the exempt activities of the organization"; these events usually have no relationship to a charitable organization's exempt purposes and activities, and are engaged in largely to generate some funds and favorable publicity which, in turn, help the organization advance its tax-exempt activities. Finally, a fundraising activity is rarely an end in itself, yet many charitable organizations and institutions have major, ongoing fundraising and development programs that are permanent fixtures among the totality of the organizations' functions.

Special events figure prominently in a charitable organization's annual reporting to the IRS. In determining whether an annual information return (Form 990) is required, only net receipts (not gross receipts) from special events are used in determining the $25,000 filing threshold. (Organizations, other than private foundations, with gross receipts that are normally not in excess of $25,000 need not file annual information returns.[667]) Part VII-A of the annual information return requires a tax-exempt organization to identify each income-producing activity; a separate line is provided for special fundraising events.[668]

It has been the view of the IRS for years that charitable organizations that conduct special events have the obligation to notify the participants in these events of the amount (if any) expended for their participation in the event that is deductible as a charitable gift.[669] Also, legislation that was enacted in 1993 requires charitable organizations to make a good-faith estimate of the value of benefits, services, and/or privileges provided to a donor as the consequence of a gift, and to notify the donor that only an amount in excess of that value is deductible.[670]

---

[664] Greenfield, *Fund-Raising: Evaluating and Managing the Fund Development Process, Second Edition* (New York: John Wiley & Sons, Inc., 1999).

[665] *U.S. CB Radio Association, No. 1, Inc. v. Commissioner, supra* note 333, at 1444.

[666] *Id.*

[667] IRC § 6033(a)(2)(A)(ii).

[668] For more detail on the federal reporting requirements for charitable organizations in the fundraising setting, see *supra* § 9.

[669] See *supra* §§ 1 and 2.

[670] See *supra* § 4.

(b) Donor Recognition Programs

(i) Introduction.   The IRS caused a substantial stir, in 1991, by determining that a payment received by a college bowl association from a for-profit corporation sponsoring a bowl football game was taxable as unrelated business income, because the payment was for a package of valuable services rather than being a gift. This IRS pronouncement was a Technical Advice Memorandum (TAM) passing on the federal tax consequences of *corporate sponsorships*, where the sponsoring business has the corporate name included in the name of the event.[671] The associations involved contended that the payment were gifts, but the IRS held that the companies received a substantial quid pro quo for the payments. This determination raised the question, once again, as to whether a payment is a "gift" when the "donor" is provided something in return.[672]

Charitable organizations throughout the United States became concerned about this IRS initiative—and properly so, because it had implications far beyond college and university bowl games. The IRS bowl-game TAM raised, once again, the question as to when the extent of donor recognition renders a payment not a gift.

This donor-recognition problem festers to this day. Initially, the IRS attempted to quell the controversy by proposing, in early 1992, guidelines for its examining agents to use when conducting audits of charitable organizations.[673] Before these guidelines could be finalized, Congress legislated on the subject later in the year; this legislation (the Revenue Act of 1992) was vetoed. Nonetheless, this legislative development introduced the concept of the *qualified sponsorship payment*. On January 19, 1993, the IRS proposed regulations in this area.[674] These regulations, however, never matured to final form; the regulation project was superseded by the enactment, in 1997, of legislation, as discussed next.

(ii) Qualified Sponsorship Payments.   Enactment of legislation in 1997 added to the federal tax statutory law the concept of the *qualified sponsorship payment*.[675] These payments received by tax-exempt organizations and state colleges and universities are exempt from the unrelated business income tax. That is, the activity of soliciting and receiving these payments is not an unrelated business.[676]

From the standpoint of fundraising, these rules differentiate between a *qualified sponsorship payment*, which is a deductible charitable contribution and as to which there is merely an acknowledgment, and a payment for services that are, or are in the nature of, advertising.

[671] Tech. Adv. Mem. 9147007.
[672] See *supra* § 14(a).
[673] IRS Ann. 92-15, 1992-6 I.R.B. 51. In general, Simpson, "When Will Corporate Sponsorship Create UBIT Liability?," 4 *J. Tax'n Exempt Org.* (No. 3) 3 (Nov./Dec. 1992); Peete, "Corporate Sponsorship Payments: Charitable Gifts Versus Income From an Unrelated Trade or Business," 6 *Exempt Org. Tax Rev.* (No. 6) 1281 (Dec. 1992).
[674] EE-74-92. In general, Roady & McDaniel, "Proposed Regulations Set New Rules for Corporate Sponsorships," 4 *J. Tax'n Exempt Org.* 10 (May/June 1993).
[675] Taxpayer Relief Act of 1997, § 965(a).
[676] IRC § 513(i)(1).

A qualified sponsorship payment is a payment made by a person engaged in a trade or business, with respect to which there is no arrangement or expectation that the person will receive any substantial return benefit other than the use or acknowledgment of the name or logo (or product lines) of the person's trade or business in connection with the organization's activities.[677] It is irrelevant whether the sponsored activity is related or unrelated to the organization's exempt purpose.[678]

This use or acknowledgment does not include advertising of the person's products or services, including messages containing qualitative or comparative language, price information or other indications of savings or value, an endorsement, or an inducement to purchase, sell, or use the products or services.[679] For example, if in return for receiving a sponsorship payment, an exempt organization promises to use the sponsor's name or logo in acknowledging the sponsor's support for an educational or fundraising event conducted by the organization, the payment is not taxable. If an organization provides advertising of a sponsor's products, however, the payment made to the organization by the sponsor to receive the advertising is subject to the unrelated business income tax (assuming the other requirements for taxation are satisfied).[680]

A qualified sponsorship payment does not include any payment where the amount of the payment is contingent on the level of attendance at one or more events, broadcast ratings, or other factors indicating the degree of public exposure to one or more events.[681] The fact that a sponsorship payment is contingent on an event actually taking place or being broadcast, in and of itself, however, does not cause the payment to fail to qualify. Also, mere distribution or display of a sponsor's products by the sponsor or the exempt organization to the general public at a sponsored event, whether for free or for remuneration, is considered a *use or acknowledgment* of the sponsor's product lines—and not advertising.[682]

This law does not apply to a payment that entitles the payor to the use or acknowledgment of the name or logo (or product line) of the payor's trade or business in a tax-exempt organization's periodical. A *periodical* is regularly scheduled and printed material published by or on behalf of the payee organization that is not related to and primarily distributed in connection with a specific event conducted by the payee organization.[683] Thus, the exclusion does not apply to payments that lead to acknowledgments in a monthly journal but applies if a sponsor received an acknowledgment in a program or brochure distributed at a sponsored event.[684] The term *qualified sponsorship payment* also does not include a payment made in connection with a qualified convention or trade show activity.[685]

---

[677] IRC § 513(i)(2)(A).
[678] H. Rep. No. 105-220, 105th Cong., 1st Sess. 69 (1997).
[679] IRC § 513(i)(2)(A).
[680] H. Rep. No. 105-220, *supra* note 678, at 68.
[681] IRC § 513(i)(2)(B)(i).
[682] H. Rep. No. 105-220, *supra* note 678, at 69.
[683] IRC § 513(i)(2)(B)(ii)(I).
[684] H. Rep. No. 105-220, *supra* note 678, at 69.
[685] IRC § 513(i)(2)(B)(ii)(II).

To the extent a portion of a payment would (if made as a separate payment) be a qualified sponsorship payment, that portion of the payment is treated as a separate payment; that is, a payment may be bifurcated as between an excludable amount and a nonexcludable amount.[686] Therefore, if a sponsorship payment made to a tax-exempt organization entitles the sponsor to product advertising and use or acknowledgment of the sponsor's name or logo by the organization, the unrelated business income tax does not apply to the amount of the payment that exceeds the fair market value of the product advertising provided to the sponsor.[687]

The provision of facilities, services, or other privileges by an exempt organization to a sponsor or the sponsor's designees (such as complimentary tickets, Pro-Am playing spots in golf tournaments, or receptions for major donors) in connection with a sponsorship payment does not affect the determination as to whether the payment is a qualified one. Instead, the provision of the goods or services is evaluated as a separate transaction in determining whether the organization has unrelated business income from the event. In general, if the services or facilities do not constitute a substantial return benefit (or if the provision of the services or facilities is a related business activity), the payments attributable to them are not subject to the unrelated business income tax.[688]

Likewise, a sponsor's receipt of a license to use an intangible asset (such as a trademark, logo, or designation) of the tax-exempt organization is treated as separate from the qualified sponsorship transaction in determining whether the organization has unrelated business taxable income.[689]

This statutory exemption from taxation for qualified sponsorship payments is in addition to other exemptions from the unrelated business income tax. These exceptions include the one for activities substantially all the work for which is performed by volunteers[690] and for activities not regularly carried on.[691]

§ 5.17 IRS COLLEGE AND UNIVERSITY EXAMINATION GUIDELINES

The IRS developed guidelines for its agents' use during their examinations of colleges and universities.[692] These guidelines, intended as a framework that agents may follow in conducting these examinations, provide the elements to be considered in determining how colleges and universities are structured. Focus is on the institutions' accounting methods, financial information,

---

[686] IRC § 513(i)(e).

[687] H. Rep. No. 105-220, *supra* note 678, at 69.

[688] *Id.*

[689] *Id.*

[690] See *supra* § 7(vi).

[691] See *supra* § 7(iv). This law became effective with respect to qualified sponsorship payments solicited or received after December 31, 1997. There is no inference as to whether a sponsorship payment received prior to 1998 was taxable. Regulations to accompany these rules were proposed in 2000 (REG-209601-92).

[692] These guidelines are part of the *Internal Revenue Manual* (*Exempt Organizations Examination Guidelines Handbook* 7(10)69 ("*Handbook*") § 342) and were published for general dissemination in Ann. 94-112, 1994-37 I.R.B.

compensation arrangements, fringe benefit issues, joint ventures, scholarships and fellowships, and unrelated business income tax issues. Charitable contributions to the institutions and their fundraising efforts are also given attention.

As to fundraising, the guidelines state that "[m]any institutions require that large contributions, especially conditional or earmarked contributions, be formally accepted by a governing board."[693] Examining agents are advised to review the minutes of meetings of such a governing board, as well as those of the "fundraising committees" (budget, finance, development, or advancement), to identify any conditional contributions that may have "questionable" terms. In an example provided, a gift to construct a building on campus is conditioned on the use of a certain architect or a specific construction firm. The guidelines state that this type of condition, which may suggest a "private benefit," might jeopardize the charitable contribution deduction if the donor and the beneficiary of the condition (in the illustration, the architect or builder) have "less than an arm's length relationship."[694]

In general, the IRS agents are to "[r]eview the institution's fundraising program to determine if donors receive benefits that might affect the deductibility of their contributions."[695] The agents are to identify the officials responsible for soliciting and accounting for gifts, and obtain a description of their activities and functions.[696] In addition, they are to review internal reports related to gifts, with emphasis on lists of contributors, restricted gifts, and in-kind gifts.[697] Also to be reviewed are agreements and correspondence, to determine whether gifts are restricted, earmarked, or conditioned on benefits being provided to donors.[698]

The agents are instructed to learn how gifts of property are being treated, that is, how items of property are valued, whether the institution secures its own appraisal, and whether a value is assigned on the receipt provided to the donor. The agents are to determine "any action taken by the institution if its valuation of the property is less than the value claimed by the donor."[699]

The examining agents are to determine whether the institution has completed its portion of the IRS form[700] that must be filed in connection with gifts of property that are claimed to be in excess of $5,000.[701] They must research whether the institution has filed any return[702] with respect to donated property that was sold, exchanged, transferred, consumed, or otherwise disposed of

---

[693] Handbook § 342.9(1).

[694] Id. Also § 342.9(2)(b).

[695] Id. § 342.9(2).

[696] Id. § 342.9(2)(a).

[697] Id. § 342.9(2)(c).

[698] Id. § 342.9(2)(d). See supra §§ 3, 4.

[699] Id. § 342.9(2)(e). This is a curious requirement, in that the law does not require the charitable organization to take any such action. Also, these examination guidelines, in proposed form (as disseminated by Ann. 93-2, 1993-2 I.R.B. 39), stated that the agents are to compare the appraised value with the value at which the property is carried on the books of the institution.

[700] Form 8283, Section B, Part IV. See supra § 13, text accompanied by notes 571–588.

[701] Handbook § 342.9(2)(f).

[702] Form 8282. See supra § 14(k).

within two years of the date of receipt.[703] Further, they are to (1) determine whether the institution is in compliance with the substantiation requirements[704] and the quid pro quo rules;[705] (2) determine whether property was accepted subject to a mortgage and, if so, any unrelated debt-financed income consequences;[706] (3) review any agency agreements that the institution may have with financial institutions for the management of various funds (to detect any private inurement or private benefit);[707] (4) evaluate the institution's compliance with the federal tax rule[708] that allows as a charitable deduction 80 percent of an amount paid by a person to or for the benefit of an educational institution, which would be allowable as a charitable contribution but for the fact that the person received, as a result of the payment, the right to purchase tickets for seating at an athletic event in the institution's stadium;[709] (5) review contributions to an institution for the purpose of acquiring or constructing institution-owned housing facilities that are rented to fraternities or sororities at rates substantially equivalent to those charged for comparable housing facilities in the institution's dormitories, to be certain that the gift is to the institution and not (with the institution as a conduit) to the fraternity or sorority;[710] and (6) determine whether the institution acknowledges contributions of books (including those by publishing companies from their inventory[711]) that are not usable in its exempt activities (because, for example, the books are outdated, damaged, or unsuitable for reading by the majority of the reading public).[712]

The guidelines instruct the agents to review trust returns in circumstances where the institution may be involved in joint ventures with unitrusts.[713] The agents are to consider a referral to the IRS Examination Division for a determination as to whether a contributor properly discounted the charitable deduction for a unitrust gift.[714] The agents are reminded that large contributions are often "channeled" through related foundations.[715]

Although designed specifically for audits of colleges and universities, the elements of these guidelines are generally applicable to an audit of the fundraising program of any charitable organization.

---

[703] *Handbook* § 342.9(2)(f).
[704] *Id.* § 342.9(2)(g). See *supra* § 3.
[705] *Id.* See *supra* § 4.
[706] *Id.* § 342.9(2)(h).
[707] *Id.* § 342.9(2)(i).
[708] IRC § 170(1).
[709] *Handbook* § 342.9(3).
[710] *Id.* § 342.9(4).
[711] IRC § 170(e)(3) places limitations on the deductibility of gifts of inventory. See *supra* text accompanied by note 575.
[712] Handbook § 342.9(5).
[713] *Id.* § 342.15(7). The examination guidelines (see *supra* note 692) instructed the agents to identify any charitable remainder trusts established for an institution.
[714] *Id.* § 342.15(7)(c). The guidelines add that the agents are to determine whether annuity income was properly reported in the case of charitable remainder annuity trusts.
[715] *Id.* § 342.15(9).

§ 5.18 POSTAL LAWS

Fundraising for charitable purposes, when undertaken by means of the mail, is regulated by the federal postal laws. This is largely accomplished by enforcement of the law concerning special mailing rates that are limited to use by qualified organizations when they are mailing eligible matter.[716]

Only qualified organizations that have received specific authorization from the United States Postal Service[717] may mail eligible matter at these special rates of postage. These organizations cannot be organized for profit, and none of their net income may accrue to the benefit of private persons.

(a) Introduction

Rates for all classes of mail are determined in rate cases, which are public proceedings administered by the Postal Rate Commission.[718] The mandate for the USPS is to recover all its operating costs from the rates it charges. The rate-making consists of assigning USPS's projected costs in two categories to each class of mail; combining the categories yields the rate. The categories are (1) *attributable costs*, which are costs that are directly measurable and traceable to a particular class of mail (such as nonprofit mailings), and (2) *institutional costs*, which are the overhead costs of the USPS, recovered by being assigned to each class in the form of a *markup*, stated as a percentage of the attributable cost.

The preferred rate for nonprofit organizations has existed because Congress, in 1970,[719] had undertaken to give the USPS an annual appropriation (*revenue forgone*) in lieu of the markup that nonprofit organizations would otherwise pay. That is, nonprofit organizations paid the attributable cost portion only (which became the nonprofit rate) and the federal government absorbed the institutional costs.

Throughout the 1980s, a steady increase in the volume of mail sent by nonprofit organizations helped increase the need for revenue forgone; this was true for all postal rate classes, which reached nearly $1 billion for the government's fiscal year 1995. Congress became reluctant to appropriate the funds necessary to support the revenue forgone subsidy. Absent *full funding,* the USPS was authorized to raise the nonprofit postal rates.

In the intervening years, nonprofit organizations faced ongoing uncertainty as to the levels of the postal rates. There have been increases from rate cases (at approximately three-year intervals) and struggles with Congress over appropriations to avoid annual increases in the nonprofit rates. Congress threatened changes to the eligibility rules; indeed, it has enacted two of them

---

[716] This authorization to mail at these special rates was enacted into law in 1951 (P.L. 82-233, 65 Stat. 672). The preferred rates for qualified nonprofit organizations were made a part of the rate structure created upon enactment of the Postal Reorganization Act of 1970, 84 Stat. 719, which created the U.S. Postal Service and the Postal Rate Commission. The prior law, including the definition of qualified nonprofit organizations, was retained as "regulations."

[717] The U.S. Postal Service is referenced in this section as the USPS.

[718] The Postal Rate Commission is referenced in this section as the PRC.

[719] See *supra* note 695.

since 1990. By 1992, all involved were anxious for a solution: Congress and the USPS did not want any more pressure from the nonprofit community about the revenue forgone amounts. Commercial mailers using the third-class rates were fearful that they would be required to assume the burden of rate increases. Nonprofit organizations were weary of these uncertainties and were concerned about the prospects of a severe increase in the applicable postal rates.

Compromise legislation was enacted in 1993: the Revenue Forgone Reform Act of 1993.[720] This measure eliminated revenue forgone and ensured continued preferred rates by establishing a favorable markup for nonprofit organizations. For fiscal 1994 and thereafter, the markup for each class of nonprofit rates was set at one-half of the comparable commercial markup amount. This legislation provided a phasing-in schedule to cushion nonprofit organizations from the effects of the new system. This schedule produces annual increases in the range of 2–3 percent (unless or until the intervention of a PRC rate case).

Today, the special rate for nonprofit organizations is termed, by the USPS, the *nonprofit standard mail rate*. This rate provides authorized organizations an opportunity to realize significant savings in postage compared with that charged at the regular standard mail bulk rates.

(b) Qualifying Organizations

The nonprofit standard mail rates are available to qualified nonprofit organizations. A qualifying organization must have a primary purpose relating to at least one of the following categories: religious, educational, scientific, philanthropic (charitable), agricultural, labor, veterans', and/or fraternal ends.[721] This purpose must be reflected in the manner in which the organization is both organized and operated. Organizations that occasionally or incidentally engage in qualifying activities are not eligible for the special mailing rates.[722]

(i) Religious Organizations. For purposes of the postal laws, a *religious* organization's primary purposes must be to (1) conduct religious worship (such as at churches, synagogues, temples, and mosques); (2) support the religious activities of nonprofit organizations, the primary purpose of which is the conduct of religious worship; or (3) further the teaching of particular religious faiths or tenets, including religious instruction and the dissemination of religious information.[723]

---

[720] Title VII of the Treasury, Postal Service, and General Government Appropriations Act for fiscal year 1994, P.L. 103-123, 107 Stat. 1267 (1993).

[721] 39 U.S.C. § 3626(a), by reference to former 39 U.S.C. § 4452 (see *supra* note 716). These organizations generally approximate those who are qualified for federal tax-exempt status by reason of IRC § 501(c)(3), (5), (10), and (19). Notably absent from this grouping of eligible organizations are some social welfare organizations (IRC § 501(c)(4) entities) and business and professional organizations, and other business leagues (IRC § 501(c)(6) entities).

[722] The criteria for qualification in this context are stated in the Domestic Mail Manual (DMM); this analysis is based on DMM Issue 55 (Feb. 10, 1999). The specific criteria are provided in DMM E670, part 2.0.

[723] DMM E670, part 2.2.

(ii) Educational Organizations. An *educational* organization's primary purpose must be instruction or training of individuals to improve or develop their capabilities, or instruction of the public on subjects beneficial to the community. An organization may be educational even though it advocates a particular position or viewpoint, as long as it presents a sufficiently full and fair exposition of the pertinent facts to permit the formation of an independent opinion or conclusion. Conversely, an organization is not considered educational if its principal function is the mere presentation of unsupported opinion.[724]

The following are examples of educational organizations:

- An organization (such as a primary or secondary school, a college, or a professional or trade school) that has a regularly scheduled curriculum, a regular faculty, and a regularly enrolled body of students in attendance at a place where educational activities are regularly carried on.

- An organization the activities of which consist of presenting public discussion groups, forums, panels, lectures, or similar programs, including on radio or television.

- An organization that presents a course of instruction by correspondence or through the use of television or radio.

- Museums, zoos, planetariums, symphony orchestras, and similar institutions.[725]

(iii) Philanthropic Organizations. A *philanthropic* organization must be an entity organized and operated to benefit the public. Examples include philanthropic organizations that are organized and operated to relieve the poor, distressed, or underprivileged; advance religion, education, or science; erect or maintain public buildings, monuments, or works; lessen the burdens of government; or promote social welfare for any of these purposes or to lessen neighborhood tensions, eliminate prejudice and discrimination, defend human and civil rights secured by law, or combat community deterioration and juvenile delinquency. The fact that a philanthropic entity organized and operated to relieve indigent individuals may receive voluntary contributions from them does not necessarily make it ineligible for the nonprofit standard mail rates as a philanthropic organization. If an organization, in carrying out its primary purpose, advocates social or civic changes or presents ideas on controversial issues to influence public opinion and sentiment to accept its views, it does not necessarily become ineligible for these rates.[726]

---

[724] A federal district court held that this regulation is invalid as being unconstitutionally vague (*National Association of Social Workers* v. *United States Postal Service,* unpublished mem. op. (C.A. 81-0574) (D.D.C. 1983), following a similar ruling as to identical language in the federal tax regulations (*Big Mama Rag, Inc.* v. *United States,* 631 F.2d 1030 (D.C. Cir. 1980)). This rule, however, continues to be adhered to by the USPS (just as the same rule continues to be in the tax regulations). See *Law of Tax-Exempt Organizations* § 7.2.

[725] DMM E670, part 2.4.

[726] *Id.,* part 2.6.

(iv) Other Categories.   The primary purpose of a *scientific* organization must be to conduct research in the applied, pure, or natural sciences or to disseminate technical information concerning these sciences.[727]

An *agricultural* organization must have, as its primary purposes, the (1) betterment of the conditions of those engaged in agricultural pursuits, the improvement of the grade of their products, and the development of a higher degree of efficiency in agriculture, or (2) collection and dissemination of information or materials about agriculture. The organization may further and advance agricultural interests through educational activities; by holding agricultural fairs; by collecting and disseminating information about cultivation of the soil and improvement of its yield, or about the harvesting of marine resources; by rearing, feeding, and managing livestock, poultry, bees, and the like; or by other activities related to agricultural interests.[728]

A *labor* organization's primary purpose must be the betterment of the conditions of workers. Labor organizations include but are not limited to organizations in which employees or workers participate; these organizations negotiate with employers on grievances, labor disputes, wages, hours of employment, working conditions, and related issues. These entities thus include labor unions and employee associations.[729]

A *veterans'* organization's membership must consist of veterans of the armed services of the United States, or an auxiliary unit or society of, or a trust or foundation for, any such post or organization.[730]

A *fraternal* organization must be primarily dedicated to fostering fellowship and mutual benefits among its members. A qualified fraternal organization must be organized under a lodge or chapter system with a representative form of government; must follow a ritualistic format; and must be composed of members elected to membership by vote of the members. Qualifying fraternal organizations include the Masons, Knights of Columbus, Elks, and college fraternities and sororities, and may have members of either or both genders.[731]

Certain political organizations are authorized to mail at the nonprofit standard mail rates.[732] *Ineligible* organizations include automobile clubs, business leagues (such as trade, business, and professional associations), chambers of commerce, citizens' and civic improvement associations, mutual insurance associations, service clubs (such as Civitan, Kiwanis, Lions, Optimist, and Rotary), social and hobby clubs, and associations of rural electric cooperatives.[733]

In general, state, county, and municipal governments are not eligible for the nonprofit standard mail rates. A separate and distinct state, county, or municipal governmental organization that meets the criteria for an eligible entity may qualify, notwithstanding its governmental status.[734]

---

[727] *Id.*, part 2.5.
[728] *Id.*, part 2.7.
[729] *Id.*, part 2.8.
[730] *Id.*, part 2.9.
[731] *Id.*, part 2.10.
[732] *Id.*, part 3.0.
[733] *Id.*, part 4.0.
[734] *Id.*

(c) Application for Authorization

In general, an organization must file an application for use of the nonprofit standard mail (Form 3623) at each post office where it wants to deposit mailings. The applicant must show on the application the qualifying category of organization under which it seeks authorization. There is no filing fee.

This application must be accompanied by evidence that the applicant meets the standards of a qualifying category and that the organization is a nonprofit entity. This evidence includes a copy of its organizing document (such as articles of incorporation), its bylaws, a financial statement prepared by a responsible independent person, a list of the activities in which the organization engaged during the previous 12 months, a statement of receipts and expenditures for the past fiscal year, a copy of its budget for the current year, and documentation that illustrates the operations of the organization (such as bulletins, minutes of meetings, and brochures).[735]

This evidence also includes a copy of any determination letter or ruling from the IRS as to the entity's tax-exempt status. Because the USPS and the IRS are independent agencies, however, recognition of tax exemption is not required to qualify for the special bulk third-class rates. This recognition of exemption is considered as evidence of qualification for preferred postal rates but is not the controlling factor in the USPS decision. When an organization submits a copy of an IRS determination that it is a religious, educational, or philanthropic (charitable) organization, or a scientific, agricultural, labor, veterans', or fraternal organization, it is considered as qualifying for the nonprofit rates, unless other evidence indicates a basis for nonqualification.[736]

This application and appropriate supporting documents are filed at the post office where the nonprofit organization intends to mail. This office reviews the application and attachments for completeness. They are then forwarded to the USPS's Nonprofit Service Center in Memphis, Tennessee. The Center notifies the applicant organization directly of its decision on the application to mail at the nonprofit standard mail rates. The Center may request additional information or evidence to support or clarify an application. Failure of an organization to furnish this information is considered a basis for denial of an application.[737]

An organization may not mail at the nonprofit standard mail rates at a post office before the application is approved. While the application is pending, postage must be paid at the applicable first-class or certain other rates. The USPS records the difference between postage paid at the regular rates and the postage that would have been paid at the nonprofit rates. A record is not maintained if postage is paid at first-class rates or at the other rates.[738]

If an authorization to mail at the special bulk rates is issued, the mailer may be refunded the postage paid at that office in excess of the special rate

---

[735] DMM E670, part 8.0.
[736] *Id.*, part 7.3.
[737] *Id.*, part 10.1.
[738] *Id.*, parts 9.1, 9.2.

since the effective date of the authorization. There is no refund where the application is denied and an appeal is not filed, or for mailings made at a post office at which a separate authorization was not filed. Also, a refund is not made with respect to the period before the effective date of the authorization. The effective date of the special rate authorization is the date of the application or the date of the eligibility of the organization, whichever is later.[739]

If an application is denied, the applicant may submit a written appeal to the postmaster where the application was filed, within 15 days of the receipt by the applicant of the decision. The postmaster then forwards the appeal, along with the supporting documentation, to the Center. After review of the file, the Center may reverse its decision and approve the application. If the Center upholds the opinion that the organization does not qualify, the appeal is forwarded to the USPS headquarters in Washington, D.C. At this point, the matter is before the Manager of Business Mail Acceptance. At this level, the final agency decision is made.[740]

The USPS may initiate, at any time, a review of any organization authorized to mail at the nonprofit standard mail rates. An organization may be asked for evidence to determine whether it remains qualified. Failure of the organization to provide this information is sufficient cause for revocation. If it is found that authorization has been given to an organization that was not qualified at the time of the application or that subsequently became nonqualified, the USPS will notify the organization of the proposed revocation and the reasons for it.[741]

A revocation takes effect 15 days from the date the organization receives the notice, unless the organization files a written appeal within that time. The USPS may ask the organization for more information or evidence to determine its eligibility. The organization's failure to provide this information is sufficient grounds for denial of the appeal. A written appeal decision is issued to the organization.[742]

The USPS revokes an authorization to mail at the nonprofit standard mail rates if no special rate mailings are made by the organization during a two-year period. An organization in this circumstance is notified of this revocation for nonuse.[743]

(d) Eligible and Ineligible Matter

An organization authorized to mail at the nonprofit standard mail rates may mail only its own matter at those rates. This matter, which generally must substantially relate to the organization's program purposes, is termed *eligible matter*. Disqualified material is known as *ineligible matter*. An authorized organization may not delegate or lend the use of its authorization to mail at the special rates to any other person. A person may not mail, or cause to be mailed

---

[739] *Id.*, parts 9.3, 9.4.
[740] *Id.*, part 10.3.
[741] *Id.*, parts 11.1, 11.2.
[742] *Id.*, part 11.1.
[743] *Id.*, part 11.4.

by agreement or otherwise, any ineligible matter at the special rates.[744] Material soliciting charitable contributions may be mailed at these rates.

Cooperative mailings—a mailing made under the auspices of two or more organizations (perhaps in the nature of a joint venture—may be made at the nonprofit rates only when each of the cooperating organizations is authorized to mail at the special rates at the post office where the mailing is deposited. Cooperative mailings involving the mailing of any matter on behalf of or produced for an organization not authorized to mail at the special rates at the post office where the mailing is deposited must be paid at the applicable regular rates.[745]

An authorized nonprofit organization's material is not disqualified from being mailed at the nonprofit standard mail rates solely because that material contains but is not primarily devoted to (1) acknowledgments of organizations or individuals who have made contributions to the authorized organization; and/or (2) references to, and a response card or other instructions for, making inquiries about services or benefits available as a result of membership in the authorized organization, if advertising, promotional, or application materials specifically concerning the services or benefits are not included.[746]

There are additional content-based restrictions on the use of the nonprofit standard mail rates by qualified organizations, in that certain types of advertisements, promotions, and offers, as well as some products, are ineligible to be mailed at the nonprofit rates. In order for material that advertises, promotes, offers, or for a fee or other consideration recommends, describes, or announces the availability of any product or service to qualify for mailing at the nonprofit rates, the sale of the product or the provision of the service must be substantially related to the exercise or performance by the organization of one or more of the purposes constituting the basis for the organization's authorization to mail at the nonprofit rates.

To be *substantially related,* the sale of the product or the provision of the service must contribute importantly to the accomplishment of one or more of the qualifying purposes of the organization. This means that the sale of the product or the provision of the service must be directly related to accomplishing one or more of the purposes on which the organization's authorization to mail at the nonprofit rates is based. The sale of the product or the provision of the service must have a causal relationship to the achievement of the exempt purposes of the authorized organization. The selling of a product or service is not a related activity simply because the resulting income is used to accomplish the purpose of the authorized organization.[747] The determination as to relatedness must be made in accordance with federal tax standards.[748]

In general, the nonprofit standard mail rates may not be used for mailing material that advertises, promotes, offers, or for a fee or other consideration recommends, describes, or announces the availability of the following:

---

[744] *Id.,* part 5.1.
[745] *Id.*
[746] 39 U.S.C. § 3626(j)(2); DMM E670, part 5.7.
[747] 39 U.S.C. § 3626(j)(1)(D)(i); DMM E670, parts 5.4d(1), 5.6.
[748] 39 U.S.C. § 3626(j)(1)(D)(i). See *supra* § 7.

- Any credit, debit, or charge card or similar financial instrument or account, provided by or through an arrangement with any person not authorized to mail at the nonprofit rates at the entry post office. This includes affinity cards.

- Any insurance policy, unless the organization promoting the purchase of the policy is authorized to mail at the nonprofit rates at the entry post office. Moreover, the policy must be designed for and primarily promoted to the members, donors, supporters, or beneficiaries of the organization, and the coverage provided by the policy is not generally otherwise commercially available (see following).

- Any travel arrangement, unless the organization promoting the arrangement is authorized to mail at the nonprofit rates at the entry post office. Moreover, the travel must contribute substantially (aside from the cultivation of members, donors, or supporters, or the acquisition of funds) to one or more of the purposes that constitute the basis for the organization's authorization to mail at the nonprofit rates, and the arrangement is designed for and primarily promoted to the members, donors, supporters, and beneficiaries of that organization.[749]

The phrase *not generally otherwise commercially available* applies to the actual coverage stated in an insurance policy, without regard to the amount of the premiums, the underwriting practices, and the financial condition of the insurer. When comparisons with other policies are made, consideration is given by the USPS to policy coverage benefits, limitations, and exclusions, and to the availability of coverage to the targeted category of recipients.[750]

There are rules allowing the mailing of low-cost items[751] and items contributed to the organization[752] at the special rates.[753] Advertisements mailed at the special rates, however, do not have to meet the substantially related test if

---

[749] 39 U.S.C. § 3636(j)(1)(A)-(C); DMM E670, part 5.4c.

[750] DMM E670, part 5.4b. These rules have a tortured history. The Revenue Forgone Reform Act (for purposes of this footnote, the Act) (see *supra* note 732) introduced major changes in the eligibility rules. The USPS published proposed regulations in this regard late in 1993 (58 *Fed. Reg.* 64918 (Dec. 10, 1993)). It extended the comment period (58 *Fed. Reg.* 65959 (Dec. 17, 1993)) and held a hearing on the proposed regulations on January 28, 1994 (as announced in 59 *Fed. Reg.* 1512). In May 1994, the USPS published what was then thought to be the final regulations, with an effective date of September 4, 1994 (59 *Fed. Reg.* (No. 86) 23159 (May 5, 1994)). On August 5, 1994, the USPS announced a delay in the enforcement of these regulations (59 *Fed. Reg.* 39967). The Treasury, Postal Service, and General Government Appropriations Act for fiscal year 1995 was signed into law on September 30, 1994 (P.L. 103-329, 108 Stat. 2432); it contained an amendment to the Act (concerning third-party advertising in the publications of qualified organizations). Another set of proposed regulations was published in early 1995 (60 *Fed. Reg.* 12480 (Mar. 7, 1995)). These proposed regulations were a republication of the "final" 1994 regulations, along with changes including those caused by the law changes created by the fiscal year 1995 appropriations act (see *supra* notes 746–747). The final regulations were published on May 5, 1995 (60 *Fed. Reg.* 22270); they took effect on October 1, 1995.

[751] See *supra* § 7, text accompanied by notes 256–258.

[752] See *id.*, text accompanied by note 243.

[753] 39 U.S.C. § 3626(m); DMM E670, part 5.6e.

the material of which the advertisement is a part meets the content requirements of a periodical publication.[754]

All matter mailed at the nonprofit standard mail rates must identify the authorized nonprofit organization. The name and return address of the authorized nonprofit organization must be either on the outside of the mailpiece or in a prominent location on the material being mailed. Pseudonyms or bogus names of organizations or other persons may not be used. If the mailpiece bears any name and return address, it must be that of the authorized nonprofit organization. A well-recognized alternative designation or abbreviation (such as "The March of Dimes" or the "AFL-CIO") may be used rather than the full name of the organization.

(e) Postage Statement

A *postage statement* must be prepared and signed by the authorized organization or its agent for each nonprofit rate mailing. This statement is a certification that (1) the mailing does not violate the postal laws; (2) only the organization's matter is being mailed; (3) the mailing is not a cooperative mailing with other persons who are not entitled to special bulk mailing privileges; (4) the mailing has not been made by the organization on behalf of or produced for another person not entitled to special bulk mailing privileges; and (5) the organization will be liable for and agrees to pay (subject to an appropriate appeal) any postage deficiency assessed on the mailing, whether due to a finding that the mailing was a cooperative one or for any other reason.[755]

§ 5.19 ANTITRUST LAWS

The antitrust laws are, in certain circumstances, applicable to charitable and other nonprofit organizations. This aspect of the law is basically embodied in the Sherman Act and the Federal Trade Commission Act. The fundamental objective of these laws is elimination of practices that interfere with free competition. These laws are intended to promote a vigorous and competitive economy in which each business enterprise has a full opportunity to compete on the basis of price, quality, and service.

The principal law in this regard, the Sherman Act,[756] prohibits contracts, combinations, and conspiracies that unreasonably restrain trade. Nonprofit organizations usually involved in antitrust law matters are business or professional associations, in that they have the interesting feature of consisting of members who are competitors. Another context in which the antitrust laws can be applicable to nonprofit organizations is standard-setting. A third aspect of nonprofit organizations' entanglement in the antitrust laws is the matter of

---

[754] 39 U.S.C. § 3626(j)(1)(D)(II); DMM E670, part 5.8.

[755] The postal laws applicable to charitable organizations, from the standpoint of fundraising, are summarized in greater detail in Hopkins, *The Second Legal Answer Book for Fund-Raisers* (John Wiley & Sons: New York, 2000), Chapter 8.

[756] 15 U.S.C. §§ 1, 2.

denial of membership to or expulsion from membership in an association. Regarding this third element, although presumably this would be a rare instance, a fundraiser could be denied membership or expelled from membership in an association of fundraisers.

The reach of the antitrust law to charities is unclear. The state of the case law is that, for the antitrust rules to apply in the charitable setting, the organization must be involved in a *commercial transaction* that has some form of a *public service aspect* to it. "Pure charity" is outside the ambit of the antitrust laws.[757]

The solicitation of funds by a charitable organization is not engaging in *trade or commerce* and thus is not covered by the Sherman Act. One court explained this point as follows:

> Not every aspect of life in the United States is to be reduced to such a single-minded vision of the ubiquity of commerce. If self-serving activity is necessarily commercial, the Sherman Act embraces everything from a church fair to the solicitation of voluntary blood donors [sic]. On this basis, every engagement or marriage would be a restraint of trade, subject to suit and defensible only by application of the rule of reason. Consensual conduct is not necessarily commercial conduct even though reciprocation is the normal accompaniment of consensual conduct. From its donations, [a charity] derives reputation, prestige, money for its officers; it does not engage in trade or commerce.[758]

Charitable organizations agreeing to use, or actually using, the same annuity rates in connection with the issuance of charitable gift annuities[759] are not in violation of the antitrust laws.[760] This protection is not confined to charities, however, and extends to lawyers, accountants, actuaries, consultants, and others retained or employed by a charitable organization when assisting in issuing a charitable gift annuity or setting charitable gift annuity rates. This antitrust law exemption also sweeps within its ambit the act of publishing suggested charitable gift annuity rates.

The history of this legislation reflects uncertainty in Congress as to whether the issuance of charitable gift annuities entails transactions that are commercial and have a public service aspect. In any event, a congressional committee concluded that giving by means of charitable gift annuities is "legitimate," particularly since the IRS "approves and regulates" these instruments.[761] Another reason for the creation of this exemption—the real stimulus for it—was the ending of litigation.[762] The case involved an allegation that the use of the

---

[757] *United States* v. *Brown University*, 5 F.3d 658, 666 (3d Cir. 1993).

[758] *Dedication and Everlasting Love to Animals* v. *Humane Society of the United States, Inc.*, 50 F.2d 710, 714 (9th Cir. 1995)).

[759] See *Tax Law of Charitable Giving*, Chapter 14.

[760] 15 U.S.C. § 37 *et seq.* This legislation was enacted as the Charitable Gift Annuity Antitrust Relief Act of 1995 (109 Stat. 687, P.L. 104-63, 104th Cong., 1st Sess. (1995)) and was supplemented by the Charitable Donation Antitrust Immunity Act of 1997 (111 Stat. 241, P.L. 105-26, 105th Cong., 1st Sess. (1997)).

[761] H. Rep. No. 104-336, 104th Cong., 1st Sess. 3 (1995).

[762] *Ritchie* v. *American Council on Gift Annuities*, 943 F. Supp. 685 (N.D. Tex. 1996), *appeal dis., Ozee* v. *American Council on Gift Annuities*, 110 F.3d 1082 (5th Cir. 1997), *reh. den.*, 116 F.3d 1479 (5th

same annuity rates by various charitable organizations, in issuing charitable gift annuities, constituted price-fixing and thus was a violation of the antitrust laws. This congressional committee offered the following as a rationale for the legislation:

> Allowing litigants to use the antitrust laws as an impediment to these beneficial activities [the issuance of charitable gift annuities] should not be countenanced where, as here, there is no detriment associated with the conduct. It is particularly difficult to see what anticompetitive effect the supposed setting of prices has in a context where the decision to give is motivated not by price but by interest in and commitment to a charitable mission.[763]

§ 5.20 SECURITIES LAWS

The applicability of the federal and state securities laws to charitable fundraising is limited. At the federal level, the principal securities laws are the Securities Act of 1933, the Securities Exchange Act of 1934, and the Investment Company Act of 1940. Generally, this body of law, including comparable state law, is designed to preserve a free market in the trading of securities, provide full and fair disclosure of the character of securities sold in interstate commerce and through the mails, and prevent fraud and other abuse in the marketing and sale of securities.

It is rare that a charitable organization or someone in the charitable fundraising profession would be offering a financial benefit or package to the public where that benefit or package is considered a security. The federal securities law broadly defines the term *security* to include not only stocks and bonds but also notes, debentures, other evidences of indebtedness, certificates of participation in a profit-sharing agreement, investment contracts, and certificates of deposit for securities.[764]

Nonetheless, a charitable organization may find itself at least within the potential applicability of the securities laws if it maintains one or more charitable income funds. The federal securities laws include rules that are designed to shield charities against the allegation that these funds are investment companies subject to the registration and other requirements of the Investment

---

Cir. 1997), *cert. gr. and judg. vac., American Bible Society* v. *Ritchie,* 118 S.Ct. 596 (1997), *on rem., Ozee* v. *American Council on Gift Annuities,* 143 F.3d 937 (5th Cir. 1998), *cert. den., American Bible Society* v. *Ritchie,* 119 S.Ct. 1454 (1999). Also *Ozee* v. *American Council on Gift Annuities,* 110 F.3d 1082 (5th Cir. 1997), *cert. gr. and judg. vac., American Council on Gift Annuities* v. *Ritchie,* 118 S.Ct. 597 (1997); *Ozee* v. *American Council on Gift Annuities,* 888 F. Supp. 1318 (N.D. Tex. 1995); *Ritchie* v. *American Council on Gift Annuities,* 1996 WL 743343 (N.D. Tex. 1996).

[763] H. Rep. No. 104-336, *supra* note 761, at 3. The antitrust laws applicable to charitable organizations, from the standpoint of fundraising, are summarized in greater detail in Hopkins, *supra* note 735, Chapter 9.

[764] 15 U.S.C. § 77b(a)(1).

Company Act. Overall, this legislation provides certain exemptions under the federal securities laws for charitable organizations that maintain these funds.[765]

A *charitable income fund* is a fund maintained by a charitable organization exclusively for the collective investment and reinvestment of one or more assets of a charitable remainder trust[766] or similar trust, a pooled income fund,[767] an arrangement involving a contribution in exchange for the issuance of a charitable gift annuity,[768] a charitable lead trust,[769] the general endowment fund or other funds of one or more charitable organizations, or certain other trusts the remainder interests of which are revocably dedicated to or for the benefit of one or more charitable organizations.[770] A charitable income fund is thus generally not an entity—an investment company—that is subject to the provisions of the Investment Company Act of 1940. This exemption is also engrafted onto the Securities Act of 1933 and the Securities Exchange Act of 1934.[771] The Securities and Exchange Commission[772] has the authority to expand the scope of the exemption provisions of this body of law to embrace funds that may include assets not expressly embraced by this definition.

A fund that is excluded from the definition of an investment company must provide, to each donor to a charitable organization by means of the fund, at the time of the contribution written information describing the material terms of operation of the fund.[773] This disclosure requirement is not, however, a condition of exemption from the Investment Company Act. Thus, where there is a failure to provide the requisite information about a charitable income fund to donors, the fund is not generally subject to the securities laws, although it may be subject to an enforcement or other action by the SEC.

Before the enactment of this statutory law, the applicability of the three federal securities laws to charitable income funds, although that term was not in use then, was addressed by the staff of the SEC. This administrative approach is traceable at least to 1972, when the SEC staff issued a *no-action letter*[774]

---

[765] This legislation was enacted, as part of an attempt to terminate litigation involving the allegation that charities were conspiring to establish uniform (and ostensibly mandatory) charitable gift annuity payout rates (see *supra* note 762), as the Philanthropy Protection Act of 1995 (109 Stat. 682, P.L. 104-62, 104th Cong., 1st Sess. (1995)). One of the arguments was that charitable income funds are investment companies subject to the purview of the Investment Company Act.

[766] See *supra* text accompanied by note 584.

[767] See *supra* text accompanied by note 584. One of the principal reasons the securities laws become implicated in the fundraising setting is that an interest in a pooled income fund technically is a security. Thus, a charitable organization with a pooled income fund is, formally, offering and selling securities. Whether an interest in another type of charitable income fund—such as a charitable remainder trust (see *supra* note 564)—is a security is less clear.

[768] See *supra* text accompanied by *supra* note 584.

[769] See *supra* text accompanied by *supra* note 584.

[770] 15 U.S.C. § 80a-3(c)(10).

[771] 15 U.S.C. §§ 77c(a)(4), 78c(e).

[772] The Securities and Exchange Commission is referred to in this section as the SEC.

[773] 15 U.S.C. § 80a-7(e).

[774] A no-action letter is a document developed by the SEC and its staff to offer advice to those seeking assistance and clarification of the securities laws from the agency. It basically is a ruling from the staff that, if a transaction is engaged in under certain facts and circumstances, the SEC will not take any adverse action against those involved in the transaction.

as to pooled income funds. This determination was predicated on the fact that these entities are the subject of federal tax law and are subject to the oversight of the IRS.[775] One of the principal conditions of this no-action assurance was that each prospective donor receives written disclosures fully and fairly describing the operation of the fund.[776]

Also, the staff of the SEC consistently maintained—and this point remains in the statutory law summarized earlier—that the antifraud provisions of the various securities laws apply to the activities of these funds and the persons associated with the operations of them. This no-action position has always been rationalized by the view that the primary purpose of those who transfer money and/or other property to these funds do so to make a charitable contribution, as opposed to making an investment.

§ 5.21 FTC TELEMARKETING RULE

The Federal Trade Commission[777] acquired a role in the realm of federal regulation of fundraising when the Telemarketing and Consumer Fraud and Abuse Prevention Act (Act) was signed into law in 1994.[778] As directed by the Act, the FTC prescribed rules prohibiting deceptive and other abusive telemarketing acts or practices.[779]

The rules as finalized were, as to charitable fundraising, substantially narrower than the initially proposed version.[780] They basically do not apply to charitable organizations engaged in charitable solicitations, although they are applicable to commercial firms that raise funds or provide similar services to charitable and other tax-exempt organizations. In part, this is because the jurisdiction of the FTC does not extend to charitable and most other nonprofit entities.

While these rules do not generally apply in the charitable fundraising setting, they nonetheless serve as useful guidelines for proper telemarketing practices. In this regard, the rules (1) define the term *telemarketing*; (2) require clear and conspicuous disclosures of specified material information, orally or in writing, before a customer pays for goods or services offered; (3) prohibit misrepresenting, directly or by implication, specified material information relating to the goods or services that are the subject of a sales offer, as well as any

---

[775] See H. Rep. No. 104-333, 104th Cong., 1st Sess. 6-7 (1995).

[776] This is why a charitable organization maintaining a pooled income fund presents prospective contributors with a disclosure statement, in the nature of a prospectus, concerning the fund. This disclosure is mandated, in effect, by the federal securities laws, rather than the federal tax laws.

[777] The Federal Trade Commission is referenced in this section as the FTC.

[778] P.L. 103-297, 108 Stat. 1545 (103d Cong., 2d Sess. (1994)), 15 U.S.C. § 6101 et seq.

[779] These rules were published in proposed form on February 14, 1995 (60 *Fed. Reg.* (No. 30) 8313). (A summary of this proposal is at II *Fund-Raising Regulation Report* (No. 4) 4 (July/August 1995).) The comment period closed on March 31, 1995. A Public Workshop Conference was held on April 18–20, 1995, to afford FTC staff and other interested persons an opportunity to explore and discuss issues raised during the comment period. A second set of proposed regulations was issued; the comment period expired on June 30, 1995 (60 *Fed. Reg.* 30406 (June 8, 1995)). The final regulations were published on August 23, 1995 (60 *Fed. Reg.* 43842).

[780] FTC Rule § 310.3.

other material aspects of a telemarketing transaction; (4) require express verifiable authorization before submitting for payment a check, draft, or other form of negotiable paper drawn on a person's account; (5) prohibit false or otherwise misleading statements to induce payment for goods or services; (6) prohibit any person from assisting and facilitating certain deceptive or abusive telemarketing acts or practices; (7) prohibit credit card laundering; (8) prohibit specified abusive acts or practices; (9) impose calling time restrictions; (10) require specified information to be disclosed truthfully, promptly, and in a clear and conspicuous manner, in an outbound telephone call; (11) require that specified records be kept; and (12) specify certain acts or practices that are exempt from the requirements. The rules became effective on December 31, 1995.

§ 5.22 INTERNET COMMUNICATIONS

(a) Introduction

The most significant federal tax law issue today—or set of issues—facing charitable organizations and those who engage in fundraising for them arises out of use by these organizations of the Internet.[781] Certainly, recent years have brought extensive use of the Internet by charitable (and other tax-exempt) organizations; this use is expanding exponentially. Some aspects of Internet communications directly affect the federal laws pertaining to fundraising, such as the substantiation requirements[782] and the unrelated business rules,[783] and some tangentially pertain to the process, such as the lobbying and political campaign activities limitations.[784]

Despite this significance, there is no discrete law on the point, in the sense of a statute, regulation, or court opinion. The IRS has not issued any guidance; there are no answers from the agency to the many tax questions this form of Internet use is generating. It is nonetheless clear that the federal tax law does not provide any unique treatment to transactions or activities of charitable organizations simply because the Internet is the medium of communication. As the IRS quite saliently observed, the "use of the Internet to accomplish a particular task does not change the way the tax laws apply to that task. Advertising is still advertising and fundraising is still fundraising."[785]

Thus, the most that can be done, at this time, is to extrapolate from existing federal law principles to determine the aspects of Internet use that directly relate to charitable fundraising.

---

[781] In general, Johnston, *The Nonprofit Guide to the Internet, Second Edition* (John Wiley & Sons: New York, 1999).

[782] See *supra* § 3.

[783] See *supra* § 7.

[784] Charitable organizations are limited as to the extent to which they can attempt to influence legislation (see *supra* § 10) and are prohibited from participating or intervening in political campaign activities (IRC § 501(c)(3)). See *The Law of Tax-Exempt Organizations*, Chapters 20, 21. State law pertaining to Internet use by charitable organizations is discussed at § 4.13.

[785] IRS Exempt Organizations Continuing Professional Education Text for Fiscal Year 2000.

(b) IRS Request for Comments

The IRS, in late 2000, requested comment on a range of questions pertaining to Internet activities by tax-exempt organizations.[786] Here are the questions raised by the IRS that are generally relevant in the fundraising context:

- Are the gift substantiation rules, concerning written acknowledgments for contributions of $250 or more,[787] satisfied with a written Webpage confirmation or copy of a confirmation by e-mail from the donee charitable organization?

- Does an organization meet the requirements of the quid pro quo contribution rules[788] with a Webpage confirmation that may be printed out by the contributor or by sending a confirmation by e-mail to the donor?

- Are solicitations for contributions made on the Internet (either on an organization's Website or by e-mail) in *written or printed form* for purposes of the disclosure rules applicable to noncharitable organizations?[789]

Here are the questions posed by the IRS that are pertinent to fundraising for charitable organizations from the perspective of the unrelated business income rules:[790]

- To what extent are business activities conducted on the Internet regularly carried on? What facts and circumstances are relevant in making this determination?

- Are there any circumstances under which the payment of a percentage of sales from customers referred by a tax-exempt organization to another Website would be substantially related to the organization's exempt purpose?

- Does a Website constitute a single publication or other form of communication? If not, how should it be separated (fragmented) into distinct publications or communications?

- When allocating expenses for a Website, what methodology is appropriate? For example, should allocations be based on Webpages (which unlike print publications, may not be of equal size)?

Here are two pertinent questions posed by the IRS, relevant to fundraising, concerning other aspects of use of the Internet by charitable organizations:

---

[786] Ann. 2000-84, 2000-42 I.R.B. 385.
[787] See *supra* § 3.
[788] See *supra* § 4.
[789] See *supra* § 5.
[790] In general, see *supra* § 7.

- Unlike other publications of a tax-exempt organization, a Website may be modified on a daily basis. To what extent and by what means should an exempt organization maintain the information from prior versions of the organization's Website?

- To what extent are statements made by subscribers to a forum, such as a listserv or newsgroup, attributable to an exempt organization that maintains the forum? Would attribution vary, depending on the level of participation of the exempt organization in maintaining the forum (e.g., where the organization moderates the discussion or acts as editor)?

Reportedly, the IRS received thousands of responses to this request for comments. Yet, formal guidance will not be provided by the IRS, at least for the foreseeable future.

(c) Internet Communications Issues

(i) Unrelated Business Rules in General.   The Internet use that implicates the unrelated business rules concerns marketing, merchandising, advertising, and the like. In general, as noted, it may be assumed that, as the law in this area develops, that law will be consistent with existing law with respect to advertising, merchandising, and publishing in the offline world.

(ii) Links.   A significant issue in this context is the subject of charity Website hypertext links to related or recommended sites. Link exchanges may be treated by the IRS the same as mailing list exchanges. Compensation for a linkage may be unrelated business income. The purpose of the link should be determinative in determining whether it is furthering exempt purposes (a referral of the site visitor to additional [educational] information) or is part of an unrelated activity (including advertising).

(iii) Corporate Sponsorships.   Internet use can involve the corporate sponsorship rules,[791] inasmuch as tax-exempt organizations may seek corporate support to underwrite the establishment and/or maintenance of all or a portion of the organization's Website. These relationships may be short term or continue on a long-term basis. The financial support may be acknowledged by means of display of a corporate logo, notation of the sponsor's Web address and/or 800 number, a moving banner (a graphic advertisement, usually a moving image, measured in pixels), or a link. The issue is whether the support is a qualified sponsorship payment, in which case the revenue is not taxable, or advertising income, which generally is taxable as unrelated business income.

There is a question about whether the use of a link in an acknowledgment will change the character of a corporation's payment, converting it from an otherwise qualified sponsorship payment (and thus nontaxable income)

---

[791] See *supra* § 16.

to taxable advertising income. The IRS may adopt the view that a payment of this nature should retain its character as a mere acknowledgment because the Website visitor must take an affirmative action—click—to reach the corporation's Website. A moving banner is more likely to be considered advertising.

(iv) Periodicals. Qualified sponsorship payments do not include payments that entitle the sponsors to acknowledgments in regularly scheduled printed material published by or on behalf of the tax-exempt organization. Here, the issue is the characterization of Website materials. Most of these materials made available on exempt organization Websites are clearly prepared in a manner that is distinguishable from the methodology used in preparing periodicals.

Nonetheless, an online publication can be treated as a periodical. When this is the case, special rules by which unrelated business income from periodical advertising is computed become applicable. Some periodicals have online editions and some print publications are reproduced online, sometimes on a subscription basis or in a members-only access portion of a Website. These materials should be and generally are sufficiently segregated from the other traditional Website materials so that the methodology employed in the production and distribution methods are clearly ascertainable, and the periodical income and costs can be independently and appropriately determined. Presumably, "genuine" periodicals have an editorial staff, marketing program, and budget independent of the organization's Webmaster.

(v) Auctions. Regarding online auctions, the IRS will be concerned with use by charitable organizations of outside auction service providers. Although utilization of these outside entities may provide a larger audience for the auction and enable the organization to avoid difficulties in connection with the use of credit cards, the relationship might have tax implications.

The focus is on control; the IRS will consider how much control the charitable organization exercises over the marketing and conduct of the auction. The IRS will want the charity to have primary responsibility in this regard. Otherwise, the IRS may be more likely to view income from these auction activities as income from classified advertising rather than as income derived from the conduct of a fundraising event. These service providers are essentially professional fundraisers;[792] their functions and fees should be scrutinized pursuant to the doctrines of private inurement and private benefit.[793]

(vi) Co-Venture Programs. Consideration should be given to affiliate and other co-venture programs with merchants, such as arrangements with large, online booksellers. Some tax-exempt organizations display book recommendations on their Websites; others have a link to the bookseller. The exempt organization earns a percentage of sales of recommended materials and perhaps also a commission on purchases sold through the referring link. The principal issue in this setting is whether the resulting income is a tax-excludable royalty.

[792] See §§ 3.6, 4.10.
[793] See *Law of Tax-Exempt Organizations,* Chapter 19.

(vii) Online Storefronts. Another set of issues pertains to online store-fronts, complete with virtual shopping carts, on the Websites of tax-exempt organizations. Again, it may be anticipated that the IRS will use the same analysis that it applies in connection with sales made through stores, catalogs, and other traditional vehicles, such as that applied in the context of museum gift shop sales. In deciding whether the unrelated business rules apply, the IRS looks to the nature, scope, and motivation for the particular sales activities. Merchandise is evaluated on an item-by-item basis, with application of the fragmentation rule, to determine whether the sales activity furthers the accomplishment of the organization's exempt purposes or is merely a way to generate revenue.

(viii) Virtual Trade Shows. The *virtual trade show* generates income for business and trade associations and other tax-exempt entities from *virtual exhibitors.* This brings into play rules by which traditional trade show income is excluded from the unrelated business income tax.[794] The extent to which the traditional rules will apply to virtual trade show income will most likely depend on whether the qualifying organization is able to demonstrate that its exhibits or displays are substantially similar to those used at a traditional trade show.

This tax law exception for trade show income probably is not available for a mere listing of links to industry suppliers' Websites. Also, it is highly questionable whether income from a year-round virtual trade show is excludable from unrelated business income. Conversely, virtual trade shows with displays including educational information related to issues of interest to industry members, or those that are timed to coincide with the sponsoring organization's annual meeting or regular trade show, may qualify for the exclusion.

In anticipation of the issuance of the request for comments on questions posed by it concerning application of the tax law to the Internet activities of tax-exempt organizations,[795] the IRS wrote: "It is hoped that all members of the exempt organizations [community] will be involved in the development of new policies which will build upon principles developed over time and adapted to allow exempt organizations to take advantage of the technological innovations of the new millennium."[796]

§ 5.23   HEALTH INSURANCE PORTABILITY AND ACCOUNTABILITY ACT REGULATIONS

Privacy regulations promulgated by the Department of Health and Human Services[797] concerning the use of health information relate to charitable fund-raising by health care entities.

---

[794] IRC § 511.

[795] See *supra* § 22(c)(ii).

[796] IRS Continuing Professional Education Text, *supra* note 765. In general, Livingston, "Tax-Exempt Organizations and the Internet: Tax and Other Legal Issues," 31 *Exempt Org. Tax Rev.* (No. 3) 419 (Mar. 2001); Reaves and Bennet, "UBIT.COM? Can the Old Laws Apply in the New Cyber Frontier?," 27 *Exempt Org. Tax Rev.* (No. 2) 251 (Feb. 2000).

[797] The Department of Health and Human Services is referenced in this section as the DHHS.

Passage of the Health Insurance Portability and Accountability Act (HIPAA) in 1996[798] required that Congress develop rules, or in the absence of Congress to act, that the DHHS promulgate regulations that address the protection of individually identifiable health information that is transmitted by electronic media.

The DHHS published its final regulations[799] regarding the privacy of this type of health information, generally defined as *protected health information* (PHI), and has allowed a two-year implementation period, except for small health plans, which have three years. In appreciating the importance of these privacy regulations, one must understand to whom they apply. The regulations go well beyond those parties transmitting PHI by electronic means.

The parties involved in these regulations are termed *covered entities* and include health care providers, health care clearinghouses, and health plans. Each of these covered entities is defined in the regulations. As an overriding principle, the basic requirements of the privacy standards are stated as follows: "A Covered Entity may not use or disclose an individual's Protected Health Information, except as otherwise permitted or required by [these regulations]."

With respect to health care providers who conduct fundraising efforts, those health care providers are covered under HIPAA and the fundraising activities are covered. In addition, a third party who provides services to a covered entity is also subject to the regulations through the concept of *business associate*. The regulations make a distinction between (1) *consent* given by an individual to a health care provider to arrange for the treatment, payment of that health care, or *health care operations,* and (2) *authorization,* which is a separate procedure by which the individual receiving health care authorizes the release of PHI to third parties not otherwise included within the consent given to the health care provider or providers.

The term *health care operations* is defined in the regulations and includes a lengthy list of activities such as peer review and quality assurance. In addition, the regulations require that a covered entity provide a *notice of privacy practices* (NPP), which notifies the individual as to how that party intends to use the PHI received from that individual.

If a covered entity wishes to use PHI for fundraising purposes, it must include a statement in the NPP of that intended use or disclosure. In addition, any fundraising materials must describe how the individual can "opt out" of solicitations for funds. These privacy standards define fundraising as part of a health care operation that is part of the consent procedure. Therefore, any provider intending to use information gained through its relationship in providing health care treatment, payment, or health care operations must obtain patient consent before sending any solicitations for contributions.

There are a myriad of exceptions and exclusions from the requirements for consent and authorization, such as utilizing *de-identified* information. There

---

[798] P.L. 104-191, 104th Cong., 2d Sess. (1996).

[799] The Final Rule on Standards for Privacy of Individually Identifiable Health Information was published by DHHS on December 28, 2000 (65 *Fed. Reg.* (No. 250) 82463). This body of law took effect on April 14, 2001.

are certain requirements for meeting the definition of what constitutes de-identified information.

An elaborate procedure involving fundraising efforts is not in the regulations. The basic requirement is that the party seeking to use the PHI gained through the consent process must disclose in its NPP that it intends to use such information for solicitation of funds and provide an opportunity for that party to opt out. Where complications may arise would be in the use of PHI by related entities, such as supporting organizations, or by unrelated entities, such as professional fundraising organizations. These relationships need to be reviewed in the context of the requirements for business associates.

CHAPTER SIX

Prospective Federal Regulation of Fundraising: Proposals and Issues

§ 6.1 Introduction
§ 6.2 Major Legislative Proposals
    (a) Wilson Bill
    (b) Mondale Bill
    (c) Luken Bill
    (d) Metzenbaum Proposal
§ 6.3 Emerging Issues
    (a) Necessity of More Rules
    (b) Mode of Disclosure
    (c) Disclosure of Fundraising Costs
    (d) Uniform Accounting Principles

(e) Federal Agency Jurisdiction
(f) Exemptions
(g) Federal Preemption of State Law
(h) Sanctions
(i) Filer Commission Recommendations
(j) Ford Administration Treasury Proposals
§ 6.4 Contemporary Developments and Prospects

As the previous chapter reflects, meaningful federal regulation of fundraising by and on behalf of charitable organizations has come into being in recent years, and its reach is expanding. As yet, nonetheless, Congress has not given serious thought to enactment of a federal charitable solicitation act.

If only because of the complexity and inconsistency of the state charitable solicitation acts, and the compliance and enforcement problems generated by multistate fundraising, it is somewhat surprising that, in the modern era, there is no federal law regulating interstate fundraising for charitable purposes—a law that would preempt or at least overlay (like the federal securities and antitrust laws) the crazyquilt of state statutes. These issues, difficult as they were just a few years ago, are exacerbated by charities' use of the Internet to raise funds. Present law stresses disclosure; future law may include registration and reporting.

There have been attempts over the years to produce a wide-ranging federal fundraising regulation law. Each of those efforts have been dismal failures. The lack of enthusiasm—let alone consensus—in Congress regarding the appropriate features and reach of this type of law is an important factor that has precluded enactment of a federal fundraising regulation law. Also, in general, Congress does not often pass laws that preempt state statutes. There is always an enormous adverse reaction to such a proposal, with the opposition spearheaded by the states' attorneys general, secretaries of state, and the like.

There may well be more federal statutory law governing fundraising. When speculating about possible future enactments, it is essential to recall the proposals made to date, despite their lack of success.

§ 6.1 INTRODUCTION

Historically, the responsibility for regulating and otherwise monitoring the process by which organizations solicit contributions for charitable purposes has been left to the states, with some collateral regulation by counties and cities. The present manner of state and local regulation of interstate charitable solicitations, however, has produced considerable confusion and has, in many respects, been ineffective. For example, the fundraising activities of the New Era for Philanthropy Foundation went undisturbed by state regulatory officials—despite a massive charitable solicitation act in its home state—who belatedly acted only in the aftermath of media reports. These statutes and ordinances involve a bewildering myriad of different laws, forms, due dates, and accounting requirements. At the same time, state regulation of fundraising has enjoyed some successes in monitoring and curbing abuses in intrastate fundraising practices.

It is, of course, difficult for a charitable organization that is soliciting financial assistance across the states to comply with or even be aware of each of the various state statutes and local ordinances. As discussed previously,[1] the exemptions are unclear and inconsistent, the requirements for registration and reporting are different, the deadlines are dissimilar, and, in general, the compliance effort can be time-consuming and confusing. Indeed, the survey of these state requirements[2] does not disclose what can be the most difficult aspect of the entire process: the multiplicity of varying application, registration, and reporting forms, which contain a wide range of questions, differing accounting requirements, and more—all of this somewhat ameliorated, to be sure, by the growing use of uniform forms.

Frankly, the only factor that is keeping the present multifarious system of differing requirements from becoming totally impossible to adhere to is a lack of enforcement by a sizable number of regulatory agencies. There are indications, however, that the enforcement attitude is changing, in part because of the more frequently used technique of soliciting funds by mail and the attendant abuses that are finding their way into media exposés. Today, a charitable organization takes a calculated risk when it ignores a charitable solicitation regulation requirement in the expectation or hope that the prohibited activities will escape the notice of the enforcement authorities.

One solution to the present jumble of conflicting and complicated requirements for complying with governmental regulation of fundraising activities would be to bring uniformity to these requirements. Despite intensive,

---

[1] See Chapter 4.
[2] See Chapter 3.

excellent, and repeated efforts, state governments have been unwilling (with minor exceptions) to voluntarily adopt common accounting principles, exemptions, and the like. Modest success has, as noted, been achieved with the use of uniform forms. Nor has a model state statute generated any appreciable interest, although contributions by the accounting profession and nonprofit organizations in developing standardized legislative provisions have been extensive. Consequently, a federal statute may be the sole feasible solution, in part because of insufficient progress toward the establishment of systems of uniform reporting and, perhaps, enforcement.

As may be expected, many insist that a federal government entry into this field is unwarranted. This position is usually based on a belief that federal regulatory authority over charitable organizations is already too pervasive, or that present state and local law enforcement with respect to charitable solicitations is sufficient, or that the abuses in fundraising for charitable purposes that have surfaced to date are isolated instances that do not warrant remedial action by means of national law.

A statute at the federal level in the field of fundraising for charity was one of the recommendations of the Commission on Private Philanthropy and Public Needs.[3] This type of a law was advocated by the Department of the Treasury in the waning days of the Ford Administration.[4] A specific proposal may be anticipated should Congress call for the views of the Department of the Treasury and the IRS on the subject or if there is a public outcry (such as in response to a well-publicized scandal) for remedial action.

Consequently, a working assumption—palatable or not—may be that a federal charitable solicitations statute is forthcoming. Therefore, it is appropriate to anticipate the possible components and extent of such a law.

The design of a charitable fundraising supervision bill necessarily depends on the motives of those formulating it. Some proponents seek to expose to the public those organizations that are "inefficiently" managed and/or that have "excessive" fundraising costs. Others endorse a more encompassing objective; they perceive the appropriate purpose of this type of law to be "consumer protection," which becomes translated into a proposed scheme of disclosure on a much more extensive, and at the same time more specific, scale. For still others, the matter of regulating fundraising costs, and otherwise regulating fundraising, is viewed as merely part of a much larger purpose—the regulation of public charities (i.e., charitable organizations other than private foundations[5]) in relation to the conduct of their programs and other practices. Some of the individuals in this last category, including some in the legislative and executive branches of the federal government, desire not only a national charitable solicitations regulation law but also the imposition of some or all of the vast panoply of laws at present applicable to private foundations (principally, the prohibitions on self-dealing, excess business holdings,

---

[3] See *infra* § 3(i).
[4] See *infra* § 3(j).
[5] See § 5.11.

and jeopardy investments, and the rules mandating minimum payout of funds and restricting the uses of these funds) on the affairs of public charities.[6]

This chapter assumes that a federal charitable solicitations law will at some time be accorded serious consideration, and projects the potential components and scope of this type of law.

§ 6.2 MAJOR LEGISLATIVE PROPOSALS

Over the years, several bills have been introduced in Congress on this subject. The measures that have directly pertained to fundraising regulation are discussed in this section. Each is identified with the name of its legislative sponsor.

(a) Wilson Bill

As introduced in various forms by then-Congressman Charles H. Wilson (D-Cal.),[7] the Wilson bill would have engrafted federal fundraising regulation onto the postal laws. The U.S. Postal Service would be invested with authority to monitor fundraising for charitable purposes as part of its mail fraud investigative and enforcement functions.

The legislation would be generally applicable to "[a]ny charitable organization which solicits, in any manner or through any means, the remittance of a contribution by mail." An organization to which the proposed law would apply would have to disclose certain specified information in the literature used in the solicitation process, including the amount expended for charitable

---

[6] *Id.* Progress toward this goal was made when the intermediate sanctions rules were enacted (see § 5.6).

[7] This legislation originated as H.R. 9584, 93d Cong., 1st Sess. (1973), and was reintroduced as H.R. 5269, 94th Cong., 1st Sess. (1975). Following a hearing on July 30, 1975, the measure emerged as H.R. 10922, 94th Cong., 1st Sess. (1975), which was reported by the then-named House Committee on Post Office and Civil Service (H.R. Rep. No. 94-1135, 94th Cong., 2d Sess. (1976)). The bill was again reintroduced as H.R. 41, 95th Cong., 1st Sess. (1977), and, in March 1977, underwent three days of hearings before the House Subcommittee on Postal Personnel and Modernization (of which Representative Wilson then was chairman). For lack of support in the philanthropic community and in Congress, H.R. 41 (as amended in the subcommittee on July 25, 1977) progressed no further during the 95th Congress and died upon its adjournment in 1978. The measure was again introduced as H.R. 875, 96th Cong., 1st Sess. (1979), but no further action was ever taken on it.

A somewhat comparable bill was H.R. 11991, 93d Cong., 2d Sess. (1974), introduced by then-Congressman Lionel Van Deerlin (D-Cal.), and reintroduced as H.R. 1123, 94th Cong., 1st Sess. (1975). Hearings were held on the Van Deerlin legislation on January 14, 1975. This legislation would have vested fundraising regulation authority in the Department of Commerce.

Legislation titled the "Charitable Solicitation Disclosure Act," which would have required disclosure of information in the course of fundraising by mail, was introduced as H.R. 2130, 100th Cong., 1st Sess. (1987), by Congressman Major R. Owens (D-N.Y.). The measure was reintroduced in the next Congress as H.R. 1257, 101st Cong., 1st Sess. (1989). Referred to the Subcommittee on Postal Personnel and Modernization of the House Committee on Post Office and Civil Service, the bill has not advanced. A commentary on this legislation appeared in XX *Phil. Monthly* (No. 5) 21 (1987).

purposes during its preceding fiscal year, expressed as a single percentage. (The percentage rule would not, however, become effective until three years after the effective date of the act.) Comparable rules would apply to audio and visual communications. A soliciting organization would be required, within 30 days after the request, to provide a person with a financial statement for its most recent full fiscal year, prepared in accordance with generally accepted accounting principles.

Exceptions would be available for solicitations of organizations' "constituencies," such as solicitations by bona fide membership groups (including local religious congregations or parishes) exclusively of their members; by schools, colleges, and universities (and their supporting foundations) exclusively of their students, alumni, faculty, trustees, committee members, and family members of these individuals; and by hospitals or other health care facilities (and their supporting foundations) exclusively of their professional staff, other personnel, trustees, committee members, and family members of these individuals.

Although enforcement of this proposed law would be a responsibility of the Postal Service, there was considerable desire by the author of the measure to not create a massive regulatory bureaucracy. Thus, the final versions of the bill expressly prohibited the Postal Service from requiring charitable organizations to furnish it at regular intervals with audit reports, accounts, or other information, or from prescribing any rules or regulations to carry out the provisions of the statutory law.

The Wilson bill basically addressed the matter of federal charitable fundraising regulation as a consumer protection effort, emphasizing public disclosure by charitable organizations rather than governmental regulation of them.

(b) Mondale Bill

The Mondale bill, as originally authored by then-Senator Walter F. Mondale (D-Minn.),[8] reflected an attitude that charitable organizations and their solicitations need to be strenuously regulated by the federal government.

The Mondale proposal would have added requirements to the Internal Revenue Code pursuant to which certain types of publicly supported charities and related entities would have to distribute at least 50 percent of their gross revenues each year for charitable purposes. Expenditures for salaries (except for persons performing services in furtherance of charitable programs), outlays for office facilities, administrative expenses, and fundraising expenses would not qualify as expenditures for charitable purposes.

Public charities subject to the Mondale bill's requirements would be those receiving a substantial part of their support from the general public or

---

[8] This legislation, titled the "Truth in Contributions Act," was originally introduced as S. 1153, 94th Cong., 1st Sess. (1975), following hearings in 1974 before the Senate Subcommittee on Children and Youth (of which Senator Mondale then was chairman). It was introduced in the House of Representatives by Congressman Joseph E. Karth (D-Minn.) as H.R. 4689, 94th Cong., 1st Sess. (1975), and subsequently by Congressman William Lehman (D-Fla.) as H.R. 478, 95th Cong., 1st Sess. (1977). The measure was not introduced in subsequent Congresses.

organizations supportive of them.[9] Thus, the measure would not apply to institutions such as churches, colleges, universities, hospitals, and medical research organizations. Also, the bill's requirements would not apply to any organization with revenues of $25,000 or less in a tax year.

Charitable organizations subject to the Mondale bill's provisions would have to annually prepare and file with the IRS information (in addition to that required in the annual information return) for determination by the IRS as to whether the 50 percent payout requirement has been met. These data would have to be prepared by a certified public accountant in accordance with approved uniform accounting principles. This annual report would also have to be filed with the appropriate officials in each state where a solicitation of contributions is made.

A public charity subject to these requirements would have to furnish prospective contributors with adequate information regarding its revenues and expenditures for charitable purposes and for other purposes during the previous year. This information would have to be disclosed at the time of the solicitation, regardless of the manner or the medium used. A "disclosure statement," approved (or at least not disapproved) by the IRS, would be required. This statement would have to be mailed within 15 days to any person who requests it, and it would have to be filed with the appropriate officials in each state where a solicitation is undertaken.

These requirements would be enforced by a system of excise taxes, in imitation of the present enforcement scheme underpinning the private foundation rules.[10] The measure would extend the termination rules, now applicable only to private foundations, to this category of public charities, and would impose civil and criminal penalties on organizations or persons responsible for a failure to comply with these various requirements.

The bill would direct the Department of the Treasury to develop standard accounting principles for public charities. The department would also be required to encourage state and local governments to accept filings made in compliance with this law in lieu of separate local reports.

Thus, the Mondale bill approached the matter of federal law applicability to charitable solicitations by the proposed establishment of rather stringent regulatory authority.

(c) Luken Bill

An effort once was under way to invest the Federal Trade Commission (FTC) with authority to investigate and regulate fundraising for charitable purposes. On July 28, 1989, hearings on this subject were held before the Subcommittee on Transportation, Tourism, and Hazardous Materials of the House Committee on Energy and Commerce. This subcommittee was interested in charitable fundraising because it has jurisdiction over the FTC, and the then-chairman of the subcommittee, Congressman Thomas A. Luken (D-Ohio), was of the view

[9] Specifically, this law would apply to those organizations whose public charity status is derived from IRC § 170(b)(1)(A)(vi), 509(a)(2), or 509(a)(3). See § 5.11.
[10] IRC Chapter 42.

that the FTC should investigate and curtail certain direct mail fundraising efforts, such as the use of misleading sweepstakes.

The regulatory community has been showing renewed interest in direct mail sweepstakes as a fundraising form, in part because, all too often, little of the money raised goes for charitable purposes and in part because the promised prizes rarely materialize. Some state attorneys general have sued direct mail promotion firms over the issue, and the U.S. Postal Service has become involved. The bases for these actions are allegations of fraud and other deceptive practices.

The history of this matter includes an inquiry to the FTC from then-Congressman Edward F. Feighan (D-Ohio) in December 1987, requesting information about certain fundraising programs, including a sweepstakes appeal. The FTC response and subsequent action were less than satisfactory to the House members, thus prompting a more formal inquiry.

The present jurisdiction of the FTC in these matters is not clear. The FTC has some jurisdiction over nonprofit organizations, but the extent of its reach is uncertain. The FTC also has jurisdiction over direct mail companies and other for-profit fundraising entities. Under existing law, the FTC must go through the exercise of determining its jurisdiction in a case before it can review the case on its substantive merits. One of the goals of the congressional inquiry was to determine whether the FTC's jurisdiction should be clarified in relation to charitable fundraising, so that the agency's resources would not be depleted in precomplaint investigations. The ability of the FTC to investigate, make rules, and enforce law in this field is dubious.

At the hearings, the FTC representatives testified that the agency welcomes the clarification as to its jurisdiction and responsibility for investigating abuses in the field of fundraising for charitable purposes.

Thereafter, Congressman Luken introduced legislation that would have amended the Federal Trade Commission Act to empower the FTC to regulate the fundraising activities of charitable organizations.[11] The proposal would accord the FTC jurisdiction over nonprofit organizations. The bill would require a charity that uses a professional fundraiser[12] in connection with the solicitation of funds to provide to each person solicited, at the time of the solicitation, a "clear and conspicuous" statement that the fundraising is "being conducted by" the fundraising professional, containing the name and address of the fundraiser. The FTC would be required to promulgate uniform accounting principles governing the costs of fundraising for charitable purposes. A professional fundraiser would be required to report annually to "appropriate State agencies the amounts charged each charity for its services and the amount raised for each charity." It would prevent a charitable organization[13] from having an individual serve as an officer or director, if he or she is also an officer,

---

[11] H.R. 3964, 101st Cong., 2d Sess. (1990), titled the "Fair Fund-Raising Act of 1990."

[12] The term *professional fundraiser* would be defined as "a person who engages in solicitation for a charity for compensation and who is not an employee of the charity for whom the solicitation is made."

[13] As defined in this legislation, a "charitable" organization is one that has its federal income tax exemption based on IRC § 501(c)(3) or § 501(c)(4).

director, or agent of a "professional fundraising organization" that is employed by the charity. The requirement of a statement to prospective donees and the prohibition on interlocking directorates between charities and professional fundraisers would preempt any state or local law that is "inconsistent" with the requirements, although a state or political subdivision would be able to secure a waiver of the preemption where the FTC determined that the requirement of state or local law "affords an equal or greater level of protection to the public" than would be afforded by the preemptive requirements.

When introducing the legislation, Congressman Luken said that the measure "will help stamp out modern peddlers of deceit, who use sophisticated technology to raise money in a way that cheats many people, particularly the elderly, and injures legitimate charities by siphoning off much needed money."[14]

(d) Metzenbaum Proposal

The most recent effort in Congress to enact a fundraising regulation bill was initiated by then-Senator Howard Metzenbaum (D-Ohio), who contemplated introduction of a "Truth in Fund-Raising Act."

This proposal would have utilized federal tax rules to create a new disclosure requirement.[15] The disclosure rule would be applicable to nearly all tax-exempt organizations. Technically, this law would be applicable to all organizations that are required to file annual information returns with the IRS, other than those that have annual gross receipts that normally are not more than $50,000.[16]

The specific rule underlying this proposed legislation was that a fundraising solicitation by or on behalf of a tax-exempt organization must contain an "express statement (in a conspicuous and easily recognizable format) setting forth the exempt purpose expenditure percentage."

The term *fundraising solicitation* would be the same as that under certain disclosure rules.[17] That is, it is a solicitation of contributions that is made in written or printed form, by television or radio, or by telephone.

The term *exempt-purpose expenditure percentage* would be determined by using the figures for the year immediately preceding the year in which the solicitation took place. For example, if the disclosure was to take place in 2002 and the organization uses the calendar year as its fiscal year, the organization would compute the percentage using 2001 figures. If this organization received $1 million in gifts in 2001 and had a fundraising cost of $100,000, its exempt-purpose expenditure percentage used in 2002 would be 90 percent. Thus, this organization, in all of its fundraising during 2002, would be required to conspicuously state that 90 percent of its gift support went to program. The same would be true for an organization that had a 2001 fundraising cost of 60 percent, except that its exempt-purpose expenditure percentage would be 40 percent.

---

[14] News Release dated Feb. 6, 1990. See Suhrke, "Do We Need More Federal Fund Raising Oversight Added to State Regulation?," XXII *Phil. Monthly* (No. 6) 4 (1989).
[15] Proposed IRC § 6115.
[16] IRC § 6033.
[17] IRC § 6113(c). See § 5.5.

The legislation would not allow for the allocation of costs between program and fundraising. The draft bill stated that the "cost of any solicitation shall include the entire cost of preparing and disseminating the written or printed form, television or radio advertisement, or telephone call of which it is a part." This would prevent the cost of, for example, a direct mail letter from being allocated partly to program (education) and partly to fundraising.

In computing gift support, an organization would not be able to include funds derived from a grant from a governmental unit or from any tax-exempt organization.

The penalty for violation of this law would be $1,000 for each day on which a failure to comply occurred or continued.[18]

This legislative proposal was endorsed by some state officials at a hearing held before the Senate Judiciary Subcommittee on Antitrust, Monopolies, and Business Rights on December 15, 1989. The subcommittee was chaired by Senator Metzenbaum, who retired in 1994. The proposal was never formally introduced.

* * *

Each of these members of Congress, and others, have found to their chagrin that this area of law is a political and legal quagmire. The issues are difficult and the politics intense. Many a politician, motivated perhaps at the outset by high ideals, has regretted entry into the murky world of charitable fundraising regulation. Influenced no doubt by the angst experienced by their predecessors, it has been well over a decade since a member of the House of Representatives or Senate has proposed a federal charitable solicitations act. Yet, other attempts seem inevitable.

§ 6.3 EMERGING ISSUES

The prospect of a federal law regulating charitable solicitations raises a host of issues for philanthropy. These include:

- The necessity of promulgating more rules; that is, whether the federal government should be confined only to disclosure or granted more extensive (private-foundation-like) regulatory powers

- The mode of disclosure

- The requirement to disclose fundraising costs

- The impact of this type of legislation on the already existing pressure for uniform accounting principles for nonprofit organizations

- The appropriate enforcement agency or agencies, for example, the IRS, Department of the Treasury, Department of Commerce, Postal Service, FTC, or some newly created agency

---

[18] IRC § 6710(a),(d).

■ The appropriate category or categories of charities or other tax-exempt organizations to be encompassed or exempted by this type of statute

■ The extent of any federal preemption of state and local laws and responsibilities

■ The nature of any sanctions to be applied

Each of these issues is discussed as follows.

(a) Necessity of More Rules

As noted, many observers are skeptical of the need for more law in the charitable solicitations field. If, however, the issue concerns the appropriateness of a law requiring the disclosure or availability of pertinent information concerning a charitable organization to those individuals who have been solicited for a charitable contribution to that organization (and who lack another means for obtaining that information, such as membership status in the organization), it is difficult to find a basis for contending against this type of a law. It is equally difficult to argue against a law designed to eliminate the criminal, fraudulent, and/or unscrupulous solicitor from the marketplace of charitable giving. One can argue against the specifics of these laws but not against the concept; many precedents for this approach are embedded in the U.S. legal system, and this type of emphasis on disclosure is being expanded as part of consumer protection efforts.

This assumes, of course, that one can make the case that a sufficient number of charitable solicitations are being conducted by the abusive and the unscrupulous to warrant corrective action at the federal level. Because of the exploits of a few, there is widespread belief that this case can be made. It must also be assumed that self-regulation by the philanthropic community cannot generate the requisite degree of disclosure to the public of the activities and financial practices of charitable organizations.[19]

Assuming, then, that this type of law—as a concept—is necessary, the next question must be whether there should be laws at the state and local levels or (perhaps preemptive) law on the federal level. For the most part, the answer to this question will depend on one's philosophy about the system and role of government in the United States, and about whether federal law would preempt state and local law.

Many believe that a scheme of well-written uniform state laws, if fairly and uniformly enforced, would be preferable to federal law. Others contend that the existing state and local law picture is one of a battery of burdensome statutes and ordinances that are poorly conceived, poorly written, and poorly enforced. Thus, some assert that the entire system should be scrapped as far as solicitations in interstate commerce are concerned and replaced by a well-written effective federal

---

[19] In an analogous circumstance, the matter of disclosure to donors as to the extent of nondeductibility in the case of quid quo pro contributions, Congress lost patience with the plodding efforts of the nonprofit community to rectify the situation and summarily imposed sweeping legislation (see §§ 5.3, 5.4).

law. By contrast, others would argue that the solution lies with uniform requirements, accounting standards, reporting forms, and the like.

(b) Mode of Disclosure

The previously discussed bills embody the point-of-solicitation disclosure concept. For example, the Wilson bill would have required the solicitation to include a statement of the "purpose of the solicitation and the intended use of the contribution solicited." The Wilson bill also would have required the information to be included with a written solicitation to be "presented in language which is readily understandable by those persons to whom the solicitation is directed, . . . be located in a conspicuous place on such solicitation, and . . . appear in conspicuous and legible type in contrast by typography, layout, or color with other printed matter on such solicitation." The Metzenbaum bill reflects a penchant for the use of percentages.

The point-of-disclosure solicitation approach is also often accompanied by a requirement that the charity supply additional information (including a financial statement) to the public upon request, with notice of the availability of this information to accompany the solicitation. Under the Wilson bill, this additional information would have to be provided within 30 days after receipt of a request for it. Under the Mondale bill, a disclosure statement would have to be mailed within 15 days to any person upon request. Provision of information to the federal enforcement agency would be still another disclosure and data dissemination requirement.

Under the disclosure-on-demand approach, the solicitation material would have to contain a statement notifying the recipient of his or her right to information about the soliciting charitable organization. For example, a recipient of a charitable solicitation might have 180 days to request the information and the organization might have 30 days within which to respond.

One can argue that all that is required is a federal statute mandating every charitable organization to provide, in response to every request received, a copy of an annual report containing financial statements which, among other elements, would state fundraising costs. A notice of the availability of this report could accompany the solicitation. Perhaps this report could be the information return that charitable organizations annually file with the IRS (Form 990), although the contents of that filing might then have to be expanded.

(c) Disclosure of Fundraising Costs

A federal charitable solicitations law would likely provide for disclosure of a charitable organization's fundraising costs. A principal issue, however, is the appropriate format and method of this disclosure.

The question of format is entangled in the issue of whether disclosure in general is to be accomplished by the point-of-solicitation or disclosure-on-demand approach, as discussed earlier. As to method, this issue has become narrowed to two positions: presentation of fundraising costs as a line item within a general financial statement or expression of fundraising costs as a single percentage of receipts. The Mondale bill utilized the first approach; the Wilson and Metzenbaum bills had, as one of their key provisions, the second approach.

The Wilson bill would have required a charitable organization to state its outlays for charitable purposes as a percentage and to do so on the solicitation materials. This type of a percentage would be based on the prior year's financial data. The Metzenbaum proposal was based on a comparable approach. The deficiencies of this requirement are discussed in a previous section.

The ultimate resolution of the matter of the method of fundraising costs disclosure will probably be a byproduct of the point-of-solicitation versus disclosure-on-demand conflict. If the single fundraising cost percentage became a requirement of a federal charitable solicitations law, however, consideration should be given to the use of a three- or four-year moving average rather than a single year's performance. As noted, Congress at present requires the utilization of such a computation in assessing a charitable organization's eligibility for non–private-foundation status.[20]

(d) Uniform Accounting Principles

A federal charitable solicitations law would be a major force for adoption of uniform accounting principles throughout the nonprofit organization community. (It may be noted that uniform accounting principles for nonprofit organizations seem inevitable for other reasons.) At present, colleges and universities, hospitals, voluntary health and social welfare organizations, and other organizations observe varying accounting standards.[21]

The issue of the proper method of disclosure of fundraising costs will likely depend on the requirements of the applicable set of generally accepted accounting principles. This matter transcends current federal legislative developments because of the ferment—which is coincidental but exceedingly pertinent—taking place at this time within the accounting profession. These developments are far from incidental, inasmuch as federal law may require that the financial statements of covered philanthropic organizations be prepared and/or be the subject of a favorable opinion by a certified public accountant. This means that these statements will have to be prepared in accordance with generally accepted accounting principles.

The American Institute of Certified Public Accountants (AICPA) promulgates rules by which financial statements are to be prepared if they are to conform with generally accepted accounting principles. For voluntary health and welfare organizations, colleges and universities, and hospitals, the AICPA has issued such rules in the form of three separate "audit guides."[22] (A fourth audit guide applies to state and local government units.) The AICPA also has developed

---

[20] IRC §§ 170(b)(1)(A)(vi)/509(a)(1) and 509(a)(2). See § 5.11.

[21] In general, see Gross, Jr., Larkin, and McCarthy, *Financial and Accounting Guide for Not-for-Profit Organizations, Sixth Edition,* Part Three (New York: John Wiley & Sons, 2000).

[22] *Industry Audit Guide—Audits of Voluntary Health and Welfare Organizations* (1974); *Industry Audit Guide—Audits of Colleges and Universities* (1973); and *Industry Audit Guide—Audits of Hospitals* (1972).

a set of accounting principles and reporting practices for nonprofit organizations not covered by an existing audit guide (such as private schools, clubs, civic associations, and political organizations).[23] Many regard these principles and practices as the beginning of development of a single package of accounting standards to be uniformly adhered to by all categories of nonprofit (including philanthropic) organizations.

Congressman Wilson repeatedly stated that it was not the intention of his legislation to have the Postal Service itself design accounting principles for charitable organizations but rather to incorporate by reference existing accounting standards in its enforcement of this law. These standards would presumably include not only those in the AICPA audit guides and the principles for other nonprofit organizations but also other standards. Thus, the Wilson bill contemplated the retention and use of uniform accounting standards for different categories of charitable organizations.

The Mondale bill would have imposed much more detailed obligations in this regard. As part of the annual information return (Form 990) filing requirements, a public charity (as defined) would be mandated to report its annual gross income "on a fund accounting basis in which restricted and unrestricted sources of revenue are clearly distinguished, broken down into such categories as are appropriate for their organization." Expenses would be reported "on a functional basis in which program costs, administrative and fundraising expenses are reported separately, and in which the program expenses are also broken down to show each of the major programs carried out by the organization together with expenses applicable to more than one program or functional category being allocated as appropriate in accordance with generally accepted accounting principles or standards."[24]

This and other information would have to be accompanied by a statement by a certified public accountant that the return was prepared in conformance with generally accepted accounting principles. The Treasury Department would be authorized to require reporting of additional information that is determined to be "necessary to inform prospective contributors of the activities and fiscal policies of the public charity, and to present fairly the financial status of the public charity." Moreover, the Mondale bill, as part of the requirement of a separate annual report, would mandate preparation of that document in conformance with generally accepted accounting principles and a statement by a certified public accountant to that effect.

The matter of disclosure of fundraising costs is very much intertwined with the matter of the applicable accounting standards. Of great concern must be the manner in which the pertinent accounting standards define the term *fundraising costs.* In many instances, such as programs and publications of schools, colleges, and universities for distribution within their alumni and membership organizations, it may be difficult to ascertain the extent to which the costs of these endeavors are properly regarded as being for fundraising.

---

[23] Statement of Position 78-10 (1978).

[24] Without waiting for any legislative authority, the IRS embodied the functional method of accounting requirements in the annual information return. See § 5.9(d).

The interplay of fundraising costs' disclosure and accounting principles becomes crucial when viewed in light of proposals that such costs be displayed as or reflected in a percentage of the charitable organization's annual gross receipts.[25] As noted, the Wilson and Metzenbaum bills would have required such a percentage on the solicitation materials, and the Mondale bill would have required it as part of the disclosure statement. The fundraising cost percentage is highly dependent on the accounting rules, for that is how the amounts to be used as the numerator and denominator of the ratio are determined.

For example, the AICPA statement of accounting principles for organizations not covered by an audit guide require those organizations to report on the accrual basis of accounting. But the Wilson and Mondale proposals appear predicated on use of the cash basis accounting method. The AICPA statement contemplates a category of receipts to be characterized as "deferred revenue," which includes donor support when tendered in the form of pledges, bequests, and perhaps other types of gift transactions. The AICPA statement would not permit the deferral of fundraising expenses that are associated with the deferred gift support. Thus, for many organizations, the result may be mandatory disclosure of a fundraising cost percentage that is much higher than is actually the case, with a consequent deleterious effect on subsequent giving by the general public.

As discussed, the Mondale measure would have the Department of the Treasury promulgate uniform accounting principles; the Luken bill would have the FTC do this.

The inconsistencies and dilemmas may well be the result of a deficiency in the proposed federal laws rather than in the accounting principles. Nonetheless, as the federal law proposals evolve, the relationship between their requirements and the applicable accounting standards will have to be carefully monitored and closely studied.

(e) Federal Agency Jurisdiction

The prospect of federal government involvement in the establishment or recognition of accounting principles for philanthropic and other types of nonprofit organizations raises still another important question in this area: Which agency of the government should assume the responsibility for administering and enforcing the charitable solicitations law?

Many advocates of a federal charitable solicitations law contend that the appropriate agency must be the IRS, because of the agency's experience and expertise in the field of tax-exempt organizations and charitable giving, guided by regulations promulgated by the Department of the Treasury. This was the approach of the Mondale bill.

The Postal Service is an unlikely candidate for the task. The Wilson bill, however, would assign such a role to the Postal Service, specifically the Postal Inspection Service, with its existing investigatory and enforcement authority, the latter including the ability to institute mail stops.

---

[25] See § 4.1.

The Department of Commerce does not want the assignment. Some, like Congressman Luken, proposed this role for the FTC. Others raise the possibility of creation of a new federal agency to regulate solicitations and perhaps other activities of charitable organizations.

The only independent analysis of this subject to date is contained in the Filer Commission report.[26] The commission, in urging the establishment of a system of federal regulation of interstate charitable solicitations, recommended that all charitable organizations be required to disclose solicitation costs to the IRS and that a special office be established somewhere in the federal bureaucracy to oversee and regulate charitable solicitations.[27] It is clear, however, that the creation of such a new agency is not to be reasonably expected any time soon. Evidence of this was manifested in 1977, at the outset of the Carter Administration, when then-Treasury Secretary Michael Blumenthal disbanded the Advisory Committee on Private Philanthropy and Public Needs, only weeks after it was assembled by the Ford Administration. This type of a commission or committee has never been reestablished.

In relation to legislation actually introduced in this field to date, the federal agency named in the particular bill as the enforcement agency has been a matter of happenstance: a member of Congress becomes interested in the subject and introduces what he (only, to date) perceives to be a remedial bill, naming in it a federal agency that is subject to the jurisdiction of the legislative committee of which the representative or senator is a member. Thus, Senator Mondale and Representatives Karth and Lehman picked the Department of the Treasury; Representative Wilson opted for the Postal Service; Representative Van Deerlin selected the Department of Commerce; and Representative Luken chose the FTC.

A possible compromise would be to assign principal jurisdiction in this field to the IRS and Treasury Department, which would develop regulations and to which reporting would be made. Collateral enforcement authority could be vested in the Postal Service, which has available to it sanctions (principally, the mail stop) that could be more effective than those available to the IRS (principally, imposition of subsequent penalties and revocation of tax exemption).

(f) Exemptions

Another controversial question is whether or to what extent one or more categories of charitable organizations should be exempted from coverage by a charitable solicitations regulation law.

One school of thought is that a federal charitable fundraising law should apply only to those charitable organizations (and their fundraisers) that extensively engage in fundraising activities as the principal means of deriving their financial support. (Whenever an abuse in this field surfaces in the media, the charity involved inevitably is heavily engaged in fundraising, usually by direct mail.) An opposing contention has it that a charitable solicitations law should

---

[26] *Giving in America—Toward a Stronger Voluntary Sector* (1975). See *infra* text accompanying notes 42–44.
[27] *Id.* at 176.

apply to every philanthropic organization simply because it engages in charitable activities or to the extent it solicits funds from the public irrespective of its other sources of financial support.

If a federal charitable solicitations law is not to apply to all categories of charitable organizations, the question becomes how to distinguish between the charitable organizations that warrant coverage by a fundraising regulation statute and those that do not. An answer to this question lies in existing federal tax law, inasmuch as Congress has enacted an extensive statutory scheme that categorizes charitable organizations in a way that could be extremely useful for this purpose and adaptable to it. This body of law[28] is that which differentiates private foundations from other categories of charitable organizations.[29] These provisions specifically reference operating institutions (such as churches, schools, colleges, universities, and hospitals)[30] and charities heavily supported by charitable contributions[31] (publicly supported organizations).

Consequently, in formulating a charitable solicitation law that applies only to organizations that derive most of their financial support from fundraising campaigns targeted to the general public, application of the law could be confined to publicly supported organizations. These are charitable entities that, for the most part, receive at least one-third of their support from the general public. (One flaw in this effort to distinguish between publicly supported charities and operating institutions is that the statutory definition of publicly supported charities includes such "operating institutions" as some libraries, museums, orchestras, theaters, and the like.) The Mondale bill would have utilized these rules, exempting such organizations from its definition of a "public charity."

By contrast, the Wilson, Metzenbaum, and Luken bills would not have exempted any category of charitable organization from all of the stated requirements. Instead, for example, the Wilson legislation offered only a limited exemption from the point-of-solicitation disclosure requirement and then only where the individuals solicited have a relationship with the organization by which they already receive or can obtain sufficient information about the organization by reason of that relationship. These partial exemptions were for membership organizations soliciting gifts from among their bona fide members; schools, colleges, and universities soliciting contributions from their alumni, students, faculty, trustees, advisory committee members, and family members of such individuals and supporting foundations of these institutions to the extent they are soliciting those individuals; and hospitals soliciting contributions from their trustees and employees and supporting foundations of these institutions to the extent they are soliciting those individuals.

Institutions such as schools, colleges, universities, and hospitals infrequently solicit the general public for financial support and rarely engage in direct mail appeals, particularly on a nationwide scale. For the most part, these institutions solicit only those individuals who constitute a relatively well-defined group that has an ongoing relationship with the institution. These

---

[28] IRC §§ 170(b)(1)(A) and 509.
[29] See § 5.11.
[30] See IRC §§ 170(b)(1)(A)(i)-(v) and 509(a)(1).
[31] See IRC §§ 170(b)(1)(A)(vi) and 509(a)(1) and (a)(2).

individuals collectively share two common characteristics: (1) they are already in a position to secure the same information from the institution that any solicitations law could reasonably require, and (2) they are not solicited as members of the "general public." Similar observations may be made as respects the fundraising practices of other operating institutions.

The Wilson bill's partial exemption for membership organizations would have encompassed churches, synagogues, and temples soliciting their congregations. (The Wilson bill did not contain a general exemption for religious organizations.) Also, the Wilson bill would have created a total exemption for a written solicitation by an individual of a small number of persons who are presumably personal acquaintances of the correspondent.

A difficult aspect of the exemption question is the unavoidable fact that when one category of charitable organization is granted an exclusion, other categories of organizations immediately lay claim to a comparable exemption, making the issue a divisive one within the philanthropic community. The exemption for solicitations of a group of acquaintances or an organization's natural constituency is not actually an *exemption* at all, however, but is instead a reflection of the legitimate scope of charitable solicitations regulation. That is, law in this field should be designed to encompass solicitations of the general public and hence need not and should not apply to personal, private, and constituent-oriented types of solicitations. This little-discussed aspect of these proposed laws deserves treatment in the legislative history of any federal statute in this field.

One other aspect of appropriate classification of organizations for purposes of fundraising regulation requires brief mention: the proper treatment of religious organizations. First Amendment problems lurk here.[32] It has proved impossible (and would be unconstitutional in any event) for any agency of the government to comprehensively define the term *religion*. At the same time, some of the most vigorous, remunerative, and abusive fundraising takes place in the name of religion.

It may be that a fundraising regulation law that is made applicable to religious organizations (as would have occurred pursuant to the Wilson bill), particularly to churches, would be unconstitutional as "prohibiting the free exercise" of religion. It may also be that this type of a law, if made applicable to charitable organizations but not to religious organizations (solely because of their religious orientation), would be unconstitutional as law "respecting an establishment of religion." (A law of the latter variety may also be constitutionally infirm as a denial of equal protection of the laws under the Fourteenth Amendment.) The outcome of this issue may also be of particular consequence to institutions operated by direction of a church or church denomination (integrated auxiliaries of churches).

The answer to this dilemma was hinted at by the Supreme Court in 1970 when it upheld the constitutionality of tax exemptions for religious organizations for properties used solely for religious worship.[33] This exemption, said

---

[32] See § 4.7.

[33] *Walz v. Tax Commission*, 397 U.S. 664 (1970).

the Court, is "benevolent neutrality";[34] the exemption was seen as simply sparing the exercise of religion from the burden of property taxation as is done for
a broad class of charitable organizations. Therefore, the standard for the exemption may be that it is constitutional where the religious organization is
treated no differently from its counterparts in the law of tax-exempt organizations. The legal questions on this point could be clarified somewhat if a challenge is ever mounted against the extension to churches of the tax on income
from an unrelated trade or business. It may also be noted that nearly every
state with a charitable solicitation statute exempts religious entities from some
or all of its requirements.[35]

(g) Federal Preemption of State Law

Another key, and the most controversial, issue with respect to federal charitable
solicitations legislation is whether this type of law should preempt state and
local laws where solicitations using a means of interstate commerce are involved.

A federal statute cannot preempt state law unless it (or, perhaps its legislative history) explicitly states that it is doing so, assuming the preemption is
constitutionally permissible. Rarely does Congress preempt state law on a subject, although it will where circumstances warrant. For example, this was done
in connection with the expansion of laws governing campaign financing and
reporting practices where elections for federal office are involved, and the establishment of a regulatory system concerning the trading of commodity fu-
tures. By contrast, in what may serve as a close model to any federal law
regulating fundraising—the federal laws regulating interstate offers and sales
of securities—Congress has permitted the states simultaneously to legislate
and enforce laws in this field.

Nonetheless, some people believe that a federal law regulating solicitations for charitable purposes should expressly preempt comparable state and
local law. This means that the federal government would assume the basic responsibility for regulating solicitations for charity where a means of interstate
commerce is used. (None of the bills introduced in Congress in this area to date
carried a preemption feature.) This approach would leave to the states and perhaps local governments the responsibility for monitoring intrastate charitable
solicitations and prosecuting cases of charitable (other than mail) fraud involving violations of general civil and criminal laws.

The calls for federal law preemption of this field clearly stem not from
any belief that federal government responsibilities require expansion but
rather as a means of affording relief from the existing hodgepodge of state laws
and local ordinances regulating charitable solicitations.

This type of a preemptive federal statute would have the virtue of enabling charities and their fundraisers to comply with only one set of requirements: one law, one due date, one form, and the like. Aside from the inherent
advantage of having to cope with only one law instead of many, there is a substantial savings of time and money to be achieved in effecting compliance.

---

[34] *Id.* at 676.
[35] See § 3.5(a), (b).

Also, the danger of running afoul of enforcement authorities is minimized; many philanthropic organizations and their agents seem to be soliciting support across the country without much awareness of the states' and other jurisdictions' legal requirements for doing so. Finally, an obvious virtue of a preemptive federal law in this area would be the substitution of one statute for dozens of varying statutes and ordinances.

Another solution to the problem would be, of course, for the states to adopt uniform laws or, on a less extensive scale, uniform reporting requirements, forms, and due dates. Even the use of standardized registration and reporting forms among the states would go a long way toward easing the costs and other burdens of compliance with these laws. In several states, the legislatures have explicitly authorized the regulators to agree reciprocally with their counterparts in other jurisdictions to exchange information for enforcement purposes and to accept filings and grant exemptions on a uniform, multistate basis where the requirements are substantially similar. Recently, fortunately, some progress has been made in this area.[36] In most instances, express statutory authority to achieve uniformity is not even required, since the enforcement officials (attorneys general, secretaries of state, and the like) have ample authority within the scope of their regulatory powers to work toward and achieve a standardized registration and reporting system. In fact, it would seem that this uniformity would breed an increase in charitable organizations' compliance with these laws, thereby enhancing the regulatory function.

A measure along the lines of a Wilson bill, emanating from a postal law-writing committee, could be a vehicle for a preemptive law in this field, unless it is sequentially referred to another committee for amendment for this purpose. The same is true for the other proposals discussed earlier; however, other legislation may be introduced to this end, under the combined jurisdiction of the judiciary, interstate commerce, and/or taxation committees in Congress.

Realistically, however, there is not much likelihood of a preemptive federal statute in this area. The attorneys general of the states covet too greatly their present authority to investigate abuses in charitable solicitations; they can be expected to strongly oppose such a feature.[37] Thus, Congress will probably elect to continue to rely on the states as the principal vehicle to monitor charitable fundraising, with the federal government playing a supervisory but secondary role. If this happens, the provisions of the Mondale bill, by which the Secretary of the Treasury would be directed to "encourage the appropriate officers of State and local governments to accept copies of the annual information returns and annual reports [as would be required by the bill] in satisfaction of the requirements of the States and local laws for similar reports from such organizations" (i.e., "public charities"), may represent the extent to which

---

[36] See § 3.4.

[37] During its annual meeting in 1977, the National Association of Attorneys General adopted a resolution stating, *inter alia*, that the "Association unalterably opposes [federal] legislative preemption of the state Attorneys General from enforcement of state charitable trust regulations and fiduciary obligations of charitable trustees and fund-raisers," although it also did express support for a "comprehensive uniform registration and reporting system" as to which the federal and state governments would have concurrent regulatory authority.

the federal government may reasonably go in securing, by statute, uniformity of reporting in this field.

At a minimum, however, coordination among federal, state, and local law and enforcement in this field is essential. Perhaps, with the cooperation of federal and state officials and representatives of interested organizations, the practical equivalent of preemption can be realized: adoption of a federal reporting form that could be filed, in lieu of separate state reports, in those states where a solicitation is undertaken and made available to the interested public.[38]

(h) Sanctions

Still another major issue with respect to a federal law regulating the solicitation of charitable contributions is the nature of the sanctions to be imposed.

Mention has been made of the possibility of invocation of the mail stop by the U.S. Postal Service as a means of circumscribing solicitations by mail that are not in compliance with the federal requirements. Other potential sanctions include those usually levied as part of the federal tax system: monetary penalties, injunctions, and criminal penalties (including imprisonment) for violations of the law. Also, some conceive of a point-of-solicitation disclosure requirement as a type of sanction.

A proposal prepared for the United Way of America[39] suggested fashioning sanctions parallel to those underlying the private foundation rules, namely, a series of excise taxes imposed in the event of the payment of "unreasonable" fundraising fees. This approach would track existing tax law,[40] by which foundation directors, officers, and other insiders who receive unreasonable compensation become subject to an initial 5 percent excise tax on the amount of compensation in excess of what is reasonable, and a 200 percent additional tax if that excessive amount is not timely repaid to the foundation, with additional sanctions available in the case of willful, repeated, or flagrant violations. As the proposal stated, "[t]his pattern could be applied to unreasonable fundraising expenditures, providing (1) a relatively modest initial excise tax on the recipient of excessive compensation, (2) a much larger excise tax if the excessive amount is not repaid within a correction period, and (3) recourse to the federal district courts for the traditional battery of equitable remedies (injunctions, removal of trustees, surcharge of trustees, and the like) in the case of repeated or serious violations."[41] The proposal also suggested

---

[38] The National Association of State Charity Officials was established in 1978 to improve communications between those who administer and enforce state charitable solicitation acts, and between the regulators and the regulated. An analysis of its genesis appears as Alexander, "State Regulators Seek New Super Organization," XI *Phil. Monthly* (No. 11) 13 (1978). Among its projects is the development of a uniform reporting form for use by all of the states. A discussion draft of such a report, distributed under the auspices of NASCO and the National Association of Attorneys General, appears at XIII *Phil. Monthly* (No. 3) 18 (1980). Another eventual NASCO project is the development of a uniform charitable solicitation act for adoption by the states.

[39] Troyer, "Proposal for Federal Legislation on Charitable Solicitations," X *Phil. Monthly* (No. 10) 30 (1977).

[40] See IRC § 4941(d)(2)(E).

[41] Troyer, *supra* note 39, at 33.

that this approach could be applied to other types of payments by private foundations where the payments exceed the level of reasonableness.

In explanation of this proposal, it was pointed out that the term *reasonable* is often employed in the Internal Revenue Code, such as the limitation on the deductibility of salaries and other business expenses. Thus, this approach would look to actual practices and comparable data in assessing whether a particular fundraising or other expenditure is in fact reasonable. The principal difficulty with this idea is the absence of meaningful information and understanding about how to assess the reasonableness of fundraising costs, although this set of rules could well serve as an incentive for the development of that information.

As an alternative to this excise tax system, the proposal advocated point-of-solicitation disclosure of information, including fundraising expenses, to prospective donors and others. Pursuant to this approach, charities could report their fundraising costs as an average of four years' experience (five years for new organizations), and most solicitations for churches would be exempted from the requirements.

(i) Filer Commission Recommendations

One of the recommendations of the Filer Commission was that a "system of federal regulation be established for interstate charitable solicitations and that intrastate solicitations be more effectively regulated by the state governments."[42] The commission's specific recommendations for federal regulation of charitable solicitations are as follows:

> In the Commission's sample survey of taxpayers, 30 per cent of those questioned said they did not like the way their contributions were used and one out of seven respondents specifically complained of excessive fundraising or administrative costs. This wariness undoubtedly has been heightened in many minds by recent cases, including those uncovered in congressional investigations, where some costs of charitable fundraising absorbed most of the funds raised, leaving the impression that some charitable solicitations are more for the benefit of the solicitors than for the charitable causes involved. In some other instances, contributions have been recurrently solicited and raised that are far in excess of the organization's operating outlays.

> The Commission believes that the vast majority of charitable solicitations are conscientiously and economically undertaken. Nonetheless, cases of unduly costly or needless fundraising point to the absence of any focused mechanism for overseeing such activity and, if need be, applying sanctions. One Commission study finds, in fact, that only one half of the 50 states regulated the solicitation of funds and that "the coverage and scope of" those that do regulate "vary widely." State regulation of intrastate solicitations, the Commission believes, should be strengthened, but because many solicitations spread over many states at once, state regulation is

---

[42] *Giving in America, supra* note 26.

inevitably limited in its effectiveness. Clearly, the federal government and federal law must play the major role in assuring the integrity of charitable solicitations, a role that they just as clearly do not play today. The Commission recommends specifically that all charitable organizations should be required by law to disclose all solicitation costs to the Internal Revenue Service, in accordance with accepted accounting principles; that all solicitation literature should be required to carry a notice to the effect that full financial data can be obtained from the soliciting organization on request; that any such requests be required to be rapidly answered; and that a special office be established in the Internal Revenue Service or in some other federal agency or regulatory body, such as the Federal Trade Commission, to oversee charity solicitation and take action against improper, misleading or excessively costly fundraisings. This special office might be supplemented by and guided by an accrediting organization, which would review the finances of and certify all exempt organizations whose solicitation practices are found to merit approval.

The Commission considered but rejected proposals that solicitation costs be legally limited to a fixed percentage of receipts because, unless such a ceiling were so high as to be an ineffective restraint on most fundraising, it would risk being too low to account for the often justifiably high costs of solicitation for new or unpopular causes. On the other hand, state as well as federal agencies concerned with regulating solicitations should be required to establish clear qualitative criteria as to what constitutes "excessively costly" fundraising (or improper or misleading solicitation, as well). Such criteria should be widely publicized so that both soliciting organizations and the contributing public would clearly understand the limits within which fundraisers operate.[43]

These recommendations, however, drew the following dissent from commission member Raymond J. Gallagher:

State governments already adequately police the solicitations of charitable contributions. There is no hard data in the material collected by this Commission that warrants a recommendation that the federal government assume a new policy role in this area. The Commission indicates that it believes that the vast majority of charitable solicitations are conscientiously and economically undertaken. The Commission, however, is concerned about the impression of many taxpayers that charity solicitations cost more than they should. I do not believe that the effective remedy for this impression is the creation of a new federal bureaucracy or the expansion of an existing one. Potential donors who have doubts about the efficiency of charitable solicitations can inquire directly of the organizations they are concerned about; and if they are not satisfied with the answers they are given, they have the most effective remedy of all: not making the contribution.[44]

[43] Id. at 176–178.
[44] Id. at 220–221.

(j) Ford Administration Treasury Proposals

When outgoing Treasury Secretary William E. Simon, on January 14, 1977, sent a package of legislative proposals to Congress to "improve public accountability and prevent abuses" in private philanthropy, the proposals included a recommendation that interstate solicitations be subject to federal legislation that would be administered by the Treasury Department. The Treasury also recommended disclosure of financial information about the soliciting organization, particularly with respect to its fundraising and administrative costs.[45]

In assessing the present situation, the Treasury proposals contained the observation that "[t]here is no supervision or monitoring of interstate solicitation [of charitable contributions] by the Federal government, and the State laws affecting it vary considerably, making it easy, particularly for large fundraising drives, to circumvent tough enforcement by any one state."

This is a curious statement. In fact, the exemption application filed by charitable organizations (Form 1023) requests information concerning charitable solicitation activities. Also, the IRS and Treasury are fully empowered to request more information about solicitation activities in the application for recognition of exemption and in an organization's annual information return (Form 990) than is at present required. Further, it is an understatement to say that the state laws relating to charitable solicitations vary considerably. In fact, they vary widely, and the accompanying regulations, forms, and enforcement efforts are even more divergent. It does not follow from this observation, however, that this variation contributes to lack of enforcement of these laws. Additionally, "large fundraising drives" are able to "circumvent tough enforcement by any one state" only by refraining from soliciting contributions in that jurisdiction (unless the state law is simply violated); at the same time, the tradeoff resulting from such a decision is that the organization deprives itself of the financial support otherwise available to it from the citizens of the particular state.

In connection with its recommendations, the Treasury Department suggested that Congress (specifically, the House Committee on Ways and Means and the Senate Committee on Finance) conduct hearings on the "appropriate methods" for regulating charitable solicitations, with "emphasis" on the following issues:

- The extent of financial data concerning the soliciting organization that must be supplied with the solicitation material

- The need for administrative review of solicitation material before dissemination (as opposed to relying solely on criminal and equitable sanctions for misleading or incomplete material)

- The appropriate method for regulating oral solicitations (e.g., by telephone and television) and the extent of disclosure required for them

- The need for limitations on fundraising and administrative costs

---

[45] Dept. of the Treasury News Release, Jan. 18, 1977.

- The preemption of varying state reporting requirements for interstate solicitations, with a uniform federal report to be filed with all requesting states

The Treasury Department recommendations went far beyond the supervision and monitoring of charitable solicitations. In related areas, the recommendations also included a proposal that every private foundation, every public charity that makes grants, and every public charity or social welfare organization with annual gross receipts of at least $100,000 (other than a church or integrated auxiliary thereof or a convention or association of churches) be required to make available to the public an annual report on its finances, programs, and priorities. Also, the Treasury recommended that certain of the restrictions on private foundations be extended to public charities. These restrictions involve the present Internal Revenue Code Chapter 42 requirements with respect to self-dealing, minimum payout, jeopardy investments, and taxable expenditures.

This proposal for an annual report by most public charities has considerable merit. This type of report could be the document that a soliciting charity would have to send to the public upon request and also file with the Postal Service, and perhaps with the states where the solicitation is to take place. The prospects of preparation of another major document for filing with the federal tax authorities (in addition to the Form 990), however, would generate protests if only because of the increased costs. Another reason that such a proposal would be resisted is that the recently imposed federal disclosure requirements[46] may have the effect of converting the annual information return into a type of public annual report.

Regarding other aspects of federal involvement in the private philanthropic processes, the Treasury Department has recommended a variety of revisions of the tax laws with respect to the charitable contribution deduction and an investment of U.S. district courts with equity powers sufficient to remedy any violation of the substantive rules concerning philanthropic organizations in such a way as to minimize any financial detriment to the organization and to preserve its assets for its philanthropic purposes.

§ 6.4   CONTEMPORARY DEVELOPMENTS AND PROSPECTS

As noted, several years have passed since a fundraising regulation proposal was introduced in the U.S. Congress. There has been a lack of interest in the subject by politicians at the federal level, and the IRS's increased activity in this area has lessened any perceived need for new law.

Nonetheless, interest in further regulation of public charities has remained high, with the emphasis shifting away from fundraising, and to unreasonable compensation and other forms of private benefit. This new focus involves fundraising issues, such as the tax consequences of payments to professional fundraisers.

[46] See § 5.9(i).

When reviewed from this perspective, it is remarkable how much law in this area has been enacted in recent years. Certainly the most dramatic of these enactments is the intermediate sanctions rules.[47] Other developments include the advent of various disclosure and document dissemination rules,[48] and the increase in monetary penalties.[49]

A study illustrating how charitable fundraising regulation can evolve, sometimes rather quickly, is provided by means of developments initiated in 1993.

One of the first items of legislation introduced in the 103d Congress (1993–1994) was a bill bearing this imposing and ambitious title: the "Federal Program Improvement Act of 1993."[50] The principal and powerful sponsors of this measure were the then-Chairman of the House Committee on Ways and Means (to which the bill was referred), Representative Dan Rostenkowski (D-Ill.), and the then-Chairman of the Subcommittee on Oversight, Representative J. J. Pickle (D-Tex.).

This proposal evolved out of an investigation and a hearing on May 14, 1992, held by the Subcommittee on Oversight and the House Subcommittee on Social Security. The subject of the hearing was "deceptive solicitations." On June 18, 1992, the two subcommittees approved a report and submitted it to the Ways and Means Committee.[51]

A letter of transmittal accompanying this report stated that the Subcommittees found "that there are continuing problems with deceptive mailings and solicitations" related to programs within the jurisdiction of the Committee.[52] The Subcommittees "identified a pattern of deceptive solicitation" in areas such as efforts to sell Social Security–related services by mail; mailings, sent by consumers, that appear to be official correspondence from the federal government; and solicitations implying that the organization involved is tax-exempt under federal law.[53] This "pattern" included the following "tactics":

- An offer by a direct mail advertiser, for a fee, of "services which the Government provides for free or at only a nominal charge"; the solicitations "often fail to mention that these services are provided at no charge by the Federal Government."[54]

- The use of "mailings which appear to be from the Department of the Treasury (Treasury). The most common are mailings that purport to be

---

[47] See § 5.6.

[48] See §§ 5.2–5.5.

[49] See §§ 5.6, 5.9.

[50] H.R. 22, 103d Cong., 1st Sess. (1993).

[51] "Deceptive Solicitations," Oversight Initiative Report No. 9, Ways and Means Committee Print 102–45, 102d Cong., 2d Sess. (1992) ("Deceptive Solicitations Report"). For purposes of this analysis, the House Committee on Ways and Means is referred to as the "Committee" and the two subcommittees that prepared this report as the "Subcommittees."

[52] Deceptive Solicitations Report, at iii.

[53] Id.

[54] This practice is a violation of the federal tax law (IRC § 6711). This law imposes penalties for a failure by a tax-exempt organization to disclose, when offering services for a fee, that the information or services are available for free from the federal government (see § 5.5).

from the Internal Revenue Service (IRS). To make these mailings look as realistic as possible, advertisers often use the words 'Internal Revenue Service,' or the initials 'IRS,' and tax identification numbers in the return address."

- "[S]ome businesses that have not been granted Federal tax-exempt status use solicitations claiming the group is a 'non-profit' association, which misleads the consumer into believing that the organization is tax-exempt and serves the public in a charitable manner."[55]

In addition, the Subcommittee on Oversight found that "some tax-exempt organizations have refused to disclose their Forms 990 and other required documents to the public, and many of the organizations that did comply made public review difficult, by forcing the individual to copy the information by hand."[56]

The findings of the Subcommittee that most closely relate to fundraising by charitable organizations were those pertaining to mailings that appear to be from government agencies and mailings from organizations that imply that the soliciting organization is a "tax-exempt" entity.

As to the first of these findings, the Subcommittees reported:

> Direct-mail advertisers often use mailings that appear to be from . . . [government agencies, such as the IRS] in order to confuse consumers. . . . The purpose of these deceptive mailings often is to get consumers to open the direct-mail letter, and to pay careful attention to the enclosed material. In some cases, the solicitation includes a "disclaimer" or language which supposedly alerts the reader that the mailing is not from a Federal agency. However, such disclaimers are generally inadequate in clarifying matters for the recipient of the mailing, and have been used by direct-mail solicitors as a defense against claims that the solicitation activities are intended to deceive.
>
> To make these mailings appear as realistic as possible, advertisers sometimes use the words "Internal Revenue Service" or the initials "IRS" in the return address location on the envelope. . . . Frequently, the envelope used by the advertiser is the same paper color and stock that is used by [the Department of the] Treasury to mail Federal checks, such as IRS tax refund checks. In some cases, advertisers use window envelopes and design the enclosed letter to look like a Federal check. Sometimes the advertiser will use additional phrases, such as "Important Information Enclosed: Do Not Forward" or "Buy United States Savings Bonds," to further aid in the deception. Another technique employed to make these envelopes appear official is to include citations to various postal regulations concerning the delivery and forwarding of mail. All of these techniques, used individually or in combination, are calculated to give the false impression that the letter is official Government business. Such deception potentially

---

[55] Deceptive Solicitations Report, at iv.

[56] *Id.* This requirement is the subject of IRC § 6104, which requires a tax-exempt organization to make available for public inspection and dissemination a copy of its annual information returns for the previous three years, applications for recognition of federal tax exemption, and any papers, letters, or documents issued by the IRS with respect to the application (see § 5.9(i)).

interferes with the ability of the Government to effectively correspond with the public and increases the likelihood that true Government mailings will be destroyed without being opened.[57]

As the following indicates, tax-exempt organizations were specifically identified as being part of this problem:

> Tax-exempt organizations have used direct-mail solicitation practices that mislead the consumer about the source and nature of the solicitation. For example, tax-exempt organizations have used their employer identification tax number in the return address section of the envelope in a manner which implies the mailing is from the IRS. In one example, the mailing was a solicitation from a 501(c)(3) organization soliciting memberships and promoting the humane treatment of animals. . . . In the other instance, the solicitation was from a political organization seeking contributions for the group's political activities.[58]

The practice of misleading consumers as to an organization's tax status was described as follows:

> [O]rganizations which do not have Federal tax-exempt status have developed solicitations which mislead the consumer into believing that the organization is tax-exempt and serves the public in a charitable manner. For example, one organization described itself in its brochures as "a nonprofit association" which, among other things, was "formed to mobilize

---

[57] Deceptive Solicitations Report, at 5.

[58] *Id.* The Subcommittees were not the only congressional committees concerned in 1992 with deceptive solicitations by tax-exempt organizations. The Senate Select Committee on POW-MIA Affairs investigated the "touchy subject of groups that have seized upon the emotional issue of missing Americans [in Southeast Asia] to raise tens of millions of dollars from contributors who believe they are financing rescue efforts"; one senator termed the solicitations "fraudulent, disingenuous, [and] grotesque" (see "Select Committee on POW/MIA Affairs Investigates Fund-Raising Abuse," 7 *Exempt Org. Tax Rev.* (No. 1) 53 (Jan. 1993); also "Senate Select Committee Recommends Congressional Action to Address Fund-Raising Abuses," 7 *Exempt Org. Tax Rev.* (No. 5) 721 (May 1993); "Senators Target POW/Mail Fund-Raisers as Deceptive," *Wash. Post,* Dec. 3, 1992, at A1).

Senator David Pryor (D-Ark.) joined the ranks of members of Congress who were unhappy with the tactics of some direct mail fundraising solicitors. His displeasure in this regard was triggered by the United States Seniors Association, an organization he lambasted as "modern-day snake-oil salesmen" and as having directors who "are experts in fund-raising, not the problems of the elderly" (press release dated May 24, 1993). The Senator, on May 24, 1993, introduced a bill (S. 1011) to amend several provisions of the Social Security Act to tighten penalties for deceptive mailings, such as those that take advantage of senior citizens. (Senator Pryor was Chairman of the Senate Special Committee on Aging and of the Senate subcommittee that oversees the Postal Service.) This bill would have eliminated the current $100,000 annual cap on penalties for mailers who misuse the words, letters, symbols, or emblems of federal agencies. It would also have considered each individual piece of improper mail to be a separate violation and, under a new definition of deceptive mailing, would prohibit a person from using agency names or symbols in a manner that could "reasonably be interpreted or considered as conveying" a relationship with those agencies. (In general, "Government Aims to Get Tough on Fraudulent Mailings," V *Chron. Phil.* (No. 17) 28 (June 15, 1993); and "Pryor Plans Curb on Mail Appeals Aimed at Elderly," *Wash. Post,* May 25, 1993, at A4.)

members for charitable work." (In addition, the organization had an "Office of Benefits Administrator," a Washington, D.C. address, and used the acronym "SSA" in describing the benefits provided to its members, a practice to which the Social Security Administration objected.) . . .

When the organization was asked if it was tax-exempt and, if so, what 501(c) status had been granted to it, the organization continued to assert that it was tax-exempt. However, when asked to supply a copy of the organization's application for tax exemption and its annual Forms 990, as required to be disclosed to the public under IRC section 6104, the organization finally admitted it was, in fact, a taxable corporation associated with an insurance company.[59]

As to the level of compliance by tax-exempt organizations with the requirement that their annual information returns be accessible by the public, the Subcommittees reported as follows:

> This law was intended, in part, to provide the public with a mechanism for checking and evaluating the operations of tax-exempt organizations, particularly organizations which solicit contributions and other funds through the mail. The Subcommittee on Oversight recently attempted to obtain such documents from eleven tax-exempt organizations and six refused. (These results are consistent with recent surveys conducted by Members of the Subcommittee and the press.) Furthermore, many of those that did make copies of their Forms 990 available to the press and the public did not allow the individuals to photocopy the information requested. Thus, the information had to be copied by hand.[60]

Legislation to implement the Subcommittee's findings was introduced on January 5, 1993.[61] Here are the most pertinent elements of this proposal:

- A tax-exempt organization would have to provide a copy of its annual information return (usually, Form 990) to any individual who requests it at the organization's office. (Under the law at that time, the return need only be made available for inspection.) The only charge could be a reasonable fee for the cost of photocopying (and not postage). Where the request is made in person, the copy would have to be provided immediately; otherwise, the copy would have to be provided within 30 days.[62]

---

[59] Deceptive Solicitations Report, at 6. There are two notable aspects to this quotation. First, it illustrates the point that there is a considerable difference between being a *nonprofit* organization and a *tax-exempt* organization (or, for that matter, being a tax-exempt organization and a *charitable* organization); a nonexempt, nonprofit organization is taxable (see *Law of Tax-Exempt Organizations* pp. 3–6). Second, not all tax-exempt organizations have to have a ruling from the IRS recognizing them as being exempt from tax; only charitable organizations and certain types of employee benefit funds must have this determination (*id.*, pp. 733–737 and 742). Thus the organization referenced in the quotation may well have been tax-exempt as a matter of law. Nonetheless, it still would have to file annual information returns (Forms 990).
[60] Deceptive Solicitations Report, at 6.
[61] See *supra* note 50.
[62] H.R. 22, *supra* note 50, § 6102(a). This proposal is now law (see § 5.9(i)).

- Every advertisement or solicitation by, or on behalf of, a tax-exempt organization would have to contain an express statement (in a conspicuous and easily recognizable format) that its annual information return will be provided to individuals upon request.[63]

- Where an organization, in an advertisement or solicitation by it, or on its behalf, makes reference to the fact that it is "nonprofit," and the organization is not tax-exempt under federal law, the organization would have to include in the advertisement or solicitation an express statement (in a conspicuous and easily recognizable format) that the organization is not exempt from federal income taxes.[64]

- Penalties for noncompliance with these three proposals would be enacted.

This study demonstrates, among other aspects of law development in this area, that law directly and indirectly impacting on charitable fundraising can come into being in response to forces that have little, if anything, to do with this type of fundraising. As noted, this effort initiated in 1993, spawned considerable law. One cannot predict when or why the next of these impulses will occur.

Thus, due to a convergence of several trends and developments, public charities are destined for greater governmental involvement in their affairs. To recapitulate: the converging forces and trends are (1) the movements toward increasing consumer protection, disclosure, and public accountability; (2) the predilection of Congress to impose penalties on persons who cause charitable organizations to violate tax laws, thereby lessening the likelihood of revocation of tax exemption;[65] (3) those who wish to encompass nearly all types of charitable organizations within the scope of the existing rules governing private foundations; and (4) those who are seeking to expand government regulation of the process of soliciting financial support. The outcomes of this convergence will say much about the nature of philanthropy in the United States in coming years. It will also say much about the shape and scope of the emerging federal tax and other law that will directly and indirectly further regulate the process of generating contributions of money and property for charitable organizations.

---

[63] *Id.* § 6102(b).
[64] *Id.* § 6101.
[65] See, e.g., IRC §§ 4911, 4912, 4955, and 4958.

CHAPTER SEVEN

Overviews, Perspectives, and Commentaries

§ 7.1 **Charitable Fundraising and the Law**
(a) Constitutional Law Background
(b) Fundraising Cost Percentages
(c) Fundraisers and Solicitors: Defining the Difference
(d) Bond Requirements
(e) Other Features
(f) Scope of Statutes
(g) Conclusion

§ 7.2 **Defining a Fundraising Professional**
(a) Definitions
(b) Defining *Solicit*
(c) Reasons for Avoiding Solicitor Status
(d) Amending the Statutes

§ 7.3 **Professional Solicitors: Role of Telemarketing**

§ 7.4 **Charitable Sales Promotions**
(a) Terminology
(b) Scope of Regulation
(c) State Laws' Definitions
(d) Forms of Regulation
(e) Some Practical Problems

§ 7.5 **Regulation Unlimited: Prohibited Acts**
(a) Basic Prohibitions
(b) Extraordinary Prohibitions
(c) Focus on Solicitors
(d) Unusual Provisions
(e) Duplicative Rules
(f) Conclusion

§ 7.6 **Fundraiser's Contract**
(a) Basic Elements
(b) Specific Elements
(c) Fee Arrangements
(d) Solicitor Status
(e) State Laws
(f) Conclusion

§ 7.7 **A Model Law**
(a) Introduction
(b) Model Law Elements
(c) Preapproval
(d) Reporting
(e) Definitions
(f) Contracts and Bonds
(g) Compensation
(h) Exemptions
(i) Other
(j) Prohibited Acts
(k) Sanctions
(l) Commentary

§ 7.8 **State Charity Officials' Concerns about Fundraising Laws**

§ 7.9 **Studies of Fundraising by Professional Solicitors**
(a) California Studies
    (i) 1993 Report
    (ii) 1994 Report
(b) Other Studies
(c) Commentary

§ 7.10 **Charity Auctions**
(a) Charity Auctions as Businesses
(b) Charitable Contribution Deductions—Donors of Items to Be Auctioned
(c) Charitable Contribution Deductions—Acquirers of Items at an Auction
(d) Substantiation Rules
(e) Quid Pro Quo Rules
(f) Sales Tax Rules
(g) Reporting Rules

§ 7.11 **Court Opinion Concerning Sliding-Scale Registration Fees**

§ 7.12 **Fundraising and Private Inurement Doctrine**

§ 7.13 **IRS and Gifts of Used Vehicles**

§ 7.14 **Some Proposals for Relief**　　　　(c) Uniform Annual Report
　　(a) Model Law　　　　　　　　　　　　(d) Other Forms of Uniformity
　　(b) Reciprocal Agreements　　　　§ 7.15 **A Look Ahead**

The previous chapters summarize the federal and state statutes, court opinions, regulations, rules, and other factors that combine to form the law of fundraising as it is applied with respect to charitable solicitations. This chapter offers some perspectives and commentaries on the subject of the laws of charitable fundraising.

§ 7.1 CHARITABLE FUNDRAISING AND THE LAW

The law of fundraising for charitable purposes is based on federal, state, and local statutes and ordinances, which are accompanied, interpreted, and expanded by a myriad of regulations, rules, forms, instructions to forms, and court opinions. The resulting total mass of law comprises an extensive set of requirements that the managers of a charitable organization, those who advise them, and those who raise funds for them, should generally understand. Lawyers and accountants who advise soliciting charities should, of course, comprehend this law in some detail; knowledge of generalities, coupled with specific advice from these advisors from time to time, may suffice for managers.

A sizable majority of this statutory and other law is enacted and promulgated at the state level. There, the process of raising funds for charitable purposes is heavily regulated. Thus, the amount of this law that will be encountered by a charitable organization engaged in fundraising will depend substantially on the number of states in which solicitations for charitable gifts take place. A charitable organization that is raising funds in every state and wants to comply with all applicable laws has before it a monumental task.

Consequently, the greatest problem created by the law for the charitable fundraising community is the barrage of registration, reporting, disclosure, and other requirements demanded by the various state charitable solicitation acts—what one court termed the "apparatus" of each of the states for regulating charities.[1] As a result, one of the chief governmental relations challenges for the field as the 21st century begins is to arrest the expansion of this form of regulation. It is antithetical to the legitimate fundraising process, if only because of the extraordinary expenses and other burdens it imposes on philanthropy.[2]

---

[1] *Center for Auto Safety, Incorporated* v. *Athey,* 37 F.3d 139, 143 (4th Cir. 1994).

[2] This regulatory burden has been described quite colorfully by commentators. In one instance, the "charitable solicitation regulatory apparatus of the states" was portrayed as a half-centipede with 51 feet, with 47 of them outfitted with "shoes . . . of different styles, shapes, materials, and construction" (Heckman, "Another Shoe Falls: Idaho," XXVIII *Phil. Monthly* (No. 2) 38 (Mar. 1995)). In another instance, the situation was analogized to state law requiring drivers' licenses: "Imagine how difficult it would be [for someone living on the East Coast] to visit one's family on the West Coast if one had to obtain a driver's license in every state along the way;" because of the states' unwillingness to cooperate with each other in this regard, "charities often spend large sums of money on administrative expenses just to satisfy the patchwork of laws and

§ 7.1   CHARITABLE FUNDRAISING AND THE LAW

Despite some major and impressive successes by the philanthropic world in the courts, states are continuing their interventionist policies in this arena, creating new laws and otherwise expanding the scope of their involvement in the charitable fundraising process.

Reasonable people agree that some form of regulation in this area is quite appropriate. There are instances of fraudulent and other bogus fundraisers and fundraising in the land. Donors, like consumers, deserve some guidance and protection against misleading fundraising. Wrongdoers should be aggressively prosecuted and punished. The integrity of the charitable dollar is vital to a strong philanthropic sector. Fundraising scandals taint the process for everyone.

At the same time, balance is required. The subject is, after all, charitable giving—an act of generosity that is voluntary. Moreover, fundraising is constitutionally protected, principally through the doctrine of free speech.[3] Charitable solicitations are the lifeblood of the sector. It is wonderful—and sometimes colorful—for a state to occasionally nab a solicitor engaged in fraud, but these accomplishments bear a price tag of enormous expense to and administrative burdens on all others in the fundraising world. Many ask: Are all of these requirements for paperwork, disclosure, record keeping, bonding, and the like necessary? Are they doing much good?

During a conference in the fall of 1994, Helmer Ekstrom, then-president of the American Association of Fund Raising Counsel, lamented that he could not find any empirical evidence to back up the immense depth of the charitable solicitation "problem" as it is being depicted by state regulators and watchdog groups.[4] (That is because there is no such evidence.) His imagery, referred to earlier, deserves a verbatim quote: "Does all of this activity amount to hunting flies with an elephant gun or chasing elephants with a flyswatter?" (The former is the case.)

Mr. Ekstrom believed that the states are taking a shotgun approach to regulation in this field. He advocated a more focused, "surgical" strategy and advised against expending inordinate amounts of money and time on what he called "low-risk" problems. There was much wisdom there; as is so often the case, the trick is in the implementation.

In fact, this approach to regulation does little to deter wrongdoing and substantially frustrates legitimate charitable solicitations. Do these laws, as one federal court of appeals pretended, rid the country of "illegitimate charities," enhance public confidence in the charitable sector, and generate higher levels of giving to the charities that remain?[5] Of course not. Instead, they are nonproductive overkill, another administrative burden imposed on charities, a justification to bloat a bureaucracy, a rationalization to hunt flies with an elephant gun. These laws are actually counterproductive in that they sap charitable resources and send the message to the public that the charitable sector,

---

regulations in the 50 states and the District [of Columbia]" (letter to the editor from the Executive Director of the Nonprofit Mailers Federation, *Wash. Post*, May 11, 1992, at A18).

[3] See § 4.3.

[4] Remarks of Helmer Ekstrom at the Third Annual Conference on "Fund-Raising and the Law," presented by the Georgetown University Law Center, Washington, DC, Oct. 26, 1994.

[5] *Center for Auto Safety, Incorporated* v. *Athey, supra* note 1, at 144, note 9.

which is so important to the nation, is merely a pack of cheats and scoundrels, and only massive regulation by the states can protect citizens against them.

State regulation in this area is out of control. It is expanding for the sake of expansion; the very process of law-writing has become little more than a contest among the state legislatures to determine which can come up with the most grandiose charitable solicitation act. The laws just get lengthier, more intricate; there is constant revision of them. The states are trying to micromanage charitable solicitations in ways that are patronizing to the charitable organizations involved, such as by dictating the contents of their contracts with fundraisers and solicitors.[6] Substantial law revision in this field is an ongoing and escalating phenomenon. Compliance with any one of these laws—assuming one can keep up with the changes—is often difficult, and compliance with the batch of them can be impossible.

There has to be a better system. Present law needs to be reformed to accommodate the legitimate fundraising process and allow it to prosper—for the benefit of society—while protecting the public and restraining the few outlaws. As discussed next, charitable fundraising is among the highest acts of free speech. When constitutional law rights are in play, government regulation is to be minimal, even if some wrongdoing has to be tolerated. Today's philosophy underlying state-law regulation of fundraising is infected with a regulatory mindset that follows precisely the opposite approach: Maximum regulation even if it is harmful to the innocent.

(a) Constitutional Law Background

Legitimate charitable organizations and their fundraising professionals generally do not object to reasonable registration and reporting obligations in connection with their charitable solicitations. Few *like* government regulation, but it has come to be accepted within appropriate bounds. Even if charities and fundraisers do complain (and they have been known to vociferously do so), it is irrelevant, because the law is clear that these and other forms of government regulation of fundraising may be imposed. Each state inherently possesses and exercises the *police power,* and this authority enables it to look out for the interests of its citizens (who are actual or potential contributors) and strive to protect its populace from unscrupulous charitable solicitations.[7]

The problem, as seen through the regulatory prism, is well reflected in the "legislative declaration" preceding the fundraising regulation statute in Colorado. That state's legislature concluded that "fraudulent charitable solicitations are a widespread practice in this state which results in millions of dollars of losses to contributors and legitimate charities each year." This sweeping declaration continues with the observation that "[l]egitimate charities are harmed by such fraud because the money available for contributions continually is being siphoned off by fraudulent charities, and the goodwill and confidence of contributors continually is being undermined by the practices of unscrupulous solicitors." This legislature thus found that the law it enacted

---

[6] See § 3.11.
[7] See § 4.3.

was "necessary to protect the public's interest in making informed choices as to which charitable causes should be supported." (It is hard to believe that fundraising rapaciousness can be so replete in a state; it can be surmised that this declaration was made on the basis of little, if any, evidence.)

Still, when undertaken for charitable ends, the fundraising process is, as noted, an act of free speech. Indeed, charitable fundraising is among the highest forms of free speech, fully protected by the First and Fourteenth Amendments to the U.S. Constitution, meaning that governmental enforcement of it must be confined to the narrowest of means.[8] These distinctions cause great tension and conflict in the writing and enforcement of the state charitable solicitation acts. The law requires that the police power be exercised in a manner that includes the appropriate restraints on enforcement of these laws as called for in the preservation of free speech rights. Regrettably, state legislators repeatedly violate these principles, writing laws that are overbroad, unduly burdensome, imprecise, and content-based. For example, as discussed later, states not so long ago were trying to regulate charities' solicitations by means of fundraising cost percentages, in the face of repeated declarations by the U.S. Supreme Court and other courts that they may not do so.[9]

The Supreme Court made it clear, in a trilogy of opinions issued during the 1980s, that the regulation of the process of fundraising for charitable purposes must be undertaken only by the most restrictive means because the solicitation of these gifts is a free speech right of the charities and those who raise funds for them.[10] Two of these cases were launched by fundraisers for charities, rather than the charitable organizations themselves.[11] The Court held that free speech and charitable fundraising are inextricably intertwined, so that the fundraiser, as well as the charity, can assert the constitutional law protection.

In the first of these cases, the Court laid down the fundamental principle that a state government may constitutionally limit speech in serving a legitimate state interest as long as it does so "by narrowly drawn regulations designed to serve those interests without unnecessarily interfering with First Amendment freedoms."[12] That is, a state government may regulate the content of constitutionally protected speech to promote a compelling interest it has, if the government confines itself to the least restrictive means of furthering the articulated interest. Otherwise, a form of regulation of charitable fundraising is to be voided as being unconstitutionally overbroad, as a transgression of free speech or other protected rights.

---

[8] By contrast, a lesser form of free speech, known as *commercial* speech, may be regulated by any approach that is reasonable. Those who dissent from the view that charitable fundraising is a high form of free speech assert that it is merely a type of commercial speech. See § 4.3(b)(iv).

[9] See *infra* text accompanied by notes 15–21.

[10] *Village of Schaumburg* v. *Citizens for a Better Environment,* 444 U.S. 620 (1980); *Secretary of State of Maryland* v. *Joseph H. Munson Co., Inc.,* 467 U.S. 947 (1984); *Riley* v. *National Federation of the Blind of North Carolina, Inc.,* 487 U.S. 781 (1988). These three opinions and the dissents are summarized in detail in § 4.3(b).

[11] *Secretary of State of Maryland* v. *Joseph H. Munson Co., Inc., supra* note 10; *Riley* v. *National Federation of the Blind of North Carolina, Inc., supra* note 10.

[12] *Village of Schaumburg* v. *Citizens for a Better Environment, supra* note 10, at 637.

In one of the federal court cases decided in the aftermath of this trilogy, an appellate court held that a state law requirement that a professional solicitor must submit the script of an oral solicitation to the state for its examination at least 10 days before the commencement of the solicitation was unconstitutional.[13] The court found that the requirement was an inappropriate prior restraint on free speech, being overly broad in its scope. The state contended that the law was the most effective means of monitoring telephone solicitations, but the court dismissed that argument with an observation that resonates throughout the entirety of the law on this subject: The First Amendment "does not permit the State to sacrifice speech for efficiency."[14]

Thus, the posture of the law today, regarding the validity of a state charitable solicitation act, is that any provision of the law that impedes the charitable fundraising process is unconstitutional unless it is the most narrow form of regulation; however—and some in the fundraising profession remain in denial about this—in general, the basic components of a charitable solicitation act, such as those requiring registration, fees, bonds, reporting, disclosure, record keeping, and prescribed contracts, are constitutional. This is the case irrespective of whether the entity being regulated is the charitable organization, a professional fundraiser, a professional solicitor, or a commercial co-venturer.

(b) Fundraising Cost Percentages

The most frequent application of this aspect of constitutional law concerns the attempts of the states to bar charitable fundraising where the expense of the solicitation, stated as a percentage of receipts, of the charitable organization involved is deemed to be excessive or unreasonable. Another variant is an attempt to prohibit compensation paid to a professional fundraiser or professional solicitor where the amount involved exceeds a particular percentage. Both of these types of laws have uniformly been struck down as being facially unconstitutional, overbroad, and not serving a legitimate governmental interest.

This subject is addressed elsewhere in the book in greater detail.[15] The point to be made here is that a charitable organization's fundraising is, for these purposes, held up by the state legislators and regulators as the sole means for determining the charity's worth or validity in the eyes of a prospective donor. "High" fundraising costs are perceived to be an indicia of fraud.[16] The fallacy of this underlying premise seems so obvious as to not merit analysis.

Yet it must be said: The thought that the merits of a charity can be distilled to nothing more than a percentage of fundraising costs is a conception that is based on a wholly invalid premise. That is the case because many variables can account for the fundraising expense of a charity in a particular year, and some of these variables have little or nothing to do with the merits of the charity or its cause.[17]

---

[13] *Telco Communications, Inc.* v. *Carbaugh*, 885 F.2d 1225 (4th Cir. 1989).
[14] *Id.* at 1233.
[15] See §§ 4.1, 4.2.
[16] An analysis of this phenomenon in the context of the use of professional solicitors appears *infra* § 11.
[17] See § 4.1.

The trilogy of cases referenced previously, and subsequent lower-court opinions, proclaim the principle that the touchstone of a charitable organization is not its fundraising expense; they stand for the principle that high solicitation costs are not an accurate measure of the presence of fraud. Laws that focus so intently on fundraising expenses are rules that attempt to limit access to fully protected speech based solely on dollar "efficiency"; the cost of speech has never been found to be a constitutionally appropriate measure of regulation.

Some fundraising methods are inherently more expensive than others. There are organizations whose programs are so controversial as to impede fundraising and thus increase costs. Usually, fundraising costs are higher in the early years of an organization's existence. An organization may have higher costs at the outset of fundraising, then reduce them over the years. A charitable organization with a well-developed constituency is likely to have much lower fundraising costs than one that does not. Legitimate charitable organizations do not deliberately strive to have "high" fundraising costs. There is no uniform way to measure these expenses. Indeed, there is disagreement about what is embraced by the term *fundraising* and controversy about when and how to allocate costs between program and fundraising activities.

Several variables account for fundraising expenses in any particular instance. A practical aspect of analysis of these variables shows that it is unfair to focus on the charity's costs or the fundraiser's fee. The success or failure of a campaign in a financial sense is likely to depend on such a multitude of factors as to be incalculable until completion of the campaign. Thus, the fundraising costs or the solicitor's fee (stated as a percentage) may not be known until the fundraising effort is completed—with a risk of violation of a law of this nature arising only after the fact.

Many factors, other than fundraising costs, should be taken into account in judging the efficacy of a charitable organization. Fundraising costs may be a factor in evaluation, but they should be judged in context, rather than as an isolated element inflated as to importance and distorted as to meaning.

It is a measure of the states' zeal to regulate charitable solicitations on the basis of fundraising costs that they have been driven—again and again—to enact blatantly unconstitutional laws. The two most recent examples have been those enacted in California and Kentucky. The Kentucky law was struck down as unconstitutional in 1994;[18] the California law was restrained by a permanent injunction issued in 1995.[19] One must ask: Why do the state regulators continue to press for these laws, why do legislatures enact them, and why do governors sign them into law instead of vetoing them—even when advised by the state's

---

[18] *Kentucky State Police Professional Association* v. *Gorman*, 870 F. Supp. 166 (E.D. Ky. 1994), concerning a statute providing that, if a professional solicitor for a charitable organization was "allowed to or will receive more than 50% of the gross receipts of the funds solicited as his compensation," the solicitation would be deemed "false, misleading or deceptive."

[19] *National Federation of Nonprofits* v. *Lungren* (N.D. Cal., order issued Mar. 29, 1995), concerning a statute barring an individual or business entity who, for compensation, solicits funds or other property in the state for charitable purposes from retaining more than 50 percent of the net proceeds collected as a fee for fundraising services.

attorney general that they are unconstitutional?[20] These misguided, all-too-frequent forays into this morass of lawmaking fly directly in the face of well-settled constitutional law and represent gross misapplications of state resources.

The element of fundraising costs remains a wholly arbitrary and ineffective means of evaluating a charitable organization's efficiency or program worth. It is a factor that only superficially appears to have any connection with a charity's "value." Those (too frequently, politicians) who point to it as an indicator of the merits of a charity often know better and thus are guilty of pandering. Over the decades, governors, attorneys general, and legislators (federal and state) have shamelessly postured on the issue of charities' fundraising costs.[21]

(c) Fundraisers and Solicitors: Defining the Difference

Another major problem with the state charitable solicitation acts is the failure of the legislators and regulators to divine an adequate definition of the terms *professional fundraiser* and *professional solicitor* (or equivalent terminology).[22] In the past, the definitions and distinctions written into the various state acts sufficed; today, they are so out-of-date, unrealistic, and inconsistent as to be nearly worthless.

In earlier, simpler times, the law viewed the fundraising professional as a consultant, one who assisted charitable organizations in planning a solicitation program or campaign, although the charity actually sought the gifts. The professional solicitor, by contrast, was a person who, in lieu of but on behalf of a charity, solicited gifts. At best, the latter had a poor reputation as one who begged door-to-door or on a street corner, or—worse—solicited by telephone from the proverbial boiler room.

Those distinctions have been blurred and sometimes erased by the advent of developments such as direct mail solicitations, telemarketing, and Internet communications. The bright line of distinction between consultants and solicitors has evaporated. The dichotomy started to fade with the massive use of direct mail fundraising, where those who consulted on the design of the literature also physically introduced it into the mails, thereby arguably becoming part of the solicitation process. Soliciting by telephone in recent years has come out of hiding and into respectability, with the callers regarded as solicitors. Some of those who previously were solely solicitors began adding fundraising planning

[20] *Id.* The attorney general of the State of California, by letter dated September 7, 1994, advised the governor to veto the legislation on the ground that, "under federal case law, the bill is unconstitutional." The attorney general wrote that the Supreme Court has repeatedly held that "using percentages to determine the legality of the fundraiser's fee is an unwarranted limitation on protected speech as reflected in charitable fundraising activities, and is not narrowly tailored to the state's interest in preventing fraud."

[21] *Id.* In his letter to the state's governor, the attorney general of the State of California observed that the unconstitutional statute was nonetheless "laudable as public policy." How can an attorney general or any other lawyer maintain that a law, which the Supreme Court and other courts have held time and time again to be flagrantly unconstitutional as a violation of fundamental rights of free speech, is somehow nonetheless "laudable as public policy"? Moreover, as to public policy, analyses have shown that there is no correlation between the merits of a charity and the level of its fundraising costs (see § 4.1).

[22] See § 4.1; *infra* § 2.

to their services. The demarcation line was irreversibly crossed when telemarketing came into vogue as a fundraising medium, causing the easy distinction between fundraising executives and solicitors to be lost forever.

Under contemporary legal precepts, many of those who are, generically, professional fundraising consultants are considered professional solicitors. This results in two problems. First, despite recent changes in practice, professional solicitors still suffer from the stigma of the past—the image of being the underbelly of philanthropy. Consequently, professional fundraising executives are loath to be viewed—by charities or their colleagues—as professional solicitors.

Second, the state charitable solicitation acts nearly uniformly treat professional solicitors more harshly than is the case with professional fundraisers. Registration fees and bond requirements are higher, and more disclosure and reporting are required. Fundraisers are forced to go through great legalistic contortions and acrobatics to avoid being classified under the law as solicitors, even though their services often partake of the functions of both. But the law does not accommodate this hybrid form, except to treat consultants and solicitors the same—as solicitors—which only compounds the problem and magnifies inherent unfairnesses. Indeed, some state charitable solicitation acts have essentially abandoned the distinction, regarding just about everyone who assists charities in the fundraising process as a solicitor.

Even if the assumption is granted that the professional solicitor is the bane of the field, reasonable individuals should somehow be able to conjure up a definition of the two categories. The distinction between those who have some role in the solicitation process and those who do not is, for the most part, obsolete. It makes little or no sense to regard a consultant as a solicitor simply because among the bundle of services performed is the function of helping to place fundraising literature in the mail. A more appropriate differentiation would be between those who first receive the donated funds and remit a net amount (if any) to the charities and those whose services are paid for by charitable organizations that received the contributions directly. What is needed is a definitional distinction that allows the states to monitor and prosecute the weekend bandits without unduly and unnecessarily regulating the legitimate fundraising executives and consultants.

(d) Bond Requirements

Traditionally, state charitable solicitation acts impose on professional fundraisers and professional solicitors the requirement that they procure a bond before commencing with their services.[23] The purpose of the bond is to offer some protection to the citizens of the particular state who have donated to charity, or what they thought was charity, under circumstances in which they may have been bilked.

The problem with bond requirements in this setting stems from the aforementioned failure of the law to make a meaningful distinction between fundraising consultants and solicitors, in that bonding only makes sense when it pertains to those who have direct and initial access to the donated funds.

[23] See §§ 3.6, 3.7.

Although today's definitions are at best vague on the point, one of the basic generic distinctions between a professional fundraiser and a professional solicitor is the handling of contributions. Basically, where the services of a professional fundraiser are provided to a charitable organization, the *charity*—not the fundraiser—is the solicitor and the recipient of the gifts. Usually, where a professional solicitor is involved, the gifts are made to the solicitor; the solicitor is reimbursed for expenses and paid a fee; and the net amount is paid to the charity involved. Therefore, a bond (or similar form of security) has some logic when required of a professional solicitor; it is of no utility when applied to a professional fundraiser.

Why, then, do some state laws extend the bond requirements to professional fundraisers? It is because the writers of these laws often do not understand the distinction between a professional fundraising consultant and a professional solicitor. This is partially a function of the matter discussed earlier; it is also partially a misconception about the workings of the charitable solicitation process, in the sense of understanding who is receiving the charitable dollars.

Procuring and maintaining these bonds can be expensive and time-consuming. There are preferable alternatives, such as use of a certificate of deposit, letter of credit, or U.S. obligation, filed in lieu of a bond. This approach allows investment assets to be pledged while not disturbing the underlying investment. It eliminates the expense of premiums and reduces the time and costs associated with renewals of bonds. This is an idea all states should embrace, whether for professional fundraisers or professional solicitors.

(e) Other Features

Other features of the states' charitable solicitation acts also pose problems for charitable organizations and professional fundraising consultants.

Most of the state laws contain several types of *prohibited acts* that apply to charities and fundraisers.[24] These prohibitions often go far beyond the scope of fundraising regulation as such, and violations of these rules can bring heavy penalties.

Some laws require complex and onerous disclosures by professional solicitors.[25] Although these laws are designed to drive solicitors out of the states and keep them out, they often also apply to professional fundraisers, thereby causing many compliance problems. Some of the states require burdensome confirmations of donors' gifts.

These laws impose hefty registration, reporting, record-keeping, accounting, and other requirements on charitable organizations and professional fundraisers.[26] They often patronizingly dictate the content of contracts between charitable organizations and professional fundraisers and/or professional solicitors.[27] A growing practice is to require legends that are far from

---

[24] See § 3.13; *infra* § 5.
[25] See § 3.17.
[26] See §§ 3.3–3.6.
[27] See § 3.11.

uniform and that clutter an otherwise carefully designed written charitable solicitation.[28] Some allow private lawsuits against fundraising consultants. The statutes are filled with injunctive, civil, and criminal penalties and carry sanctions of fines and/or imprisonment.[29] The attorneys general, secretaries of state, and other officials are given nearly unfettered authority to launch investigations, pursue injunctions, and prosecute those who (allegedly) have violated these laws.[30]

A growing number of these laws contain requirements pertaining to what are termed either *charitable sales promotions* or *commercial co-ventures*.[31] Many go so far as to have elaborate rules concerning the sale of tickets for charitable events.[32] The list of limitations and prohibitions in some of these laws seems nearly limitless.

(f) Scope of Statutes

Every statutory law has its boundaries; a statute can reach only so far. What are the outer limits of a charitable solicitation act? Oddly, there is almost no law on the point. Given that the applicability of these acts almost always arises in the context of *fundraising,* which commonly entails the request for *contributions,*[33] and inasmuch as the other principal terms employed are *charitable* and *solicitation,*[34] it would not be unreasonable to assume that the state charitable solicitation acts do not extend beyond the realm of the solicitation of gifts (and perhaps grants). Yet, at least in some states, that assumption might be erroneous.

One of the most extreme—if not the most extreme—states on the point is Michigan. There, the state's attorney general asserts, the state's fundraising law also embraces the *sale* of goods or services by or on behalf of charitable organizations where it is advertised that some or all of the proceeds of the sale will be paid over for charitable purposes.[35] This position is manifested in an attorney general opinion, holding that a person who solicits funds for a charitable organization, representing that a portion of the proceeds will be used for charitable purposes, must be licensed as a professional fundraiser, even though the transaction embodying the "solicitation" is wholly a sale.[36] In the case, an individual solicited advertisements for a book, to be published by a charitable organization, representing to prospective advertisers that part of the funds so earned would be used for charitable purposes.[37]

---

[28] See § 3.15.

[29] See § 3.21.

[30] See § 3.19.

[31] See § 3.8; *infra* § 4.

[32] See § 3.8.

[33] See § 3.2(e).

[34] *Id.* § 2(b), (c).

[35] This involves situations other than those concerning commercial co-ventures (see § 3.8).

[36] 1981-1982 Mich. OAG No. 5850 (Feb. 4, 1981). The opinion was issued, notwithstanding the fact that the preamble to the state statute provides that it is an act "to regulate organizations and persons soliciting or collecting *contributions* for charitable purposes" (emphasis supplied).

[37] The attorney general was considerably aided in the position by dint of the fact that the statute's definition of the word *contribution* generally is the "promise, grant, or payment of

In the analysis underlying this opinion, there is considerable discussion about circumstances in which a transaction is partly a gift and partly a purchase; there should be no question that transactions of this nature invoke the statute.[38] Yet, the opinion extends to transactions in which there is no element of a gift (nor solicitation of a gift in the context of the purchase). The state's statutory definition of a contribution excludes most dues; the attorney general read the exclusion to mean that all other forms of purchases of services (or goods) are to be treated as contributions.[39] Despite this opinion, it is hard to believe that a state's charitable solicitation act applies to sales transactions simply because some proceeds of the transactions will be devoted to charitable ends. This would mean that a charitable organization that generates revenue only through the sale of goods or services (such as a theater or home for the elderly or a charity raising money by means of a car wash or bake sale) would have to comply with one or more charitable solicitation acts. In actual practice, the laws are not being enforced in that manner.

Regarding the matter of the boundary, this opinion also asserted that, if "simply because the donor [note the term] was provided some benefit, such a payment could not be deemed a charitable contribution, then all of the safeguards established in [the act] could easily be circumscribed by an organization or fund-raiser." In fact, the matter is precisely the opposite: if a payment is not a charitable contribution, the transaction would fall outside the reach of the statute. The "safeguards" of these laws would be "circumscribed," but only because they simply do not apply.

In one instance, an attorney general's office attempted to apply the state's charitable solicitation act to the solicitation of corporate sponsors for a marathon conducted to generate proceeds for a charitable organization. The matter found its way into court, where it was held that the statute was inapplicable. The court concluded that the transaction was a "commercial" one and that it did not involve "gifts." As the court succinctly stated, the solicitation had "nothing to do with philanthropy."[40] That is the correct statement of the law generally: These statutes do not apply where the charitable "fundraising" does not entail the soliciting or making of any contributions.[41]

money or property of any kind of value." No mention is made of *charity* or *gifts*; it is not clear why the state's legislature assigned the word *contribution* to the definition.

[38] Examples of these transactions are quid pro quo contributions (see § 5.4), bargain sales, and forms of planned giving (such as a gift by means of a charitable remainder trust).

[39] It is quite reasonable to assume that the exclusion for dues is in the statute to resolve any confusion about whether dues are gifts (they are not)—and for no other reason. The opinion also gratuitously observes that one who contends that the statute is not applicable is doing so because the person "fears public scrutiny of its financial affairs." There surely is authority for the proposition that a person is not presumed to be a wrongdoer if the person does not voluntarily comply with an inapplicable law.

[40] *Attorney General* v. *International Marathons, Inc.,* 467 N.E.2d 51, 54 (Mass. 1984)).

[41] What this matter comes down to is that, at the end of the day, a purchase is not a contribution; only as contribution is a contribution. As one court sagely observed: "But at the end of the day, even if you put a calico dress on it and call it Florence, a pig is still a pig" (*Bradshaw* v. *Unity Marine Corporation, Inc. et al.,* 147 F. Supp. 2d 668, 671 (S.D. Tex. 2001)). An attorney general or other state official can put a dress on a purchase and call it a gift, but what the objective analysis ends up being is that a purchase is not a gift.

Thus, notwithstanding the state of the "law" in this one jurisdiction, the better view is that the state charitable solicitation acts apply only where the transaction involved entails, in whole or in part, a contribution. If a state legislature wanted to expand its charitable solicitation act to encompass all sales of goods and services by and for charities, presumably it could do so; such an expansion of the law, however, might prove impolitic.

(g) Conclusion

A considerable majority of the states have significant charitable solicitation acts.[42] A fundraising charitable organization that is located in one of these states, and/or is soliciting in one or more of these states, faces (unless exempted) a formidable array of requirements. It is one of the many anomalies of the law that a person can engage in many forms of behavior that are potentially harmful to society—and face far less regulation. For example, in some states, regulation is far more stringent for solicitation of a charitable gift than for purchase of a firearm.

Why this mountain of law came into being is not clear. This circumstance is particularly mysterious when played off against the fact that the activity that is heavily regulated is an exercise of a constitutional right and the response to it is a voluntary act. As to the latter, charitable giving is, of course, not mandatory. If a person is uncertain about making a contribution to a charitable organization, the putative donor can simply defer the gift until the uncertainty is resolved (as, for example, by obtaining wanted information). (If a donor is giving at the last minute for tax purposes, a "safe" donee—perhaps a college, hospital, or the donor's own private foundation—can be selected.)

Not only is the rationale for all of this law a mystery, so too is whether any of it is accomplishing anything of consequence. (This rationale is not to be confused with the purpose underlying these laws, which is to protect the public against unscrupulous fundraisers and unworthy charities.) Are there many fraudulent and other misrepresenting charitable solicitations? Are there many unscrupulous charities? Or ill-meaning fundraising efforts? Are individuals really being protected?—and, if so, from what?

The truth is that no one knows.

Those who portray the charitable sector as riddled with abuse are those who have a vested interest in portraying the sector, or selected entities in it, in as negative a perspective as possible: the regulators, the watchdog agencies, and the media. Even in those quarters, it appears, an authentic case is not being made: grand extrapolations from a few bits of anecdotal evidence do not prove anything.

So, the charitable community watches and struggles with these charitable solicitation acts. While conceding a legitimate purpose for these laws (protection of the citizenry), one may ask just what task or tasks all these "apparatuses" are accomplishing. Might not the energy and public money (tax

---

[42] See § 3.1.

revenues) consumed by these apparatuses be better used elsewhere (in or out of government)?[43]

§ 7.2 DEFINING A FUNDRAISING PROFESSIONAL

The various state charitable solicitation acts pose many problems for the fundraising professional. Overviews of this understatement can be found throughout this book.[44]

(a) Definitions

Among the headaches is the threshold definitional one: what is a *fundraising professional?* At a simplistic level (the historical one), a fundraising professional is either an employee of a charitable organization or a consultant, one who assists charities in planning and implementing a solicitation campaign. Generally, only the latter type of fundraising professional is subject to state regulation. The actual asking for gifts is, according to this level of analysis, the province of the charities, who do this using volunteers.

To continue this line of analysis, there are exceptions, of course, and sometimes charities obtain contributions through paid solicitors. This practice has been generally frowned on by fundraising professionals. Indeed, it was once thought throughout the world of philanthropy that "self-respecting" charities did not use paid solicitors and "proper" professional fundraisers did not associate with them.[45]

The laws among the states were written with this dichotomy in mind: the consultant and the solicitor. Thus, today, the predominant definition of a *professional fundraiser* is this:

> Any person who for a flat fixed fee under a written agreement plans, conducts, manages, carries on, advises or acts as a consultant, whether directly or indirectly, in connection with soliciting contributions for, or on behalf of, any charitable organization, but who actually solicits no contributions as a part of such services.[46]

As can be seen, there are two principal elements of this definition: the professional fundraiser does not solicit gifts and is paid for the service provided (the definition thus excludes volunteers). This definition (or a similar version of it) of the term *professional fundraiser* is used in most of the states,[47] with some of these states using the term *professional fundraising counsel.* Other states use the term *fundraising counsel.*

---

[43] In general, Pinto and Gardner, "How State Governments Regulate Charitable Fundraising," 3 *J. Tax'n Exempt Org.* (No. 3) 16 (Fall 1991).

[44] See §§ 3.6, 4.1; *supra* § 1.

[45] The author recalls serving on a task force, many years ago, that was drafting a prototype charitable solicitation act. Someone suggested adding a paid solicitor to the group, to gain his or her perspective, but none of the task force members seemed to know one.

[46] This language is from the Virginia statute.

[47] See § 4.10.

The usual definition of the term *professional solicitor*—that found in the law in most of the states[48]—is this:

> [A] person who, for financial or other consideration, solicits contributions for, or on behalf of, a charitable organization, whether such solicitation is performed personally or through his [or her] agents, servants, or employees or through agents, servants, or employees specially employed by, or for a charitable organization, who are engaged in the solicitation of contributions under the direction of such person, or any person who, for a financial or other consideration, plans, conducts, manages, carries on, advises, or acts as a consultant to a charitable organization in connection with the solicitation of contributions but does not qualify as a professional fundraising counsel.[49]

This definition has three principal elements: the solicitor asks for contributions, is paid for the service, and is anyone in the solicitation process (excepting volunteers) other than a professional fundraiser. A few states use the term *paid solicitor*.

Some states excuse from the status of either a professional fundraiser or professional solicitor those who are employees or officers of the soliciting charity, as well as lawyers, investment counselors, and bankers.

Over the years, there have been two problems with these definitions:

1. They increasingly do not work.

2. The derogation associated with being a professional solicitor has continued, with the law often being far more stringent with respect to solicitors than fundraisers.

(As to the latter point, this aspect has been somewhat ameliorated, in that courts have struck down some of the harsher provisions as being unconstitutional.)

Before discussing why these definitions do not work very well, it is important to note that there are other definitions of these terms. Consequently, considerable confusion exists in this area of the law at present. Some states so broadly define *professional fundraiser* that the definition includes a *professional solicitor*. For example, one state[50] defines a professional fundraiser as "any person who for financial compensation or profit participates in public solicitation in this state of contributions for, or on behalf of any charitable organization." In another state,[51] the term *professional fundraising firm* is used to describe what is usually defined, in other states, as a professional solicitor; two other state statutes[52] contain the same anomaly. In one state,[53] the term *professional solicitor* is so broadly defined that it encompasses what is normally defined as a professional

---

[48] See § 4.10.
[49] This language is from the Virginia statute.
[50] Minnesota.
[51] Oregon.
[52] Those in Louisiana and Utah.
[53] Tennessee.

fundraiser. Another state uses the term *professional commercial fundraiser* to describe what most states define as a *professional solicitor*.[54]

Some states define a *professional solicitor* as "any person who is employed or retained for compensation by a professional fundraiser to solicit contributions for charitable purposes in this state."[55]

In recent times, the relatively easy-to-define dichotomy between professional fundraisers (i.e., as consultants) and professional solicitors has evaporated. This phenomenon started with direct mail fundraising, where those who consulted about the design of the literature began physically introducing it into the U.S. mails, thereby becoming part of the solicitation process. Soliciting by telephone has come out of the boiler room and become respectable, with the callers regarded as solicitors. The lines of demarcation were further blurred when telemarketing became a staple of fundraising.[56] The distinctions between consultants and solicitors are, today, all too antiquated.

(b) Defining *Solicit*

Part of the problem lies in the definition of the term *solicit*. (A search of case law on this subject yielded only cases concerning barratry—lawyers illegally soliciting business—or prostitution.) The state charitable solicitation acts define the term broadly. For example, the statute in one state[57] defines the term *solicit* as meaning "to request, directly or indirectly, money, credit, property, or other financial assistance in any form on the plea or representation that the money, credit, property, or other financial assistance will be used for a charitable purpose." This is, obviously, a most encompassing definition of the word, although it is typical.

In part, this becomes a line-drawing exercise, with the question being: At what point does a consulting service become a solicitation service? As referenced earlier, direct mail fundraising presents the dilemma. A firm that assists a charity in designing fundraising literature and does nothing more is a professional fundraiser. Yet, if this firm provides an additional service, such as mailing the literature for the charity, does it become a professional solicitor? Technically, the answer must be yes, because the act of mailing a letter requesting a gift is a *solicitation*. This is, however, an exceedingly technical application of the term.

The better view is to regard the firm in this instance as the agent of the charity. Nonetheless, several years ago, this issue was before the Pennsylvania Charities Commission. The fundraising firm involved designed the literature and further assisted the charity by physically introducing the literature into the U.S. mail. The literature was mailed using the charity's preferential postal rate, the envelopes contained the charity's return address, the gifts were returned to the charity, and there was no mention of the firm in the literature. Yet, because the firm had the service of taking the bags of mail to the post

---

[54] Iowa.

[55] This language is from the Kansas statute. In general, see § 4.10.

[56] See *infra* § 3.

[57] Maryland.

office on behalf of the charity, the commission ruled that the entire operation of the firm was that of a professional solicitor.[58] So much for the "better view."

(c) Reasons for Avoiding Solicitor Status

There are several reasons why a firm or individual would prefer to not be regarded as a professional solicitor. One of them is simply that of image. Solicitors are differentiated from consultants; they are characterized as those who go door to door, stand on street corners, or telephone during private time, seeking gifts. They are also portrayed as those who consume a large portion of the contributions intended for charitable ends.

From a law point of view, professional solicitors are often treated more harshly under the state charitable solicitation acts than professional fundraisers. As an extreme example, the statute in one state[59] is applicable only to those who solicit contributions (as noted, this law terms such persons *professional fundraisers*); apparently, persons who function only as consultants are not covered at all by the statute. Another illustration is the law in a state[60] where a fundraising counsel has to register with the state only where he, she, or it has custody or control of contributions from a solicitation.

In some states, professional solicitors must be bonded, although professional fundraisers need not be. In various states, professional solicitors are required to adhere to certain requirements about disclosure, confirmations, and receipts that do not apply to professional fundraisers. For example, in one state,[61] professional solicitors must provide receipts to donors. As another illustration, in two states,[62] extensive point-of-solicitation disclosure requirements are applicable to paid solicitors but not to professional fundraisers.

(d) Amending the Statutes

The most obvious way to resolve this dilemma is to amend the statutes. One would think this a rather reasonable way to proceed. Yet there is nearly total resistance to this approach, out of fear by the regulators that a loosening of the definition will allow solicitors, generically defined, to escape regulation. State regulators are so concerned about the weekend solicitors that their mindset is expansion of the concept of the professional solicitor, rather than dilution of it.

Nonetheless, there are at least two ways to proceed in this regard. One is to provide certain exceptions to the definition of the term *professional solicitor* to exclude, for example, organizations that mail fundraising literature where the mailing is in the charity's name and otherwise under its auspices. Another way would be to build the concept of principal and agent into the statutory definition.

---

[58] See § 4.10, note 374.
[59] Utah.
[60] Connecticut.
[61] Rhode Island.
[62] Massachusetts and New Hampshire.

Probably a more radical approach is needed. This approach would entail abandonment of these traditional definitions and a fresh start. The new definitions would recognize that many individuals and firms are now hybrids of consultants and solicitors. One of the elements to distinguish one from the other would be, as noted earlier, the matter of which person would receive the charitable gifts. Reasonable individuals can surely conjure up definitions that allow the states to engage in effective regulation of the process of fundraising for charity without overly regulating the authentic fundraising consultant.

The law in one state[63] comes the closest to this approach. That statute differentiates among *fundraising counsel, professional fundraiser,* and *professional solicitor.* Under this law, a *fundraising counsel* is one who, for compensation, only consults or otherwise assists charities with respect to fundraising but "who does not have access to contributions or other receipts from a solicitation or authority to pay expenses associated with a solicitation. . . . " The term *professional fundraiser* is defined in accordance with the majority approach, and a *professional solicitor* is one who solicits gifts as an employee of a professional fundraiser. (Among other things, under this law, a fundraising counsel is not required to procure a bond.)

There is a project here—members of the fundraising profession need to develop definitions of those who practice in the field and collateral to it. These definitions could then be submitted to the states in an effort to procure amendments of the state charitable solicitation acts on the point. At present, these definitions (and laws) are too often being written by legislators who do not understand the functions of the fundraising profession.[64]

§ 7.3 PROFESSIONAL SOLICITORS: ROLE OF TELEMARKETING

An aspect of state regulation of charitable fundraising that borders on foolishness is the impact of the various solicitation acts on telemarketers who assist charitable organizations in fundraising.

As noted,[65] one of the greatest defects in the usual state charitable solicitation act lies in the section containing the definitions of terms used in the statute. There is found the meaning of words such as *professional fundraiser, professional* (or *paid*) *solicitor,* and *solicit.*

Most of the fundraising regulation zealotry is being directed at the quickie promoters, those who roll into town for a weekend with a circus or some other attraction and roll out of town with most of the money collected, leaving the

---

[63] New York.

[64] While working on a dictionary of fundraising terms, a project of the Association of Fundraising Professionals, the Chair of the Dictionary Task Force, Barbara Levy, ACFRE, observed that "[t]hat kind of ambiguity [in defining a professional fundraiser] leads others to make decisions that negatively affect fund raising" ("Fund Raising, Defined," XXXI *NSFRE News* (No. 2) 1 (1994)). In general, Flessner, "Defining the Professional Fund-Raiser," XVI *The Journal* (No. 1) 16 (National Society of Fund Raising Executives, Spring 1991). The American Association of Fund-Raising Counsel, Inc., New York, published an untitled booklet describing the functions of a fundraising consulting firm.

[65] See § 4.10; *supra* §§ 12.

charitable beneficiary with a pittance. (It is a scandal that all of fundraising, be it capital, annual giving, direct mail, or planned giving programs, is heavily regulated so that purveyors of tickets to vaudeville acts can be monitored.) Yet the statute writers cannot seem to write law regulating only these types. Instead, they rely on the traditional, but antiquated, definitions of the terms *professional fundraiser* and *solicitor.*

To reiterate, the term *professional fundraiser* is usually defined as a person who, for compensation, plans, manages, advises, or consults with respect to the solicitation of contributions by a charitable organization, but who does not solicit contributions. In a word, a professional fundraiser is thought of as a consultant. A *solicitor* is defined as a person who, for compensation, performs for a charitable organization any service in connection with which contributions are solicited. Throw in the fact that the term *solicit* is defined to include seeking of contributions over the telephone,[66] and logic seems to lead inextricably to the conclusion that a telemarketer is a solicitor.

The fact is, generically, a telemarketer is not a solicitor because the telemarketer does not receive the funds from the solicitation. That is an important distinguishing characteristic. A true professional solicitor is one who requests a contribution on behalf of a charity, receives all of the gifts, retains the fee and the amount to cover expenses, and remits the (perhaps slim) balance to the charity. Frequently, another characteristic of a solicitor is that compensation is fixed as a percentage of funds received. Further, the transactions usually are such that the donor realizes that the solicitor is not an employee of the donee/charity but is functioning in an independent capacity.

Under normal circumstances, when a gift is made to a charity as the result of a telemarketing effort, the gift is—literally—made to the charity. Compensation is usually on a set fee basis, rather than as a function of contributions received. Furthermore, those called usually believe that the caller is a direct representative of the charity, not some independent taker of most of the gift amount. In fact, a telemarketer is such a representative, functioning as an agent of the soliciting charity.

Except for the disparaging connotation usually associated with the term *solicitor,* there would be no harm done to telemarketers to be classified as solicitors if it were all a matter of definitions. The matter, however, involves much more than definitions simply because, in their zealous efforts to drive out the circus promoters, the statute writers have made life miserable for those who are categorized as solicitors.[67]

What is to be done? First, there needs to be adequate recognition of the law warp that the telemarketers are in. (Direct mail consultants are basically in this same spot.) The states are overreacting and overregulating, and the telemarketers are caught up in statutory definitions that, in real life, have no bearing on what they do. Generically, telemarketers are not solicitors.

Second, there must be some organized effort to change these laws. A single telemarketing firm is unlikely to do it single-handedly. An association or coalition must spearhead the project. It will be difficult, however, because

[66] See § 3.2(c).
[67] See § 3.7.

fundraisers have no political constituency (at least not like the constituency for charities), and the presumptions are against them.

Third, any such remedial effort must not repeat the same mistake that many legislatures have recently made. That is, drafting sweeping definitions (or exemptions) will not do. The corrective legislation must be narrow and precise enough to rectify this particular problem but not at the same time excuse the weekend promoters from the light of disclosure and stringent regulation.

§ 7.4 CHARITABLE SALES PROMOTIONS

Traditionally, the state charitable solicitation acts impose registration and reporting requirements on charitable organizations, professional fundraisers, and professional solicitors. Most of the present-day state fundraising regulation statutes embody one or more of these elements.

A more recent phenomenon, however, is regulation of charitable sales promotions, involving *commercial co-venturers*.[68] Like professional fundraisers and solicitors, these co-venturers are almost always for-profit organizations. Unlike fundraisers and solicitors, however, they are not paid for their role in the fundraising process.

(a) Terminology

In short, a commercial co-venturer is a business that, for differing reasons, wishes to help a charity. To this end, the business agrees to be a part of a promotion—indeed, to be the enervating and principal part—to benefit a charity. The motive may be purely charitable; more likely, it is a blend of motives: part charitable intent, part marketing, and part the development of goodwill in the community or across the country.

The enterprise is termed *commercial* because a business is involved. The business is a *co-venturer*. The other party to the co-venture is, of course, the charity or charities involved in the promotion. Most of the states define this type of promotion as a *charitable sales promotion.*

Commercial co-venturing occurs when a business announces to the general public that a portion (a specific amount or a specific percentage) of the purchase price of a product or service will, during a stated period, be paid to a charitable organization. When properly structured, this activity results in a charitable gift, the amount of which depends on consumer response to the promotion, by the business sponsor.

The term *commercial co-venture* is, in some respects, unfortunate. First, it suggests that the charitable organization involved is engaged in a co-venture (joint venture) with the participating for-profit organization. Second, the term implies that the charitable organization involved is doing something *commercial.* Both connotations have potential adverse consequences in law,

---

[68] See § 3.8.

particularly in the unrelated business income setting.[69] Consequently, the phrasing *charitable sales promotion,* while not ideal, is preferable.

Thus, a commercial co-venture works best for all parties concerned when the charity's role in the "venture" is passive. If, however, the charity's participation in the venture is an active one, it could be characterized as a true joint venture, with the charity seen as providing marketing services to the business. The consequence of this could be that the charity is not receiving a tax-free gift but is receiving taxable unrelated business income. Should this be the outcome, the business involved would not be entitled to a charitable contribution deduction (but would be able to deduct the amount paid as a business expense).

(b) Scope of Regulation

A few states regulate commercial co-venturing. Why do these states do this? In substantial part, they engage in this form of regulation as part of a consumer protection mentality. But, another aspect of this regulation of philanthropy exists as an attempt to save charities from themselves.

The usual dismay of a business when facing this type of regulation is understandable. The situation involves a business, wanting to do something for charity; at the same time, a state regulator is insisting that the business register with his or her office, file accountings and other reports, and perhaps even become bonded. The resulting outrage is predictable; one would think that the business would simply decline to be part of the promotion and thus spare itself the burdens of regulation.

Yet this does not happen because more is going on here than pure charity. A charitable sales promotion entails advertising, an opportunity for the business to associate itself with a charitable cause. Its reputation becomes enhanced because of the charity's reputation. The public sees the business doing something for charity, and the image of the business is improved. In turn, the public purchases the business's products or services, knowing that they are advancing charity in the process. (The consumers receive no charitable contribution deduction, however.) Consequently, charity is benefited and the business is benefited.

But the states want to be certain that the promised monies make it to charitable ends; they want to be satisfied that the business's promise to make a charitable gift is valid. They want to protect the charity by making certain that a bad bargain is not struck and that the terms of the arrangement are memorialized in a written contract.

(c) State Laws' Definitions

Several states have some form of regulation of commercial co-venturing. Disclosure, record-keeping, accounting requirements, registration requirements, and the mandated content of contracts are the principal forms of regulation; a few states require the business to register and acquire a bond. In some states, the concept of the commercial co-venture is stated as a *sales solicitation for charitable*

---

[69] See § 5.7.

purposes or a *charitable sales promotion*.[70] Oddly, one state[71] defines the term *commercial co-venturer* in its charitable solicitation act, but the concept is not thereafter used in the statute. In another state,[72] to be a commercial co-venturer, the entity must act in that capacity on an "infrequent basis"; if it does so on a "regular" basis, it is a *commercial fundraising firm*. Another state[73] defines a *charitable promotion*, but accomplishes its regulation by means of a lengthy inventory of prohibited acts.

The definitions of the term *commercial co-venture* are not uniform—as befits the general state of this area of law. One of the better approaches[74] defines a commercial co-venturer as "[a]ny person who for profit is regularly and primarily engaged in trade or commerce other than in connection with the raising of funds or any other thing of value for a charitable organization and who advertises that the purchase or use of goods, services, entertainment, or any other thing of value will benefit a charitable organization."

The law of another state[75] more broadly defines a *commercial co-venturer* as "any person who for profit or other commercial consideration, conducts, produces, promotes, underwrites, arranges or sponsors a performance, event, or sale to the public of a good or service which is advertised in conjunction with the name of any charitable organization or as benefiting to any extent any charitable purpose."

In another state,[76] the term *commercial co-venturer* is defined as "any sole proprietorship, partnership, corporation or any other legal entity, organized for profit or formed as a nonprofit mutual benefit corporation, who is regularly and primarily engaged in trade or commerce in this state other than in conjunction with the raising of funds for nonprofit purposes and who conducts commercial fund raising solicitations on an infrequent basis."

The more common way to reference a commercial co-venture is represented by the law of a state,[77] where the statute defines a *commercial co-venturer* as a "person who for profit is regularly and primarily engaged in trade or commerce in this state other than in connection with the raising of funds for charitable organizations or purposes and who conducts a charitable sales promotion." A *charitable sales promotion* is defined as "an advertising or sales campaign, conducted by a commercial co-venturer, which represents that the purchase or use of goods or services offered by the commercial co-venturer are to benefit a charitable organization or purpose." One state takes a slightly different approach, defining a *charitable sales promotion* as "an advertising campaign sponsored by a for-profit entity which offers for sale a tangible item or provides a

---

[70] One state (Florida) uses the term *sponsor sales promotion* when the charitable organization involved in what the other of these states would term a charitable sales promotion operates for the benefit of emergency service employees (such as firefighters and ambulance drivers) and law enforcement officers.
[71] North Carolina.
[72] Oregon.
[73] Pennsylvania.
[74] New York.
[75] Massachusetts.
[76] Oregon.
[77] Connecticut.

service upon the representation that all or a portion of the purchase price will be donated to a person established for a charitable purpose."[78]

One state[79] regulates commercial co-venturing, not by its charitable solicitation act, but through application of its fraudulent advertising law. That law relates to the practice of a person who "sell[s] merchandise" or "solicit[s] programs or any other advertising when any part of the proceeds will be donated to any organization or fund." Another state's rule is found in its business and professions code, where a *sales solicitation for charitable purposes* is detailed as "the sale of, offer to sell, or attempt to sell any advertisement, advertising space, book, card, chance, coupon device, magazine subscription, membership, merchandise, ticket of admission or any other thing or service in connection with which" there is an appeal for charitable purposes, or the name of a charity is used "as an inducement" for making the sale, or any statement is made that all or any part of the proceeds of the sale will be used for a charitable purpose.[80]

As noted, one state's law does not contain any provisions expressly relating to commercial co-venturers (although one of the drafts of the statute did).[81] Nonetheless, the attorney general's office in the state interprets the term *professional fundraiser* to embrace a commercial co-venturer (the for-profit business) where the company guarantees a sum of money to the charitable organization involved, irrespective of the number of products or services sold during the course of the promotion. Thus, a commercial co-venturer in this circumstance would have to register with the state and satisfy the other requirements applicable to professional fundraisers (see previous discussion). This attorney general's office is also of the view that where the for-profit business in the venture agrees to pay a fixed amount to the charitable organization for each product or service purchased (a usual feature of a commercial co-venture), the company is functioning as a charitable trustee and, therefore, must comply with the state's Charitable Trust Act. This requirement entails registration with the attorney general's office. As one commentator so correctly stated the point, this interpretation of the law "is strained at best and would probably not withstand legal challenge."[82]

One state[83] is unique in that it expressly exempts commercial co-venturers from the scope of its charitable solicitation act.

(d) Forms of Regulation

Once a promotion is defined as a commercial co-venture, then what? In one state,[84] for example, a commercial co-venturer is required to maintain "accurate and current" records during the promotion and for three years thereafter, have a written contract with the charity, and file reports with the state,

---

[78] North Carolina.
[79] Wisconsin.
[80] California.
[81] Illinois.
[82] Tesdahl, "Improved Fund-Raising through Commercial Co-venturers," 7 *Exempt Org. Tax Rev.* (No. 4) 619, 621 (Apr. 1993).
[83] Arizona.
[84] New York.

including an accounting of the funds received and disbursed. Moreover, in this state, the charity involved must annually report to the state about the commercial co-ventures it has authorized, the terms and conditions of each contract, and a statement about whether it received the requisite accounting.

The law of another state[85] contains similar requirements and adds registration, payment of a fee, and (as noted) a bond. Some states mandate certain elements in the contract.

In one state,[86] disclosure to the public is the principal requirement of the law. (This statute is applicable only where the commercial co-venturer expects that more than half of the proceeds of the solicitation will be derived from transactions within the state.) In this state, where the rule applies, a commercial co-venturer must disclose in each advertisement for the promotion the dollar amount or percent per unit of goods and services purchased or used (or, in some instances, a reasonable estimate) that will be transmitted to charity.

In two states,[87] much of the foregoing applies. That is, there are rules about the content and filing of the agreement between the charity and the commercial co-venturer, record keeping, and public disclosure.

The state laws that force contracts between charitable organizations and commercial co-venturers to contain various provisions are useful, in that certain requirements are essential in any agreement between these parties. These elements include (1) the goods or services to be offered to the public, (2) the geographic area where the offering is to be made, (3) the starting and final dates of the offering, (4) the representation to be made to the public about the amount or percent per unit of goods or services purchased or used that will benefit the charitable organization, (5) a final accounting by the commercial co-venturer, and (6) the date when and the manner in which the benefit is to be conferred on the charitable organization.

(e) Some Practical Problems

State regulators in jurisdictions with charitable solicitation acts often do not insist on compliance with their laws in every case. Some fundraising events or campaigns are so clearly proper that intervention by the regulators is not warranted—even though the fundraising is not in conformity with the state law requirements. These regulators are often overburdened; if "selective nonenforcement" is the result, so be it. The regulators might regulate in these circumstances if asked (such as by complaint), otherwise the fundraising is ignored.

This is often the case with a commercial co-venture, particularly a national promotion. With a national campaign, the business involved is often a well-known and respected enterprise; the charity is equally well known and well perceived. There is no particular nexus with the state. (The definition of a commercial co-venturer in one state[88] includes the point that the business

---

[85] Maine.
[86] Colorado.
[87] Connecticut and New Hampshire.
[88] Connecticut.

involved be one that is primarily functioning "in this state.") Regulation would likely achieve only unnecessary paperwork for all parties concerned. So the regulators do not enforce the law, although technically they should.

Sometimes it is not clear whether the promotion is really a commercial co-venture. Perhaps a product is purchased but another company makes the gift. Or, there may be two businesses involved, and one does not comply, thinking that any compliance with state law is the responsibility of the other.

In some situations, there is overregulation. Requiring commercial co-venturers to take out bonds, for example, seems unnecessary.

Some in philanthropy do not care for commercial co-ventures. They believe that co-ventures can be demeaning for the charities and that the businesses are interested only in benefiting by association with the charities rather than having any true charitable motive. While there is truth in these beliefs, they are not the entire story. These ventures can be advantageous for charities. As is so often the case in this area of the law, if there must be regulation, it should be undertaken in a way that does not discourage the practice of commercial co-venturing.

§ 7.5   REGULATION UNLIMITED: PROHIBITED ACTS

Other portions of this book summarize the more well-known features of the state charitable solicitation acts: the registration, reporting, bonding, and similar requirements imposed on charitable organizations, professional fundraisers, professional solicitors, and commercial co-venturers, as well as certain other rules pertaining to contents of contracts, record keeping, appointment of registered agents, and disclosure.

There is, however, an element of most of these solicitation statutes that all too many overlook: the provisions containing the *prohibited acts*. These provisions, which appear in most of these statutes, encompass a dimension of charitable fundraising regulation that can carry this body of law far beyond the bounds of registration and reporting.[89]

Prohibited acts are those in which a charitable organization (and perhaps a professional fundraiser and/or professional solicitor) may not lawfully engage. The more common of these several prohibitions will be reviewed first.

Every person with a role in the fundraising process should review the law of each state involved, to be certain that some prohibited act is not about to be transgressed.

(a) Basic Prohibitions

In most of these states, a person may not, for the purpose of soliciting contributions, use the name of another person without the consent of that other person. Usual exceptions concern the use of the names of officers, directors, or trustees of the charitable organization by or for which contributions are solicited. This prohibition extends to the use of an individual's name on

---

[89] See § 3.13.

stationery or in an advertisement or brochure, or as one who has contributed to, sponsored, or endorsed the organization.

A person may not, for the purposes of soliciting contributions, use a name, symbol, or statement so closely related or similar to that used by another charitable organization or governmental agency that it would tend to confuse or mislead the public.

A person may not use or exploit the fact of registration with the state to lead the public to believe that the registration in any manner constitutes an endorsement or appeal by the state.

A person may not misrepresent or mislead anyone, by any manner, means, practice, or device, to believe that the organization on behalf of which the solicitation is being conducted is a charitable organization or that the proceeds of the solicitation will be used for charitable purposes, where that is not the case.[90]

A person may not represent that the solicitation is for or on behalf of a charitable organization or otherwise induce contributions from the public without proper authorization from the charitable organization.

(b) Extraordinary Prohibitions

Some state's laws contain prohibitions that go far beyond the foregoing and reach into domains normally covered by other bodies of law—such as those pertaining to tax-exempt status or deductible charitable giving—or not addressed by other law at all. These prohibitions are extraordinary and, were it not for the fact that they are rarely enforced, would play havoc with the functions of many charitable organizations and the fundraising professionals whose services they utilize. In many instances, these rules apply even in the absence of any fundraising.

What follows are examples from various state laws. Although specific state statutory provisions are cited, other states may well have the same provisions. As noted, it is essential that the laws in each applicable state be reviewed in relation to a charitable fundraising undertaking.

For example, in one state,[91] it is a prohibited act for a charitable organization to "expend an unreasonable amount of money for solicitation or management." While this is probably the rule for tax-exempt status in general, it is, in the state regulation setting, fraught with free speech and due process implications. Every charity should strive for this result, but how are *unreasonable* expenses determined and who makes the determination?

As another example, under the law of the same state, it is a violation of law for a charitable organization to "engage in any financial transaction which is not related to the accomplishment of its charitable purpose, or which jeopardizes or interferes with the ability of the charitable organization to accomplish its charitable purpose." This type of prohibition accords the regulators carte

---

[90] This type of law was upheld in *Church of Scientology Flag Services Org., Inc.* v. *City of Clearwater*, 756 F. Supp. 1498, 1523–1524 (M.D. Fla. 1991).
[91] Connecticut.

blanche authority to scrutinize everything a charity does in the state—and raises additional due process concerns.

In another state,[92] it is unlawful for any person to "use or permit the use of the funds raised by a charitable solicitation for any purpose other than the solicited purpose or the general purposes of the . . . organization on whose behalf the solicitation was made." Directors, officers, and employees of charitable organizations, take heed.

In this state, it is also illegal for a charitable organization to represent or imply that a contributor to it will be entitled to a charitable contribution deduction for the gift unless the charity has first obtained a determination from the IRS that the gifts are deductible or a letter of opinion from a lawyer on the point. This type of law can be troublesome (and/or perhaps expensive) for a charitable organization that does not need a ruling from the IRS, such as a religious organization or an organization that is tax-exempt pursuant to a group exemption.

It is also contrary to law in this state for anyone to indicate that any portion of a membership fee or sales price paid to a charitable organization is a deductible gift unless the IRS has so ruled. This prohibition does not apply where the payor is notified in writing that the amount is not deductible. Further, in this state, a charitable organization violates the law if it accepts a contribution of cash or tangible property with a value exceeding $5.00 unless, at the donor's request, a written receipt is provided.

(c) Focus on Solicitors

State laws often use the concept of the prohibited act to further regulate the activities of professional solicitors. (These prohibitions are among the many reasons it is usually important for a company or individual to be classified as a professional fundraiser rather than a professional solicitor, if at all possible.)

For example, in one state,[93] it is a prohibited act for a professional solicitor to solicit for a charity without written authorization of two officers of the charity and without exhibiting a copy of the authorization, along with "personal identification," to persons solicited. This authorization must state a period of time for which it is valid, and a copy of it must be filed with the state.

(d) Unusual Provisions

Given the scope of the states' prohibited acts and the penchant of the states for avoidance of uniformity, it is to be expected that some states will have some rather unusual laws in this field. Here is a sampling.

In one state,[94] a person may not, when soliciting contributions for charitable purposes, "impede or obstruct, with the intent to physically inconvenience the general public or any member thereof in any public place or any place open

---

[92] Virginia.
[93] Maryland.
[94] Hawaii.

to the public." Presumably, everyone is a member of the general public, so this rule has universal application (at least in this state). The difference between a "public place" and a "place open to the public" is not clear. Nonetheless, it is clear that this rule, where applicable, is designed to restrain the more aggressive approaches to fundraising.

In another state,[95] a charitable organization, or anyone acting on behalf of one, may not solicit contributions using any "uniformed personnel of any local, state or federal agency or department." There is, however, an exception for firefighters' solicitation in uniform. This rule is obviously designed to eliminate the pressure that is inherent when someone in governmental uniform solicits charitable gifts. Sometimes the distinction between charitable giving and "protection" is facially difficult to discern.

In another state,[96] it is a violation of law for a person to "[v]ote or use personal influence" as an officer or director of a charitable organization, where a majority of the board members of the charity are professional fundraisers or their designees, "on matters on which such officer or member has a financial or material conflicting interest."

In still another state,[97] one who solicits charitable contributions may not use the words "police," "law enforcement," "fireman," or "firefighter" unless a "bona fide police, law enforcement, rescue squad or fire department authorized its use in writing."

In yet another state,[98] the law provides that a charitable organization, professional fundraiser, or professional solicitor may not, in connection with a charitable solicitation, engage in a "deceptive act or practice." This term embraces an act or practice which "[h]as a capacity to mislead whether by affirmative representation or omission" and "[i]s misleading in a material respect in that it concerns information that is important to a person's decision to make a contribution or concerns information that is likely to affect a person's decision to make a contribution." This law also contains prohibited acts relating to the awarding of prizes, offering of sweepstakes and other promotional efforts, and use of advertising and promotional material.

In still another state,[99] an employee of a nonprofit corporation organized in the state or of a corporation authorized to do business in the state may not "own or operate or have any pecuniary interest, directly or indirectly, with any business enterprise relating to the product, aims, goals or purposes of the corporation as set forth in its charter." This rule prohibits, among other aspects of this matter, a nonprofit organization to which the rule is applicable, from having a for-profit subsidiary and having individuals work for both organizations. This prohibition flies in the face of the federal unrelated business income tax rules which, under today's law, encourage the "spin-off" of unrelated activities into separate, taxable organizations.

---

[95] Minnesota.
[96] New York.
[97] North Carolina.
[98] Maryland.
[99] Tennessee.

(e) Duplicative Rules

In some states, the list of prohibited acts includes acts that are violations of the charitable solicitation statutes in any event. For example, some states' laws make it a prohibited act for a charitable organization to use the services of an unregistered professional fundraiser or professional solicitor. Likewise, these states make it a violation of the law for a professional fundraiser or professional solicitor to provide services for an unregistered charity.

(f) Conclusion

For the most part, there is nothing wrong with the foregoing prohibitions. (As noted, some bump up against constitutional law barriers.) It may be supposed that the general public would agree with these restrictions. Thus, they are politically sound, which explains why many of them appear in several state charitable solicitation acts.

These rules, nonetheless, once again raise the question of uniformity. As fundraising becomes more and more national (and, for that matter, international), is philanthropy, and thus the country in general, served by these rules? The answer for some of them clearly is yes; the law is not going to tolerate fundraising for charity that openly misuses the name or symbol of another or otherwise engages in some form of misrepresentation. At the same time, these rules are being deployed to drive paid solicitors out of certain states, and in some instances micromanage the programmatic and financial affairs of charitable organizations.

These prohibitions, then, can amount to traps, subjecting a charitable organization—solely because it engages in fundraising—to rules that have little or nothing to do with fundraising. In some situations, these rules seem overly broad and inconsistent with free speech principles, yet there is no recorded instance of a challenge to them.

§ 7.6   FUNDRAISER'S CONTRACT

The term *professional fundraiser* is specifically defined under the charitable solicitation statutes of many states.[100] A one-word generic definition of a regulated professional fundraiser, however, is *consultant*—or, more formally in legal parlance, *independent contractor*. The latter term is used in law to differentiate someone from an *employee*. But, a key word in the term is *contractor*.

Almost all consultants have a written agreement with their clients. It is axiomatic, then, that a professional fundraiser should have a written contract with each client. In fact, several state laws require that the relationship between a charitable organization and a professional fundraiser (and/or professional solicitor) be the subject of a written contract.[101]

---

[100] See § 3.2(g); *supra* § 2.
[101] See § 3.11.

The reasons for a written agreement are obvious. The principal one is to avoid disagreements later about what each party to the arrangement is expected or required to do. At the other extreme, a written memorialization gives the substantive basis for litigation, should that prove necessary.

(a) Basic Elements

What are the basic elements that should be in a contract between a charitable organization and a professional fundraiser? The place to begin in answering that question is to enumerate the nine elements that any contract of this nature should contain. These are:

1. A description of the services to be provided by the party designated as provider of the services.

2. A statement of the fees to be paid by the party designated to receive the services.

3. A provision indicating legal ownership of any property that may be utilized or created in the contractual relationship.

4. A provision stating the duration of the agreement.

5. A provision stating the parties' ability to terminate the agreement.

6. A provision stating the state's law that governs interpretation of the agreement.

7. An indemnification clause, whereby one party agrees to absorb the costs of certain liabilities found against the other party.

8. A provision stating that the contract memorializes the entire agreement between the parties and cannot be amended except in writing by the parties.

9. A statement of the effective dates of the agreement.

These items, then, should be reflected in any contract between a charitable organization and a professional fundraiser. Many of the specific clauses will vary, of course, depending on the type of fundraising involved. But, irrespective of whether the fundraising involved will utilize direct mail, special events, annual campaign, planned giving, or whatever, or whether the fundraising is in the context of a capital campaign, the advice is the same: the professional fundraiser and the charitable organization are best served by a reasonably detailed statement of services to be provided, and of amounts and schedules of fees to be paid.

(b) Specific Elements

A clear statement about the amount and timing of payment of fees to the professional fundraiser will minimize, if not eliminate, the likelihood of fee disputes. If the fees are to be paid in phases, and the charitable organization is to make payment following the close of a phase, the professional fundraiser should be certain that the charity's payment obligations along the way are clearly stated. If the fundraiser desires timely payment, some monitoring and prodding of the charitable client may be necessary.

A full statement of services to be performed is the trick to avoiding breach-of-contract litigation. The professional fundraiser must thread a way between two extremes: not promise to do more than should or can be done, yet not make the statement of services so skimpy as to cause the charitable client to wonder what it is paying for.

The professional fundraiser should be cautious about verbal statements that may heighten expectations of the client. This type of statement may later arguably become part of the contractual relationship. Because of the potential validity of oral agreements, a clause confining the agreement to its written form is essential.

As noted earlier, it is important to state in a contract who owns each particular property that is to be used in connection with, or may be created as the result of, the provision of services. In the specific context of the professional fundraiser's contract, the ownership of these properties should be addressed: mailing lists, intellectual property, artwork, and photographs. Additional properties may also be the subject of an ownership clause.

It is rarely a good idea for a professional fundraiser to guarantee results to a charitable organization client. If this is done, however, the fundraiser should be certain that the guarantee—and any accompanying conditions—is well stated.

A charity's contract for professional fundraising assistance is a contract for what the law terms *specific performance*. This is particularly true where the charity is contracting with one or more individuals. The charitable organization involved should insist that the contract be nontransferable. These conditions are generally present when the professional fundraiser is a company. The charity is contracting with the particular firm and presumably has no interest in having the obligation to perform services transferred to another company (or to an individual). Indeed, the charity may insist that the contract specify the provision of services by one or more named fundraising professionals who are employed by or otherwise affiliated with the company.

When the fundraising professional is an individual, the contract should state that he or she is rendering services as an independent contractor, rather than as an employee.

If the agreement states that the charitable organization client is to provide an approval (e.g., of the text of a letter or the graphics of a brochure), the agreement should also state that the approval shall be in writing. The professional fundraiser should subsequently be certain that the approval is obtained on a timely basis, in writing.

(c) Fee Arrangements

Caution should be exercised by the fundraising professional in describing the fee arrangement. It is considered, in many quarters, to be unprofessional or even unethical for a fundraiser to be compensated on a contingent, percentage, commission, or similar fee basis. The antitrust laws, however, prevent enforcement of this type of prohibition, which usually is in a code of ethics. In general, a fee arrangement under these terms is by no means illegal, although in extreme instances a contingent fee arrangement may jeopardize the tax-exempt status of the client charity.[102]

Contingent fee arrangements exist in many ways in addition to a stated percentage of contributions received. For example, compensation tied to the number of solicitation letters mailed, where the fundraiser controls the timing and extent of the mailing, is a form of contingent compensation.[103]

A percentage limitation, in state law, on the amount of compensation that can be paid by a charitable organization to a professional fundraiser is unconstitutional.[104]

(d) Solicitor Status

Some state laws preclude a fundraiser from treatment as a professional fundraiser where the compensation is other than a "flat fixed fee" arrangement. If the compensation is otherwise, the professional may be classified as a professional solicitor. This adverse result can, in turn, lead to more stringent governmental regulation.[105] A trend in charitable lawmaking is to stringently monitor and restrict the activities of solicitors. This is being done by means of strenuous precampaign contract reviews, greater disclosure and reporting requirements, and more.

The description of services in the contract should be reviewed from this definitional standpoint. One of the essential elements of the definition of a professional solicitor is that the solicitor is an active participant in the solicitation process.[106] A professional fundraiser can all too easily fall into this trap by agreeing to, for example, mail the solicitation letters or place the solicitation telephone calls.

Another characteristic of a professional solicitor often is that this type of a person receives the gifts directly from the donors and remits the net amount to the charity. A professional fundraiser should be paid a fee by the charity, with the charity having received the gifts directly, and the contract should make that feature clear, or at least avoid any language contemplating the receipt of gift funds by the professional fundraiser.

(e) State Laws

It goes without saying that parties to a contract are expected to obey all applicable laws. It is not necessary, however, for the contract to contain language expressly reflecting that general obligation.

---

[102] See § 5.13.

[103] In Maryland, however, "[f]und-raising counsel shall not receive compensation from a charitable organization if the consideration or pecuniary benefit depends in whole or in part upon the number or value of contributions made as a result of the efforts of the fund-raising counsel."

[104] See §§ 4.1, 4.2.

[105] See § 3.7.

[106] See § 4.10.

Nonetheless, among the laws that directly relate to both the professional fundraiser and the charitable organization client are the various charitable solicitation acts. These laws impose registration, reporting, bonding, and other requirements on both professional fundraisers and their charitable clients.[107] Because the registration and reporting forms for both parties cross-refer, the professional fundraiser should at least contemplate a clause in the contract that requires both parties to notify each other of the states in which they are registered and of any adverse regulatory developments that may arise.

Many states mandate that certain elements be in the contract that a charitable organization has with a professional fundraiser and/or with a professional solicitor.[108] These laws usually also require retention of the contract in the records of the parties for a stated period of time (often three years after the conclusion of the solicitation) and often require filing of the contract with the state. (It must be reiterated that a charitable organization, professional fundraiser, and/or professional solicitor involved in a solicitation in one or more of these states is expected to comply with the requirements of each of them. Thus, for example, a contract with respect to a solicitation intended to take place in all of the states should contain all of the provisions mandated by each of these laws.)

Usually, this contract content requirement is more extensive with respect to a contract involving a professional solicitor.[109] For example, in one state,[110] the rule involving a charitable organization's contract with a professional fundraiser is that the contract must "contain such information as will enable . . . [the regulatory office] to identify the services the . . . [professional fundraiser] is to provide and the manner of his [or her or its] compensation." By contrast, under the law of this state, the contract between a charitable organization and a professional solicitor must "clearly state the respective obligations" of the parties, and "state the minimum amount which the charitable organization shall receive as a result of the solicitation campaign, which minimum amount shall be stated as a percentage of gross revenue."

One of the most extensive contract content requirements applicable to agreements between charitable organizations and professional solicitors is that of the state[111] in which the contract must contain provisions as to (1) an "estimated reasonable budget disclosing the target amount of funds to be raised over the contract period"; (2) the type and amount of projected expenses for the period; (3) the amount projected to be remitted to the charitable organization; (4) the period of duration of the agreement; (5) the "geographic scope" of the fundraising; (6) a description of the methods of fundraising to be employed; (7) a clause assuring "record keeping and accountability"; (8) if the contract provides that the fundraiser will retain or be paid a stated percentage of the gross amount raised, an estimate of the "target gross amount" to be raised and to be remitted to the charitable organization; (9) if the contract

---

[107] See §§ 3.3, 3.4, 3.6.
[108] See § 3.11.
[109] This is one of many reasons why it is critical for the fundraising professional to be certain of the states' distinctions between professional fundraisers and professional solicitors.
[110] Connecticut.
[111] Illinois.

provides for payment at an hourly rate for fundraising, the total estimated hourly amount and the estimated number of hours to be spent in fundraising; (10) the amounts of all commissions, salaries, and fees charged by the fundraiser, and its agents and employees; (11) the method used for computing these commissions, salaries, and fees; (12) if the fundraiser, its agents and employees, or members of the families of these persons own an interest in, manage, or are a supplier or vendor of fundraising goods or services, disclosure of that relationship; (13) if the foregoing rule is applicable, the method of determining the related supplier's or vendor's charges; and (14) the fact that the contract was approved and accepted by a majority of the directors of the charitable organization and by the president of the organization.[112]

One state[113] has a law prohibiting two provisions from appearing in a contract between a charitable organization and a professional fundraiser and/or professional solicitor: (1) the charitable organization may not use contributions from a solicitation for its charitable purposes until some or all fundraising expenses have been paid; and (2) the fundraiser or solicitor may engage in a direct mail or other solicitation in the name of the charitable organization for the purpose of "paying or offsetting preexisting fundraising expenses."

In one state,[114] the contract between a charitable organization and a professional fundraiser and/or professional solicitor (or commercial co-venturer) may be canceled by the charitable organization within 15 days after the date the contract is filed with the state; this right of cancellation must be stated in the agreement.

In another state,[115] if this type of a contract involves a "possibility" that the charitable organization "might ultimately receive" less than 50 percent of the gross receipts of the solicitation involved, that fact must be "specifically and prominently" disclosed in the contract (and orally, before execution of the contract).

(f) Conclusion

As is the case with all laws, everyone involved is presumed to know them. In the fundraising context, both the contracting charity and the professional fundraiser are expected to know and conform with the state charitable solicitation acts. Some of these laws mandate the contents of contracts between charities and fundraisers. These are independent obligations, bearing potential liabilities (e.g., civil penalties and/or injunctive relief) for both parties. Neither party should assume that the other is in compliance with these laws.

A professional fundraiser should have a solid, comprehensive, and professional-looking prototype agreement to present to prospective charitable clients. With a suitable agreement, a professional fundraiser can concentrate on development work without fear of the consequences of a defective contract.

---

[112] If a professional fundraiser "materially fails" to comply with this contract content requirement, the fundraiser is not entitled to collect or retain any compensation, commission, fee, or salary received in connection with the solicitation.
[113] Maryland.
[114] New York.
[115] North Carolina.

§ 7.7   A MODEL LAW

Fundraising regulation is experiencing great surges. More states are getting involved in charitable solicitation regulation, imposing registration, reporting, and a myriad of other requirements on charities and on those who assist them in the fundraising process. States that have formerly forgone the need for a fundraising law have suddenly decided their citizens now need one. States with fundraising regulation laws are making them tougher. Those who administer these laws—the state regulators—are often applying them with new-found vigor.

(a) Introduction

These state laws require compliance by charitable organizations that engage in fundraising. They apply to these charities by the law of the state in which the organization is located and by the law of the other states in which the organization solicits contributions. Further, these laws directly affect charities by reason of the regulation of those who help them raise funds, namely, professional fundraisers, professional solicitors, and commercial co-venturers.

Without doubt, these charitable solicitation acts are well intentioned. Fundraising abuses are taking place, and the public needs and deserves a place to lodge complaints and be assured that the frauds are prosecuted and punished. The law is clear that each state, in the exercise of its police power, has the authority to enact and enforce this type of law.[116] Indeed, the states' attorneys general have considerable inherent ability to regulate in this field even without the statutory backup.

Sometimes, however, the cure is worse than the disease. Fundraising regulation, as currently written, is one of those instances. The standard contemporary state charitable solicitation acts are unnecessarily complex, onerous, stringent, and burdensome. They are all too often prompted by a motive to "get" someone or are otherwise ill conceived. The laws are often written by legislators with a dim view of what they are doing and administered by bureaucrats with a negative view toward philanthropy. In too many states, the fundraising regulation zeal is leading to the creation of regulatory empires, staffed at taxpayers' expense by lawyers and investigators whose skills are sorely needed in far more important arenas of governmental service. The paperwork and the costs imposed on charities and their professional consultants often exceed any value these overreaching laws may provide.

The ridiculousness of this situation can be readily seen when one stops to think about what is being regulated. This is not a matter of public health and safety. This is not drug trafficking or nuclear waste disposal. This is charitable giving! Some public education and disclosure would go a long way toward solving the problems in this area. If individuals are uncertain about a particular charity and cannot obtain some wanted information, they have a simple solution: do not give.

---

[116] See § 4.2.

The shame of it all is that the legislators and regulators have lost sight of what they are regulating. Philanthropy is the lifeblood of the American system. Billions of dollars are annually provided for services that government cannot and will not supply. Giving to charity is what fuels this machine. But fundraising regulation is retarding the legitimate fundraising process, although gift solicitation is a constitutionally protected act of free speech. In short, fundraising for charity is overregulated—often unnecessarily, harmfully, and counterproductively.

Some believe that one answer to all of this regulation is a model charitable solicitation act.

(b) Model Law Elements

For a variety of reasons,[117] any uniformity and simplicity to be achieved in the field of fundraising regulation for charity are not likely to be the result of enactment of a model charitable solicitation act. Nonetheless, the idea of a model charitable solicitation act lingers in some quarters. Thus, this concept is worth a brief look.

A prototype charitable fundraising regulation law is, obviously, a matter of judgment. The preferred scope of such a law is in part dependent on one's view of the appropriate role of government. One person's thoughts about the components of a fundraising law are likely to be anathema to someone else. Thus, the elements presented here constitute one view. Having said that, it must be noted that all things are relative—these elements are not presented from the standpoint of what is ideal but from the standpoint of what is realistic. For some, the preferential situation is no regulation of charitable fundraising at all. The fact is that charitable fundraising regulation will continue, however, so the question is not whether this type of regulation should exist but what form it should take.

The dual concepts at play in the area of regulation of fundraising for charitable purposes are preapproval and disclosure.

(c) Preapproval

The core of the typical state charitable solicitation act is preapproval, in the sense that registration in advance of fundraising is required. This registration may be in the form of a license or permit, but the fundamental principle is the same: a charitable organization must acquire permission from the state before it can engage in fundraising within the jurisdiction. There is no reason to believe that this basic requirement will be eliminated; indeed, it is a quite reasonable requirement.

The objective to be obtained here is balance, this being the area where one requirement of registration can be more onerous than another because of the complexity of the application process. The number of questions asked and the substance of the answers requested are extremely relevant. What is reasonable in this setting is, again, a matter of judgment, but the model act would ask for

---

[117] See *infra* § 14.

only basic information needed to assure the state regulators of compliance with the overall statute.

The model charitable solicitation act would likewise require registration of professional fundraisers and professional solicitors. The model act would not require registration of commercial co-venturers, however, because this type of regulation places unnecessary burdens on the business involved and should be a matter of registration (and reporting) by the charitable organization.[118]

(d) Reporting

The model act would not have reporting separate from the registration requirement. Instead, the prototype law would provide that each registration (whether for charitable organizations, professional fundraisers, or professional solicitors) have a duration of one year. Reregistration each year would supply the state regulators with ample information required to enforce the statute.

Again, the contents of the reapplication should be reasonable, so as not to overly burden the regulated while still providing adequate and meaningful information to the regulators.

(e) Definitions

The typical state charitable solicitation statute opens with a series of definitions, and the model law would be no different.

A model statute in this field, however, would have a definition of the term *charitable organization* that is not so broad as to embrace entities and purposes that, in other law contexts, are not "charitable."[119] Likewise, the statute would be clear as to its scope: it would apply to the solicitation of charitable contributions, not to the sale of goods and services where some or all of the proceeds will be devoted to charitable ends.[120]

The model statute would also wrestle with and resolve the difficult matter of the proper definition of the terms *professional fundraiser* and *professional solicitor*.[121] These definitions would differentiate the consultant from the true solicitor, yet simultaneously avoid placing fundraising counsel in the category of solicitor simply because of use of the telephone and/or the mails in the raising of contributions for charitable purposes.

(f) Contracts and Bonds

The model charitable solicitation act would mandate written contracts between charitable organizations and professional fundraisers, professional solicitors, and/or commercial co-venturers. This requirement is for the benefit and protection of charitable organizations, if for no other reason. The mandatory

---

[118] See *supra* § 4.
[119] See §§ 2.1, 3.2(a).
[120] See *supra* § 1(f).
[121] See §§ 3.6, 3.7, 4.10; *supra* § 2.

contents of these contracts would be minimal, however, trusting the parties to strike a fair bargain.

Entities or individuals that have access to the contributed funds would have to be bonded (or otherwise deposit adequate security with the state). Thus, this requirement would not normally be imposed on professional fundraisers and commercial co-venturers.

(g) Compensation

The model law would not (indeed, lawfully, could not) contain a percentage limitation on allowable fundraising costs incurred by charitable organizations and/or on the amount payable to professional fundraisers or professional solicitors.[122] Nor would such a provision be made mandatory as part of contracts.

The model law would require the parties to disclose all compensatory arrangements as part of the registration process. This law, however, would not require a charitable organization, when soliciting contributions, to disclose fundraising costs at the point of solicitation, nor would it mandate disclosure of the use of professional fundraising counsel or a professional solicitor. The law would, nonetheless, require a charity to state on its solicitation materials that additional information is available from the charity on request and would require the charity to promptly respond to this type of inquiry.

(h) Exemptions

The model charitable solicitation act would have exemptions. Bona fide religious organizations; colleges, universities, and schools; most health care organizations; and foundations related to these entities would be exempt from the entirety of the statute. This can be done without becoming entangled in equal protection violations[123] and should be done to eliminate from the regulatory process those charitable organizations that simply are not "part of the problem."

Other types of entities may be exempted from the registration and reporting requirements because information about them is otherwise readily available in other ways. This exemption would extend to fraternal, veterans', and other membership groups that confine the solicitations to their membership.

The model law would not make availability of the exemptions conditioned on not using professional fundraisers or professional solicitors. This type of limitation is discriminatory, often petty, and in many instances counterproductive, because often these organizations should be encouraged to use, not penalized for using, professional assistance.

(i) Other

The model law should contain other provisions that could induce simplicity and uniformity, such as the reciprocal agreement provisions, uniform accounting

[122] See § 4.1.
[123] See § 4.5.

principles, use of other states' (and perhaps the federal government's) reporting forms, and simultaneous reporting dates.

(j) Prohibited Acts

One of the most difficult aspects of the states' charitable solicitation acts is the number of prohibited acts.[124] Some prohibited acts are reasonable and would be included in the model law. These include misrepresentation of the purpose of a solicitation, implied assertions of endorsement by the state, implied assertions of endorsement of the charity involved by others when that is not the case, use of names of others without consent, use of the name of a similar charitable organization, and making false or misleading statements.

The prototype statute would not, however, attempt to regulate collateral matters, such as the amount of money expended for fundraising or management, or the application of the funds raised in ways that may interfere with the ability of the charitable organization to further its charitable purposes. These matters are more appropriate for the inherent investigatory efforts of a state's attorney general or for the process of obtaining and retaining tax-exempt status.

(k) Sanctions

The model act would authorize the usual range of sanctions, including investigations, use of subpoenas, revocation of registrations, injunctions, civil penalties, and criminal penalties. It would not interfere with the usual and other inherent enforcement options for the states' attorneys general. It would not, however, authorize private actions.

(l) Commentary

The objective in constructing a model charitable solicitation act would be to achieve a balance between the exercise of a state's police power (to protect its citizens against fraudulent or otherwise misleading solicitations for gifts) and the free speech right of charitable organizations to solicit contributions for their support (and thus not unduly impede the process of funding programs that are vital to the very same citizens). There is no need to flood charitable organizations with paperwork requirements or to force fundraising consultants to adhere to rules meant for solicitors, when no useful purpose is achieved by doing so. Fundraising outlaws must be caught and punished, but not at the expense of hobbling bona fide charity.

The fact is that, all too often, these laws are not well thought out. The ideal would be a uniform and minimal prototype law in each of the states. The charities could then comply with the rules rather readily, and enforcement could focus on the true offenders.

Unfortunately, a model law does not seem feasible as a practical matter. Resolution of the present-day mess may be achieved through reciprocal agreements, uniform accounting principles, similar registration and reporting

---

[124] See § 3.13; *supra* § 5.

forms, and/or a company to facilitate compliance by charitable organizations and others. Still, when legislating in this area, some model framework is important, if only to minimize the more egregious provisions.

§ 7.8 STATE CHARITY OFFICIALS' CONCERNS ABOUT FUNDRAISING LAWS

The American Association of Fund-Raising Counsel, under the auspices of its Government Relations Committee, conducted a study among state charity officials.[125] One of the purposes of this study was to "[g]ather information about present laws affecting charities and charitable solicitation in the states and concerns of the State Charity Officials which the American Association of Fund-Raising Counsel Government Affairs Committee may use as it assists in the development of federal and state rules, laws, and regulations."[126] The study involved the laws of 25 states.[127]

Twenty-three of these states had laws requiring charitable organizations to register (including states where registration was governed by a charitable trust law). Twenty-two of these states required professional solicitors to register. Nineteen of these states required the registration of fundraising counsel. Four of these states required the registration of commercial co-venturers.[128]

Nineteen of these twenty-five states changed the laws governing charitable organizations and their activities. Fifteen of these nineteen states changed their laws in this regard during the five years preceding the study. The primary changes these states made to their laws expanded the registration and reporting requirements, brought the law into compliance with recent Supreme Court decisions (particularly in the area of disclosure requirements), and provided for increased enforcement of these laws.[129]

The state charity officials who were interviewed expressed two basic concerns. They involved (1) enforcement of these laws, including the ability to prosecute violations, and (2) provision of information to the public and protection of the public from deceptive fundraising practices.[130]

Two-thirds of the state charity officials interviewed would have changed their charitable solicitation laws if they could. The desired changes determined by this study included the following:

---

[125] "State Charity Officials' Concerns About State Laws Governing Charitable Organizations, Activities of Charities, and Charitable Solicitations," published by the American Association of Fund-Raising Counsel, Inc. (Mar. 1992) ("AAFRC Survey").
[126] *Id.* at 1.
[127] Alabama, California, Connecticut, Florida, Idaho, Illinois, Indiana, Kansas, Maryland, Massachusetts, Michigan, Minnesota, Missouri, New Hampshire, New Jersey, New Mexico, New York, North Carolina, North Dakota, Ohio, Pennsylvania, Rhode Island, South Carolina, Vermont, and Virginia.
[128] AAFRC Survey, at 4.
[129] *Id.*
[130] *Id.* at 5.

- Clarify definitions and, in some cases, expand the groups covered by the definitions

- Regulate commercial co-venturers

- Increase the reporting requirements

- Require accounting of all campaigns

- Eliminate the requirement of bonds for professional fundraising counsel

- Increase bonds for professional solicitors

- Increase the registration and reporting requirements for telemarketers

- Place a limit on fundraising costs

- Require disclosure of all fundraising costs

- Increase fines and penalties available as sanctions

- Increase registration fees

- Clarify charitable organizations' role in fundraising[131]

These state charity officials saw their role as collectors of information and enforcers of the law. As to the former, emphasis was placed on the registration and reporting requirements for charitable organizations, professional fundraising counsel, professional solicitors, and commercial co-venturers. As to the latter, the officials singled out investigating complaints, inaccuracies in registrations and reports, and abuses; working with local district attorneys; and litigating cases.[132]

The concerns of these state charity officials ranged over the following: fundraising costs, fraudulent solicitations, lack of accountability of charitable organizations, diversion of funds, telemarketing practices, direct mail design, and compliance with the laws.[133]

This study reflected some confusion by state charity officials over the role of fundraising counsel and solicitors. Frequently, professional fundraising counsel were identified as persons who plan and manage fundraising efforts for charitable organizations. They were also characterized, however, as persons who do not receive percentage compensation and as legal advisors. Characterizations of professional solicitors included telemarketers, direct mail suppliers, organizations "that conduct the campaign and do not involve the charitable organization," and persons who receive a percentage of the funds collected.[134]

The study produced some notable quotes from state charity officials. One observed that the distinction between professional fundraising counsel and professional solicitors "is very blurred." Another said that the term *professional*

---

[131] *Id.*
[132] *Id.* at 6.
[133] *Id.*
[134] *Id.* at 7–8.

solicitor is a "misuse of the word 'professional.' " Another defined a business involved in a commercial co-venture as a "[c]ommercial enterprise that hopes to make money by representing itself as benefiting charity."[135]

The study compiled a profile of the state charity officials, reflecting the following characteristics:

- Almost one-half of them have lived in the state in which they work for at least 30 years; another 20 percent of them have lived in the state for 10 to 20 years.

- Almost one-half of them have held their present position for less than five years; 16 percent have held the position for more than five years.

- These officials took their present position primarily because it was a promotion or career opportunity; other reasons given included the opportunity to return to the state, personal interest in public service, or personal interest in consumer issues.

- Fifty-six percent of the state charity officials have held other state positions.

- One-half of these officials report to the attorney general or to the person next in line to the attorney general.

- These officials have some combination of six types of employees reporting to them, namely, lawyers, investigators (who sometimes are law students), paralegals, financial analysts or certified public accountants, administrative assistants, or clerical personnel.

- Most of these officials have a staff of one to five persons; the actual range includes officials without a staff person and others with a staff of 31.

- Twenty of these officials have a law degree.

- Two of these officials have been employed by a nonprofit organization (one by a charitable organization).

- Ten of these officials presently sit or have sat on a board of trustees of a charitable organization.

- More than one-half of these officials have raised funds for a charitable organization.

- More than three-fourths of these officials contribute to charitable organizations.[136]

Other notable comments from these officials included a plea for teaching in law schools more information and law concerning charitable organizations; an observation that understaffing in the states means that the state regulators can address only a "small portion of the problem"; a view that the fundraising

---

[135] *Id.* at 9.
[136] *Id.* at 10–11.

industry "drives charities to the 90% cost fundraisers"; a request for organizations that represent fundraising professionals to "work more closely and more frequently with the Attorneys General"; and a lament about "charities that aren't charities: those which provide salaries to people and provide lucrative sources of business to direct mail houses."[137]

A subsequent survey of state officials, published early in 1994, concluded that "[w]hen it comes to charitable regulation, there are as many strategies as there are states."[138] The problems, as seen from the standpoint of the regulators, include inadequate staffing and other resources of the regulatory agencies, interstate regulation of charitable fundraising, and telephone scams.

Here are some of the responses to this survey by regulatory officials:

- Alabama—"Solicitation is basically unregulated in this state. We can prosecute [charitable organizations] using fraud statutes."[139]

- Arizona—The biggest problems are "[p]rofessional fundraisers who keep most of the money, as well as fake charities."[140]

- Arkansas—"Charities don't oversee their fundraisers."[141]

- California—"If you can't compel point-of-solicitation disclosures, then you don't have an effective way of communicating to the public any information about solicitations at the most critical point."[142]

- Connecticut—"As far as managers of these funds go, there is an enormous amount of self-dealing and personal enrichment."[143]

- Florida—The attorney general's office has "taken legal action with organizations that haven't registered when they are required to. We have taken legal action against organizations using the name of other organizations in their soliciting."[144]

- Georgia—One of the problems is the "small amount that goes to charity versus what goes to [the] solicitor."[145]

- Kansas—"There's been an increase in the number of complaints about telefunders."[146]

- Louisiana—"We hope the state will see the need for firmer legislation."[147]

---

[137] Id. at 12–14.
[138] Mehegan, Bush, and Nacson, "Charity Regulation Today: How the States See It," 8 *Nonprofit Times* (No. 3) 1 (Mar. 1994).
[139] AAFRC Survey, at 12.
[140] Id.
[141] Id.
[142] Id. at 12–13.
[143] Id. at 13.
[144] Id. at 13.
[145] Id. at 14.
[146] Id.
[147] Id.

- Maryland—The biggest problem is "[d]eceptive solicitations—especially direct mail and telemarketing."[148]

- Massachusetts—"There are a number of global questions we've faced with regard to board stewardship."[149]

- Minnesota—A major problem is "[t]rying to force organizations to report accurately on their financial statements," in that "[t]here's a lot of creative accounting going on."[150]

- Mississippi—"We are primarily dealing with day-to-day noncompliance resulting from people not knowing about the laws."[151]

- New Hampshire—"We have a very rigorous prosecution program. Whenever there's any telephone solicitation by registered or nonregistered groups, we investigate and take statements."[152]

- North Carolina—The state is "finding that a lot of small and medium-sized charities are being run like businesses—that is, run by one or two people rather than a board, or the board is not involved, or there is self-dealing in terms of benefits."[153]

- South Carolina—"It is tragic, but there are many organizations soliciting money in our state that give as little as 10 percent to the cause they claim to represent."[154]

- Tennessee—"Professional fundraisers are not making appropriate disclosures when soliciting."[155]

- Utah—"The people fundraising by phone are very crafty, very bright people, and the public tends to be very unsuspecting."[156]

- West Virginia—"There are some organizations that misrepresent what they stand for, what their major objective is, and they use the major part of their money for salaries and administration."[157]

It is evident from this survey that (1) despite all of the fundraising law at the federal and state level, many regulators want more; (2) the regulators are properly concerned about the amount of funds solicited that is actually devoted to charitable ends; and (3) the regulators believe that the boards of directors of the charitable organizations involved either are abusing the resources of the organization or fail to adequately oversee the solicitation process.

---

[148] *Id.* at 14–15.
[149] *Id.* at 15.
[150] *Id.*
[151] *Id.*
[152] *Id.* at 16.
[153] *Id.* at 17.
[154] *Id.* at 18.
[155] *Id.*
[156] *Id.*
[157] *Id.* at 19.

§ 7.9   STUDIES OF FUNDRAISING BY PROFESSIONAL SOLICITORS

Over recent years, there have been several studies of the results of fundraising by means of professional solicitors. They all lead to the same conclusion: a substantial portion of the funds raised, in the name of charity, were not devoted to charitable purposes. This conclusion was immediately followed by another: something inappropriate, immoral, or even illegal is occurring.

(a) California Studies

The office of the attorney general in California published two reports on charitable solicitations by *commercial fundraisers,* which emphasized the "generally high costs" of fundraising by these companies. The state's law defines a commercial fundraiser as an individual or noncharitable organization (usually a corporation) that is engaged in business for profit and that solicits charitable gifts in the name of a charitable organization. This person is what most states term a *professional solicitor.*[158]

(i) 1993 Report.   The first of these reports, dated December 1993, found that, during 1992, less than one-third of the total $88 million contributed to charities in California by means of commercial fundraisers was transferred to the charities. It stated that the "vast majority" of California's 63,000 registered charities did not use commercial fundraisers to solicit the public, relying instead on volunteers and staff. It further stated that most registered commercial fundraisers were operating within California law, which requires financial reporting to the attorney general and bonding.

These 63,000 charitable organizations in the state reported collections of over $32 billion in 1993. The $88 million figure previously noted was the collection total for 121 commercial fundraisers during 1992.

The report concluded: "One problem is that some commercial fundraisers who contract with charitable organizations for fundraising exact such high fees and costs that little of the funds remain for distribution to charity. Most alarming is the fact that every year, some portion of the donations intended for worthy charitable causes is siphoned away from legitimate charities by solicitors who mislead and defraud the public." Since 1990, the attorney general's office had prosecuted several commercial fundraisers, resulting in injunctions against continued solicitation, recovery of more than $850,000 in damages and restitution, dissolution of "sham" charities, and other corrective action.

The report's message was this: "[T]wo out of every three dollars donated by Californians [in 1992] to charities which used these commercial fundraisers did not go to charity at all, but instead went to solicitation expenses and to fundraiser profits."

Included as part of this report were three tables listing data with respect to individual charities and fundraisers. One table listed each charitable organization that sponsored a commercial fundraising campaign where 15 percent or

---

[158] See §§ 3.2(h), 4.10.

less of the funds raised actually went to charity. The total revenue involved in these campaigns was a little over $25 million, with the charities receiving a total of $2.5 million (an overall average of 10 percent). Twenty-three campaigns totaled exactly 15 percent for a charity; seven campaigns yielded 100 percent for the commercial fundraiser; in three campaigns, the fundraiser received all of the funds and the charity involved remained in debt to the fundraiser. In the worst of the cases, the commercial fundraiser received $53,623 and the charity still owed the fundraiser $25,574.

Another table listed all charitable organizations (483 of them) that were involved in commercial fundraising campaigns and ranked them by the percentage of donated money that went to charity. In five campaigns, 100 percent of the funds raised went to the charities; in less than 2 percent of the campaigns, 90 percent of the funds went to charities; in 13.46 percent of the campaigns, 90 percent of the funds raised went to commercial fundraisers. In 30 campaigns, 75 percent of the funds went to charities; in 252 campaigns, 75 percent went to commercial fundraisers.

The third table provided an alphabetical list of all charitable organizations that were involved in solicitations conducted by commercial fundraisers; for each campaign, it listed total revenue, revenue to charity, and the percentage of the funds that went to the charity.

The report was also being used by the attorney general's office as a public education effort. It contained this advice to prospective donors:

- Ask the solicitor if he or she works for a commercial fundraiser and is being paid to solicit.

- Ask [for] the name of the commercial fundraiser and for proof of registration.

- Ask the solicitor what percentage of your donation will actually go to charity.

- Ask for written information about the charity's programs and expenses to be mailed to you so that you can study it and decide if it merits your contribution.

- Contribute by writing a check to the name of the charitable organization.

- Do not give a credit card number to a telephone solicitor.

- Do not be pressured by the solicitor into giving money if you feel uncomfortable about the pitch or are being threatened.

- In case of threats or suspicious solicitations by telephone, hang up and report the solicitation to the consumer fraud division of the local district attorney's office.

The report encourages those who have been solicited in this manner to also report the solicitation to the local Better Business Bureau. It pointed out that multiple complaints will be forwarded by the district attorney's office and the Better Business Bureaus to the attorney general's office for investigation. It further noted that general information about charitable organizations can be obtained by contacting the Philanthropic Advisory Service in Arlington, Virginia.

What conclusions should be drawn from this study? Assuming the numbers are accurate, the report stated that the funds that went to commercial fundraisers "went to solicitation expenses and to fundraiser profits." The report, however, did not break out those separate amounts. That fact, coupled with references to "fraudulent or misleading charitable solicitations," "siphoning away" of charitable gifts, "prosecutions," and other inflammatory language, suggests to the casual reader that two-thirds of the $88 million donated in 1992 was wasted or stolen.

This cannot be true. These forms of fundraising are expensive, and a commercial business is entitled to make a reasonable profit. The wise giving guidelines presented by the attorney general are useful—along with the proposition that "a healthy dose of common sense utilized by the prospective donor is indispensable."

The tone of the report gave away the bias. For example, the report repeatedly stated that "less than one third" of the $88 million in contributions went to charity. The amount that went to charity was $29 million, which works out to 32.954 percent. Although that is, literally, less than one-third of the total, an objective presentation would have cast the $29 million as plain "one-third." Likewise, one table listed charities that used commercial fundraisers where "less than 15%" of the funds went to charity. A close look at the table, however, reveals that, in 23 instances, precisely 15 percent of the funds went to charity. These are, admittedly, somewhat minor differences, but they are part of a portrayal of commercial fundraisers that makes them look as rapacious as possible.

These observations are not offered as an apology for all commercial fundraisers. There undoubtedly is waste and fraud in some instances, but waste and fraud can take place within charitable organizations as well; was there no waste or fraud in any of the $32 billion raised without the services of commercial fundraisers? Charities that lawfully and by necessity use the services of commercial fundraisers are being unfairly singled out and implicitly disparaged. A more balanced report would have noted that not all commercial fundraisers are crooks and that a charitable organization doing this type of fundraising directly might likely incur the same or higher costs.

Thus, the problem, once again, comes down to reasonable costs of fundraising. The problem is not whether commercial fundraisers are used. Constitutional law forbids California from outlawing fundraising by means of professional solicitors. California thus tries to achieve the same end by publicizing (embarrassing?) the charities that use solicitors and by issuing misleading "public education" efforts such as this report. (Other states are doing the same thing by other means, such as stringent disclosure and other laws aimed only at solicitors, and/or high registration and reporting fees for them.[159])

---

[159] See § 3.7.

(ii) 1994 Report. The second of these reports on charitable solicitations by commercial fundraisers was published in December 1994. The purpose of this report was "to alert the public to a growing trend—solicitation for charitable causes by commercial fundraisers." It contained "data that informs the public about the generally high costs of solicitation by commercial fundraisers."

The report concluded that, during 1993, less than one-third of the total $192 million contributed to California charities by means of commercial fundraisers went to charities. The balance, the report stated, went to pay the fundraisers' expenses and salaries. It also observed that the "vast majority" of the state's 68,000 registered charities do not use the services of commercial fundraisers.

The percentage of solicited funds that commercial fundraisers returned to charity in 1993 varied from 100 percent to 0 percent. The study focused on 161 fundraisers. The total amount of charitable contributions received by the state's charities in that year was $36 billion.

As was the case with the previous study, this report was not objectively presented. It is literally true that "less than one-third" of the amounts received went to charity. The amount that went to charity ($63.38 million), however, was 33.01 percent. So the "less than" element entails a minuscule sum. An objective report would have said that "one-third" of the gifts went to charity, rather than implying that the amount was significantly less than one-third. If the amount that went to charity had been 34 percent, the attorney general probably would have reported that "nearly two-thirds" of the funds went for noncharitable purposes.

The report was silent about how the other two-thirds of the funds were spent; there was only vague reference to "solicitation expenses" and "fundraiser profits." The bias showed when it was stated that "only" $63 million went for charitable purposes. How much of the two-thirds went for actual expenses? What percentage of the $192 million went for fundraiser profits? Why should a commercial fundraiser not have a reasonable profit? Most likely, given this type of fundraising, it costs about $129 million to net $63 million. A fair report would have had some discussion of the fact that fundraising expenses are a fact and that reasonable fundraising expenses are permissible. But the two-thirds number just hangs in the air and suggests great impropriety. That is one of the reasons the free speech rules prohibit regulation of charitable fundraising using percentages.

The report failed to note that in only five instances was the amount to charity 0 percent. (In 12 situations, the charity ended up owing the fundraiser.) Indeed, on two occasions, the charity received 100 percent. (The same fundraising company was involved.) The rankings in the report, by percentile, are shown in Exhibit 7-1.

In another example of the unbalanced nature of this report, the attorney general prepared a table listing each situation where a charitable organization using a commercial fundraiser received less than 15 percent of the funds raised. This ostensibly entailed 134 instances. In fact, 16 of these situations concerned charities that received precisely 15 percent; they should not have been listed in this table. So, in truth, in 118 instances, charities received less than 15 percent of the contributions collected. This is 23 percent of the total

Exhibit 7.1.   Summary of California 1994 Report on Charitable Fundraising: 516 Campaigns

Amounts to Charity: Rankings by Percentile	Number of Campaigns
90 percent range	7
80	10
70	38
60	71
50	50
40	25
30	32
20	97
10	129
10–0	45
Less than 0	12

number of instances. Where is the table showing the instances—126 in number—where at least 60 percent of the funds raised went to charity? This is an extraordinary percentage, by the way, given this type of fundraising.

The report is filled with language such as "charity solicitation fraud." This is shrill and misleading terminology. The report does not make the case for one instance of "fraud." It presents only the income side; there is no discussion whatsoever about a basic truth in fundraising: there are expenses involved. This report is more than a clumsy manipulation of statistics; it is a misrepresentation of fact, a distortion of the realities of charitable fundraising, and a waste of the taxpayers' money. A follow-up investigation might well reveal that more public funds were diverted in the collection of these data and the publication of the report than were inappropriately paid to commercial fundraisers.

These two reports have useful and instructive elements; with minimal effort, they could also have been made more balanced and fair.

(b) Other Studies

Reports filed with the attorney general in the State of New York showed that commercial solicitors received more than 70 percent of money raised in charitable solicitations, according to an analysis published in early 2001. The data was for 1999; it reflected solicitor collections of $184.1 million and a net to charity of $55.3 million (or 26.5 percent). Of the 581 campaigns involved, about one-fourth of them resulted in less than 20 percent of the contributions passing to charity; the highest percentage was 95 percent.

This analysis also reported that, according to reports filed with the attorney general and secretary of state in the State of Washington, slightly less than one-half of funds raised was transferred to charitable organizations. Again, for 1999, professional solicitors reported raising about $223 million, of which $112 million were retained by the solicitors. Of the 90 solicitors involved, 23 generated less than 20 percent or less for charities; the highest percentage was 97 percent.[160]

A subsequent study, viewing the data from a national perspective, concluded that annual contributions to charity by means of professional solicitors total about $1 billion, with approximately one-third of that amount passing to charitable organizations.[161] This data was derived from the records of nine states[162] and covered the period 1995–1999. Some of the findings were as follows:

- Overall, the charitable organizations using the services of professional solicitors garnered about 35 percent of the contributions.

- The smallest charities—those with annual revenue of less than $1 million—received a median of 29 cents per dollar raised.

- The largest charities—those with annual revenue of at least $10 million—received a median of 34 cents per dollar raised.

- Midsize charitable organizations received a median of 34 cents per dollar raised.

- Charities that received the lowest level of gifts were those that provide human services, including veterans' organizations (17–18 percent).

- Charities that received the highest level of gifts were colleges and universities (62 percent), public broadcasting stations (60 percent), and arts groups (49 percent).

- About two-thirds of the money raised by professional solicitors came from campaigns conducted locally or statewide.

(c) Commentary

These and other analyses often employ the word "only," as in the smallest charities "received a median of only 29 cents for every dollar raised."[163] That perception obviously reflects a bias. The factors affecting fundraising costs have been discussed.[164] Two of the principal factors are the size of the charitable organization and the extent to which the charity is known to the public. It may be that for a small charity a 29 percent net gift amount is reasonable. By contrast, colleges and universities received a 62 percent net amount, which is amply reasonable for this type of fundraising. (The percentages for special events, for example, can be much lower.) The larger charities also usually have better records, including donor lists, rendering the work of the solicitor far

---

[160] These reports were summarized at XIII *Chron. of Phil.* (No. 6) 33 (Jan. 11, 2001). The New York report is, not exactly objectively, titled "Pennies for Charity."
[161] "Calling Solicitors to Account," XIII *Chron. of Phil.* (No. 12) 1 (April 5, 2001).
[162] California, Connecticut, Minnesota, New Hampshire, New York, North Carolina, Ohio, Pennsylvania, and Virginia.
[163] "Calling Solicitors to Account," *supra* note 161, at 1.
[164] See § 4.1.

more efficient. Indeed, the most recent of the studies summarized previously stated that it "supports the idea that many charities with broadly popular, high profile missions, such as colleges and big arts groups, tend to have contracts under which they collect a significant portion of the money raised by commercial solicitors."[165]

What the studies do not show is the amount or percentages of expenses and profits. Telemarketing, for example, entails telephone equipment, compensation to callers, telephone and mailing expenses, and check handling costs. Regardless, this study concluded—without providing any statistics—that "some" solicitors pay "low" returns to charities, while "minimizing" expenses and obtaining "healthy" profits. Instances of "unscrupulous" solicitors were cited.

This study observed that the "average person ends up thinking that all commercial solicitors are engaged in scams."[166] How can that be otherwise, given the tone and language used in government reports and media analyses?

§ 7.10 CHARITY AUCTIONS

Considerable confusion and misunderstanding surround the federal tax law applicable to the conduct of charity auctions, particularly regarding application of the charitable gift substantiation and quid pro quo contribution rules.[167] This uncertainty was manifested in two articles in a personal finance magazine, where it was written that a "special circle of tax hell has been carved out for you if you're involved in one of today's hottest fundraising activities: charity auctions."[168]

This body of law has seven elements:

- The tax treatment, with respect to the charitable organization, of the funds expended by the patrons at the auction

- The charitable contribution deduction available to those who contribute something to be auctioned

- The charitable contribution deduction that may be available to those who acquire an item at a charity auction

- The substantiation rules

- The quid pro quo contribution rules

- The state sales tax rules

- The federal tax rules for reporting the event to the IRS

---

[165] *Id.* at 27. Note that the observation using the word "only" is on page 1, while this observation is tucked away on page 27. Also note use of the word "idea," as opposed to, say, "fact." Indeed, a subheadline for the analysis was: "Small Charities Are Most Apt to Be Swindled by Solicitors" (*id.* at 30).

[166] *Id.* at 31.

[167] See §§ 5.3, 5.4.

[168] "Taxing new rules for charitable giving," 48 *Kiplinger's Pers. Fin. Mag.* (No. 5) 140 (July 1994).

(There can be different and additional complexities when the fundraising event is a lottery, raffle, or other game of chance.)

(a) Charity Auctions as Businesses

The federal tax law envisions a tax-exempt organization as being a bundle of *businesses.* For this purpose, a *business* is any activity that entails the production of income from the sale of goods or the performance of services.[169] An activity does not lose its identity as a business merely because it is carried on within a larger aggregate of similar activities or within a larger complex of other endeavors of the organization.[170]

Some businesses are *related* ones, in that the conduct of them helps advance the organization's exempt purposes (other than simply through the generation of funds). Other businesses are *unrelated,* because the conduct of them does not relate to achievement of a charitable, educational, or similar purpose; this type of business usually is carried on solely for the purpose of generating income.[171]

Thus, a charity auction is a business; it is the performance of a service (selling items). These auctions are not inherently exempt functions; in the case of private schools, for example, the conduct of an auction is not an educational undertaking. Consequently, the conduct of a charity auction is the conduct of an unrelated business by the charitable organization.

The net revenue of a charity auction would, therefore, be taxable as unrelated business income were it not for one or more exceptions. The principal exception relates to the fact that, for an unrelated business to create taxable income, it must be *regularly carried on.*[172] An annual auction held by a charitable organization is not an activity that is regularly carried on; thus, the net income is not taxable. (If a charity were to hold an auction every weekend, however, this exception would not be available.)

Another important exception is the one for businesses that constitute the sale of merchandise, substantially all of which has been donated to the exempt organization.[173] This exception was written for thrift shops, but it is available in the case of auctions, irrespective of their frequency.

The third exception is for businesses in which substantially all the work in carrying it on is performed by volunteers.[174] If a charity auction is conducted entirely by volunteers, the net income from it is not taxed. (Some charity auctions are able to rely on all three exceptions.)

Thus, it is almost inconceivable that the "net income" realized as the result of a charity auction would be subject to unrelated income taxation, but only because of some specific statutory exceptions.

---

[169] IRC § 513(c). See § 5.7(a)(iii).
[170] *Id.*
[171] See § 5.7(a)(iv). Chapter 5 § 7(a)(v).
[172] IRC § 512(a)(1). See § 5.7(a)(iv).
[173] IRC § 513(a)(3). See § 5.7(a)(vi).
[174] IRC § 513(a)(1). See § 5.7(a)(vi).

(b) Charitable Contribution Deductions—Donors of Items to Be Auctioned

In general, the contribution of an item to a charitable organization, for the purpose of being auctioned, creates a charitable contribution deduction. The usual rule is that the deduction is equal to the fair market value of the contributed property.[175] (This analysis is based on the assumption that the charity holding the auction is a public charity and not a private foundation.[176])

There are, however, some wrinkles here. If the item donated is tangible personal property that has appreciated in value, the charitable deduction is confined to the donor's basis in the property.[177] This is because the gift was made for an unrelated purpose—resale by the donee.[178]

If the item donated has a value in excess of $5,000, the deduction depends on a bona fide appraisal.[179] An appraisal summary must be included with the donor's tax return. The charitable organization must report the sale to the IRS (assuming the auction took place within two years of the gift).[180]

There is no charitable deduction for a gift of the right to the use of property.[181] Thus, for example, if someone contributes the opportunity to use his or her vacation property for two weeks, there is no charitable deduction equal to the fair rental value of the property. (Moreover, the period of time the property is used by the winning bidder must be considered by the donating individual(s) as personal time for purpose of the rules regarding the deductibility of business expenses in connection with the property.[182])

There is no charitable deduction for a gift of services.[183] Thus, for example, if a lawyer donates his or her will-drafting services, there is no charitable deduction equal to the hourly rate the lawyer would charge for his or her time in preparing the will. Notwithstanding this rule in the regulations, there would be no deduction in any event because there is no deduction for gifts of property created by the donor.[184]

Further, special rules apply when a business makes a charitable contribution of items from its inventory,[185] a charitable contribution of scientific property used for research,[186] and a charitable contribution of computer technology and equipment for elementary and secondary school purposes.[187]

[175] See § 5.14.
[176] See § 5.15.
[177] IRC § 170(e)(1)(B)(i).
[178] Reg. § 1.170A-4(G)(2)(ii).
[179] Reg. § 1.170A-13(c).
[180] IRC § 6050L.
[181] Reg. § 1.170A-7(a)(1).
[182] Rev. Rul. 89-51, 1989-1 C.B. 89.
[183] Reg. § 1.170A-1(g).
[184] IRC §§ 170(e)(1)(A), 1221(3).
[185] IRC § 170(e)(3).
[186] IRC § 170(e)(4).
[187] IRC § 170(e)(6).

The substantiation rules (see following discussion) apply with respect to gifts of items that have a value of $250 or more and are auctioned by a charitable organization.[188]

(c) Charitable Contribution Deductions—Acquirers of Items at an Auction

The law in the area of charitable giving in general once was that, for a payment to a charitable organization to be deductible as a gift, the payor had to have a *donative intent.* The law, however, has shifted to a more mechanical computation: in general, deductible payments to a charity are those that exceed the fair market value of anything that the "donor" may receive in return, other than items of insignificant value. Nonetheless, in the auction and comparable contexts, the *donative intent* rule still applies: no part of a payment to a charitable organization that is in consideration for goods or services can be a contribution unless the person intended to, and did, make a payment in an amount that exceeds the fair market value of the goods or services.[189]

Whether one who acquires an item at a charity auction is entitled to a charitable contribution deduction is another matter. Thus, it was correct to observe that, regarding the enactment of the substantiation and quid pro quo rules (see following discussion): "it was widely assumed that Congress was after folks who buy stuff at auctions and then deduct most or even all of the price as a charitable contribution."[190]

There are two schools of thought here; both are facially valid. One is that the auction is the marketplace, so that whatever is paid for an item at an auction is its fair market value at that time. Pursuant to this view, the transaction is always a purchase in its entirety; there is no gift element and thus no charitable deduction.

The other school of thought is that an item auctioned at a charity auction has a fair market value, irrespective of the amount expended for it at an auction. This approach would allow a charitable deduction for an amount paid at a charity auction that is in excess of the value of the property.

In actual practice, most items disposed of at a charity auction are acquired for a value that does not involve any gift element (because the amount paid is roughly equal to the value of the item or perhaps is less), and thus there is no charitable deduction. If a person wants to claim a charitable deduction, the burden of proof is on the putative donor, who must prove that the amount paid was in excess of the property's fair value.

This burden of proof can probably be met when it is relatively easy to prove the fair market value of the item, such as an appliance or automobile. Where the value of an item is difficult to discern, however, it will be arduous for a patron of the auction to convince the IRS that a portion of the amount paid was a deductible gift.

---

[188] In general, see § 5.3.
[189] Reg. § 1.170A-1(h)(1).
[190] "Taxing new rules for charitable giving," *supra* note 168, at 140.

The determination of the fair market value of an item is the work of appraisers. Essentially, they look at comparables. If a house sold for $200,000, all other factors being equal, that is the value at the time of sale of the neighboring houses. Thus, the critical factor is the determination of the *market*. This involves geographical, economical, and timing elements.

Some disparage the idea that the value of an item sold at a charity auction is set at the time of that purchase.[191] There cannot be any dispute, however, that the auction is a market. Thus, one must logically assume that the price paid for an item at a charity auction is its fair market value. This is particularly the case where the value is difficult to ascertain commercially. For example, if a charitable organization auctioned an automobile with a sticker price of $30,000, and received $35,000 for the vehicle, it is reasonable to assume that the individual who acquired the vehicle is entitled to a charitable deduction of $5,000. If, however, a charitable organization auctioned a football, signed by members of the team, which the organization valued at $500 and which sold for $2,000, who is to say what the value of that package was at the time of the auction? The organization may have made a good-faith estimate of $500 of value, but that may not necessarily be the true value of the item under the circumstances of its sale. If the auction was the marketplace, the fair market value of the football was $2,000, not $500.

The substantiation rules (see following discussion) apply with respect to gifts made in the context of acquiring an item auctioned by a charitable organization, assuming the gift element is $250 or more.

(d) Substantiation Rules

The position of the IRS on charity auctions can be found in rulings as far back as 1967.[192] There is little question, however, that charitable organizations and their donors have not, over the intervening years, understood the IRS's stance, which, frankly, has been quite clear and sensible. Consequently, Congress believed it had to enact legislation in this area and, in 1993, it did.

At this point in the analysis, it is necessary to place the subject in a context. Can it honestly be said that an individual who attends an auction sponsored by a charitable organization is there to make a gift? Someone who wants to contribute to the charitable organization can obviously do so, without attending the charity's auction. Individuals participate in the auction to help support the charitable organization *and* to purchase items.[193]

The statutory substantiation rule is this: A donor who makes a separate charitable contribution of $250 or more in a year must, to be able to deduct the gift, obtain the requisite written substantiation from the donee charitable organization.[194] This substantiation must be an acknowledgment of the gift and

---

[191] *Id.* at 142–143.
[192] See § 5.2.
[193] This is reflected in "Update: Charity Auctions," 48 *Kiplinger's Pers. Fin. Mag.* (No. 7) 8 (July 1994); at the beginning, the reference was to "participants at charity auctions"; toward the close of the article, there was reference to "the object purchased."
[194] IRC § 170(f)(8).

must contain the following information: (1) the amount of money and a description (but not the value) of any property other than money that was distributed; (2) whether the donee organization provided any goods or services in consideration, in whole or in part, for any money or property contributed; and (3) a description and good-faith estimate of the value of any goods or services so provided.[195]

These rules are applicable with respect to gifts of items to be auctioned (assuming a charitable contribution deduction is available or desired). Also, as far as acquisition of an item at a charity auction is concerned, if there is no gift element, it is clear that the rules do not apply.

Where, however, (1) the patron at a charity auction believes that he or she had made a charitable contribution in the course of acquiring an item, (2) the ostensible gift element is $250 or more, and (3) a charitable deduction is desired, the rules come into play. The "donor" must notify the charitable organization that he or she believes that a gift was made at the auction, with the intent of receiving the necessary acknowledgment. If the charity agreed that a gift was made, it would issue a written substantiation showing the amount that was "contributed" (here, the full amount of the winning bid) and a description and good-faith estimate of the value of the item acquired. The difference, then, would be the amount deductible as a charitable gift.

The process would not function so smoothly if the charitable organization believed that no part of the payment is a charitable gift. It might refuse to issue the acknowledgment or refuse to commit itself to a good-faith estimate of the value of the item auctioned. As a practical matter, however, relations with donors and patrons are such that a charity usually cannot be that cavalier.

These rules will place considerable pressure on charitable organizations. To return to the previous example, is the organization willing to issue a substantiation acknowledgment that the auctioned football has a value of $2,000, so that the winning bidder can claim a charitable deduction of $1,500? A charitable organization that knowingly provides a false written substantiation to a donor may be subject to the penalty for aiding and abetting an understatement of tax liability.[196]

(e) Quid Pro Quo Rules

Congress has required this: when a person makes a gift to a charitable organization in excess of $75 and receives something of material value in return, the charitable donee is to make a good-faith estimate of the value of the item and notify the donor that only the difference between the fair market value of the item and the amount paid for it (if any) is deductible as a charitable contribution.[197]

Here, the application of the tax rules in the charity auction context becomes less pellucid. Superficially, the quid pro quo rules would seem to apply in the charity auction setting where the amount transferred exceeds $75 and there is a gift element.

[195] IRC § 170(f)(8)(B).
[196] IRC § 6701.
[197] IRC § 6115.

A *quid pro quo contribution* is a payment "made partly as a contribution and partly in consideration for goods or services provided to the payor by the donee organization."[198] Thus, it can be argued that the purchase of an item at an auction, at a price known to be in excess of the fair market value of the item, is both a contribution and a payment made in consideration of something (a purchase).

Nonetheless, if the donor and the donee are in harmony, and if the amount paid at an auction exceeds $75, the charitable organization can make the necessary disclosure, notifying the donor that the deductible amount is confined to the payment less the value of the item. It is important that the charitable organization be correct in these regard, because of the penalties imposed.[199]

(f) Sales Tax Rules

As discussed, every transaction at an auction is, in whole or substantial part, a *purchase.* Thus, the charity is engaging in *sales,* which can trigger application of the state's sales tax. This is a state-by-state matter, and thus it is difficult to generalize on the point, other than to say that the law of the applicable state should be reviewed.

A state is likely to exempt charitable organizations from having to pay the state's sales tax. This exemption, however, does not mean that the entity is exempt from the requirement of collecting the sales tax.

(g) Reporting Rules

A charity auction is a charitable organization's fundraising event; it is a *special event.* As such, it is reported on Form 990, Part I, line 9, as a *special fundraising event* (unless Form 990EZ is used or the organization is exempt from the requirement of filing an annual information return).[200]

Line 9a is where the gross revenue from the auction (other than any amounts the charity is treating as contributions) is reported. Direct expenses are reported on line 9b. Net income from the event is reported on line 9c.

For purposes of computing the $25,000 filing threshold, only the amount of net income need be taken into consideration.

§ 7.11 COURT OPINION CONCERNING SLIDING-SCALE REGISTRATION FEES

The U.S. Court of Appeals for the Fourth Circuit ruled, in 1994, that where a state charitable solicitation act[201] requires a sliding-scale registration fee based on a charitable organization's nationwide level of public contributions in the

---

[198] IRC § 6115(b).
[199] IRC § 6701. According to the tax regulations, a patron at a charity auction can rely on the charity's estimation of value of an item unless the patron knows or has reason to know that the estimate is unreasonable or is otherwise in error (Reg. § 1.170A-1(h)(4)(ii)).
[200] In general, see § 5.9.
[201] In this instance, the one in effect in Maryland.

prior year, the requirement is lawful.[202] The Fourth Circuit let the charitable community down with this court opinion.

First, this appellate court cast the ability of a charitable organization to solicit funds in a state as a "privilege."[203] That is not true; charitable fundraising is the exercise of a "right," and that right is protected by constitutional law principles.[204] The court's overall analysis was flawed because of this faulty lens through which it viewed the facts.

The court found that the registration fee structure was a "constitutionally sound" user fee, representing a "fair, if imperfect, approximation of the cost of using . . . [the state's] facilities and services for the charity's benefit."[205] The facts were said to show that the state's costs of "monitoring charities increase with larger charities."[206] This cost increase, the court observed, "arises because larger charities generally generate more registration and renewal documents to review, require more research relating to administrative, management, and membership activities, and give rise to more public inquiries, more paperwork requiring data entry, and more investigative effort."[207] Thus, "because a charity's fee is directly related to the workload the charity is expected to create for the Secretary, the sliding-scale fee is a fair, if imperfect, approximation of . . . [the state's] costs."[208]

This lame rationalization for the sliding-scale fee does not make sense. Why did the court passively accept the assertion that larger charitable organizations generate more paperwork for the bureaucracy than smaller ones? The opinion is silent about any supporting facts for this conclusion, and the conclusion seems counterintuitive. It stands to reason just as soundly that the larger charitable organizations will be better known, better organized and staffed, and better advised.

Might not the "facts" relied on by the court be precisely the opposite? The larger, more recognizable charities may elicit less inquiry from the public and thus require less investigative effort. The larger charities are likely to entail less "research." Their registration and renewal documents are likely to be more properly prepared and complete, causing fewer review and follow-up problems. How can larger amounts reflected in numbers cause more "data entry" time? It takes as much time to enter into a database "$100,000" as it does "$900,000." There will always be exceptions, of course, but these generalities are at least as valid as those placidly accepted by the court.

The court did not address the point of what would happen to soliciting charities if all states were to adopt this fee approach. Fifty-one jurisdictions (including the District of Columbia) charging $200 a year is an annual cost of $10,200.

---

[202] *Center for Auto Safety, Incorporated* v. *Athey, supra* note 1. (This court opinion is summarized in § 4.12.)
[203] *Id.* at 144.
[204] See, principally, § 4.3.
[205] *Center for Auto Safety, Incorporated* v. *Athey, supra* note 1, at 143.
[206] *Id.*
[207] *Id.*
[208] *Id.*

The court's treatment of the user fee rationale is the most ludicrous. Conceding that the state's fee, "although not the typical user fee, nonetheless fits comfortably within the user fee category," the court held that "charities seeking to solicit in . . . [the state] use the state's apparatus for regulating charities."[209] This, the court ascertained, is a "benefit,"[210] in the form of the "privilege of soliciting in . . . [the state] where donor confidence is enhanced owing to the state's regulation of charities."[211]

Where does one begin to assess these laughable conclusions? How about the thought that charities soliciting in the state "use" the state's "apparatus for regulating charities"? Forced on them while they kick and scream is the reality; "use" is not. The regulation is compulsive and burdening; it is not a "benefit."

The amorphous definition of *user fee* wrought by the court is nonsensical. The law is that this type of fee is one collected by a government as reimbursement for use of government-owned or government-provided facilities or services. The court wrote that the registration fee structure is a user fee because it represents a "fair, if imperfect, approximation of the cost of using . . . [the state's] facilities and services for the charity's benefit."[212] If these "benefits" combine to warrant a user fee, then every tax is a user fee. In contorting this registration fee into a user fee, the court basically nullified any meaningful distinction between user fees and general revenue taxes.

How about the precept that the state's regulation of charities "enhances donor confidence," so that the "apparatus" is a "benefit?"[213] Oh, were that the case! The fact is that the state's statute and the rest of the charitable solicitation acts do no such thing. If "donor confidence" is so great, why the need for higher registration fees to pay for responses to public inquiries, investigations, and research? There is no evidence whatsoever that these laws enhance donor confidence. If anything, they undercut donor confidence by fooling the citizenry into thinking something meaningful is being done; they enhance donor cynicism.

A footnote in this opinion states that the state law provides charities with another benefit: "eliminating illegitimate charities."[214] Come again? Then why all the need for the state administration, monitoring, investigations, and enforcement? In a separate (and wholly inconsistent) footnote, the court observes that the "largest single activity in the Office of the Secretary of State is the administration and enforcement of [the state's] laws governing charitable solicitations."[215] With all these illegitimate charities gone, who is the state regulating?

Courts are supposed to rule based on facts, not suppositions. The absurdity continued as the court wrote about still another putative "benefit" to charitable organizations from this "apparatus": this law is causing the level of charitable giving to increase, "as citizens are likely to donate to charities that have been investigated and found to be reputable."[216] There is absolutely no

---

[209] *Id.*
[210] *Id.*
[211] *Id.* at 144.
[212] *Id.* at 143.
[213] *Id.* at 144.
[214] *Id.* at 144, note 9.
[215] *Id.* at 143, note 8.
[216] *Id.* at 144, note 9.

factual basis for this silliness. Is a charitable organization considered "reputable" and thus more entitled to gift support if it has weathered an investigation by a state agency?

The court offers one more appalling assertion—another "benefit." The charities soliciting in the state "may" find that their "share of available funds" will increase.[217] Why? Because, "as illegitimate charities are weeded out, the amount of available funds will be spread among a smaller pool of charities."[218] This type of factless analysis and writing is not respectable for a first-year law student, let alone judges of a federal court of appeals.

As charitable organizations around the country struggle under the annual registration, reporting, disclosure, and other burdens the many state charitable solicitation acts impose, they will draw no comfort from the thought that they are in fact being "benefited."

7.12 FUNDRAISING AND PRIVATE INUREMENT DOCTRINE

As discussed,[219] the U.S. Court of Appeals for the Seventh Circuit reversed the U.S. Tax Court, concluding that a fundraising company was not an insider, for private inurement purposes,[220] with respect to the public charity known as the United Cancer Council (UCC).[221]

The facts of this case were summarized earlier. Basically, UCC was (it has since become bankrupt) a public charity, so recognized by the IRS in 1969. In 1984, UCC entered into a five-year direct mail fundraising contract with the company. While UCC received about $2.25 million as the result of the fundraising, the company received more than $4 million in fees. The parties had co-ownership rights in UCC's mailing list.

The Tax Court held that UCC paid the fundraising company excessive compensation, that the company exploited its rights over the list for its private gain, that the company was an insider with respect to UCC, and that this relationship created private inurement. The court upheld the IRS's retroactive revocation of UCC's exempt status in 1990, to the date in 1984 when the contract began.

The Court of Appeals grounded its findings on the premise that the "Tax Court's classification of [the fundraising company] as an insider of UCC was based on the fundraising contract."[222] That is, the focus was on the contract's terms. The Tax Court and the IRS were characterized as contending that the "contract was so advantageous to [the fundraising company] and so disadvantageous to UCC that the charity must be deemed to have surrendered the control of its operations and earnings to the noncharitable enterprise that it had hired to raise money for it."[223]

---

[217] Id.
[218] Id.
[219] See § 5.6, note 170.
[220] See § 5.13.
[221] United Cancer Council, Inc. v. Commissioner, 165 F.3d 1173 (7th Cir. 1999).
[222] Id. at 1176.
[223] Id. at 1175.

The appellate court wrote that "[f]undraising has become a specialized professional activity and many charities hire specialists in it."[224] It continued: "If the charity's contract with the fundraiser makes the latter an insider, triggering the inurement clause of section 501(c)(3) and so destroying the charity's tax exemption, the charitable sector of the economy is in trouble."[225]

UCC's "sound judgment" in entering into the contract with the fundraising firm was questioned by the appellate court. The court wrote that UCC "drove (so far as the record shows) the best bargain that it could, but it was not a good bargain."[226] Nonetheless, the court continued, the private inurement proscription "is designed to prevent the siphoning of charitable receipts to insiders of the charity, not to empower the IRS to monitor the terms of arm's-length contracts made by charitable organizations with the firms that supply them with essential inputs, whether premises, paper, computers, legal advice, or fundraising services."[227] The Tax Court and IRS's position, wrote the court, "threatens to unsettle the charitable sector by empowering the IRS to yank a charity's tax exemption simply because the Service thinks its contract with its major fundraiser is too one-sided in favor of the fundraiser, even though the charity has not been found to have violated any duty of faithful and careful management that the law of nonprofit corporations may have laid upon it."[228]

The court said it could not find anything in the facts to support the "theory" that [the fundraising company] seized control of UCC and by doing so became an insider."[229] Said the Court: "There is nothing that corporate or agency law would recognize as control."[230] It wrote that the Tax Court used the word *control* "in a special sense not used elsewhere, so far as we can determine, in the law, including the federal tax law."[231] (The Tax Court defined an *insider* as a person who has "significant control over the [charitable] organization's activities."[232])

The appellate court concluded that "[t]here was no division of charitable revenues to an insider here, nothing that smacks of self-dealing, disloyalty, breach of fiduciary obligation or other misconduct of the type aimed at by a provision of law that forbids a charity to divert its earnings to members of the board or other insiders."[233]

The Seventh Circuit remanded this case to the Tax Court for consideration in light of the doctrine of private benefit. Regarding this remand, the court wrote that the "board of a charity has a duty of care . . . and a violation of that duty which involved the dissipation of the charity's assets might (we need not decide whether it would—we leave that issue to the Tax Court in the first instance) support a finding that the charity was conferring a private benefit, even

---

[224] *Id.* at 1176.
[225] *Id.*
[226] *Id.* at 1178.
[227] *Id.* at 1176.
[228] *Id.* at 1179.
[229] *Id.* at 1178.
[230] *Id.*
[231] *Id.*
[232] *United Cancer Council, Inc.* v. *Commissioner,* 109 T.C. 326, 388 (1997).
[233] *United Cancer Council, Inc.* v. *Commissioner, supra* note 221, at 1179.

if the contracting party did not control, or exercise undue influence over, the charity. This, for all we know, may be such a case."[234] The case was ultimately settled, so the private benefit doctrine was never applied to its facts.

This opinion, as these things go, is extraordinary; it is wrong in so many ways, both procedurally and substantively. Regarding procedure, it is common for a federal appellate court opinion to begin by discussing the appropriate standard for the court's review. It is noteworthy that the Seventh Circuit skipped this step in its *UCC* opinion.

Yet here is what this same court had to say on the subject in 1984: "The Tax Court's holding [that an organization was not entitled to exemption] must be sustained on appeal unless clearly erroneous."[235] The *UCC* case should also have been reviewed under the "clearly erroneous" standard.

The Seventh Circuit is not alone in adhering to this standard. Here is the Fifth Circuit: "A finding that a corporation is not operated exclusively for charitable purposes cannot be disturbed unless clearly erroneous."[236] Second Circuit: "We review the Tax Court decision [finding an organization not entitled to exemption] for clear error."[237] Ninth Circuit: "[The] factual finding [that an organization is operated for a substantial non-exempt purpose] [is] reviewable under the clearly erroneous standard."[238] D.C. Circuit: "[O]ur review [of a denial of tax exemption] is on a clearly erroneous basis."[239]

It thus was outside the province of the Seventh Circuit to decide whether the Tax Court was right or wrong. The most it should have done was determine if the Tax Court was clearly erroneous in its *UCC* decision. Certainly, right or wrong, the Tax Court's judgment in this case was not clearly erroneous.

Regarding substance, many in the nonprofit sector are being cheered by this finding that a fundraising company was not functioning as an insider with respect to a charitable organization, for purposes of the private inurement proscription. Those who support this outcome do so because they like what the court said. Unfortunately, the court lacked the authority to say what it said, and what it said does not have much to do with the facts of this case, which admittedly are extreme. Radical facts often elicit radical decisions (which probably is one reason why the IRS litigated this one).

Everyone likes to win; no one likes to lose. This is certainly true in litigation. Here, the nonprofit sector won (at least in the short run) and the government lost. Yet there are wins and there are wins. Some wins rest on reason; they are correct outcomes. Indeed, most wins are in this category. Other wins, however, are flukes, oddball results that are not deserved. This opinion from the Seventh Circuit—this disappointing excuse for an appellate court opinion, this rambling and nonsensical collection of paragraphs, this veritable parataxis—is

---

[234] *Id.* at 1180.

[235] *Granzow* v. *Commissioner*, 739 F.2d 265 (7th Cir. 1984).

[236] *Nationalist Movement* v. *Commissioner*, 37 F.3d 216 (5th Cir. 1994).

[237] *Orange County Agricultural Society, Inc.* v. *Commissioner*, 893 F.2d 529 (2d Cir. 1990).

[238] *Church by Mail, Inc.* v. *Commissioner*, 765 F.2d 1387 (9th Cir. 1985).

[239] *Fund for the Study of Economic Growth & Tax Reform* v. *Internal Revenue Service*, 98-2 U.S.T.C. ¶50,908 (D.C. Cir. 1998).

in the oddball category. The court, in trying to help the nonprofit sector, distorted or strayed widely from the facts of the case and the applicable law.[240]

This appellate court, obviously, was fearful of the IRS. It saw the agency poised to run amok in this area, out to revoke the tax-exempt status of every charity that gets entangled in what in hindsight is a bad business deal. The IRS was viewed as "yanking" charitable exemptions for those who enter into "one-sided" contracts. The court mused that if the "charity's contract with the fundraiser makes the latter an insider, . . . the charitable sector of the economy is in trouble."[241]

An argument does not get any more disingenuous than that. The Tax Court never made any such statement. In fact, the Tax Court said: "We are not holding that an arm's-length arrangement that produces a poor result for an organization necessarily would cause the organization to lose its tax-exempt status."[242]

The fact is that the Seventh Circuit's position rests on a false premise. It was wrong for it to write that the "Tax Court's classification of [the fundraiser] as an insider of UCC was based on the fundraising contract."[243] Rather, the conclusion about insider status was based on the actual relationship between the parties that arose as the *consequence* of the contract. The facts are crystal clear that the fundraising company had UCC in its clutches and exploited the charity for its private ends. It is nothing short of unbelievable for this appellate court to sweepingly assert that this contract was an arm's-length one and regard it as typical of fundraising contracts.[244]

In its anti-IRS diatribe, the Seventh Circuit faulted the IRS for being "ignorant" of contract law.[245] The reverse is true: the court was ignorant of the law of tax-exempt organizations. How else to explain the astoundingly erroneous statement that the Tax Court's use of the word *control* is "not used elsewhere, so far as we can determine, in the law, including federal tax law"?[246] To what extent did the court make a determination? It could have looked in the Internal Revenue Code, where the term *disqualified person,* as applied with respect to public charities like UCC, is defined as any person who was "in a position to exercise substantial influence over the affairs of the organization."[247] That is almost identical to the Tax Court's definition.

How about the assertion that "nothing [here] smacks of self-dealing"?[248] Again, a mere glance at the Code would have been enlightening to the court. Although the self-dealing rules do not apply in this case, the appellate court brought them up. Self-dealing includes furnishing of services between a char-

---

[240] Many individuals who are not lawyers, and thus are not versed in the niceties of what appellate court opinions are supposed to look like, are quite favorably taken with the Seventh Circuit's opinion. One of these nonlawyers observed, articulating a view that is unassailable, that the opinion was written with *attitude.*
[241] *United Cancer Council, Inc.* v. *Commissioner, supra* note 221, at 1176.
[242] *United Cancer Council, Inc.* v. *Commissioner, supra* note 232, at 388.
[243] *United Cancer Council, Inc.* v. *Commissioner, supra* note 221, at 1176.
[244] See *supra* § 6.
[245] *United Cancer Council, Inc.* v. *Commissioner, supra* note 221, at 1177.
[246] *Id.* at 1178.
[247] IRC § 4958(f)(1)(A). See § 5.6, text accompanied by note 148.
[248] *United Cancer Council, Inc.* v. *Commissioner, supra* note 221, at 1179.

ity and a disqualified person, payment of compensation by a charity to a disqualified person, and use of the assets of a charity by or for the benefit of a disqualified person.[249] Contrary to the Seventh Circuit's belief, the facts in this case reflect rampant self-dealing (in the generic sense).

This case was to have been resolved by application of the private benefit doctrine. This could have amounted to quite a mess. The Seventh Circuit never really addressed the question of whether there was private inurement in this case; it essentially focused on the question of whether the fundraising company was an insider in relation to UCC. If there was private inurement (and there was) and that inurement was not insubstantial (and it was not), how could there not be private benefit? (The Tax Court has previously held that all forms of private inurement are also forms of private benefit.[250] Perhaps the appellate court did not know that.)

There is very little law on the private benefit doctrine (a byproduct of the operational test, which stipulates that organizations, to be charitable, must primarily engage in charitable activities[251]). One of the principal court opinions in the realm of the private benefit doctrine was wrongly decided.[252] The UCC case could have brought some illumination of the reaches of the private benefit doctrine—because of the Seventh Circuit's opinion, itself being an embarrassingly wrong decision.

In short, the Seventh Circuit had the opportunity to nicely solidify the law in this area and interlace the private inurement doctrine with the excess benefit transaction rules. The court, by mischaracterizing the facts and misstating or overlooking law, wasted this opportunity and unnecessarily injected considerable confusion with respect to the matter of vendors as insiders.

§ 7.13   IRS AND GIFTS OF USED VEHICLES

The IRS can be strikingly lyrical; it can produce fine literature. Thus, the agency has analogized to *A Tale of Two Cities* and the *Star Wars* epic in concluding

---

[249] IRC § 4941(d)(1).

[250] *American Campaign Academy* v. *Commissioner*, 92 T.C. 1053 (1989).

[251] Reg. § 1.501(c)(3)-1.

[252] The case concerned an otherwise tax-exempt school that trained individuals for careers as political campaign managers or consultants. The court was troubled by the fact that nearly all of the school's graduates became employed by or consultants to candidates of the Republican Party. To reason to the conclusion that the school could not be tax exempt, the court invented the dichotomy of *primary* private benefit and *secondary* private benefit. The beneficiaries of the primary private benefit were the school's students; the provision of benefits of this nature could not be a basis for denial of exemption because it was an exempt function. The beneficiaries of the secondary private benefit were the employers of the school's graduates—Republican Party candidates and entities. The latter category of beneficiaries was portrayed as a "select group" representing a "particular targeted private interest" (*American Campaign Academy* v. *Commissioner, supra* note 250, at 1074, 1076). The problem with this analysis is that every exempt school benefits persons, such as employers, on a "secondary" basis. For example, the senior partners of law firms enjoy, as the consequence of employing recent law school graduates as associates, far greater private benefit than that engendered by any school for political campaign professionals.

that "there is a dark side in the Exempt Organizations Universe."[253] Indeed, the IRS believes itself under siege from evildoers in the realm of charitable organizations and fundraising: the agency "in recent years has been confronted with a number of aggressive tax avoidance schemes."[254]

There is no question that the IRS has seen considerable creativity in and about the charitable sector in recent years. Some of this ingenuity has, admittedly, been abusive. Just a few of the techniques confronting the IRS recently are abuses of charitable remainder trusts, abuses of charitable lead trusts, the explosive rise in the use of donor-advised funds, inappropriate uses of supporting organizations, gifts of interests in limited family partnership, and questionable split-interest charitable insurance programs. Oddly, however, none of these bursts of creativity has irked the IRS more than the matter of solicitation of contributions to charity of used vehicles.

The IRS is of the view that the matter of vehicle (mostly cars) donation programs is a "growing area of noncompliance."[255] The IRS is not concerned with charities that occasionally receive cars by gift and resell them. It likewise is not concerned with charities that obtain cars by gift and use them in their program (such as sheltered workshops) or refurbish them for the benefit of the needy. What the IRS is principally troubled about is the use of "third-party entrepreneurs"—who receive the cars directly, dispose of them (such as by auction or sale to scrap dealers), and pay to the charity a flat fee or set amount (often a small amount) per month. These latter situations the IRS has dubbed— and here is perfect evidence of the agency's ability to generate great literature— "suspect vehicle donation plans or programs." There are ten—believe it or not—issues of law caught up in this matter of suspect vehicle donation plans.

Clearly, for the donor, a critical issue is valuation. The value of a car can be ascertained by reference to various industry compilations. Still, the value will vary depending on factors such as condition and mileage. Some car donation plan advertisements state that donors can claim a charitable deduction based on full Blue Book value, even if the car is not running (or maybe missing an engine or transmission). At best, then, the deduction is confined to the actual fair market value of the vehicle.

This matter of valuation is not confined to the donor. If the gift has a value of $250 or more, the charity must—if the deduction is to be allowed— substantiate the gift.[256] This includes providing the donor with a description of the property contributed. If the value exceeds $5,000, the donor must obtain an independent appraisal of the vehicle. Both parties should proceed cautiously, in that there are penalties for aiding and abetting in the preparation of a false tax return.

Where cars are given to a charity and the charity disposes of them, the activity is not taxable as an unrelated business because of the *donated goods exception*.[257] If the car is transferred directly to a third-party entrepreneur, that

---

[253] IRS Exempt Organization Continuing Professional Education Text for Fiscal Year 2000, Topic P.
[254] *Id.*
[255] *Id.*, Topic T.
[256] See § 5.3.
[257] IRC § 513(a)(3). See § 5.7.

exception is not available. In some instances, the payments to the charity may be properly characterized as tax-excludable royalties. The IRS, however, has staked out the position that, even if the payments would otherwise constitute royalties, the payments would not be excludable from the unrelated income tax because the charity is providing services in conjunction with the transactions—by providing the necessary substantiation documents and acknowledging appraisals.

These suspect vehicle donation plans raise another issue. To be deductible, a gift must be *to* or *for the use of* a charitable organization. To be to a charity, the gift must be made under circumstances where the donee has full control of the donation and discretion as to its use. In these instances, the "gift" often is to the third party, not the charity, in which case there is no charitable deduction to begin with. A gift for the use of a charity means that the donation is made in trust or similar arrangement—and that is not likely to be the case in this context.

The IRS has raised the issue of applicability of the *private benefit doctrine.* The agency posits situations where an automobile dealer or some other third party is the "true beneficiary" of the plan. The charity is cast as "lending" its tax-exempt status to facilitate the transactions. If the private benefit is more than insubstantial, the tax exemption of the charity may be at risk.

The IRS has also raised the possibility of applicability of the *private inurement doctrine.*[258] Where the third party is an insider, that doctrine could be implicated. The position of the IRS is that there is no such thing as incidental private inurement, so transgression of that doctrine also may endanger the organization's tax-exempt status.

The intermediate sanctions penalties[259] may be applicable, where the transaction constitutes an *excess benefit transaction* and the charity's dealings are with a *disqualified person.*

There is a penalty for aiding and abetting in the preparation of false or fraudulent tax documents that result in an understatement of tax liability.[260] There also is a penalty for organizing and selling abusive tax shelters.[261] The latter penalty can be imposed on promoters, salespersons, and their assistants.

Thus, if a charity attempts to delegate its paperwork obligations pursuant to the substantiation requirements and/or its obligations with respect to qualified written appraisals, and the result is one or more documents that an individual can use to understate income tax liability, these penalties could be applicable to the charity. The factual issue would be: Did the charity know (or have reason to believe)[262] that its actions resulted in a tax understatement? Even if the charity did not delegate any obligations, there may still be penalties if, as the IRS put it, "no deduction is appropriate."

Finally, the IRS pointed out that, even where some contribution deduction is appropriate, there may be an overstatement of a tax deduction, which also can trigger penalties. The IRS wrote of a "failure to properly supervise

[258] See *supra* § 12.
[259] See § 5.6.
[260] IRC § 6701.
[261] IRC § 6700.
[262] IRC § 6701(a)(2).

excessive claims concerning deductibility." This could happen if a charity permits a third-party entrepreneur to make claims of that nature, such as advertising full Blue Book value deductions for gifts of cars lacking motors.

§ 7.14   SOME PROPOSALS FOR RELIEF

One of the purposes of this book is to summarize the vast amount of government regulation of the process of raising funds for charitable objectives.

With most forms of government regulation, a balance is struck between the scope of the regulating and the ongoing health of the regulated. That is, usually the regulating is not so strenuous that it severely retards the growth and viability of the process that is being regulated.

When it comes to state regulation of philanthropic fundraising, however, the law has pushed to the point where matters are out of balance: the regulatory process is impeding the fundraising process. Lack of compliance with and of enforcement of these laws is one of the principal factors keeping government regulation from consuming, frustrating, and/or discouraging fundraising for charity. This is not a proper state of affairs, for the regulated or the regulators, and it should be remedied.

(a) Model Law

But, what to do? One solution that has been touted over the years is a model charitable solicitation statute.[263] The thought underlying this proposal is that charitable organizations could more easily comply with the laws in all of the states if these laws were the same. There is some truth to this, although many of the compliance burdens would not change and could even increase. As to the latter, a lobbying effort to enact a model law could result in the substitution of a more strenuous statute for a weaker one in some states, or the adoption of a rigorous statute in a state where previously there was none.

The proposal simply has too many flaws, which is probably why it is still only a proposal. To date, the charitable organizations have not been able to agree on the contents of a model charitable solicitations act because the issue is too divisive (starting with the question of exemptions). Furthermore, the state regulators cannot agree on a uniform statute in this area. Thus, there is little likelihood that both the regulated and the regulators will agree on a law.

Also, the lobbying effort involved would be prodigious and enormously costly. It would probably take millions of dollars to formulate a law and then see it through to enactment in every state. Who would coordinate that effort? Where would the funds come from? Would simplicity really result from uniformity, or would it lead to more regulation in more states? These and other questions and dilemmas make the enactment of a uniform charitable solicitation act in every state unrealistic.

---

[263] See *supra* § 7.

(b) Reciprocal Agreements

As discussed, several of these state laws contain reciprocal agreement provisions.[264] These provisions are considerably underutilized.

Here is an opportunity to breathe some uniformity into these laws and reduce the regulatory burdens, while simultaneously inducing more compliance in this area of law. This approach does not require amendment of the statute, only application of it. Pursuant to these provisions, a state regulator can allow a charitable organization to file, as its registration and/or annual report, a copy of the documents as filed in the home state. Many of these provisions also enable regulators to grant exemptions from compliance where the exemptions are part of the law in the home state.

Therefore, it is not so much uniformity of law that is required as it is unification of the process of complying with the law. How much easier it would be on charities that want to comply, but are overwhelmed by the complexity, if they could prepare documents in their home states and file copies of them in other states. The process would also be advanced and enhanced if there were greater uniformity regarding exemptions.

(c) Uniform Annual Report

Another proposal is the idea of a uniform annual report. This proposal is likewise grounded on the thought that it is not the laws that need changing so much as the process of complying with them. It truly would be simpler for all concerned if a charity required to file annually in several states could file the same document.

Once again, however, reality intrudes and spoils the potential. The fact is that the state regulators, until recently, have not been able to agree on the contents of an annual report. (An effort was undertaken once to create a uniform annual report that reflected the requirements of every state; the resulting document was so large and unwieldy that the project collapsed, literally of its own weight.)

A task force of the National Association of State Charity Officials has developed a uniform registration form, and several states and the District of Columbia have agreed to accept it. The task force has prepared an information chart stating the addresses of state regulators, the fees to be paid, whether a state supplemental form will be required, and who must sign the form. There are additional instructions for completion of the form for different states. It is not clear how the forms and state supplements will be distributed or how the information chart will be kept up to date.

This, then, is the most promising of the simplification approaches. Even here, however, the forces of division and complexity have quickly intervened, with some states not being able to avoid the temptation—or, in some instances, statutory mandate—to require additional information by means of supplemental forms.

---

[264] See § 3.16.

(d) Other Forms of Uniformity

Still other forms of uniformity are possible. The states could strive for uniform rules and regulations by introducing some commonalities into such subjects as definitions and cost allocations, but the regulators cannot agree.

Even uniformity of enforcement would help. Some states are known to be strict in their enforcement of these laws; others have a reputation for being lackadaisical. This state of affairs creates an atmosphere of cynicism and law-breaking, where some charities register only in the "tough" states, waiting to register in the others when and if they "get caught."

Another possibility lies with the Internet. The process of registering in and reporting to many states could obviously be alleviated by means of this medium. Yet, to date, there has been no effort—by a for-profit or nonprofit organization—to implement such a program.[265]

§ 7.15   A LOOK AHEAD

This chapter is appropriately closed with speculation about what is likely to happen in and to the world of fundraising and philanthropy, in both the short and long run, with regard to the development of law and regulation.

It is easy to predict that the nonprofit world will, in the coming months and years, labor under more regulation by government. This will be true at both the federal and state levels. There are many reasons for this phenomenon.

Sheer extrapolation from what has already occurred is a primary reason. At the federal level over the past 30-plus years, the fundraising community has seen enactment of the Tax Reform Act of 1969 (which brought most of today's statutory charitable giving rules, and the public charity and private foundation rules); growing sophistication in application of the unrelated business income rules; increasing emphasis on reporting and disclosure (including expansion of and public access to the annual information returns); more involvement of the tax law in administration of the fundraising process; Congressional decisions to make public a wider variety of IRS pronouncements (including private letter rulings, technical advice memoranda, and general counsel memoranda),[266] to make it easier to litigate charitable organizations' tax issues in federal court,[267] and to become more involved in the realm of planned giving;[268] and the emergence of agencies other than the IRS—the U.S. Postal Service and the Federal Trade Commission, for example—in fundraising regulation.

---

[265] There has not been much recently published on these points. Nonetheless, for the thoughts of others on revisions of or ease of compliance with state charitable solicitation statutes, see Suhrke, "Are We 'Abandoning the Quest for Informed Charitable Giving?'," XXIV *Phil. Monthly* (No. 3) 6 (1991); Suhrke, "Enforcement Costs and Strategies," XXIII *Phil. Monthly* (No. 3) 19 (1990); Suhrke, "What Can State Fund Raising Regulators Try Next?," XXIII *Phil. Monthly* (No. 2) 5 (1990); Suffern, "Where Do The States Go From Here?," XXI *Phil. Monthly* (No. 6) 5 (1988); "The Serious Problems of State and Local Barriers to Fund Raising," XX *Phil. Monthly* (No. 7) 5 (1987).
[266] IRC § 6110.
[267] IRC § 7428.
[268] IRC § 7520.

This type of regulation is founded on the belief that too much abuse is taking place in the charitable fundraising setting. The prime illustrations in this regard are the substantiation and quid pro quo contribution rules. But other emerging practices of charitable organizations are being found noxious (or at least taxable): corporate sponsorships, special events, gambling (such as raffles and sweepstakes), tours and cruises, product endorsements, affinity cards, mailing list exchanges, valuation of property, and practices that trigger the intermediate sanctions penalties.

The IRS sees "scandal" in fundraising and is particularly annoyed at what its officials perceive as "misleading" solicitations. Targeted particularly is the practice of some charitable organizations of advising prospective "donors" that "gifts" are deductible as charitable contributions when they in fact are not (because they are not gifts at all) or when there is only a partial deduction (because the payments are partly a purchase of a service or product). Although their revenue implications are not enormous, these fundraising practices are causing unhappiness within the IRS and are tainting that agency's attitude about charitable fundraising in general and enforcement of charitable solicitation acts.[269] Thus, even as regulation of charitable fundraising increases, some state regulators find the scope of regulation inadequate. For example, with respect to one of the most expansive charitable solicitation statutes in the nation,[270] the state's secretary of state said in 1992 that "[t]here aren't enough strong teeth in the law" and the "oversight doesn't reach the level I would like to see."[271]

In general, then, for the short term, federal and state regulation of the charitable fundraising process will continue to intensify.[272]

Matters are far less clear for the longer term. Federal tax policy plays a critical role in determining the environment for charitable fundraising. In the past, when tax considerations have been involved, the subjects have usually been income tax rates and similar topics. While it remains true that the magnitude of income and capital gain taxation is important, circumstances are uniquely different as the 21st century begins.

The foregoing observations have focused on what is coming, in the realm of law and regulation, for fundraising professionals and the charitable organizations they represent. It is written as though all of this new trouble at the

---

[269] E.g., "Philanthropy and the Law—Is There a Charitable Solicitation Problem?," XXIII *Phil. Monthly* (No. 8) 5 (1990); Hopkins, "Coming: More Law, More Regulation," 20 *Fund Raising Mgmt.* (No. 11) 28 (1990); Hopkins, "Is New Regulation Really Needed?," 17 *Fund Raising Mgmt.* (No. 8) 52 (1986).

[270] Maryland.

[271] "Some Charities in Md. File Misleading Accounts," *Wash. Post,* Apr. 26, 1992, at B1. Also, "Official Proposes Tighter Scrutiny for Md. Charities," *Wash. Post,* July 22, 1992, at A14; "Md. Official Restricts Five Charity Groups," *Wash. Post,* Oct. 6, 1992, at C10.

[272] E.g., Hopkins, "A Look Ahead: Fund Raising and Charity," 25 *Fund Raising Mgmt.* (No. 2) 14 (1994); Hopkins, "Federal Regulation: More Is Coming," 20 *Fund Raising Mgmt.* (No. 3) 60 (1989); Hopkins, "Fund Raisers and the Tax Law: 20 Years' Experience," 20 *Fund Raising Mgmt.* (No. 2) 32 (1989); Hopkins, "Fund Raising and the Law," 19 *Fund Raising Mgmt.* (No. 10) 54 (1988); Hopkins, "Fund Raising and the Law: What's Ahead in 1988," 18 *Fund Raising Mgmt.* (No. 10) 52 (1987).

hands of the law is wholly unavoidable and/or that the fundraising world must passively accept this new regulatory environment.

Most certainly, this is not the case. Earlier, it was noted that the most important question is not *What is coming?* but *What should fundraisers be doing about it?* The fundraising profession does not have much of a record in the field of government relations,[273] although matters are improving in that regard.[274] If nothing is done in this area, more adverse law and regulation for fundraisers and the charities they serve will be the order of the day, but much can be done to forestall or shape these coming changes.

Here are some suggestions:

1. *More lobbying.*   The fundraising profession must increase its visibility on Capitol Hill and in many of the state legislatures. Most legislators do not understand charitable fundraising; this ignorance, unless corrected, will be reflected in new laws. The lawmakers need to learn about fundraising from charitable organizations at the grass-roots level, as well as from coordinated lobbying efforts in Washington, D.C.

A fundamental lobbying tip: Legislators and their staffs need to be contacted and informed at a time when nothing is being requested of them. For example, lawmakers and/or their staffs should be provided tours of the charitable facilities in their districts or states and honored in various ways. They are thereafter likely to be more receptive to pleas for help when the inevitable crisis develops.

An immediate goal for the profession should be the identification and cultivation of members of Congress who are willing to champion the causes of charitable giving and those professionals who help charities receive necessary funds.

There are those in the philanthropic community who protest that, because of the federal tax laws, charitable organizations are not allowed to engage in government relations activities as proposed. That is usually not the case; charitable organizations often can lobby far more extensively than they do or realize.[275] The outcome of this legislative battle will be critical to the fundraising programs of charitable organizations in the future; a charity that is concerned about its status in this regard can, if all else fails, elect the expenditure test and fully utilize the self-defense exception.[276]

---

[273] Two commentators stated: "If it appears that fund-raising executives have been absent from the development of fund-raising regulation, that, sadly, has been the case" (Perlman and Bush, "State Fund-Raising Regulation: An Overview for Fund-Raising Executives," XVI *The Journal* (No. 2) 8, 14 (National Society of Fund Raising Executives 1991)).

[274] For example, the Association of Fundraising Professionals (AFP) created the position of Senior Vice President, Resource Development and External Affairs, which encompasses government relations activities.

[275] See Hopkins, *Charity, Advocacy, and the Law,* Chap. 5 (New York: John Wiley & Sons, Inc., 1992).

[276] A charitable organization that has elected the expenditure test (which is one of two ways of measuring allowable lobbying by public charities (see *id.*) can avail itself of several exceptions from the definition of what constitutes "influencing legislation" for these purposes, including the exception pertaining to "appearances before, or communications to, any legislative body with respect to a possible decision of such body which might affect the existence of the organization, its powers and duties, tax-exempt status, or the deduction of contributions to the organization" (IRC § 4911(d)(2)(C)).

2. *More coordination.* The fundraising world needs to construct more effective systems for lobbying federal and state legislative bodies. Mechanisms for in-tandem lobbying by the principal national associations with fundraising professionals as their members would be products of these systems.

3. *More networking.* Many effective government relations programs are in place and functioning well. Several of these are assembled by coalitions, both transient and permanent. These coalitions need more infiltration and utilization by fundraising interests.

4. *More engagement of the IRS.* The IRS is open to greater understanding of charitable fundraising and input from fundraising professionals. Historically, however, the fundraising professional, as such, has stayed out of this agency's corridors. The IRS needs and wants to hear from professional fundraisers, and the regulatory future of the profession will be directly shaped by the extent to which this engagement occurs and is successful.

5. *More engagement of the Treasury Department.* What was said about the IRS is equally true for the Department of the Treasury. Here, more policymaking takes place and thus the Treasury Department is another incubator of the law of charitable fundraising. For example, in the context of development of the regulations concerning lobbying by public charities,[277] Treasury wrote the first federal tax law definition of the term *fundraising;* however, the fundraising profession had no communication with Treasury about the content and scope of this very important and encompassing regulatory definition.

6. *Political action efforts.* The fundraising world should develop a political action committee (PAC), either as an adjunct to a qualified membership association or as an independent (freestanding) PAC. Those interested in the cause, and future, of professional fundraising would, presumably, gladly give in support of positive law changes and the prevention of adverse law changes.

7. *Alteration of state charitable solicitation acts.* The proliferation of strenuous and, in some instances, absurd charitable solicitation acts is reaching an alarming state. Something must be done to terminate these offenses by state legislators, while at the same time curbing abuses by the unscrupulous. A legislative project in this regard is long overdue; who better to spearhead it than fundraising professionals?

At this juncture in the nation's development of law and regulation, then, here are the legal trends directly and indirectly bearing on fundraising for charitable purposes:[278]

---

[277] See § 5.10.

[278] This summary of the legal trends is based on Hopkins, "Legal Trends Affecting Philanthropy," Chap. 32 of Worth (ed.), *New Strategies for Educational Fund Raising* (American Council on Education/Oryx Press, 2002). Another way to look at this is that boom times lie ahead for lawyers representing charitable organizations—those that engage in fundraising or otherwise—and that is telling for everyone else.

- As noted, federal, state, and local regulation of philanthropy and fund-raising for it will intensify.

- Use of the Internet by philanthropic organizations will engender much new law and consideration regarding application of existing law principles.

- More law will be introduced in response to the upsurge in entreprenurialism by philanthropic organizations.

- The intermediate sanctions rules will be expanded and enforced in ways that will directly and indirectly affect fundraising for philanthropy.

- The concept of the persons who are considered insiders or disqualified persons with respect to philanthropic organizations will be extended.

- Additional emphasis will be placed on reporting and disclosure.

- Ongoing, and perhaps increasing, abuse of planned giving techniques will occur.

- Some of the private foundation rules will be extended to public charities.

- Philanthropic organizations will increase use of joint ventures and limited liability companies.

- Use of appendages such as supporting organizations and title-holding companies will increase.

- Federal government examination of supporting organizations will increase.

- Government scrutiny of donor-advised funds will increase.

- The private benefit doctrine will emerge as a major force in the law concerning philanthropic organizations.

- More law will be developed regarding what constitutes an unrelated business.

- The doctrine of commerciality will be emphasized.

- The term *charitable* will be redefined for purposes of tax exemption.

- The watchdog agencies will meet their demise.

- The law affecting philanthropic organizations will become more complex.

- The true rationale underlying tax exemption for philanthropic entities and the income, gift, and estate tax charitable contribution deductions will be lost.

- Policy developments involving the "surprise attack"—the sudden emergence of a body of law affecting philanthropic organizations created by statute or regulations—will continue.

So, that is where matters stand, at least to the extent that one can reasonably predict them. It must be assumed that the future—short-term and long-term—will bring several additional attempts to regulate, restrain, and retard fundraising for charitable purposes. This view is not meant to inject too much gloom into the forecast, for generally—at least in the short run—the regulatory climate will not be particularly inhospitable to fundraising for charity. But, much is impending, and policymakers' attitudes are not always favorable. Adversity can bring opportunity and, as usual, the extent of new law and regulation depends in considerable part on the degree to which the charitable community, including the fundraising profession, wishes to exert itself and influence outcomes.[279]

---

[279] "The enormous amount of activity in this area [fundraising regulation] is likely to continue unabated for the next few years. We urge NSFRE [now AFP] and its chapters to become key players in this area, because their participation could go a long way toward reducing the state regulatory burdens currently imposed on nonprofit organizations and fundraising professionals. The aims of [AFP] members and state officials are really much the same: the well-being of the philanthropic sector and the citizens nonprofit organizations serve" (Perlman and Bush, *supra* note 273).

CHAPTER EIGHT

Standards Enforcement by Watchdog Agencies

§ 8.1 Nongovernmental Regulation

§ 8.2 Role of an Independent Third-Party Monitoring Organization

§ 8.3 Standards Applied by Watchdog Agencies

§ 8.4 Philanthropic Advisory Service Standards
    (a) Public Accountability
    (b) Use of Funds
    (c) Solicitations and Informational Materials
    (d) Fundraising Practices
    (e) Governance

§ 8.5 Evangelical Council for Financial Accountability Standards
    (a) Board of Directors
    (b) Audited Financial Statements

    (c) Conflicts of Interest
    (d) Fundraising

§ 8.6 American Institute of Philanthropy Standards
    (a) Fundraising Expenses
    (b) Asset Reserves

§ 8.7 Standards Enforcement

§ 8.8 Commentary

§ 8.9 A Watchdog Agency's Response to Commentary

§ 8.10 Reply to Response

§ 8.1 NONGOVERNMENTAL REGULATION

A phenomenon in the realm of regulation of fundraising for charitable purposes is the role of nongovernmental regulation by a variety of independent *watchdog* agencies. Regulation by these groups continues, but their influence is being diminished by the increase in disclosure of information about charitable organizations and the rise in accessibility to this type of information by means of the Internet. Also, the number of these entities has declined.[1]

This type of regulatory function is undertaken in three ways. One is the establishment and application of standards applicable to philanthropic groups engaging in fundraising. The second is the distribution of ratings of these organizations, based on the extent of their compliance with these standards. The

---

[1] In general, "Can Self Regulation Work?," XII *Phil. Monthly* (No. 6) 21 (1979); "Can Self Regulation Work in Philanthropy?—Part 2," XII *Phil. Monthly* (No. 7) 18 (1979).

third of these regulatory functions is the preparation and dissemination of reports on selected charitable organizations.

Donors—individuals and corporations—rely on the ratings of and reports on charitable groups by these agencies in deciding whether to make gifts, as do some grantors, such as private foundations. The media frequently relies on the pronouncements of these organizations in evaluating entities in the philanthropic sector.[2] Thus, the status of a charitable organization in relation to one or more sets of these ratings and reports can have material economic consequences.

It is appropriate to consider the role of the watchdog monitoring agencies in the context of government regulation of fundraising for charity because (1) the standards promulgated by the agencies, and the interpretations accorded the standards by them, have much in common with the provisions of state charitable solicitation acts; and (2) state regulators work closely with these agencies in evaluating charitable groups, and, concurrently, the status of a charity in relation to an agency's rating can have an impact on its status in relation to a state charitable solicitation act. (The reverse is also true.) Further, the IRS has been known to rely on the treatment by these agencies of specific charitable organizations in formulating its own evaluation of them. Further, as discussed later, the courts are likely to pass judgment, sooner or later, on the validity of these standards and their enforcement. These judicial determinations may well be of significance when applied to the provisions and applicability of state charitable solicitation acts.

The principal promulgator, monitor, and enforcer of standards is the Philanthropic Advisory Service of the Council of Better Business Bureaus (PAS).[3] Others of the watchdog groups include the Evangelical Council for Financial Accountability[4] and the American Institute of Philanthropy (AIP).

The rationale for and role of the watchdog agencies have been well expressed in an analysis prepared by the PAS, which follows.[5]

---

[2] As an illustration, the July 20, 2001, edition of *USA Today* explored the fundraising and other activities of a charitable organization established by athletes; a portion of the analysis was based on this organization's compliance (or lack of it) with a watchdog agency's standards.

[3] Another of the principal watchdog agencies, the National Charities Information Bureau (NCIB), merged with the PAS. An analysis of the work of the NCIB appeared in "Rating Charities," IX *Phil. Monthly* (No. V) 19 (1976); "Rating Charities—Part II," IX *Phil. Monthly* (No. VI) 14 (1976); and "Rating Charities—Part III," IX *Phil. Monthly* (No. VII) 31 (1976).

[4] For discussion of other voluntary standards, see, e.g., Peavey, "The Self-Regulation Alternative," XII *Phil. Monthly* (No. 9) 5 (1979); "New Fund-Raising Rules in the Catholic Church," X *Phil. Monthly* (No. 11) 25 (1977). As may be expected, with the advent of various sets of voluntary standards, there are elements of competition and discord among the self-regulators. E.g., the NCIB Report on the Church League of America, dated October 31, 1977, reporting that the organization was refusing to provide information to the NCIB because it is a standards-setting agency providing information to the public; and the PAS Report on The Fund Raising Council of the United States, dated February 1977, which held itself out as the "recognized accrediting body for organizations involved in fund raising as a means of financial support in whole or in part."

[5] This analysis, prepared by Ruth M. Atchison, then Assistant Director of the Philanthropic Advisory Service, for the Philanthropy Monthly Forum on Standard Setting, Monitoring and Enforcement, held on April 23, 1979, and edited for use as part of this chapter, is reproduced with

§ 8.2 ROLE OF AN INDEPENDENT THIRD-PARTY MONITORING ORGANIZATION

A brief look at how and why the Council of Better Business Bureaus (CBBB) got into the "business" of developing standards and monitoring charitable solicitations is required at the outset. The explanation, in two short words, is public demand. Since the first BBBs were formed in 1911, and increasingly over the years, the public has turned to the Bureaus for verification of the "legitimacy" (as the question was most often posed) of soliciting charities. Turning to a BBB in this area seemed to stem naturally from the public habit of asking a BBB about marketplace experience with particular businesses. Many Bureaus became active in monitoring and reporting on solicitations, in some cases working jointly with local government or other organizations, and in a few instances serving as the official registering body in a community. Many local BBBs developed "Guides for Giving," listing a few basic standards for groups soliciting in their areas, in response to the public demand for reports incorporating some kind of evaluation. When the national organization was formed, it logically assumed, at the request of the Bureaus (and along with many other national functions), the job of developing information and reports on nationally soliciting organizations, for use by the 143 BBBs in answering their public inquiries. The Bureaus retained their important role in monitoring local and regional solicitations, and provided input to the CBBB on national groups located in their areas.

As public interest and inquiries increased at a rapid pace, the CBBB invited Helen O'Rourke to assume directorship of the national program, which expanded rapidly beginning in 1971 and which is now administered by the Philanthropic Advisory Service (PAS), a division of the CBBB. Increasingly, the BBBs, public inquirers, and corporate members pressed for some type of evaluative conclusion to CBBB reports, based on objective criteria. This demand, plus the realization that local "Guides for Giving" were far from uniform, led the Council to consult widely with nonprofit organizations, their "umbrella" groups, and related professionals about the possibility of working together to develop basic, realistic standards that would apply to a wide range of types of groups. The encouraging response resulted in a series of formal meetings, informal discussions, and written responses in 1973 and 1974. Several drafts were produced and, finally, the BBB Standards for Charitable Solicitations were issued in the fall of 1974.

The PAS is often described as a "watchdog agency" and "donors' representative." While not inaccurate, the descriptions are a little harsher, in the first instance, and more limited, in the case of "donors' representative," than our conception of our role.

We start from the admittedly rather obvious premise that any standards, and particularly voluntary standards, will be much more effective if they have the general support and cooperation of the particular group to which they will be applied. This is especially true of what is, fortunately for all of us, the

the permission of the Council of Better Business Bureaus, Inc. Despite the passage of time, this analysis remains a classic explication of the rationalization of these agencies. Her contribution is gratefully acknowledged by the author.

independent-minded and diverse voluntary sector. (Our thinking stems rather logically from the traditional BBB role of developing basic service standards in cooperation with both business and consumers, monitoring advertising for accuracy, attempting to resolve consumer complaints, and reporting to consumers when firms either fail to cooperate in the resolution of complaints or refuse to abide by basic advertising and performance standards.)

In a general sense, then, we see our role as a kind of partnership with donors, philanthropic organizations, and the various regulatory and self-regulatory mechanisms in pursuit of the goals we all share: strengthening the voluntary sector, private giving, and public confidence by promoting responsible use of funds for the purposes intended by the donor.

It follows that we do not see our role as an adversarial one. When it does become adversarial, as it inevitably does with a few groups, we see that partly as a failure on our part. In practical terms, this viewpoint affects the way we develop and apply standards, and the spirit in which we deal with individual organizations in daily meetings and discussions. It means (1) that we do everything we can to help a cooperative "noncompliance" group meet the standards as quickly as possible, and (2) that we place a primary emphasis, in developing and applying standards, on the collective advice of responsible representatives of philanthropic groups and allied professions, donor representatives, and state and local monitoring agencies.

In our view, the most productive role of a "third-party" monitoring and reporting agency can be summarized in the following functions:

1. Education and counseling on how to meet standards, when invited.

2. Objective application of standards which are basic enough to:

   a. Incorporate the principal provisions of more detailed self-regulatory standards developed by and for specific categories of groups;

   b. Be applicable also to most nationally soliciting organizations, which are not covered by accrediting bodies of self-regulatory "umbrella" groups; and

   c. Complement state and federal governmental monitoring, which is primarily concerned with prevention and detection of fraudulent activities; and try, along with other groups, to preclude any need for additional legislation, by promoting self-regulatory action to meet donors' reasonable expectations (e.g., responsible policymaking procedures and fundraising practices, use of funds for the purposes given, financial accountability through external audits, and truthful information materials).

3. Provide advisory services, and reports on individual groups, to potential donors and other inquirers such as the media and state regulatory agencies. In providing these services, the monitoring group should try to communicate, when necessary, an understanding of extenuating factors that may produce unavoidably high fundraising costs, and other special circumstances that should be considered in evaluating, for

example, new organizations. In addition, all reporting of noncompliance with standards should explain the reasons, so readers may evaluate independently and make their own decisions about giving.

In its relations with charitable groups, the monitoring/reporting agency does act as the donors' "stand-in," since it is trying to help ensure that tax-exempt charities, with their privileged status in society, carry out their "trustee" responsibilities in a manner consistent with their stated purposes and donors' reasonable expectations about how their contributions will be used.

To represent the donors' interests most effectively, and also deal fairly with philanthropic organizations, the monitoring or "watchdog" agency must ensure that:

1. The standards applied are attainable by responsible organizations operating in the "real world," rather than idealistic goals that might produce unjust "ratings" discouraging socially useful efforts. Put another way, they must be reasonable enough to encourage well-intentioned groups to cooperate in trying to meet them, thus contributing to an overall improvement in operating standards and more effective use of many millions of the donors' dollars.

2. The standards are applied consistently and objectively to all groups, yet incorporate enough flexibility to take into account genuine and unavoidable extenuating circumstances (not an easy balance, which is why we continually seek input and advice from a wide variety of sources).

3. The standards, and supplementary guidelines, are specific and detailed enough so that (a) interested organizations can readily determine what is required to meet them, and (b) potential donors may use them as practical guides to independent evaluations.

4. The monitoring agency works cooperatively rather than punitively with inexperienced or uninformed organizations, so that potentially valuable efforts are encouraged rather than squelched.

Perhaps the most fruitful path to more effective monitoring and enforcement of standards is greater communication and coordination among all groups involved in these efforts. Our efforts in this area have been concentrated thus far in these activities:

1. Involvement of charities, accountants, legal experts, professional fundraisers, donors, and others in the development of standards.

2. Establishment of an Advisory Committee on Standards Application, representing the same categories, to advise us on guidelines for applying the standards as equitably as possible. It is important for the monitoring agency to establish formal mechanisms for continual communication and feedback from both donors and the philanthropic community. To provide this kind of input, we also consult with our Corporate Advisory Committee on the needs and expectations of this

donor category, and a Better Business Bureau Advisory Committee to keep us in touch with the needs and views of the Bureaus' public inquirers across the country, as well as BBB problems and needs as local monitoring/reporting groups.[6]

3. Regular consultations with professionals such as nonprofit accounting specialists, as well as daily exchanges of information with many state regulatory agencies.

We see a need to increase communication with the other standard-setting and self-regulatory organizations. We are developing a file of existing sets of standards, and plan to help identify the broad areas of agreement among them (as well as divergences), to pinpoint areas where focused communication may prove fruitful.

§ 8.3 STANDARDS APPLIED BY WATCHDOG AGENCIES

A charitable organization that is made subject to standards set and enforced by a watchdog agency has certain rights with respect to the standards themselves and the manner in which they are applied.

For the most part, these rights cannot rise to the level of constitutional protections, such as are accorded pursuant to the principles of due process enunciated in the Fifth and Fourteenth Amendments to the U.S. Constitution and in comparable provisions in the constitutions of the states. This is because due process rights are generally granted only with respect to actions by a government. The *state action doctrine*, however, can mandate the adherence to due process requirements by a nongovernmental organization when there is sufficient entanglement between government and the nongovernmental group, such as in the form of support or activities in tandem.[7]

---

[6] [*Author's note:* This Advisory Committee, long since disbanded, proved to be a misstep for the PAS. It refused to confine its work to matters presented to it by the PAS and persisted in looking into issues (particularly pertaining to the assessment of fundraising costs) that the PAS staff preferred to leave unexplored. The committee was abolished within two years of its formation, to stifle the substantive inquiries into various PAS assumptions and practices that the committee was pursuing.]

[7] E.g., *Brentwood Academy* v. *Tennessee Secondary School Athletic Association*, 531 U.S. 288 (2001); *McGlotten* v. *Connally*, 388 F. Supp. 488 (D.D.C. 1972). Thus, the state action doctrine could mandate applicability of due process standards to action by a watchdog agency where it is shown that, for example, an organization's status in relation to the standards is relied on by a state governmental agency in reaching a determination, under the state's charitable solicitation act, about the charitable organization.

In one instance, a state regulatory official with responsibility for administering a charitable solicitation act that then contained a rebuttable percentage limitation on the compensation of professional fundraisers advised a charitable organization that its fundraising costs were not in conformance with the state's statutory requirements solely because he understood that the organization had been found not to satisfy the fundraising cost standard promulgated by the Council of Better Business Bureaus.

The federal government as well relies on the pronouncements of these watchdog agencies. An illustration of this was the IRS's citation of the failure of an organization to meet the

Nonetheless, where a nongovernmental organization promulgates and enforces standards, there are two situations where the law requires that the standards and the application of them be *fair.*

The first of these situations is the presence of an economic factor. That is, where the power of the standards enforcement agency becomes so great as to cause adverse economic consequences to the charity that is ranked as not meeting standards, the courts can intervene to rectify the application of unfair standards or the unfair application of standards.[8] The test in either circumstance is whether the standards and/or the administration of them are *fair* or *reasonable.*[9] There is no question that the ratings of and reports on charitable organizations by watchdog agencies have economic consequences to the affected charities: individual and corporate donors rely on the listings in determining which organizations are to receive their gifts; private foundations and other grantors similarly rely on these listings in determining their grantees; state governmental agencies take the status of charities in relation to the independent agencies' standards into account in determining the status of charities under the states' charitable solicitation acts; and the IRS from time to time relies on the rankings of these agencies.[10] Moreover, the watchdog agencies readily provide information to the media, and the resulting publicity can cause one or more of the same three results to occur.

The second of these situations is when the agency's ratings power is in an area of public concern.[11] Again, there is little doubt that these agencies envision themselves as operating in the public interest, by forcing disclosure of information to the general public and otherwise acting to benefit prospective donors. Public reliance on the watchdog agencies' pronouncements has become so great as to make a national organization's fundraising success significantly dependent on a favorable rating, or to divert gifts from a national organization that receives a negative rating. A positive rating accorded a charity by a watchdog agency may well confer on the charity a significant "competitive" advantage in relation to one or more organizations that receive an adverse rating.

The foregoing two principles have been succinctly stated elsewhere: "Self regulation programs should be based on clearly defined standards that plainly indicate what is considered proper and improper. Vague standards invite arbitrary action," and "[s]tandards once set also should be administered in a reasonable manner."[12]

The setting and application of standards by the watchdog agencies are squarely subject to both of these threshold tests, and fundamental fairness dictates that their enforcement of standards be on the basis of processes that are reasonable.

---

agencies' standards in a case involving revocation of the organization's tax exemption because of its fundraising practices (see § 5.15).

[8] E.g., *Falcone* v. *Middlesex County Medical Society,* 170 A.2d 791 (N.J. 1961).

[9] E.g., *Higgins* v. *American Society of Clinical Pathologists,* 238 A.2d 665 (N.J. 1968).

[10] As noted (*supra* note 7), these latter two circumstances may likely trigger the state action principle in which the panoply of due process responsibilities would be visited upon the watchdog agency.

[11] E.g., *Marjorie Webster Junior College* v. *Middle States Association of Colleges & Secondary Schools,* 302 F. Supp. 459 (D.D.C. 1969), *rev'd,* 432 F.2d 650 (D.C. Cir. 1970), *cert. denied,* 400 U.S. 963 (1970).

[12] MacArthur, *Associations and the Antitrust Laws* 53, 54 (1976).

§ 8.4 PHILANTHROPIC ADVISORY SERVICE STANDARDS

The PAS is the division of the CBBB that monitors and reports on nationally soliciting charitable organizations.[13] The primary goal of the division, which began substantive operations in 1971, is to promote ethical standards of business practices and protect consumers through self-regulation and monitoring activities.

PAS evaluates charitable organizations according to the "CBBB Standards for Charitable Solicitations."[14] These standards cover five basic areas: public accountability, use of funds, solicitations and informational materials, fundraising practices, and governance.

(a) Public Accountability

In the area of *public accountability*, PAS requires that a charity provide, on request, an annual report that includes various items of information about the charity's purposes, current activities, governance, and finances. A charity also must provide on request a complete annual financial statement, including an accounting of all income and fundraising costs of controlled or affiliated entities.

A charity must also "present adequate information [in financial statements] to serve as a basis for informed decisions." According to the PAS, information needed as a basis for informed decisions includes items such as significant categories of contributions and other income, expenses reported in categories corresponding to major programs and activities, a detailed description of expenses by "natural classification" (e.g., salaries, employee benefits, and postage), accurate presentation of fundraising and administrative costs, the total cost of multipurpose activities, and the method used for allocating costs among the activities.

Organizations that receive a substantial portion of their income as the result of fundraising activities of controlled or affiliated entities are required to provide, on request, an accounting of all income received by and fundraising costs incurred by these entities.

(b) Use of Funds

As to "use of funds," PAS requires that a charity spend a "reasonable percentage" of total income on programs, as well as a "reasonable percentage" of contributions on activities that are in accordance with donor expectations. In this context, PAS defines a "reasonable percentage" to mean "at least" 50 percent. Charities are also expected to ensure that their fundraising costs are "reasonable." In

---

[13] Although PAS focuses mainly on charitable organizations, it also develops and distributes information on some lobbying and social welfare organizations described in IRC § 501(c)(4) and business membership groups described in IRC § 501(c)(6).

[14] It produces other publications, including *PAS Reports on National Nonprofit Organizations; Tips on Charitable Giving;* "Give But Give Wisely," which is published bimonthly and lists the national charities generating the most inquiries to PAS; and the "Annual Charity Index," which is a reference book featuring program descriptions and financial information on many national charities.

this context, fundraising costs are reasonable if those costs do "not exceed" 35 percent of related contributions. In the area of total fundraising and administrative costs, PAS standards also provide that these costs be "reasonable." In this latter context, these costs are reasonable if they do "not exceed" 50 percent of total income. A charity must establish and exercise "adequate controls" over its disbursements.

Soliciting organizations must substantiate, on request, their application of funds, in accordance with donor expectations, to the programs and other activities described in solicitations.

(c) Solicitations and Informational Materials

In the area of "solicitations and informational materials," PAS standards require that these materials be "accurate, truthful and not misleading, both in whole or in part." These terms are not defined. Solicitation materials also must include a "clear description" of the program and other activities for which funds are requested. Solicitations that describe an issue, problem, need, or event but do not clearly describe the programs or other activities for which funds are requested will not meet the standard for accuracy and truthfulness.

Direct contact solicitations (including telephone appeals) must identify the solicitor and his or her relationship to the benefiting organization, the benefiting organization or cause, and the programs or other activities for which funds are requested. Solicitations in conjunction with the sale of goods, services, or admissions must identify, among other things, the "actual or anticipated portion" of the sales or admission price that will benefit the charitable organization or cause.

(d) Fundraising Practices

As to fundraising practices, PAS standards provide that soliciting organizations must "establish and exercise controls" over fundraising activities by their staff, employees, volunteers, consultants, and contractors, including the use of written contracts and agreements. Organizations must establish and exercise "adequate controls" over the contributions they receive. Donor requests for confidentiality must be honored, including requests that a donor's name not be exchanged, rented, or sold. Fundraising must be conducted "without excessive pressure." Examples of excessive pressure include solicitations in the guise of invoices, harassment, intimidation, coercion, threats of public disclosure or economic retaliation, and "strongly emotional appeals which distort the organization's activities or beneficiaries."

(e) Governance

In the category of "governance," PAS standards require three elements. First, there must be an "adequate governing structure." This means that the governing instruments must set forth the organization's goals and purposes, define the organization's structure, and identify the body having authority over policies and programs (including the authority to amend the governing instruments). A governing structure is defined to be inadequate if any policymaking decisions of the governing body or executive committee "are made by fewer than three persons."

Second, there must be an "active governing body." To meet this standard, the governing body must, among other things, meet formally "at least three times annually, with meetings evenly spaced over the course of the year, and with a majority of the members in attendance (in person or by proxy) on average." If the full board meets only once annually, there must then be at least two additional, evenly spaced executive committee meetings during the year.

Third, adequate governance requires that there be an "independent governing body." Organizations will not meet this standard if "directly and/or indirectly compensated board members constitute more than one-fifth (20%) of the total voting membership of the board or of the executive committee." (The ordained clergy of a "publicly soliciting church," however, are excepted from this 20 percent limitation.) Organizations will not meet this third standard if board members have material conflicting interests resulting from any relationship or business affiliation.

§ 8.5 EVANGELICAL COUNCIL FOR FINANCIAL ACCOUNTABILITY STANDARDS

Religious organizations have watchdog entities. Among them is the Evangelical Council for Financial Accountability (ECFA). Founded in 1979, ECFA states that it comprises more than 900 charitable, religious, and educational organizations. Its mission is to "help Christ-centered organizations earn the public's trust through developing and maintaining standards of accountability that convey God-honoring ethical practices." It does so by promulgating and monitoring member organization compliance with its "Standards of Responsible Stewardship." (Nonmember organizations are not monitored.)

(a) Board of Directors

ECFA standards require that member organization boards have at least five individuals, a majority of whom shall not be employees, staff, or related by blood or marriage. The board must meet at least semiannually and must appoint a "functioning audit review committee" for the purpose of reviewing the annual audit.

(b) Audited Financial Statements

Every member organization must obtain an annual audit performed by an independent certified public accountant and a financial statement prepared in accordance with generally accepted accounting principles. Every member must also provide a copy of its audited financial statement upon request.

(c) Conflicts of Interest

Member organizations may undertake transactions with related parties only if a material transaction is fully disclosed in the financial statements of the organization, the related party is excluded from the discussion and approval of the transaction, a competitive bid or comparable valuation exists, and the organization's board demonstrates that the transaction is in the best interest of the organization.

(d) Fundraising

ECFA has several requirements in the area of fundraising. Representations of fact, description of the organization's financial condition, or narrative about events must be "current, complete, and accurate"; "material omissions or exaggerations of fact" are not permitted. Member organizations "must not create unrealistic donor expectations of what a donor's gift will actually accomplish within the limits of the organization's ministry." Organizations are asked to make every effort to "avoid accepting a gift from or entering into a contract with a prospective donor which would knowingly place a hardship on the donor or place the donor's future well-being in jeopardy." When dealing with donors regarding commitments on "major estate assets," organizations must "seek to guide and advise donors so they have adequately considered the broad interests of the family and the various ministries they are currently supporting before they make a final decision."

These standards state that compensation of outside fundraising consultants based on a percentage of what is raised are prohibited. Compensation to an organization's employees on a percentage-fee basis is prohibited by ECFA. ECFA standards also state that officers and directors may not receive any royalties for any product that is used for fundraising or promotional purposes by the organization. This is apparently the case even if the royalty is reasonable and negotiated at arm's length.

§ 8.6   AMERICAN INSTITUTE OF PHILANTHROPY STANDARDS

The American Institute of Philanthropy (AIP) is, according to its Website posting, a "nationally prominent charity watchdog service whose purpose is to help donors make informed giving decisions." It provides ratings of charities, using letter grades A–F.

(a) Fundraising Expenses

Like all of the watchdog agencies, AIP believes fundraising costs should be reasonable. In this organization's view, this means that a charity should expend at least 60 percent of its outlays for charitable purposes. The balance, of course, is to be allocated to fundraising and administration. Fundraising expenses should not exceed 35 percent. These percentages are based on related contributions, not total income (thereby usually making the fundraising cost ratio higher). AIP sometimes takes it upon itself to adjust an organization's fundraising expense ratio, such as where it is allocating expenses to program in the context of direct mail fundraising.

(b) Asset Reserves

In the view of AIP, a reserve of assets to enable an organization to function without fundraising for less than three years is reasonable. Organizations with "years of available assets" of more than five years are considered the "least needy." (This fact earns an organization the grade of "F" irrespective of other considerations.)

§ 8.7 STANDARDS ENFORCEMENT

There is no law to date bearing directly on standards enforcement by watchdog agencies regarding charitable organizations involved in fundraising.[15] Analogous principles of law, however, are developing with respect to comparable membership association activities and similar activities carrying antitrust overtones (such as accreditation). It is possible to extrapolate from these parallel fields of law to arrive at some basic conclusions concerning standards setting and enforcement in the charitable context.

At the outset, it can be safely observed that the courts are reluctant to intervene in the matter of independent standards enforcement. Thus, one court observed that "[c]ourts ordinarily ought not to intrude upon areas of associational decision involving specialized knowledge" and that "[p]rivate associations must have considerable latitude in rule-making in order to accomplish their objectives and their private law generally is binding on those who wish to remain members."[16] The organizations that are rated by the watchdog agencies are not members of the agencies, but the courts—in the absence of compelling circumstances—are likely to avoid passing on the merits of independent fundraising standards.

Similarly, there is no legal obstacle to the promulgation of such standards. Again, to allude to the law of membership associations, it is clear that such an organization has the power to establish operating rules and to set guidelines for the expulsion of members.[17]

---

[15] Nonetheless, law in this field may be spawned by litigation. An example is the lawsuit, filed on January 21, 1994, and amended on June 6, 1994, by Father Flanagan's Boys Home (Boys Town) against the AIP. The organization publishes "Charity Watchdog Report and Rating Guide," with the ratings based on factors such as fundraising costs and asset levels, and assigns an overall letter grade to the charities it reviews. Boys Town was graded "F" because of its accumulated assets of $567 million; because it could operate at current levels for about six years without raising any additional funds, the Rating Guide characterized Boys Town as one of the "least needy charities." The action, filed in the U.S. District Court for the Eastern District of New York, sought damages and an injunction prohibiting dissemination of the guide. The president of AIP was quoted as saying that the "donating public has a right to know [the facts]. . . . The public could be the big loser if we stop publishing this guide" (*FRM Weekly*, Jan. 26, 1994, at p. 1). By contrast, the executive director of Boys Town said that the "watchdog has become an attack dog. Somebody has to muzzle it. It is causing great harm to worthy charities" (*id.*). This case, however, was settled.

[16] *Higgins* v. *American Society of Clinical Pathologists, supra* note 9.

[17] 7 C.J.S. Associations § 25.

Associations also possess the inherent right to suspend or expel a member or otherwise to enforce disciplinary rules.[18] Again, the point of the analogy is that watchdog agencies have the authority not only to establish standards, but also to apply them.

Just as disciplinary action by an association against one of its members must be reasonable,[19] however, so must enforcement of watchdog agency fundraising standards be fair. If there ever is intervention in this field by a court, it will undoubtedly be in this context to preclude the application of standards in a manner that will unjustly cause damage or otherwise be unfair to those to whom the standard is being applied. Thus, the courts "will relieve against any expulsion based on rules which are in conflict with public policy."[20]

Fair enforcement of these standards includes the following elements:

1. The standards must be understandable, so that an organization will have an authentic opportunity to comply with them and be on notice that certain consequences will follow where this compliance is not achieved. For example, the PAS standards require fundraising costs to be *reasonable.* As noted, this raises substantive questions as to definition and computation.[21] Yet there are no public pronouncements by the PAS as to the meaning of this requirement, although there are several cases in which organizations are on the PAS "Do Not Meet Standards" list because their fundraising costs are said not to meet the standards. Needless to say, it is difficult for any organization to rebut such a finding when it is not provided with the reasons for the finding.

2. Before any adverse action (such as publication of ratings), the agency should afford the charitable organization the opportunity to refute the charges against it. An ex parte investigation alone is insufficient in relation to the requirements of a fair procedure.[22] An organization in these circumstances "should fashion its procedure to insure a *fair* opportunity for an applicant to present his position."[23]

3. An organization must be provided with a written explanation of the reason or reasons underlying a conclusion that it does not meet one or more standards. While this is an element of the first point, it also goes beyond it. The law requires—as elements of a fair procedure—that a charitable organization be provided with a reasonably adequate written statement of the basis for the decision, a reasonably adequate description of the manner in which the decision was arrived at, and a reasonably adequate disclosure of the information and data upon

---

[18] *Cowen* v. *New York Stock Exchange,* 265 F. Supp. 462 (N.D.N.Y. 1966), *aff'd,* 371 F.2d 661 (2d Cir. 1967).

[19] *Molinas* v. *National Basketball Association,* 190 F. Supp. 241 (S.D.N.Y. 191); *State* v. *Delaware Fire Co. No. 3,* 177 A. 129 (1922).

[20] *Higgins* v. *American Society of Clinical Pathologists, supra* note 9, at 671.

[21] See § 4.1.

[22] *Wyatt* v. *Tahoe Forest Hospital District,* 345 P.2d 93 (Cal. 1959).

[23] *Pinsker* v. *Pacific Coast Society of Orthodontists,* 526 P.2d 253, 264 (Cal. 1974) (emphasis by the court).

which the agency relied.[24] That is, aside from the inherent fairness of knowing why a particular standard is ostensibly violated, this knowledge—in writing from the source—can be used to educate the organization's governing groups and perhaps be used in a process of remedying the situation. Also, a written explanation helps narrow the issue and enables the organization effectively to frame an appeal.

4. Some form of meaningful appeal mechanism should be available. This mechanism does not have to be adorned with all the trappings of appellate court procedure, but there should be an opportunity for an organization—having been advised that a standard has ostensibly been violated and why—to obtain reconsideration of that decision by an objective reviewer (or review group) or at least by one who was not a participant in the decision. Thus, in one case, after observing that these matters call for "the minimal requisites of a fair procedure required by established common law principles," a court stated that (in the face of adverse association action) "an affected individual must at least be provided with some meaningful opportunity to respond to the 'charges' against him."[25] Another court stated that "[i]t is a fundamental principle of justice that no man may be condemned or prejudiced in his rights without an opportunity to make his defense, and this principle is applicable not only to courts but also to labor unions and similar organizations."[26]

5. There must be a reasonable interval between the time a decision about a standards violation is announced to the organization and the time the next rating list of organizations is published. During this interim, the organization can review and perhaps revise or otherwise rectify the practice in question or pursue a more formal type of appeal. In too many cases, an organization is, for example, rotated from a "Meets Standards" listing to a "Do Not Meet Standards" listing at the same time it is notified of the change of status.

6. In interpreting standards, a watchdog agency should not substitute its judgment on a technical matter for that of professional advisors. One of the most egregious examples of lack of adherence to this principle is where, in a situation involving a standard requiring an organization to report its finances in conformance with generally accepted accounting principles, and the organization's financial statements are accompanied by an opinion of a certified public accountant that these principles have been satisfied, the enforcers of watchdog agency standards take issue with the organization on a matter involving one or more accounting principles or reporting practices.

---

[24] *Johnson* v. *Board of Regents of University of Wisconsin System*, 377 F. Supp. 227, 240 (W.D. Wis. 1974).
[25] *Pinsker* v. *Pacific Coast Society of Orthodontists, supra* note 23, at 256.
[26] *Cason* v. *Glass Bottle Blowers Association*, 231 P.2d 6, 11 (Cal. 1951).

7. Some watchdog agencies, in addition to formulating and enforcing standards, prepare and circulate to the general public analytical reports on the programs and practices of charitable organizations. When this is done, the agency should be certain that the information contained in the report is accurate and reasonably current. While this may seem an obvious precaution, in one instance a major watchdog agency was—in one year—circulating critical information about a charitable organization taken from the organization's financial statement for its fiscal year ending four years before, even though the matter involved was rectified in subsequent fiscal years.

A watchdog agency that attempts to apply unreasonable standards or that fails to afford procedural safeguards to an organization that is the subject of its ratings may find that it is liable for damages. As one court observed: "Groups that wield economic power or exist solely for economic purposes have almost uniformly been held to a higher standard of procedural formality and regularity than voluntary noneconomic organizations."[27] While the matter may come down to a question of proof, the agency may well be found to have acted irrationally (i.e., without a reasonable basis), acted in violation of judicially protected rights of "fairness," and maligned the organization's reputation in the philanthropic community and hence impaired its ability to attract contributions and grants. Further, it is not inconceivable that the members of the governing boards of these agencies may be found personally liable as the result of the agency's standards enforcement efforts, such as for knowingly permitting the dissemination of derogatory and damaging information known to be misleading and/or derived pursuant to illegal procedures, knowingly violating an organization's rights to a fair procedure, and otherwise willfully causing injury and damage.

§ 8.8 COMMENTARY

On balance, these watchdog agencies are counterproductive. Ideally, they should be abolished; since that will not happen, the charitable community can only hope that the courts will eventually circumscribe the range of the rules and the manner in which they are enforced.

There is nothing inherently inappropriate with the concept of watchdog agencies overseeing fundraising for charitable purposes. Some find this form of regulation preferable to regulation by government, but government regulation of fundraising has hardly been abated by watchdog groups or any other force.

The fact is, however, that these watchdog agencies have squandered the opportunities presented them and have abused the trust they have aggregated. Mysteriously, the public, media, governments, donors, and grantors—almost without exception—unquestioningly accept the pronouncements of these organizations. For example, their proclamations on the potentials for deception in

---

[27] *State Marine Lines, Inc.* v. *F.M.C.*, 376 F.2d 230 (D.C. Cir. 1967).

charitable giving and their positions on individual charitable organizations are touted in the media; they are accepted without challenge and repeated as if objective truth.[28]

Most irksome to a lawyer, these standards meddle in areas where there is specific law on the point. For example, even though some states permit a nonprofit organization to have a one-person governing board, the PAS standards proclaim a governing structure to be "inadequate" if there are fewer than three board members and the ECFA standards require at least five members. ECFA compounds this arbitrariness by requiring that board members be "responsible." (Try to measure that.) The PAS standards allow board members to vote by proxy, even though this is contrary to common law principles and is permitted in only a few states. That ECFA standards state that a member organization "shall avoid conflicts of interest," then promptly reverse course and permit transactions with related parties where a legally permissible conflict-of-interest policy exists.

Sometimes the matter is worse, in that the standard does not reflect the law. For example, the ECFA standards prohibit the use of tax-deductible gifts "to pass money or benefits to any named individual for personal use." Since every individual has a name, this literally would prohibit a member organization from making any scholarships, fellowships, or awards. Presumably, the standard frowns on the naming of recipients by donors. These standards also state that member organizations should "inform the donors of IRS reporting requirements for all gifts in excess of $5,000." Yet, the pertinent requirements are those in connection with the *substantiation* rules, where the threshold is $250; the $5,000 limitation pertains to *appraisal* rules.[29]

These agencies historically have been staffed by individuals who lack the experience and training necessary to fairly underlie ratings devices, and they disseminate the ratings far and wide with statements such as "does not meet standards" or "failed to submit adequate information." Most recipients of this material do not parse the details—an individual sees "does not meet standards" and makes his or her gift to another charity, even though the failure to meet the standards may hinge on some technicality. Thus, the AIP, not liking a charity's level of endowment, once blithely gave it an "F" rating and disseminated the classification to the public. These irresponsible actions can cause great damage to charities that depend on public goodwill and financial support.

Inasmuch as there is little likelihood that the watchdog agencies will be eliminated, a review of their functions is in order. Without question, the most inappropriate function of these entities is the rating system. It simply is not possible to, in a fair manner, condense and compare the characteristics of

---

[28] An exception to this observation occurred in response to the attempt by the PAS to impose a standard in the context of direct-mail fundraising appeals, where a charity includes an educational message to the fundraising letter and allocates a portion of the cost of the mailing to program or administration. E.g., Cook, "Aim of New CBBB Standard: To Control What Nonprofits Say," XXVII *Phil. Monthly* (No. 3) 24 (Apr. 1994); Surhke, "In Your Face 'Disclosure'," *id.* at 2; Surhke, "Reprieve on CBBB Cost Allocation Disclosures," XXVII *Phil. Monthly* (No. 5) 10 (June 1994); Cook, "Assault on Freedom—Part II," *id.* at 13–14.

[29] Lawyers will not disagree, however, with the ECFA standard that encourages donors "to use the services of their attorneys, accountants, or other professional advisors." That is good advice for donees as well.

charitable organizations on such a simplistic plane; the making and dissemination of ratings ought to be abolished. The standards, as well, are often so flawed—and inconsistent with legal requirements and good management practices—that they too should be jettisoned. There is nothing wrong with reports on charitable organizations, as long as they are objective and current. Overall, however, the most useful assignment for the agencies would be the publication of educational materials about charitable giving and fundraising, largely directed at prospective donors, rather than efforts to target specific charitable organizations and to demean the sector.

One of the many ironies associated with the operation of these watchdog agencies is that their collective portrayal of themselves is less than forthright—indeed, is most misleading to the public. That is, they loftily characterize the entities as *voluntary* organizations and their standards as *voluntary* ones. Yet, this is blatantly false. There is nothing voluntary about adherence to these standards; charitable organizations are coerced into compliance out of fear of the otherwise adverse publicity that can quickly be unleashed by these agencies, which can whip up a material negative impression of a charity in a quote to a reporter or in a single mailing.

Another dimension to this distressing dilemma is the enormous amount of credibility these groups have acquired, even though there often is no substance behind the facade. A lack of competence, skill, and understanding, often coupled with both outright and subtle bias against the sector,[30] does not deter these groups from substituting their judgment for that of accountants, fundraising executives, and lawyers, and from asserting rules that contravene sound management and legal principles for charitable organizations. It is by no means clear how this state of affairs has developed—that is, how these watchdog groups became invested with this aura of ultimate and overriding knowledge and invincibility. (The summary of the origins of the PAS observes that its image in the public mind became extrapolated from the positive reputation engendered by the CBBB because of its consumer protection services.[31])

A final thought on this matter of nonproductivity. It is sad but true that the watchdog agencies, as a justification for their existence, must constantly portray the charitable sector in the darkest of terms. For example, the PAS has been aggressively discussing the results of a survey containing a variety of conclusions, including these: one-third of the respondents believed that charities had become less trustworthy during the previous year, 74 percent of them believed that more regulation of public charities is needed, and 49 percent said they were very concerned about levels of fundraising costs.

---

[30] In some respects, subtle antipathy can be more effective. As an example, in commenting on a survey indicating that charitable organizations are paying larger salaries and benefits than previously, a spokesperson for NCIB said: "I think they're giving more money [in salaries] in order to retain the talent they have" (Associated Press, as reproduced in the *Wash. Post*, Sep. 5, 1995, at E1, E2). Note the phraseology: "giving" more money. Also: "What they also have to keep in mind, however, is that it is a public record" (*id.* at E2), suggesting that these organizations have something to hide. These insinuations may have contributed to a headline accompanying this newspaper article: "Nonprofits Generous to CEOs."

[31] See *supra* § 2.

As another illustration, in the fall of 1994, the president of the NCIB gave a speech in which he painted a disheartening picture of the charitable sector, replete with case studies and statistics showing all manner of wrongdoing (such as excessive fundraising costs) and manipulation (such as rapacious officers) involving the nation's charitable organizations. The true impact of this portrayal was to depress everyone in the room; the listeners felt somewhat cheapened and ashamed for being associated, no matter how remotely, with such nefarious activities. Fortunately, the next segment of this program provided a tonic. The speaker observed that there is no empirical evidence to back up the immense breadth and depth of the problem as it is being depicted by the watchdog groups. He asked: "Does all of this activity amount to hunting flies with an elephant gun or chasing elephants with a flyswatter?"[32] It is the former, and perhaps some day a study of the "problem" will be undertaken. It would show that only a tiny minority of charities (or ostensible charities) are causing difficulties.[33]

The believability of these groups has evolved to the point that few charitable organizations possess the fortitude to challenge them; charities meekly—and involuntarily—struggle to conform with the standards because of the immense power, including the ability to swiftly decrease giving to targeted charitable organizations, that the watchdog agencies have amassed. Attracted by its simplicity, these organizations tend to highlight the subject of fundraising costs, despite the unfairness of the approach; this seems to be where public charities are the most vulnerable, which contributes to their obsequiousness.[34]

In the meantime, the standards-setting "voluntary" agencies seize on the perception (which they assiduously foment) that much wrongdoing is occurring in charitable fundraising. Their ratings and reports continue to flow. Some day, some court—it may be hoped—will intercede and expose these groups for what they are, and trim the scope of what they do. Perhaps that is the only way to shake the public's and the media's erroneous view that these agencies are objective and are performing useful functions.[35]

There may come a time when an enterprising reporter or perceptive and bold judge will see through the watchdog agencies' skein of standards and ratings and expose the misleading rationale for the existence of these groups and the often harmful and counterproductive outcomes they thrust on the charitable sector.

Meanwhile, the reach of these agencies continues to expand. On January 22, 2002, the BBB Wise Giving Alliance (the merged PAS and NCIB) issued proposed "Standards for Charitable Accountability."

[32] *Fund-Raising Reg. Rep.* (No. 1) 8 (Jan./Feb. 1995).

[33] To date, the report that comes closest to such a study is an analysis of the overall usefulness of the Council of Better Business Bureaus (Mirable, "Better Business Bureaus are a Bust," 24 *Money* (No. 10) 106 (Oct. 1995)).

[34] The differing views on this point are explored in greater detail in Stokeld, "Charitable Watchdogs: Fair or Foul?," 68 *Tax Notes* (No. 5) 534 (July 31, 1995).

[35] On its Website, the AIP observes that "[s]electing a charity to support is a bit like playing God." Yet the watchdog agencies, in the face of this awesome responsibility, keep doing it.

§ 8.9   A WATCHDOG AGENCY'S RESPONSE TO COMMENTARY

The foregoing commentary (Commentary) attracted a response (Response) from the NCIB.[36] This Response, lightly edited to conform to the book's format, follows.

> The Commentary on the "watchdog" agencies is disappointing, distressing, and dishonest.
>
> It is disappointing to those who might have expected the evenhandedness of [treatment of] law in the book. It is distressing to those who are concerned with the health of the charitable sector, who believe in openness and accountability, and who promote supporting as generously as possible charities that do what they say they do and meet donors' expectations. And it is ultimately dishonest—you knew what NCIB has been saying and doing, and clearly chose to ignore or misstate facts that did not fit your preconceptions.
>
> You are entitled (without my or anyone's permission, of course) to express any opinion you wish about organizations such as NCIB and PAS but, in a book that purports to be a standard legal reference for those concerned with fundraising, one might have hoped that the strangely nonconforming chapter on "watchdogs" had been more clearly labeled as opinion, rather than cloaked in lawyerly sounding, morally outraged phrasing. The low road traveled in high-falutin' language remains the low road.
>
> You are so wrong in so many statements that I hardly know where to begin or end a commentary on what you have written. Let me, for the record, cite a few of the more blatant examples of your adherence to wrong opinion and incorrect fact.
>
> It is stated: "In too many cases, an organization is, for example, rotated from a 'Meets Standards' listing to a 'Do Not Meet Standards' listing at the same time it is notified of the change in status." That is an outright untruth. NCIB gives organizations prior notice of such a change in status and sends all organizations prepublication copies of new reports about them, along with an explanatory letter seeking their input. We state a future date on which we will make our new report available to the public if we do not hear back. If organizations perceive the time as too short, they may call us and seek an extension, which we always agree to, even if it is several weeks or even longer. During this waiting period, an organization is listed as "Report on Update" and is never "rotated" from a "Meets" to "Not" listing as you describe.
>
> When it was written that "it is sad but true that the watchdog agencies, as a justification for their existence, must constantly portray the charitable sector in the darkest terms," you are again stating something you know to be untrue. That is an absurd statement. NCIB has clearly and strongly stated that "the great majority of charities do their work well and merit the generous support of contributors"—a statement we have made in several ways, consistently, in print and in speaking, over an extended period, including while the book was being prepared and well before it was

[36] Letter to the author from James J. Bausch, President, National Charities Information Bureau, dated May 30, 1996.

published. You are the party with the dark paintbrush and preconceived vested interest here.

Outrage was professed in the Commentary that, in "an egregious lack of adherence to . . . principle," NCIB and PAS "take issue with the organization on a matter involving one or more accounting principles or reporting practices" after that organization has reported its finances in accordance with generally accepted accounting principles. Either the Commentary is based on a naive belief that GAAP guidance is precise, concrete, and all-satisfying, or it offers a new and definitive example of disingenuousness. If you become interested in factual candor at some future time, you may wish to begin your education about GAAP and other matters by reading Regina Herzlinger's article in the March–April issue of the *Harvard Business Review,* entitled "Can Public Trust in Nonprofits and Governments Be Restored?" You may also know of Professor Herzlinger as the senior author of *Financial Accounting and Management Control of Nonprofit Organizations.* Professor H. David Sherman's sidebar on "The Gaps in GAAP" might be enlightening to one who seeks enlightenment. The point is, as representatives of AICPA and FASB routinely state, that GAAP allows wide interpretation, and any given interpretation may not satisfy all relevant perspectives. One can reasonably assume that an expert like you already knew all of this and deliberately chose to distort the picture by ignoring it.

The Commentary harps on my talk at the "Fund Raising and the Law" meeting in Washington. Yes, I did report what reliable polls indicate concerning public opinion about the trustworthiness, efficiency, and effectiveness of the philanthropic sector and specifically about fundraisers. I did not make up the "statistics," nor did I think that playing ostrich as if people's opinions did not exist or did not matter was an appropriate exercise. I also did not think I was asked to give a pep talk—although I will freely admit that I might appropriately have put more positives into that particular presentation. My purpose was to encourage those attending the conference to adopt three courses of action: to conduct themselves professionally in accordance with such principles as those expressed in the "Donor Bill of Rights," to work hard to restore public confidence in sound charities and sound fundraising, and to drum out of the profession those who consistently bring philanthropy and fundraising into disrepute. If the effect of my words was "to depress everyone in the room," I did not succeed in my goal—although a reliable witness asserts that it was you, bad-mouthing my presentation after I left, who worked hard to convince the participants that they should be depressed. It is not a matter of either elephant guns or flyswatters, but of facing up to reality and building up the goodwill and credibility that philanthropy and fundraising must have.

Finally, as I have previously informed you more than once, I personally do not subscribe to a "dark" picture of America's charities, nor would I lead an organization that did. I have devoted three decades of my life to this sector and have been raising funds for most of that time. I firmly believe that fundraising for charitable causes is a desirable means to a desirable end. I applaud it and those who do it properly and well—and I absolutely believe that is the overwhelming majority of those involved. I condemn the small minority whose actions sling mud on good practitioners and on our sector precisely because they injure contributors, charities, and all the good fundraisers.

All these things you have known, but chose to ignore. Where, one wonders, in your definition of law, does such purposeful ignorance and misstatement as you have put forth become just plain distortion, dishonesty, and defamation? There is no need for you to try to respond, as the self-serving bias of any answer you might give is already abundantly clear.

Your readers surely hoped for more integrity and less pandering to personal prejudgments and special interests than you have shown. I write far more in sorrow than in anger at the serious disservice you have done to our sector.

§ 8.10   REPLY TO RESPONSE

By virtue of the Response, one is not confined to the watchdog agencies' reports on charitable organizations to glean examples of the literary devices they so often employ: the arrogant tone, misleading phraseology, innuendo, misstatement of fact, attention-shifting to irrelevant points, and emphasis on insignificant detail to either obscure or taint the big picture.

For arrogance, nothing can surpass the concession that commentators are entitled to express opinions on the watchdog agencies absent their prior consent. Concerns about fair process are dismissed as "lawyerly sounding" phrasing and "high-falutin'" language. The Response stated that NCIB ceased rotating charities from one category to another without notice. That was a commendable development and it was nice that the organization stopped engaging in the practice, but was a trivial point in relation to the vast panorama of due process violations routinely committed by the watchdog agencies.

The most casual comparison of the Commentary with the Response yields the fact that the latter wholly sidestepped the essence of the former. That is that (1) the watchdog agencies are self-appointed and self-styled; (2) they are accountable to no external authority or constituency; (3) they falsely portray themselves as "voluntary" agencies; (4) they are staffed by individuals who are not competent to make the conclusions they reach; (5) they wield enormous leverage over hapless charities (which often comply out of fear) because of the power of the watchdogs' ratings and reports; and (6) they have never been subject to any serious external scrutiny. The Response is silent across the board in these regards.

The one concrete example to be found in the Response is telling in two respects. This is the matter of application of generally accepted accounting principles (GAAP). There is no question that these principles are the subject of considerable interpretation. But it should be obvious that the place to begin in understanding and applying GAAP is the principles themselves and the interpretations by those who are professionally competent to interpret them, namely, certified public accountants. The bias of the NCIB in this regard was dramatically revealed when the Response stated that, to understand GAAP, one must initially turn to sources that criticize the principles. The fact is that the watchdog agencies often do not like the conclusions mandated by GAAP, and thus they openly attach themselves to any source that denigrates them. The point of the Commentary was not that the watchdog agencies interpret

GAAP; it was that they substitute their judgment for that of the professionals who possess the competence to interpret these principles.

Overall, a lawyer's concern for the procedural and substantive rights of charitable organizations caught up in the clutches of one or more of the watchdog agencies becomes characterized by the Response as pandering to "special interests." Over three decades of law practice, witnessing charities mistreated and miscast by these groups becomes "personal prejudgment" and "self-serving bias." And that is just the beginning: What to make of charges of "distortion, dishonesty, and defamation"? Probably the best approach is to simply accord these claims the credence they are due, as reflected in the fact that the source of them grandly asserts that a mere Commentary in one chapter of a book constitutes a "serious disservice" to the charitable sector. The sector is hardier than that, as evidenced by its ability to survive the pretensions of and material damages inflicted by the watchdog agencies.[37]

---

[37] It was observed in § 7 that the watchdog agencies often demonstrate outright bias against the charitable sector. A classic example of this prejudice against the sector was the reaction of the heads of the PAS and the NCIB to the court decision rendering several provisions of the Los Angeles city and county charitable solicitation ordinances unconstitutional (*Gospel Missions of America* v. *Bennett*, 951 F. Supp. 1429 (C.D. Cal. 1997)) (see §§ 4.3, 4.6, 4.7, 4.8). The former said: "The reduction of such local government regulatory activities places more of a burden on the donor to check out charities on their [sic] own"; the latter said he was disappointed in the holding: "The donor has the right to know how his [or her] donation is used" (Craig, "Judge Strikes Down Key Parts of Los Angeles's Tough Rules for Charities," 9 *Chron. of Phil.* (No. 8) 25 (Feb. 6, 1997)). These views amply illustrate that the watchdog agencies champion unchecked government regulation of fundraising by the sector even to the point of its serious damage (the charitable organization involved was unjustifiably raided by 40 county sheriffs, and subjected to search and seizure at gunpoint)—irrespective of whether the law is egregiously unconstitutional. In the case, the court found 15 provisions of the ordinances to be unconstitutional on their face in violation of free speech rights, 6 provisions to be unconstitutional because of the unbridled discretion vested in government officials, and 5 provisions to be unconstitutional for various other reasons, including vagueness and violation of the Constitution's establishment clause! It is shameful that the watchdog agencies champion this type of law.

This antipathy against the sector was revealed in another context—this time in the aftermath of publication by the accounting profession of new rules concerning joint cost allocations (Statement of Position 98-2, published by the American Institute of Certified Public Accountants as an adjustment to rules written in 1987). Many charity officials have objected to these rules, finding them to be "too strict and . . . biased against legitimate fund-raising activities" (Billitteri and Blum, "Unsettled Accounts," X *Chron. of Phil.* (No. 11) 41 (Mar. 26, 1998)). Predictably, the principal watchdog agencies decided that the "revised policy is too lenient, allowing charities to hide some fund-raising costs in other accounting categories" (*id.*). Thus, while one of the nation's premier accountants in the nonprofit field (who participated in the writing of the Statement), Richard Larkin, said that the "underlying concept" of the 1998 rules "is still the same" as that of the 1987 rules, and that the "difference is only in the details," the president of the NCIB said: "The bottom line is that contributors deserve better" (*id.* at 42).

APPENDIX A

SOURCES OF THE LAW

The law as described in this book is derived from many sources. For those not familiar with these matters and wishing to understand just what "the law" regarding fundraising by charitable organizations is, the following explanation should be of assistance.

Federal Law

At the federal (national) level in the United States, there are three branches of government as provided for in the U.S. Constitution. Article I of the Constitution established the U.S. Congress as a bicameral legislature, consisting of the House of Representatives and the Senate. Article II of the Constitution established the Presidency. Article III of the Constitution established the federal court system.

Congress

The legal structure underlying the federal law applicable to charitable organizations, fundraising by them, and those who assist them in fundraising, has been created by Congress. Most of this law is manifested in the tax law and thus appears in the Internal Revenue Code (which is officially codified in Title 26 of the United States Code and referenced throughout the book as the IRC (see Chapter 1, n. 2)). Other laws written by Congress that can affect fundraising by charitable organizations include the postal, employee benefits, antitrust, trade, labor, and securities laws.

Tax laws for the United States must originate in the House of Representatives (U.S. Constitution, Article I § 7). Consequently, most of the nation's tax laws are initially written by the members and staff of the House Committee on Ways and Means. Frequently, these laws are generated at the subcommittee level, usually the Subcommittee on Oversight or the Subcommittee on Select Revenue Measures.

Committee work in this area within the Senate is undertaken by the Committee on Finance. The Joint Committee on Taxation, consisting of members from both the House of Representatives and the Senate, also provides most of the legislation-writing assistance. Nearly all of this legislation is finalized by a House-Senate conference committee, consisting of senior members of the House Ways and Means Committee and the Senate Finance Committee.

A considerable amount of the federal tax law for nonprofit organizations is found in the legislative history of these statutory laws. Most of this history is in congressional committee reports. Reports from committees in the House of Representatives are cited as "H. Rep." (see, e.g., Chapter 1, n. 12); reports from committees in the Senate are cited as "S. Rep." (see, e.g., Chapter 5, n. 203);

conference committee reports are cited as "H. Rep." Transcripts of the debate on legislation, formal statements, and other items are printed in the Congressional Record (*Cong. Rec.*). The Congressional Record is published every day one of the houses of Congress is in session and is cited as "_____ Cong. Rec. _____ (daily ed., [date of issue])." The first number is the annual volume number; the second number is the page in the daily edition on which the item begins. Periodically, the daily editions of the Congressional Record are republished as a hard-bound book and are cited as "_____ Cong. Rec. _____ ([year])." As before, the first number is the annual volume number and the second is the beginning page number. The bound version of the Congressional Record then becomes the publication that contains the permanent citation for the item.

A Congress sits for two years, each of which is termed a session. Each Congress is sequentially numbered. For example, the 107th Congress met during the calendar years 2001–2002. A legislative development that took place in 2001 is referenced as occurring during the 107th Congress, 1st Session (107th Cong., 1st Sess. (2001)).

A bill introduced in the House of Representatives or Senate during a particular Congress is given a sequential number in each house. For example, the 1,000th bill introduced in the House of Representatives in 2001 is cited as "H.R. 1000, 107th Cong., 1st Sess. (2001)" (see e.g., Chapter 6, n. 7); the 500th bill introduced in the Senate in 2001 is cited as "S. 500, 107th Cong., 1st Sess. (2001)" (see, e.g., Chapter 6, n. 8).

Executive Branch

A function of the Executive Branch in the United States is to administer and enforce the laws enacted by Congress. This executive function is performed by departments and agencies, and independent regulatory commissions (such as the Federal Trade Commission or the Securities and Exchange Commission). One of these functions is the promulgation of regulations, which are published by the U.S. government in the Code of Federal Regulations (CFR). When adopted, regulations are printed in the *Federal Register* (*Fed. Reg.*). The federal tax laws are administered and enforced by the Department of the Treasury and the federal election laws are administered and enforced by the Federal Election Commission. Other laws in this field include those administered and enforced by the Office of Management and Budget (OMB) and the Office of Personnel Management (OPM).

One of the ways in which the Department of the Treasury executes these functions is by the promulgation of regulations (Reg.), which are designed to interpret and amplify the related statute (see, e.g., Chapter 1, n. 5). These regulations (like other rules made by other departments, agencies, and commissions) have the force of law, unless they are overly broad in relation to the accompanying statute or are unconstitutional, in which case they can be rendered void by a court.

Within the Department of the Treasury is the Internal Revenue Service (IRS). The IRS is, among its many roles, a tax-collecting agency. The IRS, while headquartered in Washington, D.C., has regional and field offices throughout the country.

The IRS (from its national headquarters) prepares and disseminates guidelines interpreting tax statues and tax regulations. These guidelines have the force of law, unless they are overbroad in relation to the statute and/or Treasury regulation involved, or are unconstitutional. IRS determinations on a point of law are termed revenue rulings (Rev. Rul.); those that are rules of procedure are termed revenue procedures (Rev. Proc.).

Revenue rulings (which may be based on one or more court opinions) and revenue procedures are sequentially numbered every calendar year, with that number preceded by a two-digit number reflecting the year of issue. For example, the fiftieth revenue ruling issued in 2002 is cited as "Rev. Rul. 2002-50." Likewise, the twenty-fifth revenue procedure issued in 2002 is cited as "Rev. Proc. 2002-25."

These IRS determinations are published each week in the Internal Revenue Bulletin (I.R.B.). In the foregoing examples, when the determinations are first published, the revenue ruling is cited as "Rev. Rul. 2002-50, 2002-_____ I.R.B. _____," with the number after the hyphen being the number of the particular issue of the weekly Bulletin and the last number being the page number within that issue on which the item begins. Likewise, the revenue procedure is cited as Rev. Proc. 2002-25, 1995-_____ I.R.B. _____." Every six months, the Internal Revenue Bulletins are republished as hard-bound books, with the resulting publication termed the Cumulative Bulletin (C.B.). The Cumulative Bulletin designation then becomes the permanent citation for the determination. Thus, the permanent citations for these two IRS determinations are "Rev. Rul. 2002-50, 2002-1 C.B. _____" (see e.g., Chapter 2, n. 11) and "Rev. Proc. 2002-25, 1995-1 C.B. _____" (see e.g., Chapter 5, n. 52), with the first number being the year of issue, the second number (after the hyphen) indicating whether the determination is published in the first six months of the year (1, as is the case in the example) or the second six months of the year (2), and the last number being the page number within that semi-annual bound volume at which the determination begins.

The IRS considers itself bound by its revenue rulings and revenue procedures. These determinations are the "law," particularly in the sense that the IRS regards them as precedential, although they are not binding on the courts.

By contrast to these forms of "public" law, the IRS (again, from its national headquarters) also issues "private" or nonprecedential determinations. These documents principally are private letter rulings, technical advice memoranda, and general counsel memoranda. These determinations may not be cited as legal authority (IRC § 6110(j)(3)). Nonetheless, these pronouncements can be valuable in understanding IRS thinking on a point of law and, in practice (the statutory prohibition notwithstanding), these documents are cited as IRS positions on issues, such as in court opinions, articles, and books.

The IRS issues private letter rulings in response to written questions (termed "ruling requests") submitted to the IRS by individuals and organizations. An IRS district office may refer a case to the IRS national headquarters for advice (termed "technical advice"); the resulting advice is provided to the IRS district office in the form of a technical advice memorandum. In the course of preparing a revenue ruling, private letter ruling, or technical advice memorandum, the IRS may seek legal advice from its Office of Chief Counsel; the resulting advice is provided in the form of a general counsel memorandum. These documents are eventually made public, albeit in redacted form.

Private letter rulings and technical advice memoranda are identified by seven-digit numbers, such as "IRS Private Letter Ruling 95126007" (see, e.g., Chapter 5, n. 49). The first two numbers are for the year involved (here, 1995), the second two numbers reflect the week of the calendar year involved (here, the twenty-sixth week of 1995), and the remaining three numbers identify the document as issued sequentially during the particular week (here, this private letter ruling was the seventh one issued during the week involved). General counsel memoranda are numbered sequentially since they have been written (e.g., General Counsel Memorandum 39457 is the thirty-nine thousandth, four hundredth, fifty-seventh general counsel memorandum ever written by the IRS' Office of Chief Counsel).

The Judiciary

The federal court system has three levels: trial courts (including those that initially hear cases where a formal trial is not involved), courts of appeal ("appellate" courts), and the U.S. Supreme Court. The trial courts include the various federal district courts (at least one in each state, the District of Columbia, and the U.S. territories), the U.S. Tax Court, and the U.S. Claims Court. There are thirteen federal appellate courts (the U.S. Courts of Appeal for the First through the Eleventh Circuits, the U.S. Court of Appeals for the District of Columbia, and the U.S. Court of Appeals for the Federal Circuit).

Cases involving tax-exempt organization issues at the federal level can originate in any federal district court, the U.S. Tax Court, and the U.S. Claims Court. Under a special declaratory judgment procedure available only to charitable organizations (IRC § 7428), cases can originate only with the U.S. District Court for the District of Columbia, the U.S. Tax Court, and the U.S. Court of Federal Claims. Cases involving tax-exempt organizations are considered by the U.S. courts of appeal and the U.S. Supreme Court.

Most opinions emanating from a U.S. district court are published by the West Publishing Co. in the "Federal Supplement" series (Fed. Supp.). Thus, a citation to one of these opinions appears as "_____ F. Supp. _____," followed by an identification of the court and the year of the opinion. The first number is the annual volume number; the second number is the page in the book on which the opinion begins (see, e.g., Chapter 1, n. 13). Some district court opinions appear earlier in the Commerce Clearinghouse or Prentice Hall publications; occasionally, these publications will contain opinions that are never published in the Federal Supplement.

Most opinions emanating from a U.S. court of appeals are published by the West Publishing Co. in the "Federal Reporter Second" series (Fed. 2d). Thus, a citation to one of these opinions appears as "_____ F. 2d _____," followed by an identification of the court and the year of the opinion. The first number is the annual volume number; the second number is the page in the book on which the opinion begins (see, e.g., Chapter 1, n. 11). (Beginning in early 1994, the "Federal Reporter Third" series was started (once volume 999 of the Federal Reporter Second series was published); thus, the citations to future opinions from the U.S. courts of appeal will appear as "_____ F. 3d _____.") Appellate court opinions appear earlier in the Commerce Clearinghouse or Prentice Hall publications; occasionally, these publications will contain opinions that are never published in Federal Second. Opinions from the U.S. Court of Federal Claims are also published in Federal Second.

Opinions from the U.S. Tax Court are published by the U.S. government and are usually cited as "_____ T.C. _____," followed by the year of the opinion (see e.g., Chapter 5, n. 47). Some Tax Court opinions that are of lesser precedential value are published as "memorandum decisions" and are cited as "_____ T.C.M. _____" followed by the year of the opinion (see, e.g., Chapter 5, n. 382). As always, the first number of these citations is the annual volume number; the second number is the page in the book on which the opinion begins.

U.S. district court and Tax Court opinions may be appealed to the appropriate U.S. court of appeals. For example, cases in the states of Maryland, North Carolina, South Carolina, Virginia, and West Virginia, and the District of Columbia, are appealable (from either court) to the U.S. Court of Appeals for the Fourth Circuit. Cases from any federal appellate or district court, the U.S. Tax Court, and the U.S. Court of Federal Claims may be appealed to the U.S. Supreme Court.

The U.S. Supreme Court usually has discretion as to whether to accept a case. This decision is manifested as a "writ of certiorari." When the Supreme Court agrees to hear a case, it grants the writ (cert. gr.); otherwise, it denies the writ (cert. den.).

In this book, citations to Supreme Court opinions are to the "United States Reports" series, published by the U.S. government, when available ("_____ U.S. _____", followed by the year of the opinion) (see, e.g., Chapter 1, n. 4). When the United States Reports series citation is not available, the "Supreme Court Reporter" series, published by the West Publishing Co., reference is used ("_____ S. Ct. _____", followed by the year of the opinion). As always, the first number of these citations is the annual volume number; the second number is the page in the book on which the opinion begins. There is a third way to cite Supreme Court cases, which is by means of the "United States Supreme Court Reports—Lawyers' Edition" series, published by The Lawyers Co-Operative Publishing Co. and the Bancroft-Whitney Co., but that form of citation is not used in this book. Supreme Court opinions appear earlier in the Commerce Clearinghouse or Prentice Hall publications.

State Law

The Legislative Branches

Statutory laws in the various states are created by their legislatures.

The Executive Branches

The rules and regulations published at the state level emanate from state departments, agencies, and the like. For nonprofit organizations, these departments are usually the office of the state's attorney general and the state's department of state. There are no references to state rules and regulations in this book (although most, if not all, of the states have such forms of law relating to the advocacy activities of nonprofit organizations).

The Judiciary

Each of the states has a judiciary system, usually a three-tiered one modeled after the federal system. Cases involving nonprofit organizations are heard in all of these courts. There are some references to state court opinions in this book (although most, if not all, of the states have court opinions relating to the advocacy activities of nonprofit organizations).

State court opinions are published by the governments of each state and the principal ones by West Publishing Co. The latter sets of opinions (referenced in this book) are published in *Reporters* relating to court developments in various regions throughout the country. For example, the *Atlantic Reporter* contains court opinions issued by the principal courts in the states of Connecticut, Delaware, Maine, Maryland, New Hampshire, New Jersey, Pennsylvania, Rhode Island, and Vermont, and the District of Columbia, while the *Pacific Reporter* contains court opinions issued by the principal courts of Arizona, California, Colorado, Idaho, Kansas, Montana, Nevada, New Mexico, Oklahoma, Oregon, Utah, Washington, and Wyoming.

Publications

Articles are not forms of "the law." They can be cited, however, particularly by courts, in the development of the law. Also, as research tools, they contain useful summaries of the applicable law. In addition to the many law school "law review" publications, the following (which is not an exclusive list) periodicals contain material that is of help in following developments concerning charitable organizations, fund-raising, and the law:

> *Advancing Philantrophy* (Association of Fundraising Professionals)
>
> *The Chronicle of Philanthropy*
>
> *Daily Tax Report* (Bureau of National Affairs, Inc.)
>
> *Exempt Organization Tax Report* (Tax Analysts)
>
> *Foundation News* (Council on Foundations)
>
> *Giving USA* and other publications of the American Association of Fund Raising Counsel's Trust for Philanthropy
>
> *The Journal of Taxation* (Warren, Gorham & Lamont)
>
> *The Journal of Taxation of Exempt Organizations* (Warren, Gorham & Lamont)

APPENDIX A

The Nonprofit Counsel (John Wiley & Sons, Inc.)
The Philanthropy Monthly (Non-Profit Reports, Inc.)
Tax Law Review (Rosenfeld Launer Publications)
The Tax Lawyer (American Bar Association)
Tax Notes (Tax Analysts)
Taxes (Commerce Clearinghouse, Inc.)

APPENDIX B

IRS FORM 1023: APPLICATION FOR
RECOGNITION OF EXEMPTION

Form **1023** (Rev. September 1998) Department of the Treasury Internal Revenue Service	**Application for Recognition of Exemption** Under Section 501(c)(3) of the Internal Revenue Code	OMB No. 1545-0056 **Note:** *If exempt status is approved, this application will be open for public inspection.*

Read the instructions for each Part carefully.
A User Fee must be attached to this application.
If the required information and appropriate documents are not submitted along with Form 8718 (with payment of the appropriate user fee), the application may be returned to you.
Complete the Procedural Checklist on page 8 of the instructions.

Part I Identification of Applicant

1a Full name of organization (as shown in organizing document)		**2** Employer identification number (EIN) (If none, see page 3 of the **Specific Instructions**.)
1b c/o Name (if applicable)		**3** Name and telephone number of person to be contacted if additional information is needed
1c Address (number and street)	Room/Suite	( )
1d City, town, or post office, state, and ZIP + 4. If you have a foreign address, see **Specific Instructions** for Part I, page 3.		**4** Month the annual accounting period ends
		5 Date incorporated or formed
1e Web site address		**6** Check here if applying under section: **a** ☐ 501(e) **b** ☐ 501(f) **c** ☐ 501(k) **d** ☐ 501(n)

7 Did the organization previously apply for recognition of exemption under this Code section or under any other section of the Code? . . . . ☐ Yes ☐ No
If "Yes," attach an explanation.

8 Is the organization required to file Form 990 (or Form 990-EZ)? . . . . ☐ N/A ☐ Yes ☐ No
If "No," attach an explanation (see page 3 of the **Specific Instructions**).

9 Has the organization filed Federal income tax returns or exempt organization information returns? . . ☐ Yes ☐ No
If "Yes," state the form numbers, years filed, and Internal Revenue office where filed.

10 Check the box for the type of organization. ATTACH A CONFORMED COPY OF THE CORRESPONDING ORGANIZING DOCUMENTS TO THE APPLICATION BEFORE MAILING. (See **Specific Instructions** for Part I, Line 10, on page 3.) See also Pub. 557 for examples of organizational documents.)

a ☐ Corporation—Attach a copy of the Articles of Incorporation (including amendments and restatements) showing approval by the appropriate state official; also include a copy of the bylaws.

b ☐ Trust— Attach a copy of the Trust Indenture or Agreement, including all appropriate signatures and dates.

c ☐ Association— Attach a copy of the Articles of Association, Constitution, or other creating document, with a declaration (see instructions) or other evidence the organization was formed by adoption of the document by more than one person; also include a copy of the bylaws.

If the organization is a corporation or an unincorporated association that has not yet adopted bylaws, check here ▶ ☐

I declare under the penalties of perjury that I am authorized to sign this application on behalf of the above organization and that I have examined this application, including the accompanying schedules and attachments, and to the best of my knowledge it is true, correct, and complete.

Please Sign Here ▶

(Signature)	(Type or print name and title or authority of signer)	(Date)

For Paperwork Reduction Act Notice, see page 7 of the instructions.   Cat. No. 17133K

APPENDIX B

Part II   Activities and Operational Information

1 Provide a detailed narrative description of all the activities of the organization—past, present, and planned. **Do not merely refer to or repeat the language in the organizational document.** List each activity separately in the order of importance based on the relative time and other resources devoted to the activity. Indicate the percentage of time for each activity. Each description should include, as a minimum, the following: **(a)** a detailed description of the activity including its purpose and how each acitivity furthers your exempt purpose; **(b)** when the activity was or will be initiated; and **(c)** where and by whom the activity will be conducted.

2 What are or will be the organization's sources of financial support? List in order of size.

3 Describe the organization's fundraising program, both actual and planned, and explain to what extent it has been put into effect. Include details of fundraising activities such as selective mailings, formation of fundraising committees, use of volunteers or professional fundraisers, etc. Attach representative copies of solicitations for financial support.

APPENDIX B

Part II Activities and Operational Information *(Continued)*

4   Give the following information about the organization's governing body:

a Names, addresses, and titles of officers, directors, trustees, etc.	b Annual compensation

c   Do any of the above persons serve as members of the governing body by reason of being public officials or being appointed by public officials? . . . . ☐ Yes ☐ No
If "Yes," name those persons and explain the basis of their selection or appointment.

d   Are any members of the organization's governing body "disqualified persons" with respect to the organization (other than by reason of being a member of the governing body) or do any of the members have either a business or family relationship with "disqualified persons"? (See **Specific Instructions** for Part II, Line 4d, on page 3.) . . . . ☐ Yes ☐ No
If "Yes," explain.

5   Does the organization control or is it controlled by any other organization? . . . . ☐ Yes ☐ No
Is the organization the outgrowth of (or successor to) another organization, or does it have a special relationship with another organization by reason of interlocking directorates or other factors? . . . . ☐ Yes ☐ No
If either of these questions is answered "Yes," explain.

6   Does or will the organization directly or indirectly engage in any of the following transactions with any political organization or other exempt organization (other than a 501(c)(3) organization): **(a)** grants; **(b)** purchases or sales of assets; **(c)** rental of facilities or equipment; **(d)** loans or loan guarantees; **(e)** reimbursement arrangements; **(f)** performance of services, membership, or fundraising solicitations; or **(g)** sharing of facilities, equipment, mailing lists or other assets, or paid employees? . . . . . . ☐ Yes ☐ No
If "Yes," explain fully and identify the other organizations involved.

7   Is the organization financially accountable to any other organization? . . . . ☐ Yes ☐ No
If "Yes," explain and identify the other organization. Include details concerning accountability or attach copies of reports if any have been submitted.

APPENDIX B

Part II **Activities and Operational Information** *(Continued)*

8 What assets does the organization have that are used in the performance of its exempt function? (Do not include property producing investment income.) If any assets are not fully operational, explain their status, what additional steps remain to be completed, and when such final steps will be taken. If none, indicate "N/A."

9 Will the organization be the beneficiary of tax-exempt bond financing within the next 2 years? . . . . ☐ **Yes** ☐ **No**

10a Will any of the organization's facilities or operations be managed by another organization or individual under a contractual agreement?. . . . . ☐ **Yes** ☐ **No**
b Is the organization a party to any leases? . . . . ☐ **Yes** ☐ **No**
If either of these questions is answered "Yes," attach a copy of the contracts and explain the relationship between the applicant and the other parties.

11 Is the organization a membership organization? . . . . ☐ **Yes** ☐ **No**
If "Yes," complete the following:
a Describe the organization's membership requirements and attach a schedule of membership fees and dues.

b Describe the organization's present and proposed efforts to attract members and attach a copy of any descriptive literature or promotional material used for this purpose.

c What benefits do (or will) the members receive in exchange for their payment of dues?

12a If the organization provides benefits, services, or products, are the recipients required, or will they be required, to pay for them? . . . . ☐ **N/A** ☐ **Yes** ☐ **No**
If "Yes," explain how the charges are determined and attach a copy of the current fee schedule.

b Does or will the organization limit its benefits, services, or products to specific individuals or classes of individuals? . . . . ☐ **N/A** ☐ **Yes** ☐ **No**
If "Yes," explain how the recipients or beneficiaries are or will be selected.

13 Does or will the organization attempt to influence legislation? . . . . ☐ **Yes** ☐ **No**
If "Yes," explain. Also, give an estimate of the percentage of the organization's time and funds that it devotes or plans to devote to this activity.

14 Does or will the organization intervene in any way in political campaigns, including the publication or distribution of statements? . . . . ☐ **Yes** ☐ **No**
If "Yes," explain fully.

APPENDIX B

Form 1023 (Rev. 9-98)   Page **5**

Part III   **Technical Requirements**

1   Are you filing Form 1023 within 15 months from the end of the month in which your organization was
created or formed? . . . .   ☐ **Yes** ☐ **No**
If you answer "Yes," do not answer questions on lines 2 through 6 below.

2   If one of the exceptions to the 15-month filing requirement shown below applies, check the appropriate box and proceed
to question 7.
Exceptions—You are not required to file an exemption application within 15 months if the organization:

   ☐ **a**   Is a church, interchurch organization of local units of a church, a convention or association of churches, or an
integrated auxiliary of a church. See **Specific Instructions,** Line 2a, on page 4;
   ☐ **b**   Is not a private foundation and normally has gross receipts of not more than $5,000 in each tax year; or

   ☐ **c**   Is a subordinate organization covered by a group exemption letter, but only if the parent or supervisory organization
timely submitted a notice covering the subordinate.

3   If the organization does not meet any of the exceptions on line 2 above, are you filing Form 1023 within
27 months from the end of the month in which the organization was created or formed?. . . . . .   ☐ **Yes** ☐ **No**

   If "Yes," your organization qualifies under Regulation section 301.9100-2, for an automatic 12-month
extension of the 15-month filing requirement. Do not answer questions 4 through 6.

   If "No," answer question 4.

4   If you answer "No" to question 3, does the organization wish to request an extension of time to apply
under the "reasonable action and good faith" and the "no prejudice to the interest of the government"
requirements of Regulations section 301.9100-3? . . . .   ☐ **Yes** ☐ **No**

   If "Yes," give the reasons for not filing this application within the 27-month period described in question 3.
See **Specific Instructions,** Part III, Line 4, before completing this item. Do not answer questions 5 and 6.

   If "No," answer questions 5 and 6.

5   If you answer "No" to question 4, your organization's qualification as a section 501(c)(3) organization can
be recognized only from the date this application is filed. Therefore, do you want us to consider the
application as a request for recognition of exemption as a section 501(c)(3) organization from the date
the application is received and not retroactively to the date the organization was created or formed?   ☐ **Yes** ☐ **No**

6   If you answer "Yes" to question 5 above and wish to request recognition of section 501(c)(4) status for the period beginning
with the date the organization was formed and ending with the date the Form 1023 application was received (the effective
date of the organization's section 501(c)(3) status), check here ▶ ☐   and attach a completed page 1 of Form 1024 to this
application.

■   464   ■

APPENDIX B

Part III   **Technical Requirements** *(Continued)*

---

7   Is the organization a private foundation?
☐ **Yes** (Answer question 8.)
☐ **No** (Answer question 9 and proceed as instructed.)

---

8   If you answer "Yes" to question 7, does the organization claim to be a private operating foundation?
☐ **Yes** (Complete Schedule E.)
☐ **No**

After answering question 8 on this line, go to line 14 on page 7.

---

9   If you answer "No" to question 7, indicate the public charity classification the organization is requesting by checking the box below that most appropriately applies:

THE ORGANIZATION IS NOT A PRIVATE FOUNDATION BECAUSE IT QUALIFIES:

a	☐	As a church or a convention or association of churches (CHURCHES MUST COMPLETE SCHEDULE A.)	Sections 509(a)(1) and 170(b)(1)(A)(i)
b	☐	As a school (MUST COMPLETE SCHEDULE B.)	Sections 509(a)(1) and 170(b)(1)(A)(ii)
c	☐	As a hospital or a cooperative hospital service organization, or a medical research organization operated in conjunction with a hospital (These organizations, except for hospital service organizations, MUST COMPLETE SCHEDULE C.)	Sections 509(a)(1) and 170(b)(1)(A)(iii)
d	☐	As a governmental unit described in section 170(c)(1).	Sections 509(a)(1) and 170(b)(1)(A)(v)
e	☐	As being operated solely for the benefit of, or in connection with, one or more of the organizations described in **a** through **d**, **g**, **h**, or **i** (MUST COMPLETE SCHEDULE D.)	Section 509(a)(3)
f	☐	As being organized and operated exclusively for testing for public safety.	Section 509(a)(4)
g	☐	As being operated for the benefit of a college or university that is owned or operated by a governmental unit.	Sections 509(a)(1) and 170(b)(1)(A)(iv)
h	☐	As receiving a substantial part of its support in the form of contributions from publicly supported organizations, from a governmental unit, or from the general public.	Sections 509(a)(1) and 170(b)(1)(A)(vi)
i	☐	As normally receiving not more than one-third of its support from gross investment income and more than one-third of its support from contributions, membership fees, and gross receipts from activities related to its exempt functions (subject to certain exceptions).	Section 509(a)(2)
j	☐	The organization is a publicly supported organization but is not sure whether it meets the public support test of **h** or **i**. The organization would like the IRS to decide the proper classification.	Sections 509(a)(1) and 170(b)(1)(A)(vi) or Section 509(a)(2)

**If you checked one of the boxes a through f in question 9, go to question
14. If you checked box g in question 9, go to questions 11 and 12.
If you checked box h, i, or j, in question 9, go to question 10.**

Part III   **Technical Requirements** *(Continued)*

10   If you checked box **h, i,** or **j** in question 9, has the organization completed a tax year of at least 8 months?

☐ **Yes**—Indicate whether you are requesting:

☐ A definitive ruling. (Answer questions 11 through 14.)

☐ An advance ruling. (Answer questions 11 and 14 and attach two Forms 872-C completed and signed.)

☐ **No—You must request an advance ruling by completing and signing two Forms 872-C and attaching them to the Form 1023.**

11   If the organization received any unusual grants during any of the tax years shown in Part IV-A, **Statement of Revenue and Expenses,** attach a list for each year showing the name of the contributor; the date and the amount of the grant; and a brief description of the nature of the grant.

12   If you are requesting a definitive ruling under section 170(b)(1)(A)(iv) or (vi), check here ▶ ☐ and:

a Enter 2% of line 8, column (e), Total, of Part IV-A . . . . _____

b Attach a list showing the name and amount contributed by each person (other than a governmental unit or "publicly supported" organization) whose total gifts, grants, contributions, etc., were more than the amount entered on line **12a** above.

13   If you are requesting a definitive ruling under section 509(a)(2), check here ▶ ☐ and:

a For each of the years included on lines 1, 2, and 9 of Part IV-A, attach a list showing the name of and amount received from each "disqualified person." (For a definition of "disqualified person," see **Specific Instructions,** Part II, Line 4d, on page 3.)

b For each of the years included on line 9 of Part IV-A, attach a list showing the name of and amount received from each payer (other than a "disqualified person") whose payments to the organization were more than $5,000. For this purpose, "payer" includes, but is not limited to, any organization described in sections 170(b)(1)(A)(i) through (vi) and any governmental agency or bureau.

14 Indicate if your organization is one of the following. If so, complete the required schedule. (Submit only those schedules that apply to your organization. **Do not submit blank schedules.**)	Yes	No	If "Yes," complete Schedule:
Is the organization a church?			A
Is the organization, or any part of it, a school?			B
Is the organization, or any part of it, a hospital or medical research organization?			C
Is the organization a section 509(a)(3) supporting organization?			D
Is the organization a private operating foundation?.			E
Is the organization, or any part of it, a home for the aged or handicapped?			F
Is the organization, or any part of it, a child care organization?.			G
Does the organization provide or administer any scholarship benefits, student aid, etc.?			H
Has the organization taken over, or will it take over, the facilities of a "for profit" institution? . . .			I

APPENDIX B

Part IV   Financial Data

Complete the financial statements for the current year and for each of the 3 years immediately before it. If in existence less than 4 years, complete the statements for each year in existence. **If in existence less than 1 year, also provide proposed budgets for the 2 years following the current year.**

A. Statement of Revenue and Expenses

		Current tax year	3 prior tax years or proposed budget for 2 years			(e) TOTAL
		(a) From .... to _____	**(b)**	**(c)**	**(d)**	
Revenue	1 Gifts, grants, and contributions received (not including unusual grants—see page 6 of the instructions).					
	2 Membership fees received . .					
	3 Gross investment income (see instructions for definition) . .					
	4 Net income from organization's unrelated business activities not included on line 3.					
	5 Tax revenues levied for and either paid to or spent on behalf of the organization					
	6 Value of services or facilities furnished by a governmental unit to the organization without charge (not including the value of services or facilities generally furnished the public without charge). . . .					
	7 Other income (not including gain or loss from sale of capital assets) (attach schedule) . .					
	8 **Total** (add lines 1 through 7)					
	9 Gross receipts from admissions, sales of merchandise or services, or furnishing of facilities in any activity that is not an unrelated business within the meaning of section 513. Include related cost of sales on line 22					
	10 **Total** (add lines 8 and 9) . .					
	11 Gain or loss from sale of capital assets (attach schedule). . .					
	12 Unusual grants.					
	13 **Total** revenue (add lines 10 through 12).					
Expenses	14 Fundraising expenses . . .					
	15 Contributions, gifts, grants, and similar amounts paid (attach schedule)					
	16 Disbursements to or for benefit of members (attach schedule) .					
	17 Compensation of officers, directors, and trustees (attach schedule)					
	18 Other salaries and wages . .					
	19 Interest					
	20 Occupancy (rent, utilities, etc.) .					
	21 Depreciation and depletion . .					
	22 Other (attach schedule) . . .					
	23 **Total** expenses (add lines 14 through 22)					
	24 Excess of revenue over expenses (line 13 minus line 23)					

APPENDIX B

Part IV Financial Data *(Continued)*

B. Balance Sheet (at the end of the period shown)		Current tax year Date.................
Assets		
1 Cash	1	
2 Accounts receivable, net	2	
3 Inventories	3	
4 Bonds and notes receivable (attach schedule)	4	
5 Corporate stocks (attach schedule)	5	
6 Mortgage loans (attach schedule)	6	
7 Other investments (attach schedule)	7	
8 Depreciable and depletable assets (attach schedule)	8	
9 Land	9	
10 Other assets (attach schedule)	10	
11 **Total assets** (add lines 1 through 10)	11	
Liabilities		
12 Accounts payable	12	
13 Contributions, gifts, grants, etc., payable	13	
14 Mortgages and notes payable (attach schedule)	14	
15 Other liabilities (attach schedule)	15	
16 **Total liabilities** (add lines 12 through 15)	16	
Fund Balances or Net Assets		
17 Total fund balances or net assets	17	
18 **Total liabilities and fund balances or net assets** (add line 16 and line 17)	18	

If there has been any substantial change in any aspect of the organization's financial activities since the end of the period shown above, check the box and attach a detailed explanation . . . . ▶ ☐

APPENDIX C

IRS FORM 990: RETURN OF ORGANIZATION EXEMPT FROM INCOME TAX

OMB No. 1545-0047

Form **990**

Return of Organization Exempt From Income Tax

Under section 501(c), 527, or 4947(a)(1) of the Internal Revenue Code (except black lung benefit trust or private foundation)

Department of the Treasury
Internal Revenue Service

► The organization may have to use a copy of this return to satisfy state reporting requirements.

2001

Open to Public Inspection

A For the 2001 calendar year, or tax year beginning _____ , 2001, and ending _____ , 20____

B Check if applicable:	Please use IRS label or print or type. See Specific Instructions.	**C** Name of organization	**D** Employer identification number
☐ Address change			
☐ Name change		Number and street (or P.O. box if mail is not delivered to street address) Room/suite	**E** Telephone number ( )
☐ Initial return			
☐ Final return		City or town, state or country, and ZIP + 4	**F** Accounting method: ☐ Cash ☐ Accrual
☐ Amended return			☐ Other (specify) ►
☐ Application pending		• Section 501(c)(3) organizations and 4947(a)(1) nonexempt charitable trusts must attach a completed Schedule A (Form 990 or 990-EZ).	**H** and **I** are not applicable to section 527 organizations.

H(a) Is this a group return for affiliates? ☐ Yes ☐ No

G Web site: ►

H(b) If "Yes," enter number of affiliates ► ....

H(c) Are all affiliates included? ☐ Yes ☐ No
(If "No," attach a list. See instructions.)

J **Organization type** (check only one) ► ☐ 501(c) ( ) ◄ (insert no.) ☐ 4947(a)(1) or ☐ 527

H(d) Is this a separate return filed by an organization covered by a group ruling? ☐ Yes ☐ No

K Check here ► ☐ if the organization's gross receipts are normally not more than $25,000. The organization need not file a return with the IRS; but if the organization received a Form 990 Package in the mail, it should file a return without financial data. **Some states require a complete return.**

I Enter 4-digit GEN ►

M Check ► ☐ if the organization is **not** required to attach Sch. B (Form 990, 990-EZ, or 990-PF).

L Gross receipts: Add lines 6b, 8b, 9b, and 10b to line 12 ►

Part I — Revenue, Expenses, and Changes in Net Assets or Fund Balances (See Specific Instructions on page 16.)

	1	Contributions, gifts, grants, and similar amounts received:		
	a	Direct public support	1a	
	b	Indirect public support	1b	
	c	Government contributions (grants)	1c	
	d	**Total** (add lines 1a through 1c) (cash $ _____ noncash $ _____)		1d
	2	Program service revenue including government fees and contracts (from Part VII, line 93)		2
	3	Membership dues and assessments		3
	4	Interest on savings and temporary cash investments		4
	5	Dividends and interest from securities		5
	6a	Gross rents	6a	
Revenue	**b**	Less: rental expenses	6b	
	c	Net rental income or (loss) (subtract line 6b from line 6a)		6c
	7	Other investment income (describe ►)		7
	8a	Gross amount from sales of assets other than inventory	**(A)** Securities 8a	**(B)** Other
	b	Less: cost or other basis and sales expenses	8b	
	c	Gain or (loss) (attach schedule)	8c	
	d	Net gain or (loss) (combine line 8c, columns (A) and (B))		8d
	9	Special events and activities (attach schedule)		
	a	Gross revenue (not including $ _____ of contributions reported on line 1a)	9a	
	b	Less: direct expenses other than fundraising expenses . .	9b	
	c	Net income or (loss) from special events (subtract line 9b from line 9a)		9c
	10a	Gross sales of inventory, less returns and allowances . .	10a	
	b	Less: cost of goods sold	10b	
	c	Gross profit or (loss) from sales of inventory (attach schedule) (subtract line 10b from line 10a) ..		10c
	11	Other revenue (from Part VII, line 103)		11
	12	**Total revenue** (add lines 1d, 2, 3, 4, 5, 6c, 7, 8d, 9c, 10c, and 11)		12
Expenses	**13**	Program services (from line 44, column (B))		13
	14	Management and general (from line 44, column (C))		14
	15	Fundraising (from line 44, column (D))		15
	16	Payments to affiliates (attach schedule)		16
	17	**Total expenses** (add lines 16 and 44, column (A))		17
Net Assets	**18**	Excess or (deficit) for the year (subtract line 17 from line 12)		18
	19	Net assets or fund balances at beginning of year (from line 73, column (A)) . . .		19
	20	Other changes in net assets or fund balances (attach explanation)		20
	21	Net assets or fund balances at end of year (combine lines 18, 19, and 20)		21

For Paperwork Reduction Act Notice, see the separate instructions.   Cat. No. 11282Y   Form **990** (2001)

APPENDIX C

Part II **Statement of Functional Expenses** — All organizations must complete column (A). Columns (B), (C), and (D) are required for section 501(c)(3) and (4) organizations and section 4947(a)(1) nonexempt charitable trusts but optional for others. (See Specific Instructions on page 21.)

Do not include amounts reported on line 6b, 8b, 9b, 10b, or 16 of Part I.		(A) Total	(B) Program services	(C) Management and general	(D) Fundraising
22 Grants and allocations (attach schedule) (cash $ _____ noncash $ _____)	22				
23 Specific assistance to individuals (attach schedule)	23				
24 Benefits paid to or for members (attach schedule)	24				
25 Compensation of officers, directors, etc.	25				
26 Other salaries and wages	26				
27 Pension plan contributions	27				
28 Other employee benefits	28				
29 Payroll taxes	29				
30 Professional fundraising fees	30				
31 Accounting fees	31				
32 Legal fees	32				
33 Supplies	33				
34 Telephone	34				
35 Postage and shipping	35				
36 Occupancy	36				
37 Equipment rental and maintenance	37				
38 Printing and publications	38				
39 Travel	39				
40 Conferences, conventions, and meetings	40				
41 Interest	41				
42 Depreciation, depletion, etc. (attach schedule)	42				
43 Other expenses not covered above (itemize): a _____	43a				
b _____	43b				
c _____	43c				
d _____	43d				
e _____	43e				
44 Total functional expenses (add lines 22 through 43). *Organizations completing columns (B)-(D), carry these totals to lines 13—15*	44				

Joint Costs. Check ► ☐ if you are following SOP 98-2.
Are any joint costs from a combined educational campaign and fundraising solicitation reported in **(B)** Program services? . . ► ☐ **Yes** ☐ **No**
If "Yes," enter **(i)** the aggregate amount of these joint costs $ _____; **(ii)** the amount allocated to Program services $ _____;
(iii) the amount allocated to Management and general $ _____; and **(iv)** the amount allocated to Fundraising $ _____

Part III **Statement of Program Service Accomplishments** (See Specific Instructions on page 24.)

What is the organization's primary exempt purpose? ► _____

All organizations must describe their exempt purpose achievements in a clear and concise manner. State the number of clients served, publications issued, etc. Discuss achievements that are not measurable. (Section 501(c)(3) and (4) organizations and 4947(a)(1) nonexempt charitable trusts must also enter the amount of grants and allocations to others.)

Program Service Expenses
(Required for 501(c)(3) and (4) orgs., and 4947(a)(1) trusts; but optional for others.)

a _____
_____
_____
(Grants and allocations $ _____)

b _____
_____
_____
(Grants and allocations $ _____)

c _____
_____
_____
(Grants and allocations $ _____)

d _____
_____
_____
(Grants and allocations $ _____)

e Other program services (attach schedule) (Grants and allocations $ _____)

f **Total** of Program Service Expenses (should equal line 44, column (B), Program services) . . . . ►

Form **990** (2001)

APPENDIX C

Part IV   **Balance Sheets** (See Specific Instructions on page 24.)

	Note:	*Where required, attached schedules and amounts within the description column should be for end-of-year amounts only.*			**(A)** Beginning of year		**(B)** End of year
Assets	45	Cash—non-interest-bearing				45	
	46	Savings and temporary cash investments				46	
	47a	Accounts receivable	47a				
	b	Less: allowance for doubtful accounts	47b			47c	
	48a	Pledges receivable	48a				
	b	Less: allowance for doubtful accounts	48b			48c	
	49	Grants receivable				49	
	50	Receivables from officers, directors, trustees, and key employees (attach schedule)				50	
	51a	Other notes and loans receivable (attach schedule)	51a				
	b	Less: allowance for doubtful accounts	51b			51c	
	52	Inventories for sale or use				52	
	53	Prepaid expenses and deferred charges				53	
	54	Investments—securities (attach schedule) ▶ ☐ Cost ☐ FMV				54	
	55a	Investments—land, buildings, and equipment: basis	55a				
	b	Less: accumulated depreciation (attach schedule)	55b			55c	
	56	Investments—other (attach schedule)				56	
	57a	Land, buildings, and equipment: basis	57a				
	b	Less: accumulated depreciation (attach schedule)	57b			57c	
	58	Other assets (describe ▶ _____)				58	
	59	**Total assets** (add lines 45 through 58) (must equal line 74)				59	
Liabilities	60	Accounts payable and accrued expenses				60	
	61	Grants payable				61	
	62	Deferred revenue				62	
	63	Loans from officers, directors, trustees, and key employees (attach schedule)				63	
	64a	Tax-exempt bond liabilities (attach schedule)				64a	
	b	Mortgages and other notes payable (attach schedule)				64b	
	65	Other liabilities (describe ▶ _____)				65	
	66	**Total liabilities** (add lines 60 through 65)				66	
Net Assets or Fund Balances		**Organizations that follow SFAS 117, check here ▶ ☐ and complete lines 67 through 69 and lines 73 and 74.**					
	67	Unrestricted				67	
	68	Temporarily restricted				68	
	69	Permanently restricted				69	
		Organizations that do not follow SFAS 117, check here ▶ ☐ and complete lines 70 through 74.					
	70	Capital stock, trust principal, or current funds				70	
	71	Paid-in or capital surplus, or land, building, and equipment fund				71	
	72	Retained earnings, endowment, accumulated income, or other funds				72	
	73	**Total net assets or fund balances** (add lines 67 through 69 OR lines 70 through 72; column (A) **must** equal line 19; column (B) **must** equal line 21).				73	
	74	**Total liabilities and net assets / fund balances** (add lines 66 and 73)				74	

Form 990 is available for public inspection and, for some people, serves as the primary or sole source of information about a particular organization. How the public perceives an organization in such cases may be determined by the information presented on its return. Therefore, please make sure the return is complete and accurate and fully describes, in Part III, the organization's programs and accomplishments.

APPENDIX C

Part IV-A Reconciliation of Revenue per Audited Financial Statements with Revenue per Return (See Specific Instructions, page 26.)

a   Total revenue, gains, and other support per audited financial statements . .. ▶ | **a**

b   Amounts included on line **a** but not on line 12, Form 990:

(1) Net unrealized gains on investments . . $_____

(2) Donated services and use of facilities $_____

(3) Recoveries of prior year grants . . . $_____

(4) Other (specify):
....
.... $_____

Add amounts on lines (1) through (4) ▶ | **b**

c   Line **a** minus line **b**. . . . . ▶ | **c**

d   Amounts included on line 12, Form 990 but not on line **a:**

(1) Investment expenses not included on line 6b, Form 990 . . $_____

(2) Other (specify):
....
.... $_____

Add amounts on lines (1) and (2) ▶ | **d**

e   Total revenue per line 12, Form 990 (line **c** plus line **d**) . . . . . ▶ | **e**

Part IV-B Reconciliation of Expenses per Audited Financial Statements with Expenses per Return

a   Total expenses and losses per audited financial statements . .. ▶ | **a**

b   Amounts included on line **a** but not on line 17, Form 990:

(1) Donated services and use of facilities $_____

(2) Prior year adjustments reported on line 20, Form 990 . . . . $_____

(3) Losses reported on line 20, Form 990 . $_____

(4) Other (specify):
....
.... $_____

Add amounts on lines (1) through (4) ▶ | **b**

c   Line **a** minus line **b** . . . . .. ▶ | **c**

d   Amounts included on line 17, Form 990 but not on line **a:**

(1) Investment expenses not included on line 6b, Form 990. . . $_____

(2) Other (specify):
....
.... $_____

Add amounts on lines (1) and (2) ▶ | **d**

e   Total expenses per line 17, Form 990 (line **c** plus line **d**) . . . . .. ▶ | **e**

Part V List of Officers, Directors, Trustees, and Key Employees (List each one even if not compensated; see Specific Instructions on page 26.)

(A) Name and address	(B) Title and average hours per week devoted to position	(C) Compensation (If not paid, enter -0-.)	(D) Contributions to employee benefit plans & deferred compensation	(E) Expense account and other allowances
----------------------------------				

----------------------------------				

75   Did any officer, director, trustee, or key employee receive aggregate compensation of more than $100,000 from your organization and all related organizations, of which more than $10,000 was provided by the related organizations? ▶ ☐ **Yes** ☐ **No** If "Yes," attach schedule—see Specific Instructions on page 27.

Form **990** (2001)

Form 990 (2001)   Page **5**

Part VI	**Other Information** (See Specific Instructions on page 27.)		Yes	No

76 Did the organization engage in any activity not previously reported to the IRS? If "Yes," attach a detailed description of each activity · · | **76** | | |

77 Were any changes made in the organizing or governing documents but not reported to the IRS? · · · | **77** | | |
If "Yes," attach a conformed copy of the changes.

78a Did the organization have unrelated business gross income of $1,000 or more during the year covered by this return? · | **78a** | | |

b If "Yes," has it filed a tax return on **Form 990-T** for this year? · · · · · · · · · · | **78b** | | |

79 Was there a liquidation, dissolution, termination, or substantial contraction during the year? If "Yes," attach a statement | **79** | | |

80a Is the organization related (other than by association with a statewide or nationwide organization) through common membership, governing bodies, trustees, officers, etc., to any other exempt or nonexempt organization? · · · | **80a** | | |

b If "Yes," enter the name of the organization ▶ ....
.... and check whether it is ☐ exempt **OR** ☐ nonexempt.

81a Enter direct or indirect political expenditures. See line 81 instructions · · · · | 81a | | | |

b Did the organization file **Form 1120-POL** for this year? · · · · · · · · · · | **81b** | | |

82a Did the organization receive donated services or the use of materials, equipment, or facilities at no charge or at substantially less than fair rental value? · · · · · · · · · · · · · | **82a** | | |

b If "Yes," you may indicate the value of these items here. Do not include this amount as revenue in Part I or as an expense in Part II. (See instructions in Part III.) · · | 82b | | | |

83a Did the organization comply with the public inspection requirements for returns and exemption applications? | **83a** | | |

b Did the organization comply with the disclosure requirements relating to quid pro quo contributions? · · | **83b** | | |

84a Did the organization solicit any contributions or gifts that were not tax deductible? · · · · · · · | **84a** | | |

b If "Yes," did the organization include with every solicitation an express statement that such contributions or gifts were not tax deductible? · · · · · · · · · · · · · · · · | **84b** | | |

85 *501(c)(4), (5), or (6) organizations.* **a** Were substantially all dues nondeductible by members? · · · · · | **85a** | | |

b Did the organization make only in-house lobbying expenditures of $2,000 or less? · · · · · · · | **85b** | | |
If "Yes" was answered to either 85a or 85b, **do not** complete 85c through 85h below unless the organization received a waiver for proxy tax owed for the prior year.

c Dues, assessments, and similar amounts from members · · · · · · · · | 85c | | |

d Section 162(e) lobbying and political expenditures · · · · · · · · · · | 85d | | |

e Aggregate nondeductible amount of section 6033(e)(1)(A) dues notices · · | 85e | | |

f Taxable amount of lobbying and political expenditures (line 85d less 85e) · · | 85f | | |

g Does the organization elect to pay the section 6033(e) tax on the amount on line 85f? · · · · · · · | **85g** | | |

h If section 6033(e)(1)(A) dues notices were sent, does the organization agree to add the amount on line 85f to its reasonable estimate of dues allocable to nondeductible lobbying and political expenditures for the following tax year? · | **85h** | | |

86 *501(c)(7) orgs.* Enter: **a** Initiation fees and capital contributions included on line 12 · · | 86a | | |

b Gross receipts, included on line 12, for public use of club facilities · · · · · | 86b | | |

87 *501(c)(12) orgs.* Enter: **a** Gross income from members or shareholders · · · · | 87a | | |

b Gross income from other sources. (Do not net amounts due or paid to other sources against amounts due or received from them.) · · · · · · · · · | 87b | | |

88 At any time during the year, did the organization own a 50% or greater interest in a taxable corporation or partnership, or an entity disregarded as separate from the organization under Regulations sections 301.7701-2 and 301.7701-3? If "Yes," complete Part IX · · · · · · · · · · · · · · · · · · · | **88** | | |

89a *501(c)(3) organizations.* Enter: Amount of tax imposed on the organization during the year under:
section 4911 ▶_____ ; section 4912 ▶_____ ; section 4955 ▶_____

b *501(c)(3) and 501(c)(4) orgs.* Did the organization engage in any section 4958 excess benefit transaction during the year or did it become aware of an excess benefit transaction from a prior year? If "Yes," attach a statement explaining each transaction. · | **89b** | | |

c Enter: Amount of tax imposed on the organization managers or disqualified persons during the year under sections 4912, 4955, and 4958. · · · · · · · · · · · · · · · · · · · ▶ _____

d Enter: Amount of tax on line 89c, above, reimbursed by the organization. · · · · · · · · · · ▶ _____

90a List the states with which a copy of this return is filed ▶ ....

b Number of employees employed in the pay period that includes March 12, 2001 (See instructions.) | 90b | _____

91 The books are in care of ▶ .... Telephone no. ▶ (........)......................
Located at ▶ .... ZIP + 4 ▶ ....

92 *Section 4947(a)(1) nonexempt charitable trusts filing Form 990 in lieu of Form 1041*—Check here · · · · · · · · ▶ ☐
and enter the amount of tax-exempt interest received or accrued during the tax year · · · ▶ | 92 |

Form **990** (2001)

Form 990 (2001)   Page **6**

Part VII   Analysis of Income-Producing Activities (See Specific Instructions on page 32.)

Note: *Enter gross amounts unless otherwise indicated.*

		Unrelated business income		Excluded by section 512, 513, or 514		(E) Related or exempt function income
		(A) Business code	(B) Amount	(C) Exclusion code	(D) Amount	
93	Program service revenue:					
a	_____					
b	_____					
c	_____					
d	_____					
e	_____					
f	Medicare/Medicaid payments					
g	Fees and contracts from government agencies					
94	Membership dues and assessments . . .					
95	Interest on savings and temporary cash investments					
96	Dividends and interest from securities . . .					
97	Net rental income or (loss) from real estate:					
a	debt-financed property					
b	not debt-financed property					
98	Net rental income or (loss) from personal property					
99	Other investment income					
100	Gain or (loss) from sales of assets other than inventory					
101	Net income or (loss) from special events . .					
102	Gross profit or (loss) from sales of inventory .					
103	Other revenue: a _____					
b	_____					
c	_____					
d	_____					
e	_____					
104	Subtotal (add columns (B), (D), and (E)) . .					
105	**Total** (add line 104, columns (B), (D), and (E)) . . . . ▶					

Note: *Line 105 plus line 1d, Part I, should equal the amount on line 12, Part I.*

Part VIII   Relationship of Activities to the Accomplishment of Exempt Purposes (See Specific Instructions on page 32.)

Line No. ▼	Explain how each activity for which income is reported in column (E) of Part VII contributed importantly to the accomplishment of the organization's exempt purposes (other than by providing funds for such purposes).

Part IX   Information Regarding Taxable Subsidiaries and Disregarded Entities (See Specific Instructions on page 33.)

(A) Name, address, and EIN of corporation, partnership, or disregarded entity	(B) Percentage of ownership interest	(C) Nature of activities	(D) Total income	(E) End-of-year assets
	%			
	%			
	%			
	%			

Part X   Information Regarding Transfers Associated with Personal Benefit Contracts (See Specific Instructions on page 33.)

(a) Did the organization, during the year, receive any funds, directly or indirectly, to pay premiums on a personal benefit contract? . . ☐ Yes ☐ No

(b) Did the organization, during the year, pay premiums, directly or indirectly, on a personal benefit contract? ☐ Yes ☐ No

Note: *If "Yes" to **(b)**, file Form 8870 **and** Form 4720 (see instructions).*

Please Sign Here	Under penalties of perjury, I declare that I have examined this return, including accompanying schedules and statements, and to the best of my knowledge and belief, it is true, correct, and complete. Declaration of preparer (other than officer) is based on all information of which preparer has any knowledge.
	▶ _____ | Signature of officer Date
	▶ _____ Type or print name and title.

Paid Preparer's Use Only	Preparer's signature ▶		Date	Check if self-employed ▶ ☐	Preparer's SSN or PTIN (See Gen. Inst. W)
	Firm's name (or yours if self-employed), address, and ZIP + 4 ▶			EIN ▶	
				Phone no. ▶ ( )	

Form **990** (2001)

APPENDIX C

OMB No. 1545-0047

SCHEDULE A
(Form 990 or 990-EZ)

Department of the Treasury
Internal Revenue Service

Organization Exempt Under Section 501(c)(3)

(Except Private Foundation) and Section 501(e), 501(f), 501(k),
501(n), or Section 4947(a)(1) Nonexempt Charitable Trust

Supplementary Information—(See separate instructions.)

▶ MUST be completed by the above organizations and attached to their Form 990 or 990-EZ

2001

Name of the organization			Employer identification number	

Part I Compensation of the Five Highest Paid Employees Other Than Officers, Directors, and Trustees
(See page 1 of the instructions. List each one. If there are none, enter "None.")

(a) Name and address of each employee paid more than $50,000	(b) Title and average hours per week devoted to position	(c) Compensation	(d) Contributions to employee benefit plans & deferred compensation	(e) Expense account and other allowances
....				
....				
....				
....				
....				

Total number of other employees paid over
$50,000 . . . . ▶

Part II Compensation of the Five Highest Paid Independent Contractors for Professional Services
(See page 2 of the instructions. List each one (whether individuals or firms). If there are none, enter "None.")

(a) Name and address of each independent contractor paid more than $50,000	(b) Type of service	(c) Compensation
....		
....		
....		
....		
....		
....		

Total number of others receiving over $50,000 for
professional services . . . . ▶

For Paperwork Reduction Act Notice, see the Instructions for Form 990 and Form 990-EZ.   Cat. No. 11285F   Schedule A (Form 990 or 990-EZ) 2001

APPENDIX C

Part III	Statements About Activities (See page 2 of the instructions.)		Yes	No

1 During the year, has the organization attempted to influence national, state, or local legislation, including any attempt to influence public opinion on a legislative matter or referendum? If "Yes," enter the total expenses paid or incurred in connection with the lobbying activities ▶ $ _____ **(Must equal amounts on line 38, Part VI-A, or line i of Part VI-B.)**

Organizations that made an election under section 501(h) by filing Form 5768 must complete Part VI-A. Other organizations checking "Yes," must complete Part VI-B AND attach a statement giving a detailed description of the lobbying activities.

	1		

2 During the year, has the organization, either directly or indirectly, engaged in any of the following acts with any substantial contributors, trustees, directors, officers, creators, key employees, or members of their families, or with any taxable organization with which any such person is affiliated as an officer, director, trustee, majority owner, or principal beneficiary? *(If the answer to any question is "Yes," attach a detailed statement explaining the transactions.)*

a Sale, exchange, or leasing of property? **2a**

b Lending of money or other extension of credit? **2b**

c Furnishing of goods, services, or facilities? **2c**

d Payment of compensation (or payment or reimbursement of expenses if more than $1,000)? **2d**

e Transfer of any part of its income or assets? **2e**

3 Does the organization make grants for scholarships, fellowships, student loans, etc.? (See **Note** below.) . . .   **3**

4 Do you have a section 403(b) annuity plan for your employees? **4**

Note: *Attach a statement to explain how the organization determines that individuals or organizations receiving grants or loans from it in furtherance of its charitable programs "qualify" to receive payments.*

Part IV	Reason for Non-Private Foundation Status (See pages 3 through 6 of the instructions.)

The organization is not a private foundation because it is: (Please check only **ONE** applicable box.)

5 ☐ A church, convention of churches, or association of churches. Section 170(b)(1)(A)(i).

6 ☐ A school. Section 170(b)(1)(A)(ii). (Also complete Part V.)

7 ☐ A hospital or a cooperative hospital service organization. Section 170(b)(1)(A)(iii).

8 ☐ A Federal, state, or local government or governmental unit. Section 170(b)(1)(A)(v).

9 ☐ A medical research organization operated in conjunction with a hospital. Section 170(b)(1)(A)(iii). **Enter the hospital's name, city, and state** ▶ --

10 ☐ An organization operated for the benefit of a college or university owned or operated by a governmental unit. Section 170(b)(1)(A)(iv). (Also complete the **Support Schedule** in Part IV-A.)

11a ☐ An organization that normally receives a substantial part of its support from a governmental unit or from the general public. Section 170(b)(1)(A)(vi). (Also complete the **Support Schedule** in Part IV-A.)

11b ☐ A community trust. Section 170(b)(1)(A)(vi). (Also complete the **Support Schedule** in Part IV-A.)

12 ☐ An organization that normally receives: **(1) more than 33⅓%** of its support from contributions, membership fees, and gross receipts from activities related to its charitable, etc., functions—subject to certain exceptions, and **(2) no more than 33⅓%** of its support from gross investment income and unrelated business taxable income (less section 511 tax) from businesses acquired by the organization after June 30, 1975. See section 509(a)(2). (Also complete the **Support Schedule** in Part IV-A.)

13 ☐ An organization that is not controlled by any disqualified persons (other than foundation managers) and supports organizations described in: **(1)** lines 5 through 12 above; or **(2)** section 501(c)(4), (5), or (6), if they meet the test of section 509(a)(2). (See section 509(a)(3).)

Provide the following information about the supported organizations. (See page 5 of the instructions.)

(a) Name(s) of supported organization(s)	(b) Line number from above

14 ☐ An organization organized and operated to test for public safety. Section 509(a)(4). (See page 6 of the instructions.)

APPENDIX C

Part IV-A **Support Schedule** (Complete only if you checked a box on line 10, 11, or 12.) *Use cash method of accounting.*

Note: *You may use the worksheet in the instructions for converting from the accrual to the cash method of accounting.*

Calendar year (or fiscal year beginning in) ..▶	(a) 2000	(b) 1999	(c) 1998	(d) 1997	(e) Total
15 Gifts, grants, and contributions received. (Do not include unusual grants. See line 28.).					
16 Membership fees received					
17 Gross receipts from admissions, merchandise sold or services performed, or furnishing of facilities in any activity that is related to the organization's charitable, etc., purpose . . .					
18 Gross income from interest, dividends, amounts received from payments on securities loans (section 512(a)(5)), rents, royalties, and unrelated business taxable income (less section 511 taxes) from businesses acquired by the organization after June 30, 1975 . .					
19 Net income from unrelated business activities not included in line 18					
20 Tax revenues levied for the organization's benefit and either paid to it or expended on its behalf.					
21 The value of services or facilities furnished to the organization by a governmental unit without charge. Do not include the value of services or facilities generally furnished to the public without charge.					
22 Other income. Attach a schedule. Do not include gain or (loss) from sale of capital assets					
23 Total of lines 15 through 22					
24 Line 23 minus line 17.					
25 Enter 1% of line 23					

26 **Organizations described on lines 10 or 11:** **a** Enter 2% of amount in column (e), line 24. . . . ▶ | **26a**

b Prepare a list for your records to show the name of and amount contributed by each person (other than a governmental unit or publicly supported organization) whose total gifts for 1997 through 2000 exceeded the amount shown in line 26a. **Do not file this list with your return.** Enter the total of all these excess amounts ▶ | **26b**

c Total support for section 509(a)(1) test: Enter line 24, column (e) . . . . ▶ | **26c**

d Add: Amounts from column (e) for lines: 18 _____ 19 _____
    22 _____ 26b _____ . . . . . . ▶ | **26d**

e Public support (line 26c minus line 26d total) . . . . ▶ | **26e**

f **Public support percentage (line 26e (numerator) divided by line 26c (denominator))** . . . . . ▶ | **26f** | %

27 **Organizations described on line 12:** **a** For amounts included in lines 15, 16, and 17 that were received from a "disqualified person," prepare a list for your records to show the name of, and total amounts received in each year from, each "disqualified person." **Do not file this list with your return.** Enter the sum of such amounts for each year:

(2000) .... (1999) .... (1998) .... (1997) ....

b For any amount included in line 17 that was received from each person (other than "disqualified persons"), prepare a list for your records to show the name of, and amount received for each year, that was more than the **larger** of **(1)** the amount on line 25 for the year or **(2)** $5,000. (Include in the list organizations described in lines 5 through 11, as well as individuals.) **Do not file this list with your return.** After computing the difference between the amount received and the larger amount described in **(1)** or **(2)**, enter the sum of these differences (the excess amounts) for each year:

(2000) .... (1999) .... (1998) .... (1997) ....

c Add: Amounts from column (e) for lines: 15 _____ 16 _____
    17 _____ 20 _____ 21 _____ . . . . . . ▶ | **27c**

d Add: Line 27a total . _____ and line 27b total . _____ . . . . . . ▶ | **27d**

e Public support (line 27c total minus line 27d total). . . . . ▶ | **27e**

f Total support for section 509(a)(2) test: Enter amount from line 23, column (e). . ▶ | **27f** |

g **Public support percentage (line 27e (numerator) divided by line 27f (denominator)).** . . . . . ▶ | **27g** | %

h **Investment income percentage (line 18, column (e) (numerator) divided by line 27f (denominator)).** ▶ | **27h** | %

28 **Unusual Grants:** For an organization described in line 10, 11, or 12 that received any unusual grants during 1997 through 2000, prepare a list for your records to show, for each year, the name of the contributor, the date and amount of the grant, and a brief description of the nature of the grant. **Do not file this list with your return.** Do not include these grants in line 15.

APPENDIX C

	Part V	Private School Questionnaire (See page 7 of the instructions.)

(To be completed ONLY by schools that checked the box on line 6 in Part IV)

		Yes	No
29 Does the organization have a racially nondiscriminatory policy toward students by statement in its charter, bylaws, other governing instrument, or in a resolution of its governing body?	**29**		
30 Does the organization include a statement of its racially nondiscriminatory policy toward students in all its brochures, catalogues, and other written communications with the public dealing with student admissions, programs, and scholarships?	**30**		
31 Has the organization publicized its racially nondiscriminatory policy through newspaper or broadcast media during the period of solicitation for students, or during the registration period if it has no solicitation program, in a way that makes the policy known to all parts of the general community it serves?	**31**		

If "Yes," please describe; if "No," please explain. (If you need more space, attach a separate statement.)

		Yes	No
32 Does the organization maintain the following:			
a Records indicating the racial composition of the student body, faculty, and administrative staff?	**32a**		
b Records documenting that scholarships and other financial assistance are awarded on a racially nondiscriminatory basis?	**32b**		
c Copies of all catalogues, brochures, announcements, and other written communications to the public dealing with student admissions, programs, and scholarships?	**32c**		
d Copies of all material used by the organization or on its behalf to solicit contributions?	**32d**		

If you answered "No" to any of the above, please explain. (If you need more space, attach a separate statement.)

		Yes	No
33 Does the organization discriminate by race in any way with respect to:			
a Students' rights or privileges?	**33a**		
b Admissions policies?	**33b**		
c Employment of faculty or administrative staff?	**33c**		
d Scholarships or other financial assistance?	**33d**		
e Educational policies?	**33e**		
f Use of facilities?	**33f**		
g Athletic programs?	**33g**		
h Other extracurricular activities?	**33h**		

If you answered "Yes" to any of the above, please explain. (If you need more space, attach a separate statement.)

		Yes	No
34a Does the organization receive any financial aid or assistance from a governmental agency?	**34a**		
b Has the organization's right to such aid ever been revoked or suspended?	**34b**		

If you answered "Yes" to either 34a or b, please explain using an attached statement.

		Yes	No
35 Does the organization certify that it has complied with the applicable requirements of sections 4.01 through 4.05 of Rev. Proc. 75-50, 1975-2 C.B. 587, covering racial nondiscrimination? If "No," attach an explanation	**35**		

APPENDIX C

Part VI-A   **Lobbying Expenditures by Electing Public Charities** (See page 9 of the instructions.)
(To be completed **ONLY** by an eligible organization that filed Form 5768)

Check ▶ a ☐ if the organization belongs to an affiliated group.   Check ▶   b ☐ if you checked "a" and "limited control" provisions apply.

Limits on Lobbying Expenditures (The term "expenditures" means amounts paid or incurred.)		(a) Affiliated group totals	(b) To be completed for ALL electing organizations
36	Total lobbying expenditures to influence public opinion (grassroots lobbying)	36	
37	Total lobbying expenditures to influence a legislative body (direct lobbying)	37	
38	Total lobbying expenditures (add lines 36 and 37)	38	
39	Other exempt purpose expenditures	39	
40	Total exempt purpose expenditures (add lines 38 and 39).	40	
41	Lobbying nontaxable amount. Enter the amount from the following table—		

If the amount on line 40 is—   **The lobbying nontaxable amount is—**

Not over $500,000 . . . . .20% of the amount on line 40. . . . . .
Over $500,000 but not over $1,000,000 . .$100,000 plus 15% of the excess over $500,000
Over $1,000,000 but not over $1,500,000 .$175,000 plus 10% of the excess over $1,000,000   **41**
Over $1,500,000 but not over $17,000,000 .$225,000 plus 5% of the excess over $1,500,000
Over $17,000,000 . . . .$1,000,000 . . . .

42 Grassroots nontaxable amount (enter 25% of line 41)	42	
43 Subtract line 42 from line 36. Enter -0- if line 42 is more than line 36	43	
44 Subtract line 41 from line 38. Enter -0- if line 41 is more than line 38	44	

Caution: *If there is an amount on either line 43 or line 44, you must file Form 4720.*

4-Year Averaging Period Under Section 501(h)

(Some organizations that made a section 501(h) election do not have to complete all of the five columns below.
See the instructions for lines 45 through 50 on page 11 of the instructions.)

Calendar year (or fiscal year beginning in) ▶	(a) 2001	(b) 2000	(c) 1999	(d) 1998	(e) Total
45 Lobbying nontaxable amount					
46 Lobbying ceiling amount (150% of line 45(e)) .					
47 Total lobbying expenditures					
48 Grassroots nontaxable amount					
49 Grassroots ceiling amount (150% of line 48(e))					
50 Grassroots lobbying expenditures					

Part VI-B   **Lobbying Activity by Nonelecting Public Charities**
(For reporting only by organizations that did not complete Part VI-A) (See page 12 of the instructions.)

During the year, did the organization attempt to influence national, state or local legislation, including any attempt to influence public opinion on a legislative matter or referendum, through the use of:	Yes	No	Amount
a Volunteers.			
b Paid staff or management (Include compensation in expenses reported on lines **c** through **h.**) . . .			
c Media advertisements			
d Mailings to members, legislators, or the public			
e Publications, or published or broadcast statements			
f Grants to other organizations for lobbying purposes			
g Direct contact with legislators, their staffs, government officials, or a legislative body			
h Rallies, demonstrations, seminars, conventions, speeches, lectures, or any other means			
i Total lobbying expenditures (Add lines **c** through **h.**)			

If "Yes" to any of the above, also attach a statement giving a detailed description of the lobbying activities.

APPENDIX C

Part VII	Information Regarding Transfers To and Transactions and Relationships With Noncharitable Exempt Organizations (See page 12 of the instructions.)

51 Did the reporting organization directly or indirectly engage in any of the following with any other organization described in section 501(c) of the Code (other than section 501(c)(3) organizations) or in section 527, relating to political organizations?

		Yes	No
a Transfers from the reporting organization to a noncharitable exempt organization of:			
(i) Cash	**51a(i)**		
(ii) Other assets	**a(ii)**		
b Other transactions:			
(i) Sales or exchanges of assets with a noncharitable exempt organization	**b(i)**		
(ii) Purchases of assets from a noncharitable exempt organization	**b(ii)**		
(iii) Rental of facilities, equipment, or other assets	**b(iii)**		
(iv) Reimbursement arrangements	**b(iv)**		
(v) Loans or loan guarantees	**b(v)**		
(vi) Performance of services or membership or fundraising solicitations	**b(vi)**		
c Sharing of facilities, equipment, mailing lists, other assets, or paid employees	**c**		

d If the answer to any of the above is "Yes," complete the following schedule. Column (b) should always show the fair market value of the goods, other assets, or services given by the reporting organization. If the organization received less than fair market value in any transaction or sharing arrangement, show in column (d) the value of the goods, other assets, or services received:

(a) Line no.	(b) Amount involved	(c) Name of noncharitable exempt organization	(d) Description of transfers, transactions, and sharing arrangements

52a Is the organization directly or indirectly affiliated with, or related to, one or more tax-exempt organizations described in section 501(c) of the Code (other than section 501(c)(3)) or in section 527? ▶ ☐ Yes ☐ No

b If "Yes," complete the following schedule:

(a) Name of organization	(b) Type of organization	(c) Description of relationship

APPENDIX C

<table>
<tr><td>

Schedule B
(Form 990, 990-EZ,
or 990-PF)
Department of the Treasury
Internal Revenue Service

</td><td>

Schedule of Contributors

Supplementary Information for
line 1 of Form 990, 990-EZ and 990-PF (see instructions)

</td><td>

OMB No. 1545-0047

2001

</td></tr>
</table>

Name of organization	Employer identification number

Organization type (check one):

Filers of: **Section:**

Form 990 or 990-EZ

☐ 501(c)( ) (enter number) organization

☐ 4947(a)(1) nonexempt charitable trust **not** treated as a private foundation

☐ 527 political organization

Form 990-PF

☐ 501(c)(3) exempt private foundation

☐ 4947(a)(1) nonexempt charitable trust treated as a private foundation

☐ 501(c)(3) taxable private foundation

Check if your organization is covered by the **General rule** or a **Special rule. (Note:** *Only a section 501(c)(7), (8), or (10) organization can check box(es) for both the General rule and a Special rule—see instructions.)*

General Rule—

☐ For organizations filing Form 990, 990-EZ, or 990-PF that received, during the year, $5,000 or more (in money or property) from any one contributor. (Complete Parts I and II.)

Special Rules—

☐ For a section 501(c)(3) organization filing Form 990, or Form 990-EZ, that met the 33⅓% support test of the regulations under sections 509(a)(1)/170(b)(1)(A)(vi) and received from any one contributor, during the year, a contribution of the greater of $5,000 or 2% of the amount on line 1 of these forms. (Complete Parts I and II.)

☐ For a section 501(c)(7), (8), or (10) organization filing Form 990, or Form 990-EZ, that received from any one contributor, during the year, aggregate contributions or bequests of more than $1,000 for use *exclusively* for religious, charitable, scientific, literary, or educational purposes, or the prevention of cruelty to children or animals. (Complete Parts I, II, and III.)

☐ For a section 501(c)(7), (8), or (10) organization filing Form 990, or Form 990-EZ, that received from any one contributor, during the year, some contributions for use *exclusively* for religious, charitable, etc., purposes, but these contributions did not aggregate to more than $1,000. (If this box is checked, enter here the total contributions that were received during the year for an *exclusively* religious, charitable, etc., purpose. Do not complete any of the Parts unless the General rule applies to this organization because it received nonexclusively religious, charitable, etc., contributions of $5,000 or more during the year.) . . . . ▶ $ _____

Caution: *Organizations that are not covered by the General rule and/or the Special rules do not file Schedule B (Form 990, 990-EZ, or 990-PF), but they* **must** *check the box in the heading of their Form 990, Form 990-EZ, or on line 1 of their Form 990-PF, to certify that they do not meet the filing requirements of Schedule B (Form 990, 990-EZ, or 990-PF).*

Cat. No. 30613X   Schedule B (Form 990, 990-EZ, or 990-PF) (2001)

APPENDIX C

Name of organization	Employer identification number

Part I Contributors (See Specific Instructions.)

(a) No.	(b) Name, address and ZIP + 4	(c) Aggregate contributions	(d) Type of contribution
———		$.................	Person ☐ Payroll ☐ Noncash ☐ (Complete Part II if there is a noncash contribution.)
———		$.................	Person ☐ Payroll ☐ Noncash ☐ (Complete Part II if there is a noncash contribution.)
———		$.................	Person ☐ Payroll ☐ Noncash ☐ (Complete Part II if there is a noncash contribution.)
———		$.................	Person ☐ Payroll ☐ Noncash ☐ (Complete Part II if there is a noncash contribution.)
———		$.................	Person ☐ Payroll ☐ Noncash ☐ (Complete Part II if there is a noncash contribution.)
———		$.................	Person ☐ Payroll ☐ Noncash ☐ (Complete Part II if there is a noncash contribution.)

APPENDIX C

Page _____ to _____ of **Part I**

Name of organization

Employer identification number

Part I   **Contributors** (See Specific Instructions.)

(a) No.	(b) Name, address and ZIP + 4	(c) Aggregate contributions	(d) Type of contribution
_____		$_____	Person ☐ Payroll ☐ Noncash ☐ (Complete Part II if there is a noncash contribution.)
_____		$_____	Person ☐ Payroll ☐ Noncash ☐ (Complete Part II if there is a noncash contribution.)
_____		$_____	Person ☐ Payroll ☐ Noncash ☐ (Complete Part II if there is a noncash contribution.)
_____		$_____	Person ☐ Payroll ☐ Noncash ☐ (Complete Part II if there is a noncash contribution.)
_____		$_____	Person ☐ Payroll ☐ Noncash ☐ (Complete Part II if there is a noncash contribution.)
_____		$_____	Person ☐ Payroll ☐ Noncash ☐ (Complete Part II if there is a noncash contribution.)

APPENDIX C

Name of organization	Employer identification number

Part II Noncash Property (See Specific Instructions.)

(a) No. from Part I	(b) Description of noncash property given	(c) FMV (or estimate) (see instructions)	(d) Date received
_____		$	......../....../..........
_____		$	......../....../..........
_____		$	......../....../..........
_____		$	......../....../..........
_____		$	......../....../..........
_____		$	......../....../..........

APPENDIX C

Page _____ to _____ of **Part II**

Name of organization

Employer identification number

Part II **Noncash Property** (See Specific Instructions.)

(a) No. from Part I	(b) Description of noncash property given	(c) FMV (or estimate) (see instructions)	(d) Date received
_____		$	........../...../..........
_____		$	........../...../..........
_____		$	........../...../..........
_____		$	........../...../..........
_____		$	........../...../..........
_____		$	........../...../..........

■ 485 ■

APPENDIX C

Page ____ to ____ of Part III

Name of organization

Employer identification number

Part III   *Exclusively* religious, charitable, etc., **individual contributions** to section **501(c)(7), (8), or (10) organizations aggregating more than $1,000 for the year.** (Complete columns **(a)** through **(e)** and the following line entry.)

For organizations completing Part III, enter the total of *exclusively* religious, charitable, etc., contributions of **$1,000 or less** for the year (Enter this information once—see instructions) ▶ $ _____

(a) No. from Part I	(b) Purpose of gift	(c) Use of gift	(d) Description of how gift is held
_____	....	....	....

(e) Transfer of gift

Transferee's name, address, and ZIP + 4	Relationship of transferor to transferee
....	....

(a) No. from Part I	(b) Purpose of gift	(c) Use of gift	(d) Description of how gift is held
_____	....	....	....

(e) Transfer of gift

Transferee's name, address, and ZIP + 4	Relationship of transferor to transferee
....	....

(a) No. from Part I	(b) Purpose of gift	(c) Use of gift	(d) Description of how gift is held
_____	....	....	....

(e) Transfer of gift

Transferee's name, address, and ZIP + 4	Relationship of transferor to transferee
....	....

(a) No. from Part I	(b) Purpose of gift	(c) Use of gift	(d) Description of how gift is held
_____	....	....	....

(e) Transfer of gift

Transferee's name, address, and ZIP + 4	Relationship of transferor to transferee
....	....

Schedule B (Form 990, 990-EZ, or 990-PF) (2001)

APPENDIX C

	Page _____ to _____ of **Part III**
Name of organization	Employer identification number

Part III   *Exclusively* religious, charitable, etc., individual contributions to section 501(c)(7), (8), or (10) organizations aggregating more than $1,000 for the year. (Complete columns **(a)** through **(e)** and the following line entry.)

For organizations completing Part III, enter the total of *exclusively* religious, charitable, etc., contributions of **$1,000 or less** for the year (Enter this information once—see instructions) ▶ $ _____

(a) No. from Part I	(b) Purpose of gift	(c) Use of gift	(d) Description of how gift is held
_____	....	....	....

(e) Transfer of gift	
Transferee's name, address, and ZIP + 4	Relationship of transferor to transferee
....	....

(a) No. from Part I	(b) Purpose of gift	(c) Use of gift	(d) Description of how gift is held
_____	....	....	....

(e) Transfer of gift	
Transferee's name, address, and ZIP + 4	Relationship of transferor to transferee
....	....

(a) No. from Part I	(b) Purpose of gift	(c) Use of gift	(d) Description of how gift is held
_____	....	....	....

(e) Transfer of gift	
Transferee's name, address, and ZIP + 4	Relationship of transferor to transferee
....	....

(a) No. from Part I	(b) Purpose of gift	(c) Use of gift	(d) Description of how gift is held
_____	....	....	....

(e) Transfer of gift	
Transferee's name, address, and ZIP + 4	Relationship of transferor to transferee
....	....

Schedule B (Form 990, 990-EZ, or 990-PF) (2001)

APPENDIX D

INFLATION-ADJUSTED INSUBSTANTIALITY—$50 TEST

Year	Amount	Rev. Proc.
1993	$62	92-102
1994	64	93-49
1995	66	94-72
1996	67	95-53
1997	69	96-59
1998	71	97-57
1999	72	98-61
2000	74	99-42
2001	76	2001-13
2002	79	2001-59

APPENDIX E

INFLATION-ADJUSTED INSUBSTANTIALITY
THRESHOLD—$25 TEST

Year	Amount	Rev. Proc.
1990	$27.26	90-12
1991	28.58	92-58
1992	30.09	92-58
1993	31	92-102
1994	32	93-49
1995	33	94-72
1996	33.50	95-53
1997	34.50	96-59
1998	35.50	97-57
1999	36	98-61
2000	37	99-42
2001	38	2001-13
2002	39.50	2001-59

APPENDIX F

INFLATION-ADJUSTED LOW-COST ARTICLE DEFINITION

Year	Amount	Rev. Proc.
1990	$5.45	90-12
1991	5.71	92-58
1992	6.01	92-58
1993	6.20	92-102
1994	6.40	93-49
1995	6.60	94-72
1996	6.70	95-53
1997	6.90	96-59
1998	7.10	97-57
1999	7.20	98-61
2000	7.40	99-42
2001	7.60	2001-13
2002	7.90	2001-59

Table of Cases

Abington School District v. Schempp, § 4.7
Adams v. City of Park Ridge, §§ 4.5, 4.6
Alumni Association of the University of Oregon, Inc. v. Commissioner, § 5.7
American Academy of Family Physicians v. United States, § 5.7
American Bar Endowment v. United States, §§ 5.7, 5.14
American Bible Society v. Ritchie, § 5.19
American Campaign Academy v. Commissioner, §§ 5.13, 5.15, 7.12
American Cancer Society v. City of Dayton, §§ 4.2, 4.6
American Charities for Reasonable Fundraising Regulation, Inc. v. Pinellas County, §§ 3.22, 4.2, 4.3, 4.12
American Charities for Reasonable Fundraising Regulation, Inc. v. Shiffrin, § 3.22
American Gold Star Mothers, Inc. v. Gold Star Mothers, Inc., § 3.13
American Library Association v. Thornburgh, § 4.3
American Target Advertising, Inc. v. Giani, § 4.3
Association of Charitable Games of Missouri v. Missouri Gaming Commission, §§ 4.3, 4.5
Attorney General v. International Marathons, Inc., §§ 3.2, 7.1
Auburn Police Union v. Tierney, § 4.5

Bates v. State Bar of Arizona, § 4.3
Bauers v. Cornett, § 4.3
Baxstrom v. Herold, § 4.5
Bellotti v. Telco Communications, Inc., § 4.3
Big Mama Rag, Inc. v. United States, § 5.18
Blake Construction Co., Inc. v. United States, § 5.7
Blenski v. State, §§ 3.5, 3.13, 4.8
Bob Jones University v. United States, §§ 2.1, 5.12
Bradshaw v. Unity Marine Corporation, Inc. et al., § 7.1
Breard v. City of Alexandria, §§ 4.3, 4.6
Brentwood Academy v. Tennessee Secondary School Athletic Association, § 8.3
Brown v. Marine Club, Inc., §§ 3.2, 4.1

Calhoun Academy v. Commissioner, § 5.12
Camps Newfound/Owatonna, Inc. v. Town of Harrison, Maine, § 4.2
Cantwell v. Connecticut, §§ 4.2, 4.3, 4.6, 4.7
Cason v. Glass Bottle Blowers Association, § 8.7
Catholic Bishop of Chicago v. NLRB, § 4.7
Caulfield v. Hirsh, § 4.7
Center for Auto Safety, Incorporated v. Athey, §§ 4.12, 7.1, 7.11
Christian Stewardship Assistance, Inc. v. Commissioner, § 5.7

Church by Mail, Inc. v. Commissioner, §§ 5.13, 7.12
Church of the Lukumi Babalu Aye, Inc. v. City of Hialeah, § 4.7
Church of Scientology Flag Services Org., Inc. v. City of Clearwater, §§ 4.2, 4.7, 7.5
Citizens for a Better Environment v. Village of Schaumburg § 4.2
City of Angels Mission Church v. City of Houston, §§ 4.3, 4.5
City of El Paso v. El Paso Jaycees, § 4.3
City of Evanston v. Evanston Fire Fighters Association, Local 742, International Association of Fire Fighters, AFL-CIO-CLC, §§ 3.13, 3.19
City of Fort Worth v. Craik, § 4.2
City of Lakewood v. Plain Dealer Publishing Co., § 4.6
City of Seattle v. Rogers, § 4.5
City of Shreveport v. Teague, § 4.10
Clarence LaBelle Post No. 217 v. United States, § 5.7
Clark v. Community for Creative Non-Violence, § 4.4
Coit v. Green, §§ 1.1, 2.1, 5.12
Commissioner v. Burnett, § 5.7
Commissioner v. Duberstein, §§ 3.2, 5.14
Commissioner v. Groetzinger, § 5.7
Commissioner v. LoBue, § 3.2
Committee for Public Education v. Nyquist, § 4.7
Common Cause v. Commissioner, § 5.7
Commonwealth v. Association of Community Organizations for Reform Now, § 3.2
Commonwealth v. Events International, Inc., §§ 3.21, 3.22
Commonwealth v. Everett, § 4.6
Commonwealth v. McDermott, § 4.5
Commonwealth v. National Federation of the Blind, § 4.2
Connally v. General Construction Co., § 4.8
Connecticut v. Cancer Fund of America, § 2.6
Continental Trading, Inc. v. Commissioner, § 5.7
Coomes v. Commissioner, § 4.7
Cornelius v. NAACP Legal Defense and Educational Fund, §§ 4.3, 6.16
Cowen v. New York Stock Exchange, § 8.7

Dayton Area Visually Impaired Persons, Inc. v. Fisher, § 4.3
Dedication and Everlasting Love to Animals v. Humane Society of the United States, Inc., § 5.19
Deputy v. duPont, § 5.7
Derby v. Hiegart, § 4.10
Disabled American Veterans v. Commissioner, § 5.7

TABLE OF CASES

Disabled American Veterans v. United States, § 5.7

Disabled Veterans Service Foundation v. Commissioner, § 5.7

Duffy v. Birmingham, § 1.1

Eagle v. Vitale, § 4.7

The Ecclesiastical Order of Ism of Am, Inc. v. Commissioner, § 5.7

Employment Division, Department of Human Resources of Oregon v. Smith, § 4.7

est of Hawaii v. Commissioner, § 5.13

Estate of Campbell v. Lepley, § 3.5

Estate of Freshour, § 4.9

Everson v. Board of Education, § 4.7

Ex Parte White, § 4.6

Ex Parte Williams, § 4.6

Executive Network Club v. Commissioner, § 5.7

Falcone v. Middlesex County Medical Society, § 8.3

Famine Relief Fund v. State of West Virginia, §§ 4.3, 5.4

Federal Trade Commission v. Superior Court Trial Lawyers Association, § 4.4

Fernandes v. Limmer, §§ 4.3, 4.4, 4.12

Fisher v. United States, § 4.8

Follett v. Town of McCormick, § 4.7

Forsyth County, Georgia v. Nationalist Movement, § 4.12

Fraternal Order of Police, Illinois State Troopers Lodge No. 41 v. Commissioner, § 5.7

Freedman v. Maryland, § 4.4

Fund for the Study of Economic Growth & Tax Reform v. Internal Revenue Service, § 7.12

General Conference of the Free Church of America v. Commissioner, § 4.7

Gillette v. United States, § 4.7

Gospel Army v. City of Los Angeles, § 4.7

Gospel Missions of America v. Bennett, §§ 3.22, 4.2, 4.3, 4.4, 4.6, 4.7, 4.8, 8.10

Granzow v. Commissioner, § 7.12

Green v. Connally, §§ 1.1, 2.1, 5.12

Greene County Medical Society Foundation v. United States, § 5.7

Hague v. Committee for Industrial Organization, § 4.3

Heritage Publishing Company v. Fishman, §§ 4, 4.3

Heritage Village Church and Missionary Fellowship, Inc. v. North Carolina, §§ 4.5, 4.7

Hernandez v. Commissioner, §§ 3.2, 4.1, 4.7, 5.14

Hernandez v. United States, § 5.3

Higgins v. American Society of Clinical Pathologists, §§ 8.3, 8.7

Higgins v. Commissioner, § 5.7

Holloway v. Brown, § 4.3

Holy Spirit Association for Unification of World Christianity v. Hodge, §§ 4.3, 4.12

The Hope School v. United States, § 5.7

Hornsby v. Allen, § 4.2

Houston Chronicle v. City of Houston, § 4.5

Huron Clinic Foundation v. United States, § 5.7

Hutchinson Baseball Enterprises, Inc. v. Commissioner, § 2.1

Hynes v. Mayor of Oradell, §§ 4.3, 4.6, 4.8

Illinois ex rel. McCollum v. Board of Education, § 4.7

In re Dart, § 4.2

Indiana Voluntary Firemen's Association, Inc. v. Pearson, §§ 4.2, 4.3

International Society for Khrishna Consciousness of Houston, Inc. v. City of Houston, Texas, §§ 4.1, 4.3

International Society for Krishna Consciousness, Inc. v. Lee, § 4.3

International Society for Krishna Consciousness, Inc. v. Rochford, §§ 4.3, 4.7

Jacobson v. Massachusetts, § 4.7

Jamison v. City of St. Louis, § 4.3

Jamison v. Texas, § 4.3

Jews for Jesus, Inc. v. Board of Airport Commissioners, § 4.3

Jimmy Swaggart Ministries v. California Board of Equalization, §§ 4.3, 4.7

Johnson v. Board of Regents of University of Wisconsin System, § 8.7

Jones v. City of Opelika, § 4.6

KJ's Fund Raisers, Inc. v. Commissioner, § 5.7

Kentucky Bar Foundation, Inc. v. Commissioner, § 2.1

Kentucky State Police Professional Association v. Gorman, §§ 3.9, 4.3, 7.1

Kirk v. Commonwealth, § 4.7

Kushnir v. American Medical Center at Denver, § 5.13

Laborer's International Union of North America v. Commissioner, § 5.7

Largent v. Texas, § 4.3

Larson v. Valente, § 4.7

League of Mercy Association, Inc. v. Walt, § 4.6

Lee v. International Society for Krishna Consciousness, § 4.3

Lefkowitz v. Burden, §§ 3.22, 4.1

Lemon v. Kurtzman, § 4.7

Lewis v. Congress of Racial Equality, § 3.13

Lindsley v. Natural Carbonic Gas Co., § 4.5

Lovell v. Griffin, § 4.3

McClure v. Salvation Army, § 4.7

McDowell v. Ribicoff, § 5.7

McGlotten v. Connally, §§ 1.1, 8.3

Make A Joyful Noise, Inc. v. Commissioner, § 5.15

Marjorie Webster Junior College v. Middle States Association of Colleges & Secondary Schools, § 8.3

Martin v. City of Struthers, § 4.6

TABLE OF CASES

Massachusetts v. Oakes, § 4.3
Miller v. Internal Revenue Service, § 5.14
Mississippi State University Alumni, Inc. v.
  Commissioner, § 5.7
Molinas v. National Basketball Association, § 8.7
Monfore v. United States, § 5.7
Moore v. City of Kilgore, Texas, § 4.3
Morey v. Doud, §§ 4.5, 4.6
Murdock v. Pennsylvania, §§ 4.3, 4.7, 4.12

National Association of American Churches v.
  Commissioner, § 5.7
National Association of Social Workers v. United
  States Postal Service, § 5.18
National Awareness Foundation v. Abrams,
  §§ 4.5, 4.12
National Collegiate Athletic Association v.
  Commissioner, § 5.7
National Federation of Nonprofits v. Lungren
  §§ 3.9, 4.3, 7.1
National Foundation v. City of Fort Worth, Texas,
  §§ 4.2, 4.3, 4.5
National Foundation, Inc. v. United States,
  § 5.13
National Water Well Association, Inc. v.
  Commissioner, § 5.7
Nationalist Movement v. Commissioner, § 7.12
New York Times Co. v. Sullivan, § 4.3
Niemotko v. State of Maryland, § 4.5

Optimist Club of North Raleigh v. Riley, § 4.3
Orange County Agricultural Society, Inc. v.
  Commissioner, § 7.12
Orange County Builders Association, Inc. v.
  United States, § 5.7
Oregon State University Alumni Association, Inc.
  v. Commissioner, § 5.7
Ozee v. American Council on Gift Annuities,
  § 5.19

P.L.L. Scholarship Fund v. Commissioner, §§ 5.7,
  5.13
Packel v. Frantz Advertising, Inc., § 3.2
Parklane Residential School, Inc. v.
  Commissioner, § 5.7
Pennsylvania v. Watson & Hughey Company,
  § 2.6
People ex rel. Brown v. Illinois State Troopers
  Lodge No. 41, § 3.13
People ex rel. Scott v. Gorman, § 3.21
People ex rel. Scott v. Police Hall of Fame,
  §§ 3.21, 4.3
People of God Community v. Commissioner,
  § 5.13
People of the State of Illinois v. Police Hall of
  Fame, Inc., § 1.3
People v. Caldwell, § 3.13
People v. Framer, § 4.10
People v. French, § 4.3
People v. Gellard, § 3.22
People v. Handzik, § 4.7
People v. Stone, § 4.1
People v. Tosch, § 4.5

Perry Education Association v. Perry Local
  Educators' Association, §§ 4.3, 6.16
Piety, Inc. v. Commissioner, § 5.7
Pinsker v. Pacific Coast Society of Orthodontists,
  § 8.7
Planned Parenthood Federation of America, Inc. v.
  Commissioner, § 5.7
Planned Parenthood League v. Attorney General,
  § 4.3
Police Department of City of Chicago v. Mosley,
  § 4.5
Pollock v. Farmers' Loan and Trust Co., § 1.1
Presbyterian Church v. Hull Church, § 4.7

Rachford v. Indemnity Insurance Co. of North
  America, § 4.8
Redlands Surgical Services v. Commissioner,
  § 5.13
Rehabilitation Center and Workshop, Inc. v.
  Commonwealth, § 4.1
Rensselaer Polytechnic Institute v. Commissioner,
  § 5.7
Reynolds v. United States, § 4.7
Riley v. National Federation of the Blind of North
  Carolina, Inc., §§ 2.6, 4.3, 7.1
Ritchie v. American Council on Gift Annuities,
  § 5.19
Robertson v. United States, § 3.2
Roemer v. Maryland Public Works Board, § 4.7

Sable Communications of California, Inc. v.
  Federal Communications Commission, § 4.3
St. Louis Union Trust Company v. United States,
  § 1.1
Salvation Mission Army Workers Holy Orthodox
  Christian Church v. Commonwealth, § 3.5
Schneider v. Irvington, § 4.3
Schneider v. State, § 4.6
Seattle v. Rogers, § 4.2
Secretary of State of Maryland v. Joseph H.
  Munson Co., Inc., §§ 4.3, 4.4, 7.1
Securities and Exchange Commission v.
  Children's Hospital, § 4.1
Senior Citizens of Missouri, Inc. v.
  Commissioner, § 5.13
Shannon v. Telco Communication, Inc., § 4.3
Sherbert v. Verner, § 4.7
SICO Foundation v. United States, § 5.7
Sierra Club, Inc. v. Commissioner, § 5.7
Smith v. California, § 4.8
Sound Health Association v. Commissioner,
  § 5.12
State v. Blakney, § 3.2
State v. Delaware Fire Co. No. 3, § 8.7
State v. Events International, Inc., §§ 4.1, 4.3
State v. Maine State Troopers Associations, § 4.5
State v. Mauer, § 4.10
State v. O'Neill Investigators, Inc., § 4.3
State v. W.R.G. Enterprises, Inc., § 4.3
State Marine Lines, Inc. v. F.M.C., § 8.3
Staub v. City of Baxley, § 4.6
Stern v. Lucy Webb Hayes National Training
  School for Deaconesses and Missionaries, § 2.6

TABLE OF CASES

Streich v. Pennsylvania Commission On Charitable Organizations, § 4.3
Suffolk County Patrolmen's Benevolent Association, Inc. v. Commissioner, § 5.7
Sylte v. The Metropolitan Government of Nashville and Davidson County, § 4.7

Taylor v. City of Knoxville, § 4.7
Telco Communications, Inc. v. Carbaugh, §§ 4.3, 7.1
Texas Farm Bureau v. United States, § 5.7
Texas Monthly, Inc. v. Bullock, § 4.7
There to Care, Inc., v. Commissioner of Indiana Department of Revenue, § 4.3
Thomas v. Collins, §§ 4.2, 4.3, 4.7
Trinidad v. Sagrada Orden de Predicadores, § 1.1
Trinity Church v. City of Boston, § 1.1
Trustees of the First Methodist Episcopal Church v. City of Atlanta, § 1.1

United Cancer Council, Inc. v. Commissioner §§ 5.6, 7.12
United Nuclear Corporation v. NLRB, § 4.8
United States et al. v. Toy National Bank et al., § 4.7
United States v. Albertini, § 4.4
United States v. American Bar Endowment, §§ 3.2, 5.1, 5.7
United States v. American College of Physicians, § 5.7
United States v. Brown University, § 5.19
United States v. Kokinda, § 4.3
United States v. O'Brien, § 4.4

United States v. Thomas, § 4.13
U.S. CB Radio Association, No. 1, Inc. v. Commissioner, §§ 5.7, 5.16
Universal Life Church, Inc. v. United States, § 5.7

Valente v. Larson, § 4.7
Valentine v. Chrestensen, § 4.3
Van Wart v. Commissioner, § 5.7
Veterans of Foreign Wars, Department of Michigan v. Commissioner, §§ 5.2, 5.7
Veterans of Foreign Wars, Department of Missouri, Inc. v. United States, §§ 5.2, 5.7
Vigilant Hose Company of Emmitsburg v. United States, § 5.7
Village of Schaumburg v. Citizens for a Better Environment, §§ 2.6, 4.2, 4.3, 8.1

Walz v. Tax Commission, §§ 1.1, 4.7, 6.3
Ward v. Rock Against Racism, § 4.4
Wendy L. Parker Rehabilitation Foundation, Inc. v. Commissioner, § 3.2
Whipple v. Commissioner, § 5.7
Wickman v. Firestone, § 4.3
Williams v. Golden, § 4.6
Wisconsin v. Yoder, § 4.7
Woodbury v. Commissioner, § 5.14
World Family Corporation v. Commissioner, § 5.13
WRG Enterprises, Inc. v. Crowell, § 4.3
Wyatt v. Tahoe Forest Hospital District, § 8.7

Zorach v. Clausen, § 4.7

Table of IRS Pronouncements

Revenue Rulings	Sections	Revenue Rulings	Sections
54-243	5.14	72-431	5.7
55-676	5.7	73-504	5.11
56-152	5.7	75-201	5.7
56-511	5.7	75-472	5.7
59-330	5.7	76-204	2.1
64-182	5.1, 5.13, 5.15	77-72	5.7
66-221	5.7	78-84	2.1
67-4	5.15	78-85	2.1
67-246	5.1, 5.2	78-144	5.7
67-325	5.12	80-108	5.8
68-432	5.3	80-200	2.1
69-268	5.7	80-286	2.1
69-545	2.1	81-178	5.7
69-574	5.7	84-132	5.14
69-633	5.7	85-184	5.14
71-477	5.12	89-51	7.10
71-581	5.7	98-15	5.13

Revenue Procedures	Sections	Revenue Procedures	Sections
72-54	5.12	93-49	App. D, E, F
75-50	5.12	94-72	App. D, E, F
82-23	5.5	95-53	App. D, E, F
83-23	5.9	96-59	App. D, E, F
90-12	App. E, F	97-57	App. D, E, F
90-27	5.8	98-61	App. D, E, F
92-58	App. E, F	99-42	App. D, E, F
92-85	5.8	2001-13	App. D, E, F
92-102	App. D, E, F	2001-59	App. D, E, F

Private Letter Rulings	Sections	Private Letter Rulings	Sections
7946001	5.7	9509002	5.7
8127019	5.7	9623035	5.3
8203134	5.7	9703025	5.7
8232011	5.7	9709029	5.7
8725056	5.7	9712001	5.7
8747066	5.7	9740032	5.7
8823109	5.7	9810030	5.7
8832003	5.2	9816027	5.7
9250001	5.7	200022056	5.7
9315001	5.6	200108045	5.7
9320042	5.7	200114040	5.13
9450028	5.7	200128059	5.7

Technical Advice Memoranda	Sections	Technical Advice Memoranda	Sections
9147007	5.7, 5.16	9712001	5.7
9502009	5.7	9723001	5.7
9652004	5.7	20021056	5.7

Table of Cases Discussed
in *The Nonprofit Counsel*

The following cases, referenced in the text, are discussed in greater detail in one or more issues of the author's monthly newsletter, *The Nonprofit Counsel*, as indicated.

Case	Book Sections	Newsletter Issues
Alumni Association of the University of Oregon, Inc. v. *Commissioner*	5.7	December 1999
American Bar Endowment v. *United States*	5.7, 5.4	April 1984, July 1985
American Campaign Academy v. *Commissioner*	5.13, 5.15, 7.12	July 1989, June 2001
American Target Advertising v. *Giani*	4.3	November 1998, March 2000
Auburn Police Union v. *Tierney*	4.3	July 1991
Bellotti v. *Telco Communications, Inc.*	4.3	May 1987
Bob Jones University v. *United States*	2.1, 5.12	July 1985
Brentwood Academy v. *Tennessee Secondary School Athletic Association*	8.3	April 2001
Camps Newfound/Owatonna, Inc. v. *Town of Harrison, Maine*	4.2	July 1997
Church by Mail v. *Commissioner*	5.13	September 1985, December 1985, June 2001
Common Cause v. *Commissioner*	5.7	August 1999
Disabled American Veterans v. *Commissioner*	5.7	April 1990
est of Hawaii v. *Commissioner*	5.13	June 2001
Executive Network Club, Inc. v. *Commissioner*	5.7	March 1995
Fund for the Study of Economic Growth and Tax Reform v. *Internal Revenue Service*	7.12	May 1998, February 1999
Hernandez v. *Commissioner*	3.2, 4.1, 4.7, 5.14	July 1989
International Society for Krishna Consciousness v. *Lee*	4.3	May 1991, August 1992
Jimmy Swaggart Ministries v. *California Board of Equalization*	4.3, 4.7	March 1990
Kentucky Bar Foundation, Inc. v. *Commissioner*	2.1	March 1985

TABLE OF CASES DISCUSSED IN *THE NONPROFIT COUNSEL*

Case	Book Sections	Newsletter Issues
Laborer's International Union of North America v. *Commissioner*	5.7	October 2001
Oregon State University Alumni Association, Inc. v. *Commissioner*	5.7	December 1999
National Collegiate Athletic Association v. *Commissioner*	5.7	April 1989, November 1990
National Foundation, Inc. v. *United States*	5.13	January 1998
National Water Well Association v. *Commissioner*	5.7	March 1989
Redlands Surgical Services v. *Commissioner*	5.13	September 1999, June 2001
Riley v. *National Federation of the Blind of North Carolina*	2.6, 4.3, 7.1	September 1998
Secretary of State of Maryland v. *Joseph H. Munson Co., Inc.*	4.3, 4.4, 7.1	August 1984, January 1985, March 1985, July 1985
Senior Citizens of Missouri, Inc. v. *Commissioner*	5.13	March 1989
Sierra Club, Inc. v. *Commissioner*	5.7	July 1993, October 1994, August 1996, May 1999
United Cancer Council v. *Commissioner*	5.6, 7.12	January 1998, April 1999
United States v. *American Bar Endowment*	3.2, 5.1, 5.7	August 1986
Veterans of Foreign Wars, Department of Michigan v. *Commissioner*	5.2, 5.7	August 1987
Veterans of Foreign Wars of the United States v. *Department of Missouri, Inc.*	5.2, 5.7	December 1984
Vigilant Hose Company of Emmitsburg v. *United States*	5.7	August 2001
Village of Schaumburg v. *Citizens for a Better Environment*	2.6, 4.2, 4.3, 8.1	January 1985, March 1985, July 1985
WRG Enterprises, Inc. v. *Crowell*	4.3	February 1989
Wendy L. Parker Rehabilitation Foundation, Inc. v. *Commissioner*	3.2	November 1986

Table of Private Letter Rulings and Technical Advice Memoranda Discussed in *The Nonprofit Counsel*

The following IRS private letter rulings and technical advice memoranda, referenced in the text, are discussed in greater detail in one or more issues of the author's monthly newsletter, *The Nonprofit Counsel,* as indicated.

PLR/TAM	Book Sections	Newsletter Issues
9502009	5.7	February 1995
9712001	5.7	June 1997
9740032	5.7	December 1997
200114040	5.13	June 2001
200128059	5.7	September 2001

Index

Abuses:
  alleged, § 2.7
  costs of fundraising as, § 1.3
Accountants and accounting:
  role of, § 2.4
  generally accepted accounting principles, § 2.4(a)
Audit guidelines, IRS, § 5.1
Administrative agencies:
  defined, § 3.1(j)
  delegation of legislative authority to, § 5.6
Advance ruling, § 5.8(c)(iii)
Advance ruling period, § 5.8(c)(iii)
Affinity card programs:
  postal rates, § 5.18(d)
  unrelated business rules, § 5.7(b)(vi)
American Association of Fund Raising Counsel, § 2.3(c), (e)
American Institute of Certified Public Accountants:
  audit guides, § 6.3(d)
  cost allocation rules, § 2.6(b)
American Institute of Philanthropy standards:
  asset reserves, § 8.6(b)
  fundraising expenses, § 8.6(a)
American political philosophy, as to charitable sector, § 1.1
Annual giving programs, § 2.2(a)
Annual information returns, § 5.9
Antitrust laws, §§ 5.13, 5.19
Appraisal requirements, § 5.14(h)
Association for Healthcare Philanthropy, § 2.3(c), (d), (e)
Association of Fundraising Professionals, §§ 1.2, 2.3(c), (d), (e)
Attorneys general, powers of, § 3.19
Auctions, charity:
  acquirer deduction, § 7.10(c)
  businesses, as, § 7.10(a)
  contribution deduction, § 7.10(b)
  Internet, on, § 5.22(c)(v)
  quid pro quo rules, § 7.10(e)
  reporting rules, § 7.10(g)
  sales tax rules, § 7.10(f)
  substantiation rules, § 7.10(d)
Audit guidelines, IRS, see IRS audit guidelines

BBB Wise Giving Alliance, § 8.8
Bingo games:
  IRS checklist, § 5.1
  limits of free speech doctrine, § 4.3(e)
Blue sky statutes, § 3.22

Boards of directors:
  Evangelical Council for Financial Accountability standards, § 8.5(a)
  Philanthropic Advisory Service standards, § 8.4(e)
Bonds:
  charitable solicitation act, model, § 7.7(f)
  fundraising professionals, §§ 3.6, 7.2
  solicitors, professional, §§ 3.6, 7.2
Boorstin, Daniel J., § 1.1
Business, concept of, § 5.7(a)(i), (iii), (b)(i)
Brauer, Robert I., § 5.1
Bulk third-class mailing rate, see Postal rates, preferred

California studies of commercial fundraisers, § 7.9(a)
Campaign committees, annual giving programs, § 2.2(a)
Cause-related marketing, § 5.7(b)(ix)
Charitable, defined, § 2.1
Charitable contribution deduction rules:
  appraisal requirements, § 5.14(h)
  deduction reduction rules, § 5.14(e)
  gift, meaning of, § 5.14(a)
  gift properties, § 5.14(c)
  partial interest gifts, § 5.14(g)
  percentage limitations, § 5.14(d)
  qualified donees, § 5.14(b)
  record-keeping and reporting, § 5.14(i), (j), (k)
  twice-basis deductions, § 5.14(f)
Charitable deduction property, § 5.14(k)
Charitable fundraising:
  and law, in general, § 7.1
  portrait of, § 1.2
Charitable organization:
  defined, § 2.1
  scope of term, § 2.1
Charitable sales promotions, See also Commercial co-venturers
  defined, §§ 3.2(i), 7.4(c)
  regulation of, § 7.4(b), (d)
  terminology, § 7.4(a)
Charitable sector, § 1.1
Charitable solicitation act, prospective federal:
  advantages of, § 6.1
  AICPA audit guides, § 6.3(d)
  Commission on Private Philanthropy and Public Needs, § 6.1
  cost of fundraising, disclosure of, § 6.3(c)
  direct mail fundraising § 6.2(c)
  emerging issues, § 6.3

Charitable solicitation act, prospective federal
    (Continued)
  enforcement, federal agency charged with,
      § 6.3(e)
  exemptions, § 6.3(f)
  Federal Trade Commission § 6.2(c)
  Filer Commission Report, §§ 6.3(e), 6.3(i)
  fundraising professionals, § 6.2(c)
  interstate solicitations, §§ 6.3(i), 6.3(j)
  jurisdiction, federal agency, § 6.3(e)
  legislative proposals, § 6.2
  mode of disclosure, § 6.3(b)
  preemption of state law, § 6.3(g)
  public charities, applicability, §§ 6.2(b),
      6.3(f)
  religious organizations, exemptions, §
      6.3(f)
  sanctions, § 6.3(h)
  state law, preemption of, § 6.3(g)
  uniform accounting principles, § 6.3(d)
Charitable solicitation act, model:
  bonds, § 7.7(f)
  compensation, § 7.7(g)
  contracts, § 7.7(f)
  definitions, § 7.7(e)
  elements, § 7.7(b)
  exemptions, § 7.7(h)
  preapproval, § 7.7(c)
  prohibited acts, § 7.7(j)
  reason for, § 7.7(a)
  registration, § 7.7(c)
  reporting, § 7.7(d)
  sanctions, § 7.7(k)
Charitable solicitation acts, state:
  administrative agency involved, § 3.2(j)
  administrative enforcement, delegation of
      legislative authority, § 4.6
  annual reports, § 3.4
    uniform, § 7.14(c)
  attorneys general, powers of, § 3.19
  charitable, defined, § 3.2(a)
  charitable organization, defined, § 3.2(b)
  churches, exemptions for, § 3.5(a)
  commercial co-venturers:
    defined, § 3.2(j)
    regulation of, § 3.8
  compliance, difficulty of, § 7.1
  contracts, § 3.11
  contribution, defined, § 3.2(e)
  costs of fundraising, limitations on, § 3.9
  deceptive acts or practices, § 3.22
  definitions, § 3.2
  delegation of legislative authority,
      administrative enforcement subject to,
      § 4.6
  disclosure statements and legends, § 3.15
  due date of annual reports, § 3.4
  due process rights, § 4.4
  duration of registration or other
      authorization, § 3.3

educational institutions, exemptions for,
    § 3.5(c)
effectiveness of, § 7.1
equal protection rights, § 4.5
exemptions, § 3.5
federated fund raising organization,
    defined, § 3.1(k)
fiduciary relationships, § 3.18
financial statement filing requirements,
    § 3.3
fundraising costs, limitations on, § 3.9
fundraising counsel, defined, § 3.1(g)
fundraising expenses, defined, § 3.1(k)
health care providers, exemptions for,
    § 3.5(f), (g)
hospitals, exemptions for, §§ 3.5(f), 6.3(f),
    7.7(h)
interstate commerce, § 4.2
investigative authority, § 4.2
libraries, exemptions for, § 3.5(d)
license requirements, § 3.2
membership, defined, § 3.2(f)
membership organizations, exemptions for,
    §§ 3.5(h), 6.3(f), 7.7(h)
miscellaneous provisions, § 3.20
model act, § 7.7
museums, exemptions, § 3.5(e)
named organizations, exemptions, § 3.5(m)
notice requirements, § 3.17
officials' concerns, § 7.8
organizations affected, § 2.1
permit requirements, § 3.3
police power, § 4.2
political organizations, exemptions for,
    § 3.5(k)
preapproval requirements, § 3.3
preemption by prospective federal act,
    § 6.3(g)
professional fundraisers:
  defined, §§ 3.2(g), 7.2
  regulation of, § 3.6
professional fundraising firm, defined,
    § 3.2(g)
professional solicitor:
  defined, §§ 3.2(h), 7.2
  regulation of, § 3.7
prohibited acts, §§ 3.13, 7.5
rationale for, § 7.1
reciprocal agreements, § 3.16
record-keeping requirements, § 3.10
registered agent requirements, § 3.12
registration, § 3.3
regulatory prohibitions, § 3.14
religious organizations, exemptions for,
    §§ 3.5(b), 6.3(f), 7.7(h)
sale, defined, § 3.2(d)
sanctions, § 3.21
scope, § 7.1(f)
small solicitations, exemptions for, § 3.5(i)
solicitation, defined, § 3.2(c)

solicitation notice requirements, § 3.17
specified individuals, solicitations for, exemptions for, § 3.5(j)
statement requirements, § 3.3
summary of, § 3.1
veterans' organizations, exemptions for, § 3.5(l)
volunteer, defined, § 3.1(k)
Charleston Principles, § 4.13(b)
Child Protection and Obscenity Enforcement Act, § 4.3(c)
Childrens' Aid International, § 1.3
Churches, exemptions, §§ 3.5(a), 6.3(f), 7.7(h). *See also Religious organizations*
Colleges and universities:
  IRS examination guidelines, § 5.17
  public charity classification, § 5.11
Commemorative giving, annual giving programs, § 2.2(a)
Commensurate test:
  application in fundraising context, § 5.15
  in general, § 5.1(c)
Commerce clause violations, § 4.2
Commercial co-ventures:
  charitable sales promotions, §§ 3.8, 7.4
  defined, §§ 3.2(j), 7.4
  unrelated income taxation, § 5.7(b)(vii)
Commercial fundraisers, California studies, § 7.9(a)
Commission on Private Philanthropy and Public Needs, §§ 1.1, 6.3(i) *Also* Filer Commission
Compensation arrangements for fundraising professionals, § 5.13
  See also Contracts with professional fundraisers
  charitable solicitation act, model, § 7.7
  commensurate test, IRS application of, §§ 5.1(c), 5.15
  commissions, § 5.13
  contract, §§ 3.11, 7.7(f)
  Evangelical Council for Financial Accountability, standards, § 8.5
  intermediate sanctions, §§ 5.6, 5.13
  limitations and antitrust laws, § 5.13
  revenue-sharing arrangements, §§ 5.6, 5.13
  unreasonable:
    private benefit doctrine, § 5.13
    private inurement doctrine, §§ 5.13, 8.12(c)
Compliance:
  difficulty of, § 7.1
  IRS annual information returns, § 5.9
Constitutional issues:
  commerce clause, § 4.2
  compensation limitations, § 5.13
  delegation of legislative authority, § 4.6
  due process rights, § 4.4
  equal protection rights, § 4.5
  establishment of religion, § 4.7

exemptions for religious organizations, § 4.7
ordinances, § 3.22
percentage compensation disclosure, § 4.3
percentage limitations, § 4.3
police power, § 4.2
Postal Service property, solicitations on, § 4.3
rebuttable percentage limitations, § 4.1
religious organizations, treatment of, § 4.7
Contemporary regulatory climate, § 1.4
Contracts with professional fundraisers:
  basic elements, § 7.6(a)
  charitable solicitation acts, model, § 7.7(f)
  content requirement, state law, § 3.11
  fee arrangements, § 7.6(c)
  solicitor status, § 7(d)
  specific elements, § 7.6(b)
  state laws, § 7(e)
Contributions:
  deductions, *see* Tax deductions for charitable contributions
  defined, § 5.14(a)
  statistics, § 1.2
Cornuelle, Richard C., § 1.1
Corporate services, § 5.7(b)(ix)
Corporate sponsorships:
  in general, §§ 5.16(b), 5.22(c)(iii)
  Internet-based, § 5.22(c)(iii)
Costs of fundraising:
  alleged abuses, § 1.3
  average gift size factor, § 4.1(f)
  California studies, § 7.9(a)
  constitutionality of percentage limitations, § 3.9
  factors used to measure, § 4.1(h)
  fallacy of high costs as fraud, § 4.1(b)
  floating average approach, § 4.1(d)
  fraudulence of high costs, fallacy of, § 4.1(b)
  limitations under state charitable solicitation acts, § 3.9
  line item approach, § 4.1(c)
  lobbying expenditures, determining, § 5.10
  percentage, expressed as, § 4.1(b)
  Philanthropic Advisory Service, standards, § 8.5
  pluralization approach, § 4.1(e)
  reasonable, *see* Costs of fundraising, reasonable
  reasons for high costs, § 4.1(b)
  regulated disclosure approach, § 4.1(g)
  state regulation, *see* Costs of fundraising, state regulation
Costs of fundraising, reasonable:
  capital campaigns, § 2.2(d)(vi)
  corporations and foundations, § 2.2(d)(iv)
  determining, factors considered in, § 4.1
  direct mail, § 2.2(d)(i)
  planned giving, § 2.2(d)(v)

INDEX

Costs of fundraising, reasonable (*Continued*)
  special events and benefits, § 2.2(d)(iii)
  unreasonable expenses, prohibited acts,
    § 3.13
Costs of fundraising:
  average gift size factor, § 4.1(f)
  bottom-line ratio, § 4.1(e)
  determining costs, § 4.1(b)-(f), (h)
  disclosure:
    dilemma, § 4.1(a)
    disclosure-on-demand, § 4.1(a)
    point-of-solicitation disclosure, § 4.1(a)
    regulated disclosure approach, § 4.1(g)
  floating average approach, § 4.1(d)
  line item approach, § 4.1(c)
  most effective means, determining, §
    4.1(h)
  percentage approach, § 4.1(b)
  pluralization approach, § 4.1(e)
  reasonableness, factors considered in
    determining, § 4.1(h)
Council for the Advancement and Support of
  Education, § 2.3(c), (e)
Council of Better Business Bureaus, § 2.4(b)
Credit cards, affinity card programs, §
  5.7(b)(vi)
Curti, Merle, § 1.1

Deceptions practices laws, § 3.22
Deceptive solicitations, § 6.4
Deductions, *see* Tax deductions for charitable
  contributions
Definitive ruling, § 5.8(c)(iii)
Delegation of legislative authority, § 4.6
de Tocqueville, Alexis, § 1.1
Direct mail fundraising:
  annual giving programs, § 2.2(a)
  costs of fundraising, reasonable, § 2.2(d)
  guidelines, § 4.11
  unsolicited merchandise, § 2.2(a)
Direct Mail Marketing Association, § 2.3(c)
Disclosure requirements:
  annual information returns, § 5.9(i)
  contracts with professional fundraisers,
    percentage compensation disclosure,
    § 3.11
  costs of fundraising, state regulation:
    disclosure dilemma, § 4.1(a)
    disclosure-on-demand, § 4.1(a)
    point-of-solicitation disclosure,
      § 4.1(c)
    regulated disclosure approach,
      § 4.1(g)
  fundraising costs, § 4.1(a)
  gift substantiation, § 5.3
  in general, §§ 5.1, 5.2, 5.9(i)
  noncharitable organizations, § 5.5
  percentage compensation disclosure,
    constitutionality, § 4.3
  point-of-solicitation, § 4.1

prospective federal legislation, § 6.3(b)
quid pro quo contributions, § 5.4
solicitors, professional, § 3.17
statements and legends, state charitable
  solicitation acts, § 3.15
tax deductions for charitable contributions,
  § 5.14
Disqualified persons, fundraising context,
  § 5.6(b)(ii)
Disregarded benefits, §§ 5.2, 5.3, 5.4
Document disclosure requirements, § 5.9(i)
Doing business in a state, concept of, §§ 3.20,
  5.9(f)
Donative intent, § 5.4
Donor clubs and associations, annual giving
  programs, § 2.2(a)
Donor recognition programs,
  acknowledgment, § 5.16(b)
Door-to-door and on-street solicitation,
  annual giving programs, § 2.2(a)
Due process rights, § 4.4

Educational institutions:
  discriminatory policies, IRS denial of
    exempt status, § 5.12
  IRS examination guidelines, § 5.17
  preferred postal rates, § 5.18(b)(ii)
  public charity classification, § 5.11
  record-retention requirements, § 5.12
Ekstrom, Helmer, § 7.1
Enforcement by administrative agencies,
  delegation of legislative authority, § 4.6
Equal protection rights, § 4.5
Establishment of religion, § 4.7(b)
Estate planning programs:
  bequests, § 2.2(c)
  charitable remainder gifts, § 2.2(c)
  life insurance/wealth replacement trusts,
    § 2.2(c)
  pooled income funds, § 2.2(c)
  wills and bequests, § 2.2(c)
Evangelical Council for Financial
  Accountability, standards:
  audited financial statements, § 8.5(b)
  board of directors, § 8.5(a)
  compensation of fundraising consultants,
    § 7.12
  conflicts of interest, § 8.5(c)
  fundraising, § 8.5(d)
Events, fundraising, §§ 5.7(b)(i), 5.9(e)
Excess benefit transactions, fundraising
  context, § 5.6(b)(iii)
Exclusivity test, § 5.7(a)(i)
Exemptions:
  application contents, § 5.8(c)
  application procedure, § 5.8(b)
  charitable solicitation acts, federal
    prospective, § 6.3(f)
  charitable solicitation acts, model,
    § 7.14(a)

INDEX

charitable solicitation acts, state, § 3.5
federal legislative proposals, § 6.2
public policy rationale for tax exemptions, § 1.1
recognition of, § 5.8(a)
religious organizations, § 3.5(a), (b)
tax exemption application process, *see* Tax exemption application process
Exempt purpose expenditure percentage, § 5.10
Exemption application process, § 5.8

Fair market value of gift, § 5.14(h)
Federal legislation, proposed:
Luken bill, § 6.2(c)
Metzenbaum proposal, § 6.2(d)
Mondale bill, § 6.2(b)
Wilson bill, § 6.2(a)
Federal Program Improvement Act of 1993, prospective, § 6.4
Federal regulation of fundraising, prospective:
agency jurisdiction, § 6.3(e)
contemporary developments, § 6.4
emerging issues, § 6.3
exemptions, § 6.3(f)
federal involvement in general, § 6.1
Filer Commission recommendations, § 6.3(i)
Ford Administration proposals, § 6.3(j)
legislative proposals, § 6.2
sanctions, § 6.3(h)
state law preemption, § 6.3(g)
uniform accounting principles, § 6.3(d)
Federal Trade Commission:
charitable solicitation act, federal prospective, role in § 6.2(c)
telemarketing rule, § 5.21
Federal Trade Commission Act, § 2.6
Fees, registration:
in general, § 4.12
sliding-scale, §§ 4.12, 7.11
Filer Commission report, §§ 1.1, 6.3(i)
First Amendment, *see* Free speech doctrine
Ford Administration proposals, § 6.3(j)
Form 990, *see* IRS annual information returns (Form 990)
Fragmentation rule, unrelated income taxation, § 5.7(a)(iii)
Fraternal organizations, preferred postal rates, § 5.18(b)(iv)
Freedom Forum International, Inc., § 1.3
Free speech doctrine:
airport terminal solicitations, § 4.3(d)
fundamental principles, § 4.3(b)
gambling, § 4.3(e)
outer boundaries of doctrine, § 4.3(e)
state of law prior to 1980, § 4.3(a)
state of law subsequent to 1980s Supreme Court cases, § 4.3(c)

Supreme Court dissenting opinions, § 4.3(b)(iv)
Supreme Court opinions, §§ 4.3(b)(i)-(iii)
Functional method of accounting, §§ 2.4(a), 5.7(b)(iv), 5.9(d), 6.3(d)
Fundraising, as free speech, §§ 4.3, 7.1
Fundraising costs:
disclosure of, in general, § 4.1
disclosure of, prospective federal legislation, § 6.3(c)
percentages, § 7.1(b)
reasonableness of, § 2.2(d)
regulation of, § 4.1
Fundraising disclosure:
by charitable organizations, § 5.2
by noncharitable organizations, § 5.5
Fundraising methods, § 2.2
Fundraising professionals:
accreditation and certification, § 2.3(d)
alteration of state charitable solicitation acts, § 7.15
associations, § 2.3(c)
bond requirements, §§ 3.6, 3.7, 7.1(d)
charitable solicitation act, federal prospective, § 6.1
compensation arrangements, *see* Compensation for fundraising professionals
contracts, *see* Contracts with fundraising professionals
definitions in state charitable solicitation acts, §§ 3.6, 3.7, 7.1(c), 7.2(a)
fund development officer, § 2.3(a)
fundraising consultant, § 2.3(a)
IRS, engagement of, § 7.15
lobbying, § 7.15
networking, § 7.15
political action efforts, § 7.15
professional solicitor, § 2.3(a)
registration under state charitable solicitation acts, § 3.6
role of, § 2.3
solicitors, differences, §§ 4.10, 7.2
standards of conduct and professional practice, § 2.3(e)
Treasury Department, engagement of, § 7.15
viewpoint on regulation, § 2.7

Gallagher, Raymond, § 6.3(i)
Gannett Foundation, § 1.3
Gibbs, Lawrence B., § 5.1(a)
Gifts:
deductions, *see* Tax deductions for charitable contributions
definition of, §§ 5.1(a), 5.14(a)
in kind, annual giving programs, § 2.2(a)
partial interest, § 5.14(g)
Government regulation of fundraising, evolution of, § 1.3

INDEX

Harassment campaigns, § 5.9(i)
Health Insurance Portability and
    Accountability Act regulations, § 5.23

Implementing Guidelines, IRS fiscal year
    2002, § 5.1(e)
Increasing federal regulation, § 1.4
Insider, fundraising company as, §§ 5.6(b)(ii),
    7.12
Inspection requirements, § 5.9(h)
Insurance laws, § 3.22
Intangible religious benefits, §§ 5.3, 5.4
Intermediate sanctions:
    basic concepts, § 5.6(a)
    in fundraising context, § 5.6(b)
International Society for Krishna
    Consciousness, § 4.3(c)
Internet:
    auctions, § 5.22(v)
    Charleston Principles, § 4.13(b)
    corporate sponsorships, § 5.22(c)(iii)
    co-venture programs, § 5.22(c)(vi)
    fundraising by means of, § 4.13(a)
    in general, § 5.22
    links, § 5.22(c)(ii)
    on-line storefronts, § 5.22(c)(vii)
    unrelated business conducted on,
        § 5.22(c)(i)
    virtual trade shows, § 5.22(c)(viii)
Interstate commerce, § 4.2
Interstate solicitations, § 7.1(a)
IRS annual information returns:
    auctions, § 7.10
    disclosure of, § 5.9(i)
    filing categories, § 5.9(a)
    functional accounting, § 5.9(d)
    income-producing activities, § 5.9(e)
    public inspection requirement, § 5.9(h)
    related organizations, relationships with
        § 5.9(g)
    special fundraising events and activities, §§
        5.9(e), 5.16(a)
IRS audit guidelines, § 5.1
IRS commensurate test, see Commensurate test
IRS information returns (Form 8282), 5.14(k)

Joint ventures, § 5.13

Labor organizations, preferred postal rates,
    § 5.18(b)(iv)
Las Vegas and Monte Carlo nights, annual
    giving programs, § 2.2(a)
Lawyers, role of, § 2.5
Legal trends, § 7.15
Legislative authority, delegation of, § 4.6
Lerner, Max, § 1.1
Libraries, exemptions, § 3.5(d)
Lobbying restrictions, § 5.10
Look ahead, § 7.15
Lotteries, § 2.2(a)

Low-cost articles, § 5.2
Luken bill, § 6.2(c)
Lyman, Richard W., § 1.1

Mail, direct, see Direct mail fundraising
Mailing list rentals, § 5.7(b)(6)
Mailing rates, see Postal rates, preferred
Marine Toys for Tots Foundation, § 1.3
Membership, defined, § 3.2(f)
Membership organizations, § 4.9
Metzenbaum proposal, § 6.2(d)
Mill, John Stuart, § 1.1
Model law:
    bonds, § 7.7(f)
    commentary on, §§ 7.7(l), 7.14(a)
    compensation, § 7.7(g)
    contracts, § 7.7(f)
    definitions, § 7.7(e)
    elements of, § 7.7(b)
    exemptions, § 7.7(h)
    in general, §§ 7.7, 7.14(a)
    preapproval, § 7.7(c)
    prohibited acts, § 7.7(j)
    reciprocal agreements, § 7.14(b)
    reporting, § 7.7(d)
    sanctions, § 7.7(k)
Mondale bill, § 6.2(b)
Museums, exemptions, § 3.5(e)

National Association of State Charity
    Officials, §§ 1.4, 2.6(b), 4.13(b)
National Council on Planned Giving,
    § 2.3(c)
Neilsen, Waldemar A., § 1.1
New Era for Philanthropy Foundation, § 6.1
Nongovernmental regulation, in general,
    § 8.1
Nonprofit corporation acts, § 3.22
Notice of solicitation requirement, § 3.7

O'Connell, Brian, § 1.1
Ordinances, city and county, § 3.22
O'Rourke, Helen, § 8.2

Pallottine Fathers, §§ 1.3, 4.7(b)
Passive income, unrelated income taxation:
    modifications, exclusions provided by,
        § 5.7(a)(vii)
    royalties, § 5.7(b)(vi)
Penalties, §§ 5.1(c), 5.5, 5.9(j)
Percentages, fundraising costs and, § 4.1(b)
Philanthropic Advisory Service standards:
    CBBB Standards for Charitable
        Solicitations, § 2.4(b)
    fundraising practices, § 8.4(d)
    governance, § 8.4(e)
    informational materials, § 8.4(c)
    public accountability, § 8.4(a)
    solicitations, § 8.4(c)
    use of funds, § 8.4(b)

INDEX

Philanthropic organizations, preferred postal rates, § 5.18(b)(iii)

Pickle, J.J., § 6.4

Police power, §§ 4.2, 7.1(a)

Political organizations, postal rates, preferred, § 5.18(b)(iv)

Postal laws, § 5.18

Postal rates, preferred:
application for authorization, § 5.18(c)
cooperative mailings, § 5.18(d)
educational institutions, § 5.18(b)(ii)
eligible and ineligible matter, § 5.18(d)
ineligible organizations, § 5.18(b)(iv)
miscellaneous organizations, § 5.18(b)(iv)
philanthropic organizations, § 5.18(b)(iii)
postage statement, § 5.18(e)
qualifying organizations, § 5.18(b)
rate determination, § 5.18(a)
religious organizations, § 5.18(b)(i)
Revenue Forgone Reform Act of 1993, § 5.18(a), (d)
revocation of authorization, § 5.18(c)
substantially related test, § 5.18(d)

Preapproval:
charitable solicitation act, model, § 7.7(c)
charitable solicitation act, state, § 3.3

Preemption of state law, § 6.3(g)

Preparatory time, § 5.7(b)(ii)

Principal-agent relationship, § 5.7(b)(v)

Private benefit doctrine:
commensurate test, and § 5.15(b)(iii)
in general, §§ 5.7(b)(iii), 5.13, 5.15(b)(iii)
private inurement compared, § 7.12

Private foundation rules, extension of, § 1.4

Private inurement doctrine:
in general, §§ 5.6(a)(ii), 5.13, 7.12
intermediate sanctions and, § 5.6(a)(x)
insider status and, § 5.13
private benefit doctrine compared, § 7.12
used vehicles, gifts of, § 7.13

Professional fundraiser, defined §§ 4.10, 7.1(c), 7.2(a)

Professional solicitor:
defined, §§ 4.10, 7.1(c), 7.2(a)
fundraising by, § 7.9
telemarketer as, § 7.3

Prohibited acts:
basic prohibitions, § 7.5(a)
duplicative rules, § 7.5(e)
extraordinary prohibitions, § 7.5(a)
in general, §§ 7.1(e), 7.5
solicitors' activities, § 7.5(c)
unusual provisions, § 7.5(d)

Property, gifts of, deductibility, see Tax deductions for charitable contributions

Public charity classification, § 5.11

Public policy rationale for tax exemptions, historically, § 1.1

Qualified sponsorship payments, § 5.16(b)(2)

Quid pro quo contribution rules, §§ 5.4, 7.10(e)

Reasonable costs of fundraising, see Costs of fundraising, reasonable

Rebuttable percentage limitations, § 4.3

Reciprocal agreements, §§ 3.16, 7.14(b)

Registration fees:
in general, § 4.12
sliding-scale, §§ 4.12, 7.11

Registration requirements, § 3.3

Regularly carried on, concept of, § 5.7(a)(iv), (b)(ii)

Regulated disclosure, §§ 3.15, 3.17

Regulated professional, viewpoint of, § 2.7

Regulation:
contemporary regulatory climate, § 1.4
system for coping with, § 2.8
views as to, § 7.1(g)

Regulators, viewpoint of, § 2.6

Regulatory climate, contemporary, § 1.4

Relief, proposals for, § 7.14

Religious organizations:
cults, § 4.7(b)
exemptions, § 4.7(b)
First Amendment, § 4.7(a)
Free Exercise Clause of Constitution, § 4.7(a)
postal rates, preferred, § 5.18(b)(i)

Reporting requirements:
disclosure requirements, § 5.9(i)
filing categories, § 5.9(a)
functional accounting, § 5.9(d)
income-producing activities, § 5.9(b)
inspection requirements, § 5.9(h)
penalties, § 5.9(j)
related organizations, § 5.9(g)

Rockefeller, John D., § 1.1

Rostenkowski, Dan, § 6.4

Royalties, as passive income, unrelated business income, § 5.7(b)(vi)

Sale, defined, § 3.2(d)

Sales tax rules, auctions, § 7.10(f)

Sanctions, intermediate, § 5.6

Schools, record-retention requirements, § 5.12

Scientific organizations, preferred postal rates, § 5.18(b)(iv)

Securities laws, § 5.20

Shultz, George P., § 1.1

Simon, William E., § 6.3(j)

Sliding-scale registration fees, § 7.11

Small solicitations, exemptions, § 3.5(i)

Solicit, defined, §§ 3.2(c), 7.2(b)

Solicitation, defined, §§ 3.2(c), 7.2(b)

Solicitors, professional:
bond requirements, § 3.7
fundraisers, differences, § 7.2

INDEX

Solicitors, professional *(Continued)*
  in general, §§ 7.2(b), 7.3
  registration, § 3.7
  solicit, defined, § 3.2(c)
  solicitation notice requirements under state
    charitable solicitation acts, § 3.17
  telemarketing, role of, § 7.3
Special fundraising events and activities:
  in general, §§ 5.9(e), 5.16(a)
  IRS annual information returns, § 5.9
Special purpose programs:
  capital campaigns, § 2.2(b)
  grants from government agencies,
    foundations and corporations,
    § 2.2(b)
  major gifts from individuals, § 2.2(b)
State action doctrine, § 8.3
State charity officials' concerns, § 7.8
State laws:
  blue sky statutes, § 3.22
  charitable solicitation acts, § 3.1
  insurance laws, § 3.22
  nonprofit corporation acts, § 3.22
State fundraising law, commentary on,
    § 7.1
State regulators, viewpoint of, § 2.6
Statistics, contribution, § 1.2
Substantially related, concept of, § 5.7(a)(v)
Substantiation requirements:
  auctions, § 7.10(d)
  charitable contribution rules, § 5.3
Support group organizations, annual giving
    programs, § 2.2(a)
Sweepstakes promotions, § 2.2(a)
System for coping with regulation, § 2.8

Tax deductions for charitable contributions:
  appraisal requirements, § 5.14(h)
  auctions, § 7.10(b), (c)
  gift, definition of, § 5.14(a)
  in general, § 5.14
  partial interest gifts, § 5.14(g)
  percentage limitations, § 5.14(d)
  qualified donees, § 5.14(b)
  quid pro quo contribution rules, § 5.4
  property, gifts of, § 5.14(c)
  receipt, record-keeping and reporting
    requirements, § 5.14(i), (j)
Tax exemption application process:
  classification as public charity or private
    foundation, § 5.11
  disclosure of application, § 5.8
  15-month rule, § 5.8(c)(iii)
  importance of proper preparation, §
    5.8(c)(iv)
  procedure, § 5.8(c)
  recognition of exemption, concept of,
    § 5.8(a)
  27-month rule, § 5.8(c)(iii)

Tax-exempt status:
  application for, § 5.8(b)
  recognition of, § 5.8(a)
Telemarketing, § 7.3
Telephone and television, annual giving
    programs, § 2(a)
Trade or business, § 5.7(a)(iii), (b)(i)
Travel arrangements, preferred postal rates,
    § 5.18(d)
Trends, legal, § 7.15

Uniform annual report, § 7.14(c)
Universities, *see* Colleges and universities
Unrelated business rules:
  affinity card programs, § 5.7(b)(vi)
  auctions, exception for, § 7.10(a)
  basic concepts, § 5.7(a)
  bingo games, § 5.7(a)(vi)
  businesses, activities characterized as,
    § 5.7(b)(i)
  cause-related marketing, § 5.7(b)(viii)
  commercial co-ventures, § 5.7(b)(vii)
  corporate services, § 5.7(b)(ix)
  deduction rules, § 5.7(a)(ii)
  exceptions, § 5.7(a)(vi), (vii), (b)(vi)
  exclusions provided by modifications,
    § 5.7(a)(vii), (b)(vi)
  financial counseling by organizations,
    § 5.7(b)(iii)
  fragmentation rule, § 5.7(a)(iii)
  fundraising, rules applied to, § 5.7(b)
  low cost articles exception, § 5,7(a)(vi)
  modifications, § 5.7(a)(vii)
  partnership rule, § 5.7(a)(viii)
  passive income, § 5.7(a)(vii)
  preparatory time for activity, IRS
    consideration of, § 5.7(b)(2)
  principal-agent relationships,
    § 5.7(b)(v)
  qualified public entertainment activity
    exception, § 5.7(a)(vi)
  regularly carried on, concept of, §
    5.7(a)(iv), (b)(ii)
  royalties, § 5.7(b)(vi)
  substantially related trade or business,
    § 5.7(a)(v)
  trade or business, defined, § 5.7(a)(iii)
Unsolicited merchandise, mailings of,
    § 2.2(a)
Used vehicles, gifts of, § 7.13
User fees, § 7.11

Vagueness, unconstitutional, § 4.8
Veterans' organizations, postal rates,
    preferred, § 5.18(b)(iv)
Viewpoints on regulation:
  fundraising professionals, § 2.7
  state regulators, § 2.6
Volunteer, defined, § 3.1(k)

Watchdog monitoring agencies:
  American Institute of Philanthropy
    standards, § 8.6
  commentary on standards, § 8.8
  commentary, response to, § 8.9
  court intervention, § 8.8
  credibility, § 8.8
  Evangelical Council for Financial
    Accountability standards, § 8.5
  function of, § 8.2
  Philanthropic Advisory Service standards,
    § 8.4
  prejudice against charitable sector, § 8.8
  problems with, § 8.8
  ratings power, public concern, § 8.8
  reply to response, § 8.10
  role of, § 8.2
  standards applied by, in general, § 8.3
  standards enforcement, § 8.7
Wilson bill, § 6.2(a)
World Wide Web, document disclosure via, §
  5.9(i)